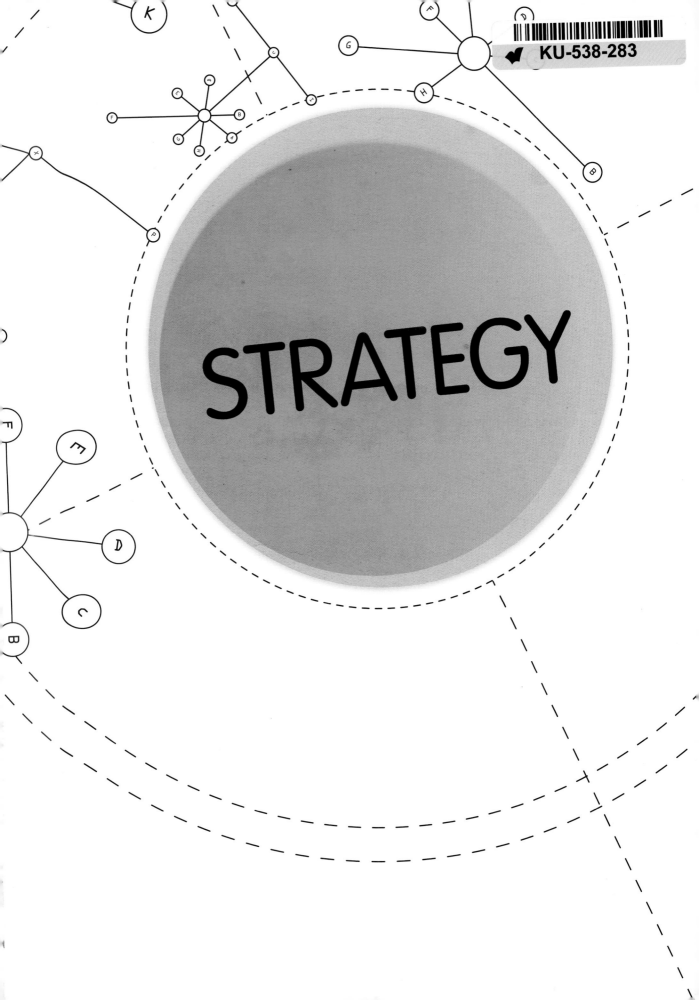

STRATEGY

All things must be examined, debated, investigated without exception and
without regard for anyone's feelings … . We must ride rough shod over all
these ancient puerilities, overturn the barriers that reason never erected, give
back to the arts and sciences the liberty that is so precious to them.

Things fall apart; the centre cannot hold.

STRATEGY
THEORY & PRACTICE

STEWART CLEGG
CHRIS CARTER
MARTIN KORNBERGER
JOCHEN SCHWEITZER

$SAGE

Los Angeles | London | New Delhi
Singapore | Washington DC

© Stewart Clegg, Chris Carter, Martin Kornberger and Jochen Schweitzer 2011

First published 2011

SAGE Publications Ltd
1 Oliver's Yard
55 City Road
London EC1Y 1SP

SAGE Publications Inc.
2455 Teller Road
Thousand Oaks, California 91320

SAGE Publications India Pvt Ltd
B 1/I 1 Mohan Cooperative Industrial Area
Mathura Road
New Delhi 110 044

SAGE Publications Asia-Pacific Pte Ltd
33 Pekin Street #02-01
Far East Square
Singapore 048763

Library of Congress Control Number: 2010929845

British Library Cataloguing in Publication data

A catalogue record for this book is available from the British Library

ISBN 978-1-84920-151-3
ISBN 978-1-84920-152-0 (pbk)

Typeset by C&M Digitals (P) Ltd, Chennai, India
Printed and bound in Great Britain by Ashford Colour Press Ltd
Printed on paper from sustainable resources

STEWART
For Lynne, Jonathan and William

CHRIS
For my wife, Ingrid, and to the memory of my grandfather,
Albert G. Carter (1912–2002)

MARTIN
For Jess

JOCHEN
For Meghan

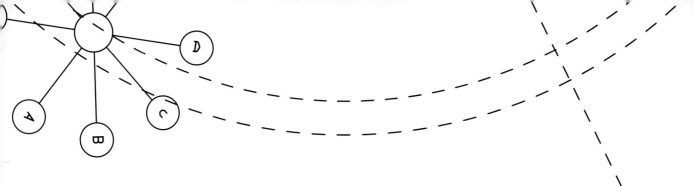

Finally, something different in a strategy text! This new volume provides a broad view of strategy covering the conventional as well as less mainstream alternatives like the growing strategy-as-practice perspective. It also does a great job of providing balanced critiques of the existing orthodoxy and provides explicit connections to some of the more accessible academic articles, providing more depth to the arguments presented. All in all, it is an excellent break from the unfortunate tendency to make strategy a narrow economic enterprise in a world that is far more complex and social than that. *Strategy: Theory and Practice* is a welcome addition to the available texts on strategy.

Nelson Phillips, Professor of Strategy and Organizational Behaviour, Imperial College of Business, UK, Co-Editor, *Journal of Management Inquiry*

This book has the critical edge that is lacking in most books on strategy, yet is very much needed – what strategy and strategizing are all about. It explains where strategy originates from and how contemporary ideas and practices facilitate or constrain decision-making and action. In particular, this book illuminates the role of power and politics in strategy – an issue that has been overlooked in most textbooks in this area. Enjoyable and inspiring reading for students, researchers and practitioners.

Eero Vaara, Professor of Management and Organization, Dean of Research Hanken School of Economics, Helsinki, Finland

This book unravels the neatness of traditional economics-based views of strategy and replaces them with much needed social, political and organizational lenses. The authors have produced a refreshing book which rightly establishes organization theory at the centre of strategic analysis and practice.

David C. Wilson, Professor of Strategy and Organization, Warwick Business School, UK

We have waited a long time for a book like this: it is eminently readable, genuinely ground-breaking and absolutely timely. Students will find it indispensable, scholars will find it thought-provoking and practitioners will find it energizing, even liberating. It revitalizes our understanding of strategy and disposes of some tired clichés and well-worn dogmas along the way.

Susan J. Miller, Professor of Organizational Behaviour, Hull University Business School, UK

Bravo! Finally, a strategy text that takes issues of power, politics and organizing seriously. Integrating concerns about ethics, corporate social responsibility and sustainability, *Strategy: Theory and Practice* provides a provocative and critically engaged approach to understanding strategy and strategizing as a complex, distributed and unpredictable activity. As such, it is an important contribution to pedagogy at the intersection of strategic management and organization studies.

Professor Michael Lounsbury, Alex Hamilton Professor, University of Alberta, Canada

This brilliant book moves away from the rational toolbox approach and highlights the organizational determinants and political outcomes of strategy. Clegg and his colleagues bring a much needed perspective to understanding how strategy impacts on society and what can be done.

Bernard Forgues, Professor of Organization Theory, EMLYON Business School, France

We've known for some time now that the discipline of Strategy is fragmenting. What I like about this book is that it not only helps us make sense of why this is happening, but it offers a coherent new framework for understanding what strategy means in the 21st century. Clegg et al. begin by revealing the dirty little secret of strategy – most of it is highly revisionist. From *In Search of Excellence* to the adulation of Enron before its collapse, by looking backward we now see that those who study strategy really do a terrible job of predicting 'winners' and 'losers' but do a great job of explaining success after the fact. Clegg et al. demonstrate the reason for this – i.e. strategy is much less about firm performance than it is about politics and power both inside and outside the firm. As such, this book provides a refreshing new perspective on strategic management. It demonstrates an awareness that firms compete not only in the material world for hard resources but also in the political world for power. It is essential reading for anyone who wants to make sense of modern (or should I say post-modern) strategic management.

Roy Suddaby, Eric Geddes Professor of Business, Alberta School of Business, Canada

This volume provides a much needed complement to traditional texts on strategy and strategic management. Its unique contribution lies in its comprehensive treatment of the history of strategic management thought and its compelling introduction to emerging strategy research informed by critical social theory. As such, it goes considerably beyond conventional strategy textbooks and should expand the horizons of students and researchers alike by deepening their understanding of the politics and social dynamics of the strategy process.

Sven Modell, Professor of Accounting, Manchester Business School, UK

At last! A strategy textbook that speaks the truth to the flatulence that is 'USDA prime' Strategy Research. 'Is that a strategic decision, or did you think about it?' managers used to say at Philips HQ in Holland. Here, finally, is a strategy book that will enable students, and their teachers, to 'think about it'.

Keith Hoskin, Professor of Strategy and Accounting, Warwick Business School, UK

The book is full of fresh approaches and lively descriptions that combine theories into sensible narratives that students and teachers can easily retain, play with, argue over – put differently, learn! The book emphasizes managerial capabilities and processes, how to think about these, see these, and how to make them better. The book also highlights new thinking in all areas and pushes these ideas forward into the future – which is very important.

Deborah Dougherty, Professor of Management and Global Business, Rutgers Business School, Rutgers University, US

This is a fabulous, groundbreaking book. When the hype is stripped away, strategy is hugely consequential – politically and ecologically. Stewart Clegg and his colleagues show us how and why. At last, a strategy text that does justice to the theory and the practice of strategy.

Hugh Willmott, Research Professor in Organization Studies, Cardiff Business School, UK

At last, a critical text on strategy that is historically informed, starting with a masterful exposition of Machiavelli and Hobbes. This historical perspective means that strategy in the present can only be understood in the context of global capitalism, and the authors build a rich picture of contemporary capitalism, drawing on a much wider range of sources than any conventional strategy text. The authors not only debunk much of the mainstream strategy literature, exposing its teleological limitations, they also set out a dazzling agenda for the study of strategy in the 21st century.

A book that lecturers and students in strategy have been waiting for, even if they didn't know it.

Michael Rowlinson, Professor of Organization Studies, Queen Mary University of London, UK

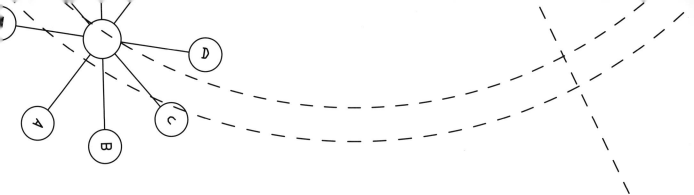

AUTHOR BIOGRAPHIES

Stewart Clegg is a prolific publisher of several hundred articles in leading academic journals in strategy, social science, management and organization theory; is also the author and editor of about fifty books, as well as a Fellow of the British Academy of Social Sciences, a Distinguished Fellow of the Australian and New Zealand Academy of Management, a Fellow of the Academy of the Social Sciences in Australia, and the recipient of significant awards from the American Academy of Management for his contributions to management theory and practice.

Professor Chris Carter is from Cornwall, he teaches strategy at the University of St Andrews and also holds a visiting fellowship at the University of Technology, Sydney. His research explores the politics of strategy and campaigns. Chris received his PhD in Organization Theory from Aston Business School. He lives in Edinburgh.

Martin Kornberger received his PhD from the University of Vienna in 2002. Currently he works as full time Visiting Professor at the Department of Organization, Copenhagen Business School. Trained as philosopher, he researches and teaches about practices of organizing, strategizing, accounting, and marketing, and explores how they shape, and are shaped by, the economy and society at large.

Jochen Schweitzer is a researcher, educator, business writer and management adviser based at the University of Technology, Sydney. With extensive professional experience and as a scholar he offers both a scientific and practical perspective on questions of strategic management, innovation, collaboration and the management of creative organizations.

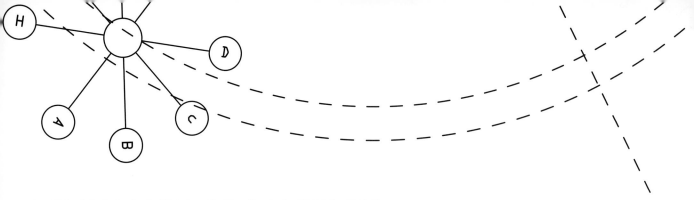

SUMMARY OF CONTENTS

Guided tour xviii
Companion website xxii
Preface xxiii

PART ONE
INTRODUCTION 1

1   The Context and Emergence of
    Strategic Thinking 3

PART TWO
CENTRAL CURRENTS IN
    STRATEGY 45

2   Strategy and Competitive
    Performance 47

3   Strategy Discovers Uniqueness: The
    Role of Resources and Knowledge 83

4   Strategy as Process and Practice 117

5   Marketing and Branding as
    Strategic Forces 149

6   Strategy and Innovation 182

PART THREE
THE POLITICS OF STRATEGY 213

7   Strategists, Top Management Teams
    and Governance 215

8   Strategic Decision-Making 259

9   Organizational Politics and
    Strategy 293

PART FOUR
GLOBAL STRATEGIES 319

10 International and Collaborative
    Strategies 321

11 Financialization, Risk and
    Accountability 359

12 Globalization and Strategy 391

References 431
Index 457

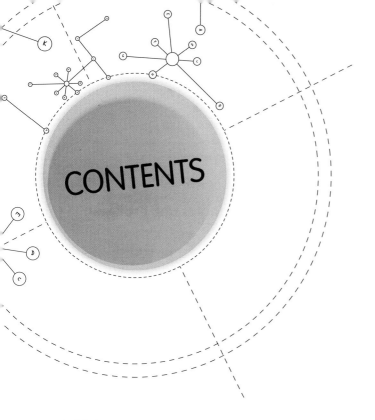

CONTENTS

Guided tour xviii
Companion website xxii
Preface xxiii

PART ONE
INTRODUCTION 1

1 The Context and Emergence of Strategic Thinking 3

Before you get started . . . 4
Introduction 4
What is strategy? 4
    What do strategists actually do when they strategize? 4
    Lineages of strategy 6
    Strategy as a paradigm 9
    Interpreting strategy 14
Elements in the dominant strategy paradigm 15
    Alfred Chandler: strategy drives structure 15
    Igor Ansoff: rational planning 16
    Edith Penrose: the theory of the firm and strategy 17
    Michael Porter: industry analysis 18
Strategy styles 18
    Evolution 19
    Revolution 20
    Complexity 23

Strategy as process and practice 25
The limitations of strategy 29
    Surprise 29
    Serendipity 33
What's wrong with this picture? 34
Summary and review 36
Exercises 39
Additional resources 39
Web section 40
Looking for a higher mark? 40
Case study 41

PART TWO
CENTRAL CURRENTS IN STRATEGY 45

2 Strategy and Competitive Performance 47

Learning objectives 47
Before you get started . . . 48
Introduction 48
Industrial organization and the structure–conduct–performance approach 49
    The basics 49
    Qualifications 50
Organizational performance and sustainable competitive advantage 52
Understanding the macro-environment 53

How different types of markets define competitive environments 56
How five forces determine competitive attractiveness 59
Another force? 63
Strategic groups 65
The value chain 66
Generic strategies 69
   Cost leadership 69
   Differentiation 70
   Focus strategies 71
   Value-creating disciplines 74
Innovation as strategic driver 75
Summary and review 76
Exercises 76
Additional resources 77
Web section 77
Looking for a higher mark? 77
Case study 78

3 Strategy Discovers Uniqueness: The Role of Resources and Knowledge 83

Learning objectives 83
Before you get started . . . 84
Introduction 84
Strategy: looking inwards 84
   The firm as a bundle of assets 84
   The foundations of the RBV 85
   Economics and the RBV 86
   Understanding resources and capabilities 86
   Barney's VRIN framework 87
Practising strategy with the RBV 88
What are the rent-generating activities of the capacities? 90
Core competencies and competitive advantage 93
What's wrong with the RBV? 95
Strategic entrepreneurship 97
Dynamic capabilities: the ghost in the RBV theory machine 98
Value creation and capture 100
Repertoires and structural poses 101
Knowledge as a crucial resource 103
   Business process reengineering (BPR) 105
   The knowledge economy 107
   The professional project of IT professionals 109
KM methods 110
   Mining knowledge: the role of intranets 110
   Stories and knowledge 111

Summary and review 113
Exercises 113
Additional resources 114
Web section 114
Looking for a higher mark? 114
Case study 115

4 Strategy as Process and Practice 117

Learning objectives 117
Before you get started . . . 118
Introduction 118
The importance of being rational 118
Strategy as emergent, grounded and not rational planning 121
   Mintzberg and managerial behaviour 121
   Mintzberg and grounded theory 125
Deliberate vs emergent strategy 126
   Andrew Pettigrew and process 128
Strategy is what strategists do, know, say … 129
   Strategy as practice (s-as-p) 129
   Strategy and learning 134
   Strategy and culture 135
   Strategy, sensegiving and sensemaking 137
Strategy as narrative 140
From strategy as competing literal representations to strategy as a constitutive discourse 143
Summary and review 145
Exercises 145
Additional resources 145
Web section 146
Looking for a higher mark? 146
Case study 147

5 Marketing and Branding as Strategic Forces 149

Learning objectives 149
Before you get started . . . 150
Introduction 150
Service-dominant logic 152
Understanding customer desire – market segmentation, targeting and competitive positioning 153
   Segmentation 154
   Targeting 156
   Positioning 157
Managing the customer relationship 158
   Relationship marketing 158
   CRM as cause-related marketing 160
Branding and identity 161

Brand capital and brand formation   163
Brand-driven strategy   166
Critical perspectives on branding   172
Summary and review   176
Exercises   177
Additional resources   177
Web section   178
Looking for a higher mark?   178
Case study   179

6   Strategy and Innovation   182

Learning objectives   182
Before you get started . . .   183
Introduction   183
Innovation: process, product and
    platform   184
Creative destruction and disruptive
    technologies   186
Theorizing innovation   189
    Rational discontinuities   189
    Incremental discontinuities   191
Which organizations innovate best?   192
Designing organizations for innovation   193
    Creativity and design thinking   193
Innovation environments   199
    Institutional innovation and
        environments   199
    The co-creation of value   200
    Open innovation and open strategy   203
    National innovation systems, learning
        networks and clusters   205
Innovation experiments   206
Social innovation   207
Summary and review   209
Exercises   209
Additional resources   209
Web section   209
Looking for a higher mark?   210
Case study   211

PART THREE
THE POLITICS OF STRATEGY   213

**7   Strategists, Top Management Teams
    and Governance**   215

Learning objectives   215
Before you get started . . .   216
Introduction   216

Strategists in practice   217
The role of leadership   222
Strategy as the work of top management
    teams   224
The reproduction of business elites
    and the centrality of strategy   226
The MBA and strategy   230
Strategy as the work of consultants   232
    Organizational surgery   233
    Organizational retooling   235
    Organizational therapy   235
    Organizational metaphysics   236
Ownership and control of strategy   237
    The debate about ownership and control   237
    Corporate governance in contemporary
        times   240
Strategy in and around the boardroom   243
Tensions in TMTs   244
Corporate codes   246
    What do codes do?   246
    Ethical codes in practice   247
Summary and review   249
Exercises   249
Additional resources   250
Web section   250
Looking for a higher mark?   250
Case study   251

8   Strategic Decision-Making   259

Learning objectives   259
Before you get started . . .   260
Introduction   260
Executive decision   261
Bounded rationality   261
Muddling through   263
Garbage cans   266
Politicized strategy: the politics of
    decisions   267
Action generators   270
On the politics of organizational
    decision-making   274
Top decisions – Bradford studies   275
Decision-making in high-velocity
    environments   277
Non-decision-making   279
Risk, bureaucracy and decisions   282
    The 1986 Space Shuttle disaster: risky
        technology and decision-making   283
Strategic decisions make the manager who
    makes strategic decisions   287
Summary and review   288
Exercises   288

Additional resources 289
Web section 289
Looking for a higher mark? 289
Case study 290

9 Organizational Politics and
Strategy 293

Learning objectives 293
Before you get started . . . 294
Introduction 294
Interests and strategy 294
Strategic interests and micro-politics 295
Strategy as a political game 297
Interests and action 297
Game stakes 299
Strategy as a game of power and
resistance 300
The dimensions of power 303
Strategy as the institutionalization
of myth 304
Politics and complex organizations 306
Multinational corporations 306
MNCs and mandates 307
The politics of strategy and structure
in different contexts 310
Summary and review 314
Exercises 314
Additional resources 314
Web section 315
Looking for a higher mark? 315
Case study 316

PART FOUR
GLOBAL STRATEGIES 319

10 International and Collaborative
Strategies 321

Learning objectives 321
Before you get started . . . 322
Introduction 322
Why collaborate? 322
Why become an MNC? 323
Market factors 323
Comparative advantage 324
Efficiency 325
Institutional factors 325
Strategies for MNCS 326
Decentralized federation; multinational
strategy 326

Coordinated federation; international
strategy 327
Centralized hubs; global strategy 327
Matrix organizations; binary strategy 329
Integrated network; transnational
strategy 330
Defining strategic alliances – key benefits
and latent issues 332
The alliance choice – to make, buy
or ally 336
Alliance organization – contractual
agreements and governance 337
Types of collaboration 339
Strategic rational 339
Completeness of contract 340
Alliance lifecycle 343
Alliance foundation 344
Development and maturity 344
Termination 345
Collaborating through polyphony 346
Alliancing and the future perfect
strategy 349
Strange conversations 351
End games and the practice of
workshopping 352
Projecting feelings, concerns and issues 353
Summary and review 355
Exercises 355
Additional resources 355
Web section 356
Looking for a higher mark? 356
Case study 357

11 Financialization, Risk and
Accountability 359

Learning objectives 359
Before you get started . . . 360
Introduction 360
The golden age of capitalism 361
The triumph of neo-liberal capitalism 362
Financialization 364
Shareholder value 364
Private equity 368
Private equity strategy 369
Strategy and the global financial
crisis 370
From buccaneers to bankrupts 370
The 2008 banking crash 371
Strategy in a crisis 377
Risk and audit 378
Rankings and reactivity: how public
measures recreate social worlds 381
Summary and review 386

Exercises   386
Additional resources   386
Web section   386
Looking for a higher mark?   387
Case study   388

12   Globalization and Strategy   391

Learning objectives   391
Before you get started . . .   392
Introduction   392
Globalization   393
Born global   395
Uneven globalization; uneven risk   397
Globalizing flows   400
Globalizing finance, procurement, people,
   and communication   402
   Financial flows   402

Procurement flows   403
People flows   405
Communication flows   407
Global strategies: convergence, divergence
   or translation?   408
   Convergence thesis   410
   Divergence thesis   411
   Translation thesis   412
Futures of globalization?   413
China   414
Summary and review   418
Exercises   418
Additional resources   418
Web section   418
Looking for a higher mark?   419
Case study   420

References   431
Index   457

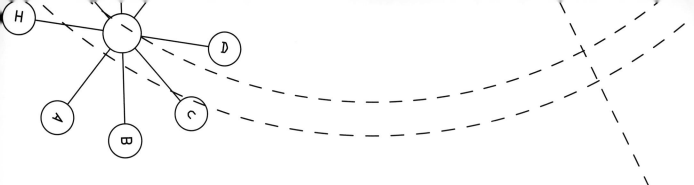

LIST OF CASE STUDIES

1   **A strategic vision for Cambodia**   41

Stewart Clegg, Miguel Pina e Cunha and Arménio Rego

2   **Competitive positioning in the Australian online apparel industry: the case of Brands Exclusive**   78

Lars Groeger

3   **Arthur Andersen**   115

Chris Carter

4   **Google**   147

Martin Kornberger

5   **Providing a service and managing the customer relationship – or how things can go wrong at TELESTAR**   179

Jochen Schweitzer

6   **Cirque du Soleil**   211

Martin Kornberger

7   **Marks & Spencer, 1990–2001: boardroom battles**   251

Chris Carter

8   **United Nations Climate Change Conference 2009**   290

Chris Carter

9   **The 1998 Australian waterfront dispute: different strategic interests, different strategies, different weapons**   316

Stewart Clegg

10 Arts collaboration: Menagerie – Contemporary Indigenous Sculpture *357*

Meghan Hay

11 Private equity unplugged: EMI, 2007–9 *388*

Chris Carter

12 Shell *420*

David Bubna-Littic and Crelis Rammelt

GUIDED
TOUR

Welcome to the guided tour of *Strategy: Theory and Practice*. This tour will take you through the main sections and special features of the text.

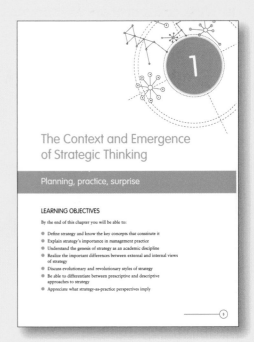

Learning objectives: A key set of learning objectives are provided for each chapter.

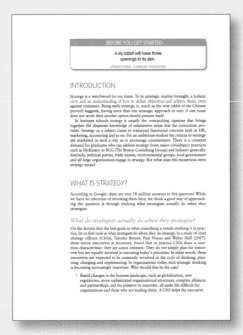

Introduction: The introduction provides you with the overall framework of each chapter.

Question time: Questions are provided to help you ensure that you have understood key points in the chapter.

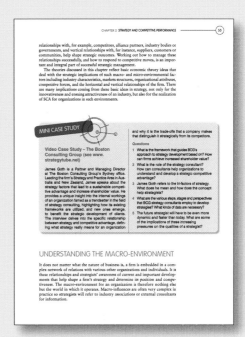

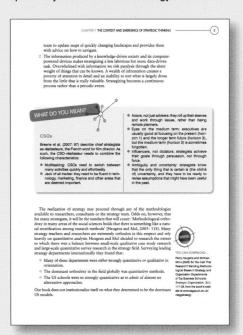

Marginal definitions: Key terms are clearly and concisely explained in the page margins of every chapter in order to aid understanding.

Mini case study: Boxed mini case studies are included for active learning and the practical reinforcement of difficult or challenging concepts. **Video case studies** are based on videos that can be accessed on a website created by the authors specifically for this text: www.strategytube.net

You can download… Full-text journal articles that enhance your understanding of a particular topic can be downloaded from the companion website: www.sagepub.co.uk/cleggstrategy

What do you mean? Within each chapter boxed text expands upon key concepts in order to facilitate learning and understanding.

Summary and review: This section simply does what it says. We review the main concepts and issues to be sure that you are clear on what was covered, and why.

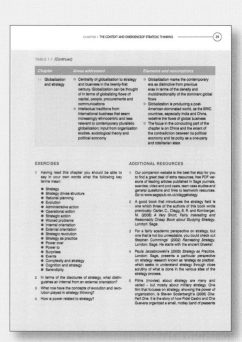

Exercises: Group and individual exercises designed to provide practical and reflective learning on key issues, concepts and phenomena covered in each chapter.

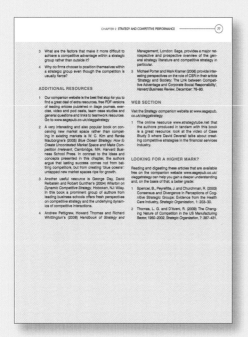

Additional resources: A selection of handpicked resources such as books and journal articles that explain and expand upon chapter contents.

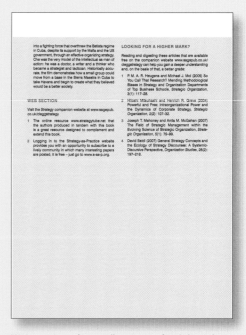

Web section: An excellent array of web-based resources such as website links and YouTube clips that illustrate and emphasize key issues covered in the book.

Looking for a higher mark? A list of engaging and challenging journal articles that can be accessed for free on our companion website are provided at the end of every chapter: www.sagepub.co.uk/cleggstrategy

Case study: Each chapter ends with an innovative case study, accompanied by questions designed for reflective learning and the reinforcement of key concepts.

COMPANION WEBSITE

Be sure to visit the companion website at **http://www.sagepub.co.uk/cleggstrategy** to find a range of teaching and learning materials for both lecturers and students, including the following:

FOR LECTURERS:

- **Instructor's manual**: Contains overviews of every chapter, along with suggested examination questions for each chapter.
- **PowerPoint slides**: PowerPoint slides for each chapter for use in class are also provided. These slides can be edited by instructors to suit teaching styles and needs.
- **Additional case studies**: These additional case studies include discussion questions.
- **Multiple choice questions**: A testbank of downloadable multiple choice questions are available for lecturers to test students or make available to students online.
- **Links to ecch case studies**: Links to relevant case studies provide lecturers with additional resources.

FOR STUDENTS:

- **Video case studies:** Online videos provide stimulating insights into the field of strategy, through interviews with professional strategists. Each video is accompanied by notes, study questions and suggested further reading.
- **Full-text journal articles**: Full access to selected SAGE journal articles related to each chapter, providing students with a deeper understanding of the topics in each chapter.
- **Links to relevant websites**: Direct links to relevant websites for each chapter.
- **Podcasts**: Podcasts provide recordings of the authors discussing different concepts, issues and debates outlined in the text.

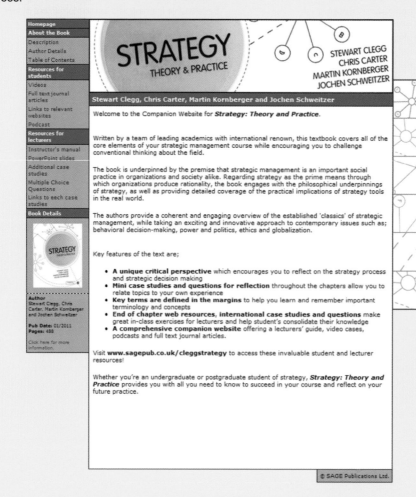

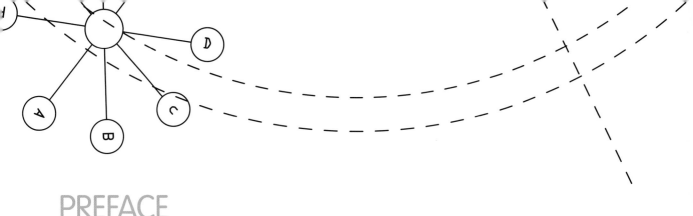

PREFACE

Why another book on strategy? After all, there are many on the market. Why spend thousands of hours on producing this text? Well, we think there is absence in the strategy literature. Quite simply, we wanted to produce a strategy book that would satisfy us as educators and the students we teach.

In many ways strategy can be seen on a continuum that draws from economic theory at one end to organization theory at the other end. The two traditions are the pillars upon which management studies are based. The economics end of the spectrum is well catered for with many books that deal comprehensively with strategy from this point of view (see Lipczynski, Wilson and Goddard, 2009). Equally, there are books that edge along the continuum, which, while still grounded in economics, gesture towards other concerns (Grant, 2009, for instance, provides an exemplary account of resource-based view [RBV] thinking). Moving into the middle ground between economics and organization theory is Johnson, Scholes and Whittington (2008), a book that is the market leader in mainstream European strategy and is presently in its eighth edition. Undoubtedly, Johnson et al.'s book has been a huge commercial success, but we are convinced that a wholly fresh start is required, which is why we have written the present book. Our book draws extensively on organization theory; unlike other texts we are explicit that strategy is inextricably bound up with issues of power and politics. While the four of us each approach strategy slightly differently, we share a sense of discontent with the textbooks that largely comprise the field.

The present book does not treat strategy as being only a set of techniques, but rather sees them as irredeemably social, organizational and political in orientation. Strategy is a cultural product that is found throughout contemporary society, not just in business organizations, NGOs or government. From our perspective, strategy is irremediably political in practice; if there were ever any doubts about this proposition, after the global financial crisis served as a reality check, it would now seem one that none could reasonably deny. The financial crisis and fall out from it necessitate a critical analysis of organization's strategies. What are the organizations doing? In whose interests are they operating? What are the intended and unintended consequences of their strategy? However, an adequate analysis of the politics of strategy that might lead to such a crisis would be difficult to make for students who had been weaned on the standard textbooks of strategy and strategic management. Few of them address the politics of strategy; none address them adequately. Moreover, strategy texts often serve up hagiographic accounts of companies and business leaders. For instance, the Harvard Business School produced 13 case studies on the Enron corporation and Gary Hamel heaped paeans of praise upon the organization in his book on revolutionary strategy. Even those accounts that have stressed the necessity of considering strategy as a practice have been limited in their account of practices as both that which happens – and that which does not. As Ezzamel and Willmott (2004) demonstrate, such accounts often write out issues of power and politics. Thus, analytic opportunities for engaging with central debates in the analysis of power and politics have been largely left begging.

Not only has a division between strategy and politics been constructed. But also there has, for too long, been an artificial divide between strategic management and organization theory, one that is an effect, very largely, of institutional histories. Strategy, from early on, was thought of in terms of rational planning oriented to criteria of performance represented through the concepts of the economics discipline. From one perspective, the economics discipline may be seen as a noticeably assured and self-referential discourse; from a different perspective it may be seen as profoundly blinkered, creating science fictions spun from the entrails of deliberately limited assumptions. These assumptions were embedded in a view of rationality that was constipated and one dimensional as well as profoundly asocial, something evident from many directions but especially from Schutz's (1967) and Garfinkel's (1967) conception of there being socially situated rationalities.

The assumptions of economic approaches tend to cut strategy and strategic management off not only from some of the most interesting and creative currents in organization theory, but also from the broader currents of social analysis, especially sociology. During the period in which strategic management and the analysis of strategy came to dominate business degrees as capstone subjects, in the United Kingdom, sociology hit a nadir in Prime Minister Thatcher's 1980s. That there was no such thing as society was an article of faith, especially for economists ill disposed to allow the social to enter into the realm of rational calculation. Such views became widely influential. Strategy emerged as a macho, testosterone-charged younger brother of economics. Analysis, rigour and a gamut of tools and techniques were in, while critique and reflection were distinctly unfashionable.

By contrast, we take sociology seriously: indeed, one of us is proud to have held a Chair in Sociology and to consider himself still a sociologist. We see no necessity to draw a line between the economic and the social and to assign strategy largely to the economic arena. We do not believe that there are universal laws that reign in abstract spheres of social and organizational life, irrespective of context. For us, as for most social theorists, the realities of organizational actions and strategies are always to be seen as profoundly embedded in the specificities of the situation.

Given this background to our project, the title of our book should be seen as a quite explicit statement. We want to create some distance from ourselves and managerialist conceptions of strategy and thus have eschewed 'strategic management' for the simpler and less managerialist 'strategy'. We believe that theory and practice are mutually implicated and always political. Our book is innovative in its political focus and its concern with the global financial crisis and globalization – hence the emphasis on 'politics' – because these processes have concentrated practical attention on the political entanglements of business strategies and society in a way that, largely, was previously missing. We draw on the work of organization theorists as much as we do on contributors to strategic management – hence we do not lionize strategy as the effect of great or charismatic leaders; instead, strategy should be seen as something that is constituted and enacted 'organizationally'. Finally, we reject any notion that strategy and strategists are absolved from a consideration of the broader social consequences of their actions – hence the concern with that much maligned signifier 'society'. In short, we think that engaging seriously with theory and practice entails a platform that sees strategy in the context: strategy as something that organizations, not individuals, make up; something in which organizational politics can never be eliminated from the picture any more than can the fact that strategy is irremediably societal. It is not a purely rational economic phenomenon that does not engage with the societal constructions and realities in which it is embedded. Thus, theory is always political, always has organizational implications and is never asocial; the same may be said for practice – there is always a social and organizational agenda behind the most seemingly benign and disinterested statement of strategy. It could not be otherwise.

Three of us, Chris, Stewart and Martin, drawing on the background sketched above, have been talking about strategy for some time. These conversations led to our releasing a test balloon of some of our ideas – in the form of *A Very Short, Fairly Interesting and Reasonably Cheap Book about Studying Strategy*. Shortly before completing that book we organized a workshop at the University of Aston (which was generously sponsored by Professor Mike West, Dean of Aston Business School), where both Chris and Stewart had been students, with an interdisciplinary group of academics who affirmed our suspicion that a social science approach to strategy was much needed, yet rarely offered. Our interest lay in an approach to strategy that placed it in the broader context of organizations and society. Enthused about these ideas we recruited Jochen and, back in Australia, Stewart, Martin and Jochen, with some funding from the University of Technology, Sydney, where they worked, started a new project in anticipation of this book: www.strategytube. net. The *StrategyTube* project was quite startling in that it taught us that practitioners did not think as the strategy textbooks taught them to – hence the dual focus of our book on practice-based approaches and strategy theory as mutually constitutive and recursively related. We realized that theory no more led to practice than practice led to theory. The two were mutually implicated.

Meanwhile, in between writing *A Very Short, Fairly Interesting and Reasonably Cheap Book about Studying Strategy* and doing the work for www.strategytube.net we wrote a paper that sought to push the envelope of strategy research and which was published in *Strategic Organization*. We pushed it to such an extent that some colleagues were upset enough to write lengthy replies to which we responded. It seems that some quarters of strategy frown at debate, with one web forum even characterizing our contribution as 'unprofessional'. We disagree. Debate, dissent and discussion are the foundation blocks of a good society and, more importantly, healthy strategy-making. We are all the more convinced of this in the wake of the recent global financial collapse. One of the problems that allowed it to happen was that people did not ask difficult questions of organizations.

On a personal level, all four of us have diverse backgrounds and experience with strategy. Stewart, a Yorkshire-born Australian sociologist and organization theorist, worked closely with Sydney Water on large-scale projects, including one that delivered the significant Sydney 2000 Olympics infrastructure, over the last decade. He discovered a strategy that he termed the future perfect, which consisted of a series of tactics such as work-shopping, imagining end games and creating space for awkward and personal questions, all oriented towards an evolving imaginary of what might be a completed project by a due project date with a process of constant revision of the means, resources and objectives in a process. The commitment to the dominant logic of the future perfect strategy certainly sustained and enhanced the prerogatives of management and negated alternative perspectives.

Chris, a Cornish farmer/accounting student turned organization theorist, researched the process of privatization of Coast Electric (a pseudonym) in the UK where he found at the outset hardly any sense of strategy at all; being a bureaucratized public sector body run by professional engineers, where there had never been any need for such strategy. When privatization occurred the engineers were displaced by managerialists and fairly soon the dominant logic of strategy provided managers with a rationalization of their successes and failures. It highlighted to Chris the importance of strategy as a language game that had far-reaching material effects within organizations. More recently, Chris worked as a strategist in the School of Management at the University of St Andrews. He, together with a colleague (Johnny Wilson), devised the strategy and wrote the documentation for the Research Assessment Exercise, one of the big competitions that UK business and management schools participate in every four of five years. He learnt a lot about strategy during this process and many of these lessons have been incorporated into this book.

Martin, an Austrian philosopher turned branding guru, came to Sydney from Austria to work with Stewart and also found some other European friends quite quickly. Together, being creative and innovative, they founded PLAY, a boutique communication agency specializing in branding and experiential marketing. PLAY practised what it signified: the approach to strategy was essentially creative. To establish itself in Sydney, PLAY organized Sydney Equisse, a unique design and art festival. Choosing everyday venues, such as shops, warehouses, cafés and galleries in the inner city, PLAY held events in 2003, 2005 and 2006 which brought over 150,000 people into an interaction with art and design. It also brought the young branding agency to the attention of many of the corporate sponsors that subsequently became clients. While not necessarily intentional, the strategy worked out well and earned PLAY two awards in the category of best experiential agency in Australia in 2008.

Jochen, a German-born Australian engineer turned strategist, has worked for the consulting practices of PricewaterhouseCoopers and IBM where he gained extensive experience in strategy development and implementation, process improvement and change management. While advising organizations in industries like automotive, mobile telecommunication, Internet services or financial services, he found that strategy consulting often follows its proprietary approach. Strategy consulting is solutions focused, which sounds great in theory but in practice could sometimes mean that different clients would receive handcrafted variants of an off-the-shelf solution to their strategic issues. Sometimes the strategic solution preceded the strategic problem depending on what solutions were current and codified in the knowledge management systems! Here the dominant logic demonstrated managerial rationality to colleagues, customers, competitors, government and significant others in the environment.

Our diverse backgrounds are reflected in our approach: rather than arguing for or against certain models we try to show them from different sides. Strategy is a heuristic, a way of making sense of the world and acting in the world; as such it must be open for revisions. And above all, we believe and argue that it is impossible to do strategy or be a strategist without being involved in politics of various kinds – this is pretty clear from the way we tackle strategy in the book. In short, politics are central to understanding strategy.

Any book admits to many readings and it would be both ridiculous and futile for authors to seek to prescribe them further than is already done by the imposition of the structure, design, and printed words and images on the pages. We have, as one might imagine, changed the title of the book, and the structural ordering of the chapters, as well as their contents, several times in the production of this volume, deciding on the present arrangement as much on grounds of convention as coherence. Other architectures are readily imaginable: for instance, for those people less inclined to follow the conventions of strategy texts and subjects, the chapters could be read as more political interventions into the field by stressing the political innovations made in the book, skipping the earlier, more orthodox chapters. In such an arrangement the increasingly political treatment of the strategy materials that is implicit in the book becomes more evident; other readers may prefer other arrangements – we would not want our imaginaries to constrain yours.

We did, however, have to settle on a design and order for the material. We think our book is quite innovative in the strategy field while still addressing much of the standard fare. We sought to signal this innovation especially with our part titles. The innovation is signalled especially in our Central Currents in Strategy, The Politics of Strategy and the focus on Global Strategies. In the Introduction and in Central Currents in Strategy you will find many of the things that would be covered in any standard strategy text – but we think not as interestingly as here. Of course, as in any text, there are omissions, some of which we are aware of and we are sure there will be others that will doubtless be pointed out. Perhaps the most obvious, as some interlocutors have pointed out to us already, is why there is no treatment of strategic human resource management (SHRM). There are two answers to this question. One answer is that we regard SHRM as a professional project of the 1990s that failed to achieve fully what its proponents envisaged (Salaman, Storey and Billsberry, 2005). HRM remains a largely operational pursuit in most organizations. The second answer is that there is a huge sub-industry in SHRM, as the aforementioned volume attests, which is self-sustaining and needs no impetus from this volume. The reason we have chosen to focus on marketing and branding strategies, which might as readily be thought operational, is simply that these play into the competitive market, the traditional locus of strategy analysis, in ways in which the personnel function rarely manages.

Finally, there are concerns with contemporary issues of ethics, corporate social responsibility and sustainability that recur throughout the book. Again, this was a deliberate strategy: it would be possible to rearrange the material so that it fell into chapters dedicated to these issues. Our concern is the risk of ghettoization – that these elements that are essential to the consideration of all issues of strategy can be bracketed and put in one place rather than being considered substantively *in situ* and in context.

ACKNOWLEDGEMENTS

The encouragement of Natalie Aguilera and Katie Metzler at SAGE, as well as Kiren Shoman, was instrumental in the materialization of the project. Along the way, we received helpful comments from friends and colleagues including Cary Cooper (Lancaster University), Miguel Pina e Cunha (Univeridade Nova, Lisboa), Arne Carlsen (SINTEF, Norway), Lisa Adiprodjo, Tyrone Pitsis, Roy Green, Siggi Gudergan, Stephen Fox, Lise Justesen and David Bubna-Litic (all at University of Technology, Sydney). At the University of St Andrews, Barbara Lessels, Alan McKinlay, Frank Mueller, Ryan Parks, Crawford Spence (now holed up in Canada) and Johnny 'the-acceptable- face-of-economics' Wilson all provided insightful commentary. Chris and Martin initially floated many of the ideas in the context of classes at St Andrews, especially in the *Management of Change* and *Strategic Management in the Information Age* modules. Jochen tested many cases and exercises in his *Marketing Strategy* and *Practice Management and Leadership* classes at the University of Technology, Sydney. The input from the students at St Andrews and UTS was invaluable in shaping parts of this book. Equally, many helped with the choice of the title of the book and in deliberations over the cover. David Belsey (EIS), Steve Conway (University of Bath), Peter Clark (Queen Mary, University of London) – who taught Chris strategy in 1993 – Thomas Diefenbach (Strathclyde University Business School), Lars Groeger (Macquarie Graduate School of Management), Matthew Haigh (SOAS), Irvine Lapsley (Edinburgh University), Neil Pollock (Edinburgh University), Mick Rowlinson (Queen Mary, University of London) and Steve Toms (University of York) have all been very helpful with their many suggestions about how to improve the text.

Inevitably 'place' has been very important in the production of this book. Three of us are domiciled in Sydney. Balmain, Surry Hills and Haberfield have provided congenial and inspiring locations for Martin, Jochen and Stewart. Chris visited Sydney in September 2009 and stayed in the Haberfield 'bunker' working on chapters with Stewart. Martin spent two months at Copenhagen Business School, and did much of his writing there, while Chris returned to his beloved Wilcove in Cornwall to write some of the remaining chapters. The master copy-editing was done at the University of Umea, Sweden, when Stewart was an Erasmus Mundus Fellow in September 2010, and in the Institute of Advanced Study at the University of Durham, when Stewart was a Visiting Fellow in late 2010, as well as in Sydney and on Bribie Island.

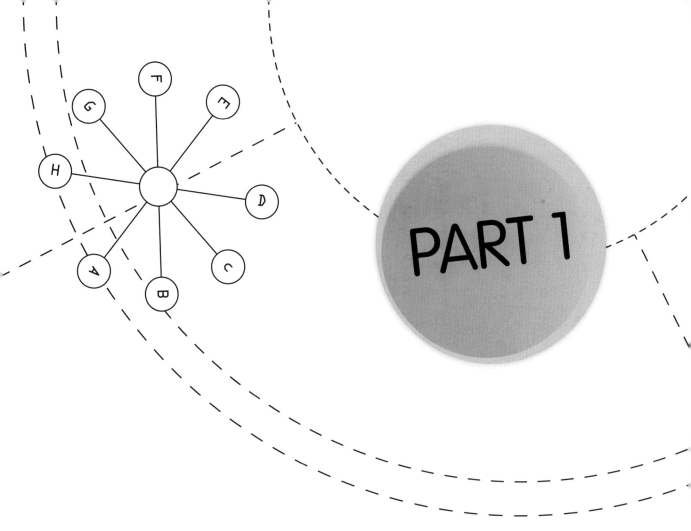

Introduction

1   The context and emergence of strategic thinking

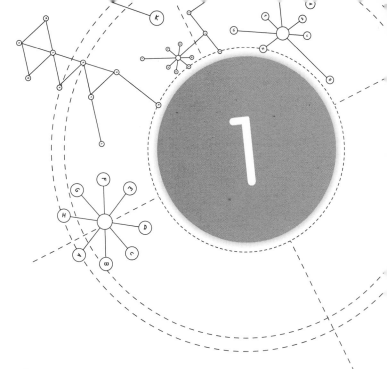

The Context and Emergence of Strategic Thinking

Planning, practice, surprise

LEARNING OBJECTIVES

By the end of this chapter you will be able to:

- Define strategy and know the key concepts that constitute it
- Explain strategy's importance in management practice
- Understand the genesis of strategy as an academic discipline
- Realize the important differences between external and internal views of strategy
- Discuss evolutionary and revolutionary styles of strategy
- Be able to differentiate between prescriptive and descriptive approaches to strategy
- Appreciate what strategy-as-practice perspectives imply

BEFORE YOU GET STARTED . . .

A sly rabbit will have three
openings to its den.

(TRADITIONAL CHINESE PROVERB)

INTRODUCTION

Strategy is a watchword for our times. To be strategic implies foresight, a holistic view and an understanding of how to define objectives and achieve them, even against resistance. Being *really* strategic is, much as the wise rabbit of the Chinese proverb suggests, having more than one strategic approach or exit: if one route does not work then another option should present itself.

In business schools strategy is usually the overarching capstone that brings together the disparate knowledge of substantive areas that the curriculum provides. Strategy as a subject claims to transcend functional concerns such as HR, marketing, accounting and so on. For an ambitious student the returns to strategy are marketed in such a way as to encourage commitment. There is a constant demand for graduates who can address strategy from major consultancy practices such as McKinsey or BCG (The Boston Consulting Group) and industry generally. Similarly, political parties, trade unions, environmental groups, local government and all large organizations engage in strategy. But what does this mysterious term strategy mean?

WHAT IS STRATEGY?

According to Google, there are over 58 million answers to this question! While we have no intention of reviewing them here, we think a good way of approaching the question is through studying what strategists actually do when they strategize.

What do strategists actually do when they strategize?

On the dictum that the best guide to what something is entails studying it in practice, let us first look at what strategists do when they do strategy. In a study of chief strategy officers (CSOs), Timothy Breene, Paul Nunes and Walter Shill (2007), three senior executives at Accenture, found that in practice CSOs share a common characteristic: they are action oriented. They do not simply plan for tomorrow but are equally involved in executing today's priorities. In other words, these executives are expected to be constantly involved in the cycle of thinking, planning, changing and implementing. In organizations today, such strategic thinking is becoming increasingly important. Why should this be the case?

1 Rapid changes in the business landscape, such as globalization, new regulations, more sophisticated organizational structures, complex alliances and partnerships, and the pressure to innovate, all make life difficult for organizations and those who are leading them. A CSO helps the executive

team to update maps of quickly changing landscapes and provides them with advice on how to navigate.

2 The information produced by a knowledge-driven society and its computer-powered devices makes strategizing a less laborious but more data-driven task. Overwhelmed with information we risk paralysis through the sheer weight of things that can be known. A wealth of information creates a poverty of attention to detail and an inability to sort what is largely dross from the little that is really valuable. Strategizing becomes a continuous process rather than a periodic event.

WHAT DO YOU MEAN?

CSOs

Breene et al. (2007: 87) describe chief strategists as *réalisateurs*, the French word for film director. As such, the CSO–*réalisateur* needs to combine the following characteristics:

● Multitasking: CSOs need to switch between many activities quickly and effortlessly.
● Jack of all trades: they need to be fluent in technology, marketing, finance and other areas that are deemed important.

● Actors, not just advisers: they roll up their sleeves and work through issues, rather than being remote planners.
● Eyes on the medium term: executives are usually good at focusing on the present (horizon 1) and the longer term future (horizon 3), but the medium term (horizon 2) is sometimes forgotten.
● Influencers, not dictators: strategists achieve their goals through persuasion, not through force.
● Ambiguity and uncertainty: strategists know that the only thing that is certain is (the cliché of) uncertainty, and they have to be ready to revise assumptions that might have been useful in the past.

The *realization* of strategy may proceed through any of the methodologies available to researchers, consultants or the strategy team. Odds on, however, that for many strategists, it will be the numbers that will count: 'Methodological orthodoxy in many areas of the social sciences holds that there is something like a natural stratification among research methods' (Heugens and Mol, 2005: 118). Many strategy teachers and researchers are extremely orthodox in this respect and rely heavily on quantitative analysis. Heugens and Mol decided to research the extent to which there was a balance between small-scale qualitative case study research and large-scale quantitative survey research in the strategy field. Surveying leading strategy departments internationally they found that:

YOU CAN DOWNLOAD...

Percy Heugens and Michael Mol's (2005) So You Call That Research? Mending Methodological Biases in Strategy and Organization Departments of Top Business Schools, *Strategic Organization*, 3(1): 117–28, from the book's website at www.sagepub.co.uk/cleggstrategy

● Many of these departments were *either* strongly quantitative *or* qualitative in orientation.
● The dominant orthodoxy in the field globally was quantitative methods.
● The US schools were so strongly quantitative as to admit of almost no alternative approaches.

Our book does not institutionalize itself on what they determined to be the dominant US models.

Lineages of strategy

For some people strategy has a long lineage, stretching back to ancient Chinese or Greek philosophy. Sun Tzu, Heraclitus and Pericles are routinely touted as founding fathers of strategy. Certainly, they are worth reviewing and are frequently on the curriculum in strategy subjects, especially in terms of military training. Others point to figures such as Hobbes, Machiavelli or Clausewitz as foundational strategists. In our estimation to draw a teleological line from the ancient Greeks to modern strategists is a stretch too far; they have been rediscovered, as it were. Hobbes, Machiavelli and Clausewitz are another matter, however, as they have long been significant figures in the field of strategy more generally from the time of their compositions to the present day. That cannot be said for the more ancient figures whose contributions have been retrospectively reconstituted as canonical.

Machiavelli, the Florentine diplomat and author who lived from 1469 to 1527, is often credited with being one of the founding fathers of strategy. Machiavelli's book *The Prince* (written around 1513) describes the forms and practices of governing a state. The fascination of *The Prince* resides in the fact that Machiavelli did not describe how government should work (as many authors before him did) but how it actually worked. He had little time for noble and normative theories and focused instead on how strategy should be done.

Machiavelli wrote the book in times of great political turmoil, when Italy was divided into many city states that either were conquered or were conquering one another, with shifting support (and success) from the German, Spanish and French kings, as well as from the Vatican. Being involved in negotiations between senior state officials, Machiavelli was less interested in the ceremony of governing than in the reality of politics. As he puts it, 'the main foundation of every state … are good laws and good arms; and because you cannot have good laws without good arms, and where there are good arms, good laws inevitably follow, I shall not discuss laws but give my attention to arms' (1961: 77). Implicitly Machiavelli criticizes theories on governance that are based on contracts, laws and notions of virtue. For him, it is the power to be able to implement a law that makes the law in the first place: policy follows power.

Machiavelli developed a deep critique of many of the established 'statecraft' texts such as those by the ancient philosophers Cicero and Seneca. Both of these writers were hugely influential and espoused that a leader should rule virtuously. Their influence was found in the advice manuals produced by some of Machiavelli's contemporaries who again emphasized virtuous and civilized behaviour. Machiavelli pointed to a series of paradoxes around virtue. For instance, he stated clearly the difficulties of a ruler being generous:

> There is nothing that is so self-consuming as generosity: the more you practise it, the less you will be able to continue to practise it. You will either become poor and despised or your efforts to avoid poverty will make you rapacious and hated; and being generous will lead to both. (Machiavelli, 1961: 57)

Machiavelli developed a practical manual of strategic and tactical advice that allowed leaders to govern their states effectively. He wrote that sensing troubles is the key to successful strategy: 'as the doctors say of a wasting disease, to start with it is easy to cure but difficult to diagnose; after a time … it becomes easy to diagnose but difficult to cure' (1961: 39). Hence, one has to take counter measures as soon as troubles are visible on the horizon. Machiavelli used the Romans as an example: they never avoided war 'because they knew that there is no avoiding of war; it can only be postponed to the advantage of others' (1961: 40). For Machiavelli power, conflict and war are at the centre of strategy.

Machiavelli portrayed Cesare Borgia, son of the Pope and feared prince of his times, as an example of extraordinary strategic foresight. Cesare was extremely successful in acquiring resources for and enlarging his state through wars. His major ally was his father, Pope Alexander VI. To demonstrate the strategic thinking of Cesare, Machiavelli explained how he guarded against the possibility of a hostile successor to the papacy that would not support him. First, he destroyed all the families of the rulers he had despoiled so the new Pope could not develop alliances with them against him; second, he made friends with all the patricians in Rome; third, he controlled the College of Cardinals as far as he could (because it controlled the Pope); finally, he acquired enough power to withstand a direct attack. Machiavelli praised Cesare as a strategic mind who focused on exactly those things that allowed him to enlarge and strengthen his empire.

From an ethical perspective we might not agree with the idea of destroying lives and whole families as a strategic move to secure power. Even though he was no sentimentalist, Machiavelli realized that what strategy dictated prudence might counsel against; yet, *realpolitik* does not allow for too much pondering. He believed that cruelty could be used well or badly: best deployed if it was employed fast, used once and for all, and one's safety depended on it being used well (1961: 65). In a similar vein he argued that it was far better to be feared than loved: 'The bond of love is one which men, wretched creatures that they are, break when it is to their advantage to do so; but fear is strengthened by a dread of punishment which is always effective' (1961: 97). A last example of the pragmatic stance that Machiavelli took towards strategy was his perspective on how a leader should honour their word. He acknowledged that it was praiseworthy to honour one's word; he continued, 'nonetheless contemporary experience shows that princes who have achieved great things have been those who have given their word lightly, who have known how to trick men with their cunning, and who, in the end, have overcome those abiding by honest principles' (1961: 99). Therefore he concluded that a ruler 'cannot, and must not, honour his word when it places him at a disadvantage and when the reasons for which he made his promise no longer exists' (1961: 100). Think of modern politicians – how true is Machiavelli's description!

Machiavelli knew how important it was to display good qualities and hide others. For Machiavelli, a ruler must not let good qualities hinder a successful rule. In fact, ethicality could be harmful. A prince should *appear* to have good qualities, however: 'men in general judge by their eyes rather than by their hands; because everyone is in a position to watch, few are in a position to come in close touch with you. Everyone sees what you appear to be, few experience what you really are' (1961: 101). Hence the representation of what a ruler is doing (in modern terms, press coverage, strategic plans, annual reports, mission statements, spin doctoring, etc.) is more important than the reality. Rhetoric creates reality; appearance is more important than action.

For Machiavelli, power games were the reality of leadership; hence, idle philosophizing about how we ought to act would be in vain. In Jeffrey Abramson's (2009) interpretation, Machiavelli's narrative poses the all-important dilemma of 'dirty hands'. Abramson, a professor of government and law at the University of Texas at Austin, argues that Machiavelli's prince, if he wants to maintain power, needs to learn how to do good *and* how to do evil – and make a decision about which action, regardless of its moral consequences, will enhance his position. In other words, sometimes leaders have to accommodate a little evil in order to do some good. Think of politicians who invade countries, accepting the civilian casualties, using as their rationale the necessity of removing a dictator in order to bring about a 'regime change'. Or think about the CEO who sacks employees in the name of a brighter future for the ones who are remaining with the firm. Both cases are examples of the 'dirty hand' problematic: in order to achieve what is promulgated and rationalized as a higher good, some ethically questionable activities in the here-and-now are legitimized and authorized. Machiavelli's answer to the dilemma was clear: to remain powerful was the highest priority; doing good or doing evil had to be determined by that overarching objective.

QUESTION TIME?

Can you recall examples of the 'dirty hand' problematic from stories you have come across in the media? Why was the situation a 'dirty hand' dilemma? Which 'evil' had to be accepted for what 'good'? What actions would you have taken? Why?

If Machiavelli affords us one early instance of a realist and non-normative approach to thinking strategically, Hobbes' *Leviathan* is one of the other great works of modern political thought. Published in 1651, just at the end of the English Civil War, Hobbes posed a specifically normative question: how might one envisage a society in which people could live together in peace and harmony? Hobbes imagined the biblical monster of the Leviathan as a sovereign who would rule the country with absolute power. Left to their own devices, in the state of nature men would frequently fight with each other and no one could enjoy the fruit of their labour as they could never be safe from someone coming and stealing what was theirs. *Homo homini lupus*: the man is a wolf to his fellow man. Hobbes had an idea about how to end the brute state of nature and ensure a more peaceful existence. In fact, his idea was so successful that it influenced almost all future political thinkers profoundly. Hobbes' answer was to imagine that people in a society would sign a contract that handed their power over to an artificial being (the Leviathan) who would from then on have a monopoly over power, including physical violence. The Leviathan would ensure that everyone would respect each other's natural rights and property.

The Leviathan was a marvellous invention indeed: as Abramson has argued (2009: 173–5), it moved the realm of politics from an organic to a mechanical metaphor. If the state was imagined as a biological body, arms and limbs and a head emerged as quasi-natural properties. The Leviathan was a monster, though, and those regularities it created were produced by design, not by nature. Hence, the state became an object of human imagination and its functioning a discipline in the canon of the humanities and social sciences. Importantly, this freed the study of the state from religion and notions of the divine right of kings or God's will. Equally important, Abramson points out that the need for a great man that was so poignant in Machiavelli's *The Prince* disappears in the Leviathan. In fact, the Leviathan is a disembodied system of governance – not a charismatic prince. With his Leviathan, Hobbes delivered the first systematic account of how systems of interacting contracts could, in theory, produce a society of people in equilibrium.

Finally in this section we will briefly consider Clausewitz, whose (1976) work *On War* was a major contribution to military strategy. It is in this book that he outlined his famous proposition that 'war is merely the continuation of policy by other means'. What was essential, he argued, was to understand that before staring or entering into any field of combat one should have a very clear sense of what one was getting into before the inevitable 'fog' of war clouded one's actions with a lack of clarity. The clash of arms and engaging in decisive conflict is one form of war but it is not the only one: strategic skirmishes can be as important as major set pieces, as can psychological warfare (Paret, 1992: 114). Clausewitz argued that we should never underestimate the role of the passions in strategy. None of these, he maintained, was as powerful as the longing for honour and renown: 'It is primarily this spirit of endeavor on the part of all commanders at all levels, this inventiveness, energy, and competitive enthusiasm, which vitalizes an army and makes it victorious' (1976: 105). Strategy, we can conclude, is not a completely rational process – passions and emotions are central to its accomplishment and our engagement in it (Gardner, 2009: 127).

Strategy as a paradigm

Strategy, in the sense in which business schools usually teach it, is a much more modern concern than a possible genealogy that includes a lineage from earlier political theorists such as Machiavelli, Hobbes and Clausewitz might suggest. Much of what counts as modern strategic knowledge has its origins in the large US corporations of the period following the Second World War. Much of what these corporations practised had been finessed by the US military in the Second World War, especially in the detailed and impressive planning that went into organizing the Normandy landings. The challenges and insights gleaned from such military organizations provided a wellspring of knowledge that formed modern strategic management. As organizations became more concerned with issues of strategy – or corporate planning as it was known – these created jobs and, in turn, a demand for strategy courses. Alternatively, one could flip this argument on its head and posit that it was actually the research and courses into strategy that created it as a function in organizations.

In disciplinary terms, the first canonical texts of strategic management come from the 1960s and 1970s, drawing mostly on economics. It was in this era, at the height of the 'organization man' and of modern organizations founded on planning and hierarchy, that strategy established itself as a discipline with its own highly regarded specialized journal, called the *Strategic Management Journal*. The discipline is now well established; it runs its own division at major conferences such as the Academy of Management in the United States and at the European Group of Organization Studies, and has its own yearly meeting organized by the Strategic Management Society. Strategic Management is a pivotal ingredient of business education (that is why you are reading this book!) and many professors in business schools would define themselves as strategy scholars.

A huge textbook enterprise now supports the discipline of strategy. Textbooks have a particular role to play in the philosophy of science – they define the 'normal science' constituting a paradigm. Thomas Kuhn (1962), the famous historian of science, defined a 'normal science' in terms of what he called a 'paradigm' – where there was relatively unanimous agreement on the central questions in a field conveyed in textbooks. Looking at the agreement and non-agreement among strategy authors served as a point of departure for Nag, Hambrick and Chen (2007), who speculated that strategy scholars might share more implicit than explicit definitions of their field. It is precisely the implicit assumptions characterizing a field that have been seen as paradigmatic by historians of science such as Kuhn (1962) although these strategy researchers studied journal articles rather than textbook knowledge. Let us consider the evidence for an implicit definition of the field constituting a paradigm: a set of normalized assumptions which frame enquiry in that field.

In order to gather evidence for their hypothesis that there was a dominant strategy paradigm, Nag et al. (2007) picked 447 journal articles from three major US journals that were published over a time span of 20 years. The three journals that were mined for articles included the *Academy of Management Review*, *Academy of Management Journal* and *Administrative Science Quarterly* (note the US-centric choice of journals – is strategy only validated in the United States?). Then Nag and his colleagues emailed 585 authors who had presented at the strategy division (more accurately, the Business Policy and Strategy Division) of the meetings of the Academy of Management. They asked their respondents to rate whether an article (presented with titles and abstracts, but no authors) was:

1 *Clearly* a strategic management article.
2 *Probably* a strategic management article.
3 *Probably not* a strategic management article.
4 *Definitely not* a strategic management article.

Surprisingly, the respondents displayed a high level of agreement with regard to what they perceived to be strategic management. Nag et al. then studied the abstracts of articles labelled strategic. Doing so, they arrived at a paradigmatic definition of strategy.

Strategy addresses major initiatives, either intended or emergent, which involve managers using resources to enhance firm performance in competitive environments, on behalf of owners.

More recently, Furrer, Thomas and Goussevskaia (2008) conducted a painstakingly detailed empirical study of the strategic management field. They analysed all the papers that had been published in the *Academy of Management Review*, *Academy of Management Journal*, *Administrative Science Quarterly* and the *Strategic Management Journal* between 1980 and 2005. They chose these four US journals because they are frequently referred to as the most influential journals in the strategy field. (Of course, once again, one has to note the absence of non-US journals. On this reckoning strategy is primarily a North American phenomenon. With their exclusive choice of journals, Furrer et al. contributed to suggestions of this bias.)

In Furrer et al's study, 2125 articles were identified that engaged with strategy. Unsurprisingly, 65 per cent of the articles were published in the *Strategic Management Journal*. Furrer and his colleagues coded the articles by identifying 26 keywords. One article could contribute to more than one keyword, so some papers counted twice. Here are their findings:

1 The most frequent keyword that was used to describe strategy research from 1980 until 2005 was *performance* (777 papers). Performance included subtopics such as wealth creation, profitability, risk and return, productivity and others. In short, strategists were occupied with how well a company did.

2 The second most frequently used keyword was *environmental modelling* (534 papers), which included a vast array of topics dealing with the interaction between the firm and its environment.

3 The third most frequently used keyword was *capabilities*, with 518 mentions. Capabilities focused on the resources inside a firm, and how they were deployed strategically.

4 Finally, the fourth was the term *organization* (492 papers), which included issues around implementation, change, learning and structure.

While performance was clearly the most important concept for strategy researchers (with a 36.6 per cent market share), the concepts of environment, capabilities and organization came in close to each other in terms of their importance (25.1, 24.4, and 23.2 per cent respectively).

During the 26-year period some interesting trends developed. Performance was the constant top concern while interest in the environment (this is interest in what strategists call the environment – an economic term referring to that which is outside the firm, not the natural environment conceived in terms of business's strategic effects on carbon footprint, climate change and so on) reduced compared with an increased concern with capabilities. Other topics closely aligned with capabilities, such as innovation, also increased in frequency of occurrence: while only 4.9 per cent of strategy researchers focused on innovation between 1980 and 1985, 22.9 per cent researched its relation with strategy between 2001 and 2005.

Having considered the implicit definition that might constitute the strategy paradigm, let us now consider some of the reasons why the paradigmatic appearance may be somewhat misleading, an effect of the artefacts considered, rather than being based on a fair sample and correct representation of the field. There are several problems with thinking that the characterization of this implicit field is equivalent to a paradigm:

- It is an effect of a particular kind of exercise: sampling a restricted range of US journals. What is odd about this from a paradigmatic perspective is that Kuhn (1962) was quite clear that a paradigm is constructed not so much through the journals as via textbook knowledge. By only focusing on journals, Furrer et al. (2008) missed the influence of books on the field. This led to the rather ironic result that Michael Porter, many people's idea of *the* strategy guru, whose packaging of knowledge is enormously influential, did not appear in the list of most influential strategists. The oddity becomes apparent when one considers that an almost parallel analysis of the development of strategic management from 1980 until 2000 by Ramos-Rodríguez and Ruíz-Navarro (2004) demonstrates that 18 of the 20 most cited works in the *Strategic Management Journal* are books. In their hit list, Michael Porter is by far the most influential strategy writer but, as someone primarily influential through writing books, he does not appear in Furrer et al.'s analysis.

- The paradigmatic appearance is also partly an effect of only looking at what gets published largely by North Americans in a small range of North American journals. Obviously, given the global dominance of English-language research by the United States, the skewed statistical sampling is not surprising. But it is skewed. It is in no way a representative sample.

- When the sample is made somewhat more representative by including European perspectives that are more recent in origin, the paradigmatic representation changes. While the largely US-centric analyses of strategy assume a coherent paradigmatic identity to the field, other, European, researchers argue that strategy represents a more fragmented picture. For instance, David Seidl (2007) suggests that strategy cannot easily be conceptualized as a unified field. It is far too diverse and has splintered into a multitude of relatively autonomous discourses in the European literature. Especially, many of these are much closer to fields such as organization studies and draw more from sociology than they do from industrial organization economics. Some of these strategic discourses have family resemblances to each other – such as those sampled in the United States – while others seem hardly related to these representations at all.

● There are evident points at which the tensions in the field are concentrated. Mahoney and McGahan (2007), writing in the same year as Seidl, see a need for future work that addresses:

(a) A focus on creative approaches that not only concentrates on markets but is also balanced by a stress on organizations. There needs to be recognition of creativity and innovation in the field. We agree entirely!

(b) Teaching assignments that should be integrated with research assignments to increase their complementarities – something we try to do throughout this book.

In part contestation about paradigmatic status arises because strategy occupies different sites, with site-specific discourses: strategy research but also consulting practice and management theories. The research arena thrives on uncertainty and contestation, testing the boundaries of what we think we know as a community of scientists, reflected in journals such as *Strategic Organization* and *Organization Studies*, as well as *Strategic Management Journal* and *Long Range Planning*. When academics consult, or when strategy is developed by consulting practices, for commercial reasons the tendency is towards the elimination of uncertainty and the production of coherent paradigmatic approaches bundled up as packaged products. While each of these different forms of representation may share terms, it should not be assumed that they share meanings; what often occurs is that some concepts become well used in one field of practice and are translated into another. Rarely is the translation perfect; with the shift from one site to another relevancies change, emphases shift and the meaning of strategies' significations takes on a local colour.

We should be careful in interpreting claims, however apparently well grounded empirically, that imply something akin to a paradigmatic consensus. As we have explained, the effect is in large part a result of the methods used to construct the field, the sampling decisions made and the exclusions that these decisions imply. There is no doubt that, given the exercises conducted, a particular representation of the field can easily be constructed as largely quantitative, economics oriented and concerned with a restricted range of issues.

In a further exercise, Stephen Cummings and Urs Daellenbach (2009) analysed all of the 2366 articles published by the end of 2006 in the journal *Long Range Planning* (*LRP*). This is particularly significant as *LRP* is by far the longest running academic journal devoted to strategy, with its first issue being published in 1968. They started off with a quote by Benjamin Franklin, 'At twenty years of age, the will reigns; at thirty, the wit; and at forty, the judgment'. Applied to strategy, Cummings and Daellenbach argued that Porter's Five Forces Model or the BCG matrix were creatures of the will. They also argued that we had entered the period of wit, marked by the fact that the 'fields of strategy and organization studies have spilled over into one another, and the focus on the noun strategy has shifted toward an interest in the verb strategizing' (2009: 234). The '"wit" in strategy analysis that we have enjoyed over the past years has also a downside: as the "wit" has gradually obscured the focus prevalent at the outset – there are now so many varied views of strategy it has become hard to be sure of what we mean when we use the term' (2009: 235). Hence, Cummings and Daellenbach suggested a new orientation towards the fourth decade of strategizing – a focus on judgement.

Before we summarize their outlook for the future it is interesting to look at the findings of their survey of past *LRP* articles. They found six reoccurring themes that represent the baseline for much of strategy research over the past 40 years:

YOU CAN DOWNLOAD...

David Seidl's (2007) General Strategy Concepts and the Ecology of Strategy Discourses: A Systemic-Discursive Perspective, *Organization Studies*, 28(2): 197–218, and Joseph T. Mahoney and Anita M. McGahan's (2007) The Field of Strategic Management within the Evolving Science of Strategic Organization, *Strategic Organization*, 5(2): 79–99, from the book's website at www.sagepub. co.uk/cleggstrategy

It is worth reading the articles by Seidl and Mahoney and McGahan as a pair.

1 First, the notion of 'corporate' has been a key aspect – signifying strategy's interest in the for-profit sector, especially large firms.

2 A second keyword was 'organization' which grew rapidly from 2000 onwards. In line with other research, we can speculate that an interest in the inner workings of firms has started to occupy strategy researchers.

3 Mergers and 'acquisitions, divestments and joint ventures' have been high on the strategist agenda.

4 Not surprisingly, 'technology' has enjoyed a prominent place in strategy research – but surprisingly it has not increased in importance over 40 years.

5 There has been a steadily growing concern with 'change', as identified by Cummings and Daellenbach – as one of strategy's master concepts.

6 Recently, notions of 'creativity and innovation' have enjoyed increased attention from strategy scholars, reflecting some of the challenges for management of the knowledge economy.

Interestingly, notions of process and practice are missing from their analysis. These two concepts become prominent only after Cummings and Daellenbach analysed the abstracts for *LRP* publications. In fact, this more detailed analysis showed 'practice/process' as the fastest growing and most important concern. They conclude that:

> Combining our key word data from *LRP* titles and abstracts enables us to interpret strategic management's most constant (and so perhaps its fundamental) themes, as *processes* and *practices* relating to the *corporate* whole, the *organizing* of resources and how the corporation responds to or manages *change*. Thinking more broadly, one could add to this set responses to or *decisions* about *technology* and other related *environmental* issues, and a recognition of the importance of *creative* or *innovative* developments. (2009: 239)

This provides a good proxy for a definition of strategy. Cummings and Daellenbach identify five emerging trends for the next decade of strategic management:

1 Strategic management will become more comfortable with eclectic approaches built on a smaller number of fundamental elements.

2 Strategists are becoming more politically astute in their practice.

3 Strategists are becoming more aesthetically aware.

4 There is increasing recognition that strategy is influenced equally by conceptions of the past and of the future, and strategic management's archive should not be dismissed as limited, simplistic and outmoded.

5 Prescriptive tools and models will become less important as scholars increasingly appreciate the uniqueness of organizations. Since a 'focus on particular cultures, practices and processes highlights ... the uniqueness of organizations (and therefore of their strategies), we are less likely to believe in the power of general prescriptions, and be more interested in rich case studies' (2009: 254).

Cummings and Daellenbach suggest that there will be a diminishing use of tools and models, which will be offset by a rise in frameworks and case studies. Interpreting Cummings and Daellenbach, we can argue that strategy is evolving from a managerial–economistic perspective towards an empirically informed social science – a shift our book contributes to.

Interpreting strategy

We should be aware that there are no 'innocent' ways of looking at the world intellectually. All the concepts we use in intellectual life are sustained by the ways in which they are used, the language games in which they figure. Their role in these language games is to focus attention – much as a microscope might. It enables us to see a small field of vision clearly but it excludes everything outside that which is focused on. All concepts are 'lenses' representing certain worldviews and enabling or impeding those who use them to see only certain things in certain ways while at the same time not seeing other things. Moreover, all concepts are built on assumptions: it could not be otherwise, so this is as true for what we will write as it is for those we write about.

We are quite explicit about what we wish to bring into strategy – a concern with power and politics, and society and organization in a global world – but how explicit are those in the implicit paradigm of strategy? We would argue that what this implicit paradigm does is to present a view of strategy whose main value is its role in producing coherent accounts of action for elites in business, organizations and society.

There is an argument in sociology known as the dominant ideology thesis (Abercrombie, Hill and Turner, 1980), which suggests that where we find patterns of values shared by elites, characterized by underlying 'ultimate values' that are rarely if ever questioned, which help to constitute a sense of common culture for the elites, then these patterns form a dominant ideology that is central to the social reproduction of accepted truths in society. Elites are able to parlay these 'truths' through their economic control of the major means for the dissemination of opinion. Within organizations, where many formal channels of communication are oriented towards the dissemination of strategic visions and mission, and the concrete strategies that these legitimate, a great deal of effort goes into framing official strategies. These are not always effective, of course: if they were they would never occasion dissent or resistance and, as we will see on many occasions in the book, strategies are rarely unproblematic in their reception by stakeholders such as customers, communities and employees.

Dominant ideologies are not necessarily *wrong* or *incorrect* representations of reality. Indeed, where elites are very successful in forming a community view, which they will use to organize themselves, they can constitute and organize reality so that, in many ways, it does in fact appear to correspond to the dominant view. We think this is how strategy works. It not only represents and organizes elite views of the world, it also shapes the world – it has world-making powers. We live in a world constructed and shaped by strategies. The organizations and businesses we work in, the shops we buy our material wants from, the universities and colleges in which we are educated, the polities that frame our roles as citizens and subjects – these all have strategies that shape the ways in which we are able to interact.

Strategies frame the reality that organizations operate in: the world that they attend to is shaped by those phenomena that not only enter into the constitution of their models but that, even more, do not enter into the construction of such models. For instance, there is a distinct absence of the state and regulation from Porter's view of the world (Carter, Clegg and Kornberger, 2008). Minimizing the role of the state is a central plank of liberal political orthodoxy. That Porter (in Porter, Takeuchi and Sakakibara, 2002, especially) sees no role for the state in his view of the world other than as a supporter of failing enterprise is, perhaps, less an accurate representation of reality and more an accurate representation of a liberal political ideology. When Porter and colleagues investigate strategy in Japan they are unable to represent the reality of business–government relations in that country as these are mediated through institutions such as *amakudari* (see Lam, 2009), the Japanese traditional practice of placing retired bureaucrats in private sectors. The term represents both a specific practice and the name given to those people who fill a specific role, such as ex-bureaucrats, who play an important role in industry development. Through such practices the elites in business and government tacitly and implicitly coordinate strategies and worldviews. In consequence, Porter et al's (2002) understanding of Japan is severely constrained.

ELEMENTS IN THE DOMINANT STRATEGY PARADIGM

Comprehensive and critical analysis is essential to well-informed debate. Debate that stays within well-worn tracks may offer a degree of reassurance to those who dominate those debates as well as those who are struggling to master and enter into them or to use the practices that they promote for practical purposes. However, such intellectual security has a way of being shattered by events in the real world. That this is the case is the thesis that our book drives towards as we consider the implications of a world of collaborating rather than merely competing organizations, the global financial crisis, and the reality of plural and multiple global flows in the era of globalization for the analysis of strategy. We believe that the centre that has been established in strategy cannot hold in these changed times (Yeats, 1921).

There are major critiques of managerialism in the social sciences generally, which are discussed in Parker (2002), but whose import for strategic management also deserves to be elaborated. Taking a leaf out of the books written by critics of managerialism, we may note that management in the contemporary age has become virtually synonymous with managerialism and it is this, in large part, which informs contemporary approaches to strategy. What is legitimated are top-down control systems oriented towards performance as the means of achieving the overarching aim of whatever goals have been specified by the top management team. The stress is on practices that are held to be efficient and effective, using rhetorical devices and the environmental modelling associated with orientations to financial and market performance, stakeholders and customer service. Efficiency and effectiveness serve as justifications for whatever human, organizational and environmental consequences ensue. Such an orientation focuses on performance, modelling, capabilities and organization in a definition that provides the field with an apparent degree of coherence and identity.

How did this consensus emerge? We will trace some key figures and moments in the coalescence of strategy as a field in what follows. Then we will address what is wrong with this picture: what does it omit that is at the cutting edge of current concerns?

Alfred Chandler: strategy drives structure

Early among those ideas that became a dominant part of strategy thinking, forming strong foundations, were the ideas that strategy drives structure and that strategy is a matter of rational planning. For most practitioners of strategy who came to the field via organization theory, economic or business history, or sociology, the key founding figure would be Alfred DuPont Chandler (yes – he is related to the DuPonts of corporate fame!). Chandler's (1962) story is quite simple. Changes in the environment create a need for new strategies. As new strategies develop, they require a new organizational structure to house them. Strategy, driven by changes in the environment, should drive the organization. Thus, Chandler built on the proposition that strategy drives structure and focused attention on the strategic plan driving, dominating and determining organizational structure.

Chandler studied nineteenth-century preindustrial, small-scale, family-owned and rudimentarily managed enterprises in the United States. He investigated their transformation into large-scale, impersonally owned and bureaucratically managed multidivisional structures by the early twentieth century. How did this happen?

The end of the nineteenth century saw the emergence of a smaller number of dominant firms that grew by incorporating suppliers, marketing outlets and so on. What had been distinct businesses were reconstituted under more centralized organizational control (Edwards, 1979: 18). Organizations grew as a strategic response to the failure of markets in those situations where contracts tended to be longer rather than shorter term; where the environment was more rather than less certain, and where the barriers to entry for new agents were high. Implicitly, these barriers were frequently organizational in that they concerned the capacity to hire labour, raise credit and secure supplies. Hence, modern organizational forms were a necessary strategic adjustment to market conditions.

The first significant change occurred as a result of the conquest of US continental space by the railways. To manage and control systems that were nationwide railway companies developed military models of bureaucracy and a modern 'multiunit' corporate form. The railways adopted strict rules of time tabling, uniforms for their staff and many other elements of a military model, especially a linear, hierarchical bureaucracy based on rank, divisions of labour and expertise.

Once railways had connected the whole country, local and regional markets became integrated into an emerging national market. The possibilities of a mass market could now be entertained. The railways made the national market possible and revolutionized logistics because firms could now source and sell beyond local markets. The railways also created opportunities for property speculation to occur around railheads, thus creating new, more concentrated, urban markets. The growth of Chicago as the abattoir of the mid-west to which pigs and cattle were shipped is a case in point; many types of secondary industries, such as canneries, food processing and glue factories, sprang up around the stockyards and slaughterhouses.

By the end of the nineteenth century and throughout the early years of the twentieth century businesses were becoming more national. They found that it was more efficient to incorporate internally the purchase of raw materials, debt financing, marketing and distribution that had previously been entrusted to regionally specialized commission agents. Administrative coordination began to replace market exchanges as the major mechanism of control because it was technically more efficient and allowed for a greater volume of business. Productivity and profits were higher and costs were lower where the fragmentation of markets was replaced with a rudimentary bureaucratization of organizations. The new organizational structures better fitted the emergent strategies; hence, structure should follow strategy.

Igor Ansoff: rational planning

A great many strategy teachers emerged from the antecedent fields of long-range planning and business policy, constructed in a systems perspective, in which the name of Igor Ansoff was magisterial. Ansoff made his important contribution to understanding strategy as a planning process in his book, *Corporate Strategy* (1965). He identified three different levels of action:

- *Operational*: the direct production processes.
- *Administrative*: a maximization of the efficiency of the direct production processes.
- *Strategic*: a concern with an organization's relation to its environment.

Ansoff's influence is echoed in management thinking that understands those at the top as the strategic thinkers of the organization. From this perspective their task is to define the big picture and to steer the organization. Top management has a role denied to lower levels of the hierarchy, since the latter lack data and strategic foresight; their role is to be the instrument that implements strategy.

While Ansoff and Chandler made strategy seem a theory-driven and elite exercise, other, more populist thinkers developed rational – or rationalized – tools and practices, showing that it was not just academics who were getting into strategy. For instance, a consultant, Albert Humphrey, devised a new form of analysis in the 1960s. This approach analysed organizations in terms of strengths, weaknesses, opportunities and threats (SWOT). The first two concepts focused on an organization's internal condition and the latter two analysed its environment. The core strategic assumption concerns the identification of opportunities that an organization can exploit better than its competitors. From this point of view, strategic management audits the environment carefully for opportunities and threats and looks internally for strengths and weaknesses. Once the strengths and weaknesses have been elaborated and the opportunities and threats have been identified, then appropriate strategies can be developed. Due to its simplicity and straightforwardness, this approach became widely recognized in the field and is still in frequent use today (Learned et al., 1969).

In his day, Ansoff was a major strategy thinker. But his day is past. Many economists would hardly acknowledge him as a founding father. Instead, they would look to a founding mother, Edith Penrose, while for many people who teach strategy, it would be hard to miss the work of Michael Porter.

Edith Penrose: the theory of the firm and strategy

For economists working in the strategy field, one of the most significant foundations is provided by the work of Penrose (1959; 2009) in *The Theory of the Growth of the Firm*. She saw the firm as a collection of productive resources, including people. These resources are administratively coordinated and controlled through managerially authoritative communication. Penrose established the firm as an object of specific economic analysis that was separate from the market.

Building on Penrose's (1959; 2009) resource-based perspective of the firm, Wernerfelt (1984) suggested that strategy should be understood in terms of the management of internal resources. He thought of the firm as a bundle of resources that represented strengths and weaknesses. These internal resources, and their configuration, would determine firm performance. The strategist's job was to manage these resources, develop them and ensure that the firm had the capabilities to compete. This view focuses on the internal management of the organization. The focus is on the firm and the dynamics related to how effectively resources are positioned, exploited and renewed.

Penrose's definition of the firm in terms of resources enables strategists to conceptualize the uniqueness of the firm in terms of the specific resources that it commands. Resources, especially managerial capabilities which are not easily copied by competitor organizations, are the real source of innovation and value for a firm, she says. It is resources, not products, which define firms: realizing this enables growth and evolution, diversification and innovation.

Firms always have more resources than they currently know, as a result of changing experiences, personnel and knowledge – which are interrelated. The knowledge a firm includes can also be the basis for a knowledge-based view of the firm (see Chapter 3). Essentially, it is a combination of the management of resources, such as knowledge, and the imagination of the entrepreneur in enacting the environment for the firm, which limits its growth.

A sustained competitive advantage depends on firms developing unique combinations of resources providing competencies that allow for flexible development in an uncertain and changing environment. Penrose provides the foundations for the resource, knowledge and dynamic capabilities perspectives that have increasingly been represented in major journals in the field, such as special issues of the *Strategic Management Journal* (1986), *Organization Science* (1996), *Journal of Management Studies* (2004) and *Organization Studies* (2008).

Michael Porter: industry analysis

Penrose, while influential, is less well known than the most eminent guru of strategy, Michael Porter, who is Bishop William Lawrence Professor of the Harvard Business School, where he leads the Institute for Strategy and Competitiveness.

Porter, whom we will get to know in more detail in the next chapter, argues that firm profitability is dependent on industry structure. For instance, if you are in the airline industry, the recent years have been tough: high oil prices, terrorism, environmental concerns, the entry of cheap airlines and a whole range of other factors have eroded the profits of most airlines. No matter how good you are in the airline industry, you have to try very hard to make a living. You can only do so at the expense of other competitor firms in the environment; you have to exercise *power over* them.

On the other hand, consider the pharmaceutical industry: higher life expectancy, better medical care for more people, and costly R&D mean that there are barriers preventing the entry of new firms and enabling its established players to generate double-digit profits. They are able to do so because they control the market *power to* innovate. Porter argues that the industry structure matters more than the firm's capabilities: crudely put, the environment determines success, not the resources controlled.

If Porter was the most significant strategy thinker after Ansoff, even he is considered a bit old hat these days. Strategy is instead likely to be seen as much more a matter of process than of rational models, planning and industry analysis.

STRATEGY STYLES

All of the material we have covered so far suggests that strategy is best considered as something that evolves rationally. Indeed, this is a dominant view, one that has given rise to an evolutionary perspective on strategy. But counterposed to this, there is also a revolutionary perspective on strategy.

We can differentiate two widely contrasting and popular styles in strategic management research. On the one hand there are those researchers who are convinced that strategy works best as a revolutionary force that radically changes the status quo. On the other hand, there is a body of knowledge that understands strategic change as evolutionary development.

Evolution

An evolutionary perspective on strategy argues that cognitive processes influence the unfolding of strategy. Cognition is not a pure and direct representation of the external world. Rather, organizational cognition is influenced by characteristics such as culture and the dominant strategic logics and embedded successful recipes. Changing these dominant strategic logics is a long-term process.

Shrivastava and Schneider (1984) discussed the way managers develop frames of reference or sets of assumptions that determine their view of business and the organization. Frames of reference may be helpful because they focus attention on what is important. But they may create patterns of habitual thought: 'as they grow more rigid, managers often force surprising information into existing schema or ignore it altogether' (Sull, 1999: 45). They form a dominant logic in the organization that is widely shared. A dominant logic may impose cognitive blinkers, which prevent the organization from seeing relevant but peripheral information (Prahalad, 2004). One of the most recent victims of this blinkered mentality is the record industry, which ignored the Internet and left it to others (including Apple's iTunes) to build new business models around the changing distribution channels. As observed by Gonzales (2003: 120):

> The design of the human condition makes it easy for us to conceal the obvious from ourselves, especially under strain and pressure. The (Union Carbide) Bhopal disaster in India, the space shuttle Challenger explosion, the Chernobyl nuclear meltdown, and countless airliner crashes, all happened in part while people were denying the clear warnings before them.

In their analysis of the state of play in strategic management, Gavetti and Levinthal (2004) identify evolutionary economics (Nelson and Winter 1982; 2002) as a new paradigm for strategic management. Before we can explore their hypothesis in more detail we have to define some of the ideas of evolutionary economics.

In 1982, Sidney Nelson and Richard Winter wrote an influential book called *An Evolutionary Theory of Economic Change*. Neither researcher was sold on the strong rational assumptions that traditional economists used to describe markets and firm behaviour. Deviating from the economics mainstream, and inspired by Simon's (1957) concept of bounded rationality, they chose 'routines' as their unit of analysis. Routines became the 'DNA' of their evolutionary model.

Nelson and Winter departed from mainstream economics in at least two ways: first, their core concept of routines did not accommodate the rational assumptions of the *Homo economicus* of the neo-classical paradigm; second, routines are not strictly individualistic activities but are developed and evolved organizationally (see Gavetti and Levinthal, 2004: 1313). For instance, the annual retreat is a routine that has a major impact on a firm's strategy. It is a routine because it has developed over time. Managers simply do strategy retreats because – well, because this is what one does as a manager! Winter puts it clearly:

> As the Alcoholics Anonymous serenity prayer puts it, 'God grant me the serenity to accept the things I cannot change, courage to change the things I can, and wisdom to know the difference.' Substitute for *courage* the words *managerial attention and related resources supporting strategic decision-making* and you have here the beginnings of a paradigm for strategic analysis, its role being to help with the wisdom part. (Winter, 1987: 162; quoted in Gavetti and Levinthal, 2004: 1314)

Focusing on those things a manager can change and those she cannot change (and, as a third perspective, insights into the differences between the two), Gavetti and Levinthal (2004) suggest, provides a potentially unifying framework for studying strategy.

Evolution's key category is survival and surviving the competition for resources, such as talented employees, and surviving as successfully as possible, in terms of performance, is the key element in strategy, from an evolutionary economics perspective. From its inception, strategic thinking has been about survival. Evolution, as ascribed to Charles Darwin, is the contest among and between populations that compete with each other for resources in a shared environment. Bruce D. Henderson, founder of the BCG, argued that '[c]ompetitors that make their living in the same way cannot co-exist – no more in business than in nature. Each must be different enough to have a unique advantage' (1989: 140). Through differentiation and specialization a firm can create and occupy a niche and live successfully in it, says Henderson. Strategy, in his words, 'is a deliberate search for a plan of action that will develop a business's competitive advantage and compound it' (1989: 141). Henderson argues that biologists are better guides to business than economists: after all, 'strategy is the management of natural competition'.

How useful is the comparison between evolution and strategy? Critically, one could argue that evolution occurs not at the individual firm level but at the level of a whole species conceived as an industry; as such, the typewriter industry goes out of the window while PC manufacturers take off; people ditch vinyl LPs and move to CDs and then swap from CDs to MP3 downloads. From the industry perspective, strategy at the organization level can seem akin to fiddling with the chairs on the deck of a sinking *Titanic*, because:

- Evolution is a functional narrative – it explains why those who are still around have been successful, which usually cannot help but be tautological. Evolution in biology assumes some kind of objective struggle for survival that is played out in Mother Nature. Organizations do not live on trees. They are part of political, social and cultural contexts, and these contexts shape them.

- In the bailout of parts of the British and American banking system during the latest global financial crisis, according to evolution they failed and should have died. But politically, especially after the consequences of Lehman Bros's demise became apparent, many world leaders agreed that some institutions were 'too big to fail' – hence they were excluded from evolution. And so are other parts of the economy that are protected by law and regulations.

- Evolutionary ideas also seem to include the idea of a progression towards higher forms of life – an assumption that one might not want to share about all developments in business. Again, the global financial crisis might provide evidence for the rather low instincts that capitalism seems to unleash in human beings.

Revolution

Unusual times require unusual strategies, suggests Gary Hamel (1996), saying that 'strategy is revolution; everything else is tactics'. What matters is being unique, different and revolutionary, overturning the industrial order, being 'industry revolutionaries' (Perhaps it was this enthusiasm for revolution that led Hamel to endorse the Enron approach to business before its dark side became evident?).

There are 10 principles of 'revolutionary' strategy according to Hamel:

1 *Strategic planning may be planning, but it is not strategic.* Planning is a rational process that resembles programming, whereas strategizing is about discovering and playfully exploring the potentials for revolution.

2 *Strategy-making must be subversive.* Strategy must question the taken for granted and the conventions that inform yesterday's business and competitor's actions. Anita Roddick (2005), founder of The Body Shop, was on record as saying that she watched where the cosmetic industry was going and then headed in the opposite direction.

3 *The bottleneck is at the top of the bottle.* Normally, senior managers define strategy. The normal organizational hierarchy is based on experience, but in fast-changing environments, successful past experience can become the obstacle to tomorrow's success. Thus, it has to be supplemented with a hierarchy of imagination, which might be inversely distributed when compared with the formal hierarchy.

4 *Revolutionaries exist in every company.* It is a fallacy to believe that the top management will be pro-change, whereas employees will always resist. Every organization has its revolutionaries who do not sit in the front row – but who have the ability to provide fresh insights. If they do not challenge the company from the inside, they will challenge it from without in the marketplace.

5 *Change is not the problem, engagement is.* Too often change is a word for routine attempts to restructure a business. However, it is more important to engage people, especially revolutionaries, in a discourse about the future and create commitment.

6 *Strategy-making must be democratic.* Instead of being a form of intellectual incest among top managers who have known each other for years and are culturally rather uniform, strategy-making must be flexible. It should include young people, outsiders and people from the margins, as they develop views that are normally unseen and unheard. They do not conform to an organization's orthodoxy and thus can provide truly revolutionary insights.

7 *Anyone can be a strategy activist.* Revolutionaries are never at the top of a hierarchy – they are spread throughout the entire organization. Giving them a voice and providing them with space to speak means transforming their anarchistic potential into activist energy.

8 *Perspective is worth 50 IQ points.* It is not easy to make people smarter, but one can provide new glasses through which the world looks different. A change of perspective leads to shifts in the things that an organization sees, which, implicitly, makes new opportunities visible.

9 *Top down and bottom up are not the alternatives.* It is not either-or but a question of organizing the communication between people who have responsibility and expertise and people who have fantasy and engagement.

10 *You cannot see the end from the beginning.* Open-ended strategy-making processes lead to surprises. The new cannot be judged on the premises of the old because it follows different rules. Moreover, a really open process leads to a future that cannot be predicted as it unfolds because people explore new avenues.

Hamel is not the only revolutionary strategist. Unlikely resonances occur as ideas travel (Czarniawska and Sevón, 2006). The Cultural Revolution, as an idea, may have begun in Beijing and travelled widely through China, but it did not end there. It had resonances in European universities in the 1960s. Surprisingly, it also had resonances in American and other business schools from the 1980s onwards.

The last place one might expect to find enthusiasm for the Cultural Revolution is in management. However, there are many echoes. Contemporary organizations and the lives of many people in them have been drastically changed as a result of the ideas of management consultants such as Tom Peters.

Peters wants to overthrow bureaucracy both substantively and in principle. However, while Mao wanted to overthrow bureaucracy by a Cultural Revolution in the interests of 'the people', seeing bureaucracy as its impediment, Peters wants to overthrow bureaucracy through a Cultural Revolution in the name not of 'the people' but of 'entrepreneurial energies'. Energized team members should replace bureaucracy; these will be people who commit themselves wholly to the goals of the organization, just as, in the Cultural Revolution, the people had to recommit, according to Mao, to the goals of the revolution as he interpreted them. Peters proselytizes constant revolutionary changes in *Re-imagine! Scorecard and Revolution Planner* and treats such a revolutionary approach as a process for sudden intuitive leaps of understanding, or an epiphany, which will unleash captive energies. Of course, it is hard not to note the paradox of a revolution planner: one could argue that a revolution is reserved for those events that defy planning! Nonetheless, in Peters' world, total commitment and identification the organization are required of members just as much as Mao demanded it of 'the people'; the problem of bureaucracy for both is that it engages less than the whole person; it encourages only the role-specific behaviour of functionaries rather than engaging whole energies.

Peters has been a frequent target of criticism in the literature, with Collins' (2007; 2008) contributions being the most encompassing and recent. From this analysis we learn that Peters' texts are dominated by narrative tales of heroic leaders whom we should admire as they battle against obstacles. Over time, the heroes have changed from the corporate bureaucrats of *In Search of Excellence* (Peters and Waterman, 1982) to small start-up entrepreneurs (Collins, 2008: 326), and increasingly to Peters himself – battling against the bureaucrats (Collins, 2008: 327).

In order to give shape to the struggle against bureaucracy, Peters identifies it with a specific reactionary figure and ethos. The figure is Robert McNamara and the ethos is that of the Harvard Business School. Peters is on frequent record as saying that his whole life has been a struggle against the legacy of Robert McNamara, which he saw as having become the essential *de facto* wisdom of the Harvard Business School, setting the pace for large American enterprise in the postwar era: 'Start with Taylorism, add a layer of Druckerism and a dose of McNamaraism, and by the late 1970's you had the great American corporation that was being run by bean counters'.[1] McNamara and Harvard merely represented the tip of an iceberg. Opposing them was not enough. Bureaucracy had to be smashed and new organization forms emerge from its ashes.

A cult of personality is entailed in the Peters' process. Peters is quite explicit about this; for him, the masses are confused and unable to find direction unless they have charismatic leaders able to project their egos in a cult of extraordinary personality. The confusion of the masses is a thesis that requires the antithesis of a great leader to lead them to the sunny uplands of a new synthesis:

> I think the Iacocca thing, the Peters and Waterman thing, the Robbins thing, the [Ken] Blanchard thing, and the Hamel-Porter thing is a very specific reaction of a whole lot of people who are confused by all the shit that's going down. When people are

---

[1]Sourced from http://www.businessballs.com/tompetersinsearchofexcellence.htm, accessed 02/08/2010

confused, they want people on white horses to lead them. Obviously it didn't have to be me and Bob, and Blanchard and [John] Naisbitt and Porter and so on, any more than it had to be Iacocca and Ted Turner. But it had to be. (Peters, quoted by Postrel, 1997)

New revolutionaries such as Peters encourage organization members to smash bureaucracy as a strategy in order to achieve emotional commitment and find authenticity in their membership of a revitalized organization. People following the enthusiasms of the moment, as these are filtered through convictions unleashed by cultural revolutionaries, which they are supposed to enact as empowered and totally committed individuals, begin to look worryingly similar to the inmates of total institutions (see Clegg, Courpasson and Phillips, 2006: Chapter 6). The main difference is that we are dealing with psychic prisons rather than steel bars and high walls. The individual as a 'psychological unity' is posited as someone with minimal friction between their character as a person and the needs of the roles that they fulfil organizationally, allowing the expansion of work and professional concerns into the entirety of their life-world.

Complexity

Traditional management thinking about strategy deals with a world of mechanistic, hence predictable, organization. Revolution would overthrow it; evolution would let it develop. Both perspectives are questionable in view of complexity thinking.

Complexity theory aids the understanding of why strategy is never complete. It is not possible to have access to knowledge in its entirety because the 'entire knowledge' is never stocked anywhere but is an emergent property of interaction, as discussions of the distributed nature of knowledge and the challenges it poses for organizational work indicate (e.g. Orlikowski, 2002).

Kauffman (1995) sees complex systems as living on the edge of chaos, having to choose strategically between preserving structure and responding to surprise. Contrary to the traditional views of strategy, such systems may not tend towards equilibrium. Indeed, they may never pass through the same state more than once (Levy, 1994).

Managers' interpretations of external complex environments may amplify, rather than control, the potential for strategic uncertainty (Starbuck, 1993). Managers may fail to attend to relevant cues or clues and thus be caught out, as would the archetypal reader of a thrilling suspense novel who, on occasions does not process adequately what is cued. A football team with ageing but costly stars has a board that does not cue that the players who attract the crowds' loyalty and support are blocking the opportunities for team renewal in the future. In a complex world of many cues it is often difficult to isolate what is significant and important; indeed, the status of events and stimuli often only becomes clear in retrospect – which is not much use for a prospective strategy!

Complexity produces wicked problems. John C. Camillus published an article in 2008 entitled 'Strategy as a Wicked Problem'. His article was based on the original contribution by two urban planners, Horts Rittel and Melvin Webber, who wrote their 'Dilemmas in a General Theory of Planning' in 1973. Camillus's rereading of the paper paired with his experience as a consultant and researcher showed that many companies saw strategic planning as an exercise in modelling and predicting the future. They crunched through data and enjoyed lengthy planning sessions. PowerPoint presentations charted the path to the future, followed by Excel spreadsheets that translated the opportunities along the way into numbers. Camillus argued that this old-fashioned approach worked as long as we were dealing with simple or trivial problems. In a world of wicked problems, however, strategy needed to change.

So what are 'wicked' problems? A wicked problem has many causes, it is hard to describe, and its solutions are neither right nor wrong, only better or worse. Global warming, terrorism or poverty, for instance, may all be considered as such. These are the characteristics of wicked problems:

1 There is no definitive formulation of wicked problems: they cannot be captured in a neat definition but are messy.

2 Wicked problems have a no stopping rule: the search for a solution never stops.

3 Solutions to wicked problems are not true or false, but better or worse: evaluation is tricky as there is no absolute right or wrong – only more or less workable compromises.

4 There is no immediate or ultimate test of a solution to a wicked problem: the unexpected consequences of solutions make evaluations a tricky task.

5 Every solution to a wicked problem is a 'one-shot operation'; because there is no opportunity to learn by trial and error, every attempt counts significantly.

6 Wicked problems do not have an enumerable (or an exhaustively describable) set of potential solutions, nor is there a well-described set of permissible operations that may be incorporated into the plan.

7 Every wicked problem is essentially unique: this means past experience does not help us to cope with it.

8 Every wicked problem can be considered to be a symptom of another problem: wicked problems are entangled and related to each other, with no single root cause.

9 The existence of a discrepancy representing a wicked problem can be explained in numerous ways. The choice of explanation determines the nature of the problem's resolution.

10 The planner has no right to be wrong: although impossible to solve, planners will be held responsible for the potentially enormous consequences of their actions.

Camillus (2008) argues that wicked problems cannot be solved – only tamed and balanced temporarily. He defines four principles:

1 Stakeholder involvement is crucial. Strategy becomes a forum in which to work out what the challenges might look like, as well as in what order or priority they should be tackled. Making sense of the situation and agreeing on the nature of the problem are paramount. Strategic conversations are a communication platform for these discussions.

2 While the strategic plans for coping with problems will change, the organization's sense of purpose and identity should not. In other words, the question of 'who are we and what is our purpose?' should be clarified before strategic plans are crafted. In this sense, identity precedes strategy.

3 Focus on action. Because wicked problems are complex, we cannot think them through and then act on the results of our reasoning. Rather, we have to experiment, put ideas forward, act on them and then adjust in the light of experience. Trial and error, learning, making experiments, adopting

YOU CAN DOWNLOAD…

Horst Rittel and Melvin Webber's (1973) Dilemmas in a General Theory of Planning, *Policy Sciences*, 4(2): 155–69, at www.uctc.net/mwebber/ Rittel+Webber+Dilemmas+ General_Theory_of_Planning. pdf pilot programmes and creating prototypes seem to be better ways forward than following grand plans.

4 Feedback is not the best way to learn; as the name suggests, it feeds *back* onto something from the past. A 'feed forward' orientation would scan the environment for weak signals. Who would have thought that the rise of the Internet would change the music industry? Feedback tells us that it *did*; feed forward could have told us that it *would*.

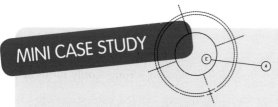

MINI CASE STUDY

Wicked problems at Wal-Mart

In organizations, most issues that are truly strategic show strong elements of wickedness. Camillus (2008) used the example of Wal-Mart to illustrate the case. Wal-Mart, the world's largest organization, deals with many different stakeholders with different values and priorities. More than 2 million employees want good working conditions and a reliable pension system; shareholders are more interested in annual dividends and the stock price; suppliers want to establish long-term relationships and struggle over standards and working practices; consumers are keen to pay as little as possible for as much as possible; many non-governmental organizations monitor Wal-Mart's behaviour, especially its environmental record, while unions abhor its anti-union orientation.

It is easy to see how these different groups have different demands that Wal-Mart can hardly satisfy with one neat strategy. The matter is further complicated by the fact that the cause of some of the problems is extremely complex. Pressure on lowering prices is handed down by Wal-Mart to its suppliers, which might not always adhere to the highest ethical or environmental standards *and* fulfil low-cost criteria. When tackling some of these challenges, Wal-Mart experiences another characteristic of wicked problems: they are moving targets. Let us say Wal-Mart decides to put its employees first and promises fair pay, good health care and a decent pension plan. Shareholders would be up in arms as they would not earn the dividend their money could earn elsewhere. Wal-Mart's stock would lose value. Consumers would also be disappointed, as they would face higher prices. They would argue that Wal-Mart was breaking its promise of 'always low prices'. What if Wal-Mart follows the shareholders' interest instead? Unions, employees, local governments and NGOs will start putting pressure on Wal-Mart. Consumers might call for a boycott to punish Wal-Mart: shares will lose value in consequence.

To make wicked problems more complicated, Camillus (2008) adds that they represent new challenges that have not been experienced before. Wal-Mart cannot simply follow someone else who has mastered the wicked problems it finds so challenging. Rather, the problems, their complexity and their configuration are novel, and might not repeat themselves. Even worse, answers to wicked problems are hard to evaluate. Often, one only develops a sense of right or wrong well after a decision has been made and the strategy is being implemented. Usually, this is too late to change the course of action.

Questions

1 Would it be the right strategy to break with the 40-year-old values of 'always low prices' and acknowledge that sustainability includes not only the financial bottom line but also ethics and environmental issues?

2 Or should Wal-Mart stay true to its formula and expand into other countries using the past successful assumptions and models?

STRATEGY AS PROCESS AND PRACTICE

Several theorists recognized that there were significant problems with overly rationalist models of the strategy process such as those developed by Ansoff or

Porter, who were disinclined to follow either evolutionary or revolutionary roads. Less interested in normatively prescribing what strategies should be, they were more interested in what, empirically, they were constructed as being in the situated actions of strategists at work. Researchers who conducted ethnographic studies of managers and executives as they were developing strategy found the process to be far more *ad hoc* and emergent than rational accounts of it suggested.

Lindblom (1959) and Cohen, March and Olsen (1972) realized that strategy-making was a fragmented process; something that takes place over time, in different venues with different participants, in a series of serial and incremental decisions. It involves a great deal of informal process in which there is much negotiation and certain degrees of randomness as problems become defined in terms of the solutions at hand.

Quinn (1978) saw strategy-making as a process of 'logical incrementalism'. Actions and events move step wise and a conscious strategy slowly emerges and changes in a fluid but controllable process. Mintzberg (1978) held views closely related to those of Quinn. Mintzberg's contribution was to make a distinction between deliberate and emergent strategy. Deliberate strategy may be what the strategy team intentionally design as they integrate data and scan the environment, but emergent strategy originates in the interaction of the organization with its environment. As events assume significance and ideas about them coalesce, emergent strategies tend to converge as ideas and actions from multiple sources integrate into a pattern.

While strategy is a powerful buzzword (e.g. *strategic* HRM, *strategic* leadership, *strategic* change, etc.) the academic field might be less influential in practice. Some critical authors (Knights and Morgan, 1991; Alvesson and Willmott, 1995; Ezzamel and Willmott, 2004; Grandy and Mills, 2004) even suggest that strategy seems to be an empty vessel that managers fill with politically important issues. For instance, Knights and Morgan's (1991) influential study discussed strategy as a powerful device that creates those problems for which it offers itself as a solution. From this perspective what is significant about strategy is its prescriptive bias. Instead of prescribing what strategy should be, we should instead study what it is that strategists actually do when they do strategy. A more analytical and descriptive approach is needed.

In many ways the ideas of authors such as Weick and Mintzberg spawned the strategy as practice approach. The latter is an approach that shares the same scepticism about the rational accounts of strategy and a similar fascination for what actually happens when strategists are engaged in the strategy process. Drawing on the seminal work of Pettigrew (1973; 1992) and Mintzberg (1973; Mintzberg and Waters, 1985) the strategy-as-practice stream of research focuses on strategizing – the active process of making and enacting strategy. It stresses the importance of attending to the structures and contexts through which the processes of enacting strategy – strategizing – are accomplished (Whittington, 1993; Hendry, 2000; Jarzabkowski, 2003; 2004; 2005; Johnson, Melin and Whittington, 2003; Whittington, 2003; Balogun and Johnson, 2004; 2005; Mantere, 2005).

Reacting against the often prescriptive nature of much of the strategy field, this approach seeks to investigate strategy and strategists anthropologically and sociologically. The focus of this perspective is on cultural contexts, discursive habits and the ways in which managers construct networks of action that entwine them together in doing strategy. It seeks to follow the actors, study their texts and capture their discourse, so as to observe how strategy is made up and describe what strategists do. It is so popular that it even has its own dedicated website. There, the following definition of strategy as practice is offered.

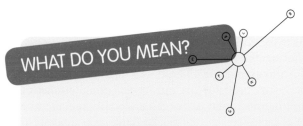

SOURCE: WWW.S-AS-P.ORG/, ACCESSED 9 MARCH 2010.

WHAT DO YOU MEAN?

Strategy as Practice

A network concerned with the everyday processes, practices and activities involved in the making of strategy.

Strategy as Practice is a community of scholars interested in the practice of strategy. As scholars we are interested in a broad spectrum of issues concerned with the making and doing of strategy and strategic change in organizations. We apply a variety of different theoretical approaches, such as practice perspectives on organizations, sensemaking, discourse analysis, and script theory. What we are agreed on is the importance of a focus on the processes and practices constituting the everyday activities of organizational life and relating to strategic outcomes, if we are to move our field forward. We see the linkage through to strategic outcomes as an important component of our research as we ultimately need to be able to link the outcomes of (multiple) strategizing activities, events and behaviours within the firm to more macro organizational, institutional and, possibly, even broader social contexts and outcomes. If we are to theorize about the link between what occurs within organizations and more macro levels of analysis we need to situate organizational activities within the broader context of action. As such, we share with traditional strategy research a concern for firm performance, but we also emphasize the significance of potentially multiple strategizing outcomes and their interactions through time. As a result, we are typically involved in in-depth qualitative research that enables us to examine the inside of strategizing processes, and marry the concern for both content and process, and for both intentional and emergent activities and outcomes. In addition, we acknowledge the role of a broad range of strategists outside of the senior management team in organizations, and the potential impact of others within the field on strategizing activities, such as consultants and business school academics.

Recent years have seen an increasing interest in this strategy as a practice perspective (e.g. Whittington, 1993; 2003; Johnson et al., 2003; Jarzabkowski, 2005) focused on the micro-analysis of strategy. Often the approach taken is discursive, capturing strategy as it is talked into practice, an approach that builds on the seminal article by Knights and Morgan (1991: 252; also see Knights and Morgan 1995; Thomas, 1998; Lilley, 2001; Levy, Alvesson and Willmott, 2003; Vaara, 2002; Grandy and Mills, 2004; Laine and Vaara, 2007; Vaara, Kleymann and Seristö, 2004).

Closely related to the strategy-as-practice views emerging from sensemaking and emergence perspectives has been the development of analyses that view strategy in narrative terms, as telling a story about an organization. Barry and Elmes (1997) examine strategy as a form of narrative. They emphasize the fictive nature of strategic narratives as well as the 'multiple realities' constructed through narration. Other authors have made related analyses. Hardy, Palmer and Phillips (2000) illustrate the strategy process through an analysis of the ways in which those who are strategizing use discursive resources involving circuits of activity, performativity and connectivity. In this way they analyse the micro-processes through which specific strategy statements gain acceptance or not. Eriksson and Lehtimäki (2001) explore strategy documents to demonstrate how strategy rhetoric often reproduces specific and problematic assumptions concerning strategy and the role of specific actors. Samra-Fredericks (2003; 2004a; 2004b) focuses on the rhetorical skills that strategists use to persuade and convince others. Ezzamel and Willmott (2004) show how the reading of strategy statements provides the basis for organizational power relationships. All of these approaches suggest that understanding strategy entails close accounting of the processes of its constitution and deployment.

Laine and Vaara (2007: 33) insist that one cannot understand specific texts and discourses without considering the social context in question, as well as important ritual elements of strategy-making. These can include routinized sensemaking patterns and behaviours used for organizational decision-making as well as explicit traditions and methods that are organizationally specific to a particular strategy processes (e.g. Jarzabkowski, 2005). Making such an analysis enables one to focus on strategy as something that is struggled over by competing groups within the organization as they seek to make their definitions of it dominant. They do so by attempting to fix meaning in ways that reproduce power relations in the organization that makes them more strategic than rivals. The result of these struggles, suggest Laine and Vaara (2007: 36), is often a dynamic relation 'between control (using a specific discourse as a means of control) and resistance (trying to cope with or directly resist specific discourses and their implications, e.g. for subjectivity)'. They refer to these as 'discursive struggles' which deal 'with competing views concerning organizational strategies, but also involve more fundamental questions related to the subjectivity of the actors involved' (2007: 36).

It is evident that the power of a strategy resides not just in what it does, or in what it seeks to do; it also inheres in the ways in which specific strategic discourses constitute a sense of ordering of the organization and its relations, both internally and externally, that have the talisman of corporate legitimacy attached to them. This is one reason why discursive struggles over strategy can be so acute: whoever 'owns' the strategy has considerable legitimacy. It will be their routines, their narratives, their interests that are deeply embedded in whatever the strategy is.

Indeed, we could say that much strategic thinking is designed to make issues and problems routine, to provide narratives linking past and future that serve specific agendas of strategic managerialism in which interests are embedded, and we can expect that the competition to establish these interests will be fierce. Strategy-making is a major arena in which power is played out through discourses and associated practices that produce specific rationalities, stabilize or change particular patterns of relations, both hierarchical and extended networks, and that position certain interests and viewpoints as more or less obligatory passage points within the organization – conduits through which rational action (and actors) have to pass if they are to be considered rational. Simultaneously, managers have to be able to:

- Bring off their actions as being in accord with the strategic objectives of the organization that employs them.
- Do so while maximizing their ability to gain access to organizational resources in order to further their own interests.
- Enhance their power relations and the prestige of their office and its contribution to the strategy-making process.

Managers who can play these politics successfully will go far in the 'turf wars' that characterize complex organizations (Buchanan and Badham, 2008), in which, according to an important US study of corporate acquisitions in the 1960s, 'top managers are actors, corporations are instruments, and top managers use these instruments to pursue their interests in proportion to their capacities' (Palmer and Barber, 2001: 110).

Mintzberg (1990) pointed out that in turbulent environments with high uncertainty the process of defining a strategy is most likely to become a messy and experimental process driven from the bottom up, seeking to capture valuable insights for strategy formulation that reside in the heads of the employees who

The notion of interests is essential to an analysis of strategy. Interests shape how we see the world, how we interpret it, and act in it, the ideas, attitudes and intentions we form towards significant phenomena in the world that link subjects and objectives, present states and future desired ones.

YOU CAN DOWNLOAD...

P. M. Laine and E. Vaara's (2007) Struggling over Subjectivity: A Discursive Analysis of Strategic Development in an Engineering Group, *Human Relations*, 60(1): 29–58, from the book's website at www.sagepub.co.uk/cleggstrategy

implement strategy as much as in the heads of those who think (they think) it. The implementation and the emerging shortcomings and insights can be the basis for tomorrow's strategy. In fact, implementation becomes a part of the strategy formulation process. A stress on implementation as being as important as planning and formulating takes us to a concern with sensemaking.

People make sense and they make it as they go about doing things. Their doings and their sensemaking are inexorably entangled. Overall, one function of strategy as an important discourse is to legitimate certain sorts of managerial actions, particularly planning and prediction, which is a mainstay of strategic concerns. Assumptions of rationality and planning act as a talisman, warding off the unexpected, the surprising and the eventful, through providing routine incantations with which to orient action. Such planning helps organizations and strategists to make sense, or, as it is called in the literature, it enables them to accomplish sensemaking.

Much of what happens in organizations entails a constant process of sensemaking, especially when it comes to strategy. There are environmental cues to be registered, enacted and reacted to; streams of data and information to interpret; politics to untangle and negotiate, and complex bodies of different knowledge to mediate.

Sense is always made in the moment, looking both backwards as well as projecting forwards. In terms of strategy the most significant element of sensemaking is that it should produce a plausible narrative, a story line that key people can buy into. All strategic sense, as we have seen, is influenced by the social context. Sensible meanings tend to be those for which there is social support, consensual validation and shared relevance. If other people think that a particular interpretation is sensible then you are more likely to do so as well. Given that people's sensemaking is patterned by things such as disciplinary formation, gender and experience, sensemaking differs with the identities of those doing the sensemaking. Different identities in organizations, in terms of regional, professional or divisional characteristics, for instance, will be important in forming different patterns of sensemaking.

Sensemaking concerns the elaboration of traces into full-blown stories, typically in ways that selectively shore up an initial hunch. An initial linkage between a particular and a category is elaborated into a more confident diagnosis through successive rounds of selective search for confirming evidence. Strategists will use cognitive maps – their sketches of what is going on and who's who – in making sense, which they have derived from their past experiences; thus they project their pasts onto their futures. Sensemaking involves bracketing, framing, isolating cues, associating, and creating new events and labels as it tries to provide an answer to the key question of what the strategic intent should be (Weick, 1995; 2008).

Weick (2007) defines sensemaking as the ongoing retrospective development of plausible images that rationalize what people are doing.

THE LIMITATIONS OF STRATEGY

Surprise

Nothing unsettles the strategist more than the unexpected because there are no cues available to make sense of unanticipated events. Unsurprisingly, strategists have devoted considerably less energy to events that surprise and are unpredictable. This is understandable because the unpredictable cannot be controlled and managing is often taken as controlling (Mintzberg, 2004). By definition, as

Habermas (1971) identified, what is controllable can be predicted. As a corollary, the unpredictable touches on the inexplicability, ineffability and indecipherability of things not yet known. To be surprised is thus to be taken unawares, without preparation, with no anticipation beforehand.

Managerial issues always involve interpretations of facts, not objective representations of reality (Thomas and McDaniel, 1990). It is probably correct to say that most managers prefer routines to surprises. On the whole, surprise is the very opposite state to that which is most frequently recommended for good management, where, from the earliest days, predictability, control and routine have been stressed (Clegg, Kornberger and Pitsis, 2008). Management strives to be as consequential and controlling as possible. However, in the memorable words of Donald Rumsfeld, when faced with the chaos of a postwar Iraq in 2004, 'stuff happens'. Indeed it does. Less prosaically, 'everything has both intended and unintended consequences. The intended consequences may or may not happen; the unintended consequences always do' (Weick, 2004: 51). Organization can be thought of as dealing with repetition and routine (Weick and Westley, 1996). Westley (1990: 339) defines organization as 'a series of interlocking routines, habituated action patterns that bring the same people together around the same activities in the same time and places'. In the interpretation process, some surprising possibilities may simply be 'normalized' and accommodated to existing schema. They may erupt later and take an organization unawares.

Difference presents a pervasive risk for strategies based on repetition and its registration – or non-registration. When singularity upstages mundane repetition we can refer to it as an event. When they occur, events disrupt the illusion of strategic control. Events are necessarily problematic for plans because they define a potential space for action within which inflections of structural rules and design are not only possible but also likely. As politicians and practitioners of statecraft have long known, events can steer or derail strategies, policies and careers. The irruption of events can act as a 'black hole' that can decentralize the structured flow of daily 'non-events' constituting the routine actions of the organization. Events are a constant source of surprise.

Events are always contextually specific and their content indeterminate. How such situations are interpreted depends on individuals' institutionalized interpretive devices for sensemaking, as these are discursively embedded in the social networks of organizations. By institutionalized interpretive devices we mean commonly shared and understood ways of making sense of events and situations; these are intersubjectively shared as a framework between members of communities of practice that constitute a dense social network of individuals embedded in an institutional field, such as that of investment banking or mortgage broking. Perhaps the most notable event that has proven surprising to strategists in recent times has been the market contagion of September 2008, which disequilibrated many taken-for-granted assumptions guiding the behaviour of the investment community.

Events can rapidly delegitimize strategies and make managers switch interpretive devices, as Gioia (1992) argued in his analysis of the failed interpretive schemes used in detecting problems with the Ford Pinto. The Pinto was a car that when involved in rear-end collisions could explode, because of the position of the petrol tank. Unfortunately the designers did not discover this until it was in use. The strategists decided that to keep the car in production and pay insurance for the accidental damage to people and property was cheaper than withdrawing the model from sale. The tendency of the Pinto to explode was a surprise; once known, it became an accident waiting to happen that, strategically, was calculable in economic (if not ethical) terms.

A surprise may be defined as any event that happens unexpectedly, or any expected event that takes an unexpected shape.

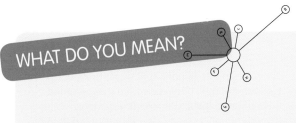

WHAT DO YOU MEAN?

Strategic surprises

Dell's mail order strategy caught the PC industry by surprise. The effectiveness of Domino's delivery strategy was a surprise to Pizza Hut. Consumers' reaction to New Coke was surprising, considering the discrepancy between predictions and actual responses to consumers. The George W. Bush administration was surprised that the citizens of Iraq did not greet an invading army as liberators and proceed in an orderly direction towards a liberal market economy and democracy.

Clearly, while all these phenomena may be deemed surprises, they are not all cut from the same cloth. The first two cases provided surprises to competitors; the second two cases proved surprising for their progenitors – it was their expectations rather than those of their rivals that were confounded.

Some surprises prefigure themselves in the form of warning signals that, for one reason or another, may go unnoticed (Wissema, 2002), while others apparently come without warning (Levy, 1994). Normal accidents, where overly complex and tightly coupled systems pose evident risks, can subsequently be seen as unsurprising accidents waiting to happen (Perrow, 1984). Some surprises, when dissected in retrospect, could have been avoided – such as the loss of life from the *Titanic*, due to an inadequate number of lifeboats (Watkins and Bazerman, 2003).

Being surprised is perceived as the opposite of 'good management' (Pondy and Mitroff, 1979). Traditional organizational wisdom, engineering based and rationality oriented, emphasized such features as objectivity, detachment and control (Shenhav, 2003). As a result, as noted by Tsoukas (1994: 3), 'in our modern societies … prevention is deeply valued; we don't like to be taken by surprise'. Organizing is reduced to predictability – to a phenomenon lacking any surprising or non-routine qualities. McDonald's is often seen as the prototype – you should never be surprised by a McDonald's burger (Ritzer, 2004).

We know that surprises happen, however: aircraft hurtle into skyscrapers; bombs explode on tube trains; stock markets go into meltdown; sport celebrities, such as Tiger Woods, are caught in personally compromising situations. Yet, events that might initially appear surprising may be less so on further reflection. Athletic and handsome billionaire sports stars have many opportunities for transgression and there are always plenty of people available to transgress with, attracted by the lure of fame, physicality and money. Those who surround such stars as strategic advisers typically try to keep such surprises out of the public eye. Others want to make sure that their surprises grab public attention spectacularly.

MINI CASE STUDY

9/11 as a surprise for strategy

Surprise is as old as warfare. The events of September 11, 2001 seemed especially shocking both because they were so destructive and because they were so unexpected. Yet, neither the fact that the attack occurred nor the form it took should have been a complete surprise. Familiarity with terrorist methods, repeated attacks against US facilities overseas, combined with indications that the continental United States was at the top of the terrorist target list, all suggested the possibility of an imminent

(Continued)

(*Continued*)

and significant attack. Take the so-called Phoenix memo as an example: in July 2001 an FBI field officer sent a report to his superiors warning of a possible attack by Osama bin Laden based on the observation that an 'inordinate number of individuals of investigative interest' were attending flight schools in Arizona. However, no one reacted and the memo was not read until after 9/11. In August 2001, another FBI agent working in Minneapolis reported a suspect person who undertook flight training. The FBI HQ did not react to the report, which frustrated the Minneapolis agent. In order to put emphasis on his suspicion he argued that he was 'trying to keep someone from taking a plane and crashing it into the World Trade Center'. The FBI HQ replied that 'this was not going to happen' and did not follow the lead.[1] The unanticipated event occurred and now Ground Zero occupies the symbolic space of what was once the heartland of US commercial might.

9/11 fits very much into the norm of a surprise caused by a breakdown of intelligence warning. In retrospect, the terrorist attacks on the Twin Towers should not have been such a surprise. There were plenty of indications that the United States in general and New York's Twin Towers in particular had been singled out for attack. They had been bombed by Islamist extremists in 1993, as were the Khobar Towers in Dahran, Saudi Arabia, in July 1996. Islamist radicals lacking sophisticated weapons had previously adopted low-technology altruistic suicide (Durkheim, 2002) in order to destroy highly symbolic targets. In retrospect, the attacks were foreshadowed by the bombing of the US Embassies in Kenya and Tanzania in August 1998 and the attack launched by a suicide boat on the USS *Cole* in October 2000.

The day before the 9/11 attacks, the Congressional Research Service published a report citing the links between bin Laden and Near Eastern terrorist groups, using suicide bombers. The signs were overlooked for four reasons:

1 Good intelligence indicators were lost in the 'noise' of disinformation.

2 There was a belief that the enemy lacked the technical capacity to undertake the action.

3 What Porch and Wirtz (2002) refer to as 'mirror imaging': 'the assumption on the part of the intelligence "consumer" that the action undertaken was unlikely because it was "illogical"'.

[1] See the official report of the 9/11 Commission which can be downloaded for free at *www.9-11commission.gov/report/911Report.pdf*

4 There were lots of cues that were not sent up the bureaucratic chain because they seemed unimportant, trivial or irrelevant to more important concerns. Local FBI agents reported that Arab students in flight schools only wished to learn how to take off, not to land. But the information's significance remained buried until informed by hindsight. Organizational 'noise' occurs when organizational jurisdictions overlap, compete and are unclear, encouraging the hoarding rather than sharing of information between rival agencies. The inability of the CIA and the FBI to communicate contributed to the failure to detect the 9/11 attacks, just as the failure of army and naval intelligence to cooperate aided the Pearl Harbor debacle. Organizations need to be able to 'spot surprises, not just to confirm expectations' (Starbuck, 1993: 83). Or, as Tsoukas (1994) put it, managers sometimes fail in transforming events into experiences. It is this gap between events and experiences, facts and expectations, that explains why signals (events) that presage a forthcoming disruption may not be properly noticed (i.e. converted into lived experience).

The 9/11 attacks on the Twin Towers forced people into a fundamental reanalysis of their assumptions and habitual behaviours; however, intelligence agencies knew that:

1 Suicide bombing was a routine Islamist strategy.

2 Tower buildings had been attacked previously.

3 Suicide bombers routinely hijacked modes of transport as vehicles of destruction, namely boats, cars and trucks.

4 High profile US targets were liable to attack.

5 The Twin Towers had been the target of a previous Islamist bombing.

6 Osama bin Laden had declared war on the Unites States.

All the threads were there but the connection had not been made because the meaning that added up the Twin Towers with altruistic suicide and vehicular attack had not made sense of the easiest way in which this might be achieved – from the air.

Question

What was the organizational impact of 9/11 on strategies dealing with homeland security in the Unites States?

Serendipity

While many events can prove problematic, not all events will be. Sometimes surprises can be happy encounters, to which the term serendipity is usually applied. Chance, luck and happenstance may be as relevant in organizational life as in other domains, however far they may appear to be from the predictable matter of science. The idea that there may be logic in disorder (Warglien and Masuch, 1995) and mess (Abrahamson and Freedman, 2006) is largely excluded from formal strategy theory. That there is a logic to disorder does not mean that organizations are irrational or incoherent but rather that there is an element of unpredictability and emergence in the fabric of organizations that needs to be considered and studied.

The logic of emergence and disorder may be found in many instances of organizational life, ranging from strategy-making to product innovation to management learning:

- Cohen et al.'s (1972) work on garbage-can-type decision-making demonstrated the role of chance, luck and timing in organizational choice through the accidental confluence of problems, solutions, participants and problems.
- Mintzberg and McHugh (1985) showed that strategy formation is to some extent the result of a spontaneous convergence by a variety of actors.
- Burgelman (1991) highlighted the role of internal experimentation travelling from bottom to top.
- Olsen (1976) referred to organizations characterized by a lack of shared and consistent goals, clear technology and member participation as 'organized anarchies'.

Serendipity has also been presented as an outcome of exploratory learning efforts (March, 1991). It is often said that highly prescribed and standardized processes lead to good products as the fruit of hard work and tight control (Cooper, 1998), yet the importance of serendipity has been seen as particularly visible in the case of innovation, especially in new product development.

Serendipity starts accidentally, when someone is looking for a solution to a given problem – problem A; in the process, the person notices something that will lead to the solution of a different problem (problem B) that may be of even greater value. For the discovery of a solution for B while looking for A, a metaphorical leap has to occur: A has to become seen as *an attribute of* or *equal to* B in some way.

WHAT DO YOU MEAN?

The role of serendipity in spicing up performance

Pfizer scientists were assessing sildenafil citrate as a medication for blood pressure and serendipitously discovered that it was effective in the treatment of a totally different problem – erectile dysfunction: an incidental discovery that led to the creation of Viagra.

Making something out of the unexpected is not purely a matter of luck. Quoting Pasteur, Merton and Barber (2004: 171) note that luck tends to favour prepared minds, those ready to benefit from it. Preparedness itself, they argue, is linked to qualities such as alertness, flexibility, courage and assiduity. There is merit in being able to reap the fruits of serendipity by connecting discoveries and needs and it is in this sense that serendipity may be viewed as capability rather than chance. Sometimes both the discovery and the need are new. The process of serendipity thus involves the relational ability to see anew, whether this ability is that of the serendipitous hero in a tale of discoveries or the surrounding networks. Attention to ways of seeing signifies the importance of cognitive processes for strategy.

WHAT'S WRONG WITH THIS PICTURE?

There is a lot missing from the conventional overview of strategy. Sure, it has moved from an outside-in, to an inside-out and even bottom-up view of strategy, as we cover in our next three chapters. But there still seems to be a lot missing.

One obvious absence is where strategy fits in the firm or organization. The assumption is that it sits at the top, in the *head*quarters, from where it is rationally dispensed to flow down and through the organization. However, there are emergent perspectives centred on 'branding', 'strategic marketing' and 'innovation' that take a very different view. While highly rationalist accounts of strategy stress its elite location, often seeing it as a closely guarded secret that emerges with great fanfares from on high, more realistic accounts of strategy stress that it concerns the whole firm, its image as a totality, as well as its important stakeholders.

One reason that these views are often not centre stage in either theory or practice is because of the politics of organizations. Marketing and strategic branding do not always have a representation in the citadel of power – the boardroom. Strangely, politics are also largely absent from the strategy perspectives of all but a few contributors such as Mintzberg and Pettigrew. From our perspective (Clegg and Haugaard, 2009), power is the central concept of the social sciences and should be the central concept of a discipline such as strategy, which, as we have explained both here and elsewhere, can draw so much from writers such as Machiavelli (Carter et al. 2008).

In contemporary times a major way in which power operates strategically is through the normalization of strategic managerialism as the dominant trope of management in everyday life. The trope is expressed through various devices of performativity; these are devices designed to measure and enhance performance, that key concept of strategic management. One thinks of auditing, assessment, inspection and evaluation conducted through everyday techniques of power embedded in strategic management such as industry and quality standards, best practice benchmarking, league tables, the balanced scorecard and so on. These devices require treatment in the literature not just as techniques and tools that can be learnt but also as material practices having a political dimension as well as one that is technological, as Diefenbach (2009) argues. There are interests, ideologies and powers wrapped up in these technologies of control that deserve analysis in terms that are broader than the merely technical.

Clearly, the power potentialities of strategic managerialism are rarely if ever fully satisfied. Employees, stakeholders, performance can all deviate from that which is modelled or planned for them. Things can go wrong – badly wrong, as we will see. But the beauty of strategy discourses is that failure or an inability to achieve targets simply becomes a basis for even more strategic planning and exhortation – this time, new strategies, the right strategies, rather than the failed ones of the past. The only answer to a strategy that is not working as desired and planned is to find another one that does. We might say, cynically, that strategy feeds on failure. Strategy requires failure to innovate and renew itself. Discursively, the major purveyors of strategy, the consulting companies, need to be able to promote new products and practices into the market and the shortcomings of existing ones become the basis for doing so.

Probably the most strategic issue and the biggest failure for business in the past three years has been the global financial crisis that began to unfold in 2007 from the US sub-prime market (Ferguson's (2008) *The Ascent of Money: A Financial History of the World*, has a good analysis of the crisis's major elements in Chapter 5, 'Safe as houses'). Interestingly, the crisis is a major example of strategies gone wrong. Some colleagues in strategy, especially those of a more quantitative bent, like to imagine themselves predictive scientists. Strangely, we do not recall any predictions of the crisis's occurrence from the major quantitative strategy schools, or related economics and finance perspectives, suggesting that strategies of financialization were hardly analysed reflexively.

Of course, we need to ask where these strategies came from: on the whole, they came from business elites and top management teams trained in the most elite business schools. Yet, this institutional location and packaging of strategy as knowledge is largely outside the remit of an enquiry into strategy's knowledge practices; additionally, as it occurs on the macro-scale and largely through instruments and devices that are difficult to access discursively, it has largely been overlooked in present studies of strategy as practice.

We need to ask also what have been the effects of the dominance of financialization, globally. While there has been the development of a huge literature on globalization in disciplines such as sociology in recent years, little of it seems to have made its way onto the strategy agenda, which is still inclined to see the global world through imperial prisms of conquest that remain very ethnocentric, under the rubric of 'international business'.

Issues of climate change, sustainability and corporate sustainability are at the top of the agenda not only for many governments and civil society organizations but also for many businesses. But to what extent have issues of strategic sustainability made it into the pages of the vast majority of strategy texts? Not much. We, however, have sought to string together issues of sustainability through this book, especially in cases and in the discussion of globalizing tendencies.

Finally, there is the question of cases. Strategy is the case-based subject par excellence. But why do so many cases have to be so boring and so constrained in leaving out of the picture the things we have mentioned here? Our cases – we hope – are not boring and they do address a wide range of issues.

In addressing these 'determinate absences' in this book, absences whose non-presence defines the usual picture, we break new ground and capture emergent realities that strategy texts hitherto have largely not addressed.

SUMMARY AND REVIEW

Strategy as a discipline is focused on questions of how organizations (or, more narrowly, firms) are able to perform better. It is an inherently practical discourse – strategy has been shaped as much by interested consultancy as by disinterested academic enquiry. The earliest versions of strategy were big on detail and stressed that rational planning informed by data and fed through models on computers would be the best basis for future actions. Unfortunately, such models often contained assumptions based on past behaviour that were not so useful in modelling a world in which those assumptions no longer held. One thing that strategists soon learn is that the future is not necessarily a linear extrapolation of the past. Given that a great deal of strategy has a prescriptive focus, stressing what should be done, it can be dangerous to assume that the ways in which the world was, and the means with which one made sense of it, will be carried through into the future.

Over its brief history the discourse of strategy has been likened to a pendulum, where the weight of ideas has oscillated between an 'external' and an internal 'focus', between an orientation to the outside competitive environment and industry conditions and an orientation to the internal capabilities of the organization, such as the knowledge and resources it can access and control. Typically, strategy has been seen as the harbinger of new routines to deal with a changing environment or with which to marshal and deploy a new mix of resources and capabilities; increasingly, however, strategy is being seen in the context of what have been termed wicked problems. Faced with wicked problems, various strategists have suggested new directions for strategy. Some, such as Gary Hamel, urge the adoption of revolutionary manifestos while evolutionary theorists abhor the idea of such a radical change; others, such as the strategy-as-practice crew, suggest moving further away from prescription towards a more fine-grained micro-description and analysis of what it is that strategists actually do when they are doing strategy.

The strategy-as-practice perspective leads us to questions that are a long way from the industrial economics roots of much strategy thinking, posing questions of culture, identity and micro-politics. But it hardly addresses the realms of surprise, complexity and cognition, with which we have concluded this introductory chapter. Surprise, by definition, is not a practice one is familiar with; additionally, complexity is not a practice but a characteristic of the environment, while cognition is not a practice that one can readily observe. We think that surprising things have been happening in the world of strategy and we think we have a newer, and better, more realist story to tell that addresses these things. In Table 1.1 we demonstrate how the structure of the book maps onto the issues that have been raised in this introduction.

TABLE 1.1 Basic elements and core assumptions in the analysis of strategy

Chapter	Areas addressed	Elements and assumptions
1 Strategy and competitive performance	• Centrality of competitive performance • Intellectual traditions from industrial organization economics	• Centrality of markets and competition • Restricted role of the state • External focus on environment conceived in market terms
2 Strategy discovers uniqueness: the role of resources and knowledge	• Centrality of unique firm-specific capabilities • Intellectual traditions from Penrose and the theory of the firm	• Centrality of how a firm does what it does • Search for capabilities that are valuable, rare, inimitable and non-substitutable • Internal focus on organization capabilities as a bundle of assets
3 Strategy as process and practice	• Centrality of emergent processes rather than rational plans • Focus on practices – what strategists do when they do strategy • Intellectual traditions from sociology, especially grounded theory, ethnomethodology and discourse analysis	• Strategy is a product and we need to study the processes and practices through which it is produced • Strategy is produced through recursive practices that feed from and sustain orthodox strategic thinking

(Continued)

TABLE 1.1 *(Continued)*

Chapter	Areas addressed	Elements and assumptions
4 Marketing and branding as strategic forces	● Centrality of branding processes to affirm an organizational identity ● Intellectual traditions from the organization studies literature concerned with identity and from strategic marketing concerned with branding, and from the sociology of consumption concerned with 'nothingness' ● Centrality of a marketing strategy to lock in customers as a central plank of strategy for competitive markets ● Intellectual traditions from marketing and actor-network theory (ANT)	● Strategy is about positioning organizations as brands with equity built into them; if the organization is branded this branding carries across all its family of different products ● There is a risk that strong branding creates nothing – products that are comparatively devoid of distinctive or substantive content apart from their branding ● Strategy concerns product segmentation, targeting and positioning as core activities ● Stabilizing a strategy in the marketplace entails recruiting and translating customers into a relationship with the strategy and the firm that is promoting it
5 Strategy and innovation	● Centrality of innovation as a means of creating incremental and discontinuous innovation market offerings of goods and services ● Intellectual traditions from R&D and product innovation research, national innovation systems literature, design thinking, sociological institutional theory and political economy	● Strategy cannot be routine; any routinized strategy will fail – innovation is constantly required, whether incremental or discontinuous or both ● Innovation is an organization-level phenomenon – it should not be thought of simply in terms of product innovation but in terms of the overall architecture of the organization and how it enables or inhibits innovative practices
6 Strategists, top management teams and governance	● Centrality of elites in organizations – the top management team – to the strategy-making process ● Intellectual traditions from s-as-p perspectives, leadership research and the social and political theory of elites, especially business elites and the various kinds of 'capital' that they can use	● Strategy has a specific location at the apex of organizations and this is a distinct milieu that requires study in its own right, in terms of issues of corporate governance, boardroom behaviour, tensions in top management teams and corporate codes ● It would be wrong to assume that strategy is either unitarily formulated or implemented: it entails the construction of complex social relations that are irremediably political
7 Strategic decision-making	● Centrality of decisions as the outputs of the strategy-making process. Decisions always involve phenomena such as bounded rationality,	● Strategy means decision-making and the common economics representation of decision-making as an overtly rational process is empirically incorrect

(Continued)

TABLE 1.1 *(Continued)*

Chapter	Areas addressed	Elements and assumptions
	muddling through, non-decision-making, mobilization of bias, garbage-can behaviours and risk analysis • Intellectual traditions include behavioural, organizational and political theories of decision-making	• Decision-making is not irrational, however, but it is conditioned not only by the models of rational choice that economists produce, but also by the realities of situated action in a flow of events
8 Organizational politics and strategy	• Centrality of interests to the production and transformation of strategies. Interests imply power • Complex organizations have complex interests and complex power as can be seen in instances of multinational corporations (MNCs) • Intellectual traditions from sociology of power, political theory, organization studies and international business	• Strategy-making means an exertion of will over diverse fields of action to stabilize social relations within the fields on preferred conduits of power • Power relations are at the centre of strategy-making, especially as organizations become more complex, as we can see through analysis of MNCs
9 International and collaborative strategies	• Centrality of collaboration for contemporary strategy demonstrates that no organization is an island and that many seek to collaborate strategically with other organizations in order to be more strategic • Intellectual traditions from international business, marketing theory and organization studies	• Organizations and firms as the isolated and atomistic competitive agents of neo-classical organization theory are a fiction that has outlived its usefulness • Organizations today follow strategies that are not only competitive but also collaborative
10 Financialization, risk and accountability	• Centrality of capitalism as the frame within which theories of strategy have been developed, applied and refined. The different stages capitalism has evolved through up to the dominance of financialization as seen in the global financial crisis (GFC) • Intellectual traditions from political economy, post-Keynesian economics, business history, managerial accounting and the sociology of risk	• The GFC is the most significant event ever to impinge on the horizon of strategy-makers, thinkers and researchers. It needs to be understood in detail • Strategies of financialization were central to the events that produced the GFC. With these strategies even firms such as General Motors that were known for making automobiles ended up making more profit from the circulation of capital • Strategy in a capitalist economy always moves through circuits of capital and understanding these is essential if we are not to see a repetition of the errors in strategy that led up to the GFC

(Continued)

TABLE 1.1 *(Continued)*

Chapter	Areas addressed	Elements and assumptions
11 Globalization and strategy	● Centrality of globalization to strategy and business in the twenty-first century. Globalization can be thought of in terms of globalizing flows of capital, people, procurements and communications ● Intellectual traditions from international business that seem increasingly ethnocentric and less relevant to contemporary pluralistic globalization; input from organization studies, sociological theory and political economy	● Globalization marks the contemporary era as distinctive from previous eras in terms of the density and multidirectionality of the dominant global flows ● Globalization is producing a post-American-dominated world, as the BRIC countries, especially India and China, redefine the flows of global business ● The focus in the concluding part of the chapter is on China and the extent of the contradiction between its political economy and its polity as a one-party and totalitarian state

EXERCISES

1 Having read this chapter you should be able to say in your own words what the following key terms mean:

● Strategy
● Strategy drives structure
● Rational planning
● Evolution
● Administrative action
● Operational action
● Strategic action
● Wicked problems
● Internal orientation
● External orientation
● Strategic revolution
● Strategy as practice
● Power over
● Power to
● Surprises
● Events
● Complexity and strategy
● Cognition and strategy
● Serendipity.

2 In terms of the discourse of strategy, what distinguishes an internal from an external orientation?

3 What role have the concepts of evolution and revolution played in strategy thinking?

4 How is power related to strategy?

ADDITIONAL RESOURCES

1 Our companion website is the best first stop for you to find a great deal of extra resources, free PDF versions of leading articles published in Sage journals, exercise, video and pod casts, team case studies and general questions and links to teamwork resources. Go to www.sagepub.co.uk/cleggstrategy

2 A good book that introduces the strategy field is one which three of the authors of this book wrote previously: Carter, C., Clegg, S. R. and Kornberger, M. (2008) *A Very Short, Fairly Interesting and Reasonably Cheap Book about Studying Strategy*, London: Sage.

3 For a fairly academic perspective on strategy, but one that is not too unreadable, you could check out Stephen Cummings' (2002) *Recreating Strategy*, London: Sage. He starts with the ancient Greeks!

4 Paula Jarzabkowski's (2005) *Strategy as Practice*, London: Sage, presents a particular perspective on strategy research known as 'strategy as practice', which seeks to understand strategy through close scrutiny of what is done in the various sites of the strategy process.

5 Films (movies) about strategy are many and varied – but mostly about military strategy. One film that focuses on strategy, showing the power of organization, is Steven Soderbergh's (2008) *Che: Part One*. It is the story of how Fidel Castro and Che Guevara organized a small, motley band of peasants

into a fighting force that overthrew the Batista regime in Cuba, despite its support by the Mafia and the US government, through an effective organizing strategy. Che was the very model of the intellectual as man of action: he was a doctor, a writer and a thinker who became a strategist and tactician. Historically accurate, the film demonstrates how a small group could move from a base in the Sierra Maestra in Cuba to take Havana and begin to create what they believed would be a better society.

WEB SECTION

Visit the *Strategy* companion website at www.sagepub. co.uk/cleggstrategy

1   The online resource www.strategytube.net that the authors produced in tandem with this book is a great resource designed to complement and extend this book.

2   Logging in to the Strategy-as-Practice website provides you with an opportunity to subscribe to a lively community in which many interesting papers are posted. It is free – just go to www.s-as-p.org.

LOOKING FOR A HIGHER MARK?

Reading and digesting these articles that are available free on the companion website www.sagepub.co.uk/cleggstrategy can help you gain a deeper understanding and, on the basis of that, a better grade:

1   P. M. A. R. Heugens and Michael J. Mol (2005) So You Call That Research? Mending Methodological Biases in Strategy and Organization Departments of Top Business Schools, *Strategic Organization*, 3(1): 117–28.

2   Hitoshi Mitsuhashi and Henrich R. Greve (2004) Powerful and Free: Intraorganizational Power and the Dynamics of Corporate Strategy, *Strategic Organization*, 2(2): 107–32.

3   Joseph T. Mahoney and Anita M. McGahan (2007) The Field of Strategic Management within the Evolving Science of Strategic Organization, *Strategic Organization*, 5(1): 79–99.

4   David Seidl (2007) General Strategy Concepts and the Ecology of Strategy Discourses: A Systemic-Discursive Perspective, *Organization Studies*, 28(2): 197–218.

CASE STUDY

A strategic vision for Cambodia

Stewart Clegg, Miguel Pina e Cunha and Arménio Rego

At the outset we remarked that strategies are as likely to be found in public organizations as they are in private organizations. In this case study we want you to consider what is perhaps the most utopian strategy that any government has tried to implement. It concerns the real-time experiment that was Democratic Kampuchea under Pol Pot.

Pol Pot's vision for Cambodia was 'to plunge the country into an inferno of revolutionary change where, certainly, old ideas and those who refused to abandon them would perish in the flames, but from which Cambodia itself would emerge, strengthened and purified, as a paragon of communist virtue' (Short, 2004: 288). In this new form of social organization, the reason for living would no longer be 'to have' but 'to be', being in a 'society without desire, without vain competition, without fear for the future' (as described in Short, 2004: 314).

The goal of the Kampuchean Communist Party was the construction of a 'clean, honest society' (Short, 2004: 247), freed of every form of exploitation, a society with no classes and no differences. The Cambodian utopia of the Khmer Rouge was expressed in different domains of language and everyday life. Change started with the country's name itself. The Kingdom of Cambodia was part of the past. The new nation would be called Democratic Kampuchea (DK), a designation that recovered the original indigenous pronunciation, rather than the Westernized form 'Cambodia'. The 'Khmer' language was now called 'Kampuchean'. Cambodia was the country of the Khmer, the heirs of Angkor Wat. The new Kampucheans included the Khmer but also the members of other ethnicities in order to avoid the impression of racial exclusion. The goal was uniformity, social, economic and even biological uniformity. Mey Mann noted that, in the future, 'everyone was (to be) exactly 1 m 60 tall' (in Short, 2004: 326). Socially, everything different or distinctive was unacceptable, for example wearing spectacles, which was something regarded as bourgeois or intellectual. Interestingly, the Issarak, who, 20 years earlier, were the precursors of the Khmer Rouge, took the same types of measure.

The Kampuchean project was to design an organizational utopia that would realize a communist society composed of peasants. However, as every organizational student has read oftentimes, changes may be difficult because old habits die hard. In this case, however, the revolutionary leaders of the Communist Party of Kampuchea (CPK) accepted that the ends justified every means, including the death of those whose ideas were opposed. To eradicate the feudal and capitalistic dimensions of Cambodian society, violent and extreme measures were taken. Members of the classes that were to be abolished were killed in large numbers. Others were 'reeducated' as peasants. In the process, of course, many also died. Money, markets and property, all emblems of capitalism, were also victims of this vision.

Two major organizational processes took place in the country: extreme collectivization and management by terror. Collectivization is core to communist ideology. Private property is viewed with suspicion and should, preferentially, be substituted by common ownership that is administered by the state. In Khmer Rouge Kampuchea, however, the process of collectivization was as radical as any ever attempted. Even Mao Zedong, and later Deng Xiaoping, expressed their opinions about what they saw as the radicalism of the measures being adopted during Cambodia in the Khmer Rouge years. Money and markets were abolished; cities – the sites of everything evil in the Khmer Rouge doctrine – were emptied and citizens force-marched to be collectively reeducated in the countryside. Instead of being reeducated many ended up being the victims of massive state killing campaigns. For the CPK everything private was undesirable. This included not only property and goods but also thoughts and emotions. These practices were too radical even for the totalitarian Chinese leaders – whose ideas heavily influenced the Cambodian revolutionaries.

The North Vietnam US War, as well as China and the Soviet Union's interests in the area, all played a decisive role in shaping Cambodian internal politics and the ascent to power of the Red Khmer. Progressively the former schoolteacher built a vision of a superior state, a pure communist society that would be a benchmark to other nations. He reinvented his own biography as a rubber plantation worker and created an organization characterized by a thirst for power and unlimited distrust.

(Continued)

(Continued)

Pol Pot practised the opposite of textbook wisdom on leadership: he led in secrecy, built a paranoid organization and was inscrutable and ruthless. Distrust and secrecy were crucial in the resistance of the Cambodian maquis but failed to work in the national government. These characteristics were adequate to a guerrilla leader but not for a national politician. As a leader and organizational actor, he was a victim of previous success, maintaining strategies that had worked well in the past, although in the face of significantly different challenges (see Miller, 1990, on the general point). In the case of the Khmer Rouge the persecutory preoccupation that was developed throughout the resistance years led to a paranoid organization of the state and a leadership style with a significant potential for self-destruction (Kets de Vries and Miller, 1986).

At the level of domestic policy, he was able to capitalize on the turmoil characterizing local Cambodian politics. The system of governance was feudal, lacking checks and balances, and the monarchy premised on obvious pre-modern traits. The nation was backward and poor. Tensions between city and forest/country constituted a defining line for societal cleavage, a potential contradiction ripe for the Marxist plucking, and a source of social explosion in their potency (see McIntyre, 1996). By defending a peasant revolution the Khmer Rouge presented themselves as the bearers of a new vision for society, based on a discourse that was extremely powerful for the poor people from the rural areas; in other words, for the majority of Cambodians. Externally, it played well to a Western intelligentsia, especially in Paris, fascinated and fooled by the trickle of information about the Cultural Revolution that had seeped out of China. For leftist intellectuals there the Kampuchean revolution seemed an even bolder strategy of counter-hegemony to that of Mao's, while seemingly based on it.

Certainly, as a leader, Pol Pot forged a utopian vision for his country; however, as discussed by Short (2004), his ideological soulmates were not so much Stalin or Mao, but rather Thomas More, the French Revolution Hébertistes and Jacobins, and the nineteenth-century Russian utopian socialists. He was a man in search of a vision. He was aware of the difficulties that such a project would entail but he was determined: it was better to go too far than not far enough. Forging a new identity, based on a fully redesigned system of power and governance, promised to bring the country back to its ancient brilliance. Angkor, the eternal reference of Cambodia's glory, could be rebuilt in the new nation of Democratic Kampuchea, described by its leaders as a new example to the world, a society of purity and equality, freed from any chains of exclusion and exploitation.

A prolonged national decline and political exclusion are powerful motivators for young elites to try something radically new. The appeal of utopia is strong for those who do not want to take an unsatisfactory status quo for granted (De Cock, 2009) and who cannot change it incrementally from within. To turn utopia into reality, during the clandestine years, the Khmer Rouge created a military force characterized by strict obedience of a traditional Khmer kind. Inside the party, the leading clique implemented a regime that has been described as militarist, dictatorial and authoritarian (Frings, 1997). After the victory, these rules were maintained. Those incurring even small errors could be heavily penalized. The obedient army, which, before ascending to power, had fought many battles with equally brutal enemies during the civil war, constituted the apparatus and force necessary for carrying out the utopian vision of an egalitarian and rural Democratic Kampuchea.

Some of the factors that explained Pol Pot's longevity as a guerrilla leader (e.g. paranoia, secrecy) became a problem when he assumed the role of national political leader. His life is a paradigmatic illustration of the possible consequences of utopian visionaries who want to impose the superiority of their worldview upon others. Pol Pot is a good example of bad utopian leadership (Kellerman, 2004) for a number of reasons.

First, being a member of the Cambodian elite with a metropolitan education, by any possible account he was bourgeois, the type of people that the revolution he led was targeting. When his position as the leader of the Khmer Rouge was finally revealed, a fictitious biography was circulated which presented him as a rubber plantation worker from the Eastern Zone. In other words, if authenticity is a necessary quality for leadership, then Pol Pot should not be considered as an example of it – authentic leadership being 'a pattern of transparent and ethical leader behavior that encourages openness in sharing information needed to make decisions while accepting followers' inputs' (Avolio, Walumbwa and Weber, 2009: 423).

Second, he was a covert leader. He acted as a member and then leader of a clandestine movement. He defended secrecy as crucial for victory: 'only through secrecy can we be masters of the situation' (Short, 2004: 337). Covert leadership is not a common topic of organizational and management

(Continued)

(Continued)

research. The case suggests that probably it should be, because these leaders undergo distinct processes of character formation whose manifestations may not be apparent because of the secrecy surrounding them. For instance, in terms of communication, he was not explicit – rather he cultivated ambiguity and obliquity.

Third, despite his likeable attitude, a disposition praised in the management literature (Casciaro and Lobo, 2005), he was cruel and ruthless. As a leader he expected submission to the worldview that he was cultivating. Difference was not tolerated. People around him started to be extremely careful about what they said to him. Any *faux pas* could be interpreted as an indication of treason. Massive killings were conducted not only to purge the country of its 'natural' enemies, but also to eliminate the traitors who were produced by the *santebal*, the secret police, whose system of interrogation resulted, inevitably, in executions. The search for 'strings of traitors' led to a state of collective paranoia in which no one should be trusted. This, in turn, reinforced the need for vigilance and stimulated further paranoia.

Fourth, Pol Pot led a life of luxury as a leader, despite his utopianism, and the oft-communicated desire that the Kampuchean reign of ideological purity and renunciation was intended to serve as an example to the world. Members of the central committee and high dignitaries of the regime actually protected themselves from the harshness of life in Cambodia. As examples of ethical leadership, they were not as pure as their vision would suggest. They had access to fine and abundant food ('all the leaders grew fat' (Short, 2004: 346); 'familyism' was a sin but not necessarily for the families of the top cadres (Short, 2004: 347); Buddhism was a reactionary religion but Nuon Chea, the regime's number two, authorized his mother to keep a Buddhist monk to recite to her the sutras; people should be selfless but cadres seduced 'attractive young women' (2004: 347) and then executed them on any accusation of moral turpitude.

As ten Bos points out, the development of a new institutional system of organizations designed to enforce a plan for the creation of a new society often progresses in ways that do not result from planning: 'one of the important features of the bureaucratic labyrinth is that it takes a while before you are going to notice that you are increasingly absorbed by its complexities' (2004: 16).

With the ascent to power of the Khmer Rouge, 'Cambodia's institutions were being turned upside down to bring them into line with the Khmer Rouge rule' (Short 2004: 331). The country now had a new name, a new leader, a new political system and new representations of itself. The revolution was such an 'extremely marvelous, extremely wonderful, prodigious leap' (Short 2004: 341), straight into full communism from a feudal society (an impossibility, according to Marx), that Pol Pot and his followers thought that Cambodia would become a model to the entire world – including the United States. The new society was a strange combination of radical reform together with deeply ingrained elements of Khmer identity. As Lanzara (1998:16) has observed:

> processes of institutional breakdown and rebuilding put contradictory requirements on individual and collective identity. On the one hand they require the capability of breaking with the past, transcending one's own identity in order to 'convert' and 'be reborn' to a new, emerging identity; on the other hand they require the capability of 'throwing a bridge' between the past (or the present) and the future, thus reestablishing a sense of continuity.

Revolutions must build on the past, even as they renounce it. Despite the strong pressure upon religion, the influence of Buddhism remained perceptible, the family was reimagined, and the monarchy's role was redesigned.

Despite the new perception of religion, many dimensions of Buddhist philosophy were still important in revolutionary Cambodia, at least as a means for its citizens to make sense of the situation. Pol Pot, when speaking to public audiences, used to carry with him a fan, a symbol of the monkhood. And his behaviour was seen to accord with the monk's progression to enlightenment. Sopheap, a cadre of the Khmer Rouge, described Pol Po as follows:

> For a monk, there are different levels. At the first level, you feel joy. And it's good. Then there's a second level. You no longer feel anything for yourself, but you feel the joy of others. And finally, there's a third level. You are completely neutral. Nothing moves you. This is the highest level. Pol Pot situated himself in the tradition of serenity. (in Short, 2004: 340)

From a citizen viewpoint, Pol Pot's place in the order of things could be accounted for using religion and superstition. A guide in Angkor Wat likened Pol Pot to Yama, the Hindu deity of the underworld (Chandler, 2000: 118). The coming of the Khmer Rouge was also anticipated in the predictions of the *Puth Tumniay*, and equated with the legendary

(Continued)

(Continued)

'500 thieves', millennial bandits who would rob everything from people, including their material possessions, their families and eventually their lives. Moreover, the whole country could now be considered a sort of Buddhist hell (Short, 2004: 315).

With Pol Pot, the traditional, bourgeois family of the past was to be substituted by a big collectivist family – the Kampuchean family of equals. Under the new order, parents should now be called by their children as 'uncle and aunt', and other adults as 'mother' and 'father'. Marriages were arranged by the Angkar (the correct organization, in fact the CPK, as recognized in 1977) – which substituted for the family in this role; also the old, 'self-centred', family institutional roles would now be performed by the Angkar. Nothing was outside the interest of this big national family united by the party. And the obligation of particular families henceforth would be to understand and accept the new state and its philosophy of the common good. Children were taken from their families to be indoctrinated and made responsible, in some cases, for some of the worst tasks in the Khmer Rouge regime, namely in the S-21 extermination centre. These were, literally, the children of the revolution.

Questions

1   What lessons do you draw for those strategists who favour revolutionary change, such as Hamel and Peters, from this case?

2   Explore what it entails to be a revolutionary in strategic terms, drawing on at least two approaches to strategy to answer the question.

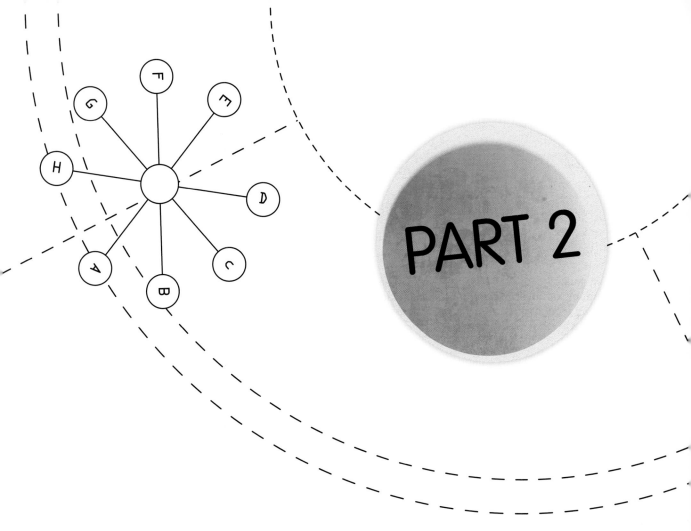

Central Currents in Strategy

2 Strategy and competitive performance

3 Strategy discovers uniqueness: the role of resources and knowledge

4 Strategy as process and practice

5 Marketing and branding as strategic forces

6 Strategy and innovation

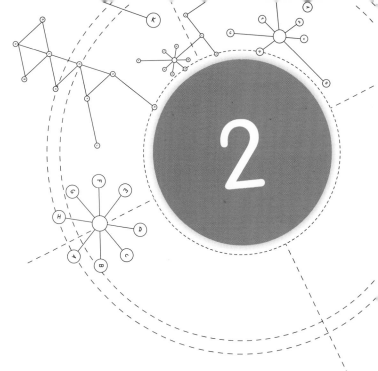

Strategy and Competitive Performance

2

Environments, markets, generic positions

LEARNING OBJECTIVES

By the end of this chapter you will be able to:

- Understand the importance of differences in competitive environments
- Explain what competitive advantage is and how it can be achieved
- Distinguish different types of markets and understand their nature
- Realize the role of industry-related forces that influence the strategy process and be able to evaluate them
- Analyse the macro-environment, value chain and strategic groups and understand how they can affect a firm's strategic choices
- Discuss the advantages and disadvantages of generic strategic positions

> ## BEFORE YOU GET STARTED . . .
>
> ### The essence of strategy is choosing what not to do.
>
> **(MICHAEL PORTER)**

INTRODUCTION

We have pointed out that early contemporary strategy theorists and practitioners focused on an outside-in perspective on strategy; that is, they gave most attention to the role and importance of the factors that were external to the firm. Strategic managers, thus, focused on the analysis and interpretation of the environment and the industry that the firm was operating in. The assumption was that the profitability of a firm is a result of the structure of its markets and the firm's ability to position itself successfully within its competitive environment. While today we know that there are also many firm-internal aspects that strategists consider when 'doing strategy', the understanding of the business environment that corporations and other organizations compete in remains a central aspect of a strategist's work.

This business environment can be conceived of in many ways: as an industry, an ecosystem, a field, an economy, or it may be thought of in terms of structural aspects such as market, institutional and legal structures. Assuming that a firm might be active in several regions and multiple markets, it becomes crucial to understand the environment in terms of the key 'rules of the game', especially those that derive from government regulations that restrict or support the business. Such rules could be, for example, antitrust laws, which in the early nineteenth century helped to avoid a monopoly-like domination in the US oil or tobacco industries, or deregulation laws which had a huge effect on the structure of the energy and telecommunication industries in many European countries. Other rules may derive from what strategists call overall demand drivers: the factors shaping the demand for an organization's goods and services in the environments in which it operates. We will explore various other factors that shape the business environment of an organization in this chapter.

A firm's interactions and relationships with other organizations, individuals, government bodies and many other institutions help shape strategic outcomes. Firms face vigorous competition in most environments but they also have to manage supplier and buyer relationships. Competition with other firms is referred to in terms of horizontal relations while the management of suppliers and buyers is referred to as vertical relationships. Working out how to shape these relationships successfully, and how to respond to competitive moves, is an important and integral part of strategic management. The theories discussed in this chapter reflect these basic ideas. They derive from a subfield known as industrial organization that has developed in economics.

INDUSTRIAL ORGANIZATION AND THE STRUCTURE–CONDUCT–PERFORMANCE APPROACH

The basics

Industrial organization (IO) is a field of economic theory that helps to explain the structure of markets, the strategic behaviour of firms, their interactions and the industries to which they belong.

The central idea of IO is that the success of an industry in producing benefits for the consumer depends on the conduct of its firms, which then depends on the factors that determine the competitiveness of the market.

Two American economists, Edward S. Mason (1939; 1949) and Joe S. Bain (1956; 1968), contributed significantly to the development of IO and gave the strategy discipline some of the underlying principles and structure that it still retains. The assumption is that a firm's performance is largely a function of the industry environment in which it competes. If that supposition holds, the industry structure will largely determine conduct, which in turn determines performance, and therefore actual managerial conduct can be ignored and performance can be explained by structure, a perspective that has been coined the structure–conduct–performance (S–C–P) approach.

Factors that influence market structures include:

- *Supply conditions.* For instance, technology and cost structures characterize a market; in a technology-driven industry, such as the computer industry, the average cost of production will tend to fall when there are improvements in the production process or lower material costs. Similarly, in other sectors, such as medicine or the military, technology has driven up costs much higher than the rate of inflation.

- *Demand for a product.* Changes in consumer taste and preferences, price, availability of substitute products and the method of purchase can influence the overall demand for a product or service. If the overall production volume increases because of increased demand, the industry will tend to have only a small number of firms that will compete with each other. Hence, the number and size distribution of buyers and sellers will indicate the market power that a firm might have in its industry. For example, the increasing demand for flights between Australia and the UK is only served by a relatively small number of international airlines.

- *The degree of differentiation of products.* Product differentiation refers to the characteristics of the product and is the way in which firms improve the quality of their offerings over time (usually by means of innovation) and subsequently affect their market share. Similarly, the launch of entirely new products by competitors can lead to shifts in their market share. For example, the introduction of Apple's iPhone has significantly changed the market structure in the mobile phone industry, taking away market share from companies such as Nokia, Samsung and Motorola.

- *Extent of vertical integration and diversification.* Vertically integrated firms, such as the fashion retailer American Apparel or many oil companies, control several steps in the production and/or distribution of their product or service; hence, they wield more power in the marketplace. Diversified firms, such as the multinational manufacturing company ITT Corporation

Industrial organization (IO) takes an external perspective and is concerned with the environmental settings within which firms operate and behave as producers, sellers and buyers of goods and services.

or General Electric, invest in a variety of different product markets to reduce their exposure to risk in single product markets, hence exerting influence in a range of markets.

● *Government policy.* National, regional and local governments as well as economic or political unions such as the European Union (EU) or the North American Free Trade Agreement (NAFTA) enforce regulations that guide and restrict competition, taxes and subsidies, employment, price controls, trade policies or environmental policies for many industries. For example, in early 2010 the EU competition authorities approved a giant merger between France Telecom's Orange UK and Deutsche Telekom's T-Mobile UK to create the largest European mobile phone operator. However, the European Commission promoted competition by requiring that the two companies had to agree to amend existing network sharing agreements with Hutchison 3G UK (3UK).

Michael Porter (1980; 1985) suggested that factors such as initial capital requirements, the threat of price cutting by established firms and the level of product differentiation represent 'barriers to entry' for new-firm entrants into markets. Hence, a thorough understanding of the market and its potential entry barriers becomes critical for organizations to determine. The concentration among competing players and the extent to which one or a few large producers dominate the market help determine whether competing in a market is economically and strategically profitable. The key issue is to define accurately the market within which one is competing. For instance:

● A narrow definition of a competitive market might be the markets for highly profitable business-class air travel on key routes such as London to Sydney or Paris to New York. In such a market there is a regulated and small number of competing players.

● A broader definition of the market as the global airline industry would mean that a firm may have more choice as to which segment to compete in, but it also means it would be more difficult for the firm to find a profitable competitive position.

The issue of barriers has been much discussed in the literature: an excellent account of the state of knowledge with regard to what drives entry is provided by Geroski (1995) while Bunch and Smiley (1992) look at the ways in which firms actively deter entry.

Qualifications

The S–C–P approach posits that market characteristics such as the ones described above influence conduct, that is the behaviour of the firm. Different firm behaviours can usually be observed in terms of overall business objectives, which might relate to the maximization of profits, increasing sales revenues, a growth in market share, or increasing operational and managerial effectiveness. Also, different pricing strategies might derive from industry characteristics and lead to firm behaviour that emphasizes, for example, pricing at cost, temporary low pricing, price leadership or price discrimination approaches. Product design, branding and marketing too are influenced by industry parameters, for example by changes in demand or a competitor's move to include a new product feature. However, product differentiation is also a conscious strategic choice for a firm. In that sense it is strategic conduct that determines the market structure. In the same way a firm's behaviour with regard to research and development, the development of organizational partnerships, collaboration or mergers and acquisitions is influenced by and influences the structure of its markets. Generally, research in the last few decades has supported the S–C–P approach while also generating some fierce criticism. The following are some important qualifications that have emerged.

● The S–C–P approach does not always specify precise relationships between market structures, firm conduct and firm performance and it is not always clear which factors belong to structure, conduct and performance. For example, while the S–C–P paradigm suggests that the individual firm's behaviour or conduct within a given market can usually be ignored, such conduct also influences market structures. A firm's effort with regard to strategic initiatives such as advertising, legal tactics, product choice, research and development, or possible ventures such as mergers and acquisitions, collaboration, collusion or major investments in production facilities, act as strategic choices (e.g. Child, 1972; Spence, 1977) that change the market conditions for competitors. Strategic choices are decisions made by the top management team (or dominant coalition as it is sometimes referred to) with respect to important factor conditions such as markets, technology and so on.

● Another example of firm conduct affecting market structure is where there is an asymmetry of information in the market. This exists when one party has more or better information than another, which can influence how the environment is enacted, shaping strategic decision-making and subsequently creating an imbalance of power, as the better-informed party gains advantage. For example, when a firm supplies competitors with specific information that shapes decision-making, perhaps through an advertising campaign informing potential customers about price and quality, companies can influence the competitive environment through the signals they send and the sense of the environment that they enact.

● Finally, firms' performance may affect the market structure: the best performing firms can dominate the market in the long term by setting the standards for prices, production efficiency and product quality or by having exclusive access to critical resources. Hence, the more firms behave strategically in a given market, the more the causal S–C–P chain will be broken. Think of the way that Arsenal, Chelsea and Manchester United have dominated English Premier League football in recent years (at the time of writing, since its formation Manchester United has won the premiership eleven times, Arsenal three times and Chelsea twice; only one other club – Blackburn Rovers – has won it during its 16-year history).

The significance of understanding the dynamics of competition between companies within an industry cannot be underestimated. The S–C–P concept can help identify opportunities for a business, especially if it is planning to enter into an industry as a new player; it helps determine if an industry is attractive, and it can provide a firm with the advantage of ways of differentiating its products or services from similar offerings. Nevertheless, strategic management theorists and practitioners alike have realized that conduct and performance will reflect back on market structures. This led to a shift away from the idea that the market structure represents the main determinant of competition within markets. More recent strategic management concepts, which are usually referred to as new industrial organization (NIO) theories (Schmalensee, 1982), emphasize the influence and importance of a firm's conduct and strategic behaviour. According to these approaches the firm is not seen as a passive participant in markets, but an active player, influencing its industries and competition through strategic decision-making and subsequent actions.

QUESTION TIME?

2 What types of organizational conduct can you observe in the global automobile industry?

3 Are there situations in which the causal chain of the S–C–P model can be reversed?

1 What is the influence of market characteristics on the firm's ability to compete?

ORGANIZATIONAL PERFORMANCE AND SUSTAINABLE COMPETITIVE ADVANTAGE

Sustainable competitive advantage (SCA) is what allows a business or corporation to maintain and improve its competitive position in a market against competitors in the long term. Achieving SCA is the purpose of strategic management since it allows a firm to make a profit. Strategists have diverging ideas about how SCA can best be achieved.

Economic rent may be defined as the situation where an organization earns above market returns. It is a measure of market power, in terms of the rate of return over and above the average available on the market.

Scholars agree that the primary purpose of strategic management is to guide the organization in achieving superior organizational performance as it develops a sustainable competitive advantage in the environment in which it operates.

While there is no one 'best way' to build a competitive advantage, the reality of business success and failure clearly indicates that some strategies work better than others. As a fundamental requirement, an organization will always try and ensure that its financial returns exceed its capital costs, meaning that the business offers a better return on an investment than leaving the money in the bank. For instance, if an organization can get a 5 per cent return on its capital by placing it on deposit with a bank, it will set a significantly higher return for it to be achieved through its business activities. Firms will often look for a 15–20 per cent return on capital employed. When a competitive advantage has been achieved, it will enable the organization to make economic rent.

While the relative extent of competitive differences may be debatable, there is no doubt that some organizations in an industry will do better than others. From a strategy perspective this suggests that, if such differences are not merely random, then they must be a result of the application of ideas from strategic management in investigating issues relating to 'competitiveness' at the firm, industry and national level. Given that there are substantial differences between businesses in an industry, competition must be analysed not only at an aggregate industry level but also at the level of the individual firms that compete with each other, the micro-economic level. Indeed, research has shown that the differences in financial returns within an industry are often considerable and will probably exceed the differences that can be seen across industries (Cool, Dierickx and Jemison, 1989; Rumelt, 1991).

What are the factors that might explain the variations in organization performance in an industry? Barnett and McKendrick (2004) argue that differences in competitive performance within an industry can be attributed to organizational attributes such as firm size. In a study of the global hard-disk drive manufacturing industry between 1981 and 1998 they found that the ability of large organizations to ameliorate competitive constraints insulated them from an important source of organizational development and protected them from being 'selected out', or disappearing from the market, if they were no longer competitive. While large organizations led the technology race in the hard-disk drive market, these firms failed to develop into competitors that were as strong as their smaller counterparts.

Another factor that seems to explain why some organizations do better than others in their industries is related to firms' interactions and relationships. Horizontal relationships with, for example, competitors, alliance partners, industry bodies or governments, and vertical relationships with, for instance, suppliers, customers or communities, help shape strategic outcomes. Working out how to manage these relationships successfully, and how to respond to competitive moves, is an important and integral part of successful strategic management.

The theories discussed in this chapter reflect basic economic theory ideas that deal with the strategic implications of such macro- and micro-environmental factors including industry characteristics, markets structures, organizational attributes, competitive forces, and the horizontal and vertical relationships of the firm. There are many implications coming from these basic ideas in strategy, not only for the innovativeness and ensuing attractiveness of an industry, but also for the realization of SCA for organizations in such environments.

MINI CASE STUDY

Video Case Study – The Boston Consulting Group (see www. strategytube.net)

James Goth is a Partner and Managing Director at The Boston Consulting Group's Sydney office. Leading the firm's Strategy and Practice Area in Australia and New Zealand, James speaks about the strategy factors that lead to a sustainable competitive advantage and increase shareholder value. He provides a unique insight into the internal workings of an organization famed as a trendsetter in the field of strategy consulting, highlighting how its existing frameworks are utilized, and new ones emerge, to benefit the strategic development of clients. The interview delves into the specific relationship between strategy and competitive advantage, defining what strategy really means for an organization

and why it is the trade-offs that a company makes that distinguish it strategically from its competitors.

Questions

1   What is the framework that guides BCG's approach to strategy development based on? How can firms achieve increased shareholder value?

2   What is the role of the strategy consultant? How can consultants help organizations to understand and develop a strategic competitive advantage?

3   James Goth refers to the tri-factors of strategy. What does he mean and how does the concept help strategists?

4   What are the various steps, stages and perspectives that BCG strategy consultants employ to develop strategies? What kinds of data are necessary?

5   The future strategist will have to be even more dynamic and faster than today. What are some of the implications of these increasing pressures on the qualities of a strategist?

UNDERSTANDING THE MACRO-ENVIRONMENT

It does not matter what the nature of business is, a firm is embedded in a complex network of relations with various other organizations and individuals. It is these relationships and strategists' awareness of current and important developments that help shape a firm's strategy and determine its position and competitiveness. The macro-environment for an organization is therefore nothing else but the world in which it operates. Macro-influences are often very complex in practice so strategists will refer to industry associations or external consultants for information.

Yet strategists need to build and base strategic decisions on their own perception of key influences in the broader environment. A thorough analysis of the macro-environment helps ensure that they have fully addressed the current and future operating environment for the firm. Such analysis is often referred to as PESTEL analysis. PESTEL analysis (Table 2.1) is an acronym that stands for the Political, Economic, Social, Technological, Environmental and Legal influences that are usually beyond the firm's control but must still be considered both as sources of competitive advantage (opportunities) and as potential sources for an erosion of competitive advantage (threats):

- *Political* influences, governments and other political bodies matter in a number of ways. Government action can foster industry creation and economic development. Mahmood and Rufin (2005), for example, consider the role of government in the process of technological development and show that its role regarding technological development varies during the development process. Other political factors that can be considered when analysing the macro-environment of the firm include the impact of corrupt governments on firm-level decision-making by managers of multinational enterprises, the attractiveness of political markets and the impacts they can have on firm-level strategies, and the role of deregulation for the competitive situation of an industry. When a country is distanced from technological frontiers, its government can spur economic development through the centralization of economic and political control, but as the economy approaches the technological frontier, the government's role must change considerably, with political and economic freedom now being necessary.

- *Economic* influences refer to macro-economic factors such as exchange rates, business cycles and economic growth rates or interest rates in the countries that the firm operates in. For example, higher interest rates may deter investment because it costs more to borrow, while a strong currency may make exporting more difficult because it raises the price in terms of a foreign currency. Other dynamics include inflation that may provoke higher wage demands from employees and raise costs, while higher national income growth may boost the demand for a firm's products. At the time of writing, commentators are speculating on the economic prospects for the global economy in the medium term.

- *Social* influences incorporate changing cultures and demographics, such as ageing populations or urbanism in many parts of the world. Such changes can impact on the market for a firm's products and the availability and willingness of people to buy from or work for companies. In the UK, for example, the ageing population has led to some firms shutting pension funds to new entrants, while at the same time the demand for sheltered accommodation and medicines for elderly people has increased.

- *Technological* influences refer to innovations such as the Internet, biotechnology and nanotechnology or the invention of new materials. Mobile phones, computer games and high-definition TVs have spawned new markets because of technological progress. Such technological developments often reduce costs, improve the quality of products and services, and provide benefits for consumers as well as the companies that make use of new technologies.

- *Environmental* influences are important 'green' issues, such as the pollution and waste that can affect industries such as farming, tourism, travel, transportation or insurance. With major climate changes occurring due to global warming, a greater environmental consciousness and changing policies, environmental factors are becoming a more significant issue for firms to consider. The growing desire to protect the environment is having an impact on consumer buying behaviour, which in turn is affecting demand patterns and business opportunities.

● *Legal* influences concern legislative constraints or changes, such as health and safety legislation, recycling regulations, equal opportunity directives or restrictions on company mergers and acquisitions. Each of these influences can have a considerable impact on a firm's costs and the demand for its products and, therefore, on its future ability to compete successfully in its markets.

TABLE 2.1   PESTEL analysis

Examples of PESTEL Factors					
Political	*Economical*	*Social*	*Technological*	*Environmental*	*Legal*
Corporate/ consumer taxation	Overall/ industry growth	Disposable income	New discoveries and developments	Environmental regulation and protection	Changes in employment law
International trade regulations	Credit availability and interest rates	Education	Speed of technology transfers		Regulation of competition
Overall government attitude	Foreign exchange	Demographics, e.g. age, ethnic mix	Internet		Health and safety regulations
Influence of political alliances	Minimum wages	Labour/social mobility of employees	Energy use and cost	Consumer awareness	Government antitrust regulations
Local inducement policies	Stage of business cycle	Overall living conditions and lifestyle changes	Technological obsolescence		Fishing quotas
Political stability	GDP and Inflation	Attitudes towards work	Decreases in transportation costs		Consumer protection
Government spending	Consumer confidence	Fashion and fads	Scientific advances		
Trade balances	Unemployment	Health and welfare	Access to raw material		

In the first mini case study in this chapter we shall look at an industry often regarded as mature – the automobile industry. Indeed, sometimes there have been suggestions that the environment is so overcrowded with firms competing for a diminishing market share because of an over supply of commodities that the market could rightly be regarded as being too full for innovative strategies to be developed.

MINI CASE STUDY

Is the global automobile industry a mature industry?

Most people would certainly answer 'yes'. Given that the industry is over 100 years old and has evolved over many decades from producing motorized carriages to today's sophisticated high-tech automobiles, we might be inclined to argue that the industry is likely to be fully mature, if not in decline, given environmental concerns and the fading availability of oil. Especially with the recent 2008–9 economic crisis in mind, few people see the auto industry as ready for further growth. Even before the damage done by the global financial crisis, motor vehicle manufacturing was considered a mature sector, with static or even eroding markets, and with existing firms subject to intense competition. The crisis has put major manufacturers, such as Ford and GM, under immense pressure, leading them to fight for their survival by offering deeply discounted products and requiring billions of taxpayer dollars to secure jobs and stay afloat.

But there are also signals that the industry's decline is very much overstated. In a recent report,

two management consultants with Booz & Company, Ronald Haddock and John Jullens (2009), argue that automakers willing to think anew about their markets and their business models will be in a position to benefit from the greatest wave of expansion that the industry has ever seen. In fact, looking beyond the current challenges, they report increasing levels of productivity and capability, significant innovations in technology and the look and feel of motor vehicles, and – most importantly – a wave of accelerating economic development in countries such as China, India, Brazil or Russia that will, sooner or later, produce an enormous new demand for personal mobility.

The 2009 launch of the Nano by the Indian firm Tata Motors Ltd, a much celebrated $3000 microcar, was not only a wake-up call for many traditional car manufactures but could also be considered the starting point for an era in the auto industry that will be characterized by significant engineering and supply-chain breakthroughs in car production as well as innovative strategies in approaching market segments that thus far have been largely ignored. While a number of other vehicle makers, such as Mahindra & Mahindra and Maruti in India, Chery in China, and some global auto companies such as Renault and Volkswagen, have been noted for the inexpensive cars they are designing for new markets, various players in the global auto industry will have to rethink their strategic position and product offerings in the face of tremendous changes in market environments.

Questions

1 What do you think are the significant recent changes in the global automobile industry environment?

2 What do you think is required from traditional automobile manufacturers today that they seemed to have ignored for too many years?

3 What do you think might be the potential advantages of newcomers such as Tata Motors in India?

Image 2.1   Tata Nano Car

HOW DIFFERENT TYPES OF MARKETS DEFINE COMPETITIVE ENVIRONMENTS

Using the PESTEL tool for analyses of the key influences of the macro-environment is a first step in understanding the organization's current and potential future situation. A second important step is a detailed analysis of the competitive situation, in other words the market structure of the different markets the firm chooses to compete within.

For an organization it is important to understand how these different competitive environments can affect its strategic choices, those crucial decisions about markets and technologies that are the preserve of the top management team. A central characteristic is the extent to which a market is homogeneous or heterogeneous, that is the extent to which it presents the same or different conditions for every firm that is competing within it. We can consider four basic market structures: the homogeneous or pure market, the monopoly, the oligopoly and the hypercompetitive.

1 In a *homogeneous* or pure market it is very easy for a firm to imitate success almost immediately because information about the market, its customers, products or production costs is available to all players. In such situations there is little need for strategy. Often, the only distinguishing variable that a firm can use to its advantage is relative price. That is also why in homogeneous (or pure) markets we see price wars that result in firms earning very little profit, an unattractive situation for any firm, and a situation that, in reality, is not often found outside economic theory. An example of a perfectly competitive market would be the international currency market. However, one can argue that even currency exchange is an imperfectly homogeneous market since the central banks will try to influence trade and countries will often peg their exchange rates.

2 At the other end of the market spectrum is the *monopoly*. It is, akin to the pure market, a special case with little need for strategy since there are no direct competitors to worry about. If an organization is in the fortunate position of having no competitors, its strategic objective will be to retain full control and protect that position. Classic examples of a commercial monopoly used to be national telephone companies such as AT&T in the United States, which, until the 1980s, controlled the phone networks for local and long-distance services and was the sole provider for telephone equipment. In some countries, such as Australia, national telephone companies that were public monopolies were privatized and effectively remained largely private monopolies. It is not only public sector organizations that have been privatized that can be effective monopolies. Today, Microsoft has often been accused of monopolizing the operating system market for computers and has been sued many times over this issue. Very few companies, however, will find themselves in a competitive environment that can be classified as either a monopoly or a pure market.

3 An *oligopoly* is characterized by a limited number of players acting in relatively predictable and coordinated ways to supply products and services. Because there are only a few players in an oligopoly, each will be generally aware of the actions of the others. Decisions by one firm will influence, and will be influenced by, the decisions of other firms. Strategic planning in an oligopoly, therefore, involves taking into account the likely moves of the other market participants. Oligopolistic industries are prime candidates for collusion. Such collusion occurs when competitors within an industry cooperate illegally for mutual benefit, for example to stabilize unstable markets or reduce the risks of these markets for investment or product development. In the United States, for instance, in the late nineteenth century, a series of antitrust laws were passed to limit such behaviour, responding to the power of the large, integrated holding companies established by Standard Oil and other companies. While it

Market structure describes the state of a market with respect to competition. Whether the market is highly competitive or not is the key question.

is possible to regulate nationally it is more difficult to regulate globally. The civil passenger aircraft industry is a good example of an oligopolistic market, since there are only a small number of manufacturers worldwide including Boeing, Airbus/EADS, Embraer and Bombardier. The oligopoly is a very common market form in developed economies as well as being an emerging market form in many sectors, because globalization allows firms to compete in markets that they did not have access to previously. Other examples of oligopolistic markets are the mobile and wireless network industries, which in many countries are heavily regulated, so that often only two or three providers are licensed to operate in the same region. The Organization of Petroleum Exporting Countries (OPEC) and other producers in the global oil and gas industry are an example of oligopolistic markets. OPEC members benefit from high profits by controlling the amount of oil that is made available.

4   Finally, *hypercompetition* depicts a market in which the sources of competitive advantage can change quickly, and maintaining above-average profits over a long time is difficult. Richard D'Aveni (1994) coined the term hypercompetition and argued that in new markets, or what was called the 'new economy' in the 1990s, technologies such as the Internet and related offerings were so new that the standards and rules were not yet developed and competitive advantages could not be sustained in the long term. Hence, any long-term SCA has to come from continually disrupting the status quo, changing the rules of the game, by taking the industry in new directions where competitors' strengths become irrelevant. A firm will, therefore, aim for a sequence of short-term advantages that can span numerous competitive arenas. For example, firms might compete over price or quality, or innovate in supply-chain management, new value creation, or raise enough financial capital to outlast other competitors. Thomas and D'Aveni (2009) link such an increase of within-industry heterogeneity of returns in the US manufacturing sector to increases in volatility and find a broad, monotonic shift towards hypercompetition. There are links to be made with earlier work carried out by economists sympathetic to the Austrian view by researchers such as Dennis Mueller, who were grappling with these issues in the late 1970s and early 1980s. A nice review of this earlier work can be found in Young, Smith and Grimm (1996).

Although oligopoly and hypercompetition are categorical simplifications of a much more complex reality, these terms help distinguish different environments, requiring different strategies, in which it is possible to realize above-average returns.

Real markets are much more complex and will usually entail a mixture of the characteristics described above. Take the Internet, which, much as any other type of *physical* market structure, is an enabling (infra)structure for buyers and sellers to exchange information, transact and complete various actions before, during and after the transaction. It is a networked information system. In that sense an online market is not that much different from a physical marketplace. Yet there are some important implications that will emerge from the fact that the marketplace is online:

YOU CAN DOWNLOAD...

L.G. Thomas and R. D'Aveni's (2009) The Changing Nature of Competition in the US Manufacturing Sector, 1950–2002, *Strategic Organization*, 7(4): 387–431, from the book's website at www.sagepub. co.uk cleggstrategy

- Typically private electronic marketplaces serve *multiple buyers and one seller*, for example when you buy a concert ticket direct from the organizers' website, or *multiple sellers and one buyer*, where, for example, a number of builders participate in a live reverse auction in response to a call for bids posted by a city council. While such variations occur in physical markets too, they can be scaled much easier in the context of the Internet.

● Another distinguishing factor is the increasingly important role of participants other than buyers and sellers in the transaction. Third parties can provide value-added services to buyers and/or sellers on the Internet, including, for example, accessing information about product quality and the price of competing brands from an infomediary rather than the seller. Infomediaries, such as Autobytel.com, BestBuy.com, or BizRate.com, offer buyers access to large amounts of data about products and companies before they make a purchasing decision, thereby acting as an intermediary between those who want the information and those who supply the information (Hagel, 1999).

● Buyers can also engage in a conversation about quality and price with past and prospective buyers and sellers. Again, while such interactions can also occur in the physical marketplace, their prevalence and scalability are greater in the electronic marketplace. Hence, online buyers are usually much better informed, resulting in a more competitive environment; eBay is an example of this.

Let us now look at some of the theories that can help us further understand the different aspects of market structures such as oligopolies and hypercompetition, since these are the most common environments a strategist would have to deal with.

QUESTION TIME?

1 Why do you think it is important for a strategist to differentiate and understand the different types of market structures?

2 What are some additional examples of homogeneous, monopoly, oligopoly or hypercompetitive industries?

3 How does the structure of an industry influence the level of competition within that industry?

HOW FIVE FORCES DETERMINE COMPETITIVE ATTRACTIVENESS

To better understand market structures and organizational conduct (behaviour) in terms of the S–C–P approach we have so far looked at the macro-environment of the firm and identified different types of markets. We now proceed to examine further what can be called the analysis of the industry's micro-environment. Turning the S–C–P approach and IO logic on their heads, Michael Porter (1980; 1985) suggested the Five Forces Model (Figure 2.1) to determine the attractiveness of an industry and construct a sustainable competitive position for the firm among competitors. This model captures the main gist of Porter's theory of SCA in that it emphasizes the five forces defining the rules of competition within a market.

FIGURE 2.1 Porter's
Five Forces Model

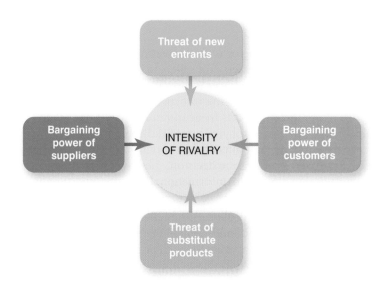

Porter argues that a competitive strategy must emerge from a refined understanding of the rules of competition that determine market attractiveness. He claims, 'The ultimate aim of competitive strategy is to cope with and, ideally, to change those rules in the firm's behaviour' (1985: 4). The crucial question in determining profitability, from this perspective, is how much value firms are really able to create for their customers, and how much of this value will be captured or competed away by rivals. While the market structure determines which players capture the value, a firm is capable of influencing the five forces through its own conduct. In that sense Porter opposes the initial S–C–P logic, suggesting that conduct influences structure as much as structure determines conduct.

The model is a very practical tool with which to analyse an industry's attractiveness. In particular, it enables a firm to construct a cogent competitor analysis since it specifies the competitive structure of an industry in a more tangible manner. In addition, it recognizes the role of firms in formulating an appropriate competitive strategy to achieve superior performance.

In the model four forces – the bargaining power of customers, the bargaining power of suppliers, the threat of new entrants and the threat of substitute products – influence a fifth force, the level of competition in an industry. Together these forces are close to a firm and will directly affect its capacity to serve its customers and thus make a profit. A change in any of the forces will normally require a firm to reassess its position in the marketplace. Each of these forces has several determinants:

1 *The bargaining power of customers.* Customer demand is the main factor that determines the power of buyers. For example, buyer power is strong when there are many firms competing for few buyers. Think of a retail supermarket chain such as Tesco in the UK or Cole's and Woolworth in Australia that has huge buyer power by deciding from which supplier to purchase tinned food to stock all the shops in that country. As buyers (customers) Tesco and Woolworth have significant power because they can compare prices and switch easily. This is different from a patient who needs a special drug for a rare disease that is only offered by one pharmaceutical company. In this case, the buyer has little power and will have to accept the price that pharmaceutical company sets. There

are various factors that help determine the relative power of customers. These include the degree of buyer concentration in relation to firm concentration within the industry, the typical volume that a buyer demands, the costs of switching to a new producer, the availability of information for buyers about products and services in an industry, the overall price structure and price sensitivity of buyers.

2 *The bargaining power of suppliers.* Supplier relationships can be complex, especially when suppliers, for example, have exclusive access to important inputs such as raw materials, technology or knowledge. Suppliers can be in a very strong position and eventually dictate the quality, volume and, most importantly, prices of goods and services. The factors that help determine supplier power in an industry include the degree of supplier concentration in relation to firm concentration, the supplier's switching costs relative to the firm's switching costs, the degree of differentiation of inputs, the availability and presence of substitute inputs, the threat of forward integration by suppliers relative to the threat of backward integration by firms, the cost of inputs relative to the selling price of the product, and the importance of the buyer's volume to the supplier. The OPEC states are important suppliers to the airline industry and wield significant power because of the limited number of potential suppliers of oil; also, think of a highly unionized firm in which suppliers (qualified labour) can call for a strike and stop production.

3 *The threat of new entrants.* When new firms enter an existing industry, this will have an impact on competition. Porter suggests that strategists should assess how easy it is for a new company to enter an industry or how easy it is for an existing firm to exit the industry. Obviously, the most attractive segments will have high entry barriers and low exit barriers. Entry barriers might include capital requirements, brand equity, product differentiation, profits based on economies of scale, switching costs for buyers, access to distribution channels, other cost advantages, experience, or government policies. Take for instance the pharmaceutical industry: entry barriers are extremely high because it takes many years to research and test drugs before they can be sold for profit. Hence, a new start-up would face huge costs and long-term investment without returns, which is not a very attractive prospect for capital. In each industry, companies and firms that are already established will seek to protect those areas where they are most profitable and attempt to prevent any additional competitors from entering the market. It is not uncommon for rivals to work together temporarily to keep new firms out. Barriers to exit the industry are often similar to barriers to entry; they limit the ability of a company to leave the market – even if it wants to do so. The consequence is that this makes competition more intense because one company that otherwise might prefer to leave is forced to stay in the industry. **Asset specificity** is a common exit barrier. The motive for creating such barriers is to keep out companies that perform poorly and sustain a situation where all existing competitors have the potential for better profits.

4 *The threat of substitute products.* Where substitute products are readily available in other industries and have the potential to satisfy a similar need for customers, they can shape the strategic context. As more substitutes become available and affordable, the competition is less intense since customers have more alternatives. Substitute products may limit the ability of firms within an industry to raise prices and improve margins. The factors

Asset specificity is an economic term used to describe a situation where a firm's assets, such as the plant and equipment required for manufacturing a product, are highly specialized and, therefore, cannot easily be sold to other buyers in another industry.

that determine this force include the buyer propensity to substitute, the relative price performance and quality of substitutes, buyer switching costs, and the perceived level of product differentiation within an industry. Take the example of CDs as a substitute for vinyl, and MP3 technology as a substitute for CDs. Or take Skype as an example of a new technology that may displace traditional telephony. In these cases the new technology does not compete with the old one but substitutes it. The danger is that strategists might benchmark themselves to other firms within their industry without realizing that the real threat is emerging from elsewhere. Typewriter companies in the 1970s competed fiercely with each other for better quality typewriters – overlooking the real threat that was coming from what was then the infant PC industry.

5 *The intensity of competitive rivalry.* At the heart of the Five Forces Model is the degree of rivalry among firms within the focal industry. The number of players, and their relative size, matters, as do other characteristics of the industry (see the discussion earlier in this chapter). A larger number of firms, for example, will increase the rivalry because more firms will be competing for the same customers and resources. This rivalry also intensifies if the firms have a similar market share, leading to a struggle for market leadership. If a market is characterized by slow market growth, firms will compete more intensely for a market share, while in a growing market firms will be able to improve revenues simply because of the expanding market. Also, if companies are facing a high level of fixed costs in producing goods and services, profits will usually stem from an economy of scale effect so that firms must produce near capacity to attain the lowest unit costs. Given that the firm must now sell large quantities, it will have to fight more aggressively to achieve a profitable market share. Other factors that increase the rivalry in an industry are low switching costs or low levels of product differentiation, whereas brand identification and loyalty tend to constrain rivalry.

The central idea of Porter's Five Forces Model is that the profitability of an organization depends on its bargaining power when negotiating prices with suppliers and customers. Logically, a strong bargaining position means that in relation to its competitors an organization pays less to its suppliers and sells at a higher price to its customers. Hence, economic market structures, such as those characterized by monopoly, oligopoly or hypercompetition, are shaped by the five forces and ultimately determine the bargaining power of the firm. Hence, strategic management, in Porter's sense, means navigating through the web of opportunities and threats framed by external competitive forces.

In a market with low barriers to entry the threat from newly competing rivals is only likely to be high when the level of profitability in this industry is also high. Therefore the strategy in an industry with a high threat of new entrants might be to limit prices that, while keeping profits low, help to avoid competitors entering the market. The Five Forces Model directs the strategist towards some of the most important aspects in achieving a long-term competitive advantage; it helps identify the sources of competition and determine their relative strength. In that sense a firm's conduct or strategic behaviour is influenced by its assessment of the five forces. However, as with the S–C–P approach, Porter's model is in essence static and to some extent underestimates the role and importance of the uncertainty and change that can occur in the competitive environment of the firm. Mere analysis of a list of forces in the competitive environment will not advance strategic management efforts until the few driving factors that can really define and bring about change within an industry are identified and understood.

WHAT DO YOU MEAN?

Industry shakeouts

A competitive clean-up

When a market is growing, the potential for high profits can encourage new firms to enter that market; at the same time current firms will be encouraged to increase production. The consequence is that the industry becomes crowded with competitors. Even a growing demand cannot support the new entrants and the increased supply from established players. In this situation competitors will have excess capacity with too many goods chasing too few buyers. An industry shakeout will occur as a result of intense competition, price wars and often company failures. An example of an industry shakeout occurred with investors and Internet businesses during the dot-com boom from 1998 to 2001. A combination of rapidly increasing stock prices, market confidence that IT and Internet companies would turn future profits, together with individual speculation in stocks fuelled by widely available venture capital, all created an environment in which many investors were willing to overlook traditional investment criteria in favour of a misguided confidence in prospectuses promising technological advancements. The industry experienced a massive decline in which a majority of the dot-coms died after swallowing up their venture capital, with many having never made a profit.

Questions

1 In the context of the global financial crisis of 2008–9, identify an industry in which there has been a competitive shakeout.

2 Analyse the micro-environment using Porter's Five Forces Model.

ANOTHER FORCE?

Recently there have been suggestions that the industry analysis should be expanded beyond the Five Forces Model that Michael Porter suggested to one that includes the analysis of additional forces in terms of the relative powers of other stakeholders.

One notable school of thought considers the sixth force to be complementors: that is, businesses offering complementary products within an industry, an idea credited to Andrew Grove (1996), the former CEO of the Intel Corporation. Grove positioned Intel as a powerful complementor of Microsoft products. Together both companies have dominated the global PC markets through their inseparable Wintel combination of Intel processors and Microsoft software. Another example is the automobile industry where companies such as Volkswagen or Fiat offer finance and insurance for newly bought vehicles as complementary services to their customers. Brandenburger and Nalebuff (1995) coined such strategies coopetition, that is the pursuit of win–win as much as win–lose opportunities jointly with substitutors or complementors. Substitutors are alternative players from whom customers can purchase products or to whom suppliers can sell their resources, while complementors are players from whom customers buy complementary products or to whom suppliers sell complementary resources. Both substitutors and complementors affect the industry since their technological advances and strategic moves can significantly change its competitive dynamics. According to these authors, coopetition can help an organization create and capture value.

Another contender as a sixth force is the state. Porter's work is impeccably neo-liberal so it is of little surprise that the role of the state is downplayed in his framework. At a prosaic level the influence of state regulations, such as network licences for mobile phone companies or fishing quotas for the fishing industry, can enhance and restrict the profitability of an industry. It is crucially important not to neglect the role of the state. For instance, in the United States, how can one ignore the role the state plays in the massive military–industrial complex?[1] If we look at some of the most innovative regions, such as Huntsville, Alabama, then the US Missile and Space Program was mother to the considerable invention that occurred, fuelled by federal funding on a grand scale, and the importation of knowledge in the form of German scientists, such as Dr Werner von Braun, whose expertise was in rocket science.

Finally, other powerful groups that possess power in Porter's terms include stakeholders such as the general public, shareholders and employees. The role and influence of employees, which is well established in countries that have works councils, such as Germany and the Netherlands, has also increased in many industry sectors of Anglo-Saxon economies. Employees generally now have more demanding requirements with regard to green management practices and corporate social responsibility. In some industries, for example the US automobile sector, employees remain highly unionized and, thus, can constitute a powerful influence that strategists have to analyse closely in order to understand a firm's competitive position.

In response to the various claims of additional forces in the model Porter argued that:

> Complements can be important when they affect the overall demand for an industry's product. However like government policy, complements are not a sixth force determining industry profitability since the presence of strong complements is not necessarily bad (or good) for industry profitability. Complements affect profitability through the way they influence the five forces … The strategist must trace the positive or negative influence of complements on all five forces to ascertain their impact on profitability. (Porter, 2008: 86)

While the specifics of competition may change, the fundamental influence of the five forces changes little. That is, although complementary products, as well as state regulations and the influence of other groups, are important phenomena, they lack a clear relationship with profitability and hence are typically looked at as factors that feed into competitive analysis through the five forces (Stonehouse and Snowdon, 2007). Where a sixth force has been added to Porter's original Five Forces Model, acceptance has been somewhat limited, because, first, there is no definite and specific sixth force in all sectors, it is different for each sector; and, second, while a sixth force could be defined for all sectors, the influence of this factor can also be captured in the other five forces and thus its necessity is less compelling.

Industry analysis is widely used and can significantly improve the strategic understanding of the competitive environment of a firm. However, there are potential problems with Porter's framework. Perhaps most importantly, the boundaries of an industry are increasingly difficult to identify. Firms will behave in ways that are increasingly strategic in their search for competitive advantage. Today's firms link their products and services in new ways that span multiple old and new industries, adding to an increasingly blurred picture of industry boundaries. Companies such as Yahoo!, eBay, MSN, Amazon or Google are redefining and blurring the differences between the markets for online shopping, news and email services, search engines, advertising, entertainment and communication. Given these dynamics, industry analysis has been criticized because it provides a static picture. It assumes the security of industry distinctions that the reality keeps challenging. The model also assumes that a firm can only profit and grow in a zero-sum game; that is, at the expense of another firm's profit and growth. Such a perspective is limited, since firms are also able to grow their returns by creating win–win relationships with suppliers and competitors alike or by innovating processes and products.

[1](see www.youtube.com/watch?v=8y06NSBBRtY)

STRATEGIC GROUPS

The presence of a strategic group in an industry has a significant effect on the industry's profitability, countering the IO economics' assumption that an industry's members differ only in market share.

Firms can be classified into categories of strategic similarities within, and differences across, groups (Hunt, 1972). For example, in the US automobile industry GM, Ford and Chrysler constitute 'The Big Three', while Toyota, Honda, Nissan and Mazda are 'The Samurai' and Mercedes, Audi and BMW belong to the 'Luxury Car' group. While IO economics considers the structural aspects of an industry, work on strategic groups is largely focused on firm groupings within an industry. Bauerschmidt and Chrisman (1993), for example, report a reduction in strategic diversity in the global microcomputer industry between 1985 and 1989 due to a consolidation from six to four strategic groups. While many survivors changed strategies, it was those firms with broader scope strategies that were more likely to be successful.

Recent studies (Porac and Thomas, 1994; Ketchen et al., 1997; Nath and Gruca, 1997; DeSarbo and Grewal, 2008) confirm that strategic groups exist across various industries and have a distinct role in explaining competitive market structures and firms' strategic postures/recipes. The existence of strategic groups influences competition because firms that utilize similar strategies compete more directly inside their strategic group than outside. As a result the competitive environment will be more distinctive with regard to the forces that determine each company's position (DeSarbo and Grewal, 2007).

Thinking in terms of strategic groups can change the way executives perceive their business in relation to others (McNamara, Deephouse and Luce, 2003). For example, managers can see a computer and software store as a meeting point for people interested in gaming or as a provider of IT services for business people. The first strategic group competes with cafés or sports facilities, the second with other more professional IT service providers. Findings in the area of strategic group identity suggest that strategic group membership is stable over time and that firms within a strategic group will co-evolve. Spencer, Peyrefitte and Churchman (2003), for example, examine the extent to which a consensus exists among managers' perception of strategic groups and explore the task and institutional factors that might influence such perceptions.

The idea of strategic groups has been incorporated within Porter's general approach to strategic analysis by explaining strategic groups in terms of mobility barriers (McGee and Thomas, 1986). Mobility barriers can be enhanced by isolating mechanisms. Strategic group analysis (SGA) (Fiegenbaum and Thomas, 1990) is useful not only because it helps identify direct and indirect competitors and their basis for competitive advantage, but often also because it clarifies how likely it is that a firm will move from one strategic group to another, or which general strategic opportunities or problems it is that an industry or strategic group is facing. In analysing strategic groups you need to identify organizations with similar strategic characteristics that follow similar strategies or compete on similar bases. Strategic groups can be identified by comparing rival firms with regard to the extent of their product diversity, geographic coverage, the amount of customer segments served, the use of distribution channels, the importance of branding and marketing, the overall product quality, or pricing strategies. The strategic group concept restores strategic decisions to the centre of analysis and reemphasizes the firm as an important unit of analysis. A detailed understanding of the industry context, the position a firm holds in relation to its competitors, the implications of strategic groups, as well as the power of suppliers and customers can all help with the creation of strategies that can lead to a competitive advantage for the firm.

Michael Porter (1980) defined a strategic group as a group of firms in the same industry that follow the same or similar strategies.

YOU CAN DOWNLOAD…

B. Spencer, J. Peyrefitte, and R. Churchman's (2003) Consensus and Divergence in Perceptions of Cognitive Strategic Groups: Evidence from the Health Care Industry, *Strategic Organization*, 1(2): 203–30, from the book's website at www.sagepub.co.uk/clegg strategy

Mobility barriers are similar to barriers to entry, but act as barriers for a group within an industry rather than for the industry as a whole. Firm-specific sources of mobility barriers include organizational structure and control systems, management skills and capabilities, the nature and extent of diversification and of vertical integration, and the nature of the firm's ownership and its connections with powerful groups such as unions, consumer groups and state regulators.

An isolating mechanism is an entry barrier or a mobility barrier to a market that can generalize the concept of mobility barriers and link them to unique firm characteristics such as the possession of idiosyncratic capital. This allows for the identification of groups based on similar clusters of isolating mechanisms on the grounds that they make competitive positions stable and defensible.

1 How might we differentiate strategic groups within the airline industry?

2 What are the factors that make it more difficult to achieve a competitive advantage within a strategic group rather than outside?

3 Why do firms choose to position themselves within a strategic group even though the competition will usually be fierce?

THE VALUE CHAIN

What has not yet been analysed is the role of the capabilities that reside inside the firm. Porter (1985) suggested using value-chain analysis (Figure 2.2) to understand these aspects better. He argued that the value chain was a most useful tool for analysing the added value of processes of production or delivery of services, shifting attention towards internal activities and the question of how, in fact, one 'creates' a competitive advantage.

A competitive advantage grows out of the way firms perform discrete activities – conceiving new ways to conduct activities, employing new procedures, new technologies, or different inputs. Hence, as a strategist you would analyse each step in this process that actually adds value to services and products and thereby map a firm into its strategically relevant activities. The added value is the difference between the cost of production and the revenues realized in the marketplace.

Think, for example, of your favourite restaurant; it transforms fresh produce into great meals. It has to source the produce from quality *providers* – procurement – and it has to set up a reliable and consistent supply of produce – inbound logistics – and then deliver it to the customer's table looking fresh, ready to eat, and delightful to the

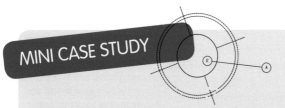

MINI CASE STUDY

Restaurant Noma: the value chain

Image 2.2　Restaurant Noma

Most foodies probably do not think of Nordic cuisine in terms of Michelin-rated restaurants. French cuisine, certainly; maybe Italian or Spanish; but Nordic cuisine seems associated in the popular imagination with pickled herrings, reindeer meat, potatoes (in many guises) – heavy food accompanied by beer and schnapps.

Restaurant Noma, jointly owned by successful food entrepreneur Claus Meyer, who provided the capital to start the business, and chef René Redzepi, is situated in an old warehouse building in Copenhagen, once the headquarters of the Royal Greenland Trade enterprises. The building now houses, in addition to Noma, Iceland's Embassy and the Home Rule representation for the Faroe Islands and Greenland.

The intention of Noma was to renovate the reputation of Nordic foods. The first step in doing this was to seek out the very best *providores* of raw materials that were recognizably indigenous to the North Atlantic region. Ingredients such as

(Continued)

(Continued)

horse mussels, deep-sea crabs and langoustines are flown in live from the Faroe Islands to be freshly killed and cooked immediately prior to serving. Halibut, cod, seaweed and curds are flown in from Iceland. Lamb, musk ox, berries and Greenland water are also sourced. If an ingredient is not in season or cannot be fished out of a nearby sea, fjord, lake or river, it does not make it onto the menu. Basic Nordic ingredients such as cereals, hulled grains and legumes are experimented with to make surprising preparations that will supplement some of these rare ingredients. Setting up reliable and trusted supply chains was essential.

Second, Noma sought to establish a culture of excellence and a preparedness to experiment. The Noma chef/cook and other joint owner René Redzepi came to Noma after having served as assistant manager at Kong Hans Restaurant in Copenhagen and had previously worked for extended stints at some of the world's most highly esteemed three-star Michelin restaurants (French Laundry, El Bulli and Jardin des Sens). He was a craftsman who had served a fine apprenticeship and learnt from master chefs. The potentials of milk and cream are explored for a modern cuisine. Different cereal grains are used in unfamiliar ways. Berries and herbs are collected on excursions to the countryside, including certain varieties that are rarely gathered; thus, some raw ingredients are used that could not be sourced through the usual *providores*. Traditional methods of preparing Nordic foods are reinterpreted. Smoking, salting, pickling, drying, grilling and baking on slabs of basalt stone are used, as are self-made vinegars and distilled spirits. In the North Atlantic's peasant antecedents these were all method of preserving and cooking foods in the long, cold, dark winters when fresh produce was scarce. Rather than Mediterranean-sourced wines for sauces and soups, systematic use is made of beers and ales, fruit juices and fruit-based vinegars as the basis for sauces and seasonings. Vegetables, herbs and spices and wild plants in season play a prominent role. Old manuscripts and recipe collections are scoured for anthropological insights into past traditions that have hardly survived in the modern world. Old ingredients, forgotten traditions and experimental methods are combined in state-of-the-art kitchens, equipped with the most modern kitchen appliances. The watchwords for Noma are purity and simplicity – both in the ingredients and in their transformation. The menu is a rich array of degustation courses, served with style and simplicity.

Third, there is ambience. Restaurant Noma has simple handcrafted cutlery with bone and horn handles, Nordic in their style and fabrication. The chairs and tables are plain local timber, beautifully aged, as are the floors and beams, reminders of the original old warehouse. Patrons are as likely to turn up on a bicycle as in a taxi or a car and will not feel intimidated by the democratic ethos of the restaurant. (Of course, while the ambience may be elegant, understated and recognizably Nordic, so is the quality!)

Fourth, unlike many restaurants, Noma has a full-time business manager, a Copenhagen Business School graduate, who is engaged not only in the day-to-day managing but also more importantly in articulating a strategic vision and mission designed to gain Noma that third Michelin star.

Fifth, the wait-staff at Noma are professionals: they are elegant, discrete, attentive and integral to the operations of the business. They are not recruited cheaply from the ranks of students or out-of-work actors or models. Of course, professional-business managers, fresh ingredients, specialist *providores* and accomplished wait-staff are not cheap.

Sixth, there is the role of the state, coordinated through the Nordic Council of Ministers, a collaborative council established by the Nordic states, which launched a New Nordic Food programme to expose the value of Nordic food and its associated culture. René Redzepi was appointed as one of the ambassadors for the programme because of his ongoing efforts to advance and promote the knowledge of Nordic food. The role of the programme should not be underestimated. There is a reciprocal relation between the Nordic Council's efforts and the culture of excellence and experimentation being developed at Noma. Redzepi's rendition of Nordic gourmet cuisine is a response to the 'challenge to play a part in bringing forth a regeneration of Nordic culinary craft, in its capacity to encompass the North Atlantic region and to brighten the world with its distinctive tastiness and special regional character'.

In April 2010, Noma was declared the best restaurant in the world by the acclaimed publication *Restaurant Magazine*, taking the top spot from the Spanish restaurant *El Buli* and the English restaurant *The Fat Duck*. Since that listing, the three-month waiting list is increasing exponentially as Noma takes a new booking every two minutes.

(Continued)

(Continued)

Questions

1. What is the strategic position of Restaurant Noma?

2. How does the concept of strategic groups apply to the fine dining industry?

3. What would you analyse as the value chain for Restaurant Noma?
   (The following websites may be useful: www. Noma.dk, www.copcap.com/composite-1487.htm, www.nelso.com/dk/place/7240/, www.clausmeyer. dk/en/the_new_nordic_cuisine_/Noma_.html)

FIGURE 2.2 Porter's concept of the value chain

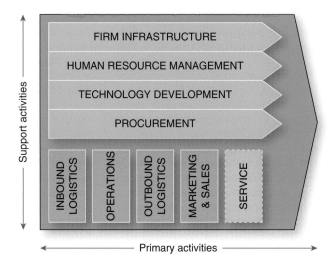

senses – the outbound logistics. In between there is the skill of the kitchen staff under the chef's supervision. If the restaurant is to flourish it will need to be marketed and represented in the various marketing channels for restaurants. How the restaurant looks, its infrastructure, as well as the way it recruits and trains its staff, the management of human resources, will also be important. The value the restaurant adds consists of the skills of the chef, the friendliness of the waiter, and the overall ambience – in short, the added value is that which exceeds the value of the sum of the parts. And at times the value added can be quite amazing. Take, for example, a restaurant recently voted the third best in the world, Restaurant Noma in Copenhagen: it is a two-star Michelin restaurant where the whole team, from the business manager, through the chefs, to the wait-staff, have focused on becoming and being number one in the world. Analysing the restaurant's value chain, we can scrutinize each of its activities as a potential source of advantage.

A firm sustains competitive advantage by performing the strategically important activities better than its competitors. The value-chain framework emphasizes that competitive advantage can come not just from great products or services but from any activity along the value chain. As can be seen in Figure 2.2, there are several primary activities (from inbound logistics to services) that describe the chain of production. Porter also includes support activities that keep the primary activities going.

Decisions about **outsourcing** often flow from a value-chain analysis. At Noma, for instance, all outsourced relations with food suppliers are with trusted and high-quality *providores*; the value chain is not something that is tightly and competitively managed to drive down costs but is managed to ensure consistent quality.

Although strategy might suggest that outsourcing can cheapen costs and thus add monetary value in an operation, Noma tells us that value is not purely about

Outsourcing means eliminating parts of the production system that do not add value to the product and can be better or more cheaply contracted ('outsourced') to another company that is a specialist in this area. For instance, instead of having their own accountancy department, companies might outsource the tasks to specialists. They could do it better and cheaper, preserving more value, than if it were internally organized. It is, hence, important to understand how a firm fits into the overall value system, which includes the value chains of its suppliers, distribution channels, outsourcing partners and buyers.

value for money: it is also about the value of innovation, quality and culture more generally.

GENERIC STRATEGIES

Another influential concept that Porter suggested is the concept of generic strategies (Figure 2.3). Remember that Porter argues that the primary determinant of a firm's profitability is a combination of its position within the industry that it operates in and the overall attractiveness of that industry. In fact, even if an industry generates below-average profitability, a firm that is positioned well can still generate superior returns. To position a firm successfully, managers have to leverage the company's strength and build SCA. In his concept of generic strategies Porter argues that a firm's strengths eventually relate to two basic types of competitive advantage: *low cost* or *differentiation*. Managers have to decide which type of competitive advantage they build their strategy on.

Noma's strategy is clearly based on differentiation. A subsequent decision is about competitive scope, a choice between targeting broad industry segments or a focus on a narrow segment. The choice of competitive advantage in combination with a broad or narrow competitive scope leads to three generic types of strategies: cost leadership, differentiation and focus, where the focus strategy can have a cost focus or a differentiation focus. Noma's strategy decided to opt for a narrow market segment, choosing discerning customers with a well-developed gastronomic appreciation.

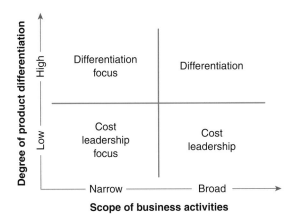

FIGURE 2.3 Porter's generic strategies

Cost leadership

One widely used strategy for competitive advantage is that of cost leadership.

The source of a cost advantage can vary for different industries, but commonly involves the pursuit of economies of scale, proprietary technology, or better access to raw materials and other production factors. A firm following a cost leadership strategy must find and take advantage of all sources of cost advantage to sustain its position; only then can it command prices at or near the industry average that will result in above-average returns. Cost leadership strategies can usually be found in broad markets. If, for example, pricing is very competitive or the industry matures and prices decline, the firm that follows a cost leadership strategy is often able to maintain profitability longer while other competitors suffers losses.

To implement a cost leadership strategy successfully a firm has to develop efficiencies with regard to the use of facilities and production processes to create the same benefit for customers at a much lower cost than competitors.

Companies that have followed a cost leadership strategy with significant success include Wal-Mart, Aldi, Toyota, Southwest Airlines and IKEA. Typical strengths of a leadership strategy include:

- Access to capital that allows a significant investment in production assets and, at the same time, represents an entry barrier that other firms may not be able to overcome.
- The ability to develop products very efficiently, for example by using only a few components or having a short assembly method.
- Access to world-class expertise in manufacturing processes, service delivery or well-organized distribution channels.

To maintain their strength, low-cost producers such as Southwest Airlines know that they must continuously improve productivity and efficiency. This may include substantial investments in, for example, acquiring the newest and youngest fleet in the industry rather than buying used aircraft. While that is costly, Southwest Airlines is able to save on pilot training, maintenance, spare parts inventory and other activities by volume purchasing only one type of aircraft, the Boeing 737. Yet maintaining a position of cost leadership in an industry is not easy, especially when other firms are also able to lower their costs because, by doing this, they gain improved access to technology, capital and knowledge enabling them to reproduce strategic production capabilities, thus eliminating competitive advantage.

Differentiation

In a differentiation strategy a firm seeks to be unique in its industry by offering products or services that stand out from the competition based on features or components that customers value most and are willing to pay for.

Another widely used strategy for competitive advantage is that of differentiation.

Difference in a firm's offering can come from various sources, including the brand image, technology, superior and additional features, better customer service, dealer networks and outstanding support. In general products and services can be differentiated on the basis of either tangible or intangible features:

- Tangible features include things such as size, colour, design and weight that are recognizably different and increase the perceived quality of the product. Other tangible differentiators are pre-sales and post-sales services such as payment options, accessories, available upgrades and spare parts that complement a product.
- Intangible differentiators represent unique characteristics that a firm is able to offer buyers, such as exclusiveness, individuality, brand image or security. The crux is to find those attributes of an offer or a combination thereof that a sufficiently large group of buyers within an industry see as important. A firm can then develop the right products and services and thereby obtain a position where it can meet exactly those customers' needs.

Firms that follow a differentiation strategy are usually rewarded for their uniqueness with the ability to charge a premium price, which should cover the extra costs incurred in offering the unique product. Even in the case where suppliers increase their prices, a firm may just be able to pass along those costs to its customers for whom it might be difficult to find substitute products.

Companies with successful differentiation strategies include the automobile manufacturer Mercedes, the audio and video equipment manufacturer Bang & Olufsen, the transport and logistics provider FedEx, and luxury fashion companies such as Chanel, Gucci and the like. The organizational strengths of these companies include access to leading research and development, very creative product developers, a smart sales force that can communicate the outstanding qualities of the product, and an overall reputation or brand recognition for quality and innovation.

To ensure long-term success these firms have to make sure that the combination of factors used to achieve differentiation is difficult, if not impossible, for rivals to imitate. This is often achieved through entry and mobility barriers or building a strong brand and a loyal customer base. At the same time companies that follow a differentiation strategy have to be aware of changes in customer tastes and preferences, since a competitive advantage can easily vanish by losing sight of what customers want.

Porter's generic strategies are generic because they are not dependent on the firm or the industry and because they characterize strategic positions at *the simplest and broadest level*. Yet they are useful in that they emphasize the implications of the strategists' decision about the type and scope of a firm's competitive advantage. There are different risks inherent in each generic strategy, but, as Porter puts it, being 'all things to all people' is a sure recipe for mediocrity – namely getting 'stuck in the middle'.

Focus strategies

The firm's choice of a narrow competitive scope within an industry defines the focus for its generic strategies. Hence, pursuing a focus strategy entails targeting a particular segment with the objective to meet the needs of this particular group and thereby achieve high levels of customer loyalty and subsequent above-average returns. The focus strategy has two variants: the differentiation focus and the cost focus. While in a differentiation focus a firm seeks differentiation in its specific target segment, the cost focus strategy seeks a cost advantage in a target segment. In other words, a differentiation focus exploits the special needs of unique buyer groups, while the cost focus strategy exploits differences in cost behaviour.

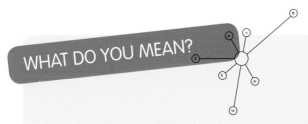

WHAT DO YOU MEAN?

Stuck in the middle

Michael Porter said firms that do not follow one of the three generic approaches, or firms attempting to pursue more than one of these strategies, would be 'stuck in the middle', meaning that they would find themselves in a position where they might be unable to realize profits above the industry average. The reason is that a firm's decisions about how to allocate its resources would become unclear, thereby not providing a competitive advantage in any of the three generic ways. Customers, suppliers and others would receive confusing impressions.

For example, if a firm aims to differentiate its offer by producing high-quality products, it might undermine the customers' perception of that quality if it seeks to become a cost leader at the same time. Even if the quality did not suffer, the firm would risk leaving a confusing impression with its customers. In fact, only few firms have sufficient resources to pursue more than one strategy at a time.

Porter wanted to emphasize the importance of strategic clarity in making these two fundamental strategic decisions: first, when taking a low-cost position or developing uniqueness in buyers' eyes; and, second, on whether to attempt to serve the entire market or a smaller segment of buyers. To be successful over the long term, a firm must select only one of the three generic strategies.

The bottom line for any firm adopting a focus strategy is to make sure that customers really do have different needs and wants. That is to say, firms have to ensure that there is a valid basis for segmentation, that customer needs can be better serviced by entirely focusing on them and that currently available products do not yet sufficiently meet those needs and wants. There are many well-known examples of a differentiation focus strategy. For instance, The Body Shop is an example of a differentiation focus strategy. While one advantage of a differentiation focus strategy is that firms may be able to pass on higher costs to customers since substitute products are hard to find, the trade-off for this strategy is that the market share is usually limited to the size of the specific segment. However, within this limitation, profits can be significant.

The Body Shop is distinctive. It takes a basic low-value-added product, cheap personal care items, and brands and sells them in specialist retail outlets. Previously, prior to the emergence of the Body Shop in the 1970s, you would have bought such items in a pharmacy or department store, choosing from a variety of well-known brands. There is a very different strategy available to manufacturers and retailers of these items, however, and that is to promote and market them based on a strategy of cost leadership. An example of cost leadership focus would be those retailers who sell own-label or discounted label products, often called 'me-too's'. Since a firm following this strategy seeks a lower cost advantage in one or a few market segments it will usually offer a more basic product, which is still acceptable to a sufficient number of consumers. This can be risky, however, because a broad-market cost leader might easily be able to adapt its product and compete directly. Think of mass retail chain store pharmacy retailers, for instance.

While Porter originally suggested that firms should avoid being unclear about their strategic intention with regard to the three generic options, over the years strategists found that various combinations of these generic strategies were possible as well as profitable. For example, a single generic strategy might not be the best option when customers seek multi dimensional satisfactions from a given product in a mixture of quality, style, convenience and price. Hence, a high-quality producer might closely follow a differentiation strategy and then suffer when another firm enters the market and offers a lower quality product that better meets the overall needs of customers. It is important to understand exactly the kind of product aspects or combinations customers will look for.

A successful combination of generic strategies is often a result of seeking an advantage on the basis of one strategy while pursuing parity on the other (Table 2.2). Alternatively, firms may pursue multiple strategies by creating separate business units for each strategy. In either case the competition will also attend to cost, differentiation and focus, to the extent that an industry will sometimes become characterized by an homogenization of strategies, which may then trigger a state described earlier as hypercompetition.

TABLE 2.2　Strategic implications of generic strategies and industry forces

	Differentiation	*Cost Leadership*	*Focus*
Buyer power	Buyers have less power to negotiate because of limited alternatives	Firms may be able to offer discounts or lower price to powerful buyers	Buyers have less power to negotiate because of limited alternatives
Supplier power	Firms may be able to pass on supplier price increases to customers	Firms are more protected from powerful suppliers	Low volumes lead to more supplier power; however, a differentiation-focused firm is able to pass on supplier price increases to customers

(Continued)

TABLE 2.2 (*Continued*)

	Differentiation	*Cost Leadership*	*Focus*
Entry barriers	Firms are better protected because customer loyalty can discourage potential entrants	The capability to cut prices deters potential entrants	A unique competency as the result of a focusing strategy can represent an entry barrier
Threat of substitutes	The threat of substitutes is reduced since customers become attached to differentiating attributes	The capability to cut prices can help defend against substitutes	Specialized products and unique competencies protect against substitutes
Rivalry	Brand loyalty can help keep customers from switching to rivals	Cost savings and production efficiencies allow competing on price	Rivals may not be able to meet differentiation-focused customer needs

MINI CASE STUDY

Strategy at IKEA and Dell

IKEA and Dell are two very successful organizations in their respective industries. What is it that sets them apart from the competition?

IKEA combines stylish furniture with affordable prices. In order to deliver this unique proposition, it innovated how furniture was displayed (in the showroom furniture is shown in mini-room displays, creating ideas about how it could be used, which inspires people); IKEA gave away attractive catalogues full of IKEA products that you could linger over at home and imagine how useful or beautiful they would be in your environment; IKEA saved money on warehousing through flat-packing its furniture; it created an aura of Swedish wholesomeness and practicality by its naming strategy – who had ever thought of calling flat-pack shelves Billy?

Additionally, IKEA makes its customers a partner in the fabrication of the furniture as it is the customers who have to put the flat-pack boxes together at home. It also added some services, such as childcare facilities or the infamous IKEA restaurant where the whole family could relax over a meal and a drink at extremely low prices and experience a little imagined Sweden with its soused herrings. IKEA is a great example of what Michael Porter calls strategic positioning, that is 'performing different activities from rivals' or performing similar activities in different ways' (1996: 62).

It becomes clear that positioning is about the creation of a unique and valuable position, involving a different set of activities. It is exactly what IKEA does. Could a competitor copy IKEA? Yes, you could build a company from scratch that is modelled on IKEA. But it would be a risky business as you would lack the learning and experience that IKEA has gained since it opened its first store in 1958 in Sweden. How about companies that are already in the furniture business – could they not simply imitate IKEA? Yes, but this means they would have to give up their current showrooms, their spacious warehouses, break contracts with their suppliers, retrain their staff and so on. They might as well start a business from scratch! The key point that Porter makes is that you cannot have it both ways: you cannot have IKEA's flat-pack system that co-opts customers into being amateur furniture assemblers and offers them a premium experience. Strategy, Porter argues, is all about choices and trade-offs. The set of activities that results from these choices creates your unique strategy. The main threat to a successful strategy is compromise: trying to be too many things to too many people.

Dell, on the other hand, is a classic example of a company that produces goods at a low cost, derives profits from economies of scale, and has a distinct competitive advantage because it can undercut its rivals predominantly on price. Dell's success is due to the company's famous build-to-order direct-sales business model, which eliminates expensive intermediaries, lowers

(Continued)

(Continued)

working-capital investments and provides real-time market information to management. The direct model also means small overhead costs and allows Dell to undercut rivals without sacrificing features or profitability. The firm has consistently improved margins and increased revenue. At the same time Dell has replicated its business model across numerous new markets, most recently by moving into consumer electronics. Meanwhile, Dell's competitive advantage in building computers, servers and notebooks at the lowest possible prices has made life extremely difficult for other manufacturers, such as Gateway GTW and HP Compaq HPQ.

Questions

1 What is IKEA's and Dell's core strategy? Which of Porter's generic strategies do the firms follow?

2 Can a firm follow more than one generic strategy? Discuss the implications of doing so!

Value-creating disciplines

Every business possesses capabilities that enable it to position products and services in a market; however, only a few of these capabilities need to be superior to those of the competition. These are the distinctive capabilities that support a value proposition that is valuable to customers and hard for competitors to match. Treacy and Wiersema (1995) suggest a generic framework for gaining such a competitive advantage. In their framework a firm will typically choose to emphasize one of three 'value disciplines':

- *Product leadership* is a strategy where a firm continuously improves the performance of its products and services to gain thereby a superior market position. Apple is a leader in PC technology, Intel is a product leader in computer chips, as are Mercedes in the automobile industry or Nike in athletic footwear. These companies achieved superior market positions through major technological advances, rapid product variation and innovation (see Chapter 6) and an ability to create products and services that serve customer needs better than competitors'. The strategy is based on a firm's ability to sense market opportunities, a fast product development and launch, technology integration and flexible manufacturing.

- *Operational excellence* describes a value discipline that focuses on providing middle-of-market products at the best price with the least inconvenience. Companies such as Aldi in groceries and Matalan in clothing, or food outlets such as McDonald's, Burger King and KFC, provide such no-frills mass-market retailing. This strategy requires a firm to achieve operational excellence in the core processes of order fulfilment, supply-chain management, logistics, service delivery and transaction processing.

- *Customer intimacy* is a value discipline that focuses on the cultivation of a close customer relationship and the delivery of very specific products and services that exactly match the need of specific customers. An example would be Dell, which produces PC to very specific customer specifications. A firm pursuing this strategy has the ability to incorporate customer needs flexibly through maintaining long-term customer relationships, while at the same time producing enough volume for the micro-segments of the markets that it is serving.

INNOVATION AS STRATEGIC DRIVER

The models of industry analysis, five forces, value-chain analysis and generic strategies have been subject to much critique. Generally it is argued that their limitations stem from the historical context in which these models were developed. During the 1980s the global economy was characterized by cyclical growth in which corporate objectives usually emphasized the need for profitability and survival. Compared with today's more dynamic markets, the development taking place in most industries at that time was comparatively stable and predictable, so that a firm had to optimize its strategies in relation to the external environment.

A central limitation of the Five Forces Model, for example, is the assumption that markets are perfect in the economic sense. In fact, governments, unions or other industry bodies regulate many industries. So the more regulated industries are, the less meaningful are the insights a model such as the five competitive forces can deliver. As a result, five-forces analysis is applicable to rather simple market structures, since a comprehensive description and analysis of five forces can be difficult in complex industries with multiple interrelations, product groups, by-products and segments. A too-narrow focus on particular segments of such industries, however, runs the risk of missing important elements.

WHAT DO YOU MEAN?

Product or process innovation

Porter (1996) argued that strategy was about doing things differently or doing different things. The strategic advantage of product innovation is that no one else can offer what you offer. An example would be Toyota's Prius car – a new environmentally-friendly product that represents innovation and is of strategic value for Toyota.

Process innovation, on the other hand, focuses on innovative ways of assembling and/or delivering products and services. Think of Dell computers. Dell did not invent a new product. Rather, it thought of a clever way of distributing PCs directly to customers over the phone or Internet. Cutting out the retailers, Dell and its customers shared the savings. Dell's innovation was process innovation because it redefined the way products were sold. Here, the strategy was based on a new way of delivering a product.

Of course, the two categories cannot always be neatly separated. Consider the example of the online telephone service Skype, founded in 2002 by the Swede Niklas Zennström and his Danish partner Janus Friis. In 2005 they sold Skype to eBay for $2.6 billion. Their innovation challenged the business model of telephony. Traditional providers try to make their customers speak as much as possible and as long as possible on the phone, maximizing their revenue through usage. Skype, on the hand, is free of charge when used online from computer to computer. So how does Skype earn an income? First, its cost base is very low as innovative software uses the individual user's hardware to run Skype. Also, Skype does not pay for the network as users are already connected to the Internet anyway. Finally, marketing costs are very low as one convinced user will encourage their friends and family to join Skype so they can talk with each other. Skype's business model relies on additional services that extend beyond the free computer-to-computer telephony. For a small fee, you can call mobile phones or landlines in foreign countries via the Internet. For Skype this works: since the cost per user is minimal, a large number of users, each spending a small amount of money on additional services, generate an attractive business. Hence, Skype's innovation is centred on a new business model.

Questions

1 What are the differences between process innovation and product innovation?

2 Can you find some more examples of firms that successfully innovated their products or process?

Another limitation is that industry analysis does not sufficiently account for today's dynamic market structures. Technological breakthroughs, innovative start-ups and other industries will often totally transform existing business models, overcome entry barriers and build relationships along the supply chain very quickly. While concepts such as the five forces and generic strategies may be useful for a later analysis of the new situation, they cannot provide sufficient guidance for preventive actions in dynamic environments.

Finally, IO and related concepts are based on the idea that a firm achieves competitive advantages over other players in the markets as well as over suppliers or customers by competition only. With this focus, however, it does not consider that a strategic advantage can come from, for example, strategic partnerships, internal efficiencies and, most importantly, innovation. Charles Baden-Fuller and John Stopford (1992), for example, argue that firm size and industry sector do not affect a firm's strategic advantage as much as its ability to innovate and adapt to market conditions. Innovation, however, is costly, risky and hard work. So why do organizations engage in innovation? And what are the strategic advantages of innovation? We examine innovation as a driver for strategic decision-making in more detail in Chapter 6.

SUMMARY AND REVIEW

Competition is a complex matter. While economies globalize and exchanges between different economic systems increase, industry definitions have become blurred by the multifaceted activities of increasingly diverse participants. In hypercompetitive environments profits are more difficult to capture and sustain. The most effective competitive strategy is always to create new sources of competitive advantage before a competitor can copy the market leader's position. These activities may allow a firm to preserve sustainable profits, but innovation is risky and failure rates are high. Hence, oligopolistic markets are often much more attractive.

In this chapter we have explored how comprehensive analysis and a thorough understanding of macro- and micro-environments can influence strategic decision-making and help strategists create sustainable competitive advantages for their organizations. Grounded in industrial organization economics and the structure–conduct–performance view, we introduced and discussed various concepts and instruments that support the strategic manager. The key learning points for the student of strategy include: different types of markets entail distinct sorts of competition; the profitability of an industry can be assessed by analysing the five forces that shape the competitive environment; value-chain analysis can help identify unique capabilities within the firm and among competitors; competing within strategic groups requires a more refined unique selling proposition; generic strategies and value-creating disciplines enable a firm to focus its strategic direction and avoid being stuck in the middle, and macro-environmental influences can be better understood using a PESTEL analysis.

EXERCISES

1   Having read this chapter you should be able to say in your own words what the following key terms mean:

- Competitive strategy
- Five forces
- Sixth force
- Industrial organization economics
- Strategic choice
- Asymmetry of information
- S–C–P model
- Sustainable competitive advantage
- Economic rent
- Homogeneous market
- Monopoly
- Oligopoly
- Hypercompetition
- PESTEL analysis
- Asset specificity
- Strategic groups
- Mobility barriers
- Isolating mechanisms
- Value chain
- Outsourcing generic strategies
- Cost leadership
- Differentiation
- Focus strategies
- Product innovation
- Process innovation.

2   How might we differentiate strategic groups within the airline industry?

3 What are the factors that make it more difficult to achieve a competitive advantage within a strategic group rather than outside it?

4 Why do firms choose to position themselves within a strategic group even though the competition is usually fierce?

ADDITIONAL RESOURCES

1 Our companion website is the best first stop for you to find a great deal of extra resources, free PDF versions of leading articles published in Sage journals, exercise, video and pod casts, team case studies and general questions and links to teamwork resources. Go to www.sagepub.co.uk/cleggstrategy

2 A very interesting and also popular book on conceiving new market space rather than competing in existing markets is W. C. Kim and Renée Mauborgne's (2005) *Blue Ocean Strategy: How to Create Uncontested Market Space and Make Competition Irrelevant*, Cambridge, MA: Harvard Business School Press. In contrast to the ideas and concepts presented in this chapter, the authors argue that lasting success comes not from battling competitors, but from creating 'blue oceans': untapped new market spaces ripe for growth.

3 Another useful resource is George Day, David Reibstein and Robert Gunther's (2004) *Wharton on Dynamic Competitive Strategy*, Hoboken, NJ: Wiley. In this book a prominent group of authors from leading business schools offers fresh perspectives on competitive strategy and the underlying dynamics of competitive interactions.

4 Andrew Pettigrew, Howard Thomas and Richard Whittington's (2006) *Handbook of Strategy and Management*, London: Sage, provides a major retrospective and prospective overview of the general strategy literature and competitive strategy in particular.

5 Michael Porter and Mark Kramer (2006) provide interesting perspectives on the role of CSR in their article 'Strategy and Society: The Link between Competitive Advantage and Corporate Social Responsibility', *Harvard Business Review*, December: 78–93.

WEB SECTION

Visit the *Strategy* companion website at www.sagepub.co.uk/cleggstrategy

1 The online resource www.strategytube.net that the authors produced in tandem with this book is a great resource: look at the video of Case Study 3 where David Deverall talks about creating competitive strategies in the financial services industry.

LOOKING FOR A HIGHER MARK?

Reading and digesting these articles that are available free on the companion website www.sagepub.co.uk/cleggstrategy can help you gain a deeper understanding and, on the basis of that, a better grade:

1 Spencer, B., Peyrefitte, J. and Churchman, R. (2003) Consensus and Divergence in Perceptions of Cognitive Strategic Groups: Evidence from the Health Care Industry, *Strategic Organization*, 1: 203–30.

2 Thomas, L. G. and D'Aveni, R. (2009) The Changing Nature of Competition in the US Manufacturing Sector, 1950–2002, *Strategic Organization*, 7: 387–431.

CASE STUDY

Competitive positioning in the Australian online apparel industry: the case of BrandsExclusive

Lars Groeger

BrandsExclusive is an Australian company based in vibrant Darlinghurst, Sydney, that sources fashion clothing, accessories and shoes directly from fashion brands and organizes online sales events. Its community of shoppers can access sales events online and purchase at significantly reduced prices – up to 70 per cent off normal retail prices. Membership is by invitation only and non-members are not able to access or buy from the website. However, membership is free of charge and there are no further commitments or obligations to buy. Sales events only last several days with limited stock exclusively available to members.

'Every brand wants to sell online, but there are a lot of reasons they can't – protecting the brand and price or existing distribution channels are some of them', says Daniel Jarosch, co-founder of Brands Exclusive. His partner, Rolf Weber, adds: 'There is strong consumer demand to buy genuine brands from a trusted online source at an affordable price.' Once you combine the two trends and find a solution to intermediate between brands and consumers a new distribution channel is created. However, no matter how obvious the market opportunity seems, it was not until May 2009 that BrandsExclusive provided a solution to meeting the needs of Australian fashion brands and consumers, creating value for both. This case describes the market environment and the challenges BrandsExclusive is facing as well as the strategic decisions it took and value propositions it created to gain a competitive advantage during the first six months of its operation.

The business idea

How did the two entrepreneurs come up with the idea in the first place? Having an international background and extensive e-commerce and fashion industry experience, Daniel and Rolf had carefully observed the development of highly successful exclusive shopping clubs in Europe over the past few years. Online private shopping clubs began in France with the launch of the vente-privee.com website in 2001. While the first three years of vente-privee.com were characterized by investment and development, an accelerated period of growth started in 2004. By the end of 2008 the company had expanded its operations to Spain, Germany, Italy and the UK, with 6.5 million registered members across Europe and estimated revenues of €510 million (A$1 billion for 2009).

The business model has since then been adopted by a number of companies globally including GILT.com, BuyVIP.com hautelook.com or ruelala.com. Succeeding entrants in the European market were able to generate high revenues within an even shorter period of time: German-based Brands4friends.de was founded in 2007 and reached the break-even point within six months, generating revenues of €30 million (A$50 million) during the first year. In the United States GILT.com was launched in 2007 and received a US$40 million investment from venture firms in a deal that now values the two-year-old company at US$400 million.

The guiding principle for the different players in the European and American market is the same: fulfil the need of apparel brands to sell excess stock quickly, without harming the brand's image or competing with other distribution channels. However, a closer look at their strategic positioning reveals key differences with regard to sourcing strategy, the scope of the target market, and the quality and exclusivity of offered goods, as well as the exclusivity of the membership community. Hence, for BrandsExclusive the question was whether the Australian market offered the same potential as the international markets, and, if so, which particularities had to be considered in order to transfer and realize a proven business model from overseas to the Australian continent.

The Australian apparel industry

'Fashion is made to become unfashionable', said Coco Chanel, and fashion by its very nature is unpredictable. Yet the Australian apparel retail industry has shown strong rates of growth in recent years and was worth A$12.8 billion in 2008. In general, clothing retailers will purchase a variety of clothing products and accessories from manufacturers and wholesalers and sell these products direct to consumers without developing or changing these further. Retailers will typically have access to both supplier groups. In addition, they will also engage in customer service, product

(Continued)

(Continued)

merchandising, advertising, inventory control and cash handling. Existing retailers can be grouped into the following categories: department stores (e.g. David Jones, Myers, etc.), major chains (e.g. Just Jeans, Jay Jays, etc.), independent stores, brand stores (e.g. Diesel flagship store etc.), direct factory outlets, off-price retailers, direct online channel of brand (e.g. skins.com.au) and discount online shopping clubs (e.g. ozsale.com. au). Retailers will differentiate themselves through styles and the range of clothes they offer. At the time of BrandsExclusive's launch there was one online retailer in the market that followed a similar approach to the private shopping clubs in Europe: ozsale.com.au. Launched in 2007 the company focused primarily on children's apparel following a self-registration membership strategy.

It is important to consider that apparel-purchasing decisions are very personal and closely linked to an individual's feelings of self-esteem, their body image and the image they wish to project. Thus, the importance of brands and the image a brand carries is tremendous. If brand loyalty exists, it is more likely to be loyalty towards the designer than to the retailer, thereby strengthening the position of the fashion manufacturer – usually towards the top end of the brand. Nevertheless, there is a growing industry for 'apparel retail' that is affordable and fashionable at the same time, as are Zara or H&M in Europe.

While creating and sustaining an exclusive brand is of the utmost importance for fashion manufacturers, there is a problem when they have large amounts of excess inventory. While manufacturers would like to use other than their regular channels, the risk of damaging the brand value by finding the premium A$250 designer jeans next to no-name brands in the bargain bin is too high. It is, hence, common practice that firms with upscale brand products would rather destroy their goods than jeopardize the premium image. In the past manufacturers have tried to sell products directly to customers by using Internet channels, thus bypassing the retailers. However, this has resulted in channel conflict since the new online channel and traditional brick and mortar channels destructively compete against each other when selling to the same markets. A prominent example is Levi Strauss & Co. When the company launched online sales of the Levi and Dockers brands in 1999, key retailers quickly told Levi that its account was in jeopardy of being cancelled if it continued to sell direct to consumers online. Within a few months Levi ceased all online advertising efforts and only a year after launching the site, Levi stopped selling Dockers and Levis online.

E-commerce in Australia

A prerequisite to entering the Australian apparel industry is that an adequate online infrastructure has to be in place. Australia is among the ranks of the most connected nations, with an Internet penetration rate of almost 80 per cent – this translates to over 17 million Internet users. Australians also make frequent use of the Internet. According to NielsenOnline, the amount of time Australians spent online in 2008 surpassed for the first time the amount of time spent watching TV. Hence, the online infrastructure for adapting the principles of the European exclusive shopping clubs to Australia looked very promising.

Market potential

Defining the market is the first step to forecasting sales. In order to define accurately the market in which to compete a number of descriptors are chosen that will characterize and set the limits of a market. Rolf and Daniel defined their market in terms of customers' needs as 'anyone who wants to buy genuine branded goods at a high discount from a trusted source online'. Thus, the market opportunity is large and broad, spanning geographic as well as demographic boundaries such as age, gender, family size, income, occupation or education. Internet access and eligibility to engage in legal transactions on the Internet act as the only main constraints on the size of the potential market.

To understand the market potential better one could also look at the size of the Australian apparel retail industry (A$12.8 billion), of which 10–25 per cent represent out-of-season or overstock products (A$1.28 billion). Assuming that 30 per cent of these goods are sold online (A$0.384 billon), and that BrandsExclusive might gain a market share of 20 per cent, this could result in revenues of A$77 million per year. Yet, Rolf Weber points out that:

> The business model doesn't necessarily need to limit itself to overstock products in apparel or the apparel category. It will eventually evolve as we see overseas. This means the opportunity increases accordingly with

(Continued)

(Continued)

more available stock and added categories depending on the preferences and needs of the consumers.

Hence, the business model is expandable. Also, the fact that the business model had already been proven successful overseas provided the two entrepreneurs with an opportunity to look at a more mature French player, vente-privee.com, and adjust the model to the specific conditions in Australia.

Challenges

Market opportunities always come with risks. During the past decade numerous e-tailing start-ups have appeared, seeking new market opportunities. But the market development has not been as successful and rapid as expected and many players vanished as quickly as they appeared. For example, after spending AU$135 million of venture capitalists' money in just 18 months and attracting few customers, boo.com became what the *Financial Times* referred to as 'the highest profile casualty among European e-tailing start-ups'. While the conditions for e-commerce have changed, it seems that the bad memories still hold back major retailers from going online. Compared with the United States and UK, BrandsExclusive, as well as other online channels in Australia, are confronted with consumers who are still wary of online shopping. The number of complaints regarding online transactions is fairly high and has undermined consumer trust and added to e-consumers' fear of falling prey to online fraud – mostly around credit cards. Furthermore, experts cite the lack of a catalogue shopping culture as another cause for consumer concerns in Australia.

Although the Internet is a convenient channel to conduct commercial transactions, apparel online shopping is associated with high levels of perceived risk and has to compete with the classic bricks and mortar channels. First, and perhaps most importantly, there is the difficulty of accurately assessing the product online. Many of the characteristics of a garment that are pivotal to the consumer decision-making process – colour, touch and feel, and fit – are difficult, if not impossible, to communicate virtually. The accuracy of colour on the Web is of particular concern to consumers. Conventional thinking held that shoppers would be reluctant to buy clothes they could not touch, feel and try on. Thus, product presentation and the website atmosphere are critical factors in evoking positive emotion and eventually increasing positive shopping responses. Furthermore, consumers do not receive instant gratification for their purchase as in a bricks and mortar store. The joy of showing off the newly purchased bargain among friends and family has to be postponed until the goods finally arrive in the mailbox.

Pure e-tailers face relatively few barriers to entry in setting up a shop online. The combination of low capital requirements and the above outlined broad and large market opportunity leads to a high threat of new entrants. With competitors being a click away for consumers, loyalty and trust are even harder to build in the web environment. Furthermore, it is of great importance to BrandsExclusive to establish relationships quickly with exclusive fashion brands, building trust and overcoming any concerns regarding possible channel conflicts or the dilution of the brand image. Although the market is viewed as having a supply surplus, it is essential for the start-up to attract quickly a large number of shopping club members by conducting sales events with premium brands. Thus, Brands Exclusive had clearly to position itself on two markets: fashion brands as suppliers on the one side and the end-consumers as buyers on the other side.

Value proposition for fashion brands

The major benefit for manufacturers is to have access to a proven online retail channel, without any extra costs or risks. This enables the supplier to generate a high sales volume through a fast clearance of excess inventory. Channel conflict is avoided, since the goods are sold to a new, exclusive and closed customer base, maybe even reaching out to previously hard-to-reach customer segments. Removing a campaign from the site as soon as it is finished with no trace that it existed protects the brand identity; sales also do not show up in Google searches. The brand stays in control and might also benefit from cross-selling in other channels. Due to the short time period of the sales event and its exclusivity, members might not be able to buy what they wanted. Following the human trait that we usually value more what is hard to get, these members might then ideally seek to purchase the brand through more usual channels. BrandsExclusive produces the campaign and executes it as well; thus, there is no effort for the brand. In addition, the fashion brand also receives a detailed sales

(Continued)

(*Continued*)

analysis report, gaining valuable consumer insights from every single campaign.

The delivery of these promises is built on the two fundamental principles of relationship management and trust. While it would be feasible to source the branded goods from China or the United States or receivership goods, BrandsExclusive only purchases the products direct from the brand itself – thus paying a higher price. This sourcing strategy clearly differentiates it from other players in the market, which purchase the goods in higher volumes from several sources. This allows the competitors to obtain better prices; however, they also have to finance and handle the stock. By contrast, BrandsExclusive only orders the aggregated consumer demand at the end of the sales event.

Whereas this ordering procedure leads to a longer waiting period for the consumer, it mitigates inventory and cash flow risks as no cash is tied up with inventory. The direct brand sourcing strategy not only differentiates BrandsExclusive from other online channels in the 'brand market', it is also a prerequisite to fulfil the end-consumers' need to buy genuine, authentic brands from a trusted source.

Value proposition for consumers

The supply of genuine brands is guaranteed through the direct sourcing strategy and the resulting continuous high quality of the goods. To overcome consumer concerns regarding the online shopping experience, BrandsExclusive acknowledged the high importance of trust and relationship building with each and every consumer. To achieve this, the founders state that there is only one way: 'To constantly deliver our promises.' Besides the authenticity of the goods, the high price discount is the second main promise they need to deliver. BrandsExclusive's main advantage compared with traditional channels is that it is able to deliver the price promise with every sales campaign. Not holding any inventory leads to no warehousing and personnel costs and the virtual showroom also reduces fixed costs. Furthermore, online marketing costs are kept to a minimum due to the invitation-only membership approach. Marketing focuses on email announcements to members and personalized customer relationship management. Satisfied members spread the news about the shopping club on behalf of the firm and provide BrandsExclusive with the most powerful marketing tool: word of mouth. To foster member referrals, BrandsExclusive provides

a range of invitation applications for the members to choose from, such as address book uploads, Facebook integration, or MSN messenger invitations applications. The highly competitive cost structure enables the start-up to pass on the savings to the fashion manufacturers in terms of attractive margins and to the club members in terms of highly discounted prices – hence the ability to constantly deliver the price promise.

Department stores and fashion retailers, on the other hand, are trapped in the sales cycle: consumers are increasingly suspicious of special sales and have learned that within short time intervals the next sales will occur – why pay the full price? Brands Exclusive creates a limited edition of the brand with every sales event due to the exclusivity, the limited time and the limited quantity of the merchandise. With a growing sense of haste in people's lives, there is also a passion about things that shout 'act now!' or you will miss out on the fleeting experience. To create a truly inspiring and natural online experience and overcome the limitations of assessing products only online, BrandsExclusive pays great attention to the presentation of the product. To create a quasi 3D effect, the visual product presentation is on human models – instead of laying the goods out flat. Detailed descriptions of the models provide further information for the consumer, for example 'our model is 175 cm tall, weighs 57 kg and is wearing a size 8 in this product'. Pictures of the models from different angles as well high-resolution zoom-in features on the merchandise further create an informative visual display. Nevertheless, the consumer is unable to try on the goods and thus might still be afraid of a mispurchase and its subsequent consequences. BrandsExclusive's answer is a returns policy with no questions asked, further underlining their commitment to excellent customer service.

Outlook

BrandsExclusive's target is to build membership to a minimum of 100,000 within the first year and have between 25 and 50 sales campaigns per month by the end of 2009, while maintaining a high conversion rate. The focus is on two key areas: membership growth and the supply of a wide and deep range of products. By the end of 2009, Daniel Jarosch expects to see at least five private shopping club operations in Australia as a result of the success of the business model. In addition, venture

(*Continued*)

(Continued)

investors have a habit of chasing the latest trend, driving up valuations and encouraging a glut of copycats, which could spoil the party, as the *Wall Street Journal* stated in July 2009. However, the importance of strategic planning for e-commerce firms cannot be overstated and will eventually lead to sustainable competitive advantage.

(This case study was written in September 2009. By December 2009 BrandsExclusive had increased the membership to 100,000 and were showcasing 30 sales events a month – accelerated even more during the first half of 2010: by July membership had reached 500,000, more than 120 sales events a month were showcased and 400 brand suppliers had collaborated with the start up. Jarosch and Weber are now well on track to reach 800,000 members by the end of 2010.)

Questions

1   Analyse the industry that BrandsExclusive operates in by using the models presented in this chapter. What is BrandsExclusive's competitive position? Who are its direct and indirect competitors?

2   Using Porter's concept of value-chain analysis, what are the value-creating steps for Brands Exclusive and to what extend can these help create a sustainable competitive advantage?

3   Which of the generic strategy options is close to the strategy that BrandsExclusive follows? What are the possible short- and long-term implications of this strategy?

4   How should BrandsExclusive address the two main challenges of membership growth and the necessary supply of a wide and deep range of exclusive goods?

5   What are the challenges of accelerated growth rates? How should the start-up overcome these challenges?

6   Which key performance indicators (KPIs) are of greatest importance for this business model?

Strategy Discovers Uniqueness: The Role of Resources and Knowledge

LEARNING OBJECTIVES

By the end of this chapter you will be able to:

- Understand the origins and assumptions of the resource-based view (RBV) of the firm
- Grasp the central concepts associated with the RBV of the firm
- Critique the RBV of the firm
- Understand the link between the RBV and knowledge-based view of organizations
- Understand the rise of knowledge management (KM)
- Understand the central concepts associated with KM

INTRODUCTION

Why do some firms repeatedly outperform others? What makes an organization successful? These are questions that go to the heart of strategy. As we have seen in the previous chapter, some strategists see market positioning as being central to having a successful strategy. We explored these perspectives using the contributions of Michael Porter and their subsequent qualifications. While Porter has been an enormously successful strategy brand, his environmental focus illuminates as it obscures. What it obscures is what goes on inside the firm. In contrast to Porter, other contributors to the strategy literature see competitive success as being attributable to the internal resources and capabilities of a firm, the premise of the resource-based view (RBV) of the firm.

Colloquially speaking, the RBV is often known as the inside-out approach to strategy. More elegantly, the perspective recognizes that, *inter alia*, important resources are inscribed in the complexity of an organization's culture, human resources and intellectual property that will provide the ingredients for a superior long-term performance beyond that of its competitors.

The main developments of the RBV took place during the 1980s up until the early 1990s. As a perspective it stands in sharp contrast to the ascendancy of Porter's external view of competitive strategy that we addressed in the previous chapter. Whereas Porter concentrates attention *externally* on markets, advocates of the RBV focus attention *internally* on an organization's capabilities.

According to the resource-based view (RBV), firms should seek to develop inimitable resources over time. It is possession of these and these alone that will help produce a meaningful and long-term competitive advantage.

STRATEGY: LOOKING INWARDS

The firm as a bundle of assets

There is a key question that stands behind the shift from an externally oriented to an internally oriented view of strategy. If we accept that markets have become far more volatile, capricious and changeable, does it make sense to orient the organization's strategy around a market that, in all probability, will change? The RBV would regard such a strategic orientation as at best misplaced and most probably a dangerous gamble that could go badly wrong if a market changes quickly.

Robert Grant (1991), a key RBV scholar, argues that in fast-changing times an external orientation does not provide a secure foundation on which to develop a successful strategy. Moreover, when a market-based strategy is successful it is likely to be copied by competitors – thus reducing any competitive advantage. Jay Barney (1986: 1232), another influential RBV scholar, noted in an early article that 'environmental analysis, by itself, cannot create the unique insights, while in the same circumstances, the analysis of a firm's unique skills and capabilities can'. Consequently, the RBV approach jettisons the strategic fixation on the market that characterizes Porter's analysis in favour of an orientation to what goes on inside the organization. Internal resources and capabilities provide the basic direction for a firm's strategy, according to RBV theorists:

> [M]anagers often fail to recognise that a bundle of assets, rather than the particular product market combination chosen for its deployment, lies at the heart of their firm's competitive position. (Dierickx and Cool, 1989: 1504)

Strategically, the RBV approach considers it better to focus on those internal factors that the organization can attempt to control – however partially – rather than on those external factors that are clearly beyond its control.

The foundations of the RBV

The RBV has been shaped by a number of different streams, according to Barney and Arikan (2006). These include the work of Edith Penrose, as well as Ricardian economics, antitrust economics and extant studies of competencies. Most of the authors central to the RBV cite Penrose reverentially in terms of the genesis of the RBV. It is widely recognized that Penrose's work has had an important influence on the development of the RBV, such that she is, in many ways, the doyenne of the RBV. Accordingly, most of the key thinkers associated with RBV – people whose ideas we will meet shortly – cite Penrose approvingly.

Edith Penrose (1914–96) was an American economist, driven from the United States by McCarthyism, whose seminal contribution was *The Theory of the Growth of the Firm*, published in 1959. At this juncture, the firm was a mysterious entity for economists; they treated it as a black box: something that contains parts that work in mysterious and inscrutable ways, rather as you might feel about the engine in your car – you know it is important but you do not actually know how it works. So it was with economists. Edith Penrose sought to prise open the black box and understand how it actually worked. She identified the firm as having important productive capacities that created resources.

In a worldview dominated by neo-classical ideas about perfect competition and markets her focus on what firms actually did was innovative and refreshing. Unfortunately, her ideas were developed largely independent of the emerging field of organization theory and thus an opportunity for economists to enrich their thinking with even greater realism than Penrose admitted was lost. Consequently, the theory of the firm and the theory of organizations developed relatively autonomous of each other.

Penrose broke decisively with neo-classical orthodoxy. According to neo-classical economics all that should exist in the economy is a free market. If free markets worked as perfectly as economists fictionalize then organizations would not be needed – all transactions would occur through market exchanges. The fact that there are organizations is proof that there are market imperfections; thus, while organization theory would view the existence of organizations as a social fact that existed empirically, for economists the existence of organizations poses an analytical problem rather than an empirical datum. As Ronald Coase (1988: 38), a prominent heterodox economist, suggested, it is strange that '[e]conomists have tended to neglect the main activity of the firm, running a business'. Penrose did not. Her ideas were in many important ways radical for economists: 'Penrose argued that one cannot even start to analyze the external environment of the firm (to include the market) without a prior understanding of the nature of the firm, which is its human and nonhuman resources, and their interaction', suggests Christos Pitelis (2007: 479). These were not part of the lexicon of the average economist at that time.

The precise influence of Edith Penrose remains open to debate, however. In recent years Alan Rugman and Alain Verbeke (2002) have argued that the intellectual role played by Penrose's work in the development of the RBV has been overstated. In contrast, authors such as Yasemin Kor and Joseph Mahoney (2004) have argued that Penrose's work played a central role in the development of the RBV, with which we tend to concur.

Economics and the RBV

In the RBV the firm is characterized primarily in terms of the resources or knowledge it embodies or commands: 'It appears obvious that the study of business strategy must rest on the bedrock foundations of the economists' model of the firm ... [the] economic concepts [of Coase and Williamson] can model and describe strategic phenomena' (Rumelt, 1984: 557). For economists, the resource-based theory is viewed as a complement to, rather than a substitute for, prevailing economic theories. Economists see the RBV as a means of adding an appreciation of the role of the firm to our understanding of markets (Penrose, 1959; Wernerfelt, 1984).

The RBV extends neo-classical views, especially in terms of the technological relationship between physical inputs and outputs embodied in the neo-classical production function. Focusing on such a problematic demonstrates how the RBV complements more conventional economics. Some central but simple ideas are stretched to accommodate the fact that firms dominate the production and distribution of goods and services. Miller and Shamsie (1996) argue that each firm's uniqueness derives from those resources it controls that are unavailable to other firms. For example, Grant (1991) distinguishes between tangible and intangible resources, and Barney (1991) distinguishes between physical capital, human capital and organizational capital resources. A central component of the RBV as it has developed from Penrose is to stress the role of these and other isolating mechanisms, a concept that we met in the previous chapter.

Kor and Mahoney (2004) singled out five isolating mechanisms identified by Penrose:

1 Path dependencies in resource development.
2 The firm-specific knowledge possessed by managers.
3 The shared team-specific experience of managers.
4 The entrepreneurial vision of managers.
5 The firm's idiosyncratic capacity to learn and diversify.

What is distinctive about these isolating mechanisms is that each one of them is the subject of strategic choices situated within the firm. Irrespective of the features of the competitive environment, these are factors that firms can manage because they are resources that managerial action can use to create specific sources of value for the organization that employs them.

Understanding resources and capabilities

An article of faith for the RBV is that *resources* and *capabilities* provide the building blocks for constructing a firm's strategy.

The terms capabilities and resources are central to the RBV. The difference between resources and capabilities is not always drawn clearly. Foss and Eriksen (1995) and Langlois and Foss (1997) draw the distinction in the definitions contained in the margin of this page and overleaf.

Barney (1991) assumes resources are distributed unevenly across firms and that it is very difficult to transfer productive resources from firm to firm. It is an expensive and organizationally difficult task to achieve such transfers.

Capabilities are not tradable and are not necessarily embodied in any particular individual. Capabilities might include a good track record in research and development, a reputation for using only high-quality inputs, a reputation for good customer service, or other aspects of the firm's culture and traditions. Through their continued use, capabilities can become stronger, more profitable and more difficult for competitors to imitate. The firm acts as a repository for the skills, knowledge and experience that have accumulated over time. Capabilities are best thought of as complex patterns of interaction, for which some organization theorists have developed the notion of organizational routines, a concept we will meet later in the chapter.

Resources tend to be either property based or knowledge based:

1 Property-based resources are legally defined property rights held by the firm, such as the physical plant, the right to the use of labour, finance, raw material inputs and intellectual property. Other firms are unable to appropriate these rights unless they obtain the owner's permission. Contracts, patents or deeds of ownership protect property-based resources.

2 In contrast, the law does not protect knowledge-based resources such as technical expertise or good relationships with trade unions, but they may still be difficult for other firms to access.

While many resources are tangible, especially property-based resources, others are intangible and more difficult to assess. For instance, an organization's culture might be an intangible resource – it is not something that can be touched or felt, yet it might be crucial to an organization's success.

The nature of the firm depends on the unique resources and relationships it controls: 'A firm's competitive position is defined by a bundle of unique resources and relationships' (Rumelt, 1984: 557). These resources and relationships generate rents: those resources that are unique in creating economic rents are the more valuable to the firm, by definition: if they are unique no one else possesses them. In a competitive market, rents arise because the initial owner and the firm that hires them have different expectations as to the value of the resource. To the owner, the value of a resource is its opportunity cost, or its value is its next best use. To the firm, however, combining and coordinating the resource hired with other firm-specific resources adds value. The fact that the firm can use the resource in ways the owner cannot envisage creates a differential between the initial owner's valuation and the firm's valuation of the resource.

Resources are tradable and uniquely tied to individuals within the organization. Resources are best understood as inputs into the production of a good or a service. The basic types of resources are financial, physical and human.

Barney's VRIN framework

It is worth reflecting upon what actually counts as a resource. For strategic purposes a resource must be something that is unique to the firm or rare. If a resource is available to all firms then it is unlikely to be a source of competitive advantage.

Jay Barney is a professor at Ohio State University. He is one of the central figures within the RBV community. His work is among the most cited in the field and he has played an important role in developing the RBV. Barney's particular focus is on how organizations actually acquire the resources they need for their strategies. He makes a strong critique of product market approaches, such as those of Porter, seen in Chapter 2. For Barney, a firm oriented to a product market strategy is unlikely to generate economic rent because other firms in the market can buy the same resources and eliminate any rent-making possibilities. Equally, the market for such resources will value the assets in such a way that they will take into account the future earnings potential, thus making the assets very expensive. In turn, this will eliminate the possibilities of earning economic rent.

Barney (1991) argues that for a resource to be a secure basis for competitive advantage, it must display four characteristics that are often referred to as the VRIN model:

1 Valuable, in that the resource enables a firm to produce a good or service in an efficient and/or effective manner to exploit opportunities and counter threats.

2 Rare, in that few organizations possess the resource.

3 Imperfectly imitable, in that it is difficult for competitors to copy the resource.

4 Non-*substitutable*, meaning that competitors cannot easily supply the resource in the market.

WHAT DO YOU MEAN?

VRIN in action

A good example of competitive advantage based on the VRIN model is the case of prestigious universities such as Harvard in the United States or Cambridge in the UK. Researchers conduct **v**aluable research and teach the next generation of scholars. This is a **r**are skill in that not many universities or other organizations can afford the costly infrastructures and networks that research is embedded in. Given the reputation that these elite universities have, they can attract funding from government, industry and donors more easily than others, allowing them to invest more in their top researchers and infrastructure. Their reputational capital is especially **i**mperfectly imitable. Finally, the value created by these institutions is **n**ot easily substitutable: in the foreseeable future, research will play an important part in the development of the knowledge society and might (hopefully, the authors want to add!) not be substituted with other activities.

The VRIN model indicates how resource-based theorists think competitive advantage is derived. If each of the VRIN conditions is satisfied then there is the possibility of a resource providing a sustainable competitive advantage. It has provided the basis for many subsequent studies that, *inter alia*, have identified resources such as organizational culture, strategic HRM, IT and trust as important resources that can provide a competitive advantage. The RBV seeks to identify those things that organizations have that cannot easily be the basis for copying, because it would be too costly for other firms to do so or because competitors are unable to access and emulate them. Thus, rather than scanning the market for opportunities, strategists should be looking inside the firm to discover the sources of a competitive advantage.

PRACTISING STRATEGY WITH THE RBV

There are two key challenges in using the RBV in strategy-making:

1 The strategist has to try and identify the resources that a firm possesses.

2 The second stage is to identify the capabilities possessed by an organization.

In some cases it is comparatively easy to identify a resource – for instance, an oil company's access to reserves (physical), its refineries (physical), its drilling operations (technological), its huge financial reserves (financial), its management expertise (human) and its long-standing experience of prospecting, drilling and refining oil and dealing with complex geopolitical situations (organizational). But equally, in high-value service organizations, such as bespoke consultancies, brand agencies and so forth, it can be difficult to identify specific resources:

> By a resource is meant anything which could be thought of as a strength or weakness of a given firm. More formally, a firm's resources at a given time could be defined as those (tangible and intangible) assets which are tied semi-permanently to the firm. (Wernerfelt, 1984: 172)

Grant (1991) discusses the problem of identifying resources, especially as their conception is limited to what is counted on a company's balance sheet. He suggests that a proxy for the resources held by a firm can be seen in the difference between the book value of a firm (which can be identified from the company accounts) and the amount at which the company is valued on the stock market. Grant has a point, although in an age of exuberant capitalism and its aftermath, a heavy dose of scepticism towards stock market valuations is probably in order.

Capabilities exist in functional areas, such as HR and marketing, and they also occur when different functional capabilities are combined and integrated. Grant (1991) identifies integrated capabilities as being a particularly potent source of competitive advantage. Of course capabilities do not make themselves immediately apparent to a strategist's observation. In many cases these capabilities may be tacit and very difficult, if not impossible, to identify.

Any capability is only a source of strength when it is stronger than those of its immediate competitors. Furthermore, what is a capability at one time can in fact become a weakness over time. A good example of this is Marks & Spencer, an organization that Grant cites approvingly in his 1991 article. There is little surprise that Grant praised Marks & Spencer (M&S), for it was a corporate icon of the time. Indeed, in the 1980s and 1990s many UK organizations had the express ambition of being the M&S of their industry. Grant identified M&S's key capability as being 'the ability to manage supplier relations to ensure a high and consistent level of product quality' (Grant, 1991: 121).

Less than a decade after Grant had lionized the strategic capabilities of M&S, the company was in serious trouble, from which it took a painful decade to recover. The key problems lay in changing tastes in consumer demand for which its much vaunted supplier network became a problem: the suppliers were good at delivering what customers had traditionally wanted but the high street was changing. Younger consumers, more style-savvy and with a growing propensity to shop for fashion goods, saw M&S as a staid store in terms of style, layout, fashions and even the appearance of its shop assistants, compared with newer brands such as Zara and H&M, which had better – that is faster and more fashion-conscious – stylists and designers who could translate the Milan and Paris catwalk looks into cheap copies within weeks of their appearance.

M&S was slow to respond to changing tastes because the innate conservatism of an organization which typically did not recruit from outside and grew its own managers through its own training programmes gave it little chance of easily understanding how competitor firms were doing things differently. Moreover, its core market was conservative – it had grown mature with M&S. It took a decade but M&S subsequently responded by establishing boutique labels aimed at different market segments inside the overall frame of the store, such as Per Una. M&S retained the conservative core products and customers but sought to capture a more fashion-conscious sector of the market as well. The problem, however, was that for many young women M&S was where their mothers shopped, so how could they be fashionably unique, rare, inimitable creatures if they dressed similarly to their mothers?

If we were to think of capabilities in other competitive fields such as sport, it would be evident that these can clearly decay with age and use. Footballers, tennis players and other sports people have unique embodied capabilities, but these can deteriorate with use or rival players can develop strategies that enable them to win in competitions. It can be the same in business.

The message seems clear: to get ahead you have to be different and being different depends on having some unique resources and capabilities. Wernerfelt (1995: 173) puts it starkly:

> Strategies which are not resource-based are unlikely to succeed ... . This is so obvious that I suspect that we soon will drop the compulsion to note that an argument is 'resource-based'. Basing strategies on the differences between firms should be automatic rather than noteworthy.

If you share Wernerfelt's certainty and are convinced by the ideas underlying the RBV, what are the practical implications? Barney and Arikan (2006) suggest that the managerial implications include the following:

- *Overcoming disadvantages.* An organization that is at a strategic disadvantage to its competitors could attempt to improve its position by 'identifying the valuable and rare resources that it currently does not possess'. Equally, by analysing the resources of competitors it will be able to assess the extent to which resources can be mimicked or substituted.
- *Realizing potential.* By analysing its own resources and capabilities a firm might be able to identify potential that is not currently being exploited.
- *Self-understanding.* The RBV can help organizations to understand more comprehensively the types of resources that actually generate a competitive advantage.

WHAT ARE THE RENT-GENERATING ACTIVITIES OF THE CAPACITIES?

The RBV idea of strategy is for a firm to generate a long-term competitive advantage and thus generate economic rents, a concept that we encountered in Chapter 2, depicting those situations in which profit is in excess of a fair market return, one that derives from a market being imperfect. Economic rents occur when reality does not look the way that neo-classical economists imagine it should. The RBV regards firms that have unique intangible assets as also having the possibility of earning such economic, or Ricardian, rents (after David Ricardo, the famous nineteenth-century economist who first conceptualized them).

According to Barney, firms following a product market strategy that earns economic rent are either *repositories of superior knowledge*, in which the strategists are far more skilled and insightful than their competitors at decoding the future of the market, or *just lucky*. Barney argues that it is difficult to believe that firms following a product market strategy would come up with wildly different assessments of the sector they operate within.

Barney points out that product market strategy tools, such as a PESTEL analysis or a five forces framework, are widely available and the stuff of common knowledge – so how can they provide a competitive advantage? Strategists using the same tools and the same data are likely to draw similar conclusions as to the future of the market. Accordingly, the product market approach to strategy-making is unlikely to yield the informational advantages required to create a competitive advantage. Similarly, luck is unlikely to last over the long term and cannot be a platform for creating competitive advantage.

Barney (1986: 1239) advocates looking inside the organization and analysing it to see what resources it already possesses. He lists potential organizational assets as comprising:

- Special manufacturing know-how.
- Unique combinations of business experience.
- The teamwork of senior managers.

Barney's approach involves determining whether resources are developed in-house or are bought from the market. In the latter case the firm might buy a company to get hold of resources that are coveted. For Barney, the resources that a firm already possesses are likely to have a greater chance of generating economic rent than those bought on the open market: 'firms that do not look inwardly to exploit resources they already control in choosing strategies can only expect to obtain normal returns from their strategizing efforts' (Barney, 1986: 1239). Consequently, Barney was cautious about the strategy of diversifying the firm through a strategy of mergers and acquisitions. Asserting that mergers and acquisitions only occasionally deliver the value that is anticipated in advance of the deal, he points out that the expected synergies rarely materialize. Part of the problem is that it is difficult for someone from the outside to understand what resources reside inside a firm. If a strategist does successfully identify a firm to acquire – one possessing synergistic resources – then they may well have to pay a high price for the assets, thus eliminating any possibility of generating economic rent.

Strategists are keen to understand the extent to which a competitive advantage is sustainable over the long term – for if it is not, it will hardly deliver economic rents. There is always the assumption that a competitive advantage will diminish over time, especially as competitors imitate and the value of the capability lessens. While the erosion of competitive advantage is to be expected, the speed with which this takes place can vary dramatically. There are four central factors determining the sustainability of a firm's competitive advantage. They are:

1 *Durability*. The extent to which a competitive advantage is long lasting depends, in part, on the durability of a firm's capabilities. In many cases, capabilities can endure over many decades, as has been the case with Coca-Cola, Guinness beer or Mars chocolate. The organizations behind these brands such as those just mentioned have strong reputational capabilities that appear to depreciate slowly, if at all. Other capabilities can be shorter lived; for instance, technological innovation can often sound the death knell for a capability's capacity to generate a competitive advantage. For instance, many high street travel agents have seen their margins slashed and viability threatened by the explosion of web-based travel booking services, such as expedia.com. Capabilities can also outlive the resources that go into them. Mercedes has been making quality cars for generations – this capability has endured long after many skilled car workers have retired. Similarly, Manchester United Football Club has been the most successful British football club in recent years. The manager Sir Alex Ferguson has built four major Manchester United teams over the last two decades. The capability to create a world-class team has endured long after once-key players have hung up their boots.

2 *Transparency*. If a set of resources and capabilities can be imitated in another context, the source of competitive advantage can be rapidly diminished. A strategist seeking to imitate a rival needs to work out how the competitive advantage is actually achieved. This can be difficult and is often referred to as the *transparency problem*. It necessitates trying to work out how to acquire/build the resources and capabilities required in order to imitate rivals. Of course, it can be difficult, or sometimes virtually impossible, to identify the resource that is most important in explaining the competitive advantage enjoyed by an organization. Furthermore, as Grant reminds us (1991: 125), 'a capability which requires a complex co-ordination between large numbers of diverse resources is more difficult to comprehend than a capability which rests on the exploitation of a single dominant resource'.

3 *Transferability*. The extent to which resources and capabilities can be easily transferred will impact upon the longevity of a firm's competitive advantage. Once the requisite resources and capabilities have been identified, a competitive advantage is likely to be short-lived. The transferability of resources and capabilities from one context to another is not, of course, as straightforward as it might seem. There can be geographic immobility, meaning that it is very difficult to transfer resources and capabilities from once context to another. Evidently this is clear when it comes to copying large production facilities such as a high-tech German or Japanese car manufacturing plant. It also applies when trying to copy a firm that functions within a richly networked cluster, such as the specialist engineering firms in the UK's Motorsport Valley, or the Internet companies based in Silicon Alley in Manhattan. Certain resources and capabilities may well be highly firm specific and will turn out to be more or less immobile. Often, when firms hire talented staff to replicate what they have achieved in another context, this will end in failure.

4 *Replicability*. Where the transferability of resources and capabilities can prove difficult, firms may instead attempt to create their own. In some cases the resources and capabilities that sustain competitive advantage in other contexts can be easily copied. UK supermarkets, for instance, are locked in a fierce competitive struggle whereby they can quickly replicate the resources and capabilities of their competitors. In other cases it can be much more difficult to replicate the required resources and capabilities. This can occur where the capabilities are particularly complex, or in cases where there appears to be highly specific cultural conditions within a firm (though it is always important to be wary of corporate fables that equate a particular culture with success; often these are self-serving myths that the leadership promulgate and propagate).

While generating a competitive advantage over the long term is one thing, Grant alerts us to the fact that it is not the same as appropriating the returns from this competitive advantage, something that may sound paradoxical. What he means is that other actors in the organization or its environment may well appropriate much of the returns. For instance, a rock group might enjoy a competitive advantage over its rivals; it might sell millions of CDs, sell out stadiums, yet end up making little or no money. Managers, record companies, 'clever' accounting and so forth will appropriate the money. These are the imperfect sources of friction in the market that stand between the artists and their audiences. Similarly, a football club might be very successful in terms of generating turnover and winning games on the pitch, yet often will make losses. The English Premier League is notorious for the number of clubs that lose money, in spite of being successful. The problem for the clubs is that the players appropriate most of the rents earned by the clubs.

An organization's ability to appropriate the rents earned from its activities may well result in its relative power *vis-à-vis* key employees. If a firm's strategy revolves around a few key people it can be very risky for that firm. For instance, Gordon Ramsey, the well-known celebrity chef, early in his career was Head Chef at the Aubergine Restaurant in London. Following a dispute with the owners he left the restaurant, which then posed major commercial difficulties for Aubergine, as it was reliant on his burgeoning reputation as *the* up and coming chef of late 1990s' London.

CORE COMPETENCIES AND COMPETITIVE ADVANTAGE

Within academic debates in the field of strategic management the RBV, as we have seen, has assumed a major position. However, being academically influential is one thing, but to what extent has the RBV had a major impact on how organizations 'do' strategy?

The chief way in which RBV thinking has gained influence within boardrooms is through the concept of core competencies. Appearing in an influential 1990 *Harvard Business Review* article C. K. Prahalad and Gary Hamel's work on core competencies has played an important role in transmitting RBV ideas from academia into the world of strategy-making. They conceptualized core competencies in a definition that has been widely used.

As both an engine and glue one might imagine that the results could be disastrous: we do not normally put glue into engines unless we want to sabotage them! The metaphors may be unfortunate but the import is fairly clear: the core competencies of an organization are what make a business more than an assemblage of parts. The specific assemblages that constitute a core competency, when working properly, power the organization's trajectory.

In a highly normative article, Prahalad and Hamel asserted that the successful organizations they studied in the 1980s (they were writing in 1990) owed their pre-eminence to the development of core competencies. What do they see as core competencies? In yet another metaphor, they conjure up the image of a tree:

> The diversified corporation is a large tree. The trunk and major limbs are core products, the smaller branches are business units, the leaves, flowers, and fruit are end products. The root system that provides nourishment, sustenance, and stability is the core competence. You can miss the strength of competitors by looking only at their end products, in the same way you miss the strength of a tree if you only look at its leaves. (Prahalad and Hamel, 1990: 4)

Trees, roots, engines, glue: the metaphors seem out of control. Still, this promiscuity and inconsistency in metaphors does not seem to have had an adverse impact on their popularity in the strategy market! Just to try and keep the metaphors under control we will attempt to explain their theory with the tree as the root metaphor (ouch!).

The health of a tree is generally determined by what is happening to the roots: Are they getting enough water and nutrients? Are they in good health? For most people, save for experienced arborists, the health of the roots of a tree only becomes clear if something goes wrong with the leaves or the bark. So it is with

Core competencies are the 'glue that binds existing businesses. They are the engine for new business development' (Prahalad and Hamel, 1990: 5).

Image 3.1 'Tree'

PHOTOGRAPHY BY STEWART CLEGG

organizations: by the time visible manifestations (falling market share, quality control problems, diminishing customer loyalty) become apparent it is very difficult to remedy the situation. Given this insight, Prahalad and Hamel emphasize a strategy that requires companies to pay careful attention to identifying and nurturing their core competencies. Three criteria for a core competence have to be fulfilled:

1 The competency must provide potential access to a wide variety of markets.
2 The competency must make a significant contribution to an organization achieving its goals.
3 The competency must be difficult to imitate.

Demonstrating how core capabilities underpin all products, they highlight how Canon – the imaging giant – can be understood to have core capabilities in precision mechanics, fine optics and microelectronics. All of Canon's product line, which is diverse, draws on at least one of the core capabilities. To return to the tree metaphor, the roots of the tree (the capabilities) underpin the health and vitality of the branches (main product lines) and leaves, fruit and berries (the actual product). Consistent with the RBV, the core capabilities approach necessitates looking deep into the organization to try to find what actually underpins that organization.

Prahalad and Hamel are particularly exercised by the way in which an organization's structure can militate against developing, nourishing and bearing the fruit from the core capabilities of the organization. They reserve particular scorn for the strategic business unit model of organizing. As a model it has it origins in the M-form and treats every part of the organization as a separate business. The ensuing turf wars and partisanship that often characterize such organizations preclude the development of capabilities across units. Often, they observe, firms are unable to see where their competencies lie; consequently, core competencies are often destroyed in corporate restructuring programmes. Infamously, this was the case with many over-hyped business process reengineering programmes, on which more will be written later in the chapter.

Complex modern firms will inevitably outsource many of their functions. As an activity outsourcing has grown exponentially in recent years. Prahalad and Hamel caution against indiscriminate or over-zealous outsourcing as this, in some circumstances, can lead to the loss of core competencies. For instance, in the 1980s the Chrysler Motor Company outsourced its engine building to Mitsubishi and Hyundai. Rover, the now defunct UK car firm, followed a similar strategy, outsourcing its engine technology to Honda. In sharp contrast, Honda was investing heavily in research and development, through sponsoring a Formula One team, to help develop its core competency. Honda survived and thrived; Rover did not.

As an antidote to outsourcing sources of value, Prahalad and Hamel advocate paying attention to the strategic architecture of the firm. This entails the following:

1 Identifying the core capabilities of an organization.

2 Deciding what core capabilities need to be built.

3 Assessing the technologies required to support the capabilities.

4 Designing an organizational structure that allows linkages to be made across different capabilities.

5 Ensuring that the core capabilities are controlled by the central organization and not by an individual strategic business unit.

6 Making resource allocation transparent.

Prahalad and Hamel (1990), those masters of the mixed metaphor, argue that strategic architecture provides a roadmap for the future. Leaving the metaphors to one side, their argument provided a powerful rationale for building a strategy around core capabilities.

WHAT'S WRONG WITH THE RBV?

It is important to remember that any theory will attract criticism. That is both inevitable and healthy. We should remember that theories within strategy are not the 'truth' but are best considered as heuristic devices or tools rather than literal representations. And tools can always be improved by thoughtful use and innovation.

As we have seen, the RBV quickly established itself as one of the central positions in strategic management. It achieved this without initially drawing much fire from critics. The situation has changed, however, and in recent years the RBV has been subject to considerable scepticism. Leading its critics are Richard Priem and John Butler who in 2001 published an important article in the prestigious pages of the *Academy of Management Review*, from where they conducted a comprehensive critique of the RBV. Their article has sparked considerable debate. Other critics include Peter Clark (2000) who argues from an organization theory perspective, John Sillince (2006) from a knowledge management perspective, and Steven Toms (2010) from an accounting viewpoint.

What follows are some of the problems with the RBV as a tool for doing strategy and some suggestions on how it might be improved:

1 *A problematic view of knowledge*. Knowledge in the form of resources and capabilities is clearly central to the RBV. The perspective has the tendency to conceptualize knowledge in an organization as an entity – as a thing – that

can be moved around. This is rather a mechanical view of knowledge and one that is at odds with much of the thinking on knowledge management, as we will see later in the chapter. Sillince (2006) suggests that it might be more apposite to treat knowledge as a process. What he is referring to is that an organization's knowledge base will consist of people, with their expertise, interacting with technology in an organizational structure. Consequently, knowledge is always in flux, it is not a tangible item. Sillince goes further by pointing out that it is difficult to attach a value to knowledge when conducting a VRIN analysis. As he puts it, 'the value of a firm's knowledge is problematic, contestable and socially constructed' (Sillince, 2006: 802). He highlights that the knowledge that is coveted in an organization will rest, in part, on the identity of that organization. For instance, an engineering organization is likely to value and privilege engineering knowledge, rather than financial or marketing acumen.

2 *Lacking a theory of the firm.* Industrial economics is premised on having a theory of the firm, which seeks to explain why a firm exists in economic terms. The RBV, according to its critics, lacks a theory of the firm and consequently cannot be considered a theory in its own right (Priem and Butler, 2001; Toms, 2010). Priem and Butler (2001: 28) became particularly hot under the collar about this, asserting: 'additional conceptual work is needed if the foundation of RBV is to meet the law-like generalization standard'. Similarly, Foss, from the Copenhagen Business School, has argued that being able to explain differences between firms, such as different resource bases, is insufficient to make these a theory of the firm. To redress this, Foss (1996) advocated an engagement with transaction cost economics. Agreeing with him partially, Toms (2010) argues that while the RBV seeks to explain competitive advantage, it fails to do so because it lacks an adequate theory of the firm. He advocates a *rapprochement* between the labour theory of value (which sees the difference between the returns to human labour for the employee and the owners of the firm as the source of all value) and the RBV as a way of achieving this.

3 *A tautological argument.* A tautology occurs where an argument is framed in such a way that it is self-referential and thus impossible to dispute. An example of this would be to say that a 'successful team will win a lot of matches'. As an argument this is difficult to dispute! Priem and Butler (2001: 28) argue that the RBV applies a similar form of tautological logic, for example: 'competitive advantage is defined in terms of value and rarity, and the resource characteristics argued to lead to competitive advantage are value and rarity'. They are trying to highlight that the RBV explains an outcome (competitive advantage) and describes what it looks like (possessing valuable and rare resources), and also highlight the inputs (valuable and rare resources) required to make this a reality. Confused? You should be. The premise of their argument is that the RBV uses a circular argument to justify itself.

In a similar vein, Sillince conducts a forensic deconstruction of the RBV and highlights its self-fulfilling properties:

> There is, thus, a self-fulfilling aspect to resource based theory. The theory states that competitive advantage follows from valuable, rare and non-inimitable and non-substitutable resources. Rationalizations constructed after the alleged success has happened look for self-serving instances of this. (Sillince, 2006: 803).

In other words, the RBV is a recursive device in which the theory is confirmed by a practice that is a redescription of the theory – thus the theory is entirely self-referential!

4 *Causally ambiguous*. A further criticism of the RBV is that it is causally ambiguous. What, in essence, this means is that it is difficult to disaggregate cause from effect. In other words, it is hard to understand the effect a particular resource has on performance. How does a strategist actually identify which resource has an impact on performance? Moreover, the RBV falls silent on the quantity of a resource that is required. How does the amount of each resource actually relate to performance? Furthermore, as Sillince points out, knowledge contains both 'substantial and rhetorical parts, making estimations of its effect on competitive advantage difficult' (2006: 806–7).

5 *Retrospective*. It is often said that hindsight has 20:20 vision. So, it would seem, does the RBV. The RBV appears to be only able to pinpoint whether a resource is valuable *after* it has actually been used. The corollary is that some critics see the RBV as an inveterate *post hoc* perspective.

6 *Resources as an all-embracing concept*. The danger with the RBV is that everything that is valuable in and around an organization gets labelled a resource. Consequently, the term can be emptied of all analytical precision, becoming a catchall term. As Priem and Butler (2001: 34) put it, '[the RBV's] overly inclusive definitions of resources make it more difficult to establish contextual and prescriptive boundaries'.

7 *Sustainable competitive advantage*. One of the premises of the RBV is that for a successful strategy a firm or organization has to create a sustainable competitive advantage. There is now some doubt among commentators on the RBV as to whether this is a realistic aspiration. For instance, Fiol (2001: 692) argues:

> I question whether it is possible to gain a sustainable competitive advantage based on a particular set of core competencies in today's environment, no matter how inimitable it may be. Both the skills/ resources and the way organizations use them must constantly change, leading to the creation of continuously changing temporary advantages.

8 *Practical usability*. The extent to which the RBV is a usable theory for managers tends to support these qualms. Notwithstanding the framework outlined by Grant (1991), critics argue that it lacks a practical application (Priem and Butler, 2001). Of course, if the central elements of the theory cannot be controlled in practice then its predictive ability will be limited, both theoretically and practically. Unfortunately, for positivists, this is the invariable fate of all those little boxes that they connect together with arrows. The infinitude of undecidable and unpredictable elements that are omitted from any schema can always be a risk to its viability.

STRATEGIC ENTREPRENEURSHIP

The frameworks that we have reviewed in this and the previous chapter have been based on a comparatively static analysis. For the RBV the firm seeks to capture rents based on the scarcity of the interior resources controlled while Porterian analysis sees rents captured when the interfirm rivalry is low. For rents to be captured there has to be an imperfect equilibrium, suggests Matthews (2010: 221), based either on imperfect markets for resources or on imperfect access to markets achieved by controlling the barriers to entry for rival firms. Market inefficiencies (barriers to entry in product markets or barriers such as inimitability in resource markets) are the source of extraordinary profits in both perspectives.

However, this is often not the case. If we think of enterprises such as Apple or easyJet, each of them can be identified with an extraordinary entrepreneur and it is the entrepreneurship of the companies that has built their business models by following hunches, testing hypotheses about markets and customers, investing in resources and activities, generating gains and incurring losses. These are the strategic calculations that entrepreneurs make, using imagination, creativity, expectation and judgements to build their firms. They do so by putting together resources, activities and routines (according to Matthews, 2010).

Resources, as the productive assets of the firm or organization, are the essential elements of business. Particular firms bundle them up in specific ways, as Penrose suggests (Barney, 1995). Entrepreneurship consists of bundling that produces extraordinary returns. Think of the iPod and its family of related products: these use much the same technologies and offer the same, and in some cases less, functionality than their rivals but have been more shrewdly marketed and branded (see Chapter 5) with more complementarities with apps than rivals possess. Creative produced the Zen, which does all that the iPod does, and more, before Apple produced the iPod – but it did not produce iTunes – and that proved to be a killer app. The firm assembled by Steve Jobs and his team became far more valuable than the sum of its parts. Likewise with IKEA and the development of flat-pack furniture which the customer has hours of fun (or frustration) assembling. There is no point in just controlling resources unless they are engaged in doing something, in activities. It is through these activities that revenues are earned. The skill of entrepreneurship is in putting activities together, combining and recombining them in a series of value chains that deliver increasing returns. What links resources and activities are the standard operating procedures that firms develop – the routines – that are progressively specialized and recombined to make up a specifically and sustainably patterned performance.

Closely related to Matthews' (2010) views are those of Pitelis and Teece (2009: 5) that it is 'the diagnosis, configuration and leveraging of knowledge assets and organization capabilities' that allow the principals of these organizations to capture value in the form of profit from both the creative and routine operations of the organization. This enables not only the minimization of transaction costs but also the combination of co-specialized assets and the capture of value from intangible assets as well. Creativity implies that acts of entrepreneurial imagination, coupled with an efficient management of the routines that underpin them, are the basis for 'organizational learning' that makes the routines more effective. As routines improve, and innovations are made and captured, increasingly sophisticated competencies can build an organization's **dynamic capabilities**.

Dynamic capabilities are the processes of a firm that are able to reconfigure resources to respond to changes in the marketplace.

DYNAMIC CAPABILITIES: THE GHOST IN THE RBV THEORY MACHINE

The dynamic capabilities approach is best seen as a development from the RBV. It shares similar assumptions but links the RBV with an understanding that market conditions are fast changing and constantly require new and different competencies. In effect followers of the dynamic capabilities approach argue that if a firm is unable to adapt to changing circumstances then over the long term it will become unprofitable. The trick, according to dynamic capabilities, is to identify the 'organizational (and individual) capabilities that enable the business enterprise to build and maintain value-enhancing points of differentiation' (Augier and Teece, 2008: 1189). The dynamic capabilities approach seeks to understand how firms develop, refresh and renew important capabilities. According to Augier and Teece (2008: 1190), this involves:

> [D]efining managerial traits, management systems, and organizational designs that will keep the enterprise alert to opportunities and threats, enable it to execute on new opportunities, and then constantly morph to stay on top, once it has put the systems in place, to capture the fruits of its first round of success.

The dynamic capabilities approach argues that it is neither resources nor knowledge but intangible assets that matter most to companies (Teece, Pisano and Sheun, 1997). These include things such as:

- Technological know-how.
- Intellectual property.
- Business process know-how.
- Customer and business relationships.
- Reputations.
- Organizational culture and values.

These can be likened to a ghost in the theory machine – something that cannot be seen but to whose agency effects can be credited. What unites this disparate list of seemingly unrelated phenomena is that mastery of these factors enables businesses to sense and seize new opportunities, and use these opportunities to reconfigure and protect existing resource-based and knowledge-based assets and competencies, as well as complementary assets, for a sustained competitive advantage. In the case of the RBV the idea of dynamic capabilities is the ghost in the theory machine.

Mastery of dynamic capabilities is seen as a three-stage process, composed of *sensing, seizing* and *managing*:

1 *Sensing* involves making innovative and creative sense from relations with customers, complementors and suppliers, as well as perceiving opportunities that may have potential in the operating and business environment. For instance, given the technological platform from which the organization operates and the current plant, equipment and likely switching costs, where should the business be heading, given its history and the drag and opportunity this legacy may pose for its future? Think of the emergence of changes in regulatory and standard-setting bodies; for instance, with the switch in many advanced economies towards a more carbon-neutral future, what opportunities or threats does this pose for present and future business lines? Clearly there will be processes of co-evolution at work: shifts in public policy will help drive shifts towards more carbon-neutral futures, for instance; thus, unlike, say, Porterian industry analysis, dynamic capabilities allow a much greater role for the state.

2 *Seizing* means using something effectively. Opportunities sensed but not seized are opportunities lost. Seizing an opportunity entails designing business models to satisfy customers and capture value; developing proficient investment protocols; gaining access to capital; and showing leadership and commitment in delivering on the capabilities. Business models need to be able to identify those market segments to address; value

propositions for customers; appropriate technology and product functions, and design a method for capturing value.

3 *Managing* means maintaining a routine control of the capability. Opportunities seized but not managed are opportunities squandered. Efficient management of dynamic capabilities increasingly requires management outwith the enterprise (see Chapter 11). It entails organizations developing co-specializations, complementarities and systemically related innovation. Co-specialization requires management of assets and their development in relation to each other in alliances and collaborations; it also requires relating strategy to both structure and process, and this needs to be done so that complementarities are managed in order that they co-evolve between the different firms seeking competitive advantage, so that, jointly, they specialize their assets while combining and integrating them.

One evident problem with the approach is that we cannot know what a dynamic capability is until we have seen it in action. We only know it is a dynamic capability because it actually enables the firm to manage change. You can only know that you have a dynamic capability when you have used it and it was successful – then you will know you have it! Of course, if you think you have one and it fails then you do not have it! The sceptical reader might be forgiven for thinking that there is an element of tautology to this strategy.

Dynamic capability approaches do not replace the insights of the RBV of the firm but add to them and transform them. The centrality of both resources and knowledge is affirmed but their orchestration in conjunction with complementary assets is seen as more important than merely possessing something unique, valuable, etc. Such orchestration requires entrepreneurial leadership to take advantage of the opportunities posed by the new global flows of finance, labour, outsourcing and communications (see Chapter 12). Most especially, it also entails innovation (see Chapter 6) as well as value creation and capture.

VALUE CREATION AND CAPTURE

Organizations that build sustainable business models need to be able to innovate, in order to outflank competitors, and to create and capture value from their innovations. Value is a difficult term to define but Pitelis (2009: 1118), in a thoughtful review, defines it in the terms shown in the marginal definition.

Value can be constituted in many ways: in terms of rarity, use value or aesthetics, for example. From an organizational strategy perspective, value must inhere in the activities, products and services offered for sale in a market economy to potential beneficiaries, such as consumers. Others may also contribute to the value proposition: purveyors of capital for instance, or suppliers that need to be enrolled in its realization. Organizational value is often conjectural: that a certain stream of activities may create it is often the basis for a decision to continue a stream of innovation – there is a belief that an innovative product or service will be produced that can be a source of value through sales in the market.

Creating value does not necessarily mean capturing value. One firm can create an innovation but its value can be captured through a competitor that copies it and delivers it more effectively. A case in point would be the original Mini: it never realized a value that exceeded that which was invested in producing it until the brand (see Chapter 5) was acquired by BMW and a version of the Mini that captured brand nostalgia in a totally new vehicle was created.

Value creation, suggests Pitelis (2009: 1121), has four generic determinants: innovation; human resources and their services; unit cost economies/returns to scale; and

> **Value** is the perceived worthiness of a subject matter to a socio-economic agent that is exposed to and/or can make use of the subject matter in question.

firm infrastructure and strategy. Innovation is one of the oldest topics in the book of economic theory, going right back to Adam Smith's (1776) observations of a pin manufactory. The stress on human factors results from the increasing stress on competencies in the capabilities literature, which recognizes that it is the creative combination of these that is essential for value creation. Unit cost economies and returns to scale are also well-established topics in the economics literature; making something at less cost than competitors who have established a benchmark price can be a potent source of value, based, perhaps, on distinctive innovations or combinations of human factors. However, it could be due to the fourth generic factor – the organization's infrastructure – its systems, routines and decision-making processes (see Chapter 9) – and structure – the way in which it configures its organizational relations as a bureaucracy, an organic structure, a heterarchy and so on. When these generic determinants are bundled together they produce what Clark (2000), in his admirable *Organizations in Action,* refers to as strategic repertoires and structural poses.

REPERTOIRES AND STRUCTURAL POSES

Peter Clark, of the University of London, is extremely significant for his development of the notion of repertoire. His work engages with the RBV but develops a different – less performance-based – perspective. Clark conceives of an organization as having a number of things that it can do – rather like an orchestra or rock band will have a repertoire of music it can play, or a professional sports team will have a number of pre-organized moves they can carry out. These can all be thought of as routines that are learned, skilled and perfomative; thus, organizations such as bands and teams may be said to have a familiar repertoire. By a repertoire Clark means a richly textured set of competencies. In other words, he is interested in what an organization can actually do.

Think of organizations that you are familiar with: what can they actually do? Universities can deliver teaching, conduct research, organize graduations, etc. Similarly, airlines can sell you a ticket, check you in and fly you from A to B, perhaps stopping off at C on the way. Would you want an airline credentialing your Bachelor's or Master's degree? Or would you want your university flying you off on holiday the next time you go away? The answer to both questions is 'probably not'. The point is that organizations have specific repertoires – akin to capabilities – things you would trust them to do.

While repertoires will evolve or diminish over time, Clark identifies three component parts of a repertoire, which he refers to as 'structural poses', a concept borrowed from social anthropology. They are:

1 *Basic operating cycle.* The basic operating cycle refers to activities that are central to an organization's normal activities, which is framed over a particular time period (such as semesters in a university, seasons for a sports team, 24-hour cycles for a production plant, several years for the development of a new pharmaceutical product).

2 *Strategic innovation cycle.* The strategic innovation cycle refers to the capacity an organization has to innovate. For instance, can an organization introduce different forms of organizing, can it adapt itself to deal with future problems, does it have the ability to innovate?

3 *Special irregular events.* This part of the repertoire is the ability of an organization's repertoire to deal with extraordinary or emergency events, such as a natural disaster. When special irregular events occur organizations must develop specialist poses for coping with them as infrequently occurring

events. A good example is provided when the Olympics come to a city: not just the city administration but also all the transport service providers, the police, fire, ambulance and other services, have to adjust their structural poses – they have to be prepared for out-of-the-ordinary events occurring because of the special event, such as a terrorist action. Often, the military and the police will spend a lot of time rehearsing for potential extreme events, in order to develop well-rehearsed strategic contingency plans.

Special irregular events are the hardest to manage and organize. The problem is that the capacity to act can lie dormant for long periods and during this interregnum can become defunct. To explain this further, Clark argues that as a means of describing firm-specific knowledge, organizations can be viewed as possessing scripts. The script determines, to an extent, the roles that can be played in a certain situation and the final script is the outcome of a range of actors – each with their own interests – such as the writer, the client, the technical staff and the producers. Hence, the script is a negotiated ordering device – its common sense is worked at and negotiated in a collective enterprise where many distinct professional knowledge capabilities are brought into play. Sometimes there will be conflict between different approaches; such conflict can be strategically creative, sparking important innovations to the script.

It is useful to think in terms of the repertoire or script of an organization, while steering clear of the positivist, 'normal science' ambitions of the RBV. For us, the knowledge script of an organization will be determined by the identity of that organization, which will constitute those things that the organization takes to be important and other things that are seen as trivial. These criteria will largely hinge on the specifics of an organization.

MINI CASE STUDY

The politics of water in Arizona

In Wendy Espeland's classic (1998) study of the politics around water in Arizona, in which she highlighted the struggle against a dam development, she identified the different identities and knowledge possessed by three key groups:

1 *Bureau of Reclamation (BR) engineers.* The BR engineers viewed themselves as working for the best engineering organization in the world. They were responsible for iconic engineering feats, such as the famous Hoover Dam. The projects they created were a means of producing electric power and, crucially, damming water, which could then be used to irrigate the arid, dry Arizonan land. Their identity emphasized the benefits of harnessing nature for the good of humankind. Their knowledge base was centred on engineering prowess.

2 *Bureau of Reclamation 'new' breed.* The new breed comprised policy analysts who entered BR following environmental legislation that required a full cost–benefit analysis of a proposed dam scheme. Analysing all the ramifications of a scheme, the new breed would then attach a number to each different factor. This process of commensuration – turning a qualitative phenomenon into a quantitative entity – allowed the analysts to apply cost–benefit models derived from public choice economics. Their identity emphasized the importance of taking a holistic and objective view of a complex problem and making a rational decision. Their knowledge base was centred on the efficacy of public choice economics.

3 *Yavapai Indians.* As residents of a reservation that would be flooded under the Orme Dam proposals, the Yavapai Indians were understandably opposed to the project. Their identity emphasized their 'oneness' with the land. Their knowledge base was inseparable from their identity and they rejected the premise held by the engineers that the dam represented

(Continued)

(Continued)

progress for humankind; similarly, they rejected the assumptions of the new breed that posited a financial value could be attached to the 'cost' of their leaving the reservation.

The three groups identified above each possessed a worldview and an attendant knowledge base. The knowledge that was relevant for each of them was incommensurable with the knowledge valued by each of the others. Consequently, we may say that the identity of an organization is likely to be in a close elective affinity with the knowledge that dominant politics privilege.

Simple questions of identity are important in knowledge management, such as:

● Who are we?
● What are our objectives?

Answers to these simple questions have an impact upon the knowledge that is taken seriously in an organization.

Questions

1 Think of the organization that you learn or earn in. How would you answer 'Who are we?' and 'What are our objectives?'? Think of your answers in terms of:

● The sub-unit, departmental or divisional level in which you are situated.

● The overall organization.

● The implications for what gets to be constituted as central and as peripheral knowledge.

KNOWLEDGE AS A CRUCIAL RESOURCE

The chapter thus far has told the story of the RBV. While it is a concept whose origins were in business schools it is, nonetheless, irredeemably linked to its industrial economics origins. While the RBV has much to commend it – looking inside an organization to see what it can actually do seems to be a sensible endeavour – its economic foundations impose serious limits. The central problem is that economists have very little insight into the workings of an organization, something they have always treated as a black box.

The idea of looking inside the black box to see what went on inside organizations, which anthropologists, sociologists and others had been doing for decades, during the 1980s, began to strike people interested in strategy as a good idea. Among subsequent researchers and theorists who investigated the knowledge-based organization were Alvesson (1993), Starbuck (1992), Conner and Prahalad (1996), Grant (1996) and Kogut and Zander (1992). Liebeskind (1996) elaborates the idea that firms apply knowledge to the production of goods and services, and that knowledge is strategically the most important of a firm's resources.

The idea of the knowledge-based organization began to emerge in the 1980s with the work of people such as Drucker (1988) and Nurmi (1988). In discussions of knowledge-based organizations an important distinction is drawn between tacit knowledge and explicit knowledge. Knowledge has been likened to an iceberg, whereby explicit knowledge is merely the tip of the iceberg; all that lies below the iceberg is tacit knowledge. The characteristics of tacit knowledge are that it is *difficult to express*, *experientially based* and *possessed by the person*. The best example of tacit knowledge that most people will be familiar with is cycling. Learning to ride a bicycle involves observation and practice, and cannot be done immediately, simply by reading a manual. Tacit knowledge is held by individuals and not by the organization as such (Grant, 1996). In fact, it is

A black box is a device, system or object that can (and sometimes can only) be viewed solely in terms of its input, throughput or transformation processes, and output without any knowledge of its internal working.

A knowledge-based organization attends to two related processes that underlie its everyday processes: the effective application of existing knowledge and the creation of new knowledge.

Tacit knowledge cannot be conveyed sufficiently quickly to be appropriated immediately by the learner.

Explicit knowledge, by contrast, is easily absorbed and can be transferred to various uses immediately.

probably better thought of as tacit knowing rather than knowledge. To be useful, this knowledge must be coordinated: what one person knows needs to be integrated with what other people know. The firm exists because its management is better able to perform this coordinating function than is the market, according to the RBV.

A trade secret might be regarded as explicit knowledge: as soon as the secret is revealed, anyone can make use of the relevant knowledge. Liebeskind (1996) suggests that firms exist in order to protect explicit knowledge. Employment contracts may specify exclusivity and confidentiality clauses, preventing the transfer of economically advantageous knowledge to rival organizations. Firms can protect their explicit knowledge by threatening the dismissal of staff who pass on information, making their departure costly through the loss of bonuses, pensions, stock options and promotion opportunities. The firm may also try to ensure that people have access to no more information than is strictly necessary for them to perform their functions.

Due to the indivisibility of certain inputs, the firm may find itself with spare capacity, which offers the potential for the development of new activities. However, growth is constrained by limits to the ability of managers to conceive and control movements into new products and markets. In other words, there are cognitive limits to growth. Similar productive activities require similar capabilities, so economies of scale and scope can be realized when firms expand into similar activities. Complementary activities require different capabilities, but as the degree of complementarity increases, the need for greater cooperation and coordination becomes more important. Joint ventures, strategic alliances or full-scale integration may assist towards achieving sufficient cooperation and coordination. If managers are rent seekers, growth is constrained by their ability to transfer the firm's resources and capabilities into these new areas.

Neo-classical theory assumes firms have complete information. In reality firms are neither fully informed about the best use of resources, nor do they know if they are properly equipped to face future contingencies. It is difficult to predict future changes in market demand, how best to respond to these changes and what the payoffs are likely to be. Consequently, there is no point in attempting to estimate with any precision a production function of the type associated with neo-classical theory. Instead, the resource-based theory focuses on how firms can develop and improve their capabilities in order to adapt to a changing market environment. Success depends on the extent to which the firm's managers can nurture adaptive capabilities. Firms whose managers are slow to innovate will eventually tend to decline. Managers' decisions will depend on their technical skills, knowledge, interpersonal and leadership skills. Different managers will use similar resources in different ways. Accordingly, over time the capability of different firms will tend to diverge, as will their performance.

A simple definition of **knowledge management (KM)** is that it is a managerial practice that seeks to identify, leverage, control and create knowledge in an organization.

Corporate interest in knowledge and its management, usually expressed as **knowledge management (KM)**, exploded in the late 1990s. A well-known KM guru, Dave Snowdon, in the *Cognitive Edge* blog at www.cognitive-edge.com/blogs/dave/2009/09/defining_km.php, defined KM's purpose as providing support for improved decision-making and innovation throughout the organization via the effective management of human intuition and experience augmented by the provision of information, processes and technology together with training and mentoring programmes. Ideas are generally of their time, so how can we understand the conjunction of factors that led to the emergence of KM? We see the rise of KM as the result of four separate but interrelated factors: business

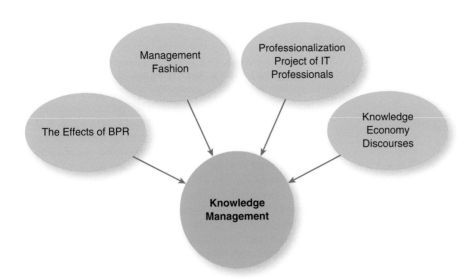

FIGURE 3.1 Factors driving the rise of knowledge

process reengineering; the knowledge economy; the professional project of IT specialists, and management fashion (see Figure 3.1).

Business process reengineering (BPR)

BPR was a highly acclaimed managerialist initiative which, during the 1990s, was widely adopted across the organizational world. BPR aimed to ignore the history of an organization and redesign it as if one was starting afresh, from a blank sheet of paper, as it were. A BPR consultant would invite people to design an organization as if one did not already exist. A large constituent part of this thinking was that if organizations were able to harness the huge processing power of IT to reengineer the corporation, a potential that was just becoming apparent, they would also be able to realize huge benefits. BPR brooked no compromise with the pre-existing organization – instead it sought to create a new organization from the ashes of the old.

The rhetoric that accompanied BPR was aggressive and violent in its tone (see Hammer and Champy, 1993, for examples; also Grint and Case, 2000). Visiting destruction on organizations through restructuring, downsizing and the removal of much of the previous mode of work organization, BPR mesmerized those in corporate elites.

BPR programmes followed a fairly predictable pattern. In the first instance, consultants would identify inefficiencies in the organization; this would be followed by a radical restructuring that, quite literally, often turned the organization on its head. Attendant to this process would be radical cuts to the labour force, with swathes of middle management, now viewed as an embarrassing anachronism, being removed from the organization. The initial results of a BPR programme generally looked positive, at least for senior executives, with it being routine for efficiency gains to be recorded and costs to be cut. Such results were trumpeted, further proof of the importance of BPR in delivering a superior corporate performance.

Unlike previous initiatives, such as total quality management (TQM), the gratification from BPR was pretty much instant. It all seemed to be going so well: executives got bonuses, consultants made money, BPR managers got promotions, management gurus sold out speaking tours and lots of books. And then it became

WHAT DO YOU MEAN?

Downsizing as a reengineering strategy

One American manager in particular, Al 'Chainsaw' Dunlap (Byrne, 1999), became infamous for downsizing and reengineering. He was the darling of Wall Street who delighted in sacking people, closing plants and ruthlessly cutting costs. He was the role model for a generation of managers, a ruthless cost cutter who sacked thousands, shut plants and bullied underlings in the pursuit of profit and shareholder value at all costs, who eventually, because of fraudulent actions as the CEO in charge of Sunbeam, was banned from ever running a company again. For a while in the 1990s CEOs such as Dunlap thrived. By cutting the head count they lowered costs and delivered short-term profits – but destroyed the long-term value. For many analysts what executives such as Dunlap did was an elixir, which would rid organizations of bad practices, anachronistic processes and generally poor performance, turning them around. But it was all short term. Often key capabilities that were not even explicitly recognized were lost.

When he was CEO at Sunbeam the cuts Dunlap demanded were so deep that the company had difficulty functioning and, in fact, many of the company's costs were even increased as a result of the cuts. Yet the company's stock soared, given Dunlap's reputation for turnarounds – until a web of fraud was uncovered that was sustaining the sales figures he posted. Dunlap was sacked, fined a paltry amount and retired to Florida to live in luxury off the gains from the misery he had inflicted on others.

clear that something was very wrong. The organizations that had BPR'd themselves discovered that in the process they had lost something; more intriguingly, it was something that they did not even know they had in the first place! What they had lost did not show up on any of the process charts that the consultants produced, or in any of the many Excel spreadsheets and PowerPoint presentations manufactured during the BPR programme. What they had lost was their organizational memory:

> Organizational memory entails understanding how past events are acquired, retained, retrieved, and even forgotten within the organization …. The structure of organizational memory is composed of a number of storage bins: individuals, culture, transformations, structure, ecology, and external archives … memory is distributed in nature; that is, the repository of organizational information is not confined to one central location (as is the case of the brain in the individual body), but, rather, it is distributed throughout the entire organization (as might be the case of memory within the human brain). Within this conceptual definition, any attempt to directly measure or assess organizational memory is doomed to be partial and incomplete, unless one examines all the bins. (Prusak, 1997: 201)

What was happening within organizations was that they were quite simply unable to perform key tasks. BPR had captured processes that consultants were able to observe and which fitted the categories that BPR used to understand the organization. In time, what became strikingly clear was that organizations that had undergone BPR had actually lost capability and organizational knowledge. This is what sociologists characterize as an unintended consequence. BPR had serious consequences for an organization that affected its ability to be able to carry out its functions. BPR rendered organizations cadaverous. One corollary was that organizations now became very aware of what they had lost. There was an urgent commercial need for them to find a means of managing their organizational knowledge base.

Knowledge loss in a global telecommunications firm

This story – as with many good stories – might be apocryphal but it speaks to the very real concerns that many large corporations had in the 1990s about their knowledge base. It was recounted by the global knowledge officer at GlobTel (a pseudonym). The organization underwent an expensive BPR programme. Hoping this would allow it to cut costs while continuing to offer high levels of customer service, GlobTel vigorously carried out the programme. Engineers, middle managers and others were retired early, costs were cut, profits went up, the City was happy and the cadre of senior managers congratulated themselves on a job well done.

Shortly after, GlobTel experienced problems with a machine in a telephone exchange. Much energy was exerted in finding a solution. The machine had never been a problem before; on enquiring into the solution the senior manager who was investigating the matter was told that old Bill always looked after that machine. The problem was that Bill had been pensioned off in the recent bout of downsizing, or rightsizing as the senior managers liked to refer

to it. Eventually, they had to concede defeat and call Bill for help. Now, Bill, a year or so previously when he had been let go, had been seen as part of the problem. In his mid-fifties and having worked in the organization since he graduated in engineering three decades before, he was deemed as surplus to requirements. BPR had demonstrated with impeccable logic that he was no longer needed by GlobTel.

Bill, a little sore from the bruising experience of being engineered into redundancy, decided to have a little fun when he took the call from GlobTel. Yes, he responded, he could come in to look at the machine but this would have to be on consultancy rates. Agreeing a fee of $20,000 plus expenses, he set off to the depot. He saw the machine, one he had worked with for 20 years, and sat and listened to it. Within minutes he was able to fix the machine. He could tell what was wrong simply by listening to the sounds emitting from the machine. The executives at GlobTel were both astonished and horrified at this story. It highlighted to them that their BPR exercise had resulted in the loss of a great deal of knowledge, with injurious effects on productivity and effectiveness. It also illustrated that the 'anachronistic' engineers were not so out of date after all. This story, according to GlobTel, was echoed in numerous other instances throughout the organization. Knowledge was then moved centre stage of its strategic priorities.

The knowledge economy

The late 1990s were an era of change. Corporations, politicians and the population at large became aware of the growing power of computers and the radical potential of the Internet. That financial euphoria, in the form of the dot-com boom, prevailed is well established. The 'Roaring nineties' – to quote Stiglitz – institutionalized many discursive shifts within the economy. (By discursive shifts we mean changes in the way that things were talked about: in the UK, for instance, the then charismatic and youthful Prime Minister, Tony Blair, even took to referring to the UK as the young country! It was Cool Britannia with no sense of irony – listen to the Bonzo Dog Doo Dah Band (1967) for the irony, an irony which in celebrating the 1960s 'Carnaby Street' era anticipated the Cool Britannia moment by 25 years.)

Perhaps the most significant shift in the new rhetoric around knowledge was the assertion that advanced Western countries were now – or on the way to becoming – knowledge economies. Authors such as David Landes argued that the crucial factor of production was now knowledge. Simply put, knowledge

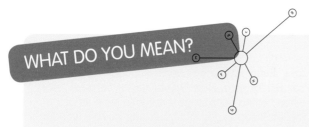

WHAT DO YOU MEAN?

Keeping abreast of fashion

The last three decades have seen the emergence of the global business consulting complex, which has had a major impact on the way in which in large corporations and governments think about themselves, and subsequently, how they organize themselves. Eric Abrahamson (1996), of Columbia University, has theorized this as management fashion. In summary, his argument is that a management ideas industry exists, its primary aim being to package, commodify, and sell new management ideas. In support of this argument, Abrahamson highlights the proliferation of management initiatives that have become popular currency in recent years: culture change, total quality management (TQM), learning organization, BPR, shareholder value (SHV), enterprise resource planning (ERP), activity-based costing (ABC), and the balanced scorecard are all prominent examples.

Knowledge management (KM) belongs to the pantheon of recent managerial initiatives. Abrahamson considers the aforementioned initiatives to be management fashions. The central reason is that the initiatives appear to follow a fashion cycle – going from being *haute couture* to *prêt-a-porter* to old hat, which follows a three- to five-year time cycle. A secondary, but important, reason is the existence of an industry – comprising large consultancies, management consultancy firms, Big 4 accountancy firms, self-styled management gurus, cutting edge companies – that actively package ideas.

The process through which ideas are developed is that the actors in the management ideas industry will be seeking out the next 'big thing' for the coming few years. In fashion parlance, they are speculating as to what will be the 'new black'. Through its deep engagement with client organizations, the management ideas industry will get a sense of what anxieties and concerns managers have at any given time. This process will allow the management ideas industry to tap into the managerial Zeitgeist. The management ideas industry then develops an initiative that can claim to be a solution to current organizational problems. The various actors within the management ideas industry will all be trying to formulate their own take on the current organizational problem – much as fashion designers working out how they are going to put their signature on this season's colours, styles and so forth.

One of the paradoxes of fashion is that while it makes claims of individuality, it relies on everyone more or less doing the same – otherwise it would not be a fashion. So it is with management ideas, as the management gurus, large consultancies, Big 4 accounting firms, IT firms all seek to put their own signature on an emerging idea. As the idea – TQM, BPR or whatever – solidifies, the various constituent parts of the management ideas industry package and commodify the new management fashion.

Abrahamson identifies two dimensions pertaining to a management fashion: the aesthetic and the technical. The aesthetic dimension relates to the packaging of the idea. This process is highly image and rhetoric intensive, it stresses that the idea must be adopted for an organization to thrive, and it backs up this assertion with a variety of war stories that highlight the efficacy of the approach. The second dimension comprises the tools and techniques that are used to implement the fashion. It might include various management techniques and computer software. For some fashions, the technical dimension can include complex methodologies.

was central to national prosperity. This message became ubiquitous as politicians, policy makers, think tanks, corporations and influential professions all got in on the act. Hyperbole flourished and distinctions were drawn between the 'new' economy and the 'old' economy. The NASDAQ quickly emerged as an important measure of how this 'new' economy was performing. Internet start-ups which had never posted a profit had market capitalizations larger than long-established blue-chip companies. At one point Amazon was worth more than Boeing, the aircraft manufacturer. Iconic companies of the time, such as lastminute.com, captured the public's imagination and seemed to be harbingers of a world to come. This helped fuel the interest in knowledge and intellectual capital that remains, in spite of the carnage that followed on the NASDAQ index, to this day.

The professional project of IT professionals

IT became inexorably more important to Western corporations. By the 1990s, IT specialists occupied well-paid positions in organizations. Yet the problem they had was that they remained peripheral to strategy-making in those organizations. They were little more than a gilt-edged support function. KM provided a convenient way of establishing a more strategic presence for IT professionals. Andrew Abbott (1988), of the University of Chicago, has theorized this behaviour as the pursuit of a professional project to gain more status and control over key decision-making areas. Abbott's work is a reminder that professional groups are constantly engaged in struggles over status and jurisdictional territory. Some professions, such as lawyers and medical doctors, have asserted themselves successfully over the last 500 years, while others, such as teachers and HR professionals, have struggled with their professional projects. The relevance of IT, as we will see, rests on the heavy use of intranets in Knowledge Management initiatives.

Many KM programmes anchor their practices in a framework developed by Japanese scholars Nonaka and Takeuchi (1995). Their bestselling book *The Knowledge-Creating Company* promulgated the four key means through which knowledge is produced in an organization. They are:

1 *Socialization (tacit–tacit).* This form of knowledge creation involves an interplay with tacit knowledge, creating tacit knowledge. A good example of this is an apprenticeship whereby the apprentice learns through doing, observing and being in the same space as the master craftsworker.

2 *Externalization (tacit–explicit).* According to Nonaka and Takeuchi, this represents the quintessential form of knowledge creation whereby tacit knowledge is taken from the mind of the worker and transformed into explicit knowledge. This form of knowledge creation has been the driving force behind most contemporary KM programmes. The premise upon which it is based is far from unproblematic. Many scholars dispute the extent to which tacit knowledge can be translated into explicit knowledge (Cook and Brown, 2002).

3 *Internalization (explicit–tacit).* This form of knowledge production occurs when someone uses explicit knowledge sufficiently often that it becomes 'second nature'. This often happens in professional work where an accountant, doctor or lawyer comes to embody the explicit knowledge.

4 *Combination (explicit–explicit).* This form of knowledge occurs where two forms of explicit knowledge combine to create a new hybridized form of knowledge. For instance, if a project team contains an accountant and strategist working together, they will be combining two forms of explicit knowledge.

Nonaka and Takeuchi's framework provokes controversy in two central ways: the first is epistemological – is knowledge that is dependent on an individual's tacit knowing transferable in the way they suggest? The second is that it ignores, perhaps because the findings are being abstracted out of the Japanese context, the issue of power in organizations – why should employees share their tacit knowledge with their employers? KM has been a hugely popular initiative. Alan McKinlay (2002) summarizes the practical impact KM has had on organizations:

1 KM has acted as a vehicle for an organization to learn about itself by answering questions such as, how do we create knowledge and how, as an organization, do we learn?

2 By attempting to capture knowledge and understand what knowledge the organization possesses, it has served as a brake on corporate forgetting.

3 KM has been an effective means of diffusing small-scale innovations across wider constituencies in the organization.

4 KM is a means of converting tacit/covert knowledge into a form that renders it a managerially regulated 'public good'.

Arguably, the dominant form of KM has been technical in nature, especially through the role of intranets, and, to a lesser extent, social, through a variety of community-based initiatives. We summarize these briefly below.

KM METHODS

Mining knowledge: the role of intranets

An intranet is a privately controlled and maintained computer system that is very similar to the World Wide Web, except it is normally restricted to use by employees inside the organization. It seeks to store knowledge but also to generate an electronic forum in which knowledge can be shared, communities created and problems solved.

The early stages of KM were dominated by organizations attempting to 'mine' their knowledge base. To do this, organizations often implemented intranet systems.

Intranets were introduced into organizations with great hyperbole but the results have, in general, failed to meet the expectations invested in them. The technicist fix has not shaped the behaviours of those using the technology. Common problems associated with intranets include:

1 Being regarded as widely irrelevant and not being used to record experiences and share knowledge.

2 Being overwhelmed with large quantities of data, some of which will be out of date or irrelevant.

3 Being viewed with suspicion by employees reluctant to share their knowledge, fearing this will erode their power base and/or make their skills redundant.

4 Rather than leading to a sharing of knowledge across the firm, the intranet can become another mechanism through which existing rivalries and tensions will play out.

5 Not being clearly linked to operational and strategic goals.

6 Imposing central solutions rather than stimulating local activity.

7 Not adapting practices to the local context by allowing a local coordination and distribution of learning.

8 Being over-centralized rather than being based on a small centralized core, with a wider distributed network.

Fifty years ago, scholars working from a socio-technical systems approach discovered that technology did not always have the intended effects. The problem was that people did not bend to the will of the new technology and failed to do what was intended by the technical designers. It would seem that intranets have, in many cases, suffered a similar fate. Some histories just keep repeating themselves – perhaps because such a gap still exists between technology strategists and social science. It is terrific to design cool systems; it is another thing to make them cool for people to use in the ways designers intended.

Stories and knowledge

In contrast to the technicist approaches towards KM, a range of other techniques has emerged. Sophisticated attempts have included using storytelling methodologies as a means of building a comprehensive understanding of the knowledge base of an organization. Social anthropologists have long ventured into the field, be it in the former colonial world or, increasingly, the Western world, to try to understand the knowledge and self-understanding of those groups they study. A storytelling approach to KM builds a thick description of the organization and through skilful analysis can provide dramatic insights into the knowledge base of an organization.

David Boje (1991; 1995), of the University of New Mexico, has developed an approach to studying stories in organizations. In addition, management scholars such as Andrew Brown (Warwick University) and Barbara Czarniawska (Gothenberg University) have developed means of analysing the narratives of organizations. The central premise of this approach is that organizations can be understood as sites characterized by talking and writing. Moreover, the stories that circulate around organizations can perpetuate and create the very reality they seek to describe. Consequently, it is fruitful to study organizations as narratives, because, among other things, this can shed light on the knowledges that exist in an organization. As Czarniawska puts it, 'Stories capture organizational life in a way that no compilation of facts ever can. This is because they are carriers of life itself, not just reports on it' (1997: 21)

Orr's (1996) study of Xerox photocopy machine repairmen is regarded as a *locus classicus* among aficionados of KM. Xerox had been at the forefront of the BPR movement, as described above: through using new communication technology it was no longer necessary for the repairmen to report to the depot each morning to pick up their jobs for the day, where they would inevitably spend time chatting, gossiping and generally hanging out with other repairmen. What Xerox found was that under the new regime of work organization productivity actually fell, rather than improved. Detailed investigations revealed that during the coffee time in the depot the repairmen gave over a good deal of their time to discussing how they dealt with particular problems, the reason being that the repair manual – while comprehensive – failed to take into account many of the local contingencies encountered by repairmen (such as climatic conditions, inclines on office floors, etc.). Much of the tacit knowledge – the knowing through doing – was shared within these morning coffee breaks. For our purposes, the central point to Orr's study is that knowledge is contained within stories.

Storytelling in organizations has extended beyond the realm of academic study. For instance, in the late 1990s, under the leadership of Steve Denning, the World Bank implemented an extensive storytelling project that aimed to share knowledge. He is normative about what makes a good story and identifies different types of story for different goals. For sharing knowledge, Denning (2004: 5) advocates the following:

- You will need a story that focuses on mistakes and shows in detail how they were corrected, with an explanation of why a solution worked.

- In telling it, you will need to solicit alternative – and possibly better – solutions.

- Your story will need to inspire responses such as: 'there but for the grace of God', 'Wow, we had better watch that from now on'. (Adapted from Denning [2004], *Harvard Business Review*)

Perhaps the area of strategy and organizations in which storytelling has been most developed is in politics. Politicians such as Barack Obama (1995; 2006) have ridden to political power on the back of inspiring stories about themselves and their lives; political parties such as New Labour employed legendary spin doctors, such as Alastair Campbell, who managed stories about the party and government that were designed to place them, strategically, in the best light and position. Of course, the very concept of 'storytelling' has a slightly questionable edge to it: storytelling is what children do when they do not want to be held accountable for their actions. There are many observers who would argue that what is true for a child also applies to the storytelling of politicians, parties and chief executives generally.

WHAT DO YOU MEAN?

How World Drug used KM

Alan McKinlay, of the University of St Andrews, conducted a detailed ethnographic study of KM in a well-known pharmaceutical company, which, for reasons of confidentiality, we will refer to as World Drug. The organization had grown in recent years through a mix of organic growth and acquisitions. It was known for selling lifestyle drugs, such as those that enhance the libido. The organization's strategy was to gain a competitive advantage through a faster 'molecule to market' time. To put this into context, in the late 1990s, when the study took place, the time it took to take a drug through the whole development, testing, regulatory process before getting it to market was 14 years. Taking a drug through this whole process was hugely expensive. World Drug has the strategic objective of reducing this time to eight years. Consequently, the organization was seeking ways to assert managerial control over the entire drug cycle. The budget for the initiative was 17 per cent of the total expenditure on a project, meaning it was generously funded to the tune of several million pounds. The initiative was developed in conjunction with an elite consulting firm. There were three dimensions to the KM programme: *social processes, technical capability* and *experiments with virtuality.*

1   *Social processes.* At the sign-off of each stage of the drug development process World Drug held a 'lessons learned' session; invariably this would take place in a luxury resort hotel as a part of the celebrations for finishing a project. World Drug was well aware that this process was unsatisfactory, providing neither a method for corporate archiving nor for making the lesson accessible in 'real time'. World Drug was aware that there was a considerable loss of operational knowledge.

As part of the KM initiative a process of capturing knowledge was introduced. Whereas 'lessons learned' had lacked structure and was irredeemably local, the KM programme was centralized and followed a methodology for capturing the learning. Three years after the introduction of KM, World Drug was disappointed: the process had become highly routinized; it became a forum for gripes about projects; it identified where standard operating procedures had been breached, and it focused on things that had delayed the process. As a process it became ritualistic and heavily bureaucratized. It reinforced the extant work organization rather than brokering innovation. It failed to engage in critical reflection or looking for deeper revelations about the nature of the drug development process. Moreover, the KM technologies generated information without control. The assemblage of the intranet, video conferencing and email meant that standard operating procedures often broke down. However, small-scale local innovations now had the potential of 'going global' through promotion on the intranet.

2   *Technical capability.* World Drug implemented an intranet that sought to turn tacit knowledge into explicit knowledge. The intranet was stocked with information from the 'lessons learned'. It aimed to capture details around both the problem and the solution. Furthermore, it sought to furnish a great deal of detail relating to the administrative procedures and decision-making processes that were contained within a project. The intranet aimed to transform the heterogeneity of work processes across World Drug into a single system, informed by best practice. The intranet was overwhelmed by the information loaded onto it. As McKinlay (2002) puts it, 'there was no mechanism for sifting through debris'. The attempts to capture tacit knowledge were, however, problematic. For reasons of pragmatism, some employees

(Continued)

(Continued)

failed to see the use of the intranet for the accomplishment of their project; others saw KM in more sinister terms in that it was an attempt by World Drug to take ownership of their knowledge. The intranet was considered a partial success in World Drug.

3 *Experiments with virtuality (Café Society).* Supporters of KM felt that the problems associated with the intranet system endangered the whole initiative. Consequently, Café Society was developed. It was a series of linked websites that aimed to be more fluid, reflexive and critical than the intranet. Café Society comprised transcribed interviews with those World Drug employees who chose to be members. A photo of the interviewee was superimposed on the interview. The interviews opened up into a chat room that aimed to provide a space for debate and dialogue. With Café Society, participation was seen as being vital – an outcome in its own right. As a designer of Café Society put it, 'Café is like

Starbucks, not McDonalds. We want people to come in relax, dream, work, and people watch' (McKinlay, 2002: 86). Café Society was an imaginative attempt to create a community of practice whereby new knowledge was created through dialogue and critique. The ideas generated from the process were more radical than the more incremental innovations associated with the social process and technological capabilities approach to KM.

Café Society is an idea that can be widely used by organizations. For instance, respected KM consultant David Gurteen runs well-attended Knowledge Cafés all around the world: see www.gurteen.com/gurteen/gurteen.nsf/id/newsletter111.

Question

1 Critically assess the extent to which a *Knowledge Café*, as outlined in the case above, might help facilitate knowledge in an organization you are familiar with.

Bringing knowledge into the picture makes entrepreneurial activity much more explicable. Profits are generated through what organizations know, how they build dynamic capabilities and develop repertoires of activities that are distinctive and organizationally efficient. We have moved a long way from the static picture of organizations as creating market inefficiencies (barriers to entry in product markets or barriers such as inimitability in resource markets) as the source of extraordinary profits to one that is more focused on a strategic entrepreneurship that seeks to bundle up resources, activities and routines in order to create distinctive dynamic capabilities and also build repertoires that tap into the knowledge that the organization is able to command.

SUMMARY AND REVIEW

In this chapter we began by reviewing the RBV, identifying its origins in the pioneering work of Edith Penrose. The chapter has considered the development of contemporary RBV theory, looking at some of its key exponents and raising some critical questions about the framework of assumptions on which it is founded. Closely related to the RBV view has been the emergence of a concern with knowledge as a unique and inimitable resource, and the growth of knowledge management, or KM. The realization of the importance of knowledge has led many strategists to consider how knowledge is actually shared – and they have ended up with the insight that humans learn by remembering stories – hence the storytelling approach.

EXERCISES

1 Having read this chapter you should be able to say in your own words what the following key terms mean:

- Resource-based view (RBV)
- A bundle of assets
- Durability
- Transparency
- Transferability
- Replicability
- Resources
- Capabilities
- VRIN framework
- Isolating mechanism
- Economic rent

- Dynamic capabilities
- Core competencies
- Repertoires
- Structural poses
- Black box
- Business process reengineering (BPR)
- Tacit knowledge
- Explicit knowledge
- Knowledge management (KM)
- Knowledge economy
- Intranet
- Storytelling
- Managerial fads and fashions.

2   What is the significance of Edith Penrose's work to the resource-based view of the firm? How does it extend classical views of the firm?

3   Explain the VRIN framework. Give some examples of firms that have profited from VRIN strategies.

4   What are the implications of the RBV for strategists?

5   Critically assess the relative merits of the RBV and the market-based view of strategy. Which would you recommend to a manager and why?

6   Why is storytelling a central element in contemporary accounts of strategy? Analyse an organization that has developed its storytelling skills – how has it done this and what have been the consequences?

7   Choose an organization that enjoys a competitive advantage based on the VRIN model. Explain what makes the organization successful.

8   Identify a management fashion and follow its spread through the media and practitioners' journals. What were its effects on organizations and their strategies?

ADDITIONAL RESOURCES

1   Our companion website is the best first stop for you to find a great deal of extra resources, free PDF versions of leading articles published in Sage journals, exercise, video and pod casts, team case studies and general questions and links to teamwork resources. Go to www.sagepub.co.uk/ clegg strategy

2   Good journals to consult for thinking about the RBV are the *Strategic Management Journal* and *Strategic Organization*.

3   Another useful resource is Edith Penrose's (1959) seminal *The Theory of the Growth of the Firm*

(it has been republished by Oxford University Press). Tim Ray and Stephen Little's (2005) *Managing Knowledge: An Essential Reader*, London: Sage in association with the Open University, is an excellent resource for exploring some of the knowledge management issues in much greater depth.

WEB SECTION

Visit the *Strategy* companion website at www.sagepub.co.uk/cleggstrategy

1   The online resource www.strategytube.net that the authors produced in tandem with this book is a great resource, especially the video featuring Alan Cadogan, who has a fascinating democratic and innovative approach to knowledge management. Watch and learn!

2   There are a great many knowledge management websites:

   (a) www.kmworld.com/
   (b) www.idea.gov.uk/idk/core/page.do?pageId=8152457
   (c) www.kmresource.com/
   (d) www.library.nhs.uk/KnowledgeManagement/
   (e) wiki.nasa.gov/cm/wiki/?id=1926
   (f) www.stevedenning.com/site/Default.aspx

3   There are also some videos online – we found this one useful: http://video.google.com/videoplay?docid=6395347688190577033#

4   For further information on Arthur Andersen: www.lrb.co.uk/v22/n21/foot01_.html

LOOKING FOR A HIGHER MARK?

Reading and digesting these articles that are available free on the companion website www.sagepub.co.uk/cleggstrategy can help you gain a deeper understanding and, on the basis of that, a better grade:

1   Constance E. Helfat and Margaret A. Peteraf (2009) Understanding Dynamic Capabilities: Progress along a Developmental Path, *Strategic Organization*, 7: 91–102.

2   Richard J. Arend and Philip Bromiley (2009) Assessing the Dynamic Capabilities View: Spare Change, Everyone?, *Strategic Organization*, 7: 75–90.

CASE STUDY

Arthur Andersen

Chris Carter

Arthur Andersen was a Big 5 accounting firm, one of the large international audit firms that in recent decades have dominated the accountancy profession. The Big 5 enjoyed a virtual oligopoly over conducting audits for large blue-chip firms. Only chartered accountants can conduct audits of large organizations and sign off their accounts. In effect the state granted the accountancy profession immense privilege – in the form of being the only group that could sign off on accounts – and in return it expected to be able to trust the company accounts that were produced. Arthur Andersen had, traditionally, demonstrated very high standards of professional integrity, something that facilitated its development into, arguably, the leading accountancy firm in the world. Headquartered in Chicago, it carried out its operations in most cities in the Western world. In addition to this it was well represented in the developing world. Arthur Andersen styled itself as the 'Marine Corps' of the accountancy profession. For several years the firm had enjoyed double-digit growth: during the 1990s its turnover quadrupled, hitting around $9 billion in 2001. At its peak, it employed in the region of 85,000 people. The business model was based on conducting audits for large blue-chip clients (Fortune 500, FTSE 100). Andersen had highly skilled senior partners in the firm who would manage client relationships. At more junior levels, bright graduates, who had been very carefully trained to follow the Andersen methodology, would conduct audits. In the process of conducting this work they built close relationships with their clients. This was strengthened further by the custom of former Andersen employees joining a client firm after a few years. The organization had an enviable brand. It possessed a deep knowledge of its clients. It also had the ability to conduct large projects, which they charged on the basis of billable hours. Andersen sought to diversify into new activity, partly as a response to the mature nature of the audit market, which was at saturation point and had little or no chance of expanding. Increasing Andersen's share within this market was problematic as few clients ever switched accounting

firm. Andersen diversified into business consulting, especially in the area of information technology applications. It established a subsidiary, Andersen Consulting, to house its consulting activities. The 1980s and 1990s saw Arthur Andersen and Andersen Consulting boom. The 1980s saw opportunities ushered in by the computerization of the industry, widespread corporate restructuring programmes, privatization programmes; the 1990s saw the rise of the Internet, the restructuring of the Soviet Union, the emergence of China and India as major world economies. Arthur Andersen provided audit and tax services to large companies, while Andersen Consulting provided a wide range of consultancy services to large corporations, governments and the public sector. The organization was seen as having the ability to provide high quality-services to its clients.

Difficulties had been growing for some time between Arthur Andersen and Andersen Consulting. They operated semi-independently of each other but both were governed under the umbrella of a global partnership. The difficulty was that Andersen Consulting had become much more profitable than Arthur Andersen, but that Arthur Andersen wielded more power in the global partnership. This led to a series of summits to discuss this problem: the result was the Dallas and Paris accords. After trying to accommodate the demands of Andersen Consulting, it was eventually agreed that the two parts of the global partnership would separate. A long battle over the 'Andersen' name was eventually settled when a court judged that Andersen Consulting would have to adopt a new name: Accenture. Arthur Andersen had been developing its own consulting operations and this was a major source of growth in the firm. There was some disquiet about accountancy firms selling consultancy, with some commentators arguing that it led to a conflict of interest: would an audit be really stringent if, at the same time, a firm was also trying to sell consultancy services? Arthur Andersen was routinely mooted by influential publications, such as *Accountancy Age*, as the leading accountancy firm in the world. The extent to which it had built its revenues and developed a fresh consulting wing was much admired. It was very close to major governments and looked forward to the new millennium as an era of opportunity.

In March 2001 the spotlight began to fall on Enron, when a financial journalist ran a story on whether its stock was overpriced. Over the summer of 2001, it became clear that Enron was in serious

(Continued)

(Continued)

trouble. By the autumn of 2001, it futher became clear that Enron was disintegrating following a total implosion of the firm's financial architecture. The problem was that Enron was Arthur Andersen's major client. The Enron account was worth up to $100 million per annum, about half of which was for the audit, while the other half was for consultancy services.

Arthur Andersen was quickly dragged into what by now was a major scandal and political issue. Why had it signed off on Enron's accounts? Why has it not signalled that Enron's 'profits' were, in fact, a fantasy, based on accounting fictions? A central factor in Enron's collapse was the way in which debt was hidden away from the balance sheet, future profits, which rarely materialized, were booked in the present, and cash flow was manipulated. This was clearly an accounting issue. If it was not already looking bad for Arthur Andersen, things got worse when it became clear that the firm was shredding documents for Enron. The suggestion was that these documents were in some way incriminating. It became open season on Arthur Andersen; while it sought to argue that the events in Houston were down to the wrongful actions of some rogue traders, analysts were less convinced. Clients, under pressure from their shareholders, sacked Arthur Andersen as auditor. Each week saw yet more high-profile clients dispense with Andersen's services.

This reached far beyond the United States, where the Enron scandal was playing out. The US State Department launched a legal action against Arthur Andersen over the shredding of documents. In a legal precedent, which three years later was to be overturned, Arthur Andersen was found guilty of obstructing justice. This meant that in the United states, it could no longer conduct accountancy audits. Elsewhere, partners were concerned – the Arthur Andersen brand, which for so long had been a strength, now became a serious liability – and sought to move to other accountancy firms. Civil lawsuits from those who had lost out in the Enron debacle mounted and Arthur Andersen folded. A once-powerful colossus of the accountancy profession was brought down in just a few short months.

Questions

1　Using the resource-based view, how would you characterize Arthur Andersen's resources and capabilities in the 1980s and 1990s?

2　Use the dynamic capabilities perspectives to explain Arthur Andersen's diversification into consulting.

3　Use the resource-based view to explain Arthur Andersen's decline and fall.

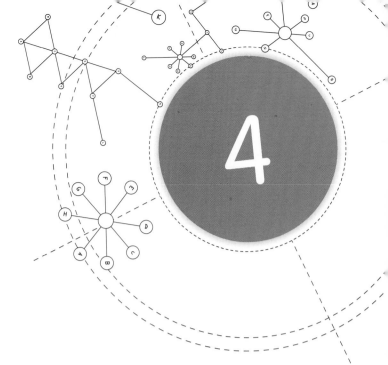

Strategy as Process and Practice

LEARNING OBJECTIVES

By the end of this chapter you will be able to:

- Understand the limitations of a rational top-down approach to strategic planning

- Appreciate Henry Mintzberg as a provocative thinker in the field of strategy

- Understand how strategies emerge from organizational processes

- Link emerging strategy back to concepts of culture, sensemaking, identity and learning

- Reflect on the implications of emergent strategy for organizational change

- Understand the constitutive and recursive relation between strategy as lay theory and practice as well as professional theory and practice

---

BEFORE YOU GET STARTED . . .

Life is what happens to you while
you're busy making other plans.

(JOHN LENNON)

INTRODUCTION

Google is a firm whose strategy does not easily fit into the frameworks we have discussed so far. Google seems to have little faith in planning but a lot of confidence in its ability to come up with the next big thing from its playful and curious culture. Google's strategy is not determined top down by executive managers but literally created in everyday trial-and-error experiments and conversations across the entire organization. Strategy at Google emerges from a web of interactions that are neither planned nor centrally controlled (for more on Google see the article by Iyer and Davenport, 2008). In this chapter we will explore how such evidently successful strategies emerge, and how they challenge old-fashioned organizational hierarchies and more traditional ways of strategizing.

In previous chapters – especially when we discussed Michael Porter's competitive strategy and where we looked at the resource-based view of the firm – we have discussed strategy as a rather rational undertaking. Remember Michael Porter's theory: he argues that firms should study the structure of the industry they are in and then position themselves within that environment. The resource-based view (RBV) offered an inverse explanation: the firm should identify its unique resources and then develop a strategy that optimizes and exploits these strengths.

Whether strategists craft their strategy from the inside out, or the outside in, in both instances they have to rely on one basic assumption: that the world exists objectively out there, waiting to be analysed. When analysed there is faith that a plan will result that, in turn, will inform action. The premise is simple: first, you think, then analyse and action follows: think, plan, do.

THE IMPORTANCE OF BEING RATIONAL

The study and practice of strategic management has followed a simple logic for most of its career. From the outset, founding fathers of the discipline, such as Igor Ansoff (1965), defined strategy as a planning exercise conducted by top managers. The metaphor that comes to mind is that of the head (top management team) that thinks, and the body (the organization) that follows. In fact, Chandler's (1962) argument that structure should follow strategy made the point succinctly: once strategy is set, and the top management team has decided on direction, the organization has to be designed, if necessary with a sharp scalpel, to follow suit. In Chandler's (1962: 314) words, 'Unless structure follows strategy, inefficiency rules'. Strategy is the corporation's *cogito ergo sum*: I think, therefore I am. Top management plans, therefore the organization is.

WHAT DO YOU MEAN?

Cogito ergo sum

The French philosopher René Descartes (1596–1650) chose *cogito ergo sum* (I think, therefore I am) as the starting point for his philosophical enquiries. He was looking for an unshakably certain basis on which he could build his philosophy. Before him, other philosophers had found their certainty in God.

Descartes doubted: he argued that life, and even religious beliefs, had to be based on our ability to think rationally. Only when we think, he pondered, can we be certain that we are not being deceived. Consequently, for Descartes, only the mind could be the source of true knowledge whereas the body could delude us. He described the senses as imperfect sources of knowledge. Although his philosophy is more complex than this brief summary, he is acknowledged as the father of rationalism. And rationalism is the father of most strategic thinking.

The rational approach to decision-making came out of the discipline of economics, with its central premise being that a three-fold process can be followed:

1 Rational actors access as much complete information as is possible pertaining to all the available alternatives.

2 All possible consequences of each of the alternatives are mapped out.

3 A comparison of different alternatives, normally done by using a cost–benefit analysis, is undertaken.

According to this rational view, after the three-fold process has been followed strategists will be equipped with the information they require to make a rational decision, one that will maximize their returns. Rational choice models – many of which were developed by the US military – had diffused widely by the 1950s.

As an indication of how such ideas travelled, it is illustrative to look at the career of Robert McNamara, the controversial 1960s US defence minister, whom we have already met as a subject of Tom Peters' loathing in Chapter 1. McNamara studied at the University of California, Berkeley, followed by graduate studies in business at Harvard, where he joined the faculty as an assistant professor (lecturer). During World War II he worked as an officer in the US military while the United States went through the process of building a large conscript army. In organizational and strategic terms this posed challenges, being a huge logistical exercise and involving the movement of millions of men and supplies. The operations group that McNamara was a member of developed a series of methodologies to facilitate effective logistics for the US military.

The know-how that developed was remarkable and US management practice was both rapidly developed by the wartime experience and garnered widespread admiration. Not surprisingly, US corporations took note. At the end of the war, the Ford Motor Company hired McNamara and many of his team, who were known in the firm as the 'whizz kids'. Young, educated and equipped with new methodologies, they had a profound impact on modernizing Ford. In 1960, McNamara served briefly as the first President of Ford from outside the family, before becoming Secretary of State for Defense in the Kennedy and Johnson administrations. During this period, he sought to apply techniques he had developed at Ford back into the military, as it was escalating the Vietnam conflict. The war was modelled as a system in which the performance measures were the number of enemy deaths recorded.

McNamara's legacy is controversial (Morris's (2003) Oscar-winning documentary provides an insight into this legacy and controversy) and for some he is reviled as a war criminal. He is, however, the fascinating embodiment of the belief in rational choice models and, more generally, in technocratic decision-making processes guiding strategic planning. Further, his personal journey illustrates the close connections between the military and large corporations, something Dwight Eisenhower, himself a five star general turned president, dubbed the military–industrial complex.

MINI CASE STUDY

Video Case Study – Watch *The Fog of War* DVD

Questions

1 What central insights can you draw from McNamara's life as a strategic decision-maker? In particular, discuss the relevance of his 11 lessons for strategic decision-making:

1 Empathize with your enemy.
2 Rationality will not save us.
3 There's something beyond oneself.
4 Maximize efficiency.
5 Proportionality should be a guideline in war.
6 Get the data.
7 Belief and seeing are often both wrong.
8 Be prepared to reexamine your reasoning.
9 In order to do good, you may have to engage in evil.
10 Never say never.
11 You can't change human nature.

For many strategists, strategic planning is important because it represents organizational rationality to its multiple stakeholders. Thus, strategic planning demonstrates how rational and modern an organization is. When looking at strategy from this perspective, it becomes an 'obligatory point of passage', the frame within which organizational rationality is produced and its sense maintained through myths and ceremonies (Meyer and Rowan, 1977). That these might be nothing but myths and ceremonies, however, is the point of this chapter. Strategic planning, in delineating a frame, constitutes a reality that fits within that frame:

● For example, take the famous SWOT analysis (Strengths, Weaknesses, Opportunities and Threats); it divides the world into four realms. These four realms are a myth produced via the ceremonial invocation of data that is thought to fill the matrix, usually by a consultant. Having such a matrix in mind, the world actually comes to be perceived as divided and consisting of only four fields. And it is precisely in this sense that strategic plans are maps that will create the territory they seek to describe.

● Think of a consumer electronics company that announces its vision in big words – being the world's leading innovator in its market. Samsung did this in 1993. Regardless of whether this was realistic or not, the statement captured the attention of young, ambitious and highly motivated scientists who hoped to realize their ambitions in this company and get hired. As a result, Samsung really did become one of the world's more innovative enterprise. By 2009 the company was widely regarded as the new Sony: it had done what its president had foreseen years earlier. In this case, the strategic intent was realized, in part, because it was announced. The strategic goal was accomplished not just because of a major planning effort but also because of smart communication, which talked the plan into reality. This is what is referred to as a self-fulfilling prophecy: the communicated plan is realized because it is communicated.

Often, consulting companies will contribute to strategic planning, acting as providers of rationality, legitimizing decisions already taken. Strategy think tanks such as McKinsey or the Boston Consulting Group have been important producers of strategy concepts and, when not originators, they have been important brokers in bringing academic concepts into practice. As such, it should not be astonishing that strategy has been crafted primarily for those who will pay the hefty fees of consultants: in fact, top managers will hire consultants because they expect them to tell stories that flatter their ability to act as powerful and decisive agents of change, as leaders who can make a difference. Much of the time they will do so. What executive would not fancy being a captain steering the ship through stormy seas, avoiding collisions and heading towards brave new future worlds? While this image might be flattering for those in the upper echelons of management, it can have negative effects on the agility of the organization as whole.

STRATEGY AS EMERGENT, GROUNDED AND NOT RATIONAL PLANNING

Bill Starbuck (1983) has argued, against overly rationalist views, that organizations are action generators that do not plan and then do; rather, in Starbuck's view, organizations act and do what they are good at, and then search for problems that look to be a justification for their action. Many writers in the strategic management literature have ignored this critical insight apart from Henry Mintzberg, who sees strategic planning as part of the problem, not the solution.

Mintzberg and managerial behaviour

Henry Mintzberg was born in Montreal in 1939 and did his undergraduate degree in engineering before he completed a Master's and PhD at MIT Sloan School of Management. He works at McGill University in Montreal, Canada. He shot to fame in 1973 when he conducted what seemed at the time a rather dull study: with a stopwatch in his left hand and a pen in his right, he meticulously recorded the daily life of five executives in different organizations, asking them to keep a diary of their doings. His suspicion was that what managers think they do would differ radically from what they actually do.

Mintzberg realized that interviewing managers about what they do would not be a reliable methodology: asking them about their jobs elicited standard, almost textbook answers stressing that managing is about planning, controlling, organizing and keeping an eye on the big picture. In this view, with which managers seem only too keen to conform, the manager can be seen as a rational planner.

Mintzberg's research told him a different story to that which managers seemed to believe about themselves: the five executives spent most of their time on mundane issues, dashing from one conversation to the next, and hardly focusing on any one issue for a long period of time; most interactions occurred on an *ad hoc* basis, dealing with problems as they arose, switching the focus every 10 minutes or so. Management was based on judgement and intuition. In short, managers did not behave as if they were rational engineers but played diverse roles and often improvised.

Equipped with thought-provoking ideas, and an engaging writing style, he remains one of the most outspoken critical voices in the field of strategic management. In a series of contributions he attacked orthodox strategy thinking. In 1990 Mintzberg published a critique of the basic assumptions of strategy in the influential *Strategic Management Journal*, provoking Igor Ansoff (1991) to reply, and thus to differentiate fundamentally opposing assumptions about rationality and structure.

Mintzberg turned Chandler's dictum that strategy followed structure on its head. The organization, with its design, its culture and its power games – these all co-shape its strategy, not the other way round. The head (top management) was held hostage by the body (the organization). Organizations should be thought of primarily in essentially local terms, as arenas of local politics, disputes, cleavages and conflicts. Strategy then becomes a grand narrative that local interests can seek to articulate to further whatever it is that they most desired to do. Often such desires are quite parochial: to gain influence, belittle their enemies in the organization, forge alliances with their preferred friends or the enemies of their enemies. Strategy is useful because it provides a rationale, a kind of camouflage, for doing these things.

Mintzberg argued that strategic planning had become a Taylorized and mechanical exercise where planning systems churned through data and set the future path. This was a paradox: while planning involved analysing data, the emergent strategy was based on synthesis, on thinking creatively and laterally, bringing things together and using the grand plans of strategy as a camouflage for doing so. Planners and their tools were badly equipped to do the job of being strategic: Mintzberg went so far as to say that planning was the opposite of strategy (1994: 333). Being strategic would often mean using the planned strategy in ways that were quite antithetical to the formal plans.

He further argued that virtually all texts about strategy-making depict it as a deliberate process in which we first think and subsequently act: 'We formulate, then we implement. The progression seems so perfectly sensible' (Mintzberg, 1989: 29). Thinking is reserved as a special task for the top management team. Again, in the words of Mintzberg:

> The notion that strategy is something that should happen way up there, far removed from the details of running an organization on a daily basis, is one of the great fallacies of conventional management. And it explains a good many of the most dramatic failures in business and public policy today. (1989: 31)

What mattered for strategy was not something static, such as the resources or knowledge possessed, it was something that evolved in the formal meetings and informal arenas of the organization. In Mintzberg's view, the distinction between strategy formulation and strategy implementation also no longer made sense: the doing of strategy and the articulating of strategy did not follow each other in a linear fashion. In fact, sometimes strategy might follow action rather than produce it and strategy is then formulated as an afterthought to a *fait accompli*. Strategy in such situations is a story that can be made to fit whatever the facts are represented as being. Strategy can be used to legitimate how and where an organization has got to rather than showing it the way to get there.

Mintzberg's (1994: 222) critical view of strategic planning unearthed five key assumptions that are routinely made in its name:

1 *Formalization*. Strategic findings must be translated into formal concepts. The processes that will lead to strategy's success can be clearly identified, anticipated and must be unambiguously communicated.

2 *Detachment*. The system does the thinking and produces strategies, which 'only' have to be implemented. A divide is presupposed between thinking and action, between strategy and implementation, between strategic planning and operational business. Management acts from a distance, based on remote control, displacement and abbreviation.

3 *Division of labour*. Management (the head) thinks, while the body of the organization has to be informed and formed following the strategic plans. Once a plan is formulated, the supplementary problem is one of implementation or pure execution.

4 *Quantification*. The strategy-making process is driven by 'hard facts' comprising quantitative representations of the organization and its environment. Knowledge of these is and must be 'objective'.

5 *Predetermination*. The context for strategy-making is stable and relies on hard data and predictable states of affairs. The strategic plan is a means to anticipate future developments and forecast coming changes.

If the five assumptions were to be replaced, there had to be something other than *formalization*, *detachment*, *division of labour*, *quantification* and *predetermination* on offer. Mintzberg is nothing if not a good marketer. In 1994 he suggested the five Ps of strategy:

1 *Perspective* is all about 'ways of seeing'. The gaze through which we see something defines the essence of that thing seen. If the gaze is fixed on the known numbers, on rational analysis and on extrapolating the future from the past, it is not likely to see far into the future: to see into the future requires an imaginative gaze rather than one that is fact grubbing. Evidence-based strategy is all very well but it will rarely lead to a breakthrough innovation, for instance. The mental models that frame and shape the ways in which we gaze at a phenomenon will define the nature of the phenomenon – they do more than just reveal it as it is, they constitute it as being what it is taken to be. Perspective is a relatively recent invention: in art it only emerges with the use of mirrors in fifteenth-century Florentine painting. Perspective gives us a sense of the depth of field in a literal, representational way. Once we see perspective in paintings, earlier art, lacking in perspective, can appear 'wrong'. Perspective makes things seem natural and correct. It provides a literal representation of the ways in which we conventionally see things. Thus, by extension, perspective in strategy provides a mental frame or cognitive structuring for the ways in which we apprehend what we take to be the real. Taking a perspective on things often means that we are applying a paradigm – a conventionally accepted and legitimate way of seeing – to the matter at hand. Perspective provides reassurance but it will never provide the shock of the new that its radical disruption through approaches such as Cubism might occasion. Perspective is inherently conservative: it reproduces what is already seen to be known.

2 *Planning* strategy is formulated prior to the actions to which it applies and it is developed intentionally, with a purpose: it is teleological in that it seeks to bring some defined end into being. While generals usually have plans for a battle they will rarely stick to them as the battle ebbs and flows:

they will modify their actions, and their plan, through emergent strategies that are shaped as much by the enemy as the planners. Unfortunately, many organizations are not as flexible as many generals – they will stick to a plan because it is still the plan long after it should have been emergently reshaped. One reason why this is so is because many plans are formulated at a great distance, literally and metaphorically, from arenas of action. The plan is supposed to be conceived on high and to unfold down and through the organization to all fields of operations. High and mighty conceptions often make nice fantasies of control and prediction but rarely survive the rough and tumble of operations on the ground in some far-flung corner of the corporate empire.

3 *Pattern* making is often a form of retrospective discovery where the journey that has been unfolding, perhaps somewhat randomly or with a degree of confusion, becomes a recognizable path followed, whether consciously or not. This path is defined by the consistency with which it emerges and has been followed. Not for nothing do social scientists refer to path dependency: the best predictor of a direction for the future is the direction in the past.

4 *Position* refers to the place of an organization within its environment. Think of a battlefield and the troops commanding a position – a ridge, fortification or landing beach. If you have a commanding position it is that much harder for the competition (or enemy) to defeat you. Position does not only have martial referents, however. It can also refer to context in ecological or economic terms. A firm may occupy a niche position in a business environment, for instance; being a boutique label or producer of a good or service would be a case in point – a small, intimate, distinctive hotel, for instance, or a retail outlet with standout individual designs unavailable in the malls and high streets. Or, conceived in economic terms, a position may be an ideal niche because it allows the company to make a profit by positioning a specific product in a specific market for which it is ideally suited. For instance, while there will be a limited market for a Maserati or Bentley among the Indian elite, there will be a far larger market for a Tata Nano.

5 As a *ploy*, strategy may be thought of as playful, as unexpected, unanticipated, sometimes even as whimsical. Marketing strategies are the best examples of ploys: think of HSBC's use of the same images with different captions – a red stiletto shoe, for instance, that is labelled 'ecstasy' in one image and 'agony' in another. The ploy is used to try and suggest to the putative HSBC client that things that appear the same often are not and that it takes deep contextual knowledge to attach the right image to the right label. In this way the ploy seeks to show that HSBC is not only a global but also a local bank.

Mintzberg favours a grassroots model of strategy-making. Initially, he suggests, strategies grow 'like weeds in a garden, they are not cultivated like tomatoes in a hothouse' (Mintzberg 1989: 214). Following this metaphor, strategy can take root in all kinds of places, with new ideas able to start anywhere in the organization if there are favourable resources. Once these strategies spread organically throughout the organization, they become collective patterns of behaviour. Management's job is to nurture and ensure fertile soil for ideas – but not to intervene and weed out the jungle. There is an Italian fable that makes the same point: a peasant patriarch, on his deathbed, tells his indolent sons that there is treasure buried on his land. On his death they begin to dig the soil everywhere, in search of it. They do not find treasure directly but indirectly they do – because they have prepared the ground for sowing and growing crops.

To think of strategy this way is to see it emerging from the roots rather than to go searching for it in the highest echelons of the organization. Strategy starts from the bottom up and gains support and energy from the everyday work of the members of the organization – as opposed to those lofty plans written by top executives during a retreat in a fancy off-site location. It is pretty hard for these documents not to feed the vanities of those participating while simultaneously demonstrating that they are often out of touch with the more mundane concerns of the business or organization.

Not surprisingly, Mintzberg's ideas created quite a stir in the small world of strategy theory. Some interpreted them as a 'humanization' of the field of strategy (e.g. Pettigrew et al., 2006): suddenly, human actors were important again, and the way they made sense of complex environments was more important than the algorithm a computer produced. Strategy was no longer a calculation but a kind of team sport in which the basic rules of the game regulated individual players' moves as they tried to out-manoeuvre their opponents.

Mintzberg and grounded theory

Mintzberg was initially a grounded researcher, in the field, closely observing how managers did what they did and how they accounted for what they were doing. Although he is rarely explicit about this, it seems evident that his ideas were influenced by the research approach popularized by Glazer and Strauss (1967) for it was they who first coined the term, emergent theory. In emergent theory understanding is not shaped a priori by a detailed hypothetico-deductive model, which functions as a plan. Instead, by being able to grasp the everyday terms and theories that are used in situated activities, such as making up strategy through systematic data collection and constant analysis of the emerging insights, discovery proceeds through direct contact with the subject's own understandings (Human, 2009: 425).

Mintzberg's thinking follows the precepts of grounded theory (Glazer and Strauss, 1967):

1 In grounded theory the researcher does not start from an a priori plan or model. Instead, one tries to discover what the relevant categories are from the data collected from a deep immersion in the research setting.

    The corollary to this disinclination to entertain models or plans in Mintzberg's emergence perspective is simple: strategists may think that strategy follows on from the plans and models that they create – but, in reality, it is being constantly interpreted, negotiated and made sense of through their own everyday actions and those of the people charged with its implementation as well as those who will resist the strategy: sometimes these can include employees, customers, stakeholders, competitors and governments.

2 Grounded theory researchers search for the meaningful categories with which they can make sense of the data they collect through the process of theoretical sensitivity. Theoretical sensitivity is achieved through the method of constant comparison where the data episodes collected are investigated for patterns of difference and sameness. These categories are captured through a process of constant coding that identifies, refines and redefines the emergent categories of concepts and the interrelationships between the categories being used and the concepts that organize these

categories. The focus is on ordinary people as practical theorists making sense of their world.

Mintzberg's emergence theory treats strategists in the same way. To understand strategy we must also understand the categories and concepts that strategists are using to make up strategy and to negotiate its interpretation in many subsequent scenes and settings. Some of these categories and concepts might, for instance, come from the strategists' MBA education in rational planning models, Porterian analysis or the RBV. However, we should bracket any a priori assumption we might have about these being literal or empirically realistic models; instead, we should look at how they become used in practice by those who deploy them. What are important are use values and effects, not any assumptions made about the extent to which models correspond with reality or any existing state of affairs. Basically, the strategy-as-practice school takes this point and runs with it.

3 Grounded theory researchers are not researching with a *tabula rasa*, of course. They are only too aware of broader social theory. However, what they try to do is to hold off from applying this until they have formed a good impression and analysis of the everyday theories in use of the subjects at hand. Then they may bring the more formal theory that they can draw on into play in order both to refine the theory through contact with the empirical data and to make more informed sense of the sense being made by the subjects in their everyday theorizing.

Mintzberg's approach to strategy is similar: strategists cannot make up strategy from nothing but have strategic thinking tools with which to work. However, as they make sense of complex unfolding realities their understanding of the use of these tools undergoes subtle modifications and negotiations. Thus, strategy is emergent: it emerges from a set of theories and tools but is constantly being redefined, reconfigured and renegotiated in practice. Strategy is a form of negotiated order – or, better, negotiated ordering.

Mintzberg's grounded theory began its career in close observation and the ethnographic analysis of managers at work. Unlike almost all prior strategy thinkers he was not prescribing what strategy should be but describing how it actually emerged in practice. In almost all respects Mintzberg is an important root for what has become known as the strategy-as-practice movement, albeit not the only advocate of the emergence perspective on strategy or the sole precursor of the strategy-as-practice school.

DELIBERATE VS EMERGENT STRATEGY

Strategy, according to Mintzberg, is best characterized as a stream of decisions made over time. In trying to understand the strategies pursued by organizations, he posits that it is useful to consider the extent to which a strategy is *deliberate* or *emergent*. Much hinges on these terms and the distinctions between them. Deliberate strategies are fairly straightforward: they are carefully articulated, then communicated widely throughout an organization, before being implemented with an express outcome in mind. A strategy analyst can then assess whether the objectives of a deliberate strategy are actually being achieved. In contrast, an emergent strategy is where an outcome is realized 'despite, or in the absence of, intentions'

(Mintzberg and Waters, 1985). The crucial difference between the two types of strategy rests on the *intent* that underpins them: a deliberate strategy is precise and preordained, whereas an emergent strategy lacks express intent. While it is comparatively straightforward to envisage what constitutes a deliberate strategy, one could be forgiven for thinking that an emergent strategy is little more than freewheeling anarchy that denotes a total lack of strategy! What strategy does not derive from intent? On this point Mintzberg and Waters have the following to say:

> Emergent strategy does not mean management is out of control, only – in some cases at least – that it is open, flexible and responsive, in other words, willing to learn. Such behaviour is especially important when an environment is too unstable or complex to comprehend, or too imposing to defy. Openness to such emergent strategy enables management to act before everything is fully understood – to respond to an evolving reality rather than having to focus on a stable fantasy. (1985: 271)

Mintzberg and Waters' (1985) contribution highlights that some strategies do, in fact, lack intent. Mintzberg cautions that few strategies, if any, are purely deliberate or exclusively emergent. Instead, strategies are likely to bear the traces of both tendencies. To elaborate on this further, Mintzberg and Waters constructed a taxonomy based on the respective degree of deliberation and emergence contained in a strategy. For those familiar with Mintzberg's broader corpus of writings, you will note that he appears to be especially fond of constructing taxonomies!

1 *Planned strategy*. This is characterized by formal planning with explicit objectives. The strategy is communicated widely by senior executives and is carefully implemented. It is a 'deliberate' strategy. The classical approaches to strategic management, such as an Ansoffian approach to strategy, would follow this approach. In this approach strategy-making is tightly controlled.

2 *Entrepreneurial strategy*. This is where the entrepreneur formulates the strategic vision. It has express intentions and a vision of the future, though it is prone to being halted or altered according to the entrepreneur's whim. It is broadly a 'deliberate' strategy and is tightly controlled by the entrepreneur.

3 *Ideological strategy*. An ideological organization – such as an extremist political organization, the military or a terrorist group – will often have a very strong culture, which socializes organizational actors into subscribing to a particular set of goals. The goals are often utopian and inspirational to members of the organization. An ideological strategy is broadly deliberate, often determining methods as well as objectives.

4 *Umbrella strategy*. This can be seen where an organization comprises a range of different interest groups and exists in an environment of uncertainty. The senior strategists will define broad boundaries allowing others discretion to adopt strategies within those boundaries. An umbrella strategy is at once deliberate – setting broad goals – and emergent – allowing experimentation to realize those goals. Often in the process of an umbrella strategy the goals themselves can change. Mintzberg and Waters cite the example of NASA in 1960s, as it attempted to 'put a man on the moon', as an example of an umbrella strategy. As a strategy it is far less controlling than the previous three examples.

5 *Process strategy*. In this case the central leadership of an organization control the process through which a strategy is formulated and the people

charged with making the strategy. The content of the strategy is, however, at the discretion of those making it. An example of this might be in a multi-divisional organization where individual sub-units are allowed to formulate their own strategies, albeit by using an established process to arrive at their strategy.

6　*Unconnected strategy.* This is where a part of an organization, enjoying considerable autonomy, is able to develop its own strategy. From the vantage point of the group making the strategy it might be deliberate or emergent, though from the perspective of the organization such strategy-making is always emergent.

7　*Consensus strategy.* This form of strategy-making is generally emergent, with an agreed consensus emerging from discussions between different interest groups in an organization. Such a form of strategy-making entails negotiation and an organization having a 'feel' for a particular issue.

8　*Imposed strategy.* This is when a powerful group or an event from outside an organization determines a strategy for an organization. An example would be the International Monetary Fund imposing budget cuts on a national government. For the government concerned, an imposed strategy is emergent in nature, although it might subsequently become the subject of deliberate intent by the organization.

Mintzberg and Waters' (1985) articulation of eight types of strategy-making is not meant to be exhaustive; instead, it is illustrative of the distinctions between deliberate and emergent strategy. Deliberate strategy is focused on pursuing a particular direction and tightly controlling the implementation of a strategy, whereas emergent strategy is more concerned with an adaptation to circumstances and strategic learning. As Mintzberg and Waters' (1985) ideas above suggest, strategies are likely to combine both deliberate and emergent features, although some, such as the planned strategy, are more overtly deliberate, while others, such as unconnected strategy, are irredeemably emergent.

Andrew Pettigrew and process

One of the most important contributors to the theory of strategy as a process came from the UK – Andrew Pettigrew. Pettigrew wrote an influential book in 1985 called *The Awakening Giant: Continuity and Change at ICI*. Pettigrew directed a whole team of British strategy academics who worked in the 1980s at the Warwick Business School's Centre for Corporate Strategy and Change (CCSC), a centre that focused on combining the fine-grained study of specific organizational contexts with an account of the strategy process (e.g. Johnson, 1987). Pettigrew's book was in many ways the pacesetter for the agenda of the CCSC. It focused on the change that occurred within ICI over long periods of time. Pettigrew was curious to understand why quite similar change initiatives had had different outcomes in the organization. He found answers to his question by looking at the history, the context and the processes of ICI.

Pettigrew's work was a critique of Porter and others who used more static approaches. For Pettigrew and his colleagues, the content of a specific strategy was the result of the strategy-making process. The process determined the outcome through the patterns of domination, the legitimization of cognitive maps and the organization of interaction in a particular way. Hence, to produce better strategies one had to be able to create a better strategy-making process. Focusing on the strategy process meant abandoning a linear, rationalistic template for strategy and instead following the complex and dynamic evolution of strategic thoughts and how they change the organization.

Pettigrew sees an organization's strategy as the result of a process embedded in a context. In this context the link between formulation and implementation is not a unilinear process of *think, plan, act, review,* but is conditioned by a complex and emergent temporality which is constantly refining the activities being undertaken as well as the stage of the process that they are being undertaken in. Hence, understanding strategic change means understanding its changing meaning as it emerges and is defined and redefined by various actors and stakeholders over time. Whose definitions of the situation prevail is always an effect of organizational power and politics. Only detailed ethnographic case studies and specific business histories, combined with the eye for detail of an anthropologist, can really grasp strategy as a flow and a process. Pettigrew is an important precursor of the strategy-as-practice perspective.

STRATEGY IS WHAT STRATEGISTS DO, KNOW, SAY …

Strategy as practice (s-as-p)

Of course, plans play an important role in organizations; we are not saying that they do not. *But plans rarely unfold according to plan.* For Mintzberg, the strategic path an organization will actually take, the realized strategy, is characterized by the interplay between bottom-up, grassroots initiatives and top-down planning that reflects management's intent. For him, realized strategies emerge out of the interaction between learning and planning (see Mintzberg and Waters, 1985). And learning can sometimes be a painful and political affair as planners learn what they do not know through the dead ends, hijacks and crashes that their plans endure and provoke.

Save for a few exceptions, the dominant strands within strategic management are based on economics. The theoretical context provided by an economist's approach to strategy engenders a reality in which numbers, equations, models, abstract frameworks and a macro-analysis of industry dynamics are dominant representations. What is left out of the picture is the work of strategy – the people whose task it is to produce strategy, the tools they use, the workshops in which strategic ideas are born, the language they deploy to make strategic sense of the world and to legitimate their views as strategic.

In short: the actual *practice* of doing strategy has been left unaccounted for in approaches inspired by economics. As Jarzabkowski and Spee (2009: 70) have observed, there 'appears to be little room in mainstream strategy research for living beings whose emotions, motivations and actions shape strategy'. Strategy, they suggest, is similar to an elaborate dance in which the moves are part crafted and part improvized from the resources and skills that the players can contribute. The metaphor of the tango suggests itself: choreographed, spontaneous, emotional and formalistic all at the same time.

A diverse group of scholars have gathered together under the umbrella of *strategy as practice* to focus on bringing human action back into strategy research (for an overview see Jarzabkowski and Spee, 2009; an early example of the approach is provided by Jarzabkowski, 2004).

YOU CAN DOWNLOAD…

Paula Jarzabkowski's (2004) Strategy as Practice: Recursiveness, Adaptation and Practices-In-Use, *Organization Studies*, 25(4): 529–60, from the book's website at www.sagepub.co.uk/cleggstrategy

Image 4.1 'Tango'

PHOTOGRAPHY BY STEWART CLEGG

Practices involve the various routines, discourses, concepts and technologies through which this strategy labour is made possible – not just obvious ones such as strategy reviews and off-sites, but also those embedded in academic and consulting tools (Porterian analysis, hypothesis testing, etc.) and in more material technologies and artefacts (PowerPoints, flip-charts, etc.). (Jarzabkowski and Whittington, 2008: 101)

The focus is on what strategists do when they do strategy – their practices.

The new approach is clearly to be understood as a systematic critique of orthodox, hegemonic and mainly North American, or North-American-inspired, strategy research with the objective being to 'break through the economics-based dominance over strategy research' (Jarzabwkowski and Spee, 2009: 70).

The venture of strategy as practice took entrepreneurial shape in February 2001 when a group of about 50 researchers convened at EIASM (the European Institute for Advanced Studies in Management) in Brussels, attending a workshop organized by Gerry Johnson, Leif Melin and Richard Whittington, to discuss developments in strategy's micro-processes. The output of the conference resulted in a special issue of the *Journal of Management Studies* (Johnson et al., 2003) and, perhaps more significantly, started a conversation about the need for a more practice-based approach to strategy-making. In the following years these key researchers, together with figures such as Paula Jarzabkowski, constructed a network of actors and actions that has led to the emergence and partial institutionalization of a 'strategy-as-practice' group. To date, the s-as-p movement has run several special issues of influential management journals, organized tracks at conferences and maintains a website with some 2700 registered members. In its short history, s-as-p has institutionalized itself quickly and effectively. As the official website www.strategy-as-practice.org states:

> Strategy as Practice is a community of scholars interested in the practice of strategy. … What we are agreed on is the importance of a focus on the processes and practices constituting the everyday activities of organizational life and relating to strategic outcomes, if we are to move our field forward.

At the core of this new approach, as the use of 'strategizing' might suggest, is a concern for what strategic actors actually do and the kinds of activities they do when they strategize (Whittington, 1996; 2002). According to Whittington (2004) the key innovation of the strategy-as-practice framework is to treat strategy as an important social practice – as something that organization members do – that requires serious analysis. The notion of strategy developed by the s-as-p approach depicts strategy as an activity: 'strategy' is not only an attribute of firms but also an activity undertaken by people. Strategy must always be treated as something that people do.

Following what people actually do when they strategize, the practice-based approach investigates the nitty-gritty details of strategy formation – the routines of budgeting, the expenditure meetings, the reports and presentations – through focusing on 'praxis, practitioners and practices' (Whittington, 2002). For instance, Dalvir Samra-Fredericks (2003) analysed the interactions of strategists and found how their linguistic skills construct strategic realities, including a shared definition of the future. She started from the observation of Barry and Elmes (1997: 430) that what is needed is a study of how language is used by strategists to establish meanings and create a 'discourse of direction'. Taking this starting point, Samra-Fredericks builds a new direction for strategy research that draws on sociology to analyse how strategizing is accomplished during 'real-time' talk-based interaction.

Much strategy work is accomplished through talk – through analysing and arguing for various discursive devices, forms of representation and favoured logics of analysis:

> [I]t is through talking that strategists negotiate over and establish meanings, express cognition, articulate their perceptions of the environment (etc.) and from this basis, legitimate their individual and collective judgements. Even knowledge, know-how and expertise must be expressed in some way and thus, 'made to count'. As Tsoukas (1996, p. 23) also suggests, knowledge such as 'industry recipes' (Spender, 1989) are 'embedded in conversations and social interactions'. It is through speaking these forms of knowledge, the competitive landscape and possibilities for one's own organization are made sense of and realized. Similarly, physical entities such as written reports and flip-chart 'musings' are always talked about and in this way, strategists *breathe life* into them and make them meaningful for their present purposes. Given this, studies of strategists' naturally occurring talk-based routines are important for understanding how they develop strategic direction and project a viable sense of the 'organization' into the future. (Samra-Fredericks, 2003: 143)

Analysing naturally occurring conversations that occurred in setting the strategy for a manufacturing company she demonstrates the ways in which the opening remarks of one strategist set the scene for what subsequently unfolded into the strategy. The analysis of naturally occurring conversations marks off Samra-Frederick's work, in general, from that of other researchers who rely on more conventional interview data and who often elide the substantive display of strategic competencies in situated actions, preferring instead more abstracted and generalized reports, such as one finds in Hardy et al. (2000) and Vaara (2002). Against these less field-based and interpretive accounts she prefers to use an ethnomethodological approach, using ideas from Garfinkel (1967) and conversation analysis (Sacks, 1992; Sacks, Schegloff and Jefferson, 1974) to undertake a systematic fine-grained analysis of strategists' linguistic skills and forms of knowledge in practice. From this perspective, the 'objective world of facts' that is presumed to exist by members is analysed in the ways in which this world is made sense of through common-sense categories and social constructions which constitute the sense of that world. Attending to the subtle flows of interaction in situated talk in action is essential to the development of this perspective.

The talk recorded and analysed was generated around a discussion of two strategic weaknesses: one in IT capability and the other in strategic thinking at the board/top management team level. She identified six factors defining interpersonal competence in strategy. These are the ability to:

1   Speak forms of knowledge – to draw on a tacit competency in using locally and situationally meaningful and typical categories to construct a compelling story of the organization.

2   Mitigate and observe the protocols of human interaction (respecting and observing the moral order). This involves achieving a political positioning of preferred analyses while respecting the 'face' of significant others. One needs to achieve a discursive dominance of one's preferred proposals in such a way that does not signal nor create needless strife and conflict in the strategy community. The skilled use of pronouns that collect or divide – 'we', 'us', the 'organization', the 'team', as opposed to 'them', the 'competition', people who are not 'team players', etc. – is particularly important.

3   Question and query: skilled strategists are able to construct what is 'reasonableness' in such a way as to curb simultaneously the possibilities for counter moves by others (because they would be outside the bounds of being reasonable), often leaving these others wondering how they had been out-manoeuvred.

4   Display appropriate emotion: strategizing is often emotional work, as signs of frustration, enthusiasm and energy are communicated in words and gestures, looks and embodiment.

5   Deploy metaphors: the use of appropriate and gripping metaphors, metaphors that subsequently frame discussion, is a vital skill for the successful strategist.

6   Put history 'to work': being able to weave the past, present and future together from discursively available characterizations, plot lines and themes, and to be able to do this improvizationally, in action, in talk.

In addition, the art of knowing *when* to do this (the 'right time') as a tacit form of *knowing* is also vital. The insight that generates these six competencies is deeply grounded in a contextual analysis. Although we might expect to find these capabilities across situations, we would not necessarily expect to find all six and only these six; other contexts may make other skills more contingent. Above all, these skills are politically, culturally and situationally relevant – they work to make and constrain sense in specific strategic situations. They demonstrate what kinds of skills in demarcating what kinds of categories constitute serious and respectable strategy talk in specific settings.

In a related paper, Samra-Fredericks (2005) combines her fine-grained analysis of everyday strategic interactions with a concern for the pragmatic validity claims that are made by skilled strategists as they strategize. Following Habermas (1984) she identifies these as concerns with *truth*, considered in a factual way; the *correctness* of what is said; the *sincerity* of claims made, in terms of their authenticity, for example; and their *intelligibility*. The latter is especially interesting; while claims regarding truth, correctness and sincerity draw on quite generic social skills (albeit that their emotional tone is observed to be masculine gendered in terms of a hardness, use of aggression and impatience), the latter is quite substantive. Intelligibility draws on an ability to speak managerially and strategically; to be able to deploy the types of analyses that characterize the doing of strategy. These are terms and tools that have a rhetorical and representational role to play that are learnt, largely, in business schools and especially in MBA courses. Hence, intelligibility occurs in a very specific learnt register – a facility with the tools of the trade for strategy as it is taught in business schools. The pragmatic validity claims of truth, correctness and sincerity are, as stated, normal and constitutive features of almost all interaction settings in which we take for granted that the other is committed to these protocols. Intelligibility is different: it involves using a technically specific vocabulary in ways that display those truths it makes up through the correctness of its categories, and the skillful use of language by the speakers and hearers. As Samra-Fredericks demonstrates, making the performance intelligible entails the use of some appropriate strategy categories for analysis as well as some subtle positioning of the dominant and subordinate speakers through the use of pronouns, but it also requires a gendered performance of some subtlety and authority. The gendered nature of the performance is to be seen in the ways that emotions are registered and displayed. A successful strategist is confident, assertive, a little emphatic, and aggressive even, while fluent in the use of some basic rhetorical devices usually learnt in the course of an MBA.

Rather than prescribing models of how strategy should be done, s-as-p scholars study the actions of managers. They do not try to understand what strategy should be in a prescriptive way by applying a formulaic model such as the five forces or the RBV, but research how strategy is actually done. The practice approach focuses on how managers 'do strategy', including how they develop ideas and inspirations, and the often-mundane routines and mechanisms that translate these inspirations into practice. As a style of research it requires the researcher to be very close to the action: ideally, they will sit in on meetings, study draft after draft of strategic documents and interact with all participants of the strategy-making process. There is no helicoptering in to produce a generic model into which the client is slotted – a diamond, for instance. It is not a very easy research approach to pull off because most companies guard their strategies as if they were hidden treasure, so researchers will often find it difficult to achieve the level of access necessary for a practice study.

Johnson et al. (2007: 7) conceive of strategy as practice 'as a concern with what people do in relation to strategy and how this is influenced by and influences their organizational and institutional context'. In this definition, strategy is inextricably linked to human action and interaction. There is an evident opposition to mainstream approaches in which performance, abstract resources, or the industrial context will determine strategy. S-as-p attempts to open the 'black box' of strategizing and analyse how strategy is made up.

While some s-as-p analysis is clearly non-prescriptive and analytic in intent, such as the corpus of Samra-Fredericks (2005), many other publications in the s-as-p area start from premises that share a mostly managerial perspective. S-as-p research is committed to developing 'more helpful models of managing' (e.g. Johnson et al., 2003: 12) which is a clear commitment to a managerial perspective. Despite its rhetoric, and in line with most conventional strategy research, non-executives are written out of the picture. Based on questions such as 'just what do managers have to do to make a difference and what is their impact? What works for them and what does not work?' (Johnson et al., 2003: 16) the s-as-p approach remains close to the traditions of mainstream, functional research. Intentionally or not, the s-as-p approach positions itself as a problem-solving tool for managerial elites. It does not emphasize the ways in which outsiders, renegades and strangers might influence strategy in practice. Nor is it a particularly coherent analysis – it combines a number of incoherent strands in its approach (see Carter et al., 2008b; also Carter et al., 2008c).

Chia and MacKay (2007) suggest that strategic practices should be seen as social skills that are culturally acquired and unconsciously absorbed. They are soaked up from the milieu within which strategy-making occurs. Such a milieu will tend to be marked by an unreflective acceptance of certain leading narratives and concepts driven by what Edgar Schein terms deep assumptions. From this perspective one

YOU CAN DOWNLOAD...

Chris Carter, Stewart Clegg and Martin Kornberger's (2008b) Strategy as Practice? *Strategic Organization*, 6(1): 83–100. The article generated a lively debate between the authors and s-as-p researchers; for the critique of the critique see P. Jarzabkowski and R. Whittington's (2008) Hard to Disagree, Mostly, *Strategic Organization*, 6(1): 101–6; for the rejoinder read C. Carter, S. Clegg and M. Kornberger's (2008c), S-A-P Zapping the Field, *Strategic Organization*, 6(1): 107–12, all of which are downloadable from the book's website at www.sagepub.co.uk/cleggstrategy

YOU CAN DOWNLOAD...

An interesting paper that updates the emergence approach by connecting it to the strategy-as-practice perspective. The paper is by Robert Chia and Brad McKay (2007) Post-processual Challenges for the Emerging Strategy-as-Practice Perspective: Discovering Strategy in the Logic of Practice, *Human Relations*, 60(1): 217–42, from the book's website at www.sagepub.co.uk/cleggstrategy

has to research the background history and practices for the deep assumptions that have made that milieu and its strategy what they are. Rather than see strategy as some sort of objective and transcendental approach that can be lifted from one context and applied to another, we should always approach it in terms of the local realities that have constituted it and which, in turn, it constitutes.

Strategy and learning

Rapidly changing technologies, hyper competition and globalization leave organizations with little chance but to build a learning organization that has resilience and an appetite for change.

A learning organization has the ability to manage knowledge. Knowledge is hard to centralize: for instance, Orr's excellent (1996) study of photocopier repairmen illustrated that local knowing, collaboration and improvisation were necessary to fix broken machines (see Chapter 3 for more details on learning and KM). The simple error message that distressed the user and greeted the repairman did not convey enough information to allow quick and simple problem solving. Rather, the repairman had to draw on collectively built experiences and narratives to know how to fix problems. The moral of the story is that knowledge is distributed across the entire organization and is often lodged in implicit knowing rather than formally codified knowledge. Think of all those Microsoft 'help' options: do you really understand most of them? We don't.

When a research and development team improve the functioning of a given device they engage in single loop learning.

Double loop learning is more strategic.

To put it metaphorically, single loop learning involves learning the competencies necessary to play a certain game successfully, whereas double loop learning requires thinking and learning about what is the most valuable game to play. Single loop learning concerns acting according to the rules of a certain game; in contrast, double loop learning involves learning what the actual rules of the game are and how they could be changed to modify the game or play a different game altogether. Single loop learning focuses on optimizing problem-solving behaviour in a given context, whereas double loop learning challenges the core assumptions, beliefs and values that frame the context. In the words of Argyris and Schön:

> When the error detected and corrected permits the organization to carry on its present policies or achieve its present objectives, then that error-and-correction process is *single-loop* learning. Single-loop learning is like a thermostat that learns when it is too hot or too cold and turns the heat on or off. The thermostat can perform this task because it can receive information (the temperature of the room) and take corrective action. *Double-loop* learning occurs when error is detected and corrected in ways that involve the modification of an organization's underlying norms, policies and objectives. (1978: 2)

Double loop learning is a core organizational capability in creating an emergent strategy. Double loop learning requires strategic changes: it challenges the core assumptions and beliefs that organizations hold dear. As such, the appetite for learning creates an ability that enables strategies to emerge and shape the organization.

Emerging strategists not only foster learning in their organization, but also nurture and, where possible, manage the culture of an organization. In fact, emerging strategies rely on organizational cultures in which curiosity and innovation are valued and practised.

Rather than having a strategy unit or a strategically minded leader at the top, the learning organization behaves, as a whole, strategically. Rather than trying to predict the future, the mantra of the emergent approach is being prepared for future challenges that cannot be summarized in neat strategy reports. Preparedness replaces predictability as the strategic imperative.

Single loop learning optimizes its knowledge of a given problem by using skills, refining abilities and acquiring the knowledge necessary to achieve a resolution of that problem. While important, this knowledge is not necessarily strategic. It might be more focused on efficiency gains and achieving operational effectiveness, a kind of learning that occurs within a given framework, where the parameters are pre-defined and the learning activity focuses on how to optimize (or maximize or increase) your capacity within this frame.

Double loop learning means changing the frame of reference that normally guides behaviour and teaches you how to change the rules of the game. It implies rethinking the task at hand and considering whether its accomplishment is beneficial or not.

Strategy and culture

Edgar Schein (1997) defines culture as the deep, basic assumptions and beliefs that are shared by organizational members.

The strategic importance of cultures resides in their pervasive impact on how organizational members make sense of opportunities and challenges, how they deal with problems and how they discuss them. Schein differentiates between three levels of culture:

1 The first level represents the level of artefacts, including visible organizational features such as the physical structure of buildings, their architecture, uniforms, interior design and logos, for instance. The playful Google logo that changes on important dates, the iconic architecture and design of the Googleplex and the campus-like furniture that adorns its interior are good examples of artefacts. One could argue that they are of strategic importance as they help to create a relaxed and playful cultural context conducive to the encouragement of fruitful conversations and new ideas.

2 Schein's second level refers to expressed values. These represent the non-visible facets of cultures, as they express the norms and beliefs that employees express when they discuss organizational issues. Mission statements and espoused values, such as Google's *Don't Be Evil*, are examples in case. Obviously, this level is the strategists' preferred playground when they are working on the strategic mission, vision and values of the organization. Strategists work to create a privileged space around an organization's preferred statements of these to solidify and make them concrete.

3 The third level of culture is the most influential one. This is where the basic assumptions of the organization are hidden beneath artefacts and expressed values. In the language of Karl E. Weick, this level includes the cognitive maps that structure the way we interpret the world. Level 3 is where we store what we take for granted, and do not want, cannot, or do not know how to question. Without being explicitly expressed, this level shapes decision-making and behaviour without being perceived as such. (Look also at Chapter 9 where you will see that these cultural levels also map onto political levels of strategy.) These deep structures of culture are the hardest to articulate and the most influential in practice. A good example drawn from literature is to be found in George Orwell's classic book, *Homage to Catalonia* (2003), where he describes how the deep assumptions of the various political factions in Barcelona during the Spanish Civil War drove their strategies (see especially Appendix II).

Emerging strategies depend on all three levels, especially the third one. From a cultural perspective, to manage strategy means understanding and, if possible, managing deeply held assumptions about the nature of the organization. An example here is Microsoft, which for rather a long time did not recognize the Internet as an important new arena for competition. Bill Gates realized its importance just before it was almost too late. Netscape had established the first successful Internet browser, and companies such as Google and Yahoo! were well ahead in the search engine business.

Given that culture is deeply rooted in an organization, the question is: can the strategist manage it to the advantage of the organization? Two McKinsey consultants, whom you have already encountered in Chapter 1, answered the question

Culture represents the taken-for-granted ways an organization perceives its environment and itself. And these ways are always plural, often fragmentary and usually emergent around the irruption and condensation of specific issues, so it is usually the case that there is a plurality of organizational cultures in any one context.

with an emphatic 'yes' – and produced the best selling management book in history. Peters and Waterman's *In Search of Excellence* (1982) propelled culture centre stage in corporate analysis. Their message was simple: great companies have excellent cultures. Excellent cultures deliver outstanding financial success. What makes a culture excellent is an agreement around its core values and presuppositions and that these are widely shared and acted on.

With the publication of *In Search of Excellence* the idea of culture became seen as a master concept for organization analysis. Indeed, this book, along with one or two other not quite as influential but still important books, including Deal and Kennedy (1982) and Schein (1997), are often seen as the innovations that made culture a popular and acceptable topic for consultants and managers alike, lifting it out of the relative business obscurity of anthropology where it had previously been largely located.

It was presumed that if you forged a strong culture – one that incorporates all organization members in shared beliefs and commitments – then everything else – good morale, performance and results – should follow. In this view, the strategist's main task was to shape a strong culture that would align all organization members. A flood of papers in strategic management resulted that argued the link between strong culture and superior performance (e.g. Hall, 1993). Strong cultures, so the story went, were the competitive advantage that made organizations unique and successful.

Relatively early in the debate, as we have seen in Chapter 3, Barney (1986) raised a question from within the RBV camp: 'Organizational Culture: Can It Be a Source of Sustained Competitive Advantage?' His answer was that firms whose culture displayed three distinct characteristics (being valuable, being rare and being imperfectly imitable) could achieve a superior financial performance. However, Barney was less optimistic that management could engineer such a culture. With Socratic grace, he argued that only if the culture of a firm cannot be engineered could it be a source of truly sustainable competitive advantage. If it could be engineered, it would be easily imitable, and hence every organization would 'have' a superior culture. Of course, there would be no competitive advantage in such a scenario. Put simply, culture did matter, but it was beyond the influence of strategists who were in search of excellence.

While Barney's critique followed the logic of the RBV view of strategy, the Stanford Professor Joanne Martin (2000) redefined the understanding of culture. In her seminal book on culture, she argued that culture might be more differentiated and fragmented than the functional perspective *à la* Peters and Waterman suggested. In their view, strong cultures are shared cultures – and what is not shared is not part of culture. It is deviance – the classical functionalist category used for explaining cases where all members do not share a central value system.

Deviations from the cultural ideal are seen as unfortunate, yet exceptional, shortcomings. Often, this approach results in culture being represented as the reflection of an organization's elite but such a shared understanding hardly comprises everyday organizational life, with its mundane routines and its vernacular sense grown over time – the everyday cultures of the organization. Note the plural once again: it is rarely the case that everyone will share the same understandings and sense of the organization and undesirable that they should, because, as we have argued, there would be no impetus for innovation if everyone thought the same way!

Martin argued that homogeneity was problematic and that in reality organizations were more differentiated and may be even more fragmented than the strategic culture theorists assumed. According to the fragmentation view she proposed, culture could neither be clearly consistent nor clearly contested. The picture was more likely to be one that represented contradictory and confusing cultures battling for the soul of the organization as much as for that of the individual. Individuals are more likely to exist in a state of competing cultural interpellations – where they are constantly under competing pressures to identify themselves and their organization with rival conceptions of what is an appropriate cultural identity. To make things more complicated, this does not mean that fragmented cultures can replace one strong integrated culture. As Martin has argued, cultures always contain elements of integration, differentiation and fragmentation at the same time.

Where does this leave the strategist? While culture is a pivotal concept in the emergence strategy perspective, the means to manage it are limited. Culture does matter, but it is hard, if not impossible, to engineer. The critique of this perspective is similar to one that can be raised in relation to Mintzberg's writing: it leaves the eager strategists with little room for action and reduces their task to creating a framework in which a viable strategy might emerge. At least, in an organization that has taken the culture of excellence ideas on board, the strategist can watch the spectacle from the comfort of some beanbags placed in the spaces for mingling and socializing to represent, and hopefully create, an informal learning culture.

Strategy, sensegiving and sensemaking

Organization theorist Karl Weick introduced the notion of sensemaking to capture what it is that strategists do when they do strategy.

Sensemaking is the ongoing retrospective development of plausible images that rationalize what people are doing.

For Weick et al. (2005: 409) 'sensemaking is an issue of language, talk and communication: situations, organizations, and environments are talked into existence'. Weick has used the notion of enactment to stress the fact 'in organizational life, people often produce part of the environment they face' (Weick, 1995: 30). Organization members organize themselves through working out the local stories in which they find themselves (Weick, 1979; 1995). In many ways, especially as they are inducted, new members of organizations are characters in search of a frame with which to guide their perception and representation of reality. Actors adopt frames for making sense in the course of communicative processes (Weick, 1995). In turn, their sensemaking becomes a 'springboard for action' (Taylor and Van Every, 2000).

Writers on sensemaking argue that there are no pure 'facts' – only interpretations of facts, and it is precisely these interpretations, these ways of making sense, that form the basis for decisions and actions. For instance, Porac and his colleagues analysed the Scottish knitwear industry and found that notions of strategy and competition were constituted by individuals' attempts to make sense of their environment. In the words of Porac et al. (1995: 224), 'market structures are constraints only because managers believe they exist. Rather than being an exogenous force acting *on* managerial minds, market structure is an endogenous product *of* managerial minds'. Whether it is the Scottish knitwear industry or Google, what managers perceive as their markets is a matter of cognition – and not a given 'fact'.

Following Weick et al. (2005: 41), strategy emerges from *local* acts of sensemaking: 'Students of sensemaking understand that the order in organizational life comes just as much from the subtle, the small, the relational, the oral, the particular, and the momentary as it does from the conspicuous, the large, the substantive, the written, the general, and the sustained'. Thus, strategy is as likely to emerge from the tacit and taken-for-granted assumptions that are shared by strategists as from the data they process if only because the data have to be made meaningful. And if there is a great deal of homogeneity between strategic actors, they are likely to make similar sense – when what is actually required is a radically different interpretation – but there is no one to provide such an interpretation. Moreover, sensemaking is an inherently *political* activity because interpretations, framing and the production of meaning are powerful forms of control. And finally, sensemaking is an *ongoing* accomplishment that is particularly important when contradicting or ambiguous events occur that question established routines (Weick, 1995). Weick (1979: 188) says, '[o]rganizations formulate strategy after they implement it, not before. Having implemented something – anything – people can then look back over it and conclude that what they have implemented is a strategy'.

If we think of strategies as symbolic devices that are effective because their sense is shared, then strategy becomes more of a social organizing device than a tool to forecast the future. Weick (1995: 54) popularized the story of a map used by soldiers lost in the Swiss Alps to make the point:

> I can best show what I think strategy is by describing an incident that happened during military maneuvers in Switzerland. The young lieutenant of a small Hungarian detachment in the Alps sent a reconnaissance unit out into the icy wilderness. It began to snow immediately, snowed for two days, and the unit did not return. The lieutenant suffered, fearing that he had dispatched his own people to death. But the third day the unit came back. Where had they been? How had they made their way? Yes, they said, we considered ourselves lost and waited for the end. And then one of us found a map in his pocket. That calmed us down. We pitched camp, lasted out the snowstorm, and then with the map we discovered our bearings. And here we are. The lieutenant borrowed this remarkable map and had a good look at it. He discovered to his astonishment that it was not a map of the Alps but of the Pyrenees.

In this story, strategy is not a precise roadmap to the future – in fact, if the soldiers had followed the map in detail, they would have most certainly been lost on the mountains in ice and snow. The map had another, more important function: it gave people hope, and it gave them the trust in their leader to get them out of a dangerous situation. Most importantly, it equipped the leader with faith in the situation. In this view, strategy is not a means to accomplish a desired end; rather, strategy is a device that allows people to make sense of a situation and coordinate their activities. Strategy, and the symbols that make it meaningful, are a crucial part of organizing. Strategy is important from the sensemaking perspective in quite different ways to the perspectives we have considered thus far.

Internally, strategies change reality not because they are implemented but because they are communicated. Planning implies an implicit theory of the organization, thinking of and picking out certain things as a central theme. Plans are maps that create the terrain they pretend to describe (Weick, 1979) – you cannot orientate yourself just through reading a map, because every attempt to understand the terrain through the map changes the sense of the map and the terrain (Clegg and Hardy, 1996). Through the creation of new maps an organization creates new terrain, new possibilities and new realities: far from being out there, waiting patiently to be discovered, 'reality' is the product of our mental constructions.

Dennis A. Gioia and Kumar Chittipeddi build on sensemaking work and apply it to strategy. According to the sensemaking perspective, strategic change can only occur when people change their mental models. Hence, strategic change means, first of all, destabilizing taken-for-granted assumptions and ideas about the world. Once the organization accepts that the old way of making sense is no longer valid or desirable, the strategist can offer new mental maps for orientation. Gioia and Chittipeddi's (1991: 446) study of how strategic change occurred in a public sector university emphasizes that 'symbols mobilize action' in the strategic management process. Their study showed that strategic change is not a matter of developing a detailed plan that is then simply implemented. Rather, a strategy is a map that helps organization members to make sense of their environment. Since the map is (at least partly) drawn up by the management team, strategic change is also a process of sensegiving.

Gioia and Chittipeddi's (1991: 433) study of strategic change illustrates how strategy is embedded in cognitive processes. Their argument is that '*strategic change involves an attempt to change current modes of cognition and action to enable the organization to take advantage of important opportunities or to cope with consequential environmental threats*'.

The idea of the 'mode of cognition' sounds more complicated than it is: just ask your lecturer how she would describe your university. Let us say she is proud of the university's excellent education programme. Her 'mental model' of what makes a good university might be grounded in the idea that teaching is the best way to educate people and contribute to society. However, another lecturer might have a different 'cognitive model': he might say that doing first-rate strategy research is the key to help organizations, as research uncovers new ways of doing things. Published in journals, the new findings are accessible to literally thousands of managers all over the world. Now imagine these two imaginary lecturers had to craft a strategy for your university: no doubt these strategies would differ because of the different assumptions both hold dear. They would not even agree on basic questions such as 'what makes a good university?' or 'what is relevant information that should inform the strategy-making process?' For the education-oriented lecturer, student evaluations might be important; for the research-driven lecturer, the number of publications in international journals would be a key reference point.

Gioia and Chittipeddi found that sensemaking and sensegiving shape strategic change. They observed four phases to this process:

1 In the *envisioning* phase the president of a university developed an embryonic strategic vision of the institution. In this phase, he and his team were trying to make sense of the current situation and identify the key drivers that would have an impact on future plans.

2 In the *signalling* phase he communicated that he intended to change the institution. This created ambiguity and anxiety as people felt threatened by the prospect of an uncertain future.

3 During the *revisioning* phase, ideas for strategic change were openly discussed. Different initiatives were also discussed with important stakeholders.

4 Finally, in the *energizing* phase, the formal strategic planning process started; meetings and consultations with staff provided space in which ideas were reinterpreted and the consequences for action were discussed.

Gioia and Chittipeddi argue that it is only this last phase that is usually captured by strategy research in terms of strategic planning. The three previous phases are pivotal, yet often overlooked. As they argue, '[t]he clear intent was to provide a viable interpretation of a new reality and to influence stakeholders and constituents to adopt it as their own' (1991: 443). The president first made sense of the organization, identified the threats and opportunities, and drew up a new map for the future; then he shared this map with the organization members, who were expected to use it to make sense of where they were. Ultimately, the new map was a tool to comprehend, accept and act on the desired strategic change (1991: 444).

A closely related study is Jane Dutton and Janet Dukerich's (1991) research into how the New York Port Authority reacted to the problem of homelessness encroaching on its domain in the 1980s. First, the organization defined itself as being in the transport business and ignored the problem. When it became too hard to ignore, because there were too many homeless people sleeping and living on its properties, the management team had to rethink the basic identity of the organization: this resulted in their providing facilities for homeless people. The key issue here is that the organization radically changed how it made sense of its environment, and how it thought of its identity (we will come back to the latter point in the next section).

The Port Authority' managers acted on a mental map of the world in which the only relevant points were stations and travellers, much as in the London Tube map: however, neither map features the social tragedies and human comedies that unfold everyday in countless stations – the dramas, lost tourists, business people who run late, happy lovers who do not care where they are, and the unfortunates for whom the Tube offers a suicide opportunity. What you make of the Tube map depends on the mental maps that you bring to bear on it: for the radical Islamist it might be a vehicle for an improvized explosive device while for the anxious lover it will be a transport to joy. Meanwhile, more prosaic managers probably see it as a means to the end of getting to an appointment or to work on time.

The basic assumption of studies on strategy and sensemaking (see Porac and Thomas, 2002, for a good overview) is that organizations are 'interpretation systems' (Daft and Weick, 1984). As such, organizations collect and interpret information, and then act on it. If we follow this perspective, it is crucial to understand how an organization identifies information, how it processes it and how it relates it to action.

Generally speaking, managers will act on the basis of those mental models that shape their mundane worldview of their work. These mental models influence what we believe is relevant, how we think of it and how we act on it. Mental models can be imagined as 'cognitive maps' that will enable organizational employees to orient themselves, decide where to go next and discuss how to get there. Cognitive maps highlight, simplify and frame what strategists perceive as strategic issues, strategic problems or strategic solutions.

STRATEGY AS NARRATIVE

We argued before that strategy is linked to sensemaking. Sensemaking happens through conversations. Hence, strategy emerges out of conversations among diverse stakeholders. Sometimes the conversations are heated, shouted, accusatory, or finger pointing, involving adversaries such as NGOs, community groups or local political actors. Strategy can emerge from the whole range of conversations: once sense is made out of the positions staked out, strategy will be created, negotiated and discussed until the dominant group in an organization (normally management) agrees with its content. Hence, strategy can be analysed as a form of storytelling. Powerful stories are usually constructed in prestigious environments such as corporate HQ, banks and treasury buildings. Other times the important conversations are more *sotto voce* and will take place in discrete clubs and restaurants, among friends or at least between people who share certain understandings, styles and background, people who belong to the business elite, who will often share similar social capital built through social networking on the boards of prestigious institutions such as galleries, opera houses, cultural centres and charities.

Image 4.2 'Powerful Buildings'

PHOTOGRAPHY BY STEWART CLEGG

In an important paper entitled 'Strategy Retold: Toward a Narrative View of Strategic Discourse', David Berry and Michael Elmes suggest that a particularly good way to understand strategy is to see it in narrative terms, as a way of constructing a likely story, a narrative fiction, about an organization. Barry and Elmes note the contemporary importance of strategy, suggesting that 'strategy must rank as one of the most prominent, influential, and costly stories told in organizations' (1997: 430). They analyse strategy as narratives or stories told in organizations about the past, present, and future.

Thinking of strategy as a series of likely stories sounds weirder than it is – think of the notion of 'blue' and 'red ocean' strategy (see Kim and Mauborgne, 2005): of course, no organization is sailing on two differently coloured oceans. Kim and Mauborgne use these coloured oceans as metaphors, encouraging us to assume that whatever lies hidden in the 'blue ocean' is advantageous for an organization, whereas 'red oceans' should be avoided. Through linking experiences and opportunities that we encounter in the world to coloured oceans (clearly a fiction) we automatically attach a negative or positive value to them. The colours red and blue make it easy to categorize things as 'good' or 'bad'. But they also shape our mental maps of the world and have an impact on what we consider to be possible actions. The metaphor gives rise to a new way of thinking about the future – a way of thinking that is deeply framed by the metaphor itself. Understanding strategy as narrative focuses on analysing how stakeholders create meaning and make sense of their environment.

Although the notion of competitive strategy is an idea that Porter once had, it has become so manifest as a widely used idea in strategy texts that it has taken on a materiality and concreteness that makes it appear as real as a misplaced fountain pen (Ezzamel and Willmott, 2008: 197). Presumably you could lose your competitive

MINI CASE STUDY

Strategic planning as storytelling at 3M

Gordon Shaw, Executive Director of Planning at 3M, and his two co-authors (Shaw et al., 1998) argue that their company has abandoned the bullet-point report and the PowerPoint presentation, and replaced them with stories. According to them, stories not only clarify one's thinking, but also capture the imagination and create excitement within 3M. Bullet points, on the other hand, make us 'intellectually lazy', they argue. Here are the reasons why (of course, in bullet points!):

● Bullet points are too generic and refer to things that could apply to a whole range of projects or organizations. For instance, to say 'engage stakeholders' is important yet the bullet point does not reveal much about the how and why.

● Bullet points leave relationships unspecified: bullet points present the world as a sea of unconnected dots. According to Shaw and his colleagues, they allow only three generic relationships: a hierarchy of what is important; a sequence of what comes first, second, third, etc; and defining an element as belonging to a group (e.g. within the European Union there are

27 countries: Austria, Belgium …). Much as in a Pointillist paining, bullet points break up the flow of experience into small, apparently unrelated units. However, relationships are crucial and have a complex make-up that bullet points do not allow you to see.

● Bullet points leave important background and contextual information unmentioned: again, to say 'engage stakeholders' reveals little about the historical connections, political issues and potential future hurdles in the collaboration.

To fight intellectual laziness, 3M encourages its employees to tell strategic stories. Stories have a stage, characters, some sort of conflict or drama that has to be resolved, and some kind of ending. This basic structure allows the communication of complex messages to happen in an emotional way that touches people's hearts and minds. A strategy that does this is the best precondition to motivate people and coordinate action.

Questions

1 What are the stories that best tell the strategy of your organization?

2 Why these stories and not others?

3 Why are they significant?

4 How are they reproduced and known?

strategy and have to find a new one. In sociological terms we would say that the idea of competitive strategy is reification, something that has become taken for granted as something real, despite its being ideational.

Alternatively, from a narrative or story perspective you might want to study 'competitive advantage' as part of an evolving 'language game through which strategy researchers and managers presently solve their problems' (Powell, 2001: 886). It is through specific discursive practices of strategizing (Knights and Morgan, 1991) that the objects which define a specific strategy are made up. Competitive advantage becomes a handy term with which to gloss corporate success or failure. For instance, Rose and Miller (1992: 175) emphasize how specific narratives connect rationalities with 'programmes, calculations, techniques, apparatuses, documents, and procedures' through which strategic ambitions are embodied and given effect.

From the perspective of rationalities being connected to techniques the success of a strategy resides in its perfomative power. Simply put, how persuasive is the strategy for its intended audience? Does it resonate with their sympathies and interests? Does it meet their concerns as they express these as analysts, bankers, employees, customers, or is the strategy that has been laboriously constructed wasted by confronting the indifference or hostility of key constituencies?

Analysing strategies as stories means analysing them as narratives with structuring powers: they frame, anticipate and cast realities. As such, strategy does not differ from other stories, such as autobiographies, biblical stories, novels or movies: these are all more or less emotional ways of making sense of the world and offering solutions to commonly experienced problems. They are scripts we can use to organize our lives. Often, as we have seen, these scripts of strategy are characterized by a high degree of rationalism constituting their deep assumptions.

YOU CAN DOWNLOAD…

Mahmoud Ezzamel and Hugh Willmott's (2008) Strategy as Discourse in a Global Retailer: A Supplement to Rationalist and Interpretive Accounts, *Organization Studies*, 29(2): 191–217 from the book's website at www.sagepub. co.uk/clegg strategy

FROM STRATEGY AS COMPETING LITERAL REPRESENTATIONS TO STRATEGY AS A CONSTITUTIVE DISCOURSE

Ezzamel and Willmott (2008: 192) suggest that the strategy debate has increasingly come to centre on whether literally 'objective' or 'subjective' approaches best capture the essence of strategic management. Mintzberg, together with other contributors such as Pettigrew (1985), had shifted the focus from one perspective to the other: from rationalist objectivism to a search for emergent subjectivism. Others interested in phenomena such as sensemaking, identity, and narrative, even revolution, have taken up the emergent subjectivism and its overall interpretive approach enthusiastically. But is this enough? What is left out? What remains to be addressed?

Excluded from analysis is a consideration of the constitutive effects of the use of strategy as a discourse even though, arguably, it is through discourse(s) that the plurality of conceptions and accounts of 'strategy' and 'strategic management' is articulated – the neglect of strategy as a discourse is a glaring omission from the study of strategy. Ezzamel and Willmott note some exceptions to this stark neglect. There is the work of Barry and Elmes (1997) and Vaara et al. (2004) as well as Chia's recognition that strategy 'works to create some sense of stability, order and predictability and thereby produce a sustainable, functioning and liveable world' (2000: 514). What strategy does is what matters from a discursive perspective, which focuses on strategy through concentrating on those things it constitutes: the world of the strategist becomes populated by the taken-for-granted materialities that strategists produce, such as competitive environments, markets, segments positioning – all the matters we have covered thus far.

Building on the work of David Knights (Knights and Morgan, 1991; Knights, 1992), which draws heavily on the French historian of ideas, Michel Foucault, Ezzamel and Willmott seek to demonstrate that analysis needs to do more than merely counterpose opposites assumed really to characterize strategy. Instead, one should look at how these opposing positions are made up. It does not matter, they suggest, whether a term such as 'competitive advantage' implies 'the effective control of some key variable(s) or with the views or meanings attributed to entrepreneurs and/or executives' (2008: 193). We should instead see such terms as elements in what Wittgenstein (1968) referred to as an evolving language game. Or, to adopt Foucault's (1972) perspective, we need to understand strategy as a practice that constructs its own objects of analysis and thus materializes them through its discourse.

In other words, whether viewed through Porter or Mintzberg, strategy terms are talked into being. Different theories merely talk different emphases and terms into being as a result of the conventional arrangements relating power and knowledge in that discourse:

> Discourses are inscribed in power-knowledge relations where power is understood to operate through a plurality of relationships to form and institutionalize knowledge claims – claims, for example, about 'organization', 'strategy', 'knowledge' and 'power' ... reality is understood to be do-able-and-knowable only through the development of diverse, partial and ultimately politically conditioned discourses. Foucauldian analysis does not claim that the practices comprising the social world are reducible to discourse. Rather, knowledge of 'strategy' or 'experts' is understood to be constituted through discursive practices. (Ezzamel and Willmott 2008: 193, 194)

The discourses of strategy are not imperfect representations of some external reality; rather, they are stories that enable those who tell them to perform strategy in different ways. The interpretivist focus on cognitive mapping in theorists such as Mintzberg merely predisposes analysts to an alternative but fallacious apprehension of reality. It is fallacious because the very things it attends to – cognitive maps – are recursively constituted by the theory itself. That strategists have cognitive maps is an effect of the theory that postulates this. Once accepted, then these maps will always be found, as the frame of cognitive mapping organizes, politically, the construction of the strategists' reality that the Mintzbergian makes:

> There is no appreciation of how interpretivist analysis is inescapably constitutive of what it claims to capture or reflect ... in order to study a social object, such as 'strategy', as a discursive practice, it is necessary to proceed as if our knowledge of this object exists independently of the discourses that enable us to identify and explore it. (Ezzamel and Willmott, 2008: 197, 198)

Using this Foucauldian analysis enables them to demonstrate not only how the mutually constituted and interpenetrated 'scientific' and 'everyday' discourses of strategy constituted a realm of privileged 'strategy objects', but also how these objects were mobilized in and made material by specific techniques of power contained within new managerial disciplines of accounting. These new disciplines of accounting brought with them a new awareness of what the essence of strategy was and who resisted strategy (those who resisted were often those political agents who were not caught up in the strategy discourse).

Theoretically, these are important points. They alert us to the fact that an analysis which takes its objects for 'real' is always tied up with the assumptions made in constituting these objects as well as the consequences of their materialization.

SUMMARY AND REVIEW

In this chapter we have introduced an emergent perspective on strategy-making. Championed by Henry Mintzberg and other process theorists, this approach to strategy critically distances itself from the rational planning approach by arguing that strategy is an emergent phenomenon. Rather than trying to predict the future, the emergent approach depicts strategy as a contested and constantly evolving outcome of the interaction between formal plans and an organization's sensemaking of it. The corollary of this insight is that strategy cannot be planned top down but relies on bottom-up (emerging) processes that introduce new ideas and unexpected views into strategy. Key concepts that become pivotal to strategy making are organizational sensegiving, sensemaking, learning, culture and identity as these aspects frame the capability to think and act reflexively.

The underlying hypothesis of much of the literature that we have addressed in this chapter is that cognitive maps frame the ways organization members perceive themselves, their environments, and the opportunities and threats they identify within it. These cognitive maps legitimate certain views while discrediting others. The task of the strategist is to shape the canvas on which an organization projects its cognitive maps; by doing so, the strategist has to reflect on self-perception, the taken-for-granted assumptions that are embedded in the organizational culture, and foster an appetite for learning and change. The strategist has to accept that the future is unpredictable; hence, the goal is to create a preparedness and agility that will enable the organization to adapt as changes unfold. And the role of researchers is to study how and in what ways the strategists do strategy in practice – rather than normatively stipulating what it should be a priori.

Well, we certainly prefer this way of doing strategy to the idea that it is merely a matter of closed-system models founded on coherent systems of concepts that mirror the real in some mysterious way – but, as Ezzamel and Willmott make clear, an approach that substitutes a one-sided subjectivism for a one-sided objectivism may not be the advance that its adherents claim. Instead, we should critically interrogate how any given discourse of strategy – whether in lay terms of 'practice' or professional terms of 'theory' – is possible. Actually, as our use of the inverted commas is meant to suggest, the opposition between theory and practice is quite problematic because ordinary practitioners of strategy are themselves theoretical actors. They are not only using their understandings of more formal strategy theories in practice to do their jobs and populate their world with categories and other devices that constitute its sense, but are also, in their everyday articulation and discourses, material exhibits for the strategy-as-practice crew to work on. In this way the recursive nature of strategy could not be clearer. Privileged in practice, its lay terms become privileged in theory, which in turn feeds into practice in a loop of recursivity that is eternally indexical and neverending. Its sense can never be made apart from the sense that its strategists – in formal theory and everyday practice – are making of it. Strategy feeds on its materialities.

EXERCISES

1 Having read this chapter you should be able to say in your own words what the following key terms mean:

● Emerging strategy
● Process
● Learning
● Sensemaking
● Identity
● Cognitive maps
● Strategy as narrative
● Strategy as practice
● Strategy as discourse
● The materialities of strategy
● Strategy as a form of power/knowledge.

2 Who are the most influential protagonists of the emergent view on strategy and how do their ideas differ from other strategy schools?

3 According to the emergent perspective, what are the means by which strategy can be influenced?

4 According to Steve Shallhorn, former CEO of Greenpeace Australia, strategy is a multi dimensional change process. How does he describe the task of the strategist? (See www.strategytube.net)

5 Imagine you go to a job interview with the Boston Consulting Group. Their Managing Partner has heard of strategy as emergent process but does not understand how such a perspective would affect their approach to consulting. How would you explain the emerging strategy approach and its potential implications for practice?

ADDITIONAL RESOURCES

1 Our companion website is the best first stop for you to find a great deal of extra resources, free PDF versions of leading articles published in Sage journals, exercise, video and pod casts, team case studies and general questions and links to teamwork resources. Go to www.sagepub.co.uk/cleggstrategy

2　A good book that introduces the strategy field is one which three of us wrote previously: Carter, C., Clegg, S. R. and Kornberger, M. (2008) *A Very Short, Fairly Interesting and Reasonably Cheap Book about Studying Strategy*, London: Sage.

WEB SECTION

Visit the *Strategy* companion website at www.sagepub.co.uk/cleggstrategy

1　The doyen of the emergent approach to strategy, Henry Mintzberg, runs a website with many interesting articles, debates and images – see www.mintzberg.org/

2　There are several useful video interviews with Henry Mintzberg on YouTube – just search for him on the site and watch him in action.

3　Finally, you can study the fascinating story of the Brazilian firm Semco, led by Ricardo Semler, who democratized the organization and shows how strategic decisions can emerge out of an open conversation – see his MIT lecture on http: mitworld.mit.edu/video/308/

LOOKING FOR A HIGHER MARK?

Reading and digesting these articles that are available free on the companion website www.sagepub.co.uk/clegg strategy can help you gain deeper understanding and, on the basis of that, a better grade:

1　Ezzamel, M. and Willmott, H. (2008) Strategy as Discourse in a Global Retailer: A Supplement to Rationalist and Interpretive Accounts, *Organization Studies*, 29(2): 191–217, provides an interesting empirical account of how strategy as narrative shapes organizations.

2　Jarzabkowski, P. (2004) 'Strategy as Practice: Recursiveness, Adaptation and Practices-In-Use, *Organization Studies*, 25(4): 529–60, offers a theoretical perspective on process and practice based strategy research.

3　Chia, R. and MacKay, B. (2007) Post-processual Challenges for the Emerging Strategy-as-Practice Perspective: Discovering Strategy in the Logic of Practice, *Human Relations*, 60(1): 217–42, develop a critical account of strategy as practice.

Google

Martin Kornberger

On 16 June 2006, the *Oxford English Dictionary* added the verb 'to google' to its repertoire. This was only eight years after Larry Page, one of the two founders of Google, had used the word as a verb for the first time: on 8 July 1998 he wrote to his friends: 'Have fun and keep googling!'[1] Google has become a crucial part of our burgeoning information society. But the iconic company did not just shape our computer culture: it was – and is – an overwhelming economic success story. On 19 August 2004, Google released stocks at $85, raising $2 billion, the biggest technology IPO to date. When we wrote these lines, the stock price was about $450. At its peak, in November 2007, its value was close to $750 per share. Even the Google brand is worth billions. In Interbrand's brand evaluation ranking, Google jumped from the 20th spot to 10th in the 2008 list, with a brand value of $25 billion, up by 43 per cent from the previous year.[2] In the 2009 Interbrand ranking, Google improved further to seventh, which equals a brand value increase of 25 per cent to a staggering $31,980 million.[3] In Fortune's 2009 ranking, Google was 117th, just below Coca-Cola. Not bad for a company that is barely 10 years old!

What strategy did Google employ to become so successful in less than a decade? Google has been open about its ambition – to organize the world's information. In order to put this mission into practice, it did not follow the recipes in strategy textbooks. Strategy as usual would not have been useful. Just imagine using a Porter-inspired environmental analysis in a rapidly shifting market where your potential allies and competitors change almost monthly: Google has been

competing for market space not only with Netscape, Yahoo!, Microsoft, Nokia, Apple, and a great many now-forgotten search engines, such as Dogpile, but also with media organizations and publishers, and start-ups such as Facebook as well as non-profits such as Wikipedia. Google competes with Apple's iPhone for mobile Internet access. Facebook offers a different challenge: as Google cannot search inside Facebook sites, Google is not able to access information that might be relevant for its online search engine. This means that the more people work with Facebook applications, the more information is inaccessible for Google – hence the competition between the two high-tech companies. Google is even moving into real estate listings – one of the most profitable areas of traditional print-based media in their move into Web-based strategies. Google has started to source listings from real estate aggregators and allows real estate agents to list their properties free on Google Maps. This puts them in direct competition with media companies such as Fairfax News and News Limited. It seems that Google may be

> moving from being a search engine to a portal …. Instead of sending you to other websites – which have paid money to be there on its listings – it is now serving up the end data itself. That then raises the question: why would you need to go to the other sites and why would they then pay Google money [for search key words?] said Simon Baker, CEO of the online classified marketing specialist, Classified Ad Ventures (Lee, 2009: http: business.smh.com.au/business/google-sparks-real-estate-listings-brawl-20090726-dxj1.html) .

How does Google develop its strategy? Its approach to strategy can be described as emergent. Rather than defining strategic plans that should predict the future, Google encourages its staff to experiment. One of Larry Page's favourite lines makes the point: 'Having a healthy disregard for the impossible' (quoted in Vise, 2005: 11). His partner and co-founder, Sergey Brin, describes Google as follows:

> We run Google a bit like a university. We have lots of projects, about 100 of them. We like to have small groups of people, three or so people, working on projects. Some of them,

(Continued)

[1]http://en.wikipedia.org/wiki/Google_(verb), accessed 26 July 2009.

[2]www.interbrand.com/best_global_brands.aspx?year=2008&langid=1000, accessed 26 July 2009.

[3]www.interbrand.com/best_global_brands.aspx, accessed 8 December 2009.

(Continued)

for example, are related to molecular biology. Others involve building hardware. So we do lots of stuff. The only way you are going to have success is to have lots of failures first. (quoted in Vise, 2005: 16).

In order to encourage employees to be playful and experiment with ideas, Google promotes a mistake-friendly culture. The Googleplex, Google's headquarters at Mountain View, near San Jose, California, looks and feels similar to a vibrant college campus, full of beanbags, toys, music, and a well-equipped kitchen where a chef prepares meals for staff.

Google's employees will explore a vast amount of different ideas at any one time. For instance, Google.org is devoted to using IT to address global challenges, such as health or clean energy. In collaboration with the bio tech entrepreneur Craig Venter, Google is working on a project to personalize medicine. The basic idea is that you could use Google's data mining and search technology to analyse your DNA. You could gain information about yourself and preventatively fight potential disease (Vise, 2005). Sounds to be almost science fiction? Yes, sure, but at Google projects like these are supported because they have the potential to lead to breakthrough insights. Another example of the bottom-up approach to developing new ideas is Google Earth. While Google has not figured out how to make money with this mind-boggling service, and ethical issues about privacy protection still spark controversy, Google happily invests and presses on with scanning and mapping our planet.

Of course, not all projects arrive at a happy end: Froogle, Google's answer to eBay, was taken offline quietly and so was Google's orkut, the social networking site, Google checkout, Google's video portal (Google bought YouTube instead), knol (Google's failed response to Wikipedia) and many others. Maybe Google real estate will go that way as well: it certainly has powerful media interests arraigned against it.

Google simply does not know in advance which idea will work, and which one will fail. Hence the experimental approach. Take the example of Google's free phone-based information service. It does not charge a service fee, nor does it make money with advertising. It is a loss-making venture. Should it be shut down? No, says Marissa Mayer, Senior Executive at Google. While the service does not make profits, it collects something much more important – phonemes. By recording literally hundreds of thousands of people Google builds up a massive library of spoken words. And this library of words is a key to future services, such as a voice interaction with computers or video search (Stross, 2008: 87). While Google's phone-based information service might look like a failure, it could become the key to a different, and strategically much more important, project. Imagine the problems a resource-based analysis of Google would run into: what we define as a valuable resource today might be useless tomorrow and vice versa.

Question

1   Google is one of the most celebrated companies on the Internet. Your mission is to identify what the key practices are that characterize its innovation strategies. How would you analyse them? What sorts of discourse analysis might you employ and how would you do this?

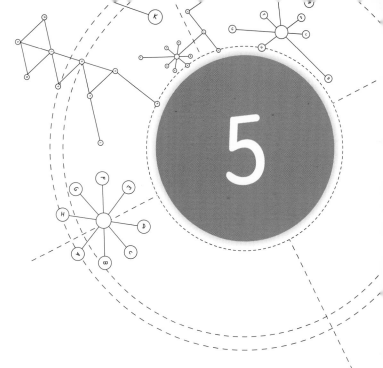

Marketing and Branding as Strategic Forces

5

Positioning, image, identity

LEARNING OBJECTIVES

By the end of this chapter you will be able to:

- Define the role and importance of marketing for strategic management
- Distinguish business and consumer markets and understand their nature
- Apply the concepts of segmentation, targeting and competitive positioning
- Explain why managing the customer relationship is so important
- Define the importance of brands for strategy-making
- Discuss how the brand can be a strategic driver that aligns organizational functions
- Understand how the brand engages with an organization's external environment
- Grasp how the brand shapes an internal culture
- Critically reflect on the limitations of branding and some of the challenges it poses

> ## BEFORE YOU GET STARTED . . .
>
> Marketing is too important to be left to the
> marketing department.
>
> (DAVID PACKARD)

INTRODUCTION

The book to date has looked at the central currents of strategy. Any strategy course pretty much anywhere in the world will reprise arguments on Porter, the RBV and Mintzberg. This part of the book reflects the experience and research interests of the authors – especially Jochen and Martin – by looking at the implications of marketing and branding for strategy. These focus on the ways in which organizations can develop distinctive strategies that are externally focused on attracting and maintaining customers. This chapter can be seen as a development of many of the preoccupations in Chapters 2–4, although it cools down the relationship with economics and draws instead on organization theory and marketing theory.

For marketers it is a central proposition that marketing must be considered central to strategy. If an organization cannot convince customers, clients and the public at large that what it offers is something that has value and therefore provides some benefit then whatever the strategy it will have failed. Recent perspectives on marketing realize its strategic centrality to the organization. Anecdotally speaking, we live in a world saturated with marketing images – not just manufacturers trying to sell their products but also governments trying to manage their message to the electorate as well as NGOs competing for attention and donations. Moving from its industrial origins, marketing as a set of practices has become inscribed in daily life. Contemporary approaches to marketing focus on intangible resources, the co-creation of value and the importance of customer relationships (Berry, 1995; Vargo and Akaka, 2009; Vargo and Lusch, 2004). These new perspectives are now converging to form a new dominant logic for marketing, one in which a strategic service provision centred on a marketing strategy rather than the provision of goods is the basis of economic exchange. In this chapter we will seek to understand marketing strategy as a body of knowledge. What is the central premise of marketing strategy? What techniques does it promote? What are the limitations of these techniques? As we have mentioned above, one of the interesting features of marketing strategy is that it has pervaded so many different aspects of everyday life. At the time of finishing this book a General Election in the UK was taking place. Each party had an election strategy that drew heavily on ideas of marketing. In fact, one of the leaders – David Cameron – had worked as a public relations strategist prior to entering politics. The point here is a general one: over the last 30 years techniques associated with marketing functions in corporations have been incorporated into politics. Often cutting edge developments – such as the use of social networking sites – will be showcased in political campaigns – such as in Barack Obama's election victory in 2008.

When thinking strategically about marketing, many common-sense factors (some of which we have already covered in previous chapters) must be considered: the extent of product diversity in and geographical coverage of the organization; the number of market segments served; the marketing channels

A marketing strategy represents an internally integrated but externally focused set of choices about how the firm addresses its customers in the context of a competitive environment.

used; the role of branding; the level of marketing effort, and the role of quality. It is also necessary to consider the organization's approach to new product development, in particular its position as a technology leader or follower, the extent of innovation, the organization's cost position and pricing policy, and its relationship not only to customers but also to competitors, suppliers and partners.

The rhetoric of strategic marketing involves understanding what customers really want and managing customer relationships to benefit the organization and its stakeholders. Building and managing a long-term customer relationship in contrast to having a short-term focus on immediate sales is a key requirement for achieving recurring customer satisfaction. The customer relationship, rather than a single transaction, is what is strategically important. Consequently, if an organization – such as a mobile phone company – is able to keep customers happy and retain them over many years then that can have huge value to the company. A firm should focus on the customer as the source of profit rather than the product. It also means that attracting new customers is an intermediate objective in the process of maintaining and cultivating an existing customer base. Of course, as organizations adopt this logic they will try increasingly to tempt new customers away from their competitors. In financial services, for example, there has been far more movement from customers than ever before – as they seek to change their credit cards, mortgage deals or current accounts. This, in turn, reinforces the logic behind strategic marketing, providing the rationale for organizations to conceive of their customers as long-term sources of profit. This is an example of what Donald Mackenzie (2006) terms Barnesian performativity, where 'real-world' behaviour emulates the theory that actually describes it.

Strategic marketing is very prescriptive in its orientation. It brooks little discussion or reflection and is best viewed as an example of managerialism (discussed in Chapter 1) in that it presumes a one-best-way of proceeding and seeks to impose its logic on the organizational world. Accordingly, there is very little internal dissent or critique within the approach. Our objective is to scrutinize the claims that strategic marketing makes for itself.

Strategic marketing involves a long-term continuous relationship with customers in contrast to having a short-term focus on immediate sales, involving a shift from transaction-oriented marketing to relationship-driven marketing. Marketing activities have significant strategic implications for an organization as a whole (Hunt and Lambe, 2000) and, as a result, marketing executives (chief marketing officers or CMOs) are more concerned now with how an organization determines its best opportunities in the marketplace given its overall objectives and resources, rather than with only promoting its offerings by creating advertising campaigns. Firms that often have several products or services spanning multiple industries will often manage their offerings in a way similar to an investment portfolio. This implies that a firm can develop sustainable competitive advantages through strategic marketing by not only taking into account its industry position, objectives, skills and resources, but also by assessing the future profit potential of each offer and considering the market growth rate and strategic fit at the individual product and service levels. Because marketing executives have important detailed knowledge about product markets, customers and the customer relationship, they can act as the intelligence agency for firms for strategic decisions such as expanding to new markets, developing new channels of distribution, offering solutions or services instead of products, and pursuing radical rather than incremental innovations.

SERVICE-DOMINANT LOGIC

Marketers posit that service is at the core of exchange and marketing, emphasizing the activity of the firm as providing a service to customers, stakeholders and employees. As such, this points out the importance of a strategic investment in people, the development of long-term relationships and quality of service, collaboration, transparency, ethical approaches to exchange and sustainability. Stephen Vargo and Robert Lusch argue that a service-dominant (S-D) logic of marketing is replacing a goods-dominant (G-D) logic in their pioneering (2004) *Journal of Marketing* article. By defining a service as an interactive process of 'doing something for someone' that is valued, they suggest that goods ultimately are part of service and acquire what they call a 'value-in-use'.

Applying S-D logic offers an integrated understanding of the purpose and nature of organizations, markets and society as being primarily concerned with the exchange of services. In S-D logic the service being offered becomes the common denominator of exchange. From an S-D point of view, all firms are service providers and service receivers; markets focus on the exchange of service, and economies and societies are service based. As a result, a service-based logic should embrace the idea of the value-in-use and co-creation of value rather than the value-in-exchange and embedded-value concepts of traditional G-D logic. The theory rests on a number of presently evolving premises that Vargo and Lusch (2008) elaborate:

- While service is the fundamental basis of exchange, it is provided through complex combinations of goods, money and institutions, so that the service basis of exchange is not always obvious.

- Goods are a distribution mechanism for service provision. Both durable and non-durable goods derive their value through use – the service they provide.

- Knowledge and skills are the fundamental source of competitive advantage. The comparative ability to cause desired change drives competition.

- The firm can only offer value propositions and the customer is always a co-creator of value. Enterprises can offer their applied resources for value creation and together with customers can create value following an acceptance of value propositions by the customer.

- Because service is defined in terms of customer-determined benefit and co-created, it is inherently customer oriented and relational.

- All social and economic actors are resource integrators, which implies that the context of value creation is collaborative and derived from networks of networks.

- Value for the beneficiary is unique, idiosyncratic, experiential, contextual and meaning laden.

Because the S-D perspective addresses competition through service, it clearly has implications for strategic management (although the strategic management literature acknowledges strategic orientations at the firm level, such as capabilities or the skill portfolio, as sources of competitive advantage and superior performance; e.g. Ramani and Kumar, 2008). Service, when nurtured effectively, can enable or support an organization to outperform its rivals. As we have seen in Chapter 3, this assumption is commonly grounded in resource- and capability-related views (e.g. Wernerfelt, 1984; Barney, 1991; Teece et al., 1997). S-D logic has the ability to explain and unify the service role of interacting partners and boundary objects, such as goods being co-produced, and has already led to new ways of looking at strategic innovation in theoretical as well as practical terms.

YOU CAN DOWNLOAD...

Stephen L. Vargo and Robert F. Lusch's (2008) Service-Dominant Logic: Continuing the Evolution, *Journal of the Academy of Marketing Science*, 36(1): 1–10, from the book's website at www.sagepub.co.uk/cleggstrategy

The concept of boundary objects was originally introduced by Star and Griesemer (1989) to refer to objects that serve an interface between different communities of practice. Boundary objects are an entity shared by several different communities but viewed or used differently by each of them. They contain sufficient detail to be understandable by different interests, and serve as points of mediation and negotiation about their meaning. They are flexible enough to adapt to local needs and have different distinct identities in different communities, but at the same time are robust enough to maintain a common identity across the boundaries to be a place for shared work.

Ingo Karpen and Liliana Bove (2008) take a prescriptive approach when they suggest specific sets of organizational practices will indicate a firm's strategic ability to co-create superior value with service beneficiaries. Organizations have to understand individual customer's needs and contexts by communicating with and relating to customers, engaging with them to influence service processes and/or outcomes so that service flows towards customers are coordinated and integrated.

While the strategic implications of S-D logic are currently evolving, they clearly emphasize the firm's ability to understand and focus on the customer as the service beneficiary. The ultimate question is always whether a competitive advantage in such a co-creation capability is beneficial and, if so, how beneficial it is for the customer and the service provider. The answer to these questions derives from the firm's strategic analysis of its markets, external environments, available resources, and the desires and characteristics of its customers.

UNDERSTANDING CUSTOMER DESIRE – MARKET SEGMENTATION, TARGETING AND COMPETITIVE POSITIONING

A key ingredient of any strategy is to know the market that is being targeted. For instance, this book is being targeted at sophisticated practitioners and students of strategy. Political parties decide whether to target their core vote or to appeal to floating voters. Strategy must, therefore, find ways to identify the underlying problems that the users of its goods and services seek to solve and the related benefits they desire from using an already-existing product or service. At its most creative, it will be oriented to imagining and designing solutions to needs that have yet to be created. Understanding customers means being oriented to their needs rather than offering them what it is convenient to produce.

For example, people do not necessarily enter a Starbucks café for the coffee *per se*. Starbucks coffee is not necessarily the best on offer, especially in countries that boast a sophisticated coffee culture, such as Australia and Italy. Still, in many, sometimes surprising places, where arguably there is lots of better coffee available, Starbucks does well. This begs the question: what does the customer get from Starbucks? How does Starbucks turn a simple commodity combining hot water, milk and coffee into its business proposition?

Starbucks' decision-makers, such as CEO Howard Schultz or CMO Terry Davenport, looked beyond the coffee to try and understand what customers really want and to create an experience that their customers would find beneficial (Pine and Gilmore, 1999). Such an experience is more than just having coffee in a relaxed atmosphere where friends and workmates can meet. Starbucks understands that what it offers is much more than coffee; it is a place where people socialize, read, study, check their emails or listen to music – Starbucks becomes a way of branding socializing time: 'let's meet at Starbucks'. The company also understands that the physical space and ambience, including plenty of comfortable seating, the aroma of coffee in the air, as well as the shop attendants' attitude, all contribute to making people feel welcome, staying longer and coming back again. Starbucks also understands that customers can be positioned as caring about more than just the coffee: they can be positioned as ecologically responsible, caring about the environment, and persuaded that drinking more coffee somehow helps serve these considerations.

By positioning its brand as environmental friendly Starbucks is able to distinguish itself from competitors (Michelli, 2007). While there are usually obvious substitutes for coffee, and for Starbucks, the real substitute for visiting a Starbucks café might not just be another café; it could be going to other places for social interaction such as a park, a public library or a bar. In the UK, Starbucks is increasingly being branded as an 'office' from which urban wannabe knowledge workers can work. Being heavily branded, going to Starbucks is as instantly recognized option. Organizations need to realize that invariably there are alternative experiences, products or services that may satisfy latent customer needs – that there is always more sizzle that can be added to the barbecue sausage and that it is the sizzle that sells the sausage.

Understanding the customer's motivation to buy, the underlying customer's needs and the benefits that a customer seeks in using a product or service is the first important step in creating a successful offer. We will now look at important differences in dealing with consumers as opposed to business customers and introduce the concepts of segmentation, targeting and positioning to address ways of better understanding customers and satisfying their needs.

Segmentation

The discourse of marketing prescribes that organizations seeking to understand customers need to think in terms of three steps: segmentation, targeting and positioning (S–T–P). In these stages the organization must first distinguish among different groups of customers in the market (segmentation), then choose which group(s) it can serve effectively (targeting), and finally communicate the central benefit it offers to that group (positioning).

A number of questions guide the segmentation of markets: Who are the customers? What do they buy and why? How, when and where do they buy? Knowing who customers are is not simply a matter of knowing who uses a product or experiences a service.

Customers can generally be divided into two categories:

Segmentation is the process of dividing a market into distinct groups with distinct needs, characteristics or behaviour who might require separate offerings or marketing mixes.

- Consumer customers, who purchase goods and services for use by themselves and by those with whom they live.
- Business customers, who purchase goods and services for use by the organization for which they work.

While there are a number of similarities between the purchasing approaches of each type of customer group and the characteristics of associated markets, there are important differences as well. Most obvious is the magnitude of transactions. Business customers typically are engaged in substantial relation-based transactions with longer time horizons than consumers.

One similarity between purchasing decisions in consumer and business markets is that individuals other than the end-user will often participate in or influence the decision process. Organizationally, several individuals may play various roles in the decision-making process (see Chapter 8, on decision-making) such as a buying centre or purchasing department. Individuals can occupy the role of end-user, influencer, buyer, decider or gatekeeper, for each of which they will have very different expectations of what the product or service should be. Variables such as price, quality, service and individual psychological processes will influence each individual role and buying behaviour.

For a major airline that is in the market for an aircraft such as the Airbus 380, many roles will be involved and consulted before arriving at a purchase decision, as we will see in Chapter 8. In this case the decision involved pilots (users), flight safety engineers (influencers), the board (deciders), the purchasing manager (buyer), key internal gatekeepers (such as secretaries) and many more.

Strategically, it is important to know the following:

- What products do certain customers tend to purchase?
- Why do they purchase the organization's products and services or why do they choose competitors' products and services?
- What needs and benefits are being met by their consumption decisions?
- What unmet needs and benefits could be met by as-yet-unimagined products?

On the last point, consider the success of microwave ovens in the 1980s and 1990s. While a conventional oven allows food to be cooked and heated conveniently, microwave oven manufacturers recognized that this need could be fulfilled even more quickly by using a technology other than that of conventional heating. By focusing on understanding what kind of problems people try to solve, rather than on the products themselves, these companies were able to gain a significant share in the food cooking and heating market. Today, as many people are more concerned with healthy and nutritious food preparation, quicker food heating seems less important. Hence 'slow food cookers' can be found in more and more kitchens around the world, replacing the microwave.

To get such a deep understanding of these questions, different approaches to segmentation are used. A firm will usually segment markets or customers according to a combination of the following types:

- *Geographic segmentation*, which includes dividing a market into different geographical units such as nations, states, regions, countries, cities or neighbourhoods.
- *Demographic segmentation*, which includes dividing the market into groups based on demographic variables such as age, gender, family size, family life cycle, income, occupation, education, religion, race, generation and nationality.
- *Psychographic segmentation*, which includes dividing a market into different groups, based on social class, lifestyle or personality characteristics.
- *Behavioural segmentation*, which includes dividing a market into groups based on consumer knowledge, attitude, use or response to a product. This is often either *occasion based*, where markets are divided into groups according to those occasions when buyers get the idea to buy, actually make their purchase or use the purchased item, or *benefit based*, where markets are sorted into groups according to the different benefits that consumers seek from the product.

Strategic marketing prescribes that organizations have to be able to analyse segments and ensure that they are measurable, in terms of size, purchasing power and profiles of segments, and accessible, in terms of being able to reach and serve the market segment effectively. In addition, the segment has to be worth serving, using whatever yardstick of value is current in the organization. In strategic terms, the segment must be differentiable, which means that it must be conceptually distinguishable and respond differently to different marketing mix elements and programmes, and it must be such that effective programmes can be designed to attract and serve the segments. There are a lot of haves and musts in the preceding sentences, something that points to the prescriptive nature of strategic marketing. It erects laws – as if it were a natural science.

Other segment-related knowledge, such as 'when', 'where' and 'how' purchases are made, is also very useful and often relatively easy to obtain through a firm's sales and accounting records. However, the usefulness of such information is lim-ited: it only tells us something about why people do buy what is on offer; it does not help our analysis of why they do not. For example, one of the many reasons for the decline of the UK-based retailer M&S in the 1980s was their long-time reluctance to accept credit cards (see the Case Study in Chapter 7). That this was the case might have been evident from sales staff encounters, but it would not have shown up in the data that head office attended to. Similarly, marketers who understand the specifics about the buying habits and preferences of existing and potential market segments are also more likely to be able to alter these.

Targeting

If all markets are segmented then there has be a choice made about which segments are best to enter: this is targeting.

> **Targeting** is the process of evaluating each market segment's attractiveness and selecting one or more segments to enter.

The evaluation of each market segment usually includes an analysis of its poten-tial to grow, its competitive intensity and the firm's ability to access and serve that particular group of customers. The growth potential can be estimated by looking at the current and predicting the future market size, growth rates, market share or the extent to which a product or service may change, for example when new tech-nologies become available. The analysis of competitive intensity includes analysing the number and strength of competitors, the ease of entry to reach a specific target segment and an evaluation of potential substitute products as well as studying other competitors' strategies. The ability to access and serve a target market depends on a familiarity with the potential target segment, the existence of marketing chan-nels such as wholesalers, outlets or the Internet, and the extent to which the target market needs are in alignment with the overall strategic direction and capabilities.

Based on such a thorough analysis of external and internal aspects, which we have discussed in much greater detail in Chapter 2 and Chapter 3, the strategist has to decide whether a target market is worth pursuing. The greater the ability of a strategy to be able to predict how current and future products and services will serve such very finely segmented groups of customers, the better it will be. Once there is a good understanding of valuable target market segments, products and services can be positioned against competitors' offerings. Think of the way that the iPhone came to dominate 3G mobile sales quite rapidly; the response of Samsung, Nokia, etc., was to create phones that were virtual iPhone clones.

There are various different target market strategies that a firm may follow:

- *Single segment strategy*. Also known as a concentrated strategy. One market segment (not the entire market) is served with one marketing-mix. A single segment approach often is the strategy of choice for smaller companies with limited resources.

- *Selective specialization*. This is a multiple segment strategy, also known as a differentiated strategy. The product itself may or may not be different – in many cases only the promotional message or distribution channels will vary.

- *Product specialization*. The firm specializes in a particular product and tailors it to different market segments.

- *Market specialization*. The firm specializes in serving a particular market segment and offers that segment an array of different products.

- *Full market coverage*. The firm attempts to serve the entire market. This coverage can be achieved by means of either a mass-market strategy in which a single undifferentiated marketing mix is offered to the entire market, or by a differentiated strategy in which a separate marketing mix is offered to each segment.

According to the logic of strategic marketing, any organization seeking to enter a market and grow is well advised to focus first on the most attractive segment that matches its capabilities. Once it gains a foothold, it may expand by pursuing a product specialization strategy, tailoring its offer to other market segments, or by pursuing a market specialization strategy and offering new products to its existing market segment. Such planning already denotes part of the final step in the S–T–P process, positioning an offer in the marketplace so that it can be clearly distinguished from the offerings of competitors.

Positioning

The key theoretical underpinnings of the competitive positioning approach include Porter's (1980) industrial economics, whose practical implications have been discussed in earlier chapters. The ideas of positioning were quickly picked up and translated by Al Ries and Jack Trout (2001/1982) as a communication tool to reach target customers in a crowded marketplace.

Positioning soon became a key aspect of communication strategies, as advertising agencies began to develop catchy positioning slogans for their clients. The key idea is that a distinguishable market position for a product only exists in the customer's mind. Hence, positioning considers the customer's perception of a product or service in relation to competing products. Ries and Trout argue that this approach is required because consumers are flooded with a continuous stream of advertising and that their reaction to such a high volume of communication is to trust only what appears consistent with what they know or have experienced before. Since it is difficult to change perceptions once they are formed, positioning strategies should focus on presenting simplified messages and achieving a consistency in communication in terms of what the target market already accepts as true.

> Positioning is the process of arranging for a product to occupy a clear, distinctive and desirable place relative to competing products in the minds of target customers.

In that sense, the corporate image and brand are too strongly influenced by the multiple messages conveyed to stakeholders. Products or services are usually positioned on the basis of an attitude or benefit, use or application, the type of user, price or quality. The same product or service can be positioned in many different ways, since the purpose of positioning is to target a specific market segment that has particular product or service needs and is willing to pay a specific price. In achieving such a position, a difference has to be established between the present and competing offers within the same market segment, selecting the differences most valued by customers and effectively signalling such differences to the target market.

From a critical standpoint, positioning focuses on the management of consumers' perceptions via promotional strategies rather more than on the authenticity of the product, service or brand. Congruence between 'what the firm says it is' and 'what it really is' represents authenticity (Pine and Gilmore, 1999). As a result, superficial positioning strategies can be problematic since the authenticity of products and the firm itself (its brands and corporate image) are vital for building customer trust and a loyal customer base in the long term. As consumers and business customers alike become better informed and increasingly aware of what organizations do or do not do, inauthenticity is easier to detect. Authenticity entails organizational communication of commitment and consistency over time.

From a corporate strategy perspective competitive positioning is the combination of choice of target market (where the firm will compete) and competitive advantage (how the firm will compete). Hooley and co-authors (2001) argue that competitive positions are created through the deployment of competitive advantage generating resources matched to the needs of target customer groups. Holding such an advantageous position is dependent on the capacity to outflank competitor imitation, together with the ability to protect the competitive position, concepts we have discussed in Chapter 2. What becomes clear is that how a firm or other organization chooses to position itself as a company as much as how it positions its products and services is central to the creation of strategy. Let us now look at the role and importance of customer relationship management.

MANAGING THE CUSTOMER RELATIONSHIP

How a firm or other organization chooses to position itself and/or its products and services is central to the creation of strategy and strategic customer relationship management (Hooley et al., 2007).

Relationship marketing

Strategic marketing asserts that managing and advancing the interaction with customers and sales prospects in both consumer and business markets is a key strategy in sustaining a competitive advantage. If a strategy is to be translated into an effective practice in the market, then it is essential that actors in that market be enrolled in the strategy, to borrow some key terms from actor–network theory (ANT; see Latour, 2005). A network needs to be constructed that implicates customers, producers and things that are produced in one action net. ANT looks at assemblages that then become a strategy relating different elements together into a network so that they form an apparently coherent whole. Such actor–networks are always unstable and transient, existing only through a constant process of making and remaking. Relations need to be repeatedly enacted or the network will dissolve. For the network to be produced routinely there has to be an accepted problematization concerning the problem that the strategy exists to solve. Defining the problem identifies the relevant actors that need to be involved in the strategy, that need to be interested, as well as the terms of their involvement. These actors need to be enrolled into the network in the roles that strategy determines for them and they also need to be mobilized as allies and accomplices of the strategy. In strategy terms the process of building such an actor–network connecting long-term customers and firms is referred to as customer relationship management (CRM).

Customer relationship management (CRM) is a business process that reaches across many organizational functions; it is concerned with achieving improved customer satisfaction through the development of effective and lasting relationships with customers.

The concept of relationship marketing was first introduced by Berry (1983) and later refined by Berry and Parasuraman (1991), Morgan and Hunt (1994), Sheth and Paravatiyar (1995) and Gronroos (1995), among others. CRM has since become one of the dominant managerialist approaches to strategy. Essentially, it seeks to enrol customers into the firm's network on the firm's terms rather than treating them as occasional and incidental purchasers of goods and services (Payne and Frow, 2005).

Firms such as Apple have been particularly good at CRM, using Apple conferences to launch eagerly awaited new projects to an assemblage of Apple devotees. Enrolled customers sell products by word of mouth as well as through more formal advertising campaigns – think of the buzz that always surrounds a new Apple product launch ever since the success of the iPod. Apple has succeeded in defining the problem of how to deliver digital capabilities into everyday life and has very successfully enrolled, translated and mobilized Apple zealots into stabilizing the appeal and success of the portfolio of emerging products. Of course, clever branding of these as an 'i' family of related products helps.

CRM is a strategic marketing tool that is of the moment. Its appeal is such that William Band, Sharyn Leaver and Mary Ann Rogan (2008) predict that companies will spend more than $11 billion per year on CRM in 2010. This colossal expenditure aims to find, attract and win new customers, nurture and retain those customers the company already has, attract former customers back into the fold; it will help to improve the customer experience, grow revenues and reduce the costs of marketing operations and customer service while increasing the efficiency of customer-facing staff.

QUESTION TIME?

What examples of CRM have you experienced personally?

To achieve these objectives, firms will usually start by taking advantage of sophisticated IT systems that will help organize, automate and synchronize not only processes such as sales-related activities but also those for marketing, customer service and technical support. Kumar and Petersen (2005) suggest linking customer data, strategic marketing objectives and the financial performance of the firm (see also Reinartz and Kumar, 2000; Rust, Leman and Zeithaml, 2004; Venkatesan and Kumar, 2004; Reinartz, Krafft and Hoyer, 2004; Reinartz, Thomas and Kumar, 2005). When IT is used in this way to create an action net the lifetime value of each customer for organization performance can be calculated. As we will see shortly, in some cases the IT system can help make an organizational brand become a focal point for managing an organization's culture (see the Ruud Poulet video on www. strategytube.net).

While IT underpins CRM strategies, it is not necessarily the factor that makes such strategies successful. Various studies (Colgate and Danaher, 2000; Gartner Group, 2003; Srinivasan and Moorman, 2005) and the experience from many failed IT-focused CRM strategy implementations show that achieving desired CRM outcomes goes well beyond the technology initiative and involves an alignment of the whole organization (including structures, processes, governance mechanisms, leadership and culture) with a focus on the customer. More generally, organization theory highlights that IT often fails, or at least is not used in the way in which it was originally intended. It is as if IT enthusiasts forget the users when dealing with technology.

The rhetoric of CRM flows directly from total quality management (TQM) and stresses that the 'customer is king'. This of course should set alarm bells ringing. TQM was hugely popular in the 1990s. It aimed to improve customer service, organizational processes and management. Raising huge expectations, it was promoted with an evangelical zeal by management consultants. Of course no initiative could deliver on such expectations and the results were at best patchy. We reserve a similar scepticism towards CRM. If we look at Ronald Hess et al.'s (2003) study into how firms' relationship with their customers affects their responses to service failure, we see that, following TQM logic, value is argued to be based on a more personalized and closer contact with customers. Consequently, Hess et al. argue that displays of organizational reliability and authenticity, combined with the seamless performance and coordination of organizational capabilities, help provide better customer service. The argument is somewhat tautological.

CRM *as cause-related marketing*

CRM can easily be criticized as manipulative of people, constituting them only as consumers in a one-dimensional mode, rather than seeing their identity as more complex. This is especially evident when CRM becomes cause-related marketing where the customer relationship is built by linking being a caring citizen and a customer of a specific firm. American Express initiated these links. In the third quarter of 1983, one cent of every dollar that US cardholders spent was dedicated to a fund to restore the Statue of Liberty, raising $1.6 million. The practice of hooking up the two CRMs rapidly spread globally, with the view that enrolling customers through ethical commitments made for a longer term relationship than merely the provision of a business good or service. Businesses such as the Body Shop became masters of the practice. Not only were you buying cosmetics, you were also helping to save the planet or provide an income to people in some developing nation.

CRM enables business to adopt a moral cloak for its activities while it reels in customers, by hooking into their broader social dimensions as concerned citizens, thus creating a basis for a sustained longer term competitive advantage. Charities have been quick to link up with businesses to practise CRM. The results, while impressive for the causes served, can be even more impressive for the businesses concerned: American Express spent $6 million on the advertising campaign that raised $1.6 million for the Statue of Liberty but issued 28 per cent more cards during the campaign. People felt good about their involvement: not only had they joined the AmEx family of customers but they had also saved a national icon – and made AmEx more profitable.

For critical theorists such as Marcuse (1964) marketing strives to construct cause–effect relationships that can be manipulated to produce an emotional commitment to goods and services. It characterizes individuals primarily as consumers. The result, as Alvesson (1994) points out, is to treat people as purely instrumental utility maximizers in terms of consumption, conjoined with a perspective from social conditioning that also positions them as subjects relationally connected to firms and causes. CRM objectifies the person primarily as a consumer. Rights are restricted to being only satisfied or complaining. While CRM seemingly makes consumption relational and ethical, it is actually deeply manipulative: 'Within CRM, ethical choices are not a matter for moral judgment but are subject to our shopping decisions' (Smith and Higgins, 2000: 314). Curious ethical juxtapositions result in consequence.

In a television campaign for American Express shown a few years ago in the United States, black-and-white shots of children appeared in slow motion. In the background, there were the strains of John Lennon's 'Imagine.' Then the voice-over, 'Imagine if every time you bought anything with your American Express card, you helped feed someone who is hungry.' The words 'Charge Against Hunger' inscribed on a white soup bowl appear on the screen, and as the picture fades to the AmEx logo, two more words appear, the plea, 'Do More.' There are some striking incongruities. Lennon's invitation to 'imagine a world without possessions' linked to a credit card. The imagery of developing world starvation linked implicitly to the well-heeled gourmet ordering a meal, via, of course, his charge card, at an expensive restaurant (Smith and Higgins, 2000: 315).

BRANDING AND IDENTITY

When CRM really works then the customer becomes allied with a brand; a part of their identity is tied up with the brand much as a football supporter's identity is allied to their team, which can then be manipulated for organizational benefit. Manchester United makes the most out of its 50 million fans worldwide by selling them everything from MU TV to MU Mobile and MU Finance (Miller and Muir, 2004: 35). Such strategies enable the exploitation of deep and meaningful relationships that willingly enable people to make a fetish out of commodities associated with those things with which they identify. It is a form of voluntary and exciting fetishism that positively alienates the self from those others who cannot or do not aspire to the positional good that is the brand, while creating a community with those who can and do.

Brands are on the rise. Fashion designers are modern-day celebrities, with Donna Karan, Karl Lagerfeld, Ralph Lauren and Paul Smith being household names. Brands – both fashion and otherwise – have hit the public consciousness in such a way that they are readily identified across the world. It is the widespread communication of brands that signifies our image-saturated world, to such an extent that comedy programmes – *Absolutely Fabulous* comes to mind – in which certain brand names such as Versace or Harvey Nicks are continuously reproduced as jokes, can be grasped by a mass audience. This popular discourse on brands is reflected in the media: if you look at the *Wall Street Journal* over the past three decades you will find a tremendous increase in the usage of the word 'branding'. Using the database ProQuest, you will find that from 1984 to 1990 only 57 documents mentioned the word branding, while between 1990 and 2000 the number increased to 580. From 2000 until 2009, the brand explosion occurred: 1446 documents dealt in one or the other way with branding. Put simply, brands are increasingly becoming part of contemporary culture. The cliché often attributed to Dave Packard of Hewlett-Packard, that many managers feel that branding is too important to be left to the marketing department, attests to the centrality of branding in contemporary organizations. Rather the brand has to be seen as having the potential to be a strategic asset of every organization. The corollary of this insight is that the brand has to be at the heart of strategic considerations.

When organizations produce things that mean something valuable, rare and intangible for the customer then the less substitutable and imitable they will be, as we have seen in our discussion of the RBV (see Chapter 3). Think of it this way: perfectly good copies of famous-name brands are available from many outlets in cities around the world yet luxury goods sales are hardly dented. The mystique of the brand and the fear of inauthenticity on the part of the consumer that signifies themselves as a part of the brand community is a possible explanation for why this should be the case. Marx saw the fetishism of commodities as a sign of alienation; today's strategists see it as a basis for community through a dual movement of inclusion and exclusion.

The goal of branding is to establish brand equity. Brand equity is established through building four relationships between the brand and the consumer.

1　Brand awareness (e.g. is the brand on the cognitive radar of people?).
2　Loyalty (e.g. does the brand have followers?).
3　Perceived quality (e.g. do people perceive the value of the brand?).
4　Brand associations (e.g. to which socio-cultural landscape do people relate the brand?).

> Brand equity is defined as 'a set of assets (and liabilities) linked to a brand's name and symbol that adds to (or subtracts from) the value provided by a product or service to a firm and/or that firm's customer' (Aaker, 1996: 7–8).

An interesting example of these elements of brand equity can be seen in fashion: UK brands such as Burberry were until relatively recently rather staid, country brands – the mark of someone respectable and upper class from the shires, someone who perhaps hunted and fished a little, and did so in sensible hats, scarves, coats and boots. However, sometime in the 1990s, the brand crossed some boundaries. Young people, often supporters of football teams, frequently rather rough, tough and vulgar heavy drinkers, started to wear Burberry checks as a conspicuous artefact; rapidly, the brand became associated with 'chavs' – young people perceived as belonging to the underclass. Burberry's appeal to chav fashion sense is an example of an up-market product being consumed *en masse* by a lower socio-economic group and, in consequence, diluting the brand equity. Now the famous Burberry tartan has become a much less stressed feature of the Burberry range although, in all its counterfeit glory, it is still widely evident on the terraces. Burberry's tartan built brand awareness, inspired long-lasting loyalty from the hunting and fishing set, and built an estimable reputation for brand quality. However, once the fashion had become widely associated with a different class of person the brand associations changed dramatically.

A brand can provide an identity: it tells people what it is by virtue of the characteristics by which it is recognized and known. It acts as a social marker. A brand identity is simultaneously about sameness and difference. It tells us what something is and, equally, what something is not. Rarely is it the case that a brand achieves the status of an 'essential' identity – one that is constant and unchanging. Once upon a time in UK retailing the sign of an exclusive brand was that it bore the Royal Warrant as a seal of approval. When an ordinary family accompanied its bacon and eggs with HP Sauce then they might fondly imagine their monarch doing the same in Buckingham Palace. Together, the Houses of Parliament and the royal seal of approval positioned the sauce as an essentially British brand, as solid as the glass bottle in which it was sold. Although it is now made in the Netherlands it might seem a little kitsch to imagine the Royal Warrant as the most effective marketing tool for a product – that is an illusion that belongs to an earlier age of loyal subjects rather than fickle consumers.

Brand identity formation today is more fluid and temporal, and although strategies may seek to stabilize it around an essential meaning, the likelihood is that any essential meaning will be highly contingent and potentially unstable. Think of product recalls. It will be interesting to see how Toyota's reputation as a maker of quality and reliable cares is damaged by the series of safety recalls that affected over 8½ million vehicles in 2010. We simply do not know at this time to what extent the brand will prevail over the operational difficulties or what the long-term damage will be. Toyota was a brand that was built on safety and reliability – significations that now seem at odds with the news that has recently been circulating about them. Of course, with the right marketing adversity can be changed into strength as Johnson & Johnson did when it introduced tamper-proof packaging after recalling every example of a product that an extortionist had announced had been randomly poisoned.

Identity is an ambivalent concept. Joanne Martin et al. (1983) studied organizations and found that what most employees thought of as organizationally unique stories were actually shared across different organizations. They labelled this the uniqueness paradox: we think we are unique, but in fact we share what makes us unique with a large number of others. It is similar to a room full of people who all agree that they want to be different. Ironically, the wish to be different might create a rather homogeneous crowd. As Barbara Czarniawska (2008) has pointed out, identity always has to refer to something different and other to itself: alterity. Alterity and identity co-constitute each other, which brings us back to the point above about brands being about sameness and difference. Put simply, without another person, there could be no I. In a similar way organizations need other organizations to define who they are. Hence, identity is a relational phenomenon: it derives from the relation between different subjects.

A rapidly growing body of knowledge has emerged around the notion of organizational identity (for an overview see Corley et al., 2006). Its significance for strategy-making is that it frames what we imagine as possible futures (Rughase, 2006). For example, a small, elite liberal arts university might baulk at a massive expansion of its management studies courses, fearing that the more traditional subjects – Greek, Latin, theology and history – will be crowded out by this *arriviste* called management. Identity fundamentally shapes the way we perceive our environment and future within it. Strategies always, implicitly or explicitly, build on the identity of an organization. This is especially visible in the promotion and positioning of commodities offering personal transport. Think of a favourite brand of car such as an Alfa Romeo and contrast it with another brand, such as a Kia. While the former denotes Italian flair and a general air of sportiness, the latter, even when it has a 'European' design, does not. One can draw on a racing and movie heritage (it was an Alfa Spyder that Dustin Hoffman drove in *The Graduate*), while the other has no such heritage: that a Korean car may have a European design is insufficient to give it a European identity. It may be a better vehicle in many ways but not in terms of the espoused identity.

Brand capital and brand formation

Identity is always intersubjective – always something that arises from a widely shared agreement about a phenomenon's uniqueness and difference. Following Pullen and Linstead (2005; also see Pullen, 2009: 630) we may say that the idea of a brand strategy creating an identity requires an account of brand capital and brand formation.

Brand capital builds on contextual resources. In the case of the Alfa Romeo, for instance, a key value is legacy. Toyota's value was built on reliability. Few would ever have bought a Toyota for its sporting and movie legacy; few would have bought an Alfa for its reliability. Think of brand strategies that evoke a retro image while at the same pointing forward, symbolically: cars such as the Mini or Fiat 500 achieve this very effectively. They trade on the nostalgia of affluent mature people for the enthusiasms of their youth, offered in a package that respects the symbols and discourse of the moment for safety and economy, while materially offering a transport solution that will only sell to customers who are socio-economically rather well off.

Brand formation, as a process of constructing an identity, involves asking a series of strategic questions:

1   *Incorporation.* What will be built into the brand identity of all the possible things that signify what the brand means? What will be left out?

For Celia Lury (2004), a brand is not a commodity but 'a set of relationships between products or services' in time. While the idea of a product as a brand might be easy to grasp, the idea of a service is slightly more difficult – but think of a premium service or a black American Express card. Lury's definition is useful as it injects dynamism into the conceptualization of branding and in the process it makes a brand a relational concept. It is the relation between signs (think logos!) that constitute the brand. Hence the strategy of building a brand identity is essentially semiotic, building on cultural references to inject meaning into products. One example is that of a surgical shoe that became a global brand. In the mid-1940s a German doctor, Klaus Maertens, developed Dr Martens Shoes, following a skiing accident (Wipperfürth, 2005: 17–18). The bouncy soles proved to be a hit; he went on to sell his shoes to elderly women who had foot problems. In the 1960s, The Griggs Company bought the licensing rights for the shoe and started to produce it in the UK, giving rise to one of the most iconic postwar brands. Initially, blue-collar workers bought the shoes as working shoes. They were strong and hard wearing, offering a value-for-money work shoe. As a first subculture, skinheads started to wear the boots as a sign of belonging to the working class. They would also wear different coloured laces – often a signifier of which right-wing faction they belonged to. In the 1970s, the punk movement made Docs their trademark of rebellion. By the 1980s the shoes had become de rigeur for young, slightly alternative people. Doc Martens became part of a uniform for grunge and indie kids (one of the authors wore his Docs most days for an entire decade! He is now a suit-wearing professor at a posh university!) and the British lesbian scene also adopted them, along with some other elements of the skinhead culture. By the 1980, the shoes had made it across the Atlantic also to be worn by the leaders and followers of their grunge and indie music scene. Doc Martens are a brand that owes its identity to the strategies of their users rather than to the company that created the brand.

2   *Disciplining the brand.* How do we ensure that the brand identity is on message and widely understood by all those associated with it, disciplining the subjectivity of organization members so that only the brand message surfaces? How do the organization's members remain on message all the time they are in the public eye and also remain consistent with it when they are not – a problem that all politicians and their parties have to face?

This is not as easy as simply creating a slogan and putting it on a badge on a uniform that all front-office staff will wear. Think of the McDonald's brand: while it might represent for some an affordable, child-friendly restaurant, others see it as an incarnation of US imperialism and the dark side of globalization. What is the 'real' meaning of the brand? This remains contested as different groups struggle over the meaning and legitimacy of its brand. In fact, the meaning of a brand might become the most strategically valuable asset of the organization. In some cases, organizations will go as far as seeing their product as solely a manifestation of the brand. Nike is a good example here. In the early days, it produced shoes for athletes. As its popularity grew, Nike realized that most customers did not need the functionality of high-tech athletic shoes. Thinking functionally, Nike concluded that its shoes were completely overengineered for everyday use and stripped the design out of them. The result was that customers were upset and stopped buying the shoes. Not that they missed the functionality; what they missed was showing that they had bought into the Nike spirit. Customers wanted to wear shoes like their idols. Learning that normal customers loved overengineered sports shoes, because such shoes communicated something that customers could not get anywhere else, fundamentally changed Nike's understanding of what it was. While the brand is core to Nike, its products are but tools to communicate the brand. Similarly, Diesel's Renzo Rosso said, 'We started selling jeans, and now we are selling a way of life' (quoted in Wipperfürth, 2005: 106). Both Nike and Diesel are lifestyle brands that craft their strategies around their brand, of which products are but one manifestation. And, of course, guerrilla counter-strategies that point out the reliance on sweatshop sub contractors, for instance in the case of Nike, are always possible. (See, for instance, the page maintained by management academic David Boje at http://business.nmsu.edu/~dboje/nikerpts.html)

3 *Positioning the brand.* Where is the brand positioned, strategically? What media will communicate it, orient it to what target audiences, and with what messages?

Defining a strategy means positioning it in a system of differences and similarities, of distinct yet connected categories. Echoing some of the ideas we heard about in the context of strategy groups, products often relate to each other in order to be able to compete. Take the carbonated soft drinks market with its two archrivals Pepsi and Coke, and relative newcomers such as 7 UP which was branded as the 'Uncola' or Mecca Cola, a cola-flavoured beverage aimed at the Muslim world. In these examples the positioning of the brand plays with well-established connotations while simultaneously ensuring its differentiation from competitors.

4 *The organizational politics of the brand.* Is there a conflict between the client and agency about brand strategy, consumer preferences and communication? Are there conflicts between planners and creative types?

Account planning develops 'marketing strategies that at least appear to be based on objective, scientific criteria derived from in-depth qualitative and quantitative data', whereas creative types 'work according to intuitive, artistic ideas that may have little actual relationship to the expressed marketing aims' (Malefyt and Moeran, 2003: 5). Because of these structural conflicts, building a brand identity means tolerating a high level of ambivalence and ambiguity.

5 *Resistance.* How do you ensure that the brand identity does not readily leave itself open to easy subversion and resistance?

For instance, when Fiat marketed one of its models with a slogan that said 'if it was a lady it would get its bottom pinched', the consumer resistance from people outraged at the sexism of the ad – on so many levels – saw a widespread campaign of defacing billboards. Equally, with the skilful use of Photoshop many brands are subverted online.

BRAND-DRIVEN STRATEGY

The brand value of the FTSE's top 100 has been estimated to amount to a third of their total value. One-third of all wealth in the world consists of intangible brands, an affirmation of their rare and valuable status. For instance, the estimated brand value of Coca-Cola and Microsoft is $134 billion, which is roughly the annual GDP of Singapore (Clifton, 2003). 'Corporate Brand Reputation Outranks Financial Performance as Most Important Measure of Success': so concluded the survey of CEOs and leaders from the World Economic Forum in Davos in 2004. According to this research, reputation is a more important measure of success than stock market performance, profitability and return on investment, a judgement that might well have been true at the time but which, perhaps, reflected some of the hubris of the boom years before the GFC (Global Financial Crisis) in 2008. [1] As history teaches us, hubris is often followed by nemesis. In this regard, brands promise but cannot always deliver. For instance, ING, the Dutch bank, made much of its branding and the way in which this was the crucial ingredient of its success. In the wake of the multi billion-euro cash injection the Dutch government had to make to rescue the bank, it is difficult to sustain the argument that it was the brand that made ING successful!

MINI CASE STUDY

ING, the brand and objective realities

One firm that has built its success on its brand is finance house ING. According to the 2009 edition of the Fortune 500 list, the International Netherlands Group (in short, ING) is the world's eighth largest business.[2] Its 125,000 employees generate a revenue exceeding $225 billion, making it the biggest banking group in the world. It looks after 85 million clients in more than 50 countries. Still, in finance, as we learned from the collapse of Lehman Brothers, size is no guarantee of health. In the wake of the current GFC, ING was forced to sell off the insurance and investment management branch of its business, reducing its balance sheet by some 45 per cent. [3] ING had to shrink in order to be eligible for EU government support. While the future of the banking industry, including ING, might

be uncertain, the brand will continue to play a strategic role in the evolution of ING.

The brand came into existence in 1991 as a result of the merger of a bank and insurance company. 'ING grew by acquisitions, buying more than 40 or 50 different brands', Ruud Polet, Global Head of Brand Marketing, says. 'We did not rebrand them; we just let them be what they were. They just used an endorsement – at the bottom it would say "Member of ING". We had a house of brands. In 2000, we started the journey to rationalise them and create one brand – ING'.

ING uses the orange national colours of the Netherlands and the lion symbol of Amsterdam to identify itself. These constitute its recognizable brand, which it used both to structure internal operations, reducing the many brands to just the one, and, at the same time, engaging ING with the world and framing its engagement with its environments. The brand has the power – both organizationally as well as conceptually – to bring together strategy (what is ING's competitive positioning in the marketplace?); people (what is ING's culture that can deliver the brand?); operations (how should we structure our IT system so it supports our brand promise?), and marketing (how do we engage with (potential) customers?). Hence

(Continued)

[2]http://money.cnn.com/magazines/fortune/global500/2009/snapshots/7700.html, accessed 11 August 2009.

[3]See www.ft.com/cms/s/o/681ffe72-c200-11de-be3a-00144feab49a.html?nclick_check=1, accessed 8 December 2009.

[1]See www.weforum.org/en/media/Latest%20Press%20Releases/PRESSRELEASES233, accessed 2 June 2008.

(Continued)

brands are increasingly becoming the strategic organizing principle of business (see Hatch and Schultz, 2008).

ING grew through mergers and acquisitions into a jumbo–sized finance house, combining retail, online, investment banking and insurance operations under one branded roof – that of ING. ING's Ruud Polet was interviewed for www.strategytube. net in the weeks immediately before the GFC became evident, following the collapse of Lehman Brothers in September 2008. Interestingly, there is no discussion or sign of the forthcoming crisis in the discussions held with Mr Polet, the Strategy Branding Director for ING, and many words of praise for the expansionist strategy that the CEO, Michel Tilmant, had followed. View the interview and read the following case as well as using the Internet to source additional information.

Prior to the GFC, ING launched a new brand strategy that focused the bank on one brand value: 'easier'. Polet explains:

> Based on a lot of research, 'easier' turned out to be a kind of complex concept: what people meant by easier was easy to contact; be able to give a clear overview of what you're doing for me; if you are transparent; if you are fast and efficient; and if you can provide me advice when I need it – then people would regard ING as 'easier'.

Research found that 'easier' was appealing and relevant for most people, as Polet explains: '40 per cent of potential prospects were willing to switch to ING if ING was easier than its competitors. That was the business case for our board to redesign the brand around one single, simple position: "easier".' 'Easier' is an overarching concept; it communicates clearly what ING stands for. HSBC's 'The World's Local Bank' is a nice concept, but it does not really help a customer to see value. It provides for witty captioning of images in airport walkways, though. 'Easier' communicates a clear advantage, a clear value for the consumer. 'In five years there will be only three global finance brands – and ING will be one of them', Polet says confidently. The brand will be the key asset towards achieving this objective, he said.

The brand is not externally focused, however. 'Before we can announce that, we have to become easier inside the company', says Polet:

> So we are going through a total change program that turns the business upside down. We're not thinking about communicating 'easier' at the moment – maybe we never will. We have to *do* it – rather than talk about it. This is what I am working on every day – to make 'easier' stick to the business, not as a buzzword but as something that changes the business. Toyota called it *Kaizen* – we simply focus on 'easier' and use it to change the business.

Research showed Polet and his team that there were two topics that are barriers to becoming 'easier'. One is a people topic, the other a business topic: implementing change and decision-making; the other and processes. 'To become "easier" we need to help all our businesses eliminate those barriers', he says:

> That's what my job as brand manager is. So it is not a branding topic but a business topic. It's a change program, not a marketing initiative. The brand becomes an integrative platform – change people, HR people, marketing people, IT people, and executives. The brand is the common territory for discussing issues and aligning solutions. For instance, our CEO banks on the brand – he is now Chief *Easier* Officer, with his key responsibility being to drive the concept of 'easier'.

Just 12 months after that interview was held, the bank had changed dramatically. These changes were formally signalled by a number of events. Immediately after the September 2008 crash on a non-trading day, Sunday 19 October, in a move to increase its core tier 1 capital ratio – the measure commonly used to rate a bank's strength – from 6.5 to above 8 per cent, ING accepted a capital injection plan from the Dutch government. The plan supplied €10 billion of credit in exchange for securities and veto rights on major operations and investments. Effectively, the Dutch government part nationalized ING by becoming major shareholders in the bank to try and prevent its collapse. The Dutch finance minister said that this was done as a means of fortifying the bank as *the* bank to weather the financial crisis. The management said that the capital injection would have no dilutive impact on existing shareholders' holdings. ING said that its banking operations were within target solvency ratios and it retained a low-risk 'AA' credit rating. Under the scheme the government bought 1 billion newly issued non-voting shares with special rights at €10 per share. The shares will earn at least 8.5 per cent interest once ING begins paying dividends

(Continued)

(Continued)

again and that amount will escalate each year. But ING can repurchase the shares for €15. Two government advisers were appointed to the supervisory board. Thus, under the rescue terms, ING could be made to pay 150 per cent of the amount put into the company, or after three years transform the figure into shares. All of the bank's top managers gave up their annual bonuses and ING agreed that its CEO Michel Tilmant and other managers would receive no more than a year's pay if they were dismissed. ING announced separately that it would cancel dividends for the rest of the year. The company's shares immediately fell by 27 per cent on the announcement of these arrangements. After the markets had closed on Friday, 20 October, ING announced that it expected to post a €500 million loss for the third quarter, blaming the global credit crisis for its woes. Prior to the crisis ING had been among the top 20 financial services companies globally in terms of market capitalization, but its stock lost nearly three-quarters of its value. In 2007 the bank had a turnover of €76.6 billion and net profit of €9.24 billion. ING was worth just €15.2 billion at Friday's closing price after the deal had been stitched up.

By January 2008 things were unravelling further. The bank announced that it was slashing millions of dollars from its Formula One programme as part of a massive cost-cutting effort triggered by the GFC. The Formula One programme had been a centrepiece of its branding. ING was in the final season of a three-year sponsorship deal with Renault. The cost cutting would come from F1-related advertising, Dutch Finance Minister Bos said. It would not have an impact on the bank's sponsorship of the Renault team or the four races that season. The company's total F1 budget was believed to be between EUR 66 and 132 million. 'We are now in the third year so we plan to evaluate and make a decision on the future this year, taking into account current market circumstances', Bos said.

ING's CEO survived at the helm into 2009, despite the fact that the Dutch finance ministry effectively seemed to be running the company. However, early in the new year, on January 26, it was announced that ING's CEO would 'step aside'.

As Tilmant left his position the company continued to struggle. The firm was not only losing its CEO but it also lost nearly 7000 ING employees on top of a fourth-quarter deficit of nearly €3 billion. The staff cuts were designed to save ING €1.32 billion in 2009 operating expenses.

The January measures did not stop the rot. A Back to Basics scheme was announced. The Back to Basics programme was intended to streamline the company and reduce risk, costs and leverage. It axed a total of 10,800 jobs, including the 7000 initially earmarked. ING's future banking activities would be based on the proven strengths of gathering savings, distribution leadership, simple propositions and strong marketing.

Restructuring measures, including steps already taken as part of the Back to Basics programme, are expected to result in a pro forma balance sheet reduction of around €600 billion by 2013, equal to approximately 45 per cent of the balance sheet at 30 September 2008. This will be achieved via divestments and through a further deleveraging of the bank's balance sheet. Including estimated organic growth, it is expected that ING's balance sheet by the end of 2013 will be approximately 30 per cent smaller than at 30 September 2008. The proceeds from divesting the insurance operations will be used to eliminate double leverage and further repay the Dutch state.

Questions

1 Research ING's current standing in the business press. How is it faring in the recovery?

2 Is the 'easier' branding mentioned anywhere as a key attribute of the banking group?

3 What do you see as the major dysfunctions that might attach, strategically, to 'easier' as a branding exercise, under the conditions of a financial crisis?

4 How would you characterize the changes in strategic direction that ING has undergone since the global financial crisis and what actors seem to have been winners and losers in these changes?

5 What conclusions would you draw for its branding strategy?

Sources

- www.welt.de/english-news/article2600863/Dutch-government-invests-Euro-10-billion-in-ING-Groep.html

- www.ing.com/group/pressdoc.jsp?docid=417610_EN

- www.france24.com/en/20081019-ing-receive-state-cash-injection-bank-netherlands-financial-crisis

- www.usatoday.com/sports/motor/formula1/2009-01-27-ing-budget-cut_N.htm

Companies buy brands in order to gain instant access to markets. When Ford bought Jaguar it was not that interested in Jaguar's factories: what Ford was after was, of course, the Jaguar brand. It has now sold this on to the Indian manufacturer Tata. The same strategy characterized BMW's takeover of Rolls-Royce cars and Mini. In these examples, brands are a weapon of conquest or the defence of market share. Hence, brand theorists, such as Aaker (1996: 21), use military metaphors to define brands as strategically important 'battleships' in the competitive seascape:

> A brand can be likened to a ship in a fleet facing an upcoming battle. ... The brand manager is the captain of the ship, who must know where his or her ship is going and keep it on course. The other brands in the firm, like other ships in the fleet, need to be coordinated to achieve the maximum effectiveness. Competitors correspond to enemy ships; knowing their location, direction and strength is critical to achieving strategic and tactical success. The perceptions and motivations of customers are like the winds: it is important to know their direction, their strength and possible changes.

Aaker and Joachimsthaler (2002) introduced the notion of brand leadership. In their model, the brand takes on the function of a strategic tool for the organization. Traditionally, brand management, at best, had been reactive, tactical, short-term oriented and local, whereas the notion of the brand leadership model that they introduced would be proactive, visionary, long-term oriented and global. While the old model had an exclusively external focus, the new leadership model focuses on the external as well as the internal environment; rather than focusing on sales, it focuses on the brand identity as a driver of strategy. Put simply, branding claims the leadership role in organizations. Far from being a function of the marketing department, branding commands an influence across all organizational units.

Branding can be used to refashion the organization to ensure that its brand hierarchy (sometimes referred to as brand architecture) maps onto the corporate hierarchy. Take Volkswagen: the brand is hierarchically split up to include VW, Porsche, Audi, Skoda, Seat, etc. These sub-brands are then differentiated again – VW is split into Lupo, Polo, Golf, Eon, Passat, Touareg, etc. The difference between the old and new hierarchy is that brands restructure the business to represent consumer preferences inside the organization. The brand creates a new hierarchy, a new order among parts of the business. Rather than following internal lines of authority or functional divisions, this structure is derived from the external environment. The discursive device of brands and sub-brands has the capacity to restructure internal business operations.

Is a brand a symbol that represents reality? Is it simply an image that expresses identity, and sometimes masks it? Consider the example of Benetton, which charged Italian photographer Oliviero Toscani with the task of developing a new global communication strategy for its identity. Benetton's identity was built over the years through a careful use of language. At the outset of Toscani's reign it was about 'all the colours in the world', celebrating diversity. Then it started to move from harmonious diversity to show the differences between black and white, poor and rich. At the beginning of the 1990s, the communication turned more pessimistic: life, disease, illness and death were shown, in an existential gesture, as being what ultimately unites humankind through compassion and care for the other. The phantasmagoria of images that followed included a dead soldier's uniform, a dying AIDS patient and an HIV stamp on naked skin. Not surprisingly, these images created controversy. It is important to point out that the actual product did not feature in any of the ads. The brand communication was never focused on fashion; what was created was identity. This begs the question: is the Benetton brand 'real' or not?

Brands, we argue, are 'real' and powerful as images. Images create identity, through language, narratives, symbols and so on. The brand is the engine at the core of identity. It performs identity: identities are not revealed or uncovered;

they have to be made. In cases such as Benetton, the associations are remote: images that shocked were not associated directly with Benetton products in their imagery – but to the extent that they produced controversy and the fact that in each discussion the brand name Benetton appeared, they built corporate brand awareness immeasurably. Benetton became widely known not for its products so much as its corporate style. Mary Jo Hatch and Majken Schultz describe such branding as a shift from promoting the product to promoting the corporate identity.

Schultz et al. (2005: 12) have argued that the corporate brand represents 'the idea that the organization and everything it stands for is mobilised to interact with the stakeholders the organization wants to reach and engage them in dialogue'. Hatch and Schultz (2001) see the corporate brand as being made up of four distinct elements:

1. A strategic vision expressing top management's aspiration for the organization.

2. An organizational culture that expresses how employees enact values, beliefs and basic assumptions.

3. Stakeholder images developed by outsiders, including customers, media and others.

4. At the juncture of these three perspectives, the brand identity emerges as a reflection of how the organization perceives itself.

MINI CASE STUDY

The brand as the soul of the corporation

At the beginning of the twentieth century American corporations were in trouble (Marchand, 1998). Rapid growth, mergers and increasing market domination brought on a legitimacy crisis resulting in anti trust legislation being passed. Although corporations were treated as persona as a consequence of the *Santa Clara County* vs *Southern Pacific Railroad* case in 1886, the persona was without a soul. Corporate empires as run by J.P. Morgan or Rockefeller controlled large parts of people' lives without having any kind of personality. The problem also spread inside those large corporate empires: with what should employees identify? The solution came in the creation of a corporate soul – or a brand, as we would say. The corporate quest for social and moral legitimacy was played out in massive public relations initiatives.

Take the example of AT&T (see Marchand, 1998). In 1894 its monopoly patent expired. Facing competition AT&T pulled all registers to undermine its much smaller, local rivals. Hence AT&T was seen as the foreign, big and heavy contender that tried to destroy the local players outright. However, its

bullying strategy was not successful. As a result, its market share reduced from 100 per cent in 1893 to 51 per cent in 1907. Additionally, it had to face public suspicion and antagonism. Because AT&T could not win this war, it started to work on its brand and in 1908 launched one of the first brand-building campaigns. The first ads appeared in June and July 1908, recasting the image of AT&T as a company that was committed to 'One Policy, One System, Universal Service'. Although the ads were long, information heavy and clumsy ('we work *with* you and *for* the public'; 'agitation against legitimate telephone business ... must disappear') they heralded a new era: building a corporate soul that would give the corporation meaning and personality. In this respect, corporate branding was always on the agenda of leaders. The quest for reputation and legitimacy was thus recognized very early on as being central to organizational survival.

Since AT&T built a soulful image for its corporation many others have followed in its footsteps. Nokia 'connects' you with your loved ones, Vodafone 'brings the world together for you' and so on.

Question

1. Research how other telecommunication brands create the image of a 'soulful' company that is there to help improve life. (There are many leads on the Internet!)

Branding advocates assume that an aligned brand culture will lead to passion and commitment, and ultimately a better performance:

> If the values are deeply rooted and coherently interlinked, then the relevance of the brand's values and the connections staff make with the brand enable them to deliver the brand promise in a more natural manner, with passion and commitment. This, in effect, brings the brand to life and enhances the likelihood of a better performance. (De Chernatony, 2002: 122)

Blending the brand and culture is supposed to turn employees into 'living brands':

> The relationship between employees and customers is at the heart of the brand experience. Just as in any successful relationship, the employee/customer relationship needs honesty, openness and a unity of interest. When the unity of interest is intuitive, with employees and consumers sharing the same passions, it is particularly powerful. (Ind, 2001: 26)

> We might think of the employee as being the brand … the norms and values based perspective builds on the premise that the personal values off the employee become congruent with the brand values. (Karmark, 2005: 108, 109)

In this view, people are the soul of a company and therefore

> constitute the soul of the brand. The first step towards creating brand authenticity is therefore to ensure that its core values are clear and have been fully internalised by those who work within the company. (Marzano, Quoted in Lury, 2004: 34)

To create such alignment is easier said than done. How could such a level of control over individuals be achieved? Moreover, one would create a homogeneous mass of employees who would think alike, which is not necessarily what an innovative and creative organization needs. From an ethical perspective, one is reminded of visions of totalitarian societies in which everyone is marching in the same direction, chanting the same songs (see the Khmer Rouge case study in Chapter 1). Organizations that possessed strong brands, such as Enron, could fulfil the criteria expounded by the quotes above. That ended in a debacle. It is important to be sceptical of such claims regarding the power of branding.

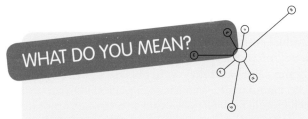

WHAT DO YOU MEAN?

The brand as strategy in the context of a law firm

Cindy Carpenter heads the marketing and HR departments at Corrs Chambers Westgarth, one of Australia's leading law firms with more than 1000 employees. Before taking on this dual role, she was a brand manager at Unilever, finished her MBA at Wharton and worked for 13 years as a strategist with the Boston Consulting Group. Cindy's portfolio heralds the advent of a new era for brand managers. In the context of a professional services firm, the brand is developed and delivered through employees. As Cindy elaborates:

'In a professional services firm, the brand is embedded in the people. The brand is really an articulation of your culture. People drive the manufacturing, the delivery, the marketing and the selling of the service. To have a powerful brand means to have a high-performing culture and invest in organizational learning that boosts the commerciality and excellence of our advice.

(Continued)

(Continued)

Branding becomes a manifestation of the behaviour of staff. Cindy's dual portfolio reflects the new challenges and opportunities: 'I feel quite privileged to sit across marketing and HR: to implement change and drive strategy you need to focus on people and how their behaviour creates the brand'. Marketing an intangible service (such as Corr's legal advice) demands a different skill as Wally Olins (2003: 75) argues: one has to get 'your own staff to love the brand and live it and breathe it so that they can become the personal manifestation of the brand when they deal with customers'. Branding works first internally, and then, as its second target, it focuses on the external market.

Question

1 Study the www.strategytube.net video of Cindy Carpenter. What are the strategic principles and practices she follows in building the Corrs Chambers Westgarth brand?

YOU CAN DOWNLOAD...

Dan Kärreman and Anna Rylander's (2008) Managing Meaning through Branding: The Case of a Consulting Firm, *Organization Studies*, 29: 103–25 from the book's website at www.sagepub.co.uk/cleggstrategy

CRITICAL PERSPECTIVES ON BRANDING

The symbolic dimension of organization and leadership is an important area for the 'management of meaning' (Pondy, 1978; Smirchich and Morgan, 1982). Kärreman and Rylander (2008: 108) argue that 'branding practice may be usefully understood as management of meaning, i.e. systematic efforts from top management to influence and shape frames of references, norms and values among employees' However, the corporate branding perspective does not take into account how consumers of the 'corporate soul' make sense of the brand. Strategists often imagine the brand as something that can be created and manipulated by top management.

Strategy is too often too top down and too much focused on the corporate level. Not only does this often make for less successful strategy, but it also has political and ethical implications. Politically, the internal and external consumers of the brand interpret the brand in their own, often idiosyncratic, ways that can provoke an effective resistance to corporate strategies.[4] We know from critical research into organizational culture how strategy attempts to achieve a congruence of identity between the corporation, its staff and customers. Brands are designed, and so are employees, who are meant to internalize the brand, to a point where they become the brand. For Casey (1995), the ultimate 'designer employee' is depicted in Singapore Airlines' flight attendants. Such a designer culture is characterized by an individual enthusiasm, dedication, loyalty, self-sacrifice and passion. However, people will often resist colonization by brand values and not always swallow the latest brand values as if they were pills. Designer employees are hard, if not impossible, to manufacture. Van Maanen's (1991) Disneyland analysis shows exactly that. In the 'smile factory', as he calls it, a strong corporate culture makes sure that every employee behaves according to Disney's philosophy. Uniforms, specific language codes (work is a 'stage', customers are 'guests', etc.), education through the Disneyland University and employee handbooks embody this spirit. Did employees turn out to be corporate clones? Although they were very much indoctrinated, they did resist the 'smile factory'. Stressed staff found their own ways for dealing with masses of visitors. They developed informal mechanisms for disciplining especially nasty customers. For instance, the 'seatbelt squeeze' on amusement rides is but a 'small token of appreciation given

---

[4]Look at www.youtube.com/watch?v=bSgTdUhfDS4, for instance, for one interesting use of Dove products; www.youtube.com/watch?v=hcadw_FrU10&NR=1 is also fun and thought-provoking.

to a deviant customer consisting of the rapid inching-up of a required seatbelt such that the passenger is doubled-over at the point of departure and left gasping for the duration of the trip' (Van Maanen, 1991: 71). Or bothersome pairs are separated into different units so that they have to enjoy a ride without each other (the so called 'break-up-the-party' gambit). These and many other unofficial and informal rules and practices are learnt and developed on the job and form a part of the culture of Disneyland – not quite what the Disney University culture and brand bible planned.

Brand interpretations will be framed by the cultural, social and political context in which readers make sense of them. Brands have meaning because people interpret them in a certain way: McDonald's Golden Arches might mean fast food to one person, be a symbol of globalization for another, and might stand for the dominance of an American way of life for a third party. The meaning we give those Golden Arches is inextricably linked with the viewer, as we have argued above. In other words, much as does beauty, one could argue, brands exist only in the eyes of the beholder. Picking up the McDonald's example again, while the Golden Arches might be seen as a symbol of liberation and progress in countries with oppressive regimes, they might also be read as the symbol of a mechanized, standardized and soulless age, as followers of the slow food movement and authors such as George Ritzer (1993), in his *The McDonaldization of Society*, argue. What really is the McDonald's brand? We argue that there is no true, eternal meaning for the Golden Arches – only a dominant reading. A dominant reading is the one that seems to be most legitimate and shared among a group of people.

The meaning of brands will be embedded in power relations and interests as different groups fight over the meaning and value of brands. Think of those protesters who fight the Nike brand as opposed to those who cherish it and feel close to their idols (earlier on Michael Jordan, not so long ago Tiger Woods) when they wear it. Both groups battle over the meaning of Nike – a struggle you can follow on literally thousands of blogs and sites such as YouTube where faithful brand disciples and insurgents hotly debate brand meaning. The brand is 'symbolically created through acts of interpretation that occur throughout the population of stakeholders who keep it alive by producing, reproducing and sometimes changing its social and cultural meanings' (Hatch and Schultz, 2008: 21).

In a recent book, Rodrigues and Child (2008) trace the history and growth of Telemig, a major Brazilian telecommunications company. Over the course of 30 years Telemig transformed its identity from a 'lumbering dinosaur to a soaring eagle' as privatization brought the organization into the twenty-first century. They make it clear that the identity of an organization should be discussed as a political phenomenon. As such, as they make apparent, it is a highly contested identity. Different interests within the organization, such as the unions versus different factions within management, and in the broader environment, such as the government versus the markets, often both opposed to the old bureaucratic management, struggle to determine the identity of the organization. There is now a privatized brand, Telemig, that emerged out of the old state bureaucracy, but, as with any brand, it is the result of identity politics. In becoming its present privatized incorporation, deep and divisive struggles to define one set of dominant values that authorized a particular way of seeing the world, while closing off other possibilities, were evident. Branding is an inherently political process.

Brands are dynamic and should be understood as a platform or arena in which negotiations about identity can take place. The brand is the interface between identity and image. This relation can be a catalyst for strategic change as different, sometimes conflicting narratives are, at least temporarily, reconciled in the brand. Andrew Brown and Ken Starkey (2000: 102) have argued that, generally, 'organizations are prone to ego defences, such as denial, rationalisation, idealisation, fantasy, and symbolisation, that maintain collective self-esteem and the continuity of existing identity'. When identity is fundamentally questioned, organizations react with identity-preserving and change-inhibiting actions: 'Information that threatens an organization's collective self-concept is ignored, rejected, reinterpreted, hidden or lost' (Brown and Starkey, 2000: 103), while information that confirms identity is highlighted and amplified. Too much focus on brand identity in terms of an organization's internal affairs results in narcissism. A narcissist identity is internally focused and equipped with defence mechanisms to block change. By contrast, hyper-adaptivity is equally problematic. Hatch and Schultz (2008) suggest that if too much emphasis is placed on the external environment, this can lead to hyper-adaption, where every fashion trend is followed. An example was LEGO in the 1990s, which opened up theme parks, went into LEGO TV, lifestyle, retail, dolls, robotics, software and so on. At the end this was a disastrous strategy because LEGO mimicked trends that did not resonate with its legacy.

We have already argued that brands have important strategic implications inside the organization. Organization members are increasingly understood as prime opportunities to express the brand. The idea is simple: the brand experience of consumers is dependent on the way they are treated by organization members. Especially in a service economy, organizations will rely on people to make their customers happy. The brand is not built around the product but around the employees who deliver the service and (ideally) create a memorable experience. Hence, so the story goes, the brand equals the behaviour of staff.

Believing that the brand equals the behaviour of the staff is an approach to employees that raises strong ethical issues. In her study of the aesthetic labour in fashion retailing, Lynne Pettinger (2004) argued that retail is located in the blurred space between production and consumption. The creation of meaning – and hence the creation of the brand – happens in the context of the store, the products on display, the overall experience and ambience, and, most importantly, the sales staff. Pettinger shows how the brand determines both the service behaviour of staff and their embodiment. For instance, staff in high-end fashion stores are called consultants, they wear suits from their own range, they are styled, wear expensive make-up, listen to trendy music – in short they represent a lifestyle that becomes part of the shopper's experience and aspirations. In other words, behaviour, action, language, dress, mannerisms and habits are expected to become brand expressions, producing one-dimensional puppets.

The case for strong brands is akin to a corporate culture redux. Whereas corporate culture evangelists promulgated that it was all about having the right culture, their contemporary brand equivalents seem to think the brand is everything. Hawking their nostrums around the organizational world, few problems, it seems, cannot be cured without recourse to a heavy dose of branding. On message, aligning the organization with the world it operates in, branding is a corporate elixir. Of course, it is not that simple. Strongly branded organizations have featured among the most spectacular corporate collapses in recent history. Enron is a classic example. Jeff Skilling (CEO), Ken Lay (Chairman) and Andy Fastow (CFO) presided over a brand that was impeccable in its adherence to the principles of branding. It was one of the most admired US companies, routinely winning *Fortune* magazine's prestigious 'Most innovative company of the year'. Wall Street analysts bought into the brand, Arthur Andersen signed off on the books, Gary Hamel, the self-styled strategy guru, wrote a book heaping paeans of praise on Enron, and the Harvard Business School produced no less than 13 case studies on the organization. It was a darling of Wall Street and seen as a blueprint for the corporation of the future. Or at least this was how it was branded. But behind the rhetoric and the carefully choreographed imagery were accounting frauds, corruption and criminality, which branding had helped disguise.

In *1984*, George Orwell's classic dystopian view of the future, the truth was constantly rewritten (newspeak), organizations said one thing, but believed another (double-think), and the richness of expression was removed from language, which became a bland form for communicating limited messages (ingsoc). There are many parallels with branding.

Branding seeks to produce a universal sign that signifies not so much the thing that it might be attached to but the hyperreality of all and any things that it might be attached to. The sign – the brand – becomes the real (Baudrillard, 1988: 166)

> that can be reproduced an indefinite number of times. It no longer has to be rational, since it is no longer measured against some ideal or negative instance. It is nothing more than operational. In fact, since it is no longer enveloped by an imaginary, it is no longer real at all. It is a hyperreal: the product of an irradiating synthesis of combinatory models in a hyperspace without atmosphere.

Ideally, the brand bears no relation to any reality whatsoever: it becomes its own pure simulacrum, something that one will find plenty of examples of in a perusal of magazines such as *Vogue*, where the brand placement in the advertisements can sometimes be more highly signified than the example of the product bearing its sign.

Branding is a response to what Baudrillard (1993: 32) refers to as 'bloatedness', where so 'many things have been produced and accumulated that they can never possible be all put to use …. So many messages and signals are produced and disseminated that they can never possibly all be read'. Branding helps us to handle this situation: we can ignore the bloatedness of choices and focus instead on the purity of the sign, seeking to be at one with those brands we choose to define us, or those brands that choose to define us.

Increasingly, as we consume brands, we consume nothing – at least according to Ritzer. Nothing refers to 'a social form that is generally centrally conceived, controlled, and comparatively devoid of distinctive or substantive content' (2004: 3). Nothing should be contrasted with something. Something is a 'social form that is generally indigenously conceived, controlled and comparatively rich in distinctive substantive content; a form is to a large degree substantively unique' (2004: 7). As he is at pains to express, his definition is not judgemental but merely descriptive. (His initial exemplar of nothing is the credit card.) Phenomena that fall towards the nothing end of the continua are largely devoid of individuality and specificity, while those that fall towards the something end are highly specific in terms of place, thinghood, persons and service; by contrast, phenomena that tend towards nothing are offered anywhere, for anything (non-things), by anyone (non-persons), and in such a way that they largely displace service elements onto the customer (non-services). Ritzer's argument is that what is increasingly being marketed and consumed, which is fuelling globalization, is the proliferation of generic and interchangeable goods and services that are suitably branded so as to be evident in the qualities of their offer as a brand identity – but this is a brand identity that lacks any specificity and embeddedness in place.

What is perhaps most worrying about a world of nothing, in which things are voraciously sought as props for identify, is that nothingness, which gains its meaning from the positional economy, is an escalator for consumption in the material economy. Hirsch (1976) distinguishes between the material and the positional economy. In the material economy Adam Smith's competitive forces may indeed produce more for everyone. With increased demand, wider markets, greater international divisions of labour and economies of scale the unit cost of goods will be lowered. But the positional economy is characterized by goods that Hirsch describes as 'social' – whose sociability becomes the very source of Ritzer's nothingness. Our enjoyment of a thing is affected by whether or not other people are consuming it as well. The key aspect of positional goods is that if everyone who wants them has them, they no longer enjoy the same value. Examples of positional goods would include Armani suits, Cartier watches, or BMW cars. Contemporary affluence in the material economy now means that more people can compete in the positional economy. But the cycle of status ascription has sped up enormously; today, in Hong Kong and Shanghai, people who a generation before were peasants can dress in the finest designer clothes that money can buy, but, of course, as soon as such designer items become widely distributed – or copied – they are no longer something so much as being on a rapid descent to becoming nothing. The globalization of nothing is driven by commercial dictates that speed up the cycle of fashionability, ensuring that more and more means less and less. It also means that more and more is consumed as the life cycle of things diminishes due to the requirements of fashion rather than the functionality of use. We consume more material goods and use more material resources simply to preserve our relative position on an escalator of consumption that only knows how to speed up. Hirsch argued that the rise of positional goods would limit growth, since by definition they had to be scarce. Yet people have proved ingenious at creating evermore sources of exclusivity. That is how the simultaneous movement of nothing being globalized and something being distinguished occurs. For as long as elites can maintain some things as 'positional goods' (Hirsch, 1976), they may mean something. But the time in which they mean this diminishes exponentially; hence nothing always threatens something. This is the paradox that branding always has to confront as a strategy. That is the whole point of luxury brands – the central message of the luxury industry is that it is exclusive, for the patricians, not for the plebeians and proletarians.

SUMMARY AND REVIEW

Departing from a shift towards an emerging paradigm in marketing theory away from a goods-dominant to service-dominant logic, we point out that a firm has to consider much more than the competitiveness of products; it has to understand the entire exchange and all related transactions involving the customer. Such perception has a number of significant implications for strategic management. Most importantly it emphasizes the value of truly understanding what customers need and affects how organizations communicate with and relate to their customers.

We then showed how insight about current and potential customer markets could be derived from the three-step concept of segmentation, targeting and positioning. First, segmentation is an approach to explore the customer base and properly understand the underlying needs of and benefits sought by customers. Organizations are generally well advised to investigate

in great detail if customer needs are being met or have not yet been fulfilled. Such analysis often presents an opportunity for the firm to develop a competitive advantage. Second, targeting a market segment denotes the managers' process of deciding whether a market segment should be pursued or not. Targeting involves a thorough financial analysis and test of potential profitability. Third, we show how positioning deals with implementing a strategy by placing an offer so that in the customer's mind it is clearly distinguishable from competitive offers. We also considered the fact that in this age of global warming and climate crisis people's demand preferences may be undergoing significant shifts. We looked at how managing the customer relationship is another important driver for creating a sustainable competitive advantage.

The brand is seen increasingly as a strategic vehicle that is used to shape and direct the organization. The brand seeks to capture and articulate an organization's values. As such it represents its identity and encapsulates what it promises to deliver to markets and employees. In fact, the power of branding lies in its two complementary faces: one is focused on the external world where it manages the relationship between the organization and its consumers and stakeholders. The second face of branding is focused on the internal organization – its identity – where it promises an alignment between strategy, identity and culture. The concept of the brand allows us to consider internal realities and external environments at the same time and address them within a coherent framework. In markets in which products are increasingly commoditized the brand is the key differentiating mechanism: the difference between a branded product and a no-name or home-brand commodity is more often than not nothing but the image that the potential buyer has in their mind. Hence, building strong brands becomes a strategic imperative: after all, what people buy are brands, not just functional products or streamlined services.

Overall, the concepts and ideas of strategic marketing and branding help the strategist identify customers and what they really want; find profitable market segments, reliable distribution channels, and a unique positioning for the company and its products or services; achieve an alignment of products and corporate brands; and develop valuable brand equity. All such considerations have important implications for what marketers call the marketing mix – that is, the definition of products/service characteristics and distribution, promotion and pricing strategies. There are critical corollaries of the movement towards becoming a brand society: the ethical implications of such moves for both consumers and employees need to be considered in any analysis of strategy.

EXERCISES

1   Having read this chapter you should be able to say in your own words what the following key terms mean:

- Product marketing perspective
- Institutional marketing perspective
- Functional marketing perspective
- Marketing strategy
- Service-dominant logic
- Segmentation
- Targeting
- Positioning
- Customer relationship marketing
- Customer lifetime value
- Brand-driven strategy
- Internal branding
- Image
- Reputation
- Brand alignment
- Potentially dysfunctional effects of branding
- Incorporation
- Disciplining the brand
- Positioning the brand
- Anticipating resistance to the brand
- Brand autonomy
- Positional goods
- Nothing as opposed to something.

2   How might we differentiate strategic groups within the airline industry?

3   What are the factors that make it more difficult to achieve a competitive advantage within a strategic group rather than outside?

4   Why do firms choose to position themselves within a strategic group even though competition is usually fierce?

5   Who are the most influential protagonists of the emergent view on brand-driven strategy and how do their ideas differ from other strategy schools?

6   According to the brand perspective, what are the means by which strategists can influence the organization?

7   According to Cindy Carpenter, Executive Director of Human Resources and Marketing at the law firm Corrs, branding is the key to managing strategically. How does she characterize the task of the strategist? (See www.strategytube.net/)

ADDITIONAL RESOURCES

1   Our companion website is the best first stop for you to find a great deal of extra resources, free PDF versions of leading articles published in Sage journals, exercise, video and pod casts, team case studies and general questions and links to teamwork resources. Go to www.sagepub.co.uk/cleggstrategy

2   The website www.strategytube.net, the online resource that the authors produced in tandem with this book, is a great resource: look at the video Case Study 7 where Cindy Carpenter provides a unique insight into how a global legal firm aligns the corporate strategy with its organizational identity and marketing strategy; also watch Ruud Polet, the global brand manager of ING, tell how the brand shaped the overall strategy of ING – before it failed spectacularly in the GFC.

3   You can watch a video of the serial entrepreneur and self-styled brand-guru Richard Branson of Virgin at www.ted.com/speakers/richard_branson.html

WEB SECTION

Visit the *Strategy* companion website at www.sagepub.co.uk/cleggstrategy

1   There is a Service Dominant Logic homepage: http://www.sdlogic.net/; also you can watch Steve Vargo talking about it on YouTube: http://www.youtube.com/watch?v=VvbMcDu_TTY and http://www.youtube.com/watch?v=7CavVNkKtFE

2   There are a huge number of branding websites availabe – you can consult the following:

- http://www.brandidentityguru.com/brand_strategy.htm
- http://www.marketingmo.com/strategic-planning/brand-strategy/
- http://www.youtube.com/watch?v=XsS5HmzYfpg
- http://www.brandchannel.com/features_effect.asp?id=66

3   Ritzer's McDonaldization thesis is discussed at: http://www.youtube.com/watch?v=bh17s9DilZw

4   In his (2007) book *The Starbucks Experience: Principles for Turning Ordinary into Extraordinary*, McGraw-Hill, New York: Joseph A. Michelli illustrates how customer service and satisfaction, employee motivation and community involvement can build a company.

5   In *The Experience Economy*, Harvard Business Press, 1999, Joseph Pine and James Gilmore argue that the service economy is about to be superseded by what they coin the experience economy. The authors make a compelling case, and consider successful companies that are already packaging their offerings as experiences.

6   In *The Future of Competition: Co-Creating Unique Value with Customers*, Harvard Business School Press, 2004, the authors C. K. Prahalad and V. Ramaswamy discuss how consumers will seek to exercise their increasing influence in every part of the business system by co-creating value that is unique to the individual.

7   In the marketing classic *Positioning: The Battle for Your Mind*, McGraw-Hill, 2000, Al Ries and Jack Trout discuss the principles of competitive positioning, using the success and failure of real products as examples.

8   In the *Handbook of CRM: Achieving Excellence in Customer Management*, Butterworth-Heinemann, 2006, Adrian Payne provides a complete coverage of the key concepts of CRM.

LOOKING FOR A HIGHER MARK?

Reading and digesting these articles that are available free on the companion website www.sagepub.co.uk/cleggstrategy can help you gain a deeper understanding and, on the basis of that, a better grade:

1   D. Kärreman and A. Rylander's (2008) Managing Meaning through Branding: The Case of a Consulting Firm, *Organization Studies*, 29: 103–25, provides a critical case study of branding as management of meaning within an organization.

2   Majken Schultz and Mary-Jo Hatch's (2005) Building Theory from Practice, *Strategic Organization*, 3(3): 337-48, offers an inspiring account of how branding can build a bridge between the theoretical ambitions of researchers and the need to produce meaningful results for practice.

3   Vargo, S. L. and Lusch, R. F. (2008) Service-Dominant Logic: Continuing the Evolution, *Journal of the Academy of Marketing Science*, 36(1): 1–10.

4   Hess, R. L., Jr, Ganesan, S, and Klein, N. M. (2003) Service Failure and Recovery: The Impact of Relationship Factors on Customer Satisfaction, *Journal of the Academy of Marketing Science*, 31(2): 127–45.

5   Kumar, V. and Petersen, J. A. (2005) Using a Customer-Level Marketing Strategy to Enhance Firm Performance: A Review of Theoretical and Empirical Evidence, *Journal of the Academy of Marketing Science*, 33(4): 504–19.

Providing a service and managing the customer relationship – or how things can go wrong at TELESTAR

Jochen Schweitzer

Kevin Cable is one of many thousands of customers of the national Internet service provider (ISP) TELESTAR. A few months ago Kevin signed up for a 24-month cable broadband contract. When he recently moved from one suburb to another within his home town he experienced very poor service. Kevin decided to write a letter to the Director of TELESTAR's Customer Service Management, Melissa Mess, and complain about the service he had (not) received:

Dear Mrs Mess

It is with great disappointment that I feel obliged to write this letter to highlight the appalling service and operations that I experienced with TELESTAR. Since I have been experiencing different ISP services here, and in a range of other countries, I feel that I am in a position to judge the difference between an acceptable and unacceptable level of service provision.

In May I decided to move. I notified TELESTAR four weeks in advance about my intention to move and the new address. I used the TELESTAR online service and only a few days later the change of address was confirmed via email and I was informed that cable Internet would be available at the new address when I moved in. I was surprised and pleased that this seemed so easy. However, I moved house on 29 May only to find that there was no working cable Internet connection available at the new place.

Monday 1 June: When I called customer service I was told that there had to be something wrong with my setup or modem since the database clearly showed that cable Internet was connected and activated. A technician was scheduled to come out the next day to help me connect.

Tuesday 2 June: I took a half-day off work to wait for the technician. When Danny, the technician, arrived it took him only a few seconds to figure out that my new residence was not yet connected to the cable. In fact, he showed me the cable in the street and how it was connected to my neighbour's house but not mine. He told me that a new job would have to be scheduled to connect the house and that he could not complete the connection. I also learned that it was only possible to initiate this process when I called customer service and requested the service – he said that he could not initiate this process on my behalf. Danny couldn't be of further help that day. I called TELESTAR and was told that a new connection would not be necessary since the records clearly show that the house was connected and activated already. It took some time to convince the customer service representative that the database was incorrect. She finally agreed to schedule a new service in two days.

Wednesday 3 June: A day before the new appointment, a message from the TELESTAR contractor was left on my answering machine confirming that TELESTAR was sending a technician tomorrow – but she cited my old address. I immediately called customer service to reconfirm the correct address. The TELESTAR representative acknowledged the mix-up and confirmed that a technician would now come to my new address.

Thursday 4 June: I took off another half-day from work to be at home when the technician arrived. At about 9am I received a call from a technician who was waiting at my old address. I called TELESTAR customer service (again) to inform them (again) about the mix-up and asking what needed to be done to get a technician to the correct address. The customer service representative told me that there had been a mix-up with the addresses and that there is unfortunately no cable Internet available at my new address. She stated that there also seemed to be a glitch in the system since she couldn't fix my new address permanently. I was advised to call back after the long weekend and request a new appointment on the following Tuesday. Nothing could be done at the current

(Continued)

(Continued)

stage and I was extremely frustrated that I didn't have access to the Internet, I'd already missed two half-days of work and I had spent a number of hours on the phone with TELESTAR waiting in queues

Tuesday 9 June: After going through the phone voice menus for the fifth time, the TELESTAR representative who I dealt with that day advised: 'The cable is still in the street and needs to be connected to the house. We can send a technician who can assess the situation and quote how much it will cost to connect the house.' For the technician to come out and quote I was advised to pay approximately $180. At this point I considered ceasing the service contract. But since I have been with TELESTAR for only 10 of 24 months of the contractual agreement I would have to pay a contract fine of $15 per remaining month. This would add up to $210. When I asked for alternative solutions the customer service representative suggested the options of ADSL Internet or wireless Internet. Both alternatives would require me entering a new 24-month contract, which, at that stage, was the last thing I wanted. Plus, both options are more expensive and don't supply the Internet bandwidth that I require. Stuck with only one option (other than leaving the contract and paying the fine) I decided to trust that TELESTAR would rectify this problem quickly and ask for a technician to give the commercial quote for the connection of my house. Subsequently a new appointment was scheduled.

Wednesday 10 June: A day prior to the new appointment I received a call to confirm the date, time and location of the visit. The person who called cited my old address and since TELESTAR technical contractors only look after certain areas I was advised to call TELESTAR and inform them about the mix-up in addresses. At this stage I had already spent about four to five hours on the phone with customer service representatives. However, I called customer service again and was told that there are various accounts in my name and that there were in fact two appointments scheduled, one for the old address and for the new address. At least that meant that one technician would come to the correct address.

Thursday 11 June: I took a third half-day off work and waited at home for the technician to arrive. The technician never showed up during the five-hour period. I called customer service three times that afternoon. First, 2.5 hours after the beginning of the scheduled appointment to reconfirm the date and place. I was told that the technician had been booked and would arrive between 12 and 5pm. I called the second time at about 4pm, knowing that even if the technician arrived he would be unlikely to connect the cable that day. I was told that nothing could be done; I could not even get the contractors' mobile phone number to find out if I could consider attending a 5.15pm appointment after having waited for five hours at home. I finally called at 5.15pm – missing my appointment – and getting forwarded to the billing department, where no one knew how to deal with late technicians or replacement bookings. While being transferred back to technical support the line failed and I had to go through the process of selecting options in the computer-managed service line again. After another 30 minutes on hold, a friendly customer service representative asked me 'What is your address again? Is it number 24 or number 74?' It, hence, appears that a technician showed up at number 74 rather than number 24, which is my address. But instead of enquiring about the correct address the technician went elsewhere.

After agreeing to schedule yet another appointment for the following Saturday between 7am and 12pm, I requested to speak to a manager. I wanted to submit a formal complaint. I was on hold for over 30 minutes before I spoke to Russell who was the customer service manager on duty. Russell is well trained, very understanding and apologetic. While I explained the occurrence of events Russell took notes and filed a complaint. Russell promised to look after this case personally and make sure that I get connected within two days.

Saturday 13 June: By 11.45am no TELESTAR technician had shown up. I had been waiting since 7am. Shortly before I am about to call customer service I received a call from the technician who said he had been booked for a 12pm to 5pm appointment, not a 7am to 12pm appointment, as I had been told. I cancelled my plans for the afternoon and at about 12.30 pm two technicians showed up at my house. It took the technicians about one hour to do the job. I now have a working Internet connection but Russell has never contacted me again.

(Continued)

(Continued)

I am extremely unsatisfied with the customer service that I have experienced with TELESTAR over the last three weeks. Your advertisements and promises of a superior Internet service experience are quite removed from the reality of your service offering to customers. Your organization failed to provide adequate levels of service on so many occasions. I urgently advise you to get your service offering and value proposition right. This whole experience is a classic case study about a company that has taken its eye off servicing the customer. I await the courtesy of your prompt response and would be interested to understand whether you consider my recent experiences with TELESTAR as being acceptable.

Yours faithfully

Kevin Cable

Questions

1   What are the underlying customer needs and service expectations for Kevin Cable?

2   What do you think went wrong in Kevin Cable's case in terms of service provision and customer relationship management?

3   What can Melissa Mess and TELESTAR learn from Kevin's letter? What are some of the strategic implications?

4   How do you think Melissa should respond to Kevin's letter?

5   How would you go about restructuring TELESTAR in order to avoid future experiences such as Kevin's?

6

Strategy and Innovation

Differentiation, co-creation, creativity

LEARNING OBJECTIVES

By the end of this chapter you will be able to:

- Understand the importance of innovation for strategic management
- Analyse the obstacles to innovation
- Discuss organization design principles and practices to overcome obstacles
- Relate open innovation to open strategy
- Understand the principles of co-creation and design thinking and their relation to strategy

INTRODUCTION

Innovation is one of the most strategic of topics. Organizations that master it are on the fast track to achieving competitive advantage. As innovation expert Jane Marceau writes:

> Many economists now view technological innovation as an endogenous factor in economic growth and see companies' growth trajectories as increasingly affected by their organizations' innovation strategies and activities, more and more firms in high-income countries depend on continuous innovation to maintain their competitiveness. How and in which ways organizational forms and strategies selected can assist or retard innovation success is thus increasingly important to companies, especially those operating in international markets: this concern has generated an important literature. (2008: 670)

Innovation is often confused with or mistaken for invention, the discovery of something previously not known. Such a definition is hardly strategic: it would not allow us to grasp the innovation that accompanied whole ways of working and living attendant on innovative developments of existing products, for instance mobile phones, MP3 players or other digital devices. The phone and music players have been around since the nineteenth century; the mobile phone and the MP3 player are not new inventions that were discovered from scratch but they are innovations because they represent a new way of delivering existing products and services – phone calls and music – in ways that create value for the people using them and the companies who complement and manufacture them.

Porter (1996), as we have seen in Chapter 2, defines strategy as being different, or doing different things. To be different means finding a set of activities, services or products that will set you apart from your rivals; thus, innovation involves learning either how to make different things or how to make things differently. The first of these is product innovation, the second is process innovation:

- Product innovation means doing new things.
- Process innovation is about doing things differently.

Product and process innovations may be radical or incremental:

- Radical innovation fundamentally changes the products offered.
- Incremental innovation makes small and continuous improvements to an existing product.

Process innovation tends to be much more usual than product innovation – in part because, once significant investments have been made in ways of doing things, they tend to stay on the same track. Otherwise, sunk costs are liquidated, existing systems made redundant and well-honed competencies disabled.

Innovation is usually defined as the creation of novelty that provides economic value through the creation of new products and services. Less often, given the origins of a great deal of innovation scholarship in a concern with new products and, to a lesser extent, services, it may entail a focus on organizational changes, including the establishment of new work practices (Marceau, 2008: 670).

INNOVATION: PROCESS, PRODUCT AND PLATFORM

Cars are one instance of an everyday product that has been subject to continuous process innovation. The automobile has not changed fundamentally in over a hundred years but has been subject to many small and incremental improvements thereby differentiating a Model-T Ford from a contemporary popular automobile.

One of the reasons that the fundamental concept of a drive train, a vehicle and four wheels has been reproduced for so long is the lock-in that the automobile platform achieved early on. Gawer and Cusumano (2002) argue that successful firms do not simply develop new products and services and compete with others in open markets. Rather, leading firms establish a platform on which new products can emerge.

Platform leaders define the rules of the game, the size of the playing field and the entry conditions for players. Of course, to be able to control the platform is a powerful position that leads to a significant competitive advantage. Platforms are important arenas in which ideas can turn into marketable products and services. Platforms manage and control demand. They create 'lock-in' paths that make it hard for customers to change their minds and for competitors to enter the game. But platforms do not always have to be designed and border-patrolled by corporate organizations.

Some platforms emerge as part of a more general institutional environment. For instance, Rao (2009: 32) argues that one key element that made the car a culturally accepted object was reliability tests. In these tests cars competed against each other to demonstrate that they were trustworthy:

> Reliability contests were credible because each race was an event that could be interpreted as evidence of the dependability of cars by the public. Since reliability contests were public spectacles, they were emotionally charged events. Finally, reliability contests had 'narrative fidelity' because they combined the logic of testing with the practice of racing and created a compelling story.

In other words, these contests made the advantages of cars tangible and visible to a large audience; they created a familiarity with a new technology and produced stories people could relate to. Henry Ford had won one of those reliability contests in 1901 against the established producer Alexander Winton, which helped to legitimize the start-up of the Ford Motor Company two years later (Rao, 2009: 32). Rao's point is that market rebels, including those who organized reliability competitions, those who attend them and those who wrote about them extensively, created an institutional environment in which car sceptics could either be convinced that the car was a symbol of progress or become marginalized.

The institutional environment within which the invention of the car could become a commercial success did not stop with reliability contests. The car represented an entirely new way of being and being free – it promised mobility as a freedom rather than a constraint, because, unlike the train, one did not have to adapt to rigid timetables. John Urry (2007) argues that the car marked a radical departure from the train, which was the great nineteenth-century transport invention. The train was public and followed a time regime set by the railway companies: it disciplined its users in terms of their adhering to schedules, timetables, platform changes, etc. In contrast, the car embodied the opposite: it created and meant *freedom* (I can go where I want), *privacy* (the car as living room on wheels) and *individuality* (from choice of model to tuning or 'pimping' up the car). These were the real innovative qualities of the car from which Ford benefited and which manufacturers exploited, starting a social movement that paved the way for a society in which the car would take on the status of a cultural object – sometimes even a cult object.

A platform is defined as an evolving eco-system that is created from many interconnected pieces. Importantly, innovations have to build on other pieces to make sense to customers. Platform leaders are those companies which control or at least shape the structure of overarching systems architecture.

As well as requiring the cultural legitimacy to become institutionalized, the car required a huge infrastructure to become useful: roads, highway networks, petrol stations, repair workshops, public licensing authorities, police, a legal framework, insurance, and so on. In the twentieth century, entire cities were being modelled to accommodate the car – Los Angeles is the example most often quoted. Once such a system takes shape, innovations against the grain of the established ecology are hard to implement because so many players benefit from the status quo. The politics of the present situation prevail: in Los Angeles they were enough to stymie any public transport rapid-transit ideas for decades because of the entrenched power of the petroleum and related products lobby (Whitt, 1982). Thus, a platform producing innovation can lock in strategies to focus on the process and incremental innovation – which is the story of the automobile.

Even though we know that cars have a negative impact on the environment and make our cities dysfunctional, and that each and every year roads produce 1.2 million dead and more than 20–50 million injured people, at an estimated cost of $518 billion, the car is still *the* preferred means of transportation. The power and diffusion of the car involved a whole network of actors who had to collaborate to create the cultural and physical conditions to turn the 'devilish contraption' into a desired object and a cultural icon. Hence, the moral of the story is that successful innovation is more than just developing an idea: it needs the active shaping of a platform in which the idea can grow and gain traction.

It is not just the automobile that springs to mind as a ubiquitous platform: think of a new application for your iPhone or computer software as examples of complex new products that have to be able to communicate with existing technology. A good example of a platform leader is Microsoft Windows: its ubiquitous operating system forces friends and foes alike to engage with its technology (Gawer and Cusamano, 2002).

MINI CASE STUDY

Gordon Ramsay's food factory

Imagine a simple case where an established restaurant decided to change its business model. The core competencies of the restaurant would be in preparing fresh meals and providing excellent service. Its platform would be a celebrity chef and a network of providers who could be relied on for high-quality ingredients. Its offer of food would be quite different from that of a McDonald's operation whose platform would be McDonaldization through a standardization of routines, ingredients and offerings.

What happens when the two platforms get mixed up when a restaurant also decides to enter the market for home delivery meals? The focus and the core competencies of the newly established home delivery unit would be the logistics, speed and know-how about preparing meals that might sit for 30 minutes in a dish before they are consumed.

Trouble can arise when the two business models become confused – which is what happened to Gordon Ramsay. As the *Sunday Telegraph* of 19 April 2009 reported:

'Gordon Ramsay is serving his pub customers ready-meals prepared in a London 'food factory' – and sold with a mark-up of 586 per cent. Dishes such as pork belly, coq au vin, braised pig cheeks and orange and bitter chocolate tart are prepared in bulk and then transported in plastic bags by unmarked vans to several of his London restaurants .... Ramsay has said in the past: 'My food hell is any ready meal. It's so easy to prepare a quick meal using fresh produce ... but people still resort to ready meals that all taste exactly the same.' The food factory is owned

(Continued)

(Continued)

and operated by GR Logistics, the catering production arm of Ramsay's umbrella business, GR Holdings. (www.dailytelegraph.com.au/news/ramsay-food-cooked-in-factory/story-e6freuy9- 1225700066902, accessed 8 September 2009)

The established business of Gordon Ramsay restaurants and gastropubs might have become accustomed to smooth operations, a stable customer base, reliable technology and steady profits and this product innovation would certainly increase profits – a 586 percent mark-up should do that! It might have been better if Gordon Ramsay's management had cut off all ties between the old gastropubs and the new mass food production unit, with the latter becoming a spin-off – but then the gastropubs would not benefit as much as they did from the parent's resources, expertise and experience.

Question

1 Using what you have gleaned from reading this book, how would you have managed, strategically, to deliver a value proposition for the gastro pub? What should its platform be?

CREATIVE DESTRUCTION AND DISRUPTIVE TECHNOLOGIES

While platforms can enable innovation they can also impede it. Innovation is a tricky business: think of the stranglehold that Microsoft has achieved as an operating system and software provider for computers. How likely is it that Microsoft will be the source of the next radical innovation on the computing platform? It would first have to destroy its conception of what it is and what it does because the platform is so ubiquitous. It would have to be creative and destructive simultaneously.

Joseph Schumpeter (1975) argued that new ideas rarely come into being because firms innovate and transform themselves; rather, capitalism develops through a process of creative destruction.

Evolutionary economists focus on creative destruction, Schumpeter's key term (Freeman and Soete, 1979). As consumers favour new technologies and products, some firms will prosper whereas others, locked into past and diminishing preferences, will die. The key role in creative destruction is reserved for technological innovations that can outflank existing products, designs and processes. Over time these will form a dominant paradigm within which the processes of production become highly efficient and there seem to be few opportunities for radical innovations within the existing paradigm. These industries are most susceptible to creative destruction by incremental innovation, often from competitors elsewhere in the world which have been more attuned to improving the product that they are competing against.

Art is a fine field in which to study the effects of creative destruction, in terms of the struggles for dominance and the rapid succession of new ways of seeing forms of representation as art. Before such radically new ways of seeing the world, for example Cubism, which sought to capture process in static representation, could be widely accepted, there had to be a creative destruction of older ways of seeing – in this case, the conventions and styles of literal representation had to be destroyed, a process that prior schools of art, such as Impressionism, had already begun. While artists often enjoy the illusion of the pure pursuit of art for art's sake, art always concerns commerce because of the platform conditions of patrons, dealers and galleries constantly seeking the 'shock of the new'. Simply reproducing the art of the past is not creative, destructive or especially profitable.

> Schumpeter defined the notion of creative destruction as a 'process of industrial mutation that incessantly revolutionizes the economic structure *from within*, incessantly destroying the old one, incessantly creating a new one'.

Image 6.1 'Creative destruction or commerce?'

In the strategy literature, creative destruction is often framed around disruptive technologies. (In the photograph, for instance, some might regard the effects of the spray paint canister as a destructive technology, one that not only despoils a public space but also devalues art, while others might see it as a source of break-through innovation. In the appropriate context and with the appropriate treatment, what is constituted as graffiti becomes art. Ever since Marcel Duchamp exhibited a porcelain urinal in a gallery the boundaries between different fields of iconography have been strategically blurred: Duchamp's 'ready mades', Tracey Emin's unmade bed, Damien Hirst's dead cows and bejewelled skulls, and many other examples of conceptual art push the boundaries – profitably.)

Strategically speaking, innovation transformations lead to major challenges for existing companies and opportunities for new organizations. Horse carriage manufacturers did not evolve into automobile producers; typewriter manufacturers did not enter the computer industry; and established software firms were slow to capitalize on the Internet. IBM did not invent Microsoft, and Microsoft did not invent Google. In each case, innovation happened outside the boundaries of the established firm.

Francis et al. (2003) have argued that there is no 'winning formula' in history for creating innovation that has outlasted time: in Stone Age societies arrowheads were made of flint by so-called knappers; they ran out of business when the new technology of bronze casting was developed, and this technology was superseded by the art of making iron arrowheads; of course, with the invention of gunpowder, arrow making was outflanked, technologically, and arrow makers had to learn new technologies or trades.

In his influential (1997) book, Clayton M. Christensen analysed why successful organizations (such as Apple, IBM and Xerox) sometimes fail when they face change and innovation. Describing this failure as the innovator's dilemma, his provocative thesis is that it is not poor but good management that is the reason for failure:

Precisely *because* these firms listened to their customers, invested aggressively in new technologies that would provide their customers more and better products of the sort they wanted, and because they carefully studied market trends and systematically allocated investment capital to innovations that promised the best returns, they lost their position of leadership. (Christensen, 1997: xii)

Christensen regards good management as the reason for failure, which he explains in the following way. Most technologies are *sustaining technologies,* meaning that they improve the performance of existing products rather than replace them. Sustaining technologies do not produce innovation. Disruptive technologies, which change the frame of technology, are the key to innovation. Disruptive technologies result in worse product performance (at least in the short term) for existing products.

Compared with established products, new disruptive technologies often perform at a lower level of perfection. For instance, top-end decks, tone arms and immaculate-quality vinyl beat early CDs hands down for tonal warmth and resonance, but CDs did not scratch as easily and were easier to use, played more music and were portable. The CDs had characteristics valued by markets: they were smaller, and they were also easier and more convenient to use. Of course, CDs have had their day in the sun: downloads now beat CDs! (And, once again, the quality of the reproduction has suffered.)

Other examples of disruptive technologies are:

- The off-road motorbike manufactured by Honda and Kawasaki. Compared with sleek BMW and Harley Davidson machines, these models were primitive, but they could go places that the big bikes, with their smooth finish, could not.
- The desktop computer. This was a disruptive technology relative to the mainframe computers developed by IBM.

The problem for established companies is that generally they do not invest in disruptive technologies because they are simpler and cheaper and thus promise less profit, or they develop in fringe markets that are not important to big players and, after the market is big enough to create serious profits, it may be too costly or too late to join. Often, the established firm's best customers do not want, and cannot use, the new, disruptive technologies, and the potential customers of the new technology are unknown. Proven marketing tools and planning skills do not necessarily work under these conditions. Hence, in many industries such as pharmaceuticals, the strategy is to buy-in innovation from smaller start-up companies in areas such as biotechnology. The capital base of the established companies can be used to pick potential winners that have been innovated external to the company.

WHAT DO YOU MEAN?

Sources of disruption

Tidd and Bessant (2009: 32) discuss different sources of discontinuity and disruptive innovation:

- New markets: take the SMS industry that grew out of nowhere into a billion-dollar industry with a profit margin of up to 90 per cent. Originally, SMS was only added to mobile phones as a minor function. It was teenage kids who started using it to avoid the peak tariffs of mobile phone providers.
- New technologies: take the advent of the computer, which posed a serious challenge to

(Continued)

(Continued)

other office equipment manufacturers (typewriter producers, etc.).

● New political rules: take the example of the tobacco industry that has to adapt to a hostile environment that regulates prices, distribution, and promotion and lawsuits from private groups.

● New business models: take companies such as eBay or Amazon that reinvent whole industries around new ways of making money.

● New needs and behaviours: take the example of the rapidly growing number of people who are health conscious and use gyms, personal trainers, fitness equipment, health food, detox holidays and so on to keep their bodies and minds in shape.

● Unthinkable events: think of 9/11 and the emerging security industry. Through the terrorist attack, a whole new business sector has taken shape. Naomi Klein's latest (2007) book on disaster capitalism critically scrutinizes this sector.

Phillips and her colleagues (2006) argue that in 'the steady state' (when 'doing what we do, just better'

is fine) good business practice will lead to innovation. This good practice includes:

● Systematic processes for progressing new ideas.
● Cross-functional teams.
● Continuous learning cycles.
● Good project management structures.

However, in discontinuous innovation, these good practices will lead to bad results. Rather, in 'discontinuous conditions' Phillips et al. (2006: 181) recommend:

● High tolerance for ambiguity as rules only emerge over time.
● Strategies need to be emergent and the organization needs to adapt and learn quickly.
● The culture should support and encourage curiosity-driven behaviour.
● Risk taking and tolerance of (fast) failures has to be high.
● Weak ties and peripheral vision are important.

THEORIZING INNOVATION

Rational discontinuities

Evolutionary economists view innovation as a result of discontinuous changes in the firm or environment. Often these changes are seen in terms of technology. New technologies emerge that allow firms to create new products: think of all the products that have been spawned by optical scanning devices, such as CD players. Xerox initially developed these in Palo Alto, California. Chesbrough (2006) analysed the value of Xerox and its spin-offs. Over the decades, Xerox's Palo Alto Research Center (known as PARC) delivered breakthrough innovations, such as important parts of the personal computer, the graphical user interface, document management software, and so on.

Most of the technologies that PARC developed were never commercialized inside Xerox. Rather, what absorbed user-interface design technology, back then, was a young start-up called Apple, and the Bravo word processor provided what became better known as Microsoft. Other companies, such as Adobe, were directly spun out of PARC.

Why did Xerox let these valuable ideas walk out of its research lab? Chesbrough (2006) argues that Xerox simply did not see the value of the technologies inside its own company. Of course, in hindsight it is easy to be smarter. At the time, though, the soon-to-be-successful technologies appeared more as ugly ducklings than graceful swans. Inside Xerox they had little value. A new business idea that would turn over a couple of million dollars in the first couple of years did not contribute to the bottom line significantly enough to justify executive attention and interest. Outside, in a new start-up firm, things were different: think of garage entrepreneurs, such as Steve Jobs in Apple's early days, for whom a million dollars would be an amazing return on investment. In comparison, a firm such as Hewlett-Packard (HP) (another garage start-up) was by 2008 making about $10 billion. An additional million would have added 0.1per cent to the bottom line. Now imagine who would try harder to earn that million – HP or the entrepreneur in the garage? This is exactly the reason why these new ideas could develop a life of their own outside their established host company. And they did. The sum of the top 10 spin-offs that emerged out of PARC came to eclipse the value of Xerox by a factor of two (Chesbrough, 2006: 10).

Tidd and Bessant (2009) differentiate between a rationalist and an incremental design for innovation strategy. The rationalist approach is influenced by military thinking and is based on a linear model: first you have to scan the external and internal environment, decide on a course of action summarized in a plan, and then implement that plan. A purely rationalist approach to innovation has severe limitations. The complexity of the external and internal environments is so high that it is hardly possible to develop a clear picture. Second, innovation is all about the future – but the rationalist approach takes the status quo as the starting point for its research. Hence, it is akin to driving forward while looking through the rear window. Obviously, this can cause serious trouble.

Following the traditional model of strategy development, goals are defined, pathways discussed and a plan for how to get where you want to be is crafted. Nowhere else in management is rationality as deeply embedded as it is in strategic planning.

March (1988) finds the planning literature not only dull and unimaginative but also bad for business. It keeps organizations in the grooves of success without their realizing that the groove is being outflanked, running out of track or getting lost. March suggested supplementing managerial rationality with a 'technology of foolishness', which is more likely to help detect interesting goals. He argues that every rational process of strategic decision-making assumes the pre-existence of a set of stable and consistent goals. March suggests that goals may sometimes change in interesting and, as he terms it, 'foolish' ways. Understanding that these goals change begs the question: how can we find new and interesting goals? Enter foolishness: 'Individuals and organizations need ways of doing things for which they have no good reason. Not always. Not usually, but sometimes. They need to act before they think' (1988: 259). Ambiguity, rapid change and uncertainty may make planning a somehow idle exercise.

In order to find new goals, one has to explore playfully and exploit circumstances and different avenues that do not lead anywhere – at first glance. 'Playfulness', according to March,

> is the deliberate, temporary relaxation of rules in order to explore the possibilities of alternative rules. … Playfulness allows experimentation. At the same time, it acknowledges reason. … A strict insistence on purpose, consistency, and rationality limits our ability to find new purposes. Play relaxes that insistence to allow us to act 'unintelligently' or 'irrationally', or 'foolishly' to explore alternative ideas of possible purposes. (1988: 261)

A high-velocity environment is characterized by 'rapid, discontinuous and simulta-neous change in demand, competitors, technology and regulation' (Wirtz et al., 2007: 297).

Small firms that are new start-ups based on a radically discontinuous idea are more likely to emerge in what Eisenhardt and Martin (2000), and more recently Wirtz and his colleagues (2007), have described as 'high-velocity environments'. Management facing a high-velocity environment has to be flexible and constantly innovative. In this high-velocity context the strategist's job is to ensure the organizations remains innovative. The essence is strategic change *and* strategic speed. Doz and Kosonen (2008) quote a former president from Nokia: 'Five to ten years ago, you would set your vision and strategy and then start following it. That does not work anymore. Now you have to be alert every day, week, and month to renew your strategy'.

In a high-velocity environment innovative strategy is not an event or a plan but a continuous process of being alert. Mintzberg (1989: 210) has observed that '[b]ecause the innovative organization must respond continuously to a complex, unpredictable environment, it cannot rely on deliberate strategy. In other words, it cannot predetermine precise patterns in its activities and then impose them on its work through some kind of formal planning process'. In a high-velocity environment, in which innovation is the best strategy, companies cannot simply rely on planning years ahead: they need experimentation to stay abreast of innovation.

Incremental discontinuities

Tidd and Bessant (2009) propose incremental design as a way of supplementing the problems of the rationalist approach. Because the world is complex and fast changing, the best way to engage in it is to deploy an incremental, step-by-step, or trial-and-error approach. Such an approach suggests small steps should be accompanied with frequent and quick feedback loops that constantly evaluate development.

The Japanese auto industry is a perfect case in point of incremental innovation: think of how it evolved over the postwar years from a perception of Japanese cars as 'Jap Crap' (which they were widely regarded as being when they first entered new markets) to possessing the quality edge that manufacturers such as Honda are now widely believed to enjoy. This edge was based on many small incremental process innovations that came from different workplace practices – closer links between R&D and production workers – and a key concern for quality. While Japanese companies copied US and European manufacturers, they also improved on their processes and products.

In the incremental approach, mistakes are seen as crucial learning opportunities. Rather than trying to avoid them, mistakes have to be made quickly and cheaply. Obviously, the incremental approach is not irrational: rather, facing a complex environment it can be seen as rational to abandon the Big Plan and substitute it with a more humble step-by-step approach, one that tolerates error and the occasional foolishness, in March's terms.

An example of foolish playfulness is the use of organizational improvisation. Kamoche and Cunha (2001: 96) define organizational improvisation as 'the conception of action as it unfolds, by an organization and/or its members, drawing on available material, cognitive, affective and social resources'. Improvisers dwell in the moment paying great attention to the subtleties of the ensemble while drawing on deep wellsprings of technique and knowledge.

The Harvard professor Rosabeth Moss Kanter (2002) has studied how pacesetter companies manage to stay ahead of the game. Her argument is that successful and innovative firms do not wait until they have developed big strategic plans that try to second-guess every possible uncertainty the future might hold. Rather, agile companies improvise: similar to March's technology of foolishness, Kanter (1992: 76) argues that firms need to act and experiment before they have a completely developed plan. They should be akin to a really creative jazz group than a well-polished orchestra following the score exactly and perfectly, such as Miles Davis's quintet. When he recorded the famous album *Kind of Blue*, he did not allow the musicians to rehearse beforehand but only create and improvise in the studio without any scores.

It is not just jazz artists such as Miles who can teach us a thing or two about strategic improvisation. One of the pioneers of strategic improvisation has been the Grateful Dead, the legendary rock band. Joshua Green (2010) notes how they pioneered ideas that are now par for the course in strategic management. Quoting the band's lyricist, John Perry Barlow, Green sees that the Dead early on had the emergent Internet economy figured before it existed:

> What people today are beginning to realise is what became obvious to us back then – the important correlation is the one between familiarity and value, not scarcity and value. Adam Smith taught that the scarcer you make something, the more valuable it becomes. In the physical world that works beautifully. But we couldn't regulate [taping] at our shows, and you can't online. The internet doesn't behave that way. But here's the thing: if I give my song away to 20 people and they give it to 20 people, pretty soon everybody knows me, and my value as a creator is dramatically enhanced. That was the value proposition with the Dead. (2010: 2)

Strategic improvisation certainly worked for the Dead – they are widely recognized as having one of the most loyal fan bases in contemporary music. And they built this on the basis of a highly flexible business model: a band democracy that incorporated the whole Dead crew, not just band members, with a revolving chair as well as making special efforts to reward loyal fans with good tickets. The Dead are often seen as throwbacks to 1960s' hippie culture and the indulgent purveyors of long meandering guitar solos – but perhaps there are some lessons to be learnt from them which have passed by more conventional observers. It is noteworthy that it is from music and musicians that business has learnt about strategic improvisation (see also Hill and Rifkin (2000) which also contains a chapter on the Dead).

Improvisation, as a 'just-in-time strategy' (Weick, 2001), might be a more suitable way of moving forward. As Weick (2001: 352) argues,

> just-in-time strategies are distinguished by less investment in front-end loading (try to anticipate everything that will happen or that you will need) and more investment in general knowledge, a large skill repertoire, the ability to do a quick study, trust in intuitions, and sophistication in cutting losses.

Such an improvisational approach to strategy-making understands that the rationality of foolishness might be better able to act and react more quickly than traditional planning.

WHICH ORGANIZATIONS INNOVATE BEST?

Some commentators argue that innovation comes from being a large organization; others suggest that most innovative ideas come from small, new businesses. The answer is probably that both are sources of innovation – but they do it differently, suggests Marceau (2008: 672).

Large organizations are able to build vast R&D capacities through the resources they command. Think of the huge laboratories maintained by the big pharmaceutical companies. However, such organizations can be notably risk averse, especially where radical innovation is concerned. Moreover, they operate in regulatory environments that militate against risk taking: pharmaceutical product innovation has to undergo years of clinical testing before regulatory authorities can approve it. One way that large, well-resourced organizations can innovate is by buying it in; they can simply take over innovative new and small firms in a merger or acquisition and thus incorporate innovations into their product line-up and innovators into

YOU CAN DOWNLOAD...

An article that shows how businesses can learn from music, namely Hatch, M. J. (1999) Exploring the Empty Spaces of Organizing: How Improvisational Jazz Helps Redescribe Organizational Structure, *Organization Studies*, 20: 75–100, which is available from the book's website at www.sagepub.co.uk/cleggstrategy

their organizations. They have the resources to be constantly scanning the environment for opportunities for acquisition or imitation.

The argument for small-firm innovation is simple: small, new, knowledge-based technology firms will be better able to take risks, which innovation always entails. Innovation is often easier to manage outside rather than inside established firms. As Pfeffer has argued, 'innovation and change in organizations requires more than the ability to solve technical or analytical problems. Innovation almost invariably threatens the status quo, and consequently, innovation is an inherently political activity' (1992: 7).

Porter (1996) suggests that innovation means doing things differently or doing different things, implying breaking with the past, with established routines and old habits which, of course, will rock the boat – and after a course is regained those who were at the helm might no longer be in charge. Hence, innovation is inherently political, even more so in established firms than new ones, where there are more vested interests at stake.

Small firms are often closer to their customers as they have to work harder to know them and provide what they want. Customers, along with suppliers and competitors, are the most important sources of learning for innovation. Close relations with customers, as end-users, can lower innovation risks, especially in service innovation. Dougherty (2006) notes that knowledge cannot be separated from the people who develop and hold it and that it is inextricably interlinked with practices and routines. This is especially the case in services firms; services are meant to solve clients' problems, meaning that the service provider has to develop a deep understanding of the client's organization, and align its own capabilities to match the current and future problems of the client. While a company such as Apple can choose suppliers for innovative products, a services firm cannot simply decide to offer new solutions. It has to develop internal capabilities, its knowledge base and practices that support learning, especially from customers, as well as engage in scanning the environment for opportunities.

YOU CAN DOWNLOAD...

Deborah Dougherty's (2004) Organizing Practices in Services: Capturing Practice-based Knowledge for Innovation, *Strategic Organization*, 2(1): 35–64, from the book's website at www sagepub. co.uk/cleggstrategy

DESIGNING ORGANIZATIONS FOR INNOVATION

Creativity and design thinking

Nobel Laureate Herbert Simon suggests focusing on the processes that we deploy to *design* the artificial world in which we live: 'Engineering, medicine, business, architecture and painting are concerned not with the necessary but with the contingent – not with how things are but with how they might be – in short, with design' (1969: xii). Quite literally, we design interfaces through which we interact with the world. What we see, how we see it and how we can see things in an innovative way depends on the design of our interfaces.

Based on these ideas from Simon, design thinking has started to develop as a concept in management (e.g. Boland and Collopy, 2004; Verganti, 2006; Beckman and Barry, 2007). In recent years, business schools all over the world have started to offer courses in design thinking. Examples include Design Thinking and Business Innovation at the University of St Gallen, Switzerland, Business Design Thinking at the Rotman School of Management, Toronto, and the Business & Design Lab at the University of Gothenburg, Sweden. Even management gurus such as Tom Peters (2005) have discovered 'design' as a concept to rethink

YOU CAN DOWNLOAD...

Mie Augier and Saras D. Sarasvathy's (2004) Integrating Evolution, Cognition and Design: Extending Simonian Perspectives to Strategic Organization, *Strategic Organization*, 2(2): 169–204, from the book's website at www. sagepub.co.uk/cleggstrategy how companies craft strategies and innovate. The assumption behind design thinking is that companies can learn from creative design practices such as those of architect Frank Gehry (see Yoo et al., 2006).

Design firms offer individual, customized products that are complex and not only solve a problem but also provide an experience. Learning from the design project with Frank Gehry for their new business school, the Weatherhead School of Management at Case Western Reserve University, Boland and Callopy (2004) introduced the notion of design attitude. This is characterized by the search for alternatives. In contrast, what most current business schools teach, and most executives enact, is a decision attitude that focuses on making the right choices. Strategy, Porter (1996) reminds us, is about tough choices. It is about analysing the environment. It is about scrutinizing internal resources. But it spends little time on imagining possible futures. A design attitude does exactly that: it focuses on developing alternatives. This is what Boland and Callopy (2004) observed during the design process of their new school: the designers questioned what learning and teaching was, they wondered why academics worked in offices, and why the university was organized in schools and faculties. These disarmingly and ostensibly simple questions are, in reality, complex and deep – and design thinking is a way to deal with those fundamental questions.

In our context, we can understand design thinking as a new way of combining innovation and strategy. Tim Brown, CEO of the innovation and design firm IDEO, defines design thinking as innovation that is 'powered by a thorough understanding, through direct observation, of what people want and need in their lives and what they like or dislike about the way particular products are made, packaged, marketed, sold, and supported' (Brown, 2008: 86). The promise behind design thinking is that designers routinely develop new ideas and innovate. Applying the principles of their thinking to management could yield a competitive advantage for organizations that fight the innovator's dilemma.

MINI CASE STUDY

How creativity becomes a strategy at Pixar (Catmull, 2008)

Pixar is one of the world's leading animation studios and has produced blockbusters including *Monsters Inc, The Incredibles, Toy Story, Finding Nemo* and, most recently, *WALL-E*. In 2006, the Disney Animation Studios bought Pixar for $7.4 billion. For the ongoing success of Pixar, creativity is the key. How does its president, Ed Catmull, understand creativity? And how does he manage it? First of all, Catmull explains that every stage of the film production is creative. The process starts with what he calls 'the high concept': this represents the master idea of the film. But the four to five years that

are needed to make the 'high concept' work are just as important. Think of an animated film: every scene, every detail in the background, every movement of the characters, every sound-bit needs to be designed. The 200–250 people that work on an animation film quite literally make up the story as they go and make hundreds of little decisions along the way. Hence, Catmull (2008: 3) explains 'creativity must be present at every level of every artistic and technical part of the organization'.

He argues that people are the key to retain the creative edge. He also argues for the 'primacy of people over ideas': if you give a good idea to a mediocre team, they will screw it up; but if you give a mediocre idea to a good team, they will make it work, he suggests. Consequently, managing creativity means managing people. Catmull defines the five principles that helped him manage innovation:

(Continued)

(Continued)

- First, the key is empowering people and giving them ownership over the process. Rather than having a development team that does the brainstorming, and an implementation team that does the doing, the boundaries between origination and implementation are blurred.

- Second, Pixar has a peer culture where people show each other their unfinished work frequently. Rather than being embarrassed about potential mistakes, they help each other develop their ideas.

- Third, Pixar staff are encouraged to talk to anyone they choose to solve a problem. This means people do not have to ask management for permission to get feedback or ideas for their projects.

- Fourth, Pixar has created the Pixar University, where people learn and share knowledge.

- Finally, Pixar uses every project as a springboard to make the next one better. Providing a safe environment in which people speak their minds, the team dissects past projects and talks about the good and the bad things that happened.

Strategy, we argue, is linked to innovation and creativity. Most organizations do not produce animation films, but they do deliver everyday products, services and experiences for their clients and stakeholders. Your university might have a mission statement ('the high concept') but the lecturers, the IT infrastructure, the classrooms, and so on, actually produce your experience of the service and ultimately determine its value. Seeing it this way, should every organization not adopt Pixar's advice?

Question

1 What and how could your organization learn from Pixar?

How does design thinking unfold? According to Brown (2008), it is less an orderly step-by-step process than a journey through three different spaces. First, one needs to understand the motivation behind the search for a solution. Second, ideation collects ideas for the process of creating, developing and testing ideas. Finally, in the implementation phase, the journey to markets is mapped out. Importantly, successful outcomes rely on a movement between these spaces, especially the first and second spaces.

Tim Brown explains how the bicycle component producer Shimano developed a new strategy through design thinking. While sales in the United States were declining, Shimano needed to develop a new strategy to increase its business. IDEO applied the principles of design thinking to solve the problem. First, IDEO researchers went out and asked some of the 90 per cent of people in the United States who did not ride a bike what kept them from doing so. Interestingly, most of them had very happy childhood memories of riding bikes, but felt uncomfortable about buying a bike in a store where only professionals seem to go, who paid a lot of money, had to deal with a complicated set-up, and endangered their physical safety on the streets. These insights into motivations came from outside of Shimano's core customer base (the 10 per cent committed bicyclists) and allowed it to reimagine a new bicycling experience – an experience that IDEO labelled 'coasting'. Coasting is done on very simple bikes, with no cables, a back-pedalling brake and a mini computer that automatically chooses the best of the three built-in gears. The bike would be comfortable, easy to ride and low in maintenance. But IDEO went further than that: it also developed a retail strategy and reinvented the consumer experience as non-threatening and fun. Together with local governments, IDEO picked safe places to ride and launched a PR campaign for bike riding. The secret to success, according to Tim Brown, is a human-centred approach that focuses on people's needs.

MINI CASE STUDY

Serious play as strategy

Johan Roos, Bart Victor and Matt Statler (2004) report on how they have used LEGO bricks as tools to make the strategy process more creative and holistic. Their core assumption is that the strategy process has effects on the content generated. In other words, the way strategists talk to each other, the tools they use to visualize their ideas, and the metaphors they deploy to express themselves all shape the content of the strategy. Building on this idea, Roos and his colleagues asked managers to play with LEGO bricks and quite literally build what they perceived as challenging and threatening. The results of their study suggest that 'serious play' integrates cognitive dimensions with emotional and social experiences. Rather than PowerPoint presentations, group workshops and flip-charts, playing with LEGO stimulated people to build their ideas, discuss with colleagues how to build the future, and have a lot of fun while doing so. Roos et al. (2004: 556) argue that play was important because it '(1) incorporates the cognitive, social, and emotional dimensions … and (2) remains intentionally open to emergent outcomes without seeking intentionally to produce them'.

Questions

1 Think about your experiences as a member of organizations – how often has play been encouraged and been productive?
2 Why do you think this is?
3 What are the consequences?

Building on design thinking, a design perspective focuses on the interaction of theory and practice in design (Romme, 2003; Romme and Endenburg, 2006). Organization theorist Deborah Dougherty, an innovation specialist (see Dougherty, 2006), has developed a 'design science' framework identifying three properties of a large and complex innovative organization: fluidity, integrity and energy:

- *Fluidity*, according to Dougherty, refers to ongoing, dynamic adaptations in product teams, among businesses, and within and across technologies and other capabilities. Fluid organizations will be more loosely rather than tightly coupled. They need to be because as Danneels (2002) shows, innovations not only draw on but also develop existing organization competencies. New technologies open up previously unthought options; changes in customer expectations privilege different aspects of performance. Innovations must open up prior decision and routines, must make issues out of what were previously non-issues, if organizations are to realize value. As Dougherty (2006) stresses, an innovative organization is not a bureaucratic organization.

- *Integrity* means that an organization prizes integration both as a principle structuring thought and action and as an outcome of that thought and action. Product innovation integrates functions because capabilities in technology, manufacturing, marketing, sales, IT (and so on) need to be aligned if innovation is to be organizationally diffused in its effects. Silos restrict alignment, confining innovations to segments. Dougherty (2008: 419) notes Clark and Fujimoto's (1991) argument that firms compete on the 'consistency between the structure and function of the product (i.e. parts fit well, components work well together) and how well a product's function, structure, and semantics fit the customer's objectives, values, production system, and use pattern'.

- *Energy* means that innovative organizations need continually to energize, enable and motivate people (Amabile and Conti, 1999). Energy is built from power resources, such as information, credibility and alliances (Kanter, 1988), and meaning making (Dougherty and Hardy, 1996). Innovating workers are autonomous workers: not under strict command and control (Damanpour, 1991), they have the opportunity to participate in strategic conversations (Westley, 1990) that energize the organization. Innovation means anticipating problems and constraints and adapting specialized knowledge to those problems that occur *in situ* – not just those that can be solved in theory.

These three core concepts can be thought of in terms of how they relate to both constraining and enabling factors.

Constraining organizational fluidity are the well-known effects of bounded rationality, as well as the fact that a great deal of organization change occurs more at the population level than intra-organizationally (new entrants on the back of new technologies) and the fact that so much of what organizations do is institutionalized – and to change that which is institutionalized threatens legitimacy. There are factors that can enable fluidity, however. The more the person's practical consciousness (formed not through the disciplines of their employment but from their extensive everyday knowledge) is oriented in organizations, the more creative they can be. They can improvise, using whatever comes to hand, to navigate a strategic path (Mintzberg and McHugh, 1985; Barney, 1986; Hutchins, 1991).

Integrity can also be conceptualized in terms of both constraining and enabling elements. Constraining innovation is the assumption that because innovation is risky, costly and requires innovation specialists, it should be kept strategically separate from more routine activities; because the coordination of these separate units is difficult and costly, businesses should be separated into congruent units, with innovation carried out in new project-based organizations. The most energized organizations will be those that most empower their members – through, perhaps, equal rights to returns on innovation through co-ownership; through collective democracy in decision-making (if the organization is small enough for direct democracy to work – usually no more than a handful of people); or through profit-sharing bonus schemes, for instance.

It is more difficult to manage innovation in larger organizations. In a series of papers, O'Reilly and Tuschman (2004) developed the idea of the **ambidextrous organization** as a device for managing innovation.

The concept of the ambidextrous organization breaks with conventional management practices. Van de Ven and his colleagues (1999: 65) found that 'managers cannot control innovation success, only its odds. This principle implies that a fundamental change is needed in the control philosophy of conventional management practices'. The ambidextrous organization characterizes an entity that is capable of simultaneous incremental *and* revolutionary innovation. The rest of the organization – the non-innovating sub-unit – can continue doing what it does well, they suggest. Successful organizations are obviously good at what they do – so good indeed that they do not want to change. Success, it seems, breeds failure: the more successful an organization is, the more it adapts to its markets, the more it aligns its internal process, and the better its strategic fit with its environments – but the harder it will be to change and innovate. Success in the short term breeds failure in the long term.

Tuschman and O'Reilly (1996: 18) explain that as 'companies grow they develop systems and structures to handle the increased complexity of the work.

Ambidextrous organizations create specialist sub-units with unique processes, structures and cultures that are specifically intended to support early-stage innovation, comprising one or more innovation teams *within* the larger parent organization. They are set up to support the unique approaches, activities and behaviours required when launching a new business or product.

These structures and systems are interlinked so that proposed changes become more difficult, more costly, and require more time to implement'.

For managers, the dynamics of innovation represent a huge strategic challenge. While they must increase the alignment and fit for short-term survival, periodically they will need also to destroy what has been created (Tuschman and O'Reilly, 1996). The strategic issue is: how can a firm be successful in the present and prepare for the future? By being ambidextrous, say Tuschman and O'Reilly, achieved through growing many small, autonomous units instead of one monstrous organization. These smaller, independent units are more agile and entrepreneurial than the parent company. Managers must create new business units to enable innovation so as not to distract existing managers and units (Christensen, 1997).

Enabling integrity draws on other organization theory logics; it suggests that emergence and minimal structuring should characterize the organization. Coordination should be through a repertoire of shared practices that function as 'seeding structures' around which they can identify and interact (Jarzabkowski, 2003). Projects, where teams dissolve and regroup, according to the dictates of the business, should be the dominant form for innovation. These enable project management tournaments to be conducted from which the next generation of senior executives can be recruited due to their success in managing the innovation battle.

Constraining energy are factors such as managers' beliefs that people are intrinsically lazy and opportunistic, keen to transact with guile, as economic theory puts it. To the extent that they believe this and create tight control structures around people and actions, then it becomes a self-fulfilling prophecy and will certainly not encourage innovation. From a structural perspective the answer is to change cultures, promote creativity, reward people for suggestions and innovation, and try to recruit innovative-oriented personalities. Focusing less on constraints and more on enabling factors leads to an emphasis on culture not as a specifically designed thing but to cultural practices that are embedded in everyday organizational life: how can people's everyday creativity be tapped in innovation? By making workplaces playful, social, enjoyable. Populate them with playful devices such as game tables, building blocks and drawing materials, and structure play time into work processes (Roos and Victor, 1999; Schrage, 2000). Innovation is not a solitary pursuit but a team sport.

The constraints perspective is drawn from a specific set of theories, as is the enabling perspective. The constraints approach derives from more structural, functional accounts of organizations while the enabling approach comes from theories that stress the action nature of organization life far more than they do the structures that constrain them. Designs for innovation should draw on both enabling and constraining perspectives on organizational design. To achieve fluidity, work should be defined and enacted as professional practices of innovation, where the constraints of situated, hands-on practice help keep people knowledgeable and build stable competencies from which change can evolve; from the enabling perspective we should realize that it is practices that drive behaviour, so the search should always be one for better practices. Integrity comes from organizing work into horizontal flows of innovation problem setting and solving.

The constraint of a common ground of coherent work makes coordination easier; different activities embedded in distinct enabling practices can flow together where there are guiding strategies within larger, loosely connected structures that possess stability and resilience. Finally, work can be energized by directly resourcing innovation. Resources feed energy but need to be controlled and structured in order to flow to the central innovation workers rather than becoming bargaining chips in endless turf wars (Buchanan and Badham, 2008).

WHAT DO YOU MEAN?

Organizations without and with ambidextrousness

General Motors, for a long time the biggest company in the world, was good at building big cars but was not ambidextrous:

● GM was actually so good at building big cars that it directed all its structures and systems to be able to exploit what it did well already and what it thought its consumers wanted. When markets changed, and it was making more money out of financing the purchase of its cars rather than building and selling them, it was impossible to change the systems and structures fast enough to catch up with the new trends for smaller cars and the collapse of the credit market in 2007 in the global financial crisis. Eventually, GM, once the proud flagship of US manufacturing, had to file for Chapter 11 and emerged from bankruptcy.

Whole industries can lack ambidextrousness but innovation can recover it:

● Take the Swiss watch industry: it dominated the market for mechanical timepieces, but was not immediately able to adjust to the challenges of the new quartz watches that were developed from the mid-1960s onwards. Then it developed the cheap, disposable and fashionable Swatch watches to catch up and compete in a segment that it had not foreseen. It won its market share back from cheap Asian digitals by the quality of its design and the economy of its production: the watches were attractive, youthful and fun, daring in design and aggressively priced, with high quality and innovative flair. They had high-tech features and a fashion and art design that changed rapidly with the seasons. Also, they used an innovative product design that lowered production costs: synthetic materials were used for the watchcases and new ultra sonic welding processes and assembly technology, which greatly reduced the number of components. Backed by the Swiss watch industry and guarantees, sold in specialist Swatch boutiques and displays, they became a cult item, with a clear product differentiation in the lines offered, such as Swatch irony – for the metal-cased watches – and Swatch Bijoux – a female-oriented jewellery line. To maintain youth appeal Swatch promotes and supports sports such as snowboarding and beach volleyball, as official timepieces. And as THESWISSCENTER'S BLOG[1] tells us, of 112 Swiss companies, Swatch comes top of the reputational list.

[1]http://theswisscenter.wordpress.com/2009/07/28/the-image-tracel/Accessed 28/06/2009

To design organizations for innovation means drawing on quite distinct design principles. Some will come from a structural perspective, stressing constraints on action; others will come from an action perspective and stress the importance of situated practices that would sometimes not seem so legitimate from a structural perspective. Organizational innovation needs designs that both constrain and enable simultaneously. (For more detail consult Dougherty, 2006.)

YOU CAN DOWNLOAD…

Deborah Dougherty's (2008) Bridging Social Constraint and Social Action to Design Organizations for Innovation, *Organization Studies*, 29(3): 415–34, from the book's website at www.sagepub.co.uk/cleggstratergy

INNOVATION ENVIRONMENTS

Institutional innovation and environments

It is sometimes suggested that it is foolish to copy if you want to innovate: the two processes seem counterintuitive to each other. However, in the literature of

Institutional entrepreneurs not only play the role of traditional entrepreneurs but also help establish new (and sometimes challenge old) institutions in the process of their activities. They do so by leveraging resources to create new institutions or to transform existing ones, according to Maguire, Hardy and Lawrence (2004: 657).

institutional theory the translation of one practice into another new one that creates a new field of enterprise is sometimes termed institutional entrepreneurship.

All organizations and their strategies occur within the context of an institutional environment in which different conceptions of what is normatively ordered and allowed will co-exist. Institutions structure what Clark (2000) refers to as organizational repertoires: the boundaries of what it is technically possible to do can always exceed those of what is normatively feasible. Organizations' institutional environments are 'characterized by the elaboration of rules and requirements to which individual organizations must conform if they are to receive support and legitimacy' (Scott, 1995: 132).

For Schumpeter (1975) entrepreneurship creates new market opportunities when gales of creative destruction transform economies and societies. To be successful entrepreneurial efforts have to gain legitimacy, if change is to be accepted; thus, entrepreneurs not only need to innovate new things, new goods and new services, but sometimes must also innovate new institutions.

An excellent example of how institutional entrepreneurship works in terms of strategy is provided by Munir and Phillips (2005) in their analysis of how, historically, Kodak created an institutional environment in which the late nineteenth-century technology of films and cameras made widespread commercial sense. Creating the technology was only part of the process; having got this new technology, there then had to be a three-fold programme of institutional entrepreneurship in order strategically to embed widespread use of the technology in the market. How was this done?

1　The roll-film camera had to be more than a technological breakthrough: it had to become useful. Kodak's strategy was to produce a great many texts – advertisements, articles and artefacts produced by the new technology in the public gaze. In this way the new technology became familiar and gained legitimacy. The key institution to which it was attached was the vacation and the extension of the eye of the tourist away from the immediate moment to the personal artefacts contained in photographs that positioned them as subjects at the centre of the vacation experience.

2　Photography was made a family pastime – anyone could use the camera because Kodak made it easy for them by loading, unloading and developing the film. Cameras were designed and made to appeal to different market segments: some were 'lady-like' and 'pretty', for instance, while others were much more functional looking.

3　The idea and practice of keeping photo albums were cultivated. Initially, the camera was marketed as easy to use, as fun; once the basic idea was accepted, product differentiation occurred as different types of technical device offering different qualities of image were promoted. The strategy now was to create distinct market segments.

In the digital age one might think this history of Kodak is all 'old school' – but this would be a mistake. Think about it – was the digital age not created in a similar way a hundred years later?

Increasingly, innovation occurs through the co-creation of value through the concerted actions of several agencies (such as disc manufacturers, lens manufacturers, chip manufacturers, etc.) rather than through the actions of individual entrepreneurs or firms.

The co-creation of value

Management and organization theorists focus on processes of innovation not only within organizations but also at the inter-organizational level, especially around phenomena such as supply chains, networks and clusters.

YOU CAN DOWNLOAD…

Kamal Munir and Nelson Phillips' (2005) The Birth of the 'Kodak Moment': Institutional Entrepreneurship and the Adoption of New Technologies, *Organization Studies*, 26(11): 1665–687, from the book's website at www.sagepub.co.uk/cleggstrategy

Recent changes in the field of information and communication technology (ICT) suggest that innovation can neither be managed nor contained inside organizations. Rather, innovations that allow organizations to develop differentiation strategies co-evolve with the environment. The reasons for the shift to co-creation are three-fold, and all three reasons have to do with the rise of the Internet and ICT (Prahalad and Ramaswamy, 2004a):

1 Consumers are more connected than before: interest group communities and other social groupings connect users with each other globally. Social networking sites such as Facebook are a good example of this shift.

2 Consumers are more informed: higher connectivity means that information travels faster and more information is accessible to more people. If you want to find out about what the best mobile phone is you go online and find literally hundreds of communities where you can read honest discussions about the pros and cons of your objects of desire. Also, other groups, such as patients, can meet in online spaces and learn about their condition and new treatments.

3 Consumers feel more empowered and are more active. Think of communities such as Linux where people produce, share and discuss how to solve problems. In the language of the strategist, core competencies cannot be owned within the firm.

These ideas of co-creation are very different from traditional perspectives on strategy. These might put a premium on innovation because this would be the best strategy to ensure you are not drawn into a price war between commodities in a highly competitive consumer goods sector, for example. Elements of the ambidextrous organization or the dual-purpose organization might be used to generate strategy. The business might have 'foolishness' seminars or away-days to encourage people to think outside the box. But the fundamental premise of the firm's strategizing would be that it is your firm that creates value and that consumers pay to enjoy what you have produced. The firm is the locus of active production; what happens outside is passive consumption. Creativity and innovation are happening inside the firm, while consumers burn up products and services. In short, value creation is company-centric.

How realistic is this company-centric view? It is not likely that Google will employ the best programmers in the world. At the beginning, the open culture, the fact that every employee can become a shareholder and the heroic David (Google) *vs* Goliath (Microsoft) struggle were a strong incentive for the best people to join Google. Today, Google is a much more bureaucratic organization and resembles more of a Goliath than a David. Hence, the best and brightest university graduates might rent their own garage and start up their own business – which is exactly what the Google founders did in the 1990s, and what Steve Jobs did with Apple when he faced a mighty IBM. The only way for companies to tap into the talent that is outside their boundaries is to open up their organization and interact with outsiders.

The strategist C. K. Prahalad and the marketer Venkat Ramaswamy have described a new phenomenon in their book *The Future of Competition*: *The Co-creation of Unique Value with Customers* (2004b). The point of departure of their thinking is to break with the old model that says firms create value unilaterally. Prahalad and Ramaswamy's idea of co-creation challenges the assumption that it is the firm that creates value. Instead, for them, innovation and value are created through the interaction between companies and their customers:

What is the net result of the changing role of the consumer? Companies can no longer act autonomously, designing products, developing production processes, crafting marketing messages, and controlling sales channels with little or no interference from consumers. Consumers now seek to exercise their influence in every part of the business system. Armed with new tools and dissatisfied with available choices, consumers want to interact with firms and thereby co-create value. The use of *interaction* as basis for co-creation is at the crux of our emerging reality (2004a: 4)

Collaboration beyond firm and industry boundaries and the engagement of consumers with internal production processes are some of the most debated new ideas in strategic innovation. Best-selling books such as *Wikinomics*, *Wisdom of Crowds* or *The Long Tail* make the case for a new era of ICT-driven collaboration between organizations and their external environments. In the words of Tapscott and Williams, the '[o]ld "plan and push economy" will give way to the new "engage and co-create economy"' (2006: 31).

Take the example of eBay whose strategy relies on creating interactions and transactions between people – and this idea has made it the second largest retailer in the world, with a turnover of $60 billion created among its 280 million customers in 2007.[1] Or think of Wikipedia, the online knowledge bank written by users. Its 75,000 active users generate almost 3 million entries in 260 different languages (and counting – we checked mid-2009). It attracts 65 million visitors per month. Wikipedia's strategy is to provide a genuine co-creation experience for its users. Now contrast its strategy with the traditional *Encyclopaedia Britannica*. In comparison, the *Encyclopaedia Britannica* offers some 80,000 articles. The most common argument against Wikipedia is its lack of accuracy. According to a study by the prestigious science journal *Nature*, a typical Wikipedia article contained four errors. On average, an article in *Encyclopaedia Britannica* contains three errors. Its main error is not commission but omission as Chris Anderson (2006) put it: it simply cannot keep up with the breadth and speed of new entries and improvements of old ones that Wikipedia's open-source model allows.

These innovative ways of organizing that are spearheaded by Wikipedia, eBay and others, it has been argued by some strategists greatly enamoured of the open-source movement, will 'eventually displace the traditional corporate structure as the economy's primary engine of wealth creation.' (Tapscott and Williams, 2006: 3). The consequences of this 'contribution revolution' (Cook, 2008), it has been suggested, are nothing short of revolutionary:

We are shifting from closed and hierarchical workplaces with rigid employment relationships to increasingly self-organized, distributed, and collaborative human capital networks that draw knowledge and resources from inside and outside the firm. (Tapscott and Williams, 2006: 240)

Management theory and practice has picked up some of these ideas. Theoretically, Zander and Zander (2005) have argued that customers should be regarded as strategic resources that can contribute to a company's growth. They base their argument on Penrose's (1959) notion of the 'insider track' suggesting that customers have deep knowledge and can contribute to problem solving.

---

[1] See the presentation at the 2008 Annual Meeting of Stockholders available at http://investor. ebay.com/index.cfm, accessed 25 August 2008.

WHAT DO YOU MEAN?

Co-creation at Procter & Gamble (Huston and Sakkab, 2006)

In their 2006 *Harvard Business Review* article, Procter & Gamble's Larry Huston, Vice President for Innovation and Knowledge, and Nabil Sakkab, the Senior Vice President for Corporate Research and Development, heralded a new era of collaboration and engagement based on co-creation.

P&G's open approach to innovation produces more than a third of its innovations and billions of dollars in revenue. For example, in 2004 P&G launched a new line of Pringles potato chips with pop culture images printed on them. Normally, P&G would have invested millions in technology to figure out how to create images in edible colours on fried potato chips. Instead, P&G wrote a brief and openly circulated it. A small bakery in Italy, run by a university professor, had actually developed a method of printing pictures on cakes. In collaboration, they quickly adapted the technology to be used on chips, and the new product hit the shelves (successfully) years earlier, and at a fraction of the development costs, than the traditional method would have allowed.

For P&G this was a long journey to arrive at an open model of co-creation for business strategy. Huston and Sakkab argue that 4–6 per cent annual growth (which equals $4 billion in the case of P&G) cannot come from inside the firm alone. They estimate that there are about 200 smart individuals out there for each of the 7500 in-house researchers they employ, totalling some 1.5 million potential innovators. To tap into their ingenuity, P&G had to change its culture from the notorious 'not invented here' attitude to 'proudly found elsewhere'. The boundaries between its in-house R&D team and the large number of external collaborators needed to be more permeable. P&G has labelled its approach 'connect and develop' – and it seems to work: R&D productivity was up by 60 per cent and the cost of innovation has fallen. The co-creation approach would not be possible without advanced ICT: websites such as www.yet2.com, www.innocentive.com, or www.yourencore.com allow global interaction between freelance researchers, retired scientists, inventive students and large corporations. Huston and Sakkab (2006: 66) are confident 'that connect and develop will become the dominant innovation model in the twenty-first century. For most companies ... the alternative invent-it-ourselves model is a sure path to diminishing returns'.

Open innovation and open strategy

In a recent *Academy of Management* Review article, Julian Birkinshaw, Gary Hamel and Michael J. Mol argued that management innovation is an important yet still relatively unexplored topic (2008; see also Hamel, 2006). Management innovation is the creation of a new management practice, process or structure that changes the state of the art. An example would be Taylor's scientific management, the divisional M-form, or teamwork: they are new ways of managing and organizing work.

If we were to think of a management innovation that rivalled these earlier examples, such as scientific management, it would probably be open-source innovation and its impact on strategic innovation inside organizations. Chesbrough (2006) talks about a paradigm shift from closed to open innovation. The paradigm of closed innovation assumes that successful innovation requires tight organizational control. According to this model, firms must create ideas, develop them, finance them and bring them all the way to market themselves. In return, they retain the intellectual property rights. Most approaches to strategy are based on a closed model of innovation. As Chesbrough and Appleyard (2007) argue, open innovation poses a challenge to strategy: strategy used to be about creating defendable positions against competitors, and constructing barriers around one's business model. Strategy usually is focused on what the firm owns and what it controls.

Models of open innovation do not follow the same rules. Applying Porter's framework to open innovation, Chesbrough and Appleyard suggest, will result in paradoxes: 'ownership, entry barriers, switching costs and intra-industry rivalry are of secondary importance in the genesis [of Linux]', they argue (2007: 62). Linux's ecosystem was worth a staggering $18 billion in 2006, yet its founders had ignored all of Porter's principles (Chesbrough and Appleyard, 2007: 61; see also Evans and Wolf, 2005). By 2008, estimates of Linux's value hit $25 billion, and it was forecast to be close to $40 billion by 2010.[2]

Open innovation is premised on allowing companies and multiple stakeholders to interact and co-create. Networks, eco systems and innovation communities become important strategic resources because they allow co-creation.

Chesbrough and Appleyard argue that organizations need not only to co-create but also to capture part of the value that is created. In other words, open innovation needs to enhance business value. The term open strategy describes this balance between creation and capture of value. Chesbrough and Appleyard (2007: 65–6) differentiate between the four 'open strategies' organizations can employ to benefit from open innovation:

1 *Deployment.* Innovation increases the user experience and user are willing to pay for the enhanced service. IBM, for instance, makes money from training and consulting on open-source software applications.

2 *Hybridization.* Firms invest in add-ons to products developed in the open and remain in control of the Intellectual Property of the add-on.

3 *Complement.* A firm sells a product or service that is related to the use of the open-source content. The example in case would be a mobile phone seller who benefits from free software for the mobile.

4 *Self-service.* In this model, the community develops a service for its own needs; no one monetizes its value.

For Chesbrough and Appleyard, all but the last model represent viable business models in an open-source environment. While self-service will produce value in general it will not produce a profit.

Not everyone agrees with Chesbrough and Appleyard's enthusiasm. Nicholas G. Carr (2007) argues that the open-source movement has severe limitations. Its benefit is based on the Easter egg hunt principle: the more children look for eggs, the sooner they will find all of them. This is an important characteristic of open source: it helps to de-bug programs and allows for lots of trial-and-error experiments. The downside is that not all problems are Easter egg hunting problems. In fact, as Carr argues, open source is based on three assumptions:

1 Participants do not have to coordinate their tasks closely.

2 Participants work for free, hence little is known about how efficiently resource allocation works in the open model.

3 Functioning open models such as Linux are not as democratic and open as they seem: Linux for instance has an inner core of programmers who safeguard the system. If there is no quality assurance, you might have to face the consequences: on Wikipedia, for instance, the entry on Homer Simpson is longer than the one on the Greek writer Homer. Homer Simpson may be a cool dude but Homer the Greek has been around a lot longer! The two Homers beg the question of how smart crowds really are.

YOU CAN DOWNLOAD...

Raymond E. Miles, Charles C. Snow and Grant Miles' (2007) The Ideology of Innovation, *Strategic Organization*, 5(4): 423–35 and take a critical look at the established (closed) models of innovation and their ideological underpinnings, on the book's website at www. sagepub.co.uk/cleggstrategy

---

[2]http://lwn.net/Articles/222336/, accessed 30 July 2009.

National innovation systems, learning networks and clusters

Co-creation at the firm level needs to be supplemented by co-creation in the national environment, suggest some researchers. The likelihood of innovation emerging increases when there is an appropriate national innovation system in place.

It is the specific configuration of relations and institutions that is important in framing the national innovation system. What matters are institutions such as the legal system, especially concerning the ownership and control of intellectual property relations, how national education and training systems are configured, the industry structure of key, competitor and surrounding organizations, the efficiency of capital markets in providing venture capital for innovation, the development of national innovation policies related to science and technology and the crucial role of universities and research centres, as well as national innovation policies (OECD, 1997) related to investments, taxation and other determinants of the 'rules of the game' that shape both public and private sector decision-making (Nelson, 2005).

At a less macro level of analysis the notion of the learning network (Bessant and Tsekouras, 2001) has been introduced to focus on the development of industry clusters. In this concept, learning is understood as a cyclical and social process of experimenting, experiencing, reflecting and conceptualizing. Clusters of firms can be found in examples such as Silicon Valley and its high-tech computer industry, Bangalore in India for outsourcing, furniture design in northern Italy, or the Midlands in the UK as home to the so-called Motorsport Valley, where many Formula one teams and crucial suppliers have development facilities. Such clusters are critical for innovation as they enable learning processes that transcend the capabilities of an isolated firm. Bessant and Tsekouras (2001: 87) mention the following advantages from shared learning:

- Potential for learning and reflection from different perspectives.
- Shared experimentation can reduce cost risks.
- Shared experiences offer space for discussion and inquiry.
- Shared learning helps to see the big-picture issues (the forest, not the trees).
- Shared learning exposes intra-organizational cognitive maps and challenges business-as-usual through confrontation with other models and ways of doing things.

Whereas learning occurs in regional clusters as a consequence of product development, learning networks are formally set up with the purpose to increase knowledge (Bessant and Tsekouras, 2001). Examples of such learning networks include professional institutions, trade or supplier associations, collaborative labs (co-labs), communities of practice, and so on. Of course, the advent of the Internet and ICT is a massive catalyst in the development of such innovation networks.

Bessant et al. (2003) conducted a case study of the South African forestry industry. *Saligna*, a species of eucalyptus hardwood that was traditionally used for mining, was rediscovered as an environmentally sustainable raw material for the furniture industry. But in order to realize this opportunity, the whole value chain of the industry needed to learn and innovate. For instance, *Saligna* was different to work with and firms had to adapt their operations; furniture production requires consistent quality, which means the raw materials have to be improved;

National innovation systems are composed of different patterns of institutions and organizational relationships (Coriat and Weinstein, 2002).

new designs that were suitable for *Salinga* wood needed to be developed; and, finally, new markets from furniture to doors, industrial products and toys emerged with the new material and competencies (Bessant et al., 2005: 26).

Birkinshaw et al. (2007) argue that innovation networks evolve through the three steps of finding, forming and performing. The key challenges that firms face are two-fold: choosing the right partner (finding) and learning how to work with them (forming). Performing, the third step, follows if the first two have been completed successfully. Of course, this sounds easier than it is. Birkinshaw et al. (2007) remind us that finding the right partner organization can be as complicated as finding the right partner in life: Where to look for the right partner? How to limit the field of your search? How should you conduct due diligence on your partner without estranging them? Similarly, forming provides challenges, including how to build relationships, how open your partner might be, how willing to share, risk and explore. Key for the performance of the innovation network are the engagement of partners, trust and reciprocity across the network, a good understanding of one's own position within the network (as opposed to attempting to control it) and, finally, learning when to let go and set your partners (and yourself) free.

Open innovation networks, as we will discuss in the next section, represent the radicalized version of the inter-organizational, co-creative innovation approach.

INNOVATION EXPERIMENTS

Given that innovation poses a formidable challenge to organizations, researchers have studied how experiments can help to overcome inertia (e.g. Davenport, 2009). Govindarajan and Trimble (2005a) suggest 10 ways to design your strategic experiment:

1   Depart from what the parent company knows. Forgetting is important!
2   Leverage assets and capabilities from your parent. Borrowing is crucial too.
3   Do not simply extend your product portfolio, your geographical reach, or refine technology. A strategic experiment has to be more fundamental.
4   Target emerging and poorly defined industries. That is where opportunities are.
5   Launch your experiment only if there is no proven formula showing how to make profit.
6   The potential for growth must be high.
7   You will have to develop some new capabilities or knowledge.
8   The strategic experiment will stay unprofitable for a while and it will be costly.
9   You cannot be sure whether the experiment is successful or not, as feedback will be ambiguous. Success might be established after the fact.
10 Leaders of experiments are generalists who face many challenges, including uncertain markets, the uncertain value proposition of products, unproven technologies, and a hazy field of potential competitors or collaborators.

Govindarajan and Trimble (2005a; 2005b) describe an organization that makes the most out of existing opportunities and is open to new ideas as a *dual-purpose organization*:

- When the new business borrows a lot from the old, and keeps close to its experience, we are dealing with innovation within an existing business model.
- If the new business has to forget a lot from its past, and borrow very little from its parent company, it is a spin-off. In this case, the relation between old and new firm might be purely financial.
- The hardest combination is one where borrowing is high, and forgetting should also be high too.

The challenge of forgetting is three-fold:

- The new enterprise must forget some of the core business definition of the old parent and it has to break with the parent's identity, its culture and its sensemaking mechanisms.
- It must forget some of the competencies of its parent. In the new market, old competencies will hold back the new firm. New competencies have to be nurtured instead.
- The new unit cannot expect the same predictability that the parent unit's business enjoys. The new business is by definition risky and uncertain, hence setbacks and failures have to be expected – in fact they will be necessary to learn and improve.

SOCIAL INNOVATION

How can we solve the great challenges of our time – such as climate change, the radicalization of cultural identities, poverty, an ageing population and rapidly rising health care costs? There is no doubt that these challenges need to be addressed in innovative ways. But who could work on holistic, complex solutions for large-scale challenges? Governments and the public sector in general seem to be too thinly resourced and too organized in silos to be able to tackle these challenges. On the other hand, corporations, the drivers of much of innovation in the past two centuries, seem to be more concerned with ensuring the survival of their existing business models and annual (if not quarterly) returns for their shareholders. Neither markets nor government planning can provide a satisfying answer. How, then, can we tackle the big challenges of our time? Who will be the innovators to solve these problems?

One answer that is frequently mentioned in the corridors of power and community movements alike is *social innovation*. Robin Murray, Julie Caulier-Grice and Geoff Mulgan define social innovation in *The Open Book of Social Innovation* 'as new ideas (products, services and models) that simultaneously meet social needs and create new social relationships or collaborations. In other words, they are innovations that are both good for society *and* enhance society's capacity to act' (Murray et al., 2010: 3). A good example for social innovation is micro-finance: in poor regions development is often stifled through the lack of access to finance. In these regions, a small amount of money could go a long way. For big banks, offering credit to poor people is not an attractive business proposition: especially after the sub-prime fiasco and subsequent global financial crisis of 2007–9, they prefer customers with big incomes who use their credit cards frequently and pay back their mortgages on time. The Grameen Bank Project founded by Muhammad Yunus, who was awarded the Nobel Peace Prize in 2006, is a good example of micro-finance. For more details see the overview at http://en.wikipedia.org/wiki/Grameen_Bank.

Two emerging forces shape social innovation: on the one hand, technology as an enabler of social networking, so that people share ideas and solutions; on the after, a growing concern with what Murray et al. call the human dimension that becomes more important than systems and structures. How does social innovation work? Murray and his colleagues have devised a six-step process:

1　Prompts, inspirations and diagnoses. Every new idea starts with the perception of a problem or a crisis. In the first stage of social innovation, the problem is experienced, framed and turned into a question that tackles the root of the problem.

2　Proposals and ideas generation: Initial ideas are developed and the proposal discussed. Importantly, wide-ranging ideas are taken into account.

3　Prototyping and pilots. Talk is cheap – so ideas need to be tested in practice. Trial and error, prototyping and testing are means of refining ideas that cannot be substituted by armchair research. The motto is *fail often, learn quickly*!

4　Sustaining. This step includes the development of structures and sustainable income streams to ensure that the best ideas have a useful vehicle to travel. Resources, networks and practices need to be organized so that innovation can be carried forward.

5　Scaling and diffusion. Good ideas have to spread – hence the scaling up of solutions is key; this can happen formally through franchising or licensing, or, more informally, through inspiration and imitation.

6　Systemic change. The ultimate goal of social innovation. This involves change on a big scale driven by social movements, fuelled by new business models, structured by new organizational forms and regulated by new public institutions and laws.

In a world in which neither big government nor big business are being seen so much as solutions but problems, there will be increasing scope for social innovation to develop new strategies for tackling entrenched problems, empowering ordinary people in the process rather than making them either clients or customers in a wholly one-dimensional way.

SUMMARY AND REVIEW

Innovation strategy is a huge and still incomplete topic. As Marceau (2008: 673) notes, there is still no overall innovation theory. Elements are to be found in different disciplines such as economics, sociology, management and organization theory, and at different levels, including the firm, region, population of organizations, nation, industry, etc. The management of innovation within organizations and firms has been slowed by a penchant for one-sided interpretations, primarily from a constraining perspective, while the insights that might flow from a more enabling perspective, rooted in action rather than structural approaches, have been relatively neglected. It is evident that an adequate practice of innovation has to draw on both perspectives and in this chapter we have followed Dougherty (2008) in suggesting that a focus on fluidity, energy and integrity allows us to do so.

There is still a great deal of work to do not only in thinking about organization design and innovation, but also in conceptualizing how such a design articulates with broader questions about the innovation environment in policy, regional, industry and institutional terms.

EXERCISES

1   Having read this chapter you should be able to say in your own words what the following key terms mean:

   ● Innovation
   ● Creative destruction
   ● Ambidextrous organization
   ● Energy, fluidity and integrity
   ● Creative destruction
   ● Organizational design
   ● Networks
   ● Open innovation
   ● Co-creation
   ● Disruptive technologies.

2   How would you design an organization to be innovative?

3   What is creative destruction and what is its role in innovation?

4   What sorts of government policies should be a concern for innovation managers and why?

5   Look at Steve Shallhorn's video on www.strategytube.net. – What are the innovative strategies that Greenpeace is developing? What levels of analysis best capture these strategies? Why would they enact strategy at these levels?

ADDITIONAL RESOURCES

1   Our companion website is the best first stop for you to find a great deal of extra resources, free PDF versions of leading articles published in Sage journals, exercise, video and pod casts, team case studies and general questions and links to teamwork resources. Go to www.sagepub.co.uk/cleggstrategy

2   You can download *The Open Book of Social Innovation* for free at www.nesta.org.uk/publications/reports/assets/features/the_open_book_of_social_innovation. See also www.socialinnovator.info

3   A good journal to consult for thinking about innovation strategies is *Creativity and Innovation Management*. There are often articles in there that can be of practical value for innovation managers.

4   Another useful resource is Mark Dodgson's (2000) *Management of Technological Innovation*, Oxford: Oxford University Press, as well as the more playful book by M. Dodgson, D. Gann and A. Slater (2005) *Think, Play, Do: Technology, Innovation and Organization*, also published by Oxford University Press.

WEB SECTION

Visit the *Strategy* companion website at www.sagepub.co.uk/cleggstrategy

1   The online resource www.strategytube.net that the authors produced in tandem with this book is a great resource: look in particular at the Video Case Study 8 where Steve Shallhorn, from the highly innovative Greenpeace organization, talks about realism and change – Look especially at the 'study questions' for this case. They are designed to complement and extend this chapter.

2   There are a great many innovation websites: some good ones include government websites such as www.innovation.gov.au/Pages/default.aspx, which has a host of innovation resources on it that you can open from downloadable PDFs.

3   www.innovationtools.com/ also has a great many resources.

4   www.innovationexchange.com/ – where creativity is the currency – is a great resource as well.

5   www.metacafe.com/watch/yt-2UDBaDtwXfI/henry_chesbrough_open_innovation/Web is where you can watch a talk by innovation guru Henry Chesbrough.

6   Interested in the Grateful Dead? Then check out the Dead archive at www.library.ucsc.edu

LOOKING FOR A HIGHER MARK?

Reading and digesting these articles that are available free on the companion website www.sagepub.co.uk/cleggstrategy can help you gain deeper understanding and, on the basis of that, a better grade:

1   Miguel Pina e Cunha and Joao Vieira da Cunha (2008) Managing Improvisation in Cross Cultural Virtual Teams, *International Journal of Cross Cultural Management*, (1)2: 187–208.

2   M. J. Hatch (1999) Exploring the Empty Spaces of Organizing: How Improvisational Jazz Helps Redescribe Organizational Structure, *Organization Studies*, 20: 75–100.

3   Kamal Munir and Nelson Phillips (2005) The Birth of the 'Kodak Moment': Institutional Entrepreneurship and the Adoption of New Technologies, *Organization Studies*, 26(11):1665–87.

4   Deborah Dougherty (2004) Organizing Practices in Services: Capturing Practice-based Knowledge for Innovation, *Strategic Organization*, 2(1): 35–64.

5   Mie Augier and Saras D. Sarasvathy (2004) Integrating Evolution, Cognition and Design: Extending Simonian Perspectives to Strategic Organization, *Strategic Organization*, 2(2): 169–204.

6   Deborah Dougherty (2008) Bridging Social Constraint and Social Action to Design Organizations for Innovation, *Organization Studies*, 29(3): 415–34.

7   Raymond E. Miles, Charles C. Snow and Grant Miles (2007) The Ideology of Innovation, *Strategic Organization*, 5(4): 423–35, takes a critical look at the established (closed) models of innovation and their ideological underpinnings.

Cirque du Soleil

Martin Kornberger

Remember going to the circus? If 'yes', you're part of a minority. Over recent decades, parents and their children have increasingly preferred to entertain themselves with television shows, PlayStations, computer games, Disneyland-like theme parks, or simply shopping. The old-fashioned circus has therefore dropped down the list of favourites. The circus seemed to be a dying business, a remnant of an earlier age, before television and a concern for the welfare of animals, a reminder of pre-modern travelling tent, medicine and freak shows. Passé, smelly, composed of low-class, sad characters, all slowly going down the pan. Not a business to invest in. Yet, one Canadian company entered the circus business, despite its ailing syndromes: Cirque du Soleil. How did the circus manage to become hugely successful, despite its depressed industry co-players? What was the strategy that made it in 2009, on its 25th birthday, so successful?

Two strategy scholars from INSEAD, in France, W. Chan Kim and Renée Mauborgne (2005) argue that the secret to its success is the Cirque's ability to create a new, uncontested market space where growth is profitable and rapid. They call such new market space Blue Oceans. In contrast to Blue Oceans, Red Oceans are the old, competitive and unprofitable markets in which most companies are stuck. In these Red Oceans, firms largely offer similar products to the same pool of customers. Hence, competition moves inevitably towards a struggle to be a low-cost provider, leading to a downward spiral, where the cheapest provider will succeed. Blue Oceans, on the other hand, are those market spaces that do not yet exist. Think of 20 or 30 years ago – there was no eBay, no Google and no Amazon; no mobile phone industry to speak of; no digital cameras – the list is long. What these industries share is that they are all multi billion-dollar markets and that they came into existence reasonably recently. Firms that focused on these new, uncontested spaces were better off than firms that focused on existing markets. But how do you move into these new, uncontested spaces? The answer is: innovate!

Cirque du Soleil is a good example of innovation: from the beginning, it set out to 'reinvent the circus' (see Kim and Mauborgne, 2004: 77). It defined its mission as to 'to invoke the imagination, provoke the senses and evoke the emotions of people around the world'.[1] Rather than showcasing caged animals that are expensive to look after, that create considerable mess and smells, and were becoming increasingly a point of critique for concerned environmental activists, the Cirque focuses on three iconic ingredients of the circus to create an innovative experience: clowns, tents and acrobats.

The tent was reinvigorated as the symbol of the circus, and redesigned with more luxurious features; clowns moved away from doing silly things, such as throwing buckets of water over each other and the audience, to a more sophisticated sense of humour; acrobats were redefined as artists who did amazing things with their bodies both individually and in an ensemble. The Cirque added ideas from the theatre and offered its visitors a coherent storyline, rather than a collection of individual acts. A great deal was imported from non-European and non-North American traditions of theatre and circus, especially from China and Japan.

For over 25 years the Cirque has performed in front of more than 90 million people in over 200 different cities. The reason why it does not share the fate of most other failing circuses is its capacity to imagine and create new, uncontested markets by basic product innovation. The Cirque took the product of the circus and totally reimagined how it might be. In order to do this, to reimagine a basic and tired product, you have to be innovative.

Question

1   The Cirque du Soleil has been reviewed and written about extensively. Basing your analysis on the available material, use the Cirque du Soleil as a prototype for imagining innovation in some other traditional and not innovative field of practice. How would you use what the Cirque du Soleil did strategically?

---

[1] www.cirquedusoleil.com/en/about/intro/intro.asp, accessed 7 August 2009.

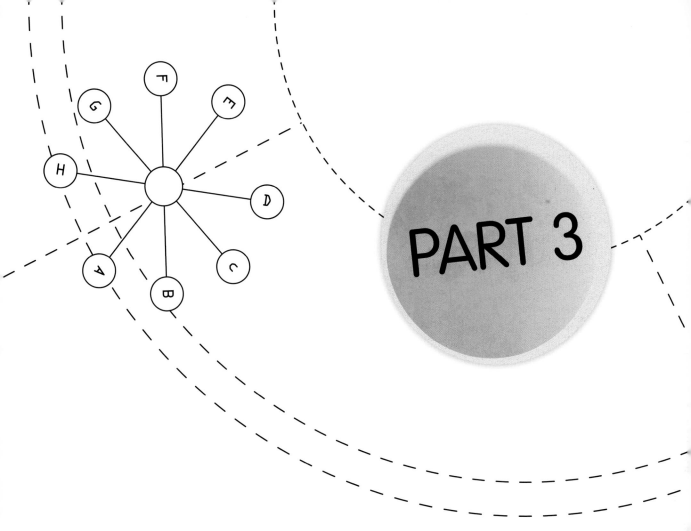

The Politics of Strategy

7   Strategists, top management teams and governance

8   Strategic decision-making

9   Organizational politics and strategy

PART 3

Strategists, Top Management Teams and Governance

Governance, stakeholders, business elites

LEARNING OBJECTIVES

By the end of this chapter you will be able to:

- Grasp the implications of the separation of ownership and control
- Explain agency, transaction and stewardship approaches to governance
- Understand current views on leadership
- Identify who the business elites are and how they are reproduced
- Critically reflect on the role of strategy champions
- Explain the role of the top management team in strategy formulation
- Identify different ways in which consultancy generates strategies

INTRODUCTION

Strategy, as we have seen in the chapters above, takes many forms. Yet, for the most part, strategy in organizations is associated with top management teams. This has many consequences, which we will explore in this chapter. To an extent the activities that are actually termed strategic are often labelled as such due to the fact that they are done by senior executives. Reflect on this: what is it that makes some action strategic while another may be only operational? Often it seems to depend on who is doing a particular task that defines whether it is strategic or operational.

The annals of strategy are replete with the strategic significance of small operational things. For instance, the late Lord Louis Mountbatten, while serving as the last British Viceroy of India, was undoubtedly a strategic decision-maker. Ultimately he decided on the partition of India into India and Pakistan, respectively, faced with the implacable opposition of Jinnah, the leader of the Muslim League, to a united India. Accounts of his tenure as viceroy highlight the inordinate amount of time he gave to organizing seating plans for formal dinners, planning menus for these dinners and, more generally, obsessing over issues of protocol. Is such behaviour strategic? In normal circumstances it would almost certainly not be thought so. But these activities were carried out by the viceroy and were important to diplomatic activity, because in the tense situation leading up to independence and the complex rivalries that attended the founding of India and Pakistan seating arrangements and who was to speak to whom were definitely strategic. Moreover, there was the little matter of his wife's romantic relationship with Pandit Nehru, the leader of the Congress Party and the man who became India's first prime minister. Strategy is, therefore, very much in the eye of the beholder.

In politics, much as in corporate life, leaders are happy to take credit for successful strategies but loathe to accept responsibility for the unsuccessful ones. Mountbatten did not hold himself responsible for the bloodbath of community violence and displacement of populations that accompanied India's partition, even though the maps were drawn up under his leadership. Whatever the strategy, odds are that it will have been the strategists and sometimes the top management team who claim the credit for it and have to carry the responsibility for its implementation. There is no better representation of this than in the world of soccer. Coaches come under pressure if they have a string of bad results. They become the embodiment of the success or failure of a strategy. In the English Premier League, which comprises 20 teams, several managers will lose their job each season, a dismissal rate mirrored in other sports that serves as an exaggerated reflection of organizational life in general. Performance counts and senior managers are generally held responsible for poor performance. Equally, they are feted for strong performances.

STRATEGISTS IN PRACTICE

The presumption is that strategy is carried out – for the most part – by those in senior positions. In an important contribution to the burgeoning strategy-as-practice literature, Finnish researcher Saku Mantere looked at who was championing strategy. By a champion of strategy he means individuals who try to:

1 Influence strategic issues beyond their immediate operational responsibilities.

2 Influence the organization to affect strategically important issues crucial for the organization's success, survival or completion of its mission.

One might think such a role would be exclusively reserved for those within the corporate elite – senior executives and their advisers. What Mantere's research highlighted was that strategic champions often came from outside the senior stratum of the organization. He identifies the role of 'the champions of strategy'. We might expect champions to be only the elites. On the basis of substantial empirical evidence collected across 301 interviews within 12 medium-sized organizations in the 100–500 employee range, this suggests that we would be wrong to think so. Strategy may often be taught and thought of as an elite practice but Mantere's (2005) data suggest that strategic champions may be found at various levels of the organizational hierarchy and are not just confined to the upper echelons.

Mantere's study not only establishes where strategic champions reside, but also proceeds to describe how they work by influencing the strategy process. As you will see in Chapter 9, influence can proceed through many paths, by people 'seeking to affect the opinions or activities of superiors, peers and subordinates, seeking to change the organization or its systems, seeking to secure resources and so on' (Mantere, 2005: 157). Such activity can be oriented as much to strategy formulation as implementation.

Championing strategy and seeking to influence a change process involves the use of 'strategic practices'. These practices comprise:

1 The deployment of tools – such as Porterian techniques for competitive industry analysis, RBV-inspired audits of competencies and competency gaps, software planning tools for project management, the balanced scorecard, etc.

2 The observance of routines – such as strategy meetings, away-days, corporate dinners, annual planning cycles and those other events which recur with cyclical frequency.

In common with the strategy-as-practice perspective outlined in Chapter 4, the focus on tools and temporally patterned events and routines situates the analysis of strategy between 'organizational macro-structures and individual activities, in the practices (routines, tools, techniques, etc.) that enable and constrain activity'. In turn these practices reproduce strategy as a result of the activities of strategists.

According to Mantere, champions can face conditions that enable their efforts to influence the strategy process or disable them, thus producing 'enabled' or 'thwarted' champions. To be enabled is to be in a power relation that allows one to do some strategic things – this might mean having the ear of the chief executive and being able to influence strategy decisively, while to be thwarted is to lack access to such power relations; that is, to be in the wilderness and not have one's ideas listened to. All of the authors of this book have, at times in their careers, felt that they were thwarted champions! These enabling and disabling strategic practices can be either adaptive, in that they will lead to some form of improvisation, or recursive, in that they will reproduce the status quo. The key questions are:

● *Which* practices enable and disable championing?
● *How* do these practices enable and disable championing?
● *Who* do these practices enable and disable?

Determining which, how and who is involved in strategy entails making powerful decisions. Power relations are central to strategy-making in a complex way. At a simple episodic level, if you cannot make happen what you have said will happen, you are not much of a strategist. More subtly, if you cannot shape the agenda from which issues emerge or through which change is implemented, or control the necessary resources, or ensure that the right people are in place to make things happen or, equally, make things not happen, then this is a strategic dereliction of duty. More subtly still, strategy is about shaping and framing vocabularies of motive, those things rationalized as needing to be done *in order to* achieve strategic goals; it concerns the discursive staking out of legitimated terms, phrases and reasoning that are tightly tied to actions that are intended to achieve strategic objectives. We might think of these as three dimensions of power at work in strategy, after Lukes (1974; 2006).

In Chapter 4 we discussed the distinction between the rational planning school and emergent strategy. One of the points of disagreement between the two approaches is the extent to which strategy should be tightly operationalized in terms of specific targets or whether it should be designed in such a way as to cut individuals some slack in interpreting and enacting it. An emphasis on the tight control and explicit operationalization of targets promotes a recursive view of strategic practices as focused on achieving defined objectives in an improved manner. As Clark (2000: 67) notes: 'Recursiveness means the socially accomplished reproduction of sequences of activity and action . . . there can be a durability about recursiveness that constrains attempts to transform the sequences'. What this means is that a recursive strategy tends to reproduce the status quo. The ways in which strategy is developed – that is, the techniques used – and the strategic objectives are likely to be very similar for this approach. In contrast, the emergence school, where the emphasis is on sensegiving and sensemaking (Gioia and Chittipeddi, 1991), places more emphasis on adaptive practices. This form of strategy-making is likely to be more fluid in the approaches it uses and more reflexive – meaning that it reflects back on itself – rather than being a tightly controlled means–end relation. Adaptive processes are more tolerant of and encourage emergence, while recursive practices are more oriented to achieving ends through controlling means. The following differences can be identified (Table 7.1).

The recursive approach stresses strategy as rational planning 'through the dissemination of information, i.e. objective knowledge, through pre-defined methods of giving feedback and through the operationalization of strategy into explicit targets' (Mantere, 2005: 169). Adaptive practices allow space for individual interpretations of strategy, 'achieved through impromptu discussions between strategists and implementers. These two are clearly distinct ideals and may often be incompatible, since there is little room for individual interpretation of strategy if it is regarded as an objective phenomenon, existing as pre-explicated targets' (2005: 169). Older, more experienced hands, embedded in social networks and shared communities of practice, are more likely to embrace adaptive strategies.

TABLE 7.1 Recursive and adaptive strategy practices

	Recursive	*Adaptive*
Strategy formation	Official feedback mechanisms Official information dissemination Strategy operationalization	Sensegiving
Organizing	Organizational design Personnel development Task definition	Cross-organizational development Continuous negotiations of responsibility
Control	Official participation Performance evaluation Resource mobilization Rewarding	Influence practices through social networks

Either the presence or the absence of recursive and adaptive strategies can aid championing or hinder it, as Table 7.2 demonstrates.

TABLE 7.2 Adaptive and recursive practices enabling and disabling championing

	Recursive		*Adaptive*	
	Enabling	*Disabling*	*Enabling*	*Disabling*
Strategy formation	Formal information dissemination practices ensure that individuals hear about strategy Formal feedback channels ensure that champions are able to voice their ideas Clearly operationalized targets and measurements allow for an understanding of strategy and result in feelings of predictability and control	Lack of explicit targets results in strategy being regarded as a platitude or conflicting, and in confusions regarding application Lack of explicit information dissemination and feedback practices result in individuals feeling disrespected, resulting in demotivation	An individual is motivated to champion strategy because it provides a purpose for their work Ownership of the interpretation of proper work practices motivates an individual Interactive communication between strategists and implementers helps the latter implementers find applications for strategy and deepens the former's understanding of implementation issues	Lack of sensegiving support of disseminated information leads to confusion regarding applications Lack of interaction between implementers and strategists leads to unrealistic objectives and demotivation Sensemaking failure concerning strategic direction leads to demotivation and feelings of insecurity and powerlessness
Organizing	Changes in organizational structure transcend talk, directing resources to proper areas	Ambiguous or dated organizational design leads to strategy being regarded as just talk	Continuous negotiation of responsibility leads to ownership of work and flexibility in the application of strategic ideas	An abundance of non-relevant development projects takes time from more crucial activities, leading to frustration

(Continued)

TABLE 7.2 (*Continued*)

	Recursive		Adaptive	
	Enabling	**Disabling**	**Enabling**	**Disabling**
	Designed career paths based on measurable strategic action motivate championing Explicit task definitions allow for the comprehension of one's role as a part of a greater unity	Overspecialization in strategic tasks undermines the feelings of responsibility of champions, leading to powerlessness and demotivation Task design not reflecting strategy creates conflict in priorities	Cross-organizational development projects challenge the status quo, leading to better cooperation between both implementers and organizational units	Individuals sticking to externally defined roles leads to poor cooperation in strategy implementation
Control	Official participation practices create a feeling of ownership of strategy Performance evaluation based on operationalized strategic targets creates a sense of control over one's success and failure Rewarding based on performance evaluation creates a feeling of championing being valued	Lacking official participation, practices result in a feeling that the strategy is being dictated, or at least in a confusion about whether participation is sought after or not Lack of rewarding of strategic action, in terms of a lacking or a faulty rewarding system, demotivates championing Lack of official practices to secure resources for strategic activities, especially in cross-functional contexts, demotivates championing	Social networks possessed by an individual champion enables them to secure resources and influence the organization, beyond official structures	Lack of a social network leaves the champion feeling helpless about this chances of making things happen

Strategy that favours recursive approaches stresses order and preplanning in strategy championing:

> Formal channels for information dissemination and feedback enable a wide audience for strategy-related matters and provide an equal opportunity to voice opinions. Operationalized targets and associated measures enable an individual to be an active player in creating strategic performance, as well as reap rewards from it. Explicit task designs and macro-structures, coupled with personnel development practices, create a

sense that strategy is a legitimate practice. Official participation practices and channels of mobilizing resources empower championing. But lack of explicitness, an oblique sense of legitimate organizing and unexplicated forms of control, the enemies of the recursive standpoint, lead to confusion, powerlessness, demotivation and cynicism. (Mantere, 2005: 171, 175)

Recursive practices draw on the champion's sense of control through predictability. Where these are disabling for champions is where they lack the ability to use the tools they have been given predictively, when they are not sure what the outcomes will be. The individual strategy champion has to have *power over* the right tools and levers to make things happen and what is disabling for champions is when they do not have this control.

By contrast, adaptive practices are much more a matter of *power to* rather than *power over*:

> Adaptive practices such as interactive impromptu discussions concerning strategy, continuous negotiation of responsibility and exerting influence through social networks enabled champions to express their ideas and create a feeling of ownership about their work. Adaptive practices, through which organizational strategy adapts to internal and external pressures, also seem to be a source of creative freedom and joy in the work of individuals interested in strategy. (Mantere, 2005: 175)

Champions are enabled because they are in a position to be able to use power creatively and innovatively to make things happen; they have a sense of psychological ownership of the agenda for these reasons.

These strategies are not randomly distributed through organizations' hierarchical structures. A lack of access to the formal tools and levers of recursive power disables many more operative employees from participating in strategy-making. At higher levels the emphasis is much more on being enabled to be adaptive rather than being constrained through a lack of access to the formal tools and thus feeling disabled. Hence, strategy in practice translates as the relative freedom and power to be able to do things for the elites and a relative powerlessness and lack of access to the tools capable of making things happen to those over whom they exercise power, with their role largely being to fulfil rational plans and targets and be rewarded and punished on this basis. Where the operatives do have access to such tools, these enable them to be strategy champions. Middle managers, in particular, lack the proper recursive control practices for such issues as rewarding, performance evaluation, resource mobilization and participation; thus, they will have recourse to adaptive strategies as ways to 'make do' and 'work round' their lack of power to make things happen using the tools available to them. Summing up, Mantere (2005: 178) suggests:

> [T]op managers seem to be enabled by many things, especially adaptive formation practices, and disabled by few. For middle managers, control is the key issue both as an enabler and disabler, while formation is a close second. The biggest obstacle for middle management championing seems to be a lack of proper control practices. Organizing seems to be a special concern for middle managers. The operative personnel are in a similar position as the middle management in terms of control, yet their greatest concern is a lack of an explicit and predictable position in strategy formation. They do not know where to get their information, where to voice their feedback and where to get clarification for objectives.

The recursive or rational planning model is clearly antithetical to the adaptive or emergence model of strategy. Both, however, describe different elements of the social reality of organizations. The closer one is to the elites in organizations, the more likely one is to encounter emergences and adaptive strategies; by contrast, the closer one is to the mass of employees, the more one is likely to encounter rational planning and recursive strategies.

Think of the organization in which you are presently employed. To what extent would you describe your knowledge as that of emergence and adaptive strategies or rational planning and recursive strategies?

YOU CAN DOWNLOAD…

Mantere, S. (2005) Strategic Practices as Enablers and Disablers of Championing Activity, *Strategic Organization*, 3: 157–284, from the book's website at www.sagepub.co.uk/cleggstrategy

Several interpretations of these findings are possible. One would be that rational plans are designed as control instruments by elites to manage those lower in the status order. Yet, as Mantere suggests, too much reliance on adaptive strategy can create a lack of ontological security – whereby someone loses confidence and belief in their ability and place in the world – for those managers accustomed to pulling levers and using rational plans to make things happen. Essentially, Mantere (2005: 179) seems to be edging towards a contingency model of strategy – albeit with political implications arising from a consideration of organizational design imperatives – in which 'championing enablers increase the performance of strategy, while disablers reduce it' and a 'champion is not likely to regard a strategy-making episode successful if he or she is not enabled in it'. We should be clear, however, that elements that increase both the specificity of recursive as well as those that allow adaptive behaviour can both enable and disable strategic fulfilment.

THE ROLE OF LEADERSHIP

If strategists are champions, then they have to lead. What does leadership consist of?[1] Commonly, leadership is seen as an influence process that is concerned with facilitating the performance of a collective task (Yukl, 2001); it has behavioural, relational and situational aspects and occurs on the individual, group and organizational level, both within the leader–subordinate interaction and in the situational environment (Sadler, 2003).

The image of top management teams as not merely managers but also leaders is integral to their image as the strategic elite. By setting the agenda and deciding on important strategic issues the top management team can be seen to exhibit leadership. Leadership is tangled up with the normalcy of the hierarchy – we ordinarily might expect that those higher up the hierarchy will lead and will normally expect that those lower down will follow, although normal expectations sometimes find disappointment in specific acts of what can be glossed as incompetence or resistance when expectations are not met. But before the fall, when doing leadership, illusions can be maintained and leader presentations of self performed by those who are the leaders, framed by the presupposition that the fate of the organization lies in their hands, to such an extent that, as Diefenbach (2009: 50) says, 'they need and deserve all the means available to carry out their

---

[1]Leadership is essential to strategy and is a fully blown field of management theory in its own right. In the context of this book we have neither the space nor occasion to delve deeply into the field; in part, there is no need to, as two of us have done so elsewhere, in collaboration with our colleague Tyrone Pitsis, and we would recommend that the interested reader investigate Chapter 3 of Clegg et al.'s (2008) *Managing and Organizations*.

selfless tasks and that their decisions must be supported, their instructions followed and their will obeyed'.

It is not only in church that the incantation 'Thy will be done' is ritually performed. Just as the will of a patriarchal god should be obeyed, so should that of the leaders of organizations: 'they must not be challenged! To criticise the leaders is to put the whole collective at risk!' (Diefenbach, 2009: 50). As he says, 'communicating such an image, acting "pro-actively" and demonstrating "strong leadership" strengthens and justifies managers' social positions, power and influence to a considerable extent'.

Management studies have been obsessed with leadership for most of the previous century. While there are numerous ideas about what constitutes strategic leadership, it remains a contested concept.

> Strategic leadership is the influence process that facilitates the performance of the top management team to achieve objectives.

Extant leadership theories emphasize different aspects of the leadership process, that is the personal qualities and characteristics of the leader in trait approaches (e.g. Miner, 1965; Bray, Campbell and Grant, 1974; Stogdill, 1974; Boyatzis, 1982; McClelland and Boyatzis, 1982; Howard and Bray, 1988), the individual behaviour or style of the leader in behavioural approaches (e.g. Fleischmann, 1953; Blake and Mouton, 1964; Bowers and Seashore, 1966; Misumi and Shirakashi, 1966; Likert, 1967), the use of different forms of power in power–influence approaches (e.g. French and Raven, 1959; Pettigrew, 1973; Kotter, 1982; Yukl and Falbe, 1991), and the situational context of the leader–subordinate relationship in situational approaches (e.g. Fiedler, 1967; 1986; House, 1971; Kerr and Jerminer, 1978; Yukl, 1989). Leadership behaviour has been linked to individual and organizational creativity, innovation and the overall strategic performance of organizations.

A more recent approach to explain the effectiveness and significance of the leadership process within organizations is full-range leadership theory (Bass and Avolio, 1995); it emphasizes the role and importance of two distinct behaviours: transformational and transactional leadership behaviour.

Transformational leadership is charismatic, inspirational, intellectually stimulating and individually considerate (Avolio, Bass and Jung, 1999). Transformational leaders help individuals to go beyond their self-interest for the sake of the larger vision of the organization. They inspire others with their vision, create excitement through their enthusiasm and question time-worn assumptions. Transformational leadership is particularly relevant in situations of change (Bass, 1985; Avolio et al., 1999) and has been linked to motivation and creativity (Burns, 1978; Sosik, Kahai and Avolio, 1998; 1999; Jung, 2001; Shin and Zhou, 2003), organizational performance (Jung and Avolio, 1999; Ogbonna and Harris, 2000; Jung and Sosik, 2002), innovation (Jung, Chow and Wu, 2003), and effectiveness in different types of organizations (Bass and Avolio, 1997). Transformational leadership has proved seductive, glamourizing leaders and their activities. We must, of course, be sceptical of such claims about leaders. For instance, Ken Lay (Chairman), Jeff Skilling (CEO) and Andy Fastow (CFO) were senior executives at the Enron corporation. President Bush socialized with and commended Kenny-boy, as he called him. Paeans of praise and adulation were heaped upon them: Gary Hamel, the strategy writer, hailed them as grey-haired revolutionaries; *Fortune* magazine gave them a variety of awards and they were seen as being at the very cutting edge of corporate America. Equally, a character such as Alan Greenspan, the long-standing former head of the American Federal Reserve, was treated with tremendous reverence for his apparently mystical control of the financial markets. Subsequently, this has all been exposed as a sham.

Transactional leadership, on the other hand, motivates individuals primarily through contingent–reward exchanges and active management-by-exception

(Avolio et al., 1999). Transactional leaders set goals, articulate explicit agreements and provide constructive feedback to keep everybody on task (Bass and Avolio, 1993; Howell and Hall-Merenda, 1999). Operating within an existing organization, transactional leaders seek to strengthen an organization's culture, strategy and structure. The theory suggests that the best leaders are those who display both transformational and transactional behaviours (Bass, 1998).

The implication of this theory is that the challenge for the top management team is to know when to exhibit transformational and when to exhibit transactional types of behaviours while implementing strategy throughout the organization. Of course, this rests on the assumption that leaders can shift from one style to another. Anecdotally, it would appear that this is a very difficult task to achieve. Doing it not only takes authenticity, it also takes into account the organizational context in which strategy is going to be implemented. Accordingly, leaders find that governance structures and mechanisms can enable and hinder the effectiveness of the leadership process.

STRATEGY AS THE WORK OF TOP MANAGEMENT TEAMS

Champions and leaders rarely work in isolation. In strategy research the top management team (TMT) has been studied as the locus of strategic decision-making. It is TMTs that ostensibly design and deliver strategy and it is their members who take the rap if it does not work well. The success of any given strategy depends on the ability of those socially constructing it to anticipate and respond to internal and external opportunities and threats. Burgelman (1983) argues that when corporate-level managers set the structural context in which strategy occurs they tend to create recursive traps for behaviour; establishing routines and developing routinized actors to manage them tends towards a more homogeneous TMT.

Research consistently demonstrates that heterogeneity in the characteristics of the TMT has advantages and that the characteristics and composition of the TMT (Hambrick and Mason, 1984; Wiersema and Bantel, 1992) can be a significant factor shaping the propensity to be able to strategize. Heterogeneity means that mindsets are not so shared; more options can be considered; relevant information can be subject to more shades of interpretation; and a broader range of potential strategies considered as a consequence. (It is for this reason that a strategy that allows more adaptive involvement by operative champions is so vital: it empowers sources of learning that would otherwise be marginalized.)

TMT researchers note the importance of ensuring that there is adequate representation of the capabilities and competencies needed to deliver on strategy within the TMT (Szilagyi and Schweiger, 1984) and that these also match the characteristics of strategic drivers in the external environment (Keck and Tushman, 1993). Strategic capacity to deal with complex heterogeneous environments is delivered by modelling the required requisite variety (Ashby, 1956) internally. Internal strategy and external environment can combine to create the need for highly heterogeneous or polyphonic TMT characteristics (Kornberger, Carter and Clegg, 2006). Adaptive behaviour, in the form of autonomous strategic initiatives, often emerges from operational-level managers located at the periphery of the organization. These managers have to maintain stability by enabling business as usual through the recursive routines even during periods of change when the emphasis is on adaptive strategies. Politically, TMT managers driving strategic change have both to try and transform operational managers' recursiveness even as they rely on them for maintaining routines.

The upper echelon approach to studying strategic change (Hambrick and Mason, 1984) follows strategic choice theory (Child, 1972) in seeing top managers as influencing the rate and type of change in organizations, emphasizing the effects of TMT heterogeneity in functional background, education and corporate tenure on the likelihood of large-scale organizational change. The initial emphasis on power relations that was so evident in Child's (1972) work has been whittled away in TMT research, however, despite the fact that work on decision-making processes regularly demonstrates the effects of power relations and deployments on decision outcomes (Pettigrew, 1973; Courpasson, 2000; Clark, 2004).

In a detailed study of the relation between CEOs, TMTs, power relations and strategic choices in the Japanese shipbuilding and robotics industries, Greve and Mitsuhashi (2007) provide empirical evidence of the links between TMT power and strategic choices. They examine how a CEO and TMT power concentration affects strategic change by examining whether CEO power over other executives affects decisions. They find that, in particular, the social capital of the CEO – for which length of service is a proxy – is particularly important: longer serving CEOs can drive through more strategic change (where diversification is the specific change being researched). In addition, they ask whether decisions are affected by a concentration of 'formal' authoritative power together with the informal power of social capital and network relations flowing from the deep embeddedness of TMTs. They find that where TMTs have concentrated formal and informal power so that there is a small clique constituting the powerful few, they are more likely to initiate strategic change (Pfeffer, 1981; Hambrick and Finkelstein, 1987). Finally, they find that a concentration of power increases the likelihood of strategic change because it provides an opportunity to redesign decision-making routines, and introduce new issues, agendas and participants, rewarding supporters and marginalizing opponents.

Strategic change strengthens the power of incumbency both in terms of actual power relations and in terms of the symbolism of these: a high level of change indicates that the TMT have an active hand in strategy-making. Change is expected of strategic managers by both external constituents and organizational members (Pfeffer, 1981; Courpasson, 2000) and builds the legitimacy of the dominant coalition (March, 1966). In addition, strategic change allows managers to try to redefine strategic priorities around those competencies and capabilities in which they can display their expertise and talents as well as impose their values and preferences on the organization. Spee and Jarzabkowski (2009) suggest that to do this the TMT use strategic tools, such as SWOT analysis or scenario planning, either instrumentally, as means to a desired end, or for their symbolic or political expediency. Such tools are useful for TMT strategy discussions, for example during workshops (Hodgkinson et al., 2006) and other strategizing activities aimed at generating ideas (Hill and Westbrook, 1997). They provide a common language with which to have a strategy conversation (Barry and Elmes, 1997; van der Heijden, 2005). They enable TMTs to play at politics by hampering shared meaning, particularly across hierarchical levels, by structuring and shaping information (Grant, 2003) and they can be used to legitimate powerful interests (Hill and Westbrook, 1997) as, for instance, when a CEO influences the use of scenario planning tools among a senior management team by stressing those scenarios regarded as viable (Hodgkinson and Wright, 2002).

YOU CAN DOWNLOAD...

One work that does not neglect the links between power and strategic choice from the book's website at www.sagepub.co.uk/ cleggstrategy by Sotirios Paroutis and Andrew Pettigrew (2007) Strategizing in the Multi-business Firm: Strategy Teams at Multiple Levels and over Time, *Human Relations*, 60(1): 91–135.

THE REPRODUCTION OF BUSINESS ELITES AND THE CENTRALITY OF STRATEGY

Effective leadership has its rewards. Corporations provide contexts in which leadership can come to the fore, be celebrated and rewarded, put on a pedestal and treated as a possession of only the elite so venerated. That there are business elites is indubitable. We find them in the gossip as well as the news columns of the financial press; on the boards not only of companies but also of great civic, arts and sporting organizations. In all countries they are honoured for their achievements and extolled for their virtues, while also occasionally lambasted for their greed and acquisitiveness in drawing down salaries and bonuses that on an annual basis will exceed most people's lifetime earnings, even in well-developed countries. These elites are the corporate titans whose time span of discretion sets the parameters for investment strategies and fortunes over something as long as a 25-year window. In all respects they stand at the centre of relations of great power, privilege, wealth and legitimacy.

While the study of elites is well established from the groundbreaking work of C. Wright Mills (1956) onwards, it is only in the last 30 years that a few researchers have begun to trace the links between corporate elites as a cohesive group and the types of strategies that they follow and capital they build.

It has been the French sociologist, Pierre Bourdieu (1973; Bourdieu, Boltanski and de St Martin, 1973; Bourdieu and Passeron, 1977; Bourdieu 1984), who has done most to clarify the different forms of capital. His writings remain central to discussions of corporate elites. He sees corporate elites as expressions of resource-based and symbolic power. Elites are rooted in what he calls a *habitus*, the sets of assumptions and underlying principles that are reproduced in daily interaction (Bourdieu, 1990). These are manifest in terms of symbolic understandings that function as sources of domination. It is not just that those who are not elites are held captive in these symbolic understanding; more importantly, as we will see in Chapter 11, symbolic understandings can operate as a dominant ideology organizing and maintaining a coherent sense of a community of 'common sense'.

This common sense is shared by elites, those people who have risen to the commanding heights of the economy, polity and society. In corporate organization terms they do so largely through their ascension to dominant, board-level positions at the top of major organizations. From these they are able to network across other elite social spaces, crating a personal field of power that intersects with already established fields of power. Bourdieu argues that the capital that elites can draw on with which to network is not only economic: there are several types existing. First, there is economic capital, in the form of monetary and other assets. Second, we need to consider **social capital**, accessed through networks of connections and social contacts.

Social capital is created by experience in school and university, as well as through specific coalitions of interest that we build within organizations. As a rule, elite schools and universities build the most valuable social capital. Some managers, by virtue of their embeddedness in elite social backgrounds, will have much more valuable social capital to draw on, while others from less privileged backgrounds will have to be more skilled at internal coalition building. In their fascinating study of elite business school graduates, Whitley, Thomas and Marceau (1981) note the role that family ties and assets, such as chateaux, ski lodges and yachts, can play in building and renewing capital and careers for younger family members.

Social capital is all the actual or potential resources that can be accessed through enduring networks of social relations.

Social capital may be found in kinship and marital ties and connections, as well as in contacts forged within specific milieux in which one is acculturated. Milieu knowledge of how things work, about the relative prestige of institutions, professions and opportunities, is invaluable in this regard. Collective family knowledge can be vital in grasping (or occluding) how these social constructions operate. Finally, there is cultural capital, in the form of both educational qualifications and the general cultural learning that is implicit, embodied and embrained, coded in quintessential gestures and modes of speech, dress and deportment.

Managers deploy social capital to construct actor networks linking the organizations they work for with others with which they deal (Coleman, 1988). Long tenure grants greater social capital to construct such networks (Barkema and Pennings, 1998; Shen and Cannella, 2002). In the longer term, social capital outweighs Machiavellian tendencies and, positively, builds more power to do things, compared with the negative power over point scoring and one-upmanship.

Quite early in their development in Europe it was recognized that business schools played a particular social function in the reproduction of business elites. In a 1981 study, *Masters of Business: The making of a new elite*, Whitley et al. identified particular roles of social reproduction and translation fulfilled by elite business schools. (Wherever we use the term translation in what follows we are using it in the sense introduced by Czarniawska and Sevón (2006) as a process whereby an entity moves from one place to another, changing in the process.) The graduates of these schools, at that time largely male, were often drawn from the ranks of business families in declining branches of family-owned industries. Family fortunes and support were used to bankroll graduation from MBA programmes so that these declining family fortunes could be reinvested subsequently in more dynamic branches of industry, after graduating and pursuing a career in consulting and in leading companies in areas such as finance, consulting, marketing and strategy. The various types of capital attached to wealth, and access to elite institutions and locales, were useful to these graduates in making their credentials work for them, especially the social capital attached to being able to mingle freely, socially, with other elites in elite locales.

In earlier work by one of the present authors, with David Courpasson (and Nelson Phillips), Clegg (Clegg et al., 2006: 342) has argued that elites are 'the missing link between studies of power and studies of democracy', responsible for shaping action at the policy level. Maclean et al. (2010: 330) note that:

> Despite Scott's (1982, 1991, 1996, 2001, 2008) extensive work on elite domination and power in Britain, the USA and elsewhere, there appears to be a 'glaring invisibility of elites' (Savage and Williams, 2008: 2) in contemporary capitalism, particularly financial elites, who, lured by temptation, use money as a 'neutral veil' while insinuating themselves as key social and political agents in wider networks of influence. The study of power has focused too infrequently on the extremely powerful, at the pinnacle of very large organizations (Pettigrew, 1992; Pettigrew and McNulty, 1995, 1998). Too little attention has been paid to the 'giant firm corporate elite' (Savage and Williams, 2008: 19), the 'professionals of power', who are fundamental to the functioning of governance regimes (Clegg et al., 2006: 343). This is despite the fact that such action goes to the heart of governance systems, where the economic and social are closely enmeshed. (Clegg et al., 2006)

Social distance is the essential principle of legitimacy of the elites:

> it is by being different, it is by signalling that getting to the top is not possible for everybody, irrespective of their merits, that the elite persuades people that there are impervious worlds and that these worlds are necessary to the balance of societies – and the organization. (Courpasson, 2009: 437)

Elite members of organizations are the repositories of inter-generational forms of resilient oligarchic power (McLean and Harvey, 2006) and of interlocking inter-organizational circles of socialization and learning (Mizruchi, 1996). They form the 'inner circle' of the business world (Useem, 1986). They interpret the rules of the game of corporate strategies and power struggles. For the vast majority of organization members, as Hardy and Clegg (1996: 628) observed: 'It is not that they do not know the rules of the game so much as that they might not even recognize the game, let alone its rules'. The chief moves in the game are those of different strategies: it is through these that corporate, sectional and personal interests are fought. Sectional interests seek to capture corporate strategy; within these sectional interests personal interests will see individuals strive to advance themselves and hinder rivals. They are able to do so because:

> In propagating a legitimate vision of the social order, those in positions of authority never entirely succeed in establishing a monopoly. Within any field, subordinate organizations and agents strive to find ways to neutralize the advantages of the dominant, and at times discover ways – 'subversion strategies' (Emirbayer and Williams, 2005: 693) – to 'outflank' more capital-rich rivals (Clegg, 1989). Symbolic struggles, Bourdieu argues, possess a degree of autonomy from the structures in which they are embedded. Agents possess reflexivity (Bourdieu, 1990; Bourdieu and Wacquant, 1992), enabling the contestation of boundaries that delimit social space (Lounsbury and Ventresca, 2003), which goes some way towards explaining the 'paradox of embedded agency' (Seo and Creed, 2002: 223). Like De Certeau's (1984) 'tacticians' who find ways of outwitting dominant systems through local improvisa-tions, Bourdieu (1996: 336–9) does acknowledge the gradual transformation of the dominant system over time (Maclean et al., 2010: 333)

Elites form an inner circle by virtue of their command of resources, in an echo of the RBV. They become dominant by holding a controlling position within an organizational field through their command over large, strategically significant resources. Dominant people hold controlling positions within an organizational field through their command over large, strategically significant resources. It is this command of resources which makes them dominant. Dominant people must be members of dominant organizations. Corporate domination signifies control of the economic field by this relatively small number of powerful companies, themselves controlled by a handful of dominant agents. The economic field is itself dominated by this relatively small number of powerful companies, them-selves controlled by a handful of dominant board members. These comprise the corporate power elite, operating collectively within a field of power, conceived as an integrative domain that brings together the uppermost strata in distinctive organizational fields. The concept of the power elite refers to a network of domi-nant agents operating collectively within the field of power, social spaces which transcend individual organizations and serve as opportunities for different types of social and positional equals to mingle: elite clubs, boardrooms, cultural institu-tion boards, etc., where successful interactions and broader social networks can be constructed. Boardrooms are the ultimate loci of power in organizational set-tings (Pettigrew and McNulty, 1998) from where broader social networks can be accessed and constructed.

The organizational and political characteristics (Zald and Ash, 1966) of busi-ness elites are characterized by their striking resilience (Davis, Yoo and Baker, 2003), a resilience that cannot be based exclusively on the cohesiveness and closure of inner circles and social networks of competence and acquaintance, if only because the elites are quite capable of social reproduction through new blood. Organizational elites are open oligarchies that, as Courpasson (2009) argues, need an elite diversifica-tion to be sustained and perpetuated. New professional groups within organizations, particularly in the areas of strategy, are sub-elites from whom would-be oligarchs are monitored and recruited from the top. Organizations are contested oligarchies through which elites circulate, perpetuating and refreshing the principal oligarchy (CEOs and major directors). Organizational leaders tend to favour the development of strong and efficient internal elites, owing much to the leader, and, eventually, aspiring to become leaders. Such groups coalesce around issues of strategy – because it is here that the limits to the time span of discretion are set.

There is an extended literature on patterns of elite production (Putnam, 1976). Executives' careers can be regarded as embedded, sponsored or contested; solidified through the social dynamics of interlocking directorates (Mizruchi, 1996) and the role of specific social networks in the simultaneous production of the elite and of a perpetuation of an elite structure (Davis et al., 2003). Companies will use non-executive directorships as a learning device for those whom they want to groom for leadership and elite roles. The most valuable elite ties are with financial institutions, the purveyors of that most vital ingredient, capital. Sponsored mobility into the right clubs is also important. Courpasson (2009) suggests that each of these paths of social mobility can lead to the business elite:

- *Embedded mobility* draws on the patina of wealth and prestige that the luck of being born in the right bed delivers to many corporate leaders. Such luck in being an heir can, of course, be furthered buttressed by an education at the right elite schools and universities, and by all the social capital and networks delivered by lives of privilege. Essentially, this fraction of the business elite draws its reproductive ability from fundamental class relations and the condensation and sedimentation of class-based principles, founded on the basis of an aristocracy and all its social devices (the upper-class effect).

- Another element of the elite uses *network-based mobility* where elevation is owed less to birthright and more to the social relations that can be coordinated around personages, through marriage and membership of the right clubs and associations, and through an extensive array of interlocking directorships. This elite fraction often recruits from the ranks of the leading strategists because they have a reputation for being business-savvy and connected. Governance is the mechanism that unites the fraction. Through common exposure and experience in the governance of elite businesses they acquire cohesion and common learning. The interlock effect regards the exchange of resources between board members, notably information and learning, and the fact that these exchanges are likely to improve governance decisions and, therefore, organizational performance, as essential. In his class perspective on interlocks Zeitlin (1974) stresses how interlocking directorates produce social cohesiveness.

- The *traditional company-based elite* will move through fast-track career paths and internal education programmes within one organization. These elites are the consummate corporate professional bureaucrats – masters of the one company and organization – to which they have devoted a life of service (see the M&S case study at the end of the chapter). Here it is intra-organizational mechanisms of career management which enable selection, grooming and conformance in what can be called an organization effect. The organization effect puts the stress on the capacity of individual organizations to choose and design their own models of authority and legitimacy. Reputational capital attaches to being an organization with attractive career mechanisms; in addition these will help frame a very particular organizational identity.

Maclean, Harvey and Chia (2010: 328) observe that in France and the UK, nearly 30 years after the Whitley et al. (1981) study, there is a 'super-concentration of power in the hands of a small number of dominant agents within the corporate economy'. The empirical foundation of their research was a comparative analysis of the 100 largest French and British companies and their directors between 1998 and 2003. They reasserted the important role that Bourdieu and Whitley and his colleagues had assigned to social capital. Social capital aids the bridge building for relationships that will span 'structural holes', connecting otherwise disconnected realms (Burt, 1992; 2000). These 'boundary spanners' (Geletkanycz and Hambrick, 1997) are often senior and chief executives who are directors with multiple directorships, thereby interlocking different corporate, cultural, civic and political fields, and who are able to learn from and frame strategies across these fields. In Bourdieu's terms, they are 'multi-positional' and able to use this to trace common narratives of strategy across multiple domains, creating a common dominant ideology for dominant elites.

How elites operate is dependent on specific elements in the respective nationally constructed societal context. In the UK and France, the field of power builds and maintains an institutional solidarity, with the French cohort being more tightly coupled and endogenous than the British one (Kadushin, 1995; Burt, Hogarth and Michau, 2000), with strong corporate ties sustained and supported by the state. The British elite is both more open in recruiting talent from outside of dominant social capital networks and more loosely coupled in these networks.

THE MBA AND STRATEGY

One of the major routes to strategic success in the UK has been the MBA, perhaps more so than in France where the top *lycées* and *grandes écoles* play a more significant role. When Whitley et al. (1981) conducted their study, the role of the business schools as a strategic device in the creation of an elite was constrained by the small number of graduates that passed through them. There are changes in the MBA market today that were not evident when Whitley et al. (1981) did their research. First, the MBA is much more widely offered and achieved: consequently, there has been some devaluation of the currency for it is no longer the positional good that it once was. Second, product differentiation is evident in the increasing number of types of MBA. There has been more diversification in programmes: there are increasing numbers of younger, often foreign entrants into British and Australian programmes in particular, offered either in the domestic economy or offshore. One might say that this characterizes the mass end of the MBA market. In these portals there is less chance of acquiring the accoutrements of social and cultural capital of the host nation but every opportunity to extend social networks among compatriots and cohorts from other developing countries. Third, their career destinations are less likely to be as the custodians of family economic capital translated to a new enterprise, after a suitable learning period in a transnational, often US-based consultancy or corporation, if only because family businesses are not the force they were in the 1970s, although they are by no means extinguished. Instead, the MBA's career objectives will more likely be to join a global business as an end point, rather than a means to an end.

Today, we may say, the effects of business schools are more widespread and less contained than they were 30 years ago, although this view has been contested by some (see Pfeffer and Fong, 2002) who see business schools as not very effective. They suggest that possession of an MBA degree is no guarantee of career success and that business school research has scant influence on management practice.

Perhaps. Nonetheless, the top-tier MBA schools still turn out the financial elites that run Wall Street and the City, while the thousands of lesser schools turn out many future managers whose worldviews are partially shaped by their experiences in business school, even if they fail to make the business elite. Foundations are framed in business school; techniques and rationalizations are learnt, and vocabularies of business motives inculcated.

What is evident is that business schools are not what they were when they offered a rarely available positional good (we discussed 'positional goods' in Chapter 5). Now there are a great many business schools and hundreds of thousands of MBA students worldwide. Having an MBA today is no longer a mark of distinction, with a few very expensive exceptions from top-tier schools. Today, the panoply of business schools serves a much broader purpose than merely being finishing schools for the scions of declining branches of capital: they serve as conduits to careers that can translate young people from India, China or elsewhere into bearers of skills that can be employed globally. Translation is still occurring but increasingly it is translation from one cultural context to a more global cultural context, from employment opportunities only in a national context to opportunities to join more global enterprises or become citizens elsewhere.

Other forms of product differentiation are evident in the development of mid-range executive MBA programmes designed to capture not so much the relatively work-inexperienced overseas student whose fees are so valuable to the institutions in which they enrol, but the more seasoned middle managers who still hope to improve their lot and for whom the prospect of being in the same learning and social spaces as the youth of Asia is a less attractive proposition. A form of virtual apartheid between the older, more domestic 'suits' and the youth of Asia and elsewhere is evident. At the top end of the market there are the global MBA programmes, taught by consortia of universities in several countries, offering a global premium experience and exposure to the international world of business and business education. Here the full panoply of cultural and social capital may be explored, learnt and deployed.

MINI CASE STUDY

Bachelors/Masters/MBA origins and networks

On the assumption that many of the readers of this text will be studying strategy as part of a management degree (BA, MSc or MBA) we would like you to do a small piece of empirical research.

Questions

1 In one of your strategy classes map out the demographics of the class:

- Where do its members come from?
- What were their parents' occupations?
- What were their previous occupations?
- For Masters students, what degrees did they take before their Master's, where did they do them and for whom have they previously worked?
- Where do they dream they will be working after completing their qualification?

2 Analyse the data and discuss these in a focus group. How does your cohort map onto the representations of MBAs discussed here and how will strategy feed into to your future career plans?

With respect to business schools and their mission, some things have not changed, however. The primary function of the MBA remains to translate the person enrolled in it from whatever context they came from to one that enables them to climb up the ladder of achievement, however this is defined. Acquiring a mastery of strategy is essential to this process of translation. In the business schools strategy is nearly always characterized as a capstone subject. Here, in this one part of the curriculum, the student is expected to pull together all the distinct disciplinary and functional knowledge they have acquired and demonstrate their capacity for holistic analysis and prescriptive prowess. Strategy is the Esperanto of the business schools: it provides a way of communicating and doing being a manager that is increasingly translatable everywhere: from business to government; from the third sector to public management; from the United States to Europe and Australasia and the global world. In terms of the discussion of Mantere's (2005) work earlier in the chapter, the more polyglot and polyphonous the constituency being taught, the more recursive the strategies will tend to be, because the more adaptive approaches require a strong sense of shared context and social capital in order to be appreciated and understood. It is the premium price paid for the global MBAs and the greater homogeneity of corporate experience of their members that should ensure that this is the case, an argument that has been vigorously mounted by Mintzberg (2004).

STRATEGY AS THE WORK OF CONSULTANTS

The dream job for many management graduates is to become a strategy consultant for one of the global strategy majors. In this position they will be exposed to a great many TMT, mingle with the business elite and sometimes be challenged to dislodge recursive routines. Often the consultants will be called in when innovating new strategies while maintaining interests in and commitments to existing strategies is too much for the TMT. In fact consultants will often play the role of champion and leader during strategy-making processes. Where existing strategic choices are not breaking free of routines or failing to generate adaptive and emergent thinking, many organizations will call in the consultants. What consultants can offer are new routine ways of breaking with existing internal organization routines: in short, they offer a new recursivity to transform the old recursivity. To do this they produce and use boundary objects: tools and artefacts that span work boundaries within organizations (Spee and Jarzabkowski, 2009). Strategy tools have been defined as those 'numerous techniques, tools, methods, models, frameworks, approaches and methodologies which are available to support decision-making within strategic management' (Clark, 1997: 417). Consulting companies both produce and use these widely; the specific intellectual property embedded in particular tools and the discontinuity between these products, creating a turnover in approaches as a more or less coordinated construction of a fashion season, is the core of the business of the strategy elites in the major consultancies.

It has been argued that the success of many strategy devices is due to their simplicity: everyday managers can understand them quickly and their ease of use provides legitimacy. However, when existing legitimacies are eroding, existing routines seem no longer the appropriate ones to be designed, there is a paucity of emergent adaptive thinking, or there is a new CEO who wants to make a big splash, then consultants can be very useful.

Consulting has been addressed by a number of organization and management theorists. Researchers have analysed consultants and their methods (e.g. Canback, 1998; Werr, 1999; Dillon, 2003); their relationships to organizations (e.g. Sturdy,

1997a; 1997b; Fincham, 1999), as well as the process of consulting more generally (e.g. Schein, 1988; 1999). Consulting has come under scrutiny in its relation to managerial power and control (e.g. Grint and Case, 1998; Berglund and Werr, 2000; Clark and Fincham, 2002; Clegg, Kornberger and Rhodes, 2004; Sturdy et al., 2004), and latterly has been seen as a form of entrepreneurship trading in strategy tools as boundary objects.

Strategy tools as boundary objects are simply artefacts that enable and constrain knowledge sharing across syntactic, semantic, pragmatic and metaphysical boundaries (Carlile, 2002; 2004; Bechky, 2003). Syntactic boundaries assume that knowledge can be translated if there is a common syntax. A semantic boundary exists where common meanings still need to be developed for translation to occur. Pragmatic boundaries are more socially and politically complex, because common interests need to be developed for translation to occur. Metaphysical boundaries are the most complex because they assume the most simplicity: they assume that a universe of meaning is possible and that all can share in it, with no tendencies to Babel-like fragmentation on the grounds of pragmatic, political interests. The transition through the four stages of boundary spanning can be thought of as ever-more ambitious consulting.

The dominant and most influential models of consulting share the underlying assumption that consulting is defined by the relation between client and consultant (see McGivern, 1983; Fincham, 1999), a perspective elaborated in the seminal contributions of Schein (1988; 1999). Schein suggests that the nature of this relation is one where 'the deeper notion of the word consultation is "helping" (2002: 21), and that consultation 'means to provide help' (2002: 27). Of course, such a relationship need not be a happy one: helpers can misuse power and clients can be resentful and defensive. Emotional relief can lead to dependency and subordination. Past experiences with helpers can lead to a transference of perceptions and feelings onto the present consultant that can be followed by counter-transference and blame from the consultant, and so forth (2002: 22–4). All these potentially distracting influences are embedded in and derive from the 'psycho-dynamics of the helping relationship' (2002: 22). Schein asserts that the client is 'often completely unaware of how seamlessly the consultant's interventions have led ... to key insights' (2002: 24). Here the consultant acts *as* a therapist – the consultant structures the subconscious of the 'patients' in the organization such that while these 'patients' can only see the results, the therapist knows how they were produced. As Schein argues (2002: 24), knowledge of such production remains the consultant's secret – 'it would hardly be constructive for the consultant to point this out to the client'. What Schein's discussion also suggests is that the recognition that results from consulting interventions can be functional or dysfunctional and elicit positive or negative outcomes. The more functional the cognition, the more positive the outcomes for the organization and its actors, conceived as an organic entity. Given that consulting contains no 'necessary structures' (Fincham, 1999: 225), in practice we can differentiate between four types of consulting (see Table 7.3).

Organizational surgery

The prevalence of consultant-driven downsizing, outsourcing or rightsizing – or what Eisenberg (1997) referred to as 'dumbsizing' – is perhaps the most common means through which organizational surgery is deployed by consultants. It causes lesions as it cuts out what are being targeted as redundant organs of the corporate body. Indeed, forms of consulting advice lead to widespread practices such as 'delayering' and business process reengineering. It is a moot case how skilled

TABLE 7.3 Four types of consulting

Type of strategy	Application to organizations	Examples of tools and methods
Organizational surgery	Organizational problems can be solved by physically altering the organization's structure independent of its cognition	● Tight fiscal control ● Downsizing ● Outsourcing ● Radical reengineering
Organizational retooling	Specific consulting processes can be correctly applied to an organization resulting in improved functioning and more independent cognition, through the intervention of technology – usually IT systems	● Employee surveillance through IT ● Total quality management premised on a rigorous sampling regime ● Organizational restructuring around structure-shaping systems ● Employee retraining to create better expressiveness in terms of the new regime of structure and technology
Organizational therapy	Organizations are complex and can only be changed and improved through processes of self-reflection and image recreation directly involving the thinking and acting of the people in the organization	● Cultural change programmes ● Strategic change programmes ● Organization identity redesigned
Organizational metaphysics	The organization should have a higher purpose to which members should aspire and conform – those who fail to do so should be changed or removed	● Development of vision and mission statements ● Transformational leadership ● Social and corporate citizenship

this surgery is. The purveyors of these practices have been simplistically portrayed as 'axemen' (Sturdy, 1997b) rather than as skilled surgeons, especially where such efforts in amputating parts of the organization are thought to provide quick solutions to endemic organizational problems. Practices of portfolio management can also be seen to involve segmenting the organization such that its constituent organs can easily be augmented or divested.

In general, such consulting rests on the belief that an organization's 'pathologies' or 'psychoses' are the result of physical and structural causes that can be cured by a surgical intervention on the structure designed to attack the offending organs. In this sense adding, excising or physically altering structural elements can remedy organizational malfunctions. The organization fails to behave in ways consistent with its structural contingencies and so must be 'restructured' to regain the fit (Donaldson, 1987; 1999; 2000). The role of the consultant is thus to identify the problem, isolate that part of the system where the problem lies and then perform the necessary surgery through an operation to fix it. In this way a common syntax can be created as the non-essential elements are divested so what remains shares a common syntax and focus.

Organizational retooling

In business terms, consulting can suggest that an organization's ills have emerged because of a problem in the 'physiology' of the organization. A permanent programme of appropriate technical interventions should be used to prevent manifestations of the organization ailment. In organizational terms, just as an anti-depressant medication, as a form of technical intervention on the central nervous system, can restore a sense of well-being to a depressed patient, the consultant can apply, for example, the introduction and management of new technical interventions for the organization's central nervous system, such as its accounting system. Such a technology can become a critical part of any organization, but most people within the organization will have little knowledge or understanding of these technologies and what they mean in technical terms. Here, the consultant *qua* therapist is best regarded as a form of expert doctor who can diagnose and prescribe organizational 'medicine'. Such consultants are 'experts' who do not rely on the client organization understanding what they are doing in order for something to be done – the results produced are the necessary and sufficient test for the client, even though the client may not be able to understand fully the advice given, other than in terms of its effects (Starbuck, 1992).

Such consulting does not necessarily rely on cognitive capacities in order to be effective; rather these cognitive capacities, conceived in terms of the overall organs of the system, as the main instrument for acquiring knowledge, are the target of the intervention. Such a technology can become a critical part of any organization, but most people within the organization will have little knowledge or understanding of how technologies of accounting, ERP and business software systems work and what they mean in technical terms.

Other examples are analogous to those technologies of the self that Foucault (in Martin, 1988) addresses at the individual level: indeed, they work on the organizational selves to create more reflexive self-regarding outcomes in terms of the organization conceived as a collective enterprise of individuals whose work is bound together organically. Technologies of the self are a series of techniques that allow individuals to work on themselves by regulating their bodies, their thoughts and their conduct; for instance, quality auditing and the adoption of standards such as the ISO 9000 series, business excellence frameworks, world's best practice, and so on. These technologies require a constant auditing, consulting and administration of the selves involved in their enactment and they help organizations function with a minimum reliance on the organization's cognitive involvement in the process. They create common meanings that enable translation to occur easily. A manager does not need to understand ISO, all they need to know is if they can tick a box, or answer the question 'Today is Monday; did I do Monday's routines, yes or no?'

Organizational therapy

The aim of therapy is to uncover the deep causes of a patient's negative thoughts and emotions. In so doing, the therapist tries to get through the patient's intricate set of defence mechanisms. For Freudian therapy, this involves examining symbols and artefacts as a sign of a person's hidden psychoses and personality disorders.

For more Lacanian psychotherapists, the appropriate cure might be language based – surfacing what had been repressed through repeated discursive analysis.

A therapeutic approach regards an organization's dysfunctions as being rooted not in the body of the organization but in its collective mind. As Kets de Vries (1991) would have it, such approaches seek to put 'organizations on the couch'. One application of this in consulting is to engage an organization in a therapeutic process involving processes of reflection and the development of self-knowledge that cuts through an organization's defence mechanisms – or 'defensive routines' to use Argyris's (1990) term – in order that the organization builds a healthy self-awareness that enables it to function in a more well-adjusted manner (Brown and Starkey, 2000). The objective is to arrive at a common frame for representing different interests so that translation can occur.

In Nonaka and Takeuchi's (1995) terms, the goal is to make tacit knowledge explicit in a similar fashion to the way a psychotherapist might seek to bring the subconscious under the scrutiny of the ego. Consulting in this tradition is process driven – it emphasizes learning and the active participation of the client throughout the change process (Werr, Stjernberg and Docherty, 1997). Therapeutically, such consultants can be described as having, as one of their chief claims, the ability to reduce managerial and organizational anxiety and replace it with reassurance, control and order in accordance with an image of organizational normalcy (Sturdy, 1997a; 1997b). This might take the form of cultural change programmes that seek to modify both employee and organizational identity in the service of improved organizational functioning (Chappell et al., 2003). These types of consultants put emphasis on the relation between counselling and coaching, seeking to unleash the power of the client organization and its members.

Organizational metaphysics

Metaphysics deals with those principles of reality transcending those of any particular science. In consulting terms it concerns itself with the creation of meaning and purpose for people who will be guided and governed by a higher being or entity: the organization. An organization, it is argued, should have a 'higher' purpose than that of the mundane realities of managing and doing business. Such a utopian vision for the organization must be identified and fostered, often by charismatic and transformational leaders who will put forward a combination of visions, missions and values to guide the organization in its spiritual quest. The consultant thus becomes similar to the guru or priest who advises the leadership on how to define and achieve its 'true' purpose. A universe of meaning is promised in which all can share, with no tendencies to Babel-like fragmentation on the grounds of pragmatic, political interests. The utopianism involved in such consulting subordinates the individual to the collective: it believes in the malleability of dreams; it is a-historic and decontextualizes human beings; utopias are total and control individuals in detail; it is a radical dream that wishes to start anew and eradicate the old; utopianism excludes love, passion and sexuality as long as they are not useful (i.e. a means of reproduction); it is obsessed with purity and a strong urge for hygiene; everything should be productive; an ambiguous notion of happiness should justify utopia, and violence and power are unavoidable to keep everything under control and to ward off foreign influences (ten Bos, 2000).

When consultants work thus, what they are doing is enacting possible organizational realities. They build their own world that is made up of concepts, metaphors and language games deriving from organizational cognition. The consultants will recognize all sorts of shortcomings, abnormalities and pathologies in an organization that become the task to be resolved. They will systematically draw a pathological picture of the organization in order to make convincing the business proposition that they embody and invoke. Having defined the pathological, in a second step the consultants will imagine a healthy future as an organizational utopia. But of course, the way to paradise is never easy, nor, in these days, cheap: it is paved with myriad obstacles, as well as good intentions; it offers the prospect of a dangerous journey, where only the experienced guide – the consultant – knows how to read the signs, see the hidden dangers and finally lead one's organization into the 'Promised Land'. As part of this, the consulting process also involves the exorcising of specific individuals who do not conform to the dominant notions of worthiness.

Metaphysical consultants deal with extremes: they make reality worse than it might be in order to make the future even sunnier, brighter and more appealing. They draw a dark picture of an organization's past and a cosy one of an organization's future, but they neglect the presence of the present – they stare at the gift of being in the mirror and see nothing but the prospect of not-being, of becoming something else, spiritually informed.

Sometimes the metaphysics will become explicitly religious: for instance, Bolman and Deal (2001), no longer reframing organizations through just four frames, have discovered the overarching importance of the spiritual frame through a narrative between two fictional characters, a business leader and his spiritual guide. Others see Jesus as the explicit answer: Jones (1996) applies Jesus's CEO wisdom to more modern and mundane situations. Mitroff and Denton (1999) conclude that most organizations are spiritually impoverished and that real change and improvement in performance will come only when organizations find ways to integrate their stakeholders' personal beliefs with organizational values. Based on their 'spiritual audit' survey of 131 organizations, they identified those beliefs to which employees are most committed and presented five models for harnessing the power of spiritual energy.

QUESTION TIME?

Many organizations have had experiences with consultants. In your workgroup, discuss these experiences: which of the above characterizations seems best to capture the different experiences?

OWNERSHIP AND CONTROL OF STRATEGY

The debate about ownership and control

In this chapter we have seen that there are many folk involved in making strategy: strategists, TMTs, consultants and different fractions of the business elites. This begs one of the most pertinent questions in management: how to control and govern organizations? And what is the role of the strategist in governance? This area is of particular relevance in the contemporary organizational world, especially in light of the spate of corporate failures in recent years. More attention is now being focused on corporate governance.

Corporate governance includes the broad issues relating to the processes and relationships that affect how corporations are administered and controlled, including the incentives, safeguards and dispute-resolution processes used to order the activities of the various stakeholders recognized by the corporation, such as owners, managers, employees, creditors, suppliers, customers and communities within which business is done.

A whole subfield has developed in the literature in the wake of the long-term impact of Berle and Means' (1932) research, in *The Modern Corporation and Private Property*, creating a field that is often referred to as corporate governance.

Corporate governance represents the formal recognition that, despite whatever may inform the teaching agenda about the functional homogeneity of business and management, corporate life, riddled as its is with different interests, can, on occasion, be riven by conflicts. Ideologies of shareholder maximization are one way that corporations seek to keep the lid on these potential conflicts: if all can be made to serve this interest then it is clear what has to be done. But, theories have been developed to minimize deviations from this interest, which we will shortly encounter. On the principle that if it is not broken there is no point putting a fix in place, we may conclude that the ideology of shareholder maximization does not always do the trick of creating consensus. Different interests are tangled up in the corporation. Nowhere do these become more apparent that in action around remuneration.

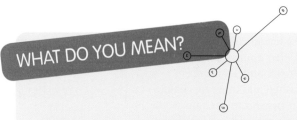

WHAT DO YOU MEAN?

Interests and remuneration

The Dean of the Rottman School of Management, Roger Martin, at Canada's University of Toronto has likened business practices that link remuneration to share value as allowing professional league sports team members to bet on the outcome of their games. He notes that both professional sports leagues such as the American NFL and publicly traded companies operate similarly. In football, players play games that are won and lost. Businesses develop products and services and sell them. If they develop and sell more products more profitably than their competitors they win; if their competitors develop and sell more products more profitably then they win.

Of course, sports fans can punt on the outcome of the sports games. They can bet that one side or the other will win, and even bet on the amount that they might win by. Similarly, business fans can punt on the outcome of the business games. They can bet on this share value going up and win a nice dividend if they are correct. The world of bets – and the world of stock markets – is one of expectations. People bet on an outcome that they think they can predict and are prepared to take a risk on. It is a world of expectations in which bookies establish 'point spreads' for each upcoming game, so people bet on how much a team will win by: will the team exceed expectations (the point spread) or not? In business, 'expectations' are traded on the stock market where prices are based not on actual product sales or performance, but on expectations of a company's future performance.

Martin says that the problem with expectations, and especially *rising* expectations, is that, at some point, they become impossible to sustain. All sports fans know this and so do teams and their coaches if they are wise. In the long term it does not really matter too much for the coach and team: they are paid on a contract basis based on their actual performance in games, not on the basis of whether or not they meet the gambling market's expectations. Anyway, legally, they are not supposed to bet on the outcomes of games for the obvious reason that if there is a large profit to be made by gambling on the result of the game, the team members face a potential 'moral hazard': they could throw the game in order to engineer a result that would maximize their value in terms of gambling returns. The integrity of the game would be compromised.

Sports team remuneration deviates from that of business. In the business world, top managerial pay is closely linked to the company's performance in the expectations (stock market) world. As a result, executives are tempted (or pressured) to make decisions will that will increase the next quarter's stock price. There is nothing wrong with that, of course – except where the values are based on unrealizable expectations, or where investment decisions are not made because they might have a negative impact on short-term share prices or dividends. Then it becomes in the short-term interests of the TMT to put off costly investments for the future in preference of strategies that will shore up or will not dilute the present value. There will be a temptation to keep expectations rising, for them to take big gambles that might well pay off, or to practise increasingly creative approaches to accounting.

What may start out as a way of aligning principal and agent interests can too easily end being dysfunctional for all parties concerned. The power of top management can lead it to favour its short-term interests in an inflated share process rather than a long-term interest in the sustainability of the business. Political questions in business, as elsewhere, usually amount to a relation between interests and actions, connected by strategies that draw on available rationalities to formulate actions designed to realize these interests. When you consider that your designs will come up against those of others who have similar designs but different rationalities and interests, then you will appreciate that crafting a coherent strategy becomes a significant political exercise of compromise, negotiation and power: sometimes others will resist, sometimes you will not be able to make them do what you want them to do and they do not want to do, and sometimes, even as you think you have succeeded, they will work to sabotage your designs. All this is normal in organizational life. Sabotage, sycophancy and secrecy are as common in organizational life as the more hallowed coordination, communication and control.

It is often assumed that if only the organization can get its corporate governance 'right', the problems of control will be solved.

Where there is a unity of ownership, control and governance, as would be the case, for instance, where a small-business proprietor runs their own business, there is little need for an explicit governance theory. The need for such theory derives from a situation where ownership and control do not necessarily coincide, as is the case with all stock-exchange-listed companies. That this is normally the case has been evident ever since Berle and Means (1932) published their book. In it they identified the following trends:

- A significant concentration of capital in enterprises of a larger scale.
- Managerial rather than owner control of the assets thus concentrated.
- A weakening of the discipline of the capital market as a constraint on managerial action where there is a separation of ownership of assets and their day-to-day control.
- The development of goals other than that of pure profit maximization as salient for managerial action.

Above all, the implications of their analysis pointed to the fact that the 'separation of ownership and control implies an inability on the part of the owners effectively to check the management of the corporation and threatens economic efficiency' (Gomez and Korine, 2008: 233). What is to stop management maximizing personal utilities rather than shareholder value?

Berle and Means (1932) were writing after the decline in dominance of the great 'robber barons' who commanded US business at the turn of the nineteenth century. It was evident that, as early as the 1920s, that control was increasingly less connected with a few dominant individuals. In part this was a result of the changing legislative environment that sought to enforce competitive and anti trust behaviour as well as the natural wastage of the barons. Moreover, property rights were increasingly being dissolved into a form of nominal ownership to which revenue rights were attached through share ownership, while the control of such assets was vested in organizationally framed relations of production and control. Real ownership was increasingly disconnected from real control. Thus, Berle and Means (1932) were addressing the widespread separation of ownership and control that characterized US business by the 1920s. In the wake of the 1929 Wall Street crash they were intrigued by why millions of people were prepared to entrust their life savings to businesses run by unaccountable managers over whom they had virtually no control. Given the high degree of fragmentation in shareholding it became apparent that the control of corporations could be achieved with quite small concentrations of shareholding. Opinions have differed about the size of the percentage, with around 4 per cent usually being sufficient to render control in the United States if the majority of the other shares are either fragmented or held by non-interventionist institutions such as pension funds (Davis and Useem, 2002: 242).

Real control can be highly concentrated even when the nominal ownership is extremely fragmented. The democratization of shareholding is not equivalent to the democratization of control. Hence, where there are significant stockholdings by executives, they may well be both agents and effective principals, to use some terms to be introduced shortly. In essence, if the stockholdings are largely passively owned by non-interventionist financial institutions that merely seek a certain rate of return, and by small shareholders, then quite small bundles of concentrated shareholding in the hands of senior executives can fuse ownership and control, which is the basis for much contemporary thinking, as we will shortly see.

Berle and Means maintained that the separation of ownership and control would mean that the managers controlled the corporation and would use its resources to pursue 'prestige, power, or the gratification of professional zeal' (1932: 122). The problematic of corporate governance – who controls the corporation and how? – flows directly from Berle and Means' (1932) work; often it has a strongly normative flavour in terms of who *should* control the corporation? The debates they initiated are important for a discussion of strategy due to three major implications:

- The growing complexity and size of the organizations that the skilled use of capital makes possible.
- The governability of this complexity.
- In whose interests the strategies that govern its use into the future will be exercised.

This control of the corporation and its strategic direction is usually referred to as the problem of corporate governance.

Corporate governance in contemporary times

Corporate governance concerns politics at large: conflicts of interests about the actions and purposes of organizations between stakeholders. That these are many and of strategic importance can be adduced from the number of official reports oriented towards producing effective corporate governance standards that will forestall these conflicts of interest, including the Organization for Economic Cooperation and Development's *Principles of Corporate Governance* and the *Cadbury Report* in the UK, as well as the California Public Employees Retirement System's *Global Principles for Corporate Governance*. In the United States, the Sarbanes–Oxley Act was introduced in an attempt to improve corporate governance in the wake of the collapse of Enron.

Part of the stimulus for these reports is theoretical: the branch of economics known as agency theory considers the shareholders as the principals of the firm for whom managers act as agents – agents who cannot be trusted unless their interests are closely aligned with those of shareholders in order to maximize shareholder value, according to leading theorists such as Fama (1980) and Jensen and Meckling (1976). In this view the firm is a bundle of assets whose value is given solely by the shareholders' return on investments. It is argued by agency theory that transparency and accountability are important: however, when firms improve their disclosure quality they tend to attract more transient institutional investors, which in turn increases the volatility of their share process in a result which is exactly the opposite of what the theory predicts. Consider the well-known case of Lehman Brothers: it was a model of agency theory, having adopted all of its corporate governance principles:

> In most (if not all) the companies that failed in the 2008 financial crisis, the majority of executive compensation packages were provided in the form of a variable, performance-based annual incentive delivered in both cash and equity awards. According to the last proxy statement presented by Lehman Brothers, its CEO received over $34 million as his annual compensation and 85 per cent of it was in the form of stock and options. ... And this is customary in the industry. Similar compensation practices have long been the norm in large financial services firms. (Berrone, 2008: 2)

Many of those large financial services firms, such as Lehman Brothers and Bear Stearns, did not survive 2008 and many other firms that still exist only do so while being deeply constrained by debt and government loans to bail them out. Although advocates of agency theory might argue that, in the long term, weak agency controls will result in poor stock valuations and thus takeovers, so that more efficient agency can be exercised and the underlying value of the assets realized, this is hardly adequate as a perspective on the excesses of 2008.

Not only does the theory not work too well in its own terms, but also its terms are far too restricted. Unfortunately for the theory, not all stakeholders are shareholders and the interests of these other stakeholders, such as employees, managers, banks, communities and unions representing the workforce, are not always paramount, especially in the short term: too strong a focus on the interests of shareholders can always be satisfied by minimizing expenditures on future-oriented activities, such as innovation, and in the short term this will return better dividends to shareholders. In the long term, however, it could consign the corporation and its shareholders to oblivion as other firms that have innovated outperform it in the market. Unfortunately for business practice, the agency perspective has been enormously influential in US and other Anglo-Saxon business circles. The consequences are evident.

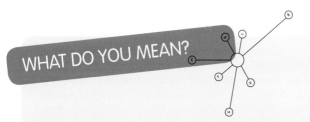

WHAT DO YOU MEAN?

Bob Tricker and Chris Mallin's blog

Banks in crisis: failures of corporate governance?

Posted February 13, 2009: http://corporategovern anceup.wordpress.com/
Corporate governance has been gaining more predominance around the world over the last decade. However the last year or so which has brought the financial crisis and the 'credit crunch' has seen an unprecedented interest in some of the areas that are central to corporate governance: executive remuneration; boards of directors, independent non-executive directors; internal controls and risk management; the role of shareholders.

However the focus on these areas has brought into sharp relief some of the failings of the present system whether these have been brought about by greed, naivety, or a lack of real appreciation of the risk exposures of banks.

Bankers' bonuses

Whilst many would agree that bankers have received huge payouts, often for seeming failing companies, bonuses appear likely to be cut, possibly

(Continued)

(Continued)

by around 40% or more. Peter Thal Larsen and Adrian Cox (*FT*, page 13, 7/8 Feb 09) in their article 'Barclays bankers braced for bonus cut' highlight that even much reduced bonuses are likely to be controversial given that feelings are running high amongst the public and politicians alike.

The generous remuneration packages of executive directors of some of the UK's largest banks have caught the headlines day after day in recent weeks. In their article 'Former executives face bonus grilling' (*FT* page 2, 9 Feb 09), George Parker and Daniel Thomas mention an interesting historical fact 'in the early 18th century, after the bursting of the South Sea bubble, a parliamentary resolution proposed that bankers be tied up in sacks filled with snakes and thrown into the River Thames'! No doubt there are those who wish the same might happen today although a grilling before the Commons Treasury Committee may prove to be almost as unpleasant an experience!

Adrian Cox's article 'Barclays executives must wait longer for bonuses' (*FT*, page 2, 11 Feb 09) highlights that Barclays is trying to design a pay structure that retains staff whilst rewarding long-term performance at a time when banks have been urged to show 'moral responsibility' in their remuneration structures. This pay restructuring will affect not just directors but also senior employees, and other banks including UBS, Credit Suisse, RBS and Lloyds are in a similar position.

Risk management

'Former HBOS chiefs accused over risk controls as bankers apologise' was the striking head of the article by Jane Croft, Peter Thal Larsen and George Parker (*FT*, page 1, 11 Feb 09). Under questioning from the Commons Treasury Committee, Lord Stevenson, Andy Hornby, Sir Tom McKillop and Sir Fred Goodwin all apologized for what had happened at RBS. Part of the questioning brought to light that a former employee had warned the board of potential risks associated with the bank's rapid expansion.

Risk management is an area that is bound to gain a higher profile given the extent of the impact of the use of toxic assets which many feel were not well understood.

Where were the institutional shareholders?

Lord Myners, the City minister, has urged shareholders to challenge banks 'Myners calls on shareholders to challenge reward cultures' by Adrian Cox and Kate Burgess (*FT*, page 3, 10 Feb 09). Lord Myners, they state, said that 'institutional investors should look at the content of remuneration reports and ask questions if the data are complex or opaque'.

My view is that it remains an ongoing debate as to what extent institutional shareholders should intervene in the affairs of the companies in which they invest (investee companies). It is widely recognised that engagement and dialogue are useful and necessary for an institutional investor to monitor the activities of investee companies. However there is a line to be drawn between what it is feasible – and desirable – for the institutional shareholders to do, and what might be seen as undesirable and restrictive.

Sophia Grene's article 'Funds say they did all they could to warn banks' (*FT*, page 9, 8 Feb 09) highlights the view of the UK's Investment Management Association that 'fund managers did all they could to prevent banks hurtling to their doom, but under the current system, shareholders cannot shout loud enough to be heard'. The IMA also indicated a possible way forward for the future: 'investors can only do so much … maybe we need to take a closer look at how investors and non-executive directors interact. They're privy to much more information than the investors'.

Walker Review of the corporate governance of the banking industry

Sir David Walker has been appointed to lead a review of the corporate governance of the banking industry which will look into remuneration and bonuses, risk management and board composition. The terms of reference can be found at: http://www.hm-treasury.gov.uk/press_10_09.htm

Bankers abroad

In the USA, President Obama has brought in reforms to limit the remuneration of executives to $500,000 at those banks that have had a bail out. Shares could also be given under incentive plans but would only kick in once government support had been repaid, 'Obama gets tough on pay for executives', Alan Beattie and Edward Luce (*FT* page 1, 5 Feb 09).

STRATEGY IN AND AROUND THE BOARDROOM

With good corporate governance in place, senior executive members comprising the TMT, under the direction of the board, should be able to shape the vision and mobilize the ranks, and make the difference between success and failure, say Tichy (1997) and Charan and Tichy (1998). Useem and Davis (2002) note also that senior selection decisions can have immediate effects on stock valuations increasing or decreasing. So can their health: for instance, Apple lost considerable share value when rumours about Steve Jobs' health began to circulate in 2009. Given these data, how much do we know of what actually goes on when and where strategy is made in the boardroom, ask McNulty and Pettigrew (1995: 847)? Not much is the answer. The boardroom is the arena in which the managerial elite struts its professional stuff and practises strategy-making, where chairmen, presidents, chief executives and non-executive directors meet and mingle purposefully in order to make decisions, operating as boards, executive committees and TMTs.

Of course, these elites are not unconstrained. Stakeholders, creditors, outside members of the board, all wield their influence on strategy-making but against this must be balanced the fact that with the exception of creditors, whose influence is often not invited, these stakeholders are chosen by the senior management as board members and that part-time board members only have a limited commitment of time and discretion to their board activities. Management, moreover, is infinitely better informed and has access to much more information and data than these external influences. Moreover, norms of board conduct often limit the influence of outsiders to little more than an advisory role (McNulty and Pettigrew, 1995: 849), despite their legal mandate. The power relations that part-time members of boards enter into when they assume board membership are constrained by the macro and structural factors shaping that context, as well as by institutionalized expectations and legal frameworks. In moments of crisis they may well be able to act outside of the 'normal' constraints and oppose executive actions, but in other circumstances they seem less likely to initiate more positive power actions, which require great 'skill' and 'will'. The ability to mobilize power increases with phenomena such as relevant experience and expertise (the usefulness of which is always contextually framed); the power that can be derived from relations with powerful external agencies; the representational role played on board committees and, most significantly, the flows of information that come from an embeddedness in networks and interlocking directorships.

In a later article McNulty and Pettigrew (1999) researched a larger sample of part-time board members than the 20 directors investigated in the previous study. Potentially, such directors can have a role in exercising strategic control and making strategic choices and changes. Not all directors will have the same say: it all depends on context, state McNulty and Pettigrew (1999: 48). The elements of context that are important are the 'public debate and policy making about corporate governance, the history and performance of the company, the conduct and process of a board and informal relations between board members'. Unfortunately, as they argue, the arena of board behaviour has been subject to much abstract theorizing in agency theory and in resource dependence theory, with the former stressing boards as arenas for conflict to be played out between owners and managers (principals and agents) while the latter stress the role that boards play as mechanisms for reducing uncertainty about the environment (Pfeffer, 1972; Pearce and Zahra, 1991). While earlier research tended not to say much about the role of boards in making strategy, it is now widely recognized that boards do in fact set the strategic direction through 'mission' and 'vision' statements.

As McNulty and Pettigrew (1999) note, earlier work by Eisenhardt and Zbaracki (1992) summarizes much of what we know about choice behaviour: it is boundedly rational, non-linear, emotional and political in character. The findings of McNulty and Pettigrew's (1999) research suggested that part-time board members do exercise some control over management with respect to strategy. Some of this involves making strategic decisions on capital investment proposals that come from management; mostly boards will agree with the proposal put forward, which of course does not mean that they are rubber stamping because the rule of anticipated reaction could well be in play. Only carefully vetted and considered proposals are likely to be accepted on the basis of rational consideration and so it is these that will tend to be placed before the board. Part-time directors shape discussions about strategic decisions in subtle ways suggest McNulty and Pettigrew (1999), especially in the early stages of formulation. Such ways are episodic, reactive and intermittent as they respond to the agendas and papers that are tabled. Hence, their role is more one of checking than initiating actions. Finally, in respect of how the context, content and conduct of strategy are shaped by part-time directors, McNulty and Pettigrew (1999) find that they will often frame strategy discussions through questioning and constructing contexts in which strategy discussions unfold, contributing to the overall normative environment of what constitutes legitimate questioning.

The sample that McNulty and Pettigrew (1995; 1999) interviewed was well laced with titled people. Certainly, the upper echelons of companies would be graced by unequivocal members of a national elite – not necessarily titles, depending on the democratic tenor of the country in question. For instance, Davis et al. (2003) found that the US corporate elite was indeed a 'small world', able to withstand environmental changes governing the nature of board composition and showing remarkable coherence and consistency in its relations and ranks. Davis and Useem (2002), two academics from the United States who research boards, note that where a US CEO has an elite MBA degree it accelerates the rapidity of their reach for the top; that the more elite the background from which they come, the more likely they are to attract high-quality external directorships and, to the extent that they hand-pick their board, that it enhances pay and perquisites (Useem and Karabel, 1986; Belliveau, O'Reilly and Wade, 1996). Overall, they note that when we extend the focus from the chief strategists to the TMT we find that companies with greater diversity at the top will gain a greater market share and operating profits (Davis and Useem, 2002).

The top management looks very different in different countries: Japanese boards rarely have outsiders on them; US boards will typically have two or three outsiders, while in German and Dutch two-tiered co-determination systems, employees will hold half of the upper tier seats; and in the UK and Switzerland it is management that dominates the board. Whatever the composition, research on teams' success suggests that when boards exceed 15 or 20 members, they become more prone to factionalism and less able to work together. In US research it has been established that companies with smaller boards had stronger incentives for their chief executive, were more likely to dismiss an underperforming CEO, and achieve a larger market share and superior financial performance, suggest Davis and Useem (2002).

TENSIONS IN TMTs

Charles Harvey, Chris Howorth, Frank Mueller and John Sillince collaborated on a fascinating study into strategy-making in a flagship British hospital, the Central

Middlesex. Harvey served as a non-executive director there and his research team provided an important glimpse into how strategy gets made in a complex professional organization such as a hospital. The one they studied, mirroring hospitals throughout the UK, had undergone a great deal of strategic change. Furthermore, there were two entrenched powerful groups represented on the hospital – the clinicians and the non-executive directors. The latter wanted change to make the firm more managerialist, while the former resisted change and asserted the traditional power of the medical profession. The boardroom was the battleground on which the two factions fought. Senior managers within the hospital sought to try and find a way of mediating between them.

While there is much talk in corporate circles of the company or organization as 'we', the unitariness of the entity in question should not be assumed. It is an empirical not an a priori matter, something that management researchers, with their eye on the upper echelons and, frequently, with interests in consulting, often miss. Not talking to many people outside the executive suites, they often miss the scorn, tension and derision surrounding strategic corporate pronouncements. Of course, not all managers are managerialist, believing in the rational mutuality of interests and their coherence as reflected in the strategic plans of the organizations. Some TMT are oriented toward pluralism. Not for them the illusion of a singular rationality that happens to coincide with their rationality and interests, but a realization that rationality is always situated and, thus, invariably a matter of plural rationalities.

Many TMT are riven with conflict. For instance, the Blair governments (1997–2001, 2001–5, 05–7) in the UK were noted for the amount of tension that existed between the PM and his Chancellor, Gordon Brown. Both factions had different agendas, different constituencies in Parliament, and both possessed highly skilled political operatives who would brief and spin against their opponents. The idiosyncratic nature of political parties means they are especially prone to such behaviour – and it should be seen as natural rather than in any way aberrant.

While conflict and dissent are inevitable in many organizations, in others they get discouraged or even suppressed. Some research that Chris, in conjunction with Frank Mueller (Carter and Mveller, 2002), carried out into strategy-making in a privatized utility identified two competing groups within the TMT: modernizing managerialists and action-based managerialists. The research chronicles the way in which the two groups saw the world differently (the modernizing managerialists were cerebral and proceeded by using theory and careful planning; in contrast, the action-based managerialists were mavericks who emphasized action over thought). Whereas in the hospital example above each of the different parties grudgingly accepted the other's existence, in the case of the utility the relationship between the two groups was hostile and antagonistic. In this instance the organization was becoming increasingly unitarist in its management.

When unitarism prevails it leads to a suppression of debate and dissent. This can become enshrined in an organization's culture as was the case with the Enron corporation. Enron in the late 1990s was corporate America's favourite company. Aggressive and highly competitive both internally and in its relations with external stakeholders, the organization prided itself on being highly successful and innovative. It set itself ambitious growth targets, which it seemed to exceed every year. While feted as a leading organization, life in Enron required employees to genuflect towards the corporate executives. One of the characteristics of Enron was that employees could only talk positively and articulate good news about the company. Tacitly, the organization had a 'no bad news' policy, whereby if anyone reported bad news to a superior they would be managed out of the company. The organization resembled a cult whereby only good news stories about Enron could be articulated. Enron, as is well known, drowned in a tsunami of

YOU CAN DOWNLOAD…

How these tensions played out on the book's website at www. sagepub.co.uk/cleggstrategy in Mueller, F., Sillince, J., Harvey, C. and Howorth, C. (2004) 'A Rounded Picture is What We Need': Rhetorical Strategies, Arguments and the Negotiation of Change in a UK Hospital Trust, *Organization Studies*, Special Issue on Discourse, 25(1): 85–103.

Pluralism is best understood as the recognition that there are equally rational, competing views in an organization.

Unitarist management is best understood as the tendency to believe that only one view is acceptable, rational and tenable.

YOU CAN DOWNLOAD…

More about the tensions surrounding unitarism on the book's website at www. sagepub.co.uk/cleggstrategy by Carter, C. and Mueller, F. (2002) The 'Long March' of the Management Modernisers: Ritual, Rhetoric and Rationality, *Human Relations*, 55(11): 1325–54.

accounting scandals. It became clear that the profits were a fiction, conjured up, as if by magic, through accounting trickery. How an organization governs itself appropriately is an important issue. In the case of Enron, one of the striking features of the organization was that there was no mechanism for dissent, critique or merely to express concern about the direction the organization was going in. Critique was heresy, a disloyalty that had to be punished. How an organization accommodates dissent and critique is an important issue.

CORPORATE CODES

What do codes do?

Increasingly, the extent to which an organization adopts a regulatory compliance system can influence its legal liability for any breaches of law that it is responsible for, as Parker and Nielsen (2009) suggest. Codes, standards and other forms of social contract are, in principle, supposed to engender better organizational behaviour. Such codes are expected not only to increase the commitment to compliance with the law, but also to build a strategic frame that acts as an insurance policy, identifying, correcting and preventing misdemeanours throughout the organization and helping support a corporate culture of ethical compliance.

Despite, or perhaps because of, the recent waves of corporate scandals, it is increasingly the case that boards adopt codes of corporate ethics for their organization members to comply with. While such codes may have obvious legitimation functions, they have also been recognized as being of real value in framing the way that the TMT, in particular, behaves. However, as Jensen, Sandström and Helin (2009) suggest, corporate codes are not static documents and their sense is never guaranteed by what they state, what they say. They are documents that are subject to constant translation in process and in use. On occasions they will be used as accounts to legitimate actions that need to be legitimated; on other occasions they will be used to try and shape actions and attitudes proactively. Their research into the introduction of a US corporate code from the parent company into a Swedish subsidiary suggests that a great deal of translation occurs in instantiating such codes. While these codes are assumed to communicate clear messages for framing ethical thinking and action, and are expected to be understood in similar ways throughout the organization, this has proved not to be the case. Codes and their interpretation are highly indexical on the context of their interpretation and their interpreters. Moreover, because of this, codes do not achieve the expressed intentions of their purpose: they do not provide an effective standardizing frame for strategic behaviour. By all means have codes, suggest Jensen et al. (2009), but do not expect too much of them and do not shy away from the fact that sometimes organization members will choose strategies that are ethically dubious, because to do so is to deny those members being exposed to the risk of making morally wrong choices. We need to be continually exposed to moral dilemmas if we are not to lose touch with morality, they suggest, in line with Giddens (1991). We should never forget that companies such as Enron won awards for their corporate codes!

In organization science the gap between rules and practice has been explored by several seminal contributions. For instance, Gouldner (1954) analysed 'indulgency patterns' in organizations that described the difference between interpretation of rules by the book and their actual interpretation in practice. For Meyer and Rowan (1977) rules are ceremonial façades to be contrasted with the reality of day-to-day organizational life, while Brunsson (1994) finds that public sector organizations institutionally maintain and capitalize on the gaps between talk, action and decision. In his words, organized hypocrisy is normal. Similarly, in the literature on business ethics several authors suggested that ethics can neither be fully understood nor managed through rule-based codes (Jackall, 1988; Victor and Cullen, 1988; Andrews, 1989; Warren, 1993; Paine, 1994; Stevens, 1994; Kjonstad and Willmott, 1995; ten Bos, 1997; Weaver, Treviño and Cochran, 1999a; 1999b). Kjonstadt and Willmott (1995: 446) capture the conclusions of this stream of literature when they say that 'the provision of codes of conduct is an insufficient, and possibly a perverse, means of recognizing the significance, and promoting the development, of ethical corporate behaviour'. Such codes of conducts might ensure compliance but they do not produce ethically sound behaviour (Munro, 1992). As Kjonstad and Willmott (1995: 449) argue, 'instead of acting to encourage and facilitate the development of moral learning and the exercise of moral judgment, [such] codes operate to promote routinized compliance'. A 'compliance mode' of ethics runs the risk of resulting in disempowerment, bureaucratization and feelings of individual irresponsibility.

Other recent empirical research supports this argument. Barker studied the standards expressed in codes of conduct at General Dynamics and found that these did not induce any fundamental change in regard to organizational ethics. Jackson (2000: 349) showed in his study of 200 companies in the UK, US, France, Spain and Germany that the 'clarity of corporate policy has little influence on managers' reported ethical decision-making. The perceived behaviour of managers' colleagues is far more important in predicting attitudes towards decision-making or managers across the nationalities surveyed'. Related research focuses on how the use of rules differs according to local culture-specific and industry-specific practices interpreted in context (Donaldson and Dunfee, 1995; Spicer, Dunfee and Bailey, 2004). This is in line with Gouldner's (1954) findings that what rules mean varies with the context of enactment; as the philosopher Wittgenstein (1968) argued, rules do not do anything by themselves but need to be interpreted and enacted situationally. It is rule *use*, not rule *existence*, which determines ethical conduct (Andrews, 1989). Jackall researched the 'moral rules-in-use that managers construct to guide their behaviour at work' and found that 'actual organizational moralities are … contextual, situational, highly specific, and, most often, unarticulated' (Jackall, 1988: 4, 6). Munro (1992) similarly captured a situation of conflicting norms embedded in different situated rationalities. Ethics are at stake when rules and norms clash and there is no meta-norm to tell one what is right from wrong. In this sense, focusing on ethics as practice requires one to pay attention to the context of organization history and its power/knowledge relations. Hence, the concepts of power and discourse become theoretically important in understanding everyday organizational ethics.

Ethical codes in practice

The pragmatic tradition of power analysis that begins with Machiavelli, moves through Nietzsche, onto Foucault, and into contemporary post-Foucauldian theories argues that it is in the micro-practices of social systems that power is played out (Gordon and Grant, 2005). Further, these micro-practices discursively and contextually frame ethics (Jackall, 1988; Kjonstat and Willmott, 1995; Keleman and Peltonen, 2001; ten Bos and Willmott, 2001; Thorne and Saunders, 2002). As Townley (1993) aptly illustrates, power relations constitute patterns of social order, including ethical order, which, over time, become embedded in dominant discourses. Beneath the surface of contextual forms of discourse and knowledge at work lurk power relations entangled in tension with explicit moral codes. It is in these tangles that ethics are constructed, organizational members and significant others make sense of them and, as a consequence, certain values can be reinforced as deeply held beliefs that shape and articulate practice.

Together with their colleague Ray Gordon, two of the authors of this book, Stewart Clegg and Martin Kornberger (2009), reported a detailed ethnographic research into the relation between newly implemented codes of conduct that had been designed by a new CEO in conjunction with change consultants in the New South Wales Police Service. They found that new codes, rather than developing new practices, became the occasion for old and ethically dubious practices to be reconstructed.

In contrast to their design, new practices aimed at changing the Police Service simply reinforced old patterns. One of these, in particular, was studied. The Operations Control and Review (OCR) was designed as a formal meeting in which the senior management team of the Police Service could coordinate and discuss the operational performance of each police Local Area Command. Disciplinary practices emerged from the commissioner and executive team's actions within these meetings, which were broadcast to every police station in the state in the interests of transparency. There, these actions were seen and internalized as a rule of anticipated reaction (Friedrich, 1937) providing clues to the consequences of non-compliant behaviour by lower level officers. Despite these operational systems being both ostensibly neutral and a technical means to achieve an objective, they framed both the exercise of power and, ultimately, whether organization members understood their own actions as ethical or not. More to the point, the established management techniques constituted potential ethical positions (Styhre, 2001).

There was a gap between discourses and practices: the new discourse of reform introduced by the commissioner and the discourse that was used by organizational members to make sense of their everyday experiences, and their actual practices, were not aligned. This was particularly evident in the use that was made of central organizational changes that were intended to empower lower order officers in the Police Service, such as the OCR. As Ford and Ford (1995) have shown, language can mask the gap between reality and image. The failure of the change effort could be seen in terms of the strong identification with an unofficial culture that members enacted in shared sensemaking processes, even after a reform of the official culture. Strong organizational identity with an old culture of police corruption not only provided members with structure and order but also reduced the uncertainties of what were often fuzzy boundaries between good and bad behaviour (Hogg and Terry, 2000). As Fiol (2001) has argued, positive identification by members with a strongly articulated organizational identity can hinder change processes. While Fiol suggests that an identity change can be accomplished through changing language, since language makes non-discursive behaviour (such as promotion systems) meaningful, the historical constitution of the NSW Police Service discourse undercut such attempts. Within the leadership and the rank and file few could imagine that, in practice, despite the Royal Commission and the reform that it precipitated, things could be done differently – and despite what the rhetoric of reform might say discursively. In short, the discourse that informed their reflection did not provide them with the language to acquire an understanding of their behaviour as potentially unethical. What we found was that the 'ostensive' aspect of routines (Feldman and Pentland, 2003) was stronger than the performative aspect that would have allowed for change: old practices moulded new initiatives in ways that paradoxically reinforced the old system.

Although the official discourse changed as new practices were implemented, at a micro level the discursive practices remained the same. Brunsson's (1994) concept of hypocrisy seemed to be operative: while the talk was adopted to comply with external pressures, the discursive actions that actually formed the practice of policing did not change. The rationality of change was a façade that masked reality rather than actually changing it (Meyer and Rowan, 1977). New strategies were assimilated into the existing patterns of the social system. Everyday interactions perpetuated existing practices, regardless of the pressure these practices were under, even when they were reconstituted in new organizational forms. In moments of enormous crisis the system, despite an organizational redesign, stuck to the old, 'default' ways of doing things such that change initiatives were quickly integrated into its old behavioural patterns. Research into resistance to change would suggest such behaviour is not unusual (Tilly, 1991; Collinson, 1994; Sewell, 1998). However, the inertia that we observed in the NSW Police Service adds an important dimension to what we know about change: members of organizations often rationalize their own versions of rationality so that actual change is hard to achieve. Everyday reasoning processes were subject to bounded rationality and led to a 'bounded morality' (Donaldson and Dunfee, 1995).

YOU CAN DOWNLOAD...

The paper by Gordon, R., Clegg, S. R. and Kornberger, M. (2009) Embedded Ethics: Discourse and Power in the New South Wales Police Service, *Organization Studies*, 30(1): 73–99 from the book's website at www. sagepub. co.uk/cleggstrategy

SUMMARY AND REVIEW

Strategy needs champions, we discovered at the outset of the chapter, and these champions can be drawn either from the top management team or from external consultancy advice. The top management team of any organization is made up of its leaders and, at least in the largest organizations, they comprise the business elite that develops strategy. Occasionally, the consultants may be called in to change things around, and we have outlined four major approaches that might be used for this kind of strategy consulting. Whatever strategies are developed and however they are developed, it is widely assumed that they will be accepted and implemented under the direction of the board of directors. Research has been conducted into boards and how they shape strategy by contributors such as McNulty and Pettigrew (1995; 1999) which complements more descriptive studies of who these elites are, how their relations are interlocked, and how cohesive they are, by investigating what it is that these boards do when they do strategy, especially the role of non-executive or part-time directors. Finally the chapter considered the question of corporate codes and the extent to which they can determine compliant behaviour. On the whole, we are sceptical about their capacity to do so, as we indicated by use of the research by Gordon et al. (2009), because the meaning of any code will always be situated and always subject to translation.

EXERCISES

1 Having read this chapter you should be able to say in your own words what the following key terms mean:

● Strategy champions
● Top management teams
● Corporate governance
● Transformational leadership
● Transactional leadership
● Business elites
● Ownership and control
● Corporate codes
● Social capital
● Dominant ideology.

2 What are some of the different approaches commonly used in consulting and how do they differ?

3 What do MBA qualifications do?

4 How do corporate codes function in practice?

5 How and why is the type of schooling and social background of managers important in determining their access to strategy-making?

6 What are the political and social implications of Bourdieu's analysis for strategy?

ADDITIONAL RESOURCES

Our companion website is the best first stop for you to find a great deal of extra resources, free PDF versions of leading articles published in Sage journals, exercise, video and pod casts, team case studies and general questions and links to teamwork resources. Go to www.sagepub.co.uk/cleggstrategy

WEB SECTION

Visit the *Strategy* companion website at www.sagepub.co.uk/cleggstrategy

1 For people who are really interested in corporate governance as a topic, the following website, which is an index to many different countries codes, might be useful: www.ecgi.org/codes/all_codes.php.

2 It is also worthwhile checking out the websites of the major consulting companies to see what kinds of offers they make in terms of their approaches to strategy consulting.

LOOKING FOR A HIGHER MARK?

Reading and digesting these articles that are available free on the companion website www.sagepub.co.uk/ cleggstrategy can help you gain deeper understanding and, on the basis of that, a better grade.

1 Gordon, R., Clegg, S. R. and Kornberger, M. (2009) Embedded Ethics: Discourse and Power in the New South Wales Police Service, *Organization Studies*, 30(1): 73–99.

2 Paroutis, S. and Pettigrew, A. (2007) Strategizing in the Multi-business Firm: Strategy Teams at Multiple Levels and Over Time, *Human Relations*, 60(1): 91–135.

3 Mantere, S. (2005) Strategic Practices as Enablers and Disablers of Championing Activity, *Strategic Organization*, 3: 157–284.

4 Maclean, M., Harvey, C. and Chia, R. (2010) Dominant Corporate Agents and the Power Elite in France and Britain, *Organization Studies*, 31: 327–48.

5 Mueller, F., Sillince, J., Harvey, C. and Howorth, C. (2004) A Rounded Picture is What We Need: Rhetorical Strategies, Arguments and the Negotiation of Change in a UK Hospital Trust, *Organization Studies*, Special Issue on Discourse, 25(1): 85–103.

6 Carter, C. and Mueller, F. (2002) The 'Long March' of the Management Modernisers: Ritual, Rhetoric and Rationality, *Human Relations*, 55(11): 1325–54.

CASE STUDY

Marks & Spencer, 1990–2001:[2] boardroom battles

Chris Carter

Introduction

As we will see in Chapter 9, on power and politics, strategy in organizations does not always proceed in a rational manner. Instead, it can be driven, in part, by the egos, ambitions and hopes of those who work within these organizations, especially when we look at behaviour in corporate boardrooms. The recent corporate history of Marks & Spencer (M&S) represents a fascinating episode within such struggles.

Founded in Cheetham Hill, Manchester, in 1894, M&S rose to a position of pre-eminence in British retailing but, from the 1980s onwards, it struggled with branding and internationalization issues, such that by the 1990s it had declined from a position of dominance in the high street to one of crisis. It was a decline that took nearly a decade – and much pain – from which to recover. While the reasons behind any corporate decline are likely to be complex, in the case of M&S it is widely accepted that problems in the boardroom contributed to the decline in fortunes of the company. This is, perhaps, all the more ironic given that Sir Richard Greenbury, the Chairman of M&S, headed up a UK government review of corporate governance.

Background context

The official culture of M&S was conservative, paternalistic, regimented and very hierarchical. It

***

[2]The case study is based on the extensive reading of numerous publications chronicling the difficulties at Marks & Spencer in the 1990s. In particular, it draws on the excellent account by Judy Bevan, which won the 2002 WH Smith Business Book of the Year award. We strongly recommend reading J. Bevan (2002) *The Rise and Fall of Marks & Spencer*, London: Profile Books. In addition to this, there are many excellent analyses produced by business journalists, available from the online archives of quality newspapers.

was an insiders' organization, in which managers joined after school or university, worked their way up and were 'looked after'. Most people stayed for the entirety of their careers and it was unusual for people to join mid-career. The organization had remained under family control until the early 1980s and in the 1990s family members remained closely linked to the organization. They cast a long shadow over M&S and in many ways set the agenda for how it should be run. People were proud to work for M&S and it possessed an iconic status with its customers. It also had very close links with its suppliers, which were tightly quality controlled to guarantee high-quality and high-reliability garments. Suppliers historically were invariably British companies that had entered into long-term contracts with M&S.

The firm was highly profitable and seemed to have an innate sense of both shaping and responding to its customers' requirements. It was renowned for delivering excellent customer service and good-quality goods at a fair price, even if the styles and fashions were a tad conservative. M&S orchestrated a mutually satisfactory set of relations between suppliers, customer, the City and staff. It was a quintessentially British firm and, aside from a few flagship stores overseas, such as in Paris and Hong Kong, never achieved much success when it ventured elsewhere. The brand did not travel well except among British expatriates and it experienced expensive misadventures in both Canada and the United States. Its growth in the UK was organic and internally generated, which saw it owning stores in high streets across the UK. Unusually for a retail firm, over the years, it had also amassed a large and valuable property portfolio.

In 1991 the outgoing Chairman, Derek Rayner, left a company that was seemingly expanding. He had taken it into North America, through the purchase of Brooks Brothers, and had increased the floor space in the UK. Yet Brooks Brothers was losing money. In the early 1990s, M&S had prevailed over the competition – Burton, Laura Ashley and Next among others – which from the 1980s had seemed to be challenging its dominance on the high street. These competitors fell prey to recessions and takeovers, while M&S remained steady. The recession in the early 1990s, which coincided with Rayner's retirement, had been severe, however, and after the high-rolling late 1980s, it caused difficulties for M&S.

(Continued)

(Continued)

New Chairman and Chief Executive

Rick Greenbury assumed control in 1991 acting as Chairman and Chief Executive, with long-standing M&S executive Clinton Silver serving as his Managing Director. Greenbury was the consummate M&S insider, being deeply socialized into the organization's sense of its culture. He had joined M&S shortly after leaving school, having for family reasons been unable to attend university, something his detractors were to claim was a source of great insecurity to him. Greenbury worked his way up from being a management trainee to head of the company. His hero was Simon Marks, a previous Chairman, and he would always approach a problem by thinking about how Marks would have approached it himself. This was to such an extent that 'whenever Greenbury hit a problem he always looked for the solution in the archives' (Bevan, 2002: 87).

Greenbury was deeply committed to the organization and was widely hailed as a retailer of exceptional ability. As a personality he was complex: many close to him were quick to point out his kindness and sensitivity; others saw him as arrogant, aggressive and over bearing. While most conceded that Greenbury was a brilliant retailer, many retained doubts about his capacity as a strategist. What was certainly clear was that Greenbury was assertive when it came to promoting M&S. For instance, a 'Rickogram' – a strongly worded letter complaining about a particular article – would, according to journalists' legend, quickly rebut any criticism in the media. Business journalists became accustomed to being on the receiving end of a Rickogram.

That Greenbury was seen as dictatorial was in keeping with the behaviour patterns of previous chairmen at M&S. Derek Rayner, the last incumbent, had been seen as even more authoritarian than Greenbury. At the time it was generally reckoned that the heads of most major retailers were mere dictators: 'Most successful retailers are run by gifted dictators, and Rick was a dictator. The problem came when, after years of success, the company began to operate only to please Rick, not the customer' (Bevan, 2002: 128). A pattern certainly existed: to rise in the organization one needed to conform, perform well and not cause any controversy. It was a context whereby one always deferred to those in power.

Out of recession

For many years M&S had successfully operated a policy of trying to satisfy both its employees and customers. It had for decades proved very successful in this endeavour. However, the business was no longer under family control and was now largely owned by institutional shareholders, such as large insurance companies and investment funds. Yet, M&S remained very insular – for instance, for most of the 1990s it refused to accept credit cards, other than its own charge card. Only in recent years had it begun to install changing rooms. This move was made, somewhat begrudgingly, in spite of the received company wisdom that this reduced the amount of available floor space for the sales of products.

The recession of the early 1990s was a difficult period for M&S. In 1992, Greenbury launched the 'outstanding value' campaign, which sought to give customers excellent value. M&S hit on some very popular lines such as 'the body' for female customers. Merchandisers (staff who decide on what quantities of a product to buy and if the product is doing well to try and acquire more) were given a free rein and were able to buy into lines they thought would be profitable. This reaped rewards, with profits in 1993 of £736 million, which by 1994 had reached £851 million. Greenbury set the target of being the first British retailer to hit £1 billion in pre-tax profit. Everything was geared towards attaining this target. The City and financial press praised Greenbury, and he scored highly in various 'most admired business man' polls that appeared in newspapers. What was behind the success of this period?

Although M&S possessed flagship stores in major cities that generated most of its profits, it also had smaller stores in provincial cities that made little or no money and, in addition, it had gradually begun to expand its 'out of town' stores. The latter – a mere 25 out of 260 stores – were generating about a quarter of all the profit for the group. Consequently, Greenbury embarked on a strategy of spending money in those stores that made money and making no investments in those that were struggling:

> In order to get to his desired £1 billion he knew he had to put maximum resources into the most profitable stores, and he had to push return on sales way above the 10% his mentor Simon Marks decreed was the maximum for sustained profits growth. (Bevan, 2002: 136)

More of the best products and a greater array of products were sent to the profit-making stores and higher margins were charged. This went against

(Continued)

(Continued)

the ethos of the firm which always emphasized the importance of charging a fair price rather than what the market could bear. These measures were combined with a more general cost-cutting and staff reduction policy. This was in line with the business process reengineering, which we discussed in Chapter 3. The strategy of cost cutting was applauded by city pundits, who generally regarded M&S as being over staffed.

Greenbury as Chairman and Chief Executive dominated the boardroom. However, in his mind, he adopted a participatory style of leadership: 'I felt that boardroom is where you make decisions and create policy', said Greenbury. 'So when we made a decision in the boardroom, that is what we would get behind. Therefore everybody had got to speak their mind. On some issues I would force people to give their views' (Bevan, 2002: 127). This view was not shared by many of the executive and non-executive directors, who felt that there was little opportunity to register any opposition. Greenbury was lauded by the City while being criticized by his executives behind his back. This is perhaps not so unusual for corporate executives, but the disjuncture between the two views was striking.

Cadbury report and a new structure

In 1993 Sir Adrian Cadbury – a member of the famous Cadbury chocolate family – authored a report for the British government into corporate governance, following a spate of corporate scandals. At the forefront of his report was the recommendation that there should be a split between the offices of chairman and chief executive, which in many organizations at the time were held by one person. The rationale was that this would make organizations more accountable, lessen the chances for criminality and reduce the power of one person being in charge. The report also recommended that at least five non-executive directors should be employed; they were seen as neutral, objective observers who could help ensure that companies were appropriately managed. While the report was advisory, along with many blue-chip companies, M&S intended to adopt it, something that was in accordance with the wishes of many of its institutional investors.

By this time, succession was beginning to be seen as an issue: who would replace Greenbury when he retired? Clinton Silver, the incumbent Managing Director, who was also retiring, would need to be replaced. In summer 1993 Greenbury devised a new

board structure which, *inter alia*, comprised the new role of deputy chairman and three managing directors – of equal standing – would run different parts of the business, the rationale being that the job was now so big it could no longer be carried out by one person. Keith Oates was appointed Deputy Chairman, while Peter Salsbury, Andrew Stone and Guy McCracken were made Managing Directors. Each of the candidates had their merits, but there was no obvious successor thus, *de facto*, the deputy chairman and managing directors in the new structure were each seen as potential successors. Greenbury, a big tennis and football fan, regarded this structure as providing a competition between the four candidates to see who would prevail. While some regarded the new structure as a means of seeing which of the four executives would emerge as *primes inter pares*, others viewed it more suspiciously, seeing it as a means of stymieing Oates' ambition to become Chief Executive. Unsurprisingly, this structure led to a great deal of tension and conflict between the four erstwhile colleagues who were now rivals.

Greenbury expanded the number of non-executive directors – a group of non-retailers that were generally loyal to him – and pursued a strategy of divide and rule among the executive directors. There was the suspicion that many directors were appointed for their loyalty rather than their ability. Succession was by now the major issue. Keith Oates emerged as a powerful figure within M&S, his power base derived from having successfully built up M&S's financial services arm. A finance expert, he was ambitious and wanted to succeed Greenbury. Against his candidacy was the fact that he was not a merchandiser – all the previous heads of M&S had been merchants – and he had come into the company, unusually, later in his career from the corporate world. Oates' detractors could simply dismiss him as a 'bean counter'. His profile was such that he was appointed Deputy Chairman in the new structure. Much to his chagrin, he soon realized that this corporate work was something of a non-role, restricted to a few ceremonial activities such as chairing meetings when the chairman was out of the country.

Oates, who regarded himself as the front-runner to become chief executive, met with Greenbury shortly after the new structure was announced and made it clear that he would not be happy working under any of the other three managing directors. Moreover, he insisted that he be made Chief Executive immediately. Greenbury was due

(Continued)

(Continued)

to stand down as Chairman in 1996, on his 60th birthday, with the expectation that someone would step up to the position a year prior to his departure. Greenbury, however, warned Oates that he could not assume that he was in pole position to become Chief Executive. In addition, he expressed his anger at, in effect, what he saw as Oates' attempt to push him into premature retirement. The relations between the two men were already strained; after this meeting they deteriorated further.

During this period Greenbury was lauded as one of the UK's leading businessmen. John Major, the Conservative Prime Minister, was a friend and invited Greenbury to head up a government report into corporate pay. This was part of the larger and ill-fated 'back to basics' campaign embarked upon by Major. That Greenbury chaired the committee was emblematic of his importance in the corporate world. His stock had never been higher. With that in mind, and perhaps in the absence of a clear successor to take over in 1996, in 1995, the M&S board invited him to continue as Chairman until he reached the age of 65 (in 2001), although subject to an annual renewal from age 62. This announcement hit Oates hard, because, being six years Greenbury's junior, he realized it made his succession to the top job unlikely. Allegedly, at this juncture Oates (Bevan, 2002: 148) became a man obsessed with prevailing in the battle for power in M&S.

In 1997, M&S became the first British retailer ever to record profits in excess of £1 billion when it posted £1.1 billion pre-tax profits. M&S had prevailed over supermarket giant Sainsbury's in the race to break the £1 billion barrier. Greenbury had delivered a 40 per cent increase in profits during his tenure as Chief Executive and Chairman. In 1998, profits edged higher still. A glance at the accounts reveals that the increase in profits came only in part, 18 per cent, from a rise in sales, the rest was realized by cutting costs. In some stores costs were cut so sharply that routine maintenance, such as changing light bulbs, became a problem (Bevan, 2002: 158). Looking more closely at the financial performance of M&S, it was clear that the top 60 major stores and the 'out of town' stores were making most of the money, with a further 160 stores doing little more than breaking even. However, this was not picked up in the media; their story was simple – it was clear that M&S was the UK's number one retailer and that its financial performance confirmed that the company was confident about the future. M&S was planning how to build on the success of the previous four years.

There were signs that the high street was changing. By 1995 Next, a challenger in the late 1980s, had recovered from the difficulties it had experienced during the recession. The British high street also saw the entrance of new names such as the US firm Gap and the European H&M and Zara. These stores offered cheap 'fast fashion' products and were emblematic of the shifts in consumption patterns and lifestyles. M&S saw itself at the pinnacle of British retailing and as above the *arrivistes* who were now populating the high street.

Greenbury was, however, looking at ways in which M&S could build on the success of the previous four years. It had always grown organically in the UK and making acquisitions was seen as against its culture. It had secret talks – dubbed 'project heaven' – with mail order giant Great Universal Stores (GUS) to merge, creating a giant retailer. Greenbury and the GUS Chairman, Wolfson, were agreed but the M&S board blocked the move. The rationale was that the respective cultures of the two firms would not gel. Oates was seen as a prime mover in blocking the deal.

Succession

At a board meeting in autumn 1997 it was formally agreed to split the office of chairman and chief executive. In discussions at previous board meetings it had been established that Greenbury would continue as Chief Executive, as well as Chairman, until 1998.

Dropping the annual renewal clause in his contract, the non-executive directors asked Greenburg to stay as Chairman until his 65th birthday, which would take him up to 2001. Before agreeing, he asked each of his directors whether they were 'with him or not'. It was, of course, difficult for members of the board to express reservations about his strategic vision or managerial style. It was easier for board members not to speak their mind and to continue to enjoy the considerable perks and prestige associated with being directors at the UK's leading retailer. Despite Greenbury's success, many of those with whom he shared the boardroom were critical. Criticisms of his personal style recurred, as did the notion that he was very limited as a strategist. As one senior critic put it, 'the further Rick was away from a knitwear checking list, the less comfortable he was' (Bevan, 2002: 138). Retrospectively, participants have likened the M&S board to a medieval court, characterized by people being afraid of the Chairman while, simultaneously, seeking to curry favour.

(Continued)

(Continued)

The challenge

Oates sought to advance his cause and courted the media, leading to a number of favourable press reports which, in effect, promoted him as the front-runner to become the next Chief Executive: 'Keith Oates is tipped to be St Michael's choice to fill Richard Greenbury's shoes' (Bevan, 2002: 163). Greenbury was appalled; the self-promotion engaged in by Oates was antithetical to M&S's culture. Oates was quite clearly making a play to become Chief Executive when Greenbury stood down from the role in 1998, while continuing to serve as Chairman. Greenbury convened a meeting with the non-executive directors, articulating the view that many of the executive directors might be in favour of Oates becoming Chief Executive. Baldock, one of the non-executive directors, volunteered to carry out an analysis of opinion in the boardroom and found that while Oates had some supporters, others were against him. In addition, he reported that there was a strong desire to split the roles of chairman and chief executive. Part of this was born out of the feeling that, currently, the Chairman was not devoting sufficient time to investor relations. The board decided to split the roles but not before 1999. Subsequently, Greenbury was asked to remain on both as Chairman and Chief Executive until the AGM in 2001.

Oates realized that this meant that the chances of him succeeding Greenbury were ebbing away. Tensions between the two mounted. Despite their offices being in close proximity, they communicated only by letter. This came at a difficult time for Greenbury – his eponymous government report was viewed as a naive failure and he was also subject to tax avoidance allegations, of which he was later completely exonerated. Institutional shareholders were expressing concern that the large cash surpluses being generated by the firm were simply sitting in bank accounts; in their view the money should be put to use (see Chapter 11). Oates, an acknowledged finance expert, was seen as having the wherewithal to leverage the cash surpluses generated by M&S. The prevailing corporate finance logic, known as the shareholder value movement, posited that the firm should increase its gearing (i.e. the ratio of its borrowing to its equity) and use the new influx of capital to expand and generate fresh profits. The new financial orthodoxy of shareholder value jarred with M&S's conservative monetary policy. Oates was pushing the agenda of shareholder value. In 1997, for instance,

Oates had purchased, for the price of £192 million, 19 city stores from Littlewoods, the retail chain. Oates' initial proposal was to purchase all of Littlewoods stores in the UK, but the board blocked this move.

He constantly asked questions of how M&S proposed to increase the returns to shareholder value. Oates was in tune with the financial *Zeitgeist* and the acquisition was widely praised by the City. He was keen to pursue a further expansion and acquisition. In particular, he wanted to move into continental Europe which, save for the Paris store, had always proved a difficult hunting ground for M&S. His strategic vision was to transform M&S into a leading global retailer. In late 1997 the company announced a £2 billion expansion plan. The City and financial press were impressed, viewing M&S's brand as strong enough to thrive overseas. Oates was behind the proposed expansion and Greenbury and the board were fully aware that this would enhance his power base. Greenbury himself was sceptical about expanding overseas; as a consummate retailer he understood the complex problems that different tastes and cultures posed for companies such as M&S. It is something of a mystery as to why Greenbury consented to Oates' plans. One measure that he did reject was Oates' proposal to streamline the balance sheet by purchasing shares in a buyback scheme, a piece of financial engineering that was too exotic for Greenbury.

In 1998 the tensions continued and after a good set of financial results in April, the half-year results for the end of the year were significantly down on the previous year. Analysts regarded them as dismal. While fashion pundits for a few years had been critical of M&S, the financial community was now starting to express its concerns. Greenbury, along with close colleagues, travelled to India on a business trip. Shortly after Greenbury took his flight to Delhi, Oates wrote to the board making the case that he should be appointed Chief Executive. There is some dispute as to whether Oates actually knew that Greenbury had left the country: his supporters claimed that Oates thought it inconceivable that Greenbury could have left the country in the wake of the poor financial results. Oates' detractors saw his behaviour as a Machiavellian power play, waiting for the chairman to be out of the country as he launched his bid for power. Whatever the truth, the letter was a clear attempt at forcing the leadership issue.

Oates' letter was faxed to an astonished Greenbury; around the same time one of the major British newspapers ran a story discussing impending

(Continued)

(Continued)

internecine warfare in the boardroom. The sources were 'friends' of board members. Greenbury cut short his visit to India and returned to the UK. In the arrivals lounge at Heathrow, he was confronted with newspaper speculation that a 'dream ticket' of Keith Oates, strategic visionary, and Peter Salsbury, retailing expert, was being lined up to assume control of M&S. Whether this was mischief making on the part of the business press or a carefully executed public relations operation remains a moot point. Greenbury convened a quick meeting with the non-executive directors he was close to, before heading, just in time, to the weekly board meeting for which he had returned. Though furious with Oates, following advice from a non-executive director, Greenbury did not challenge him directly. Instead, Baldock, one of the non-executive directors, chaired the meeting and proposed, in light of recent events, that the timetable for splitting the roles of Chief Executive and Chairman should be foreshortened. It was proposed that in the next few weeks three non-executive directors would interview all the executive directors and make a recommendation, with most executive directors being interviewed several times.

Oates met with several executive directors, promising them positions in the boardroom were he to assume control; he was also visible in the City, attending high-profile functions. In late November the non-executive directors made their decision: Salsbury was to be appointed Chief Executive and Oates was to take early retirement. Oates was stunned and left the organization that morning, leaving his solicitor to thrash out his severance package. Salsbury was characterized by many board members as a 'nice guy' (Bevan, 2002: 199) and people felt they could work with him. Greenbury was to become Non-Executive Chairman, thus Oates' challenge had, in effect, brought the former's tenure as Chief Executive and Executive Chairman to a close, although Greenbury still regarded his role as a very much hands-on one.

Salsbury and Greenbury

Greenbury and Salsbury were both steeped in M&S culture and had worked closely together. Both analysts and company insiders expected the relationship to be a harmonious one. In some respects, commentators regarded Salsbury as one of Greenbury's men. It was soon clear that this was not the case; furthermore, it became evident that Salsbury harboured a deep antipathy towards Greenbury. In 1999, M&S's financial performance was deteriorating rapidly. There were a number of factors underpinning this dramatic deterioration in performance: first, M&S was losing out to competitors such as Zara and Gap; second, the refurbishment of the Littlewoods stores had been far more expensive than had been budgeted for; third, M&S, once a byword for consumer satisfaction, had lost the confidence of its customers. The financial figures coming in from the stores suggested that profits might halve. The corollary of this for Salsbury was that he felt there was little choice but to issue a profits warning, to forewarn the City of the downturn in profits, thus halting any damaging speculation.

Salsbury and Greenbury clashed over the content of the statement to the City. Whereas the latter wanted to emphasize the one-off costs attached to integrating the Littlewoods branches, the former favoured contrition, acknowledging that the company had lost its focus and stressing that it was seeking to learn from its mistakes. Of course Salsbury's approach could be seen as little other than a damning indictment of the Greenbury years. While Greenbury objected, Salsbury pointed out that he was Chief Executive and would take the decision. This was a sign that executive power had shifted. Relations between Greenbury and Salsbury worsened following the statement to the City.

Whereas for so many years M&S had been an icon on the high street, its halo had long since fallen and it now attracted opprobrium from its stakeholders: staff were unhappy with the cost cutting, shareholders were unhappy with the fall in the share price, the City was unconvinced by the business, and customers felt badly let down by a firm they trusted and, hitherto, had treated as a national institution. Zara, Next, Gap and others were making many in-roads into M&S's core market and it found itself unable to compete. Salsbury recognized this and embarked on a change programme: 25 per cent of the management was axed, including many senior executives, earning Salsbury the nickname of Pol Pot within the company; a marketing department was established, the first time one had existed in M&S; the stores were restructured, leading to redundancies and demotions; and a defence committee was established to guard against any takeover. These changes did little to assuage the concerns of the City, for by now M&S was the subject of relentless criticism within the business press. In May 1999, the pre-tax profits had dropped by 50 per cent to £634 million. The City regarded these results as little short of catastrophic.

(Continued)

(Continued)

Salsbury and Greenbury's relationship remained poor. Greenbury requested a discussion with Salsbury over M&S's future strategy. In the executive meeting that followed Salsbury presented the new strategy – which Greenbury thought misguided – as a done deal and not open for discussion, signifying the extent to which Greenbury had lost power (Bevan, 2002: 207). After this episode the two men barely spoke. In the summer of 1999, a strategic review and the AGM were due to take place. Both of these events were to be chaired by Greenbury. The City was angry and looking for contrition. The strategic review was underpinned by a lengthy consultancy report investigating the reasons for M&S's poor performance. The consultancy report argued that the company had neglected its brand, instead concentrating on the detail of the products, and came up with recommendations that Greenbury disagreed with. He realized the time had come for him to resign. He stepped down without chairing either of the two meetings, his only request being that, in the time-honoured way, he should have a portrait painted that would hang, along with those of previous chairmen, in the boardroom. The drop in profitability and the manoeuvring by Oates had effectively ended his career at M&S. Brian Baldock stood in as Acting Chairman.

Post-Greenbury

With Greenbury out of the way, Salsbury moved quickly to distance himself from the *ancien régime*. Many of the changes were symbolic: scrapping the directors' restaurant and removing the portraits of chairmen from the boardroom, for instance. The public relations spin laid M&S's poor performance at Greenbury's door, the implication being that with him out of the way, the organization could look forward to a bright future. Substantive changes were launched: investing more in marketing; appointing a new Marketing Director, Alan McWhirter, from Woolworths; clearing out more directors; starting to take credit cards in the stores; cancelling contracts with William Baird, a long-standing supplier, and also starting to source clothes from the Far East and North Africa.

Critics argued that while it was apparent that there were lots of change for change's sake, this had not been accompanied by a clear strategic vision. People argued that Salsbury lacked a clear strategy and that all the change taking place demotivated staff, making them feel uneasy. This, in turn, led to a further deterioration in perceived customer service. From Salsbury's vantage point, the aim, far from a grandiloquent vision, was to survive, which

required tough action. The non-executive directors felt he was correct and continued to support him.

Problems continued on the shopfloor, where M&S stores were regarded as having insufficient staff and were often low on stock. Newspapers frequently regaled readers with the problems confronting M&S. This came at a time when competition was fierce and many of its rival companies – such as Debenhams and Arcadia – were struggling. In contrast, Next, Zara and Gap were doing well.

M&S's financial results continued to disappoint and, relatedly, the share price continued to slide. The non-executive directors were beginning to have their doubts about Salsbury. In particular, they felt that too many initiatives were being attempted at once, and that he was a poor communicator. They needed to decide on a new chairman; Baldock was currently serving in a temporary capacity as Greenbury's replacement. They found people were unwilling to take the job in a non-executive capacity, as under British law non-executive directors do not qualify for share options. They then decided to appoint an Executive Chairman. The City took this as non-executive disquiet about Salsbury's performance, which caused the share price to slide further. In response, Salsbury launched a further restructuring programme.

The share price collapsed in value. Some financial pundits regarded the market capitalization as being less than the value of the real estate that M&S owned. Speculation mounted that a predatory takeover, possibly to asset-strip the firm, was likely. This signalled how far the once vaunted M&S had fallen. Philip Green, the retail legend, launched a controversial and unsuccessful takeover bid. The climate in M&S remained dismal, and many talented managers left the organization to take up positions elsewhere.

The Vandevelde years

Luc Vandevelde was appointed Executive Chairman in January 2000. A Belgian national, he boasted a wealth of executive experience with American and French retailers. Having international experience and being an outsider were regarded as big advantages. The profit figures, released in May 2000, were down yet again. Vandevelde restructured the board of directors, with three directors leaving the board. The financial press speculated as to the state of relations between Vandevelde and Salsbury, his Chief Executive. Vandevelde acknowledged that the results were poor and set a two-year target to

(Continued)

(Continued)

turn things around. Salsbury stood down, and was joined by directors Freeman and McCracken. In the few years since the politicking by Keith Oates, only one director remained from that era. Vandevelde hired Roger Holmes, a 40-year-old ex-McKinsey consultant, who had been credited with turning around a number of retail operations. Vandevelde, by now, was nicknamed 'cool hand Luc' by the British press. Around the time that Holmes was appointed, a financial consultancy published a report that, *inter alia*, listed M&S as destroying more shareholder value than any other company over the previous five-year period!

In his analysis of the organization, Holmes surmised that: (1) the staff were exhausted and demoralized after several corporate restructuring exercises in less than two years; (2) the company remained very introspective and backward looking; and (3) the company had ignored its customers. Holmes' strategic objective was to improve market share, customer experience and profitability.

Holmes and Vandevelde embarked on the following strategy: with their clothing range they adopted a two-pronged approach of focusing on the core market – females between the ages of 30 and 50 – and providing them with good-quality, stylish but classic clothing and branding the ranges with a series of model shoots featuring icons familiar to the core market, such as one ex-model from the 1960s, Twiggy.

Vandevelde contracted George Davies – former owner of Next and widely acclaimed as a retailer of sheer genius – to develop his own range of clothing for M&S. Davies was not an employee but rather was contracted to produce clothing. The result was the Per Una range, up market, very fashionable and highly praised by the fashion press, and branded with a lavish set of images featuring Twiggy and other models who became recognizably the faces of M&S. Holmes also sought to rebuild M&S's tattered relations with its suppliers, as he felt they needed to be committed to the mission that M&S was seeking to achieve. He embarked on a cut-price revamping of the stores – mainly through redecorating, better lighting and new technology. One of the most dramatic changes in strategy was to halt the expansion overseas and focus instead on the UK. The ramifications of this were that investments in the United States were liquidated and the European stores were closed. Another significant shift was to sell the property portfolio and then lease it back. The rationale was that the deal would realize £1.4 billion, to be used to pay dividends to shareholders. In May 2001, profits were down further but,

importantly, perhaps not as bad as analysts had expected. Vandevelde conceded that the organization still had significant problems, although there were 'pockets of recovery'. It was popular to blame M&S's travails on Richard Greenbury, something that Vandevelde seemed content to acquiesce with. He removed all the portraits of former chairmen and gifted them to their families. In addition, he had Greenbury's office demolished and replaced with an open-plan work area!

Questions

1 Produce a chronology of the key events during the 1990–2001 period.

2 Produce a chart showing the structure of M&S's board and how it changed over time.

3 Critically assess the key problems at M&S.

4 Discuss to what extent, if any, were there signs at the peak of M&S's success that the company might encounter problems in the near future?

5 Write a short account (300 words) of the M&S story from the vantage point of one of the following: (a) Sir Richard Greenbury, (b) Keith Oates, (c) a financial journalist, (d) a shareholder, (e) an employee, or (f) a competitor.

6 Imagine you were Sir Richard Greenbury. What, if anything, would you have done differently during your reign as Chairman?

7 Based on the information available, compare and contrast the management styles of Richard Greenbury, Peter Salsbury and Luc Vandevelde.

8 Critically assess the extent to which the decline in M&S's fortunes was inevitable.

9 What is the difference between an executive and a non-executive director?

10 What would you have advised M&S to do differently?

11 Comment on the symbolic aspects of the changes in chief executives/chairmen.

12 How common do you think politicking is among senior executives? Draw on theory.

13 Imagine you were advising M&S. What board structure would you recommend? Why?

14 What can we learn from the M&S case?

15 Research what has since happened at M&S in the period from 2002 to the present day.

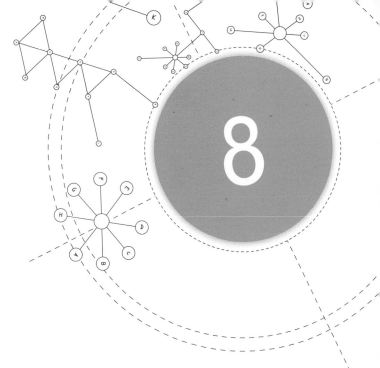

8

Strategic Decision-Making

Decisions, rationalities, garbage

LEARNING OBJECTIVES

By the end of this chapter you will be able to:

- Comprehend the difference between a decision and a non-decision
- Understand the rational, the political and the garbage-can approaches to decision-making
- Appreciate the importance of contributions by Herbert Simon, Charles Lindblom, Kathleen Eisenhardt and Louis Bourgeois to modern views on decision-making
- Discuss the central findings of the *Top Decisions* study
- Grasp how the process of decision-making unfolded during the Cuban missile crisis
- Comment critically on the role of decision-making in risky organizations
- Debate the role that superstition plays in strategic decision-making
- Assess the role of counterfactual analysis in strategic decision-making

INTRODUCTION

A strategic decision is typically defined as one that has long-term organizational implications for the future success and sustainability of an organization.

Making strategic decisions is the essential core of strategy-making.

Every organizational history is littered with missed opportunities and poor decisions. In this chapter we explain why many decisions that are entered into in good faith, accompanied by detailed analysis and invested with great hope, end, if not in disaster, then in a whimper of mediocrity. Decision-making has been seen as synonymous with strategy making: as Kathleen Eisenhardt (1999: 1) has noted, 'the ability to make fast, widely supported, and high-quality strategic decisions on a frequent basis is the cornerstone of effective strategy'. Understanding how decisions are made is central to understanding strategy making. This is all the more the case when we reflect on Paul Nutt's (1999) research finding that 50 per cent of strategic decisions end in failure! Accordingly, this chapter introduces central perspectives on strategic decision-making and addresses 'classic' studies before turning its attention to more contemporary issues.

In this chapter we will see the implications of Ezzamel and Willmott's (2008) constitutive perspectives unfold, an approach which we outlined in Chapter 4. The science of strategic decision-making has clearly emerged from a recursive and indexical relationship between what strategists do in practice and think in theory.

Image 8.1 'Field Marshall Sir Douglas Haigh'

Some strategic decisions remain controversial nearly a century after they were made.

PHOTOGRAPHY BY CHRIS CARTER

EXECUTIVE DECISION

Chester Barnard (1938), in his seminal account of executive life, highlighted the importance of decision-making. In turn, Richard Butler (1990) has highlighted Barnard's significance to the study of decision-making. Barnard had been an executive at AT&T, a major US corporation. He knew what he was writing about in theory from his experience in practice:

> It is now half a century since Barnard (1938) put decision-making at the core of organization theory and the study of managerial work. At that time, there was a good reason for this since the predominant model of industrial and commercial organization was a mechanistic-bureaucratic model against which Barnard's insights represented a break from the principles of Scientific Management. Decision-making with the attendant processes of communication and cooperation, gave a model of executive work which involved discretion, choice, delegation and the development of trust. (Butler, 1990: 11)

Richard Rumelt (1979: 196) also noted that 'one person's strategies are another's tactics – that what is strategic depends on where you sit'. So it is with decisions. According to Mintzberg, Raisinghani and Theoret (1976) strategic decisions are 'important in terms of the actions taken, the resources committed, or the precedents set'. Organizations live with the consequences of their decisions for many years because past decisions create future path dependencies. For instance, if a university decides to invest in a medical faculty, which is generally very expensive to maintain, this constitutes a strategic decision that commits considerable resources for many years. Once a medical school has been created, it would be virtually impossible to close it down, irrespective of the costs it might incur to the university, given the powerful medical stakeholders that will be strategically interested in such a school. Discursively, medical knowledge is also powerful knowledge that is capable of representing complex constellations of interest.

Strategic decisions set an organization on a particular path dependency, meaning that some outcomes are more likely than others. With hindsight some strategic decisions can appear visionary, others merely shrewd, and some will be disastrous. Of course, at the time of making them, strategic decisions are often robustly articulated and, in the context of large organizations, supported by rhetorically intensive justifications. As we will see in Chapter 9, organization relations of power vest legitimacy in people by virtue of the office they hold and the organizational resources they control. These two factors often make decisions seem more plausible in the 'here and now' than they do in retrospect (Carter and Mueller, 2006).

In Chapter 3 we discussed Wendy Espeland's (1998) study of the proposed Orme Dam development. One of the interest groups involved in this project, the Bureau of Reclamation Economists, is a typical exemplar of an organization that follows a rational decision-making process. Its approach to deciding whether a dam should be built or not was to develop a complex cost–benefit model, which attached a value to all the features associated with the dam. Based on the model a rational decision for or against the dam project was made. The Bureau's approach followed an impeccable logic, which, *inter alia*, assumed perfect information, a farsighted understanding of the causality that different alternatives offered, and their different outcomes, as well as the ability to render different alternatives commensurable and, hence, comparable. But life often does not furnish sufficient completeness as is required by rational decision-making.

BOUNDED RATIONALITY

Rational minds appreciate rational worlds. Herbert Simon, who emerged as a strong critic of rational decision-making, noted that the 'classical theory of omniscient rationality is strikingly simple and beautiful. Moreover, it allows us to predict (correctly or not) human behaviour without stirring out of our armchairs to observe what such behaviour is like' (Simon, 1978: 5). What Simon understood clearly was that the assumptions underpinning notions of rationality in decision-making were fundamentally flawed. His point was that, while perfect information might be possible to envisage in abstract terms, in practical terms it is little more than a fiction. In other words, a rational decision probably only exists in the pages of a textbook! The constraints on rational decision-making can be summarized as:

1 Real life is a bit more complicated than decision-making models might have us believe.

2 Few, if any, decisions are made under conditions of perfect rationality.

3 Issues that are being decided upon are frequently ambiguous.

4 Information about alternatives will often be incomplete.

5 The choice criteria being applied to different alternatives can often be unclear.

6 Other actors in an organization may see the issues, alternatives and choices in utterly different – sometimes antagonistic – terms to those making the decision.

7 Often the time, energy and political will to reconcile different positions may well be lacking.

If rational decisions do not exist, does that mean that all strategists are irrational? How, for instance, does one explain all the research, analysis and endless discussion that often precede a decision? Simon deals with this point directly:

> [the rejection of a priori models of rationality] should not be mistaken for a claim that people are generally 'irrational'. On the contrary, I think there is plenty of evidence that people are generally quite rational; that is to say, they usually have reasons for what they do. (1985: 297)

It is now widely accepted that people are reflexive, which means they will constantly talk about, think about and rationalize their actions. Simon's point is, therefore, not that strategists are irrational, but rather that perfect decision-making, and so perfect strategy, are simply not possible. Instead, Simon posited that rationality could only ever be a bounded rationality.

Rationality is bounded rationality when it falls short of omniscience, where the features of omniscience are largely failures of knowing all the alternatives, uncertainty about relevant exogenous events and inability to calculate consequences (Simon, 1978: 14).

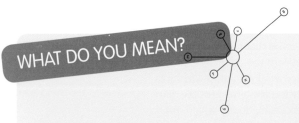

WHAT DO YOU MEAN?

Herbert A. Simon

Herbert Simon (1916–2001) was an American social scientist. Born in Milwaukee, Wisconsin, he received his Bachelor's degree and PhD in Political Science from the University of Chicago. He completed the latter while working as a research fellow at the University of California, Berkeley. In 1942 he returned to Chicago, taking up an appointment at the Illinois Institute. During this period he was part of an economics reading group that contained young doctoral scholars, including Kenneth Arrow, Milton Friedman and Franco Modigliani, who went on to become luminaries of their generation of economists. Simon referred to this as his second education. In 1949, he was appointed to a position at the Carnegie Institute of Technology, Pittsburgh (later to become Carnegie Mellon University), where he was involved in establishing a new school of industrial administration. During this period he established himself as a major thinker on decision-making in organizations. His work

(Continued)

(Continued)

had a major impact on economics, but, arguably, played an important role in the development of the field of artificial intelligence. His work was also important for the emergent field of organization behaviour. Simon's work was inter-disciplinary and established him as one of the most influential American social scientists of the twentieth century. He was honoured with the 1978 Nobel Prize for Economics. He continued to make scholarly contributions to economics, political science, computer science and management studies until shortly before his death.

Why is rationality bounded? It is bounded because of limits that are informational (i.e. perfect information does not exist) and cognitive (the ability of managers to process complex and difficult information). In reality, managers can only review a limited range of factors and possibilities in making their strategic decisions. Charles Lindblom, whose ideas are closely aligned with those of Simon's, summarized it as follows:

> Although such an approach (rational decision-making) can be described, it cannot be practiced except for relatively simple problems and even then in a somewhat modified form. It assumes intellectual capacities and sources of information that men simply do not possess, and it is even more absurd as an approach to policy when the time and money that can be allocated to a policy problem is limited, as is always the case. (1959: 80)

Decision-makers are thus only able to exercise rationality within the limits of the information that is available to them and their ability to make sense of it. James March too argued that 'human beings develop decision procedures that are sensible, given the constraints, however, even though they might not be sensible if the constraints were removed'. As a shorthand term for such procedures, Simon (1956) coined the term satisficing (March, 1978: 590).

Herbert Simon's contribution goes to the heart of the complex nature of strategic decision-making in organizations. Often, a decision is one that different interest groups in an organization can live with and that seems plausible and adequate to the task in hand. While this makes sense, it certainly seems to resonate with the authors' experiences of organizations; in the context of strategy it is startling. The ramifications of Simon's view are that organizations are, perhaps, not the rational optimizers often suggested, and that strategies – and strategic tools – are means of playing a political game between powerful actors. They privilege power and politics over rational decision-making.

Satisficing: a decision that will both 'satisfy' and 'suffice'. A satisficing decision is one where the organization does not strive to make an optimal decision, but instead chooses one that satisfies key actors in the organization and 'does the trick'. A satisficing decision is rarely ideal but it makes do with what is seen to be available and relevant.

MUDDLING THROUGH

In some cases the realities of organizations are such that it becomes very difficult for managers to make big strategic decisions, even when equipped with the categories, concepts and methods of the latest theories. Charles Lindblom (1959), for example, argued that organizations have a tendency to muddle through. Lindblom's work, resonates with Simon's notions of bounded rationality and satisficing and sought to understand how social policies were developed. It had a far-reaching influence, extending beyond the confines of social policy. While to the modern reader this perspective might seem unremarkable, when it was published it struck at the heart of the prevailing rational choice orthodoxy.

In his work Lindblom paints a picture of the way in which orthodox rational choice policy makers view the decision-making process. He uses the example of a government mandarin – whom we will term a strategist – being given the job of devising an economic policy for dealing with inflation. He is likely to proceed as follows:

1 The strategist will commence by listing all the possible values associated with inflation and place them in order of importance: 'full employment, reasonable business profit, protection of small savings, prevention of a stock market crash' (1959: 79). He makes the point that the 'clarification of values or objectives [is] distinct from and usually prerequisite to empirical analysis of alternative policies' (1959: 80).

2 The next step would be for the strategist to look at policy outcomes to see to what extent they had achieved the values identified above. This would entail research into the prevailing values held by society. That is, was full employment highly valued? Was protecting small savings important? This would be followed by the strategist calculating which value would be equal to a quantity of another value. That is, how much unemployment would be equal to what quantity of the diminishment of savings? Lindblom (1959: 81) describes the policy formulation process as following a means–ends logic: 'First the ends are isolated, then the means to achieve them are sought'. The strategist would then develop policy alternatives. However, the strategist would also seek to list all possible options, so this might produce scores of alternatives. Lindblom (1959: 81) notes that 'the test of a "good" policy is that it can be shown to be the most appropriate means to desired ends'.

3 The strategist would then analyse systematically the different policy options. The strategist would analyse 'every relevant factor' (1959: 81).

4 In conducting this decision-making process, the strategist would rely very heavily on theory – in this case economic theory on inflation.

Lindblom described this approach to decision-making as the 'root' approach. He contended that, save for relatively simple problems, such an approach is a practical impossibility. Furthermore, he pointed to a conundrum: why, in view of the impossibility of carrying out a 'root' analysis, did the textbooks and practical guides on policy making advocate such an approach? Of course, Lindblom was writing 50 years ago and ideas about policy making have moved on, but what he offered in place of 'root' decision-making still remains relevant to us today. He termed his model the *successive limited comparisons* or 'branch' method.

The premise is that in reality strategists will restrict themselves to a small number of values and merely consider a few alternative policies (1959: 80). For instance, a strategist working in a finance ministry might have the objective of trying to control inflation. There are, of course, many other values that could be factored into the objective but, following Lindblom, a strategist 'would quickly admit that he was ignoring many related values' (1959: 79).

In contrast to that which is promulgated by the 'root' approach, Lindblom argued that in reality values and policies emerged simultaneously – that is, talking about a policy necessitates one thinking about one's particular position on an issue and vice versa. Also, there may well be many disagreements – among the strategists and stakeholders – about which values should take priority. Consequently, Lindblom highlighted that decisions are more complicated than simply determining a value and subsequently devising policies to attain that value. Central to his position was the assertion that the differences between policies could often be marginal:

Two policies, X and Y, confront him. Both promise the same degree of attainment of objectives a, b, c, d, and e. But X promises him more of f than does Y, while Y promises him somewhat more of g than does X. In choosing between them, he is in fact offered the alternative of a marginal or incremental amount of f at the expense of a marginal or incremental amount of g. The only values that are relevant to his choice are these increments by which the two policies differ; and when he finally chooses between the two marginal values, he does so by making a choice between policies. (Lindblom, 1959: 82–3)

In relation to our strategist charged with controlling inflation, he would look at relatively few alternatives. In taking the decision the strategist would be likely to look closely at past experiences. For example, these might include to:

- Tackle inflation accepting that unemployment will be a consequence of this policy.
- Adopt a full employment policy, accepting that inflation will rise.
- Steer a middle course that allows some inflation and some unemployment.

The insights that would be gained by asking these questions raise an important question for strategic decision-makers: how different are the strategies under consideration? And, more specifically, on what issues do they differ? In contrast to the root method, the branch approach does not seek to establish the means and ends at the outset of a strategic decision-making process. Instead, a strategist using the branch approach regards means and ends as emerging simultaneously in the decision-making process. In relation to controlling inflation, means (unemployment) and ends (inflation) become conflated so that it is no longer easily possible to separate out the means from the end.

According to Lindblom, a good policy could be determined by whether different decision-makers were able to agree on the policy – as opposed to an alternative. In selecting a policy the decision-makers would reach agreement over the values being pursued and the instrument to pursue them. So, for instance, they may decide to steer a middle course between unemployment and inflation. A strategist using the branch approach would not expect the decision to be fully successful but should expect that it will be revised in light of experience and that fresh decisions will be taken. Consequently, the branch approach relies less on theory and more on experience.

Lindblom's approach has been dubbed the *successive limited comparisons approach* and has been extremely influential. In 1979, 20 years after it first emerged, Lindblom published a defence of his approach, even though it had been subject to serious critique (Etzioni, 1967; Dror, 1968; Self, 1975). This critique was two-fold:

1 Opponents argued that incrementalism as an approach lacked ambition and was overly limiting. The approach was irredeemably evolutionary – concentrating on making small changes. In many important respects it was a message that was resonant with the prevailing economic–political conditions of the era, one that is now rightly characterized as a golden age of capitalism.

2 For decision rationalists, the lack of a comprehensive analysis was deeply problematic. It seemed almost akin to not really trying to be rational.

However, other strategy scholars have noted the importance of Lindblom's contribution: for instance, in Langley's (1990) estimation Lindblom's work demolished the rational school of decision-making which was no mean feat. Turning to the positive aspect of his work, his argument was that 'muddling through' was how strategists actually went about forming policy in governmental organizations, positing that it 'is and ought to be the usual method of policy making' (Lindblom, 1979: 517).

By claiming that strategists should take incremental steps, was the approach not merely a means of upholding the status quo? In answering this criticism, Lindblom was resolutely pragmatic, making the point that there was often some distance between what 'is' and what 'ought' to be. In contrast, critics of Lindblom point out that to conceive policy making in terms of incremental change was to preclude the possibility of radical change. Lindblom disagreed. He pointed out that revolutionary change generally ended in failure, and instead of rejecting incrementalism, advocated 'practicing incrementalism more skilfully and turning away from it only rarely' (1979: 517). Similarly, he gave short shrift to rationalist decision-makers, saying that 'achieving impossible feats of synopsis is a fruitless, unproductive ideal ... an aspiration to synopsis does not help an analyst choose manageable tasks, while an aspiration to develop improved strategies does' (1979: 518). He continued: 'the choice between synopsis (decision rationalism) and incrementalism – or between synopsis and any form of strategic analysis – is simply between ill-considered, often accidental incompleteness on one hand, and deliberate, designed incompleteness on the other' (1979: 519).

Part of the analytical problem is to frame what we mean by incremental change. Lindblom used the following example: a central bank deciding to raise or lower the interest rate is extremely incremental (although the reductions in response to the financial crisis in 2009 might be seen as more than extremely incremental); reorganizing the banking system, such as giving the central bank independence, is still incremental; eliminating the use of money would be radical. Lindblom argued that it was useful to have a sense of a continuum from no change through to revolutionary change (see Chapter 1 on evolution and revolution).

Lindblom believed small-scale changes were less threatening. As Miller and Wilson (2006: 470) put it: 'Once each small step has been taken it gives a clearer picture of what has to be done and the future becomes more focused'. With an incremental approach to decision-making it is easier for an organization to retrace its steps and cool resistance.

YOU CAN DOWNLOAD…

A good application and discussion of Lindblom's approach in D. Collingridge and J. Douglas (1984) Three Models of Policymaking: Expert Advice in the Control of Environmental Lead, *Social Studies of Science*, 14: 343–70, from the book's website at www.sagepub.co.uk/cleggstrategy

GARBAGE CANS

The notion that decision-making does not accord with rational criteria was pushed further by Michael Cohen, Jim March and Johan Olsen (1972). They developed the notion of the garbage can. This followed in the tradition of Herbert Simon, a long-time collaborator of Jim March. The research sought to understand what happened in the decision-making process. Their premise was that many organizations were chaotic with loosely defined procedures for making strategic decisions. Seeing decision-making as taking place in situations of ambiguity, their results were a startling refutation of rational decision-making processes. Instead of a linear decision-making process being the norm what they found was that decision-making was less linear and more random.

The garbage can is a metaphor that seeks to capture the image of problems, solutions, opportunities and busy decision-makers as being adjacent to each other in a purely random fashion. The central premise of the garbage can is that specific decisions do not follow an orderly, linear process moving seamlessly from problem to solution, but, instead, are the outcomes of several comparatively independent streams of events within the organization. A decision gets made when solutions, problems, participants and choices flow around and coincide at a certain point. Like garbage in a can, these adjacencies are often purely random. Therefore, a group of senior strategists might not have strongly developed preferences prior to

Image 8.2 'Garbage can'

the decision-making process, their strategic objectives might be derived through the act of actually making a decision, there might be a very loose connection between strategic means and strategic ends, and many different actors (finance, marketing, HR, etc.) might be involved in the process.

In contrast to rational models, the garbage can emphasizes the contingent, anarchic and random nature of decision-making. For the garbage can, decisions owed a great deal to luck. Moreover, a decision-making process lacks a clear beginning and a definitive end – it is altogether a fuzzy process.

POLITICIZED STRATEGY: THE POLITICS OF DECISIONS

While decision-making may not be rational in a narrowly conceived way, it is certainly political. The authors that were introduced above provide compelling reasons as to why we should be suspicious of views that hold that rationality is completely achievable in analysing social affairs. The biggest enemy of utter rationality is the power and politics that are inscribed in every decision: different stakeholders with different interests will always try and influence a decision according to their own interests. As Eisenhardt and Bourgeois put it:

> Most strategic decision processes are ultimately political in that they involve decisions with uncertain outcomes, actors with conflicting views, and resolution through the exercise of power (1988: 737).

Consequently, organizations may be seen as arenas in which decision-making games will take place (Crozier, 1964; 1976). Cohen et al. (1972) teach us that decision-making is characterized by uncertainty and ambiguity, which, in turn, intensify the level of politics associated with the process. This is well illustrated in one of our favourite studies into strategic decision-making, that of the Cuban missile crisis.

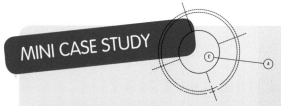

MINI CASE STUDY

Deciding nuclear Armageddon

It is generally agreed that the Cuban missile crisis, which occurred in 1962, brought the Soviet Union and the United States to the brink of war. It was a moment when the Cold War very nearly turned extremely hot. President Kennedy's leadership during the crisis has been widely praised and is seen as the pinnacle of his presidency. The incident is a classic case of strategic decision-making. Kennedy and Schlesinger (1999) and Allison (1971) documented it and it has also been made into a film, *13 Days*.

The Cold War was the contextual backdrop to the crisis: the Soviets and Americans were in a constant state of competition, with each seeking to undermine and outdo the other. While it was commonplace for the adversaries to fight through proxies, mainly in Asia and Africa, they had avoided a direct confrontation. The forces massed against each other ensured a standoff, which, if broken, would lead to MAD (Mutually Assured Destruction). While the Soviets had stronger 'conventional' forces, the Americans had a nuclear advantage. The US military presence in Europe and Turkey meant that, with the then limited range of nuclear weapons, the United States possessed a 'first-strike' capability against the Soviet Union. In contrast, continental America was out of range of Soviet nuclear missiles.

The revolutionary overthrow of the much reviled Battista government in Cuba changed the geopolitical landscape in the Americas. Led by Fidel Castro, the revolutionary government's relations with the United States quickly deteriorated. The hostile reaction of the US government to the Castro regime – especially over the nationalization of American-owned assets – soon led to the Cubans embracing communism and becoming allies of the Soviet Union. Cuba had been for most of the first half of the twentieth century a *de facto* American colony, with the American Mafia finding it a congenial home in which they could base their extensive gambling and hotel interests. The success of the Cuban Revolution was unexpected and it caught the Americans unawares. The Soviet Union took little time to exploit the golden opportunity that beckoned.

US spy planes spotted unusual activity in Cuba. Following analysis, the Americans soon realized the Soviets were installing nuclear missiles, which, once operational, would have the capacity to hit most places in the United States. This, for the first time, would give the Soviets a first-strike advantage. This sent shock waves through the Pentagon and White House. What followed were 13 days of tense decision-making.

Two dominant historical analogies, and a more recent one for the key protagonists, were drawn. President Kennedy and his entourage were haunted by events 50 years earlier, when Europe lurched, almost by accident, into the industrial slaughter that was the First World War. Many historians (Taylor, 1977) felt that an important contributory factor to the outbreak of war was the decision of the rival armies to mobilize, which made the conflict virtually inevitable. The decisions by the Tsar and the Kaiser to mobilize their troops, so Taylor's argument went, pushed Europe, inexorably, into war. Kennedy feared an aggressive US response to the missiles being made operational in Cuba would provoke the Soviets into retaliation, probably the invasion of West Berlin, which, in turn, would lead to war. Kennedy was painfully aware of how high the stakes were and that a mistake on his part could lead to Armageddon. The leaders of the military were guided by a different metaphor: they were haunted by appeasement in the 1930s, when the Western liberal democracies repeatedly made concessions to Hitler, as he breached treaties and demanded territory, on the assumption that he would be satisfied. This assumption proved to be catastrophically wrong. The military chiefs took the view that Soviet aggression and force must be matched by the countervailing power of the USA. The metaphors were drawn from experience: the military commanders had been junior officers during the 1930s; Kennedy was a keen student of history.

Matters were further complicated by the mutual distrust that existed between Kennedy, his advisers and the military. The latter felt Kennedy had stolen the 1960 presidential election, and furthermore were suspicious of his youth, privilege and inexperience. That he was regarded as a progressive politician probably did not help matters. Added to the mix was the fact that Kennedy's father, Joseph P. Kennedy, had been an influential appeaser during the 1930s while he was US Ambassador to London. To the older military chiefs the Kennedy family name was indelibly associated with the failed policy of appeasement. Kennedy and his advisers reciprocated this distrust. Kennedy's inner circle, dubbed Camelot by the media, comprised a youthful, cosmopolitan intelligentsia and viewed the military chiefs with suspicion.

(Continued)

(Continued)

A recent analogy that worried Kennedy was the Bay of Pigs disaster, whereby his government, through the CIA, had backed and funded an attempt by Cuban *émigrés* to recapture the island. Kennedy had been assured that the operation would succeed. It was, however, a badly conceived and implemented plan. The Kennedy administration was humiliated, and the military were smarting at its failure to reassert American influence over Cuba. In contrast, the incident left Kennedy suspicious of advice from the military, regarding them as overconfident and potentially hubristic.

A crisis meeting was convened by the president, and attended by his advisers and the military chiefs, when the presence of Soviet missiles on Cuba became evident. It produced two possible alternatives: bomb the missile site, followed up with an invasion; or practise diplomacy, which would mean that the missiles would be operational before any negotiation took place. There was a consensus that it was unacceptable for the Soviet missiles to be allowed to become operational, which military experts estimated would happen in 13 days. Consequently, there was a 13-day window in which the Americans could try and get the missiles out of Cuba; after that the military would have to strike to ensure their removal.

President Kennedy established a committee drawn from the National Security Council. He did not chair it and only attended when invited, giving him some distance from proceedings. The committee was dubbed ExCom and was chaired by the Attorney-General Robert Kennedy, brother of the president. ExCom was asked to: 'set aside all other tasks to make a prompt and intense survey of the dangers and all possible courses of action' (Sorensen, 1965: 675). The ExCom members were left in little doubt about the gravity of the situation.

Over the next week a number of different options were debated and discussed. The military 'hawks' preferred a military strike, followed by an invasion. In contrast, the politicians wanted to avoid conflict, unless absolutely *necessary*, and were keener on a blockade.

The military's view was that the only way to deal with the Soviets was through the use of force. In addition, they reasoned that the Soviets would not respond to a US invasion of Cuba, simply because the stakes were unthinkable. Their policy would be a means of highlighting that the United States would not tolerate a threat to its national security and would take firm and decisive action to protect itself. In contrast, the politicians felt that a strike against the Soviet missiles would lead to Soviet fatalities, which would inevitably provoke a military response: that would, in all probability, be an invasion of West Berlin, which, at the time, was a Western satellite geographically located within the Soviet Bloc. In the 13 days that followed, a small group of US politicians, advisers and military chiefs debated the action to pursue. Against the military's wishes, Kennedy decided to impose a blockade of Cuba. This was termed 'quarantine', as a blockade is officially an act of war. All ships approaching Cuba would be stopped and searched. This was to prevent more missiles getting through. In the meantime it would be made clear to the Soviet Union that the missiles had to be removed. The United States wanted this action to be taken while also wanting to avoid war with the Soviets.

At the outset, Kennedy and his team dealt with the issue in secrecy, after which he made a television broadcast to the American people outlining the problem and indicating the gravity of the situation.

Constant meetings of ExCom took place amid great confusion, as ExCom sought to second-guess the Soviet objectives. What, exactly, were the Soviets trying to achieve? Their actions and intentions could be interpreted in many different ways. Were they using the missiles as a bargaining chip? Had hardliners gained more influence? Were they looking for a confrontation? The confusion deepened when some Soviet tankers stopped at the quarantine line. Were they turning back? Or, were they waiting for Soviet submarines to protect them? As the crisis unfolded, rapid decisions were required. The naval rules of engagement allowed for firing flares above Soviet ships, something that worried Robert McNamara, the Secretary of State for Defense, as having the potential to be seen as a hostile act. The decisions were, however, very high risk. A wrong decision could have ruinous consequences.

The information available for these decisions was fragmented, incomplete and required a stream of judgements. Kennedy, as President and Commander-in-Chief, had the ultimate decision-making authority. He weighed up various viewpoints and information before taking a decision. He presided over a fractious group that was split into two factions – the military and the politicians – each of which tried to influence him. Both factions, of course, were convinced that they were right: one was seeking to protect national security, the other to prevent nuclear war.

Tensions ran high in a stressful and emotional environment, as Kennedy prepared to make his decision.

(Continued)

(Continued)

The military chiefs tried to shift the decision in their favour by engaging in an elaborate sting operation: they knew that sending in low-flying aircraft to gather further intelligence would lead to their being fired upon by the Soviets; as per their rules of engagement, they would then be able to return fire. This, they realized, would lead to a military confrontation, which they saw as inevitable. Ken O'Donnell, Kennedy's Political Adviser, spoke personally to pilots to ask them not to reveal to the military chiefs that they had been fired on. The US military did all they could to escalate the possibility of a conflict. While the crisis was unfolding they launched a large naval exercise in the Caribbean, which could reasonably be interpreted as a prelude to an invasion of Cuba; a nuclear device was tested; and a US spy plane strayed into Soviet airspace.

There were confused communications with the Soviets, including two letters from Chairman Khrushchev, the leader of the Soviet Union. The first seemed conciliatory; in contrast, the subsequent letter was more trenchant in its tone. Kennedy and his advisers speculated as to whether a coup had taken place, with Khrushchev being replaced by a hard-liner.

A political back channel between an American journalist and the Soviet Embassy was established. Robert Kennedy met secretly with the Soviet Ambassador the night before the Americans were due to begin their military operations. A deal was struck: if the Soviets withdrew their missiles from Cuba, six months hence the Americans would withdraw their Jupiter missiles which were based in Turkey. The crisis ended with the missiles being withdrawn from Cuba. It is widely agreed that the episode had brought the world to the brink of a third world war. Moreover, it is generally regarded as the most impressive part of Kennedy's foreshortened presidential career. A lesson we can take away about strategic decision-making is that judgements are rarely reached through a clear-headed, hard-nosed assessment of evidence. Instead, strategic decisions can be conflictual and reached in a tense and highly charged emotional atmosphere.

The Cuban missile crisis is a fascinating study into decision-making. Allison's (1969; 1971) analysis from the three competing perspectives of rational policy, organization process and bureaucratic politics shows how each perspective yields different insights. In an engaging account, David Buchanan and Richard Badham (2008) apply concepts from organization theory and conclude that:

● Strategic decisions are not single events based on a rational consideration of the evidence.

● Some decisions can be taken in a considered manner, while others have to be made rapidly with incomplete and ambiguous information in the face of internal disagreements.

● Information often becomes available in a fragmentary manner.

● Decisions are not the outcome of rational, linear processes but a series of influence attempts, power plays, negotiations and manipulations.

● Management decisions are more about politics and influence than rational analysis.

Question

Watch the movie 13 Days, the dramatization of the Cuban missile crisis. Prepare answers to the following questions:

1 Describe the process of strategy-making that took place in the Kennedy Cabinet.

2 What was the problem?

3 What were the options open to Kennedy?

4 Why did Kennedy and his advisors make the decisions they did?

5 What were the tensions among the decision-makers? What were the different positions?

6 How did the military try and force a particular agenda?

7 What is the relevance of this case to you as a student of strategy?

ACTION GENERATORS

One of the features of the Cuban missile crisis was how keen the US military were to invade. There were a number of reasons for this, some of which have been highlighted above. What was clear, however, was that the US military had an off-the-shelf plan to invade Cuba and overthrow Castro. This, of course, was not unusual, as it is fairly commonplace for the military and large organizations to war-game various scenarios. Bill Starbuck has commented on the tendency to apply pre-existing strategic solutions developed in one frame of analysis to problems that have not been seen through other contexts of interpretation that might have been more appropriate.

Given these tendencies to be stuck in the groove of prior frames, Starbuck (1983) argues that organizations are not so much problem solvers as action generators. What he means is that organizations spend a good deal of time generating problems to which they already have the solutions. It is not so much that the problem drives a solution, but, rather, that a solution is already at hand waiting to be applied to a variety of problems. Thus, the ways in which issues are framed become of prime importance: framed one way they will generate that solution: framed another way, another solution might be chosen. Solutions are chosen less on the grounds of their adequacy and more on their goodness of fit with the way that issues are framed. Such framing is inherently political: what faction, what disciplines, what interests, command the ears of those in seats of power? A good example of this point is the domain of US war policy in respect of Iraq.

MINI CASE STUDY

US war policy, 1991–2008

The First Gulf War was fought in early 1991. The Western allies, led by the Americans, swiftly defeated the Iraqi forces, driving them out of Kuwait, which they had invaded the year before. George H. Bush encouraged the Iraqis to rise up against Saddam Hussein, before backtracking. Scenes of carnage followed, as Hussein wreaked his revenge on those who had heeded Bush's call. Bush lost the 1992 presidential election to Bill Clinton. While psephologists largely attributed Bush's defeat to the ailing economy, the bungled end to the otherwise successful Gulf War was also held to be a factor. The Clinton administration (1993–2001) adopted a containment strategy that comprised economic sanctions and the enforcement of no-fly zones, a policy that gave some groups, such as the Kurds in the north, *de facto* independence.

Following the presidential election in 2000, which saw George W. Bush controversially awarded the presidency, attitudes towards Iraq began to change. It is widely accepted that his neo-conservative advisers – such as Dick Cheney, Karl Rove, Donald Rumsfeld and Paul Wolfowitz – had invasion plans drawn up for Iraq, long before Bush became president. The neo-cons had the solution; what they required was a reason to unleash it. Al-Qaeda, paradoxically enemies of Saddam Hussein, were to provide these neo-cons with their

opportunity. It was inevitable that the terrible atrocity of 9/11, which must count as one of the most heinous crimes seen in the West during peacetime, was going to elicit a powerful military response from the United States.

George Bush announced a 'War on Terror' against what he dubbed an axis of evil. The United States, together with its allies, invaded Afghanistan in search of Osama bin Laden. A year after 9/11 Bush began to talk about a regime change in Iraq. The neo-cons talked up the possible role of Iraq in 9/11 and spread rumours of the regime's possession of weapons of mass destruction. Unable to get UN support for an invasion, Bush's administration put together a coalition of those who were willing to grant the US-led invasion greater legitimacy: the UK, Australia, Poland and a number of other nations joined up. In March 2003, hostilities began and after a short military conflict Saddam Hussein's regime was toppled. At the time of writing, American and British troops remain stationed in Iraq. The point of this vignette is to give an illustration of a solution – invade Iraq and remove Saddam Hussein from power, installing a pro-American government in the process – that was waiting to be the answer to a problem.

Questions

1 What was the problem for which different stakeholders saw the removal of Saddam Hussein as the strategic solution?

2 Explain which of the theories encountered so far seems best able to explain the decision-making.

Strategic decision-making can be read as a game, whereby different factions manoeuvring for influence will highlight the political nature of organizations (see Chapter 9). To think of organizations, and their surrounding environment, as being political systems changes the way in which we think about strategic decision-making. Dispensing with notions of efficiency and rationality, it alerts us to the fact that strategic decisions can tell us a great deal about the power relations in and around an organization: Who is powerful? How do they see the world? What is an acceptable course of action to them and what is not?

Of course, to relax our assumptions about efficiency and rationality is not to say that these concepts are not used to justify particular strategies. By which we mean that a strategic decision is likely to be couched in terms that stress its rationality. As we will see in Chapter 9, rationality and power often go hand in hand: it is only in rare cases – such as arbitrary decision-making by a supremely confident set of power holders – that there is no reference to some form of rationality (Flyvberg, 1998).

Decision-making can tell us a great deal about an organization's strategy. For instance, deciding to buy a firm overseas might indicate the beginning of an international growth strategy; deciding to outsource all non-essential activities might indicate the adoption of a core competency strategy, and so on. If to some degree decisions involve the weighing up of alternatives, Eisenhardt and Zbaracki (1992: 18) remind us that understanding strategic decisions is central to understanding the nature of the strategy process: 'It is clear that people are rational, but only boundedly so, that power wins battles of choice, and that chance affects the course of strategic decision-making'.

Clearly, what happens and what is decided and acted on will provide important signs as to the strategy being pursued by those in control of an organization. This is evident in the case study – Go airlines – presented in the box below.

MINI CASE STUDY

Budget airlines in Europe: Go

Budget airlines are a familiar part of modern travel. easyJet and Ryanair are household names, and there are several other carriers that have emerged over the last 10 years. As a sector budget airlines came into being following EU legislation, in April 1997, that aimed to liberalize the airline industry. Prior to the legislation, routes were heavily protected and were controlled by a series of national carriers, such as BA, Air France, Lufthansa, and so on. easyJet, run by Stelios Haji-Ioannou, had commenced flying in November, while Ryanair, an Irish airline run by Michael O'Leary, began to reposition itself as a budget airline. The strategy pursued by both easyJet and Ryanair involved negotiating very

attractive landing slots with airports that had been less popular and, perhaps, were more remote from major centres of population. An airline generally pays a per capita fee to an airport for each passenger it lands, but by using Stansted, Luton, etc., the budget airlines were able to reduce this fee dramatically and hence their fares. These airports were not the buzzing hubs that they are now but were small and comparatively unused. By cutting out all unnecessary costs, the budget airlines were able to offer much reduced fares to customers. It was a paradigm shift for the airline industry.

BA was interested in the potential of budget airlines and unsuccessfully attempted to buy a stake in Ryanair and later easyJet. Bob Ayling, the then Chief Executive of BA, viewed the budget sector as being a long-term proposition and made the decision that the company should plan to create its own budget airline. Many of the senior executives at BA disagreed with this decision, regarding it as having

(Continued)

(Continued)

the potential to cannabilize their existing market and damage BA's brand. It was decided that a project would be established to design a budget airline company. Such a move came at a time when BA was going through a difficult period with its staff, who had recently been on strike, the City, who were unimpressed with BA's recent financial performance, and its customers, who were somewhat nonplussed by some of the recent branding initiatives. A low-budget airline initiative carried considerable risks.

Ayling framed the brief for the airline as follows: to avoid regulatory problems the budget airline would have to be a stand-alone operation and make a profit; the business plan should be constructed as if it were to appeal to a venture capitalist; it would be expected to make an 18 per cent return on capital employed, which was much higher than the standard BA performance expectations, and the business should add to BA's reputation rather than detract from it. Barbara Cassani, an experienced BA executive, was seconded to run the project. After much deliberation, Cassani and her team decided to call the fledgling airline Go. She made the decision that the budget airline would need to be significantly different from BA and used South West Airlines, a highly successful American low-cost operator, as a blueprint for the new airline. South West managed to offer low prices together with a good standard of customer service, something Cassani was keen to emulate.

Cassani set about establishing the design of the business, talking to specialists and marketers. Reservations from BA executives continued to be aired. Issues (see Cassani and Kemp, 2003: 60) raised included: concern about the use of the BA name and logo; concern about the damage it could do to long-standing relationships BA had with travel agents; anxiety that the initiative could further inflame industrial relations in the core business, as staff might regard it as a Trojan horse for cost cutting as well as the demand that BA should choose the routes the new airline should fly on. At board meetings executives did not challenge Ayling's decision, but they did temporize, engaging in blocking tactics.

In October 1997 at an executive meeting in Prague, Cassani made her pitch to the board. She recounts (Cassani and Kemp, 2003; 64) the item being on the bottom of the agenda and given a 20-minute slot just before lunch! The argument for establishing the airline was:

1 A significant new market sector had emerged.

2 easyJet and Ryanair were growing quickly.

3 Major airlines, such as Air France, were reputed to be planning their own budget airlines.

4 A budget airline could capitalize on these opportunities.

5 A budget airline would help defend BA against the competition that rivals such as Ryanair might pose in future.

Many on the board were sceptical but were prepared to acquiesce with Ayling's plan. Operation Blue Sky was approved and it was agreed that BA would make an investment of £25 million, with the expectation that the new airline would break even after three years. The target launch date for the airline was April 1998.

Cassani began by negotiating with airports close to London, aiming to secure a good deal. Finally, she decided on Stansted. Once the launch of BA's budget airline was announced, it attracted media intrigue, as well as coruscating attacks from the budget airline sector. Given BA's past reputation – relating to Laker in the 1970s and Virgin in the 1980s – for trying to run any competition out of business, this was perhaps not surprising. Budget operators feared that BA would cross-subsidize its new airline and then engage in a price war, in effect trying to run them out of business.

Cassani wanted to create a low-cost airline that combined good value with style, tapping into late 1990s' London cool. In many ways, what she was trying to do was the antithesis of what BA was delivering, which she characterized as follows: 'British Airways had the frustrating problem of trying to serve too many customers in different market segments. The net result was over-promising an undeliverable service to customers, watching your costs sky-rocket and then needing to charge high fares' (Cassani and Kemp, 2003: 83). She came up with what she termed the '3X + Y formula': the 3x referred to doing the basics well and cheaply, while the Y represented something that was a little surprise, such as good-quality coffee, trendy city guides and really good aircrew.

Questions

1 Studying Go, research how the airline developed and what eventually happened to it.

2 Choose one budget airline. Research its foundation, emergence and performance. What were the key strategic decisions that it had to make?

SOURCE: THIS MINI-CASE STUDY IS BASED ON THE EXCELLENT BOOK GO: AN AIRLINE ADVENTURE (CASSANI AND KEMP, 2003).

ON THE POLITICS OF ORGANIZATIONAL DECISION-MAKING

Elsewhere in this book, in Chapter 4, we recounted Andrew Pettigrew's research into organizational change at ICI (see Pettigrew, 1985). For the purposes of this chapter we are more interested in Pettigrew's early work in which he studied the IT procurement process in a manufacturing firm. What he recounted was a fascinating story of power and politics, one that remains relevant to this day. Pettigrew conceived of organizations as, in part, being communication systems. What he meant by this was that a large part of organization is about communication, but that communication might not be as clear and straightforward as one might imagine: first, different communities in an organization might have different languages, such that accountants, marketers, engineers and HR professionals may well use different terms and understand the world in very different ways; second, communication is mediated through particular structures, meetings, gatekeepers and so on. Pettigrew's study illustrates the latter point very forcefully. So what is the story?

Pettigrew researched Brian Michaels (a pseudonym), a large manufacturing firm in Scotland. The firm made four major computer-purchasing decisions in the decade between 1957 and 1968. Pettigrew studied the final decision, made in 1968. The planned expenditure was £1.5 million (£19,450,000 at 2009 prices),[1] though this eventually rose to £3.5 million (£45,489,000 at 2009 prices). The board of directors considered six different computer firms for the job. While the board were the ultimate decision-making authority, they relied on the advice of the management services division, headed up by Jim Kenny. A systems analysis department, headed up by Bill Reilly, and a programming department, led by Neil Turner, reported to Kenny. Each of the three managers quickly identified themselves with a preferred computer firm (Kenny – Mitchell computers, Reilly – Wilson Electric, Turner – STC).

Pettigrew's study chronicles how the three managers tried to mobilize in favour of their preferred supplier. By virtue of being at the 'junction of communication channels', Kenny enjoyed a considerable advantage over Reilly and Turner. He was able to exert influence in favour of his preferred solution while controlling the information revealed to the board about the preferences of his competitors. He was the central contact for the computer firms hoping to obtain the contract from Brian Michaels, which meant that all communications went through him. Pettigrew describes Kenny as playing the role of a gatekeeper:

A gatekeeper sits at the junction of a number of communication channels in a position to regulate the flow of demands and potentially control decisional outcomes (Pettigrew, 1972: 190).

> There were twelve board meetings, concerning the new computer system, in the year before the decision was taken. Kenny attended all of these meetings, whereas Reilly was only present for one and Turner for two, respectively. Pettigrew highlights how Kenny consistently spoke of his preferred supplier in overwhelmingly positive terms, while denigrating the others. (See tables 9 and 10, Pettigrew, 1972: 201)

Pettigrew saw

> decision-making as a political process in which outcomes are a function of the balancing of various power vectors. The processing of demands and the generation of support are the principle components of the general political structure through which power is wielded. The final decisional outcome will evolve out of the processes of power mobilisation attempted by each party in support of its demand. (1972: 202)

---

[1]This is calculated using the retail price index.

Pettigrew's research illustrates the way in which Kenny was able to secure his preferences with the board of directors through controlling the information flow. It is evident that information control can be an important source of power in terms of trying to secure a decision according to one's own wishes. Equally, having wide access to many contacts is also an important means of controlling information. To be a gatekeeper, it seems, can be to play an important role in strategic decision-making.

TOP DECISIONS – BRADFORD STUDIES

In the 1980s, at the University of Bradford, Richard Butler, David Cray, David Hickson, Geoff Mallory and David Wilson conducted a major research study into strategic decision-making in the UK. The study lasted a decade and sought to understand what really happened in the strategy decision-making process. The research was published in a monograph (*Top Decisions*) and via a series of articles (some of which are available on this book's website). The research produced many important insights into the nature of decision-making that remain as relevant today as when they were first published. While some of the research team have retired, David Wilson (Warwick Business School), together with Susan Miller (Hull University Business School), continue to research decision-making. The *Top Decisions* research mainly studied 150 distinct strategic decision-making episodes in 30 organizations. They were interested in answering the following questions:

- What actually happens in the process of arriving at a strategic decision?
- What differences are there in the process of making decisions?
- Why do these differences exist?

YOU CAN DOWNLOAD…

Andrew M. Pettigrew's (1972) Information Control as a Power Resource, *Sociology*, 6: 187–204, from the book's website at www.sagepub. co.uk/cleggstrategy

The answers to these seemingly straightforward questions have made a substantial contribution to understanding the way in which decisions are made. They identify independent variables that have an impact on the nature of the decision-making process. These include the type of organizational context, the levels of politics associated with a decision, and the complexity of the decision. From this they can identify three typical decision-making processes:

1 *Sporadic decisions.* As we have seen in the Cuban missile crisis, many decisions are complex and seen as very political. This can 'generate a vortex into which all are swept' (Hickson et al., 1986: 240), something associated with a sporadic decision process, summarized by Butler as follows:

> a sporadic decision involves many interests, it tends to move both horizontally and vertically in the organization and exhibits stops and starts. Where is such a decision made? Not in any once place, but it is made, nevertheless, through a diffuse and complex organizational process. … Sporadic decisions involve the highest levels in the organization, but the decision is not only made there. (1990: 13)

Sporadic decisions tended to take longer than other decisions. As Cray et al. put it: 'The decision process lurches from one impasse to the next with individuals and groups debating alternatives in the halls and cafeterias so that the decision process is drawn out' (1991: 228). Generally, Hickson et al. (1986) found the greater the level of complexity and the greater the political controversy of a decision, the more likely it will be that a decision will go back and forth and be subject to lengthy delays and revision. Topics for sporadic decisions may be complex, definitions problematic, information unavailable and/or difficult to collect, solutions hard to recognize, and the process generating headaches rather than solutions.

2 *Fluid decisions*. As a decision-making mode, this is characterized by a situation where a decision is strategic and deals with an unusual situation but is not particularly complex or political. Such decisions can be handled formally and quickly.

3 *Constricted decisions*. As a decision-making mode these are characterized by Hickson et al. (1986: 240) as ' those matters which bring familiar problems, probably least complex of all, and familiar interests, probably no more than mildly political in nature, they can be processed in a constricted [narrowly channelled] way. This is the *familiar-constricted mode*'. Such decisions are relatively smooth and straightforward and, thus, require little debate.

Hickson et al. (1986) made the point that decision-making is not necessarily linear but instead can often be iterative and feed back on itself. One of the fascinating parts of the *Top Decisions* book relates to the amount of time a decision takes to make. How long is it reasonable for a strategic decision to take? Hickson et al. found that there was huge variance over the length of time this could take. Some of the strategic decisions they studied were resolved within a month, while others were dragged out over a period of four years! In their study, the average time taken for a strategic decision was just over 12 months. Interestingly, there was

TABLE 8.1   Three decision types

Decision Type	Characterized by:
Sporadic	More delays More impediments More sources of information More variability of information More informal interaction Some scope for negotiation More time to reach a decision Decision taken at the highest level
Fluid	Fewer delays Fewer impediments Fewer sources of information Less variability of information Some scope for negotiation More formal interaction Less time to reach a decision Decision taken at the highest level
Constricted	More sources of information Less effort to acquire information Little scope for negotiation Less formal interaction Decision taken below highest level

SOURCE: CRAY ET AL. (1991: 229)

little difference between public and private sector organizations in this respect. They found that the most significant strategic decisions tend to be sporadic ones. Such decisions are characterized by political factions, a problemistic search, incremental solutions, and a dynamic non-linear reiteration and redefinition of almost all the terms in the decision mix.

DECISION-MAKING IN HIGH-VELOCITY ENVIRONMENTS

The *Top Decisions* study made a substantial contribution to our understanding of strategic decision-making. Another highly cited and important piece of research, of a similar vintage, is Kathleen Eisenhardt and Louis Bourgeois' (1988) investigation into strategic decision making. They studied eight firms in the 1980s Californian computer industry, a sector that was then changing rapidly. They formulated three questions into seven propositions (which we list A–G):

1 *Why do politics emerge?* Politics are closely associated with highly centralized organizations, presided over by a powerful CEO. This leads to executives trying to influence decisions, while the CEO engages in trying to control and withhold information. They reported behind-the-scenes attempts at co-optation (attempts to change decision-makers' minds). 'First's [one of the case study organizations] executives relied heavily on such bonding together and even held "outlaw staff meetings" in which the VPs of marketing, finance and operations met regularly outside the formal chain of command' (1988: 748). *Proposition A: 'The greater the centralization of power in a chief executive, the greater the use of politics within a TMT' (1988: 743).*

   Conflict was often a precondition of politics, but conflict alone did not necessarily lead to political behaviour. They reported conflict being resolved, often through open discussion, rather than through a recourse to politicking. Their data showed that high levels of conflict were associated with high instances of politics when the CEO was powerful and power was centralized. This was not the case when power was distributed more democratically. *Proposition B: 'Conflict is not a sufficient condition for the use of politics, conflict leads to politics only when power is centralized' (1988: 751).*

2 *What shape do politics take in a high-velocity environment?* Politics in the computer firms were organized around stable coalitions, rather than issue-based alliances coming together to pursue a specific agenda:

   > Executives do not shift allies as issues change, particularly in politically active teams. Rather they develop stable coalitions with one or possibly two other executives. They routinely seek out alliances with the same people. When the usual allies disagree on an issue, they generally do not seek out more favourably disposed executives. Rather, they either drop the issue or pursue their interests alone. (1988: 753–4)

In exploring why alliances appeared to be stable, rather than shifting and opportunistic, Eisenhardt and Bourgeois suggested the stressful nature of a highly politicized environment led 'executives to rely on habitual responses like stable coalitions' (1988: 756). *Proposition C: 'The greater the use of*

YOU CAN DOWNLOAD…

The following papers that are relevant to these studies from the book's website at www.sagepub.co.uk/cleggstrategy: Kenny, G., Butler, R., Hickson, D., Cray, D., Mallory, G. and Wilson, D. (1987) Strategic Decision-Making: Influence Patterns in Public and Private Sector Organizations, *Human Relations*, 40: 613–31; Wilson, D., Butler, R., Cray, D., Hickson, D. and Mallory, G. (1986) Breaking the Bounds of Organization in Strategic Decision-Making, *Human Relations*, 39: 309–30; Wilson, D. (1982) Electricity and Resistance: A Case Study of Innovation and Politics, *Organization Studies*, 3: 119–40.

politics within a top management team, the greater the likelihood of stable alliance patterns' (1988: 754).

The membership of alliances tended to be based on demographic factors – age, location of office and type of job – rather than being organized around a particular agenda. For instance, Eisenhardt and Bourgeois gave the following example: 'The VPs of finance and manufacturing at First formed a coalition. They were both in their early 30s and were at least 15 years younger than the rest of the team' (1988: 757). Alliances were often formed from those that had past experience of each other. Bonds included: being at school together, working together previously in a different company and joining the firm at the same time. *Proposition D: 'When the use of politics is high, the basis of alliance is likely to be similarity of demographic attributes'.*

Their findings rebutted the notion that a demographic similarity led inexorably to the formation of stable alliances. Instead, this similarity was a precondition for the establishment of an alliance. *Proposition E: 'Demographic similarity is not a sufficient condition for stable coalition formation. Rather, demographic similarity leads to stable alliance patterns only when power is centralized and the use of politics is high' (1988: 759).*

Their analysis points to the importance of the structure of an organization. Where power is centralized around a narrow clique this is much more likely to lead to the establishment of a stable alliance. Eisenhardt and Bourgeois' data suggest that once established in an organization, politics become fairly entrenched. The formation of coalitions will lag behind the centralization of power. They found that patterns of political behaviour took a long time to develop, but once they had done so the patterns were relatively durable. They also found that the formation of alliances followed, rather than preceded, changes in politics. *Proposition F: 'The formation of stable alliance patterns lags in the use of politics' (1988: 759).*

3 *How do politics affect firm performance?* While some writers posit that a level of politics in an organization is positive for a firm's performance, Eisenhardt and Bourgeois argued the opposite: politics harmed the performance of the organizations they studied. In particular they found that politicking distracted attention from the functional jobs the executives were paid to carry out. A further reason was that in the fast-moving computer industry of the 1980s, complex decisions needed to be made quickly. The information-controlling behaviour associated with politicking militated against being able to make decisions effectively. *Proposition G: 'The greater the use of politics within the top management team, the poorer the performance of a firm' (1988: 760).*

Their insights into decision-making provided important contribution to the debate. Where we would take issue with their analysis is in terms of their conceptualization of politics. Whereas Eisenhardt and Bourgeois saw politics as something that emerged as a consequence of centralization, we regard politics as being an ever-present part of organizations: simply put, without politics, organizations would not exist. In their defence, Eisenhardt and Bourgeois noted that in the fast-paced sector they were studying, often the decisions being made concerned the very survival of a firm. They pointed to the youth of the industry at the time of their research and to the major technological changes that were taking place. To lose out would have been to go out of business; consequently, they argued, there was less politics at play. Of course, as we will see in Chapter 9, politics can be at their most effective when they are not seen. Thus far, our analysis has been largely confined to visible acts of decision-making. It is now time for us to consider hidden elements of decision-making.

NON-DECISION-MAKING

Decisions are, as we have seen, crucial to the strategy-making process. Sometimes, however, what is not decided can be of equal importance. Let us explore what we mean by this statement. We can be reasonably certain that a decision tells us something about the organization and the direction it is going in. It might be a decision that quite evidently fudges the outcome, something that satisfices for two competing groups within an organization, or, alternatively, it might be a clear statement that one part of a senior management team is in control and setting the direction for the organization to take. When a strategy proceeds by favouring a dominant group this is known as the 'mobilization of bias'. Paraphrasing Schattschneider (1960), what the mobilization of bias means is that some issues are organized *into* strategy while others are organized *out* of consideration.

Dominant groups will seek to uphold the status quo, which mobilizes any bias to their benefit. According to Peter Bachrach and Morton Baratz, the 'primary method for sustaining a given mobilisation of bias is non-decision-making' (1970: 44). A non-decision means that important decisions are not made or do not even make it onto the agenda.

> A non-decision is a 'decision that results in suppression or thwarting of a latent or manifest challenge to the values or interests of the decision-maker. To be more nearly explicit, non-decision-making is a means by which demands for change in the existing allocation of benefits and privileges in the community can be suffocated before they are even voiced; or kept covert; or killed before they gain access to the relevant decision-making arena; or, failing all these things, maimed or destroyed in the decision-implementing stage of the policy process' (Bachrach and Baratz, 1970: 44).

QUESTION TIME?

Of course, power is exercised when A participates in the making of decisions that affect B. Power is also exercised when A devotes his energies to creating or reinforcing social and political values and institutional practices that limit the scope of the political process to a public consideration of only those issues which are comparatively innocuous to A. To the extent that A succeeds in doing this B is prevented, for all practical purposes, from bringing to the fore any issues that might in their resolution be seriously detrimental to A's set of preferences (Bachrach and Baratz, 1970: 7).

Discuss the importance of this statement for understanding strategic decision-making. Provide an example from the press or your own experience when this has occurred.

The idea of non-decision-making came from research done by Bachrach and Baratz, American social scientists who set out to study the strategies through which the political, commercial and professional elite of the City of Baltimore retained an iron group on power. As they put it: 'The white-dominated political system in Baltimore systematically and consistently produced a city-wide distribution of benefits and privileges that was highly unfavourable to the black poor' (Bachrach and Baratz, 1970: 70).

In particular, they were interested in the way in which the interests of the city's poor, a majority of voters, who were also majority black, were deflected. There were three strategies that were followed in particular:

1 Appointing influential members of the city's ethnic community to sinecure appointments.

2 Establishing a special task force, whose remit was to look at ways to reduce poverty.

3 Introducing some welfare provision for the city's poor.

YOU CAN DOWNLOAD…

Ad van Iterson and Stewart R. Clegg's (2008) The Politics of Gossip and Denial in Inter-organizational Relations, *Human Relations*, 61(8): 1117–37, which provides some pointers for the question time above, from the book's website at www.sagepub.co.uk/cleggstrategy

For Bachrach and Baratz (1970) the city elite effectively marginalized the city's poor. Strategic decision-making processes might work to the advantage of some groups in the organization, to the detriment of others. David Buchanan and Richard Badham (2008: 54) explain how non-decision-making can take place:

1 The more powerful will deal with the grievances of the less powerful by ignoring them, by dismissing them as minor, unsubstantiated, or irrelevant, or by subjecting them to an endless and inconclusive consideration by committees and enquiries.

2 Anticipating the consequences, the less powerful may see that their grievances and demands will be ignored or dismissed, and will not raise them in the first place.

3 The powerful will define which matters are legitimate and discussible, and the forums and procedures through which such issues are raised, thus stifling the articulation of some issues and demands, while encouraging 'acceptable' or 'safe' topics and themes.

It was scenarios such as this which led one political scientist, Matthew Crenson, to argue for the importance of studying 'political inactivity' (1971: 26) when looking at strategic decisions. Some strategists (see Jarzabkowksi and Whittington, 2008) have struggled with the concept of studying things that do not happen. In political science, however, doing this is a well-established approach (see the van Iterson and Clegg [2008]). Our view is that it constitutes an important part of the strategist's toolkit. The implication is that by taking non-decision-making seriously, we are compelled to study strategic decisions that are not made, in addition to those that are: 'the proper object of investigation is not political activity [strategic decisions] but political inactivity [strategic non-decisions]' (Crenson, 1971: 26). Crenson, Emeritus Professor of Political Science at Johns Hopkins University, is an important writer for our purpose of trying to understand strategic decision-making.

Matthew Crenson set out to understand non-decision-making in what has become a classic study. To do so he studied the way in which air pollution was treated at different junctures in two American cities. He contrasted Gary and East Chicago. The two were in all important respects very similar: they were neighbouring cities not far from Chicago, both were steel towns and both suffered from high levels of pollution. However, they differed in one vital respect: East Chicago introduced air pollution regulation in 1949, whereas Gary did not do so until 1962. Their similarity opened up the possibility of studying non-decision-making – something that does not happen – empirically in a natural experiment. East Chicago operated differently from Gary, providing a relevant counterfactual.

A relevant counterfactual makes a claim, a hypothesis, or proposes some other conditions that are contrary to the facts; thus a conditional statement would be one in which the conditional clause is false and relevant, as in 'If the train had arrived on time the accident would not have happened', where there was a train accident and it was caused by the failure of the train to conform to the timetable.

Crenson's use of counterfactual reasoning followed his interest in finding out why there was such a difference in policy between the two cities, in spite of the striking parallels between them. Why was East Chicago so much more advanced in its efforts to tackle air pollution than Gary? Analytically, he set about trying to explain what did not happen. His argument was that by studying inaction it was possible to glean important insights into the conduct of city politics in Gary. Gary was a one-company city, with US Steel enjoying huge influence there: it had actually built the city. In addition, it was also characterized by strong political organization. In contrast, East Chicago was populated by a number of smaller steel companies and lacked strong political organization. In the early stages, US Steel's influence was such that the local population did not even raise the issue of regulating pollution. This, according to Crenson, was because of the anticipated

WHAT DO YOU MEAN?

Using counterfactuals for strategy

Some business historians have started to use counterfactuals as a means of looking back on decisions and asking 'what if?' A counterfactual approach, which remains controversial among historians, is a means of trying to explore how history might have been different if a key event had or had not happened. Recall Chapter 3, where we explored the manner in which the RBV is tautological. Charles Booth (2003), at the University of the West of England, cites the following examples:

- What if Hitler had defeated the Soviet Union in the Second World War?
- What if Nazi Germany had developed an atomic bomb in 1942?
- What if John F. Kennedy had lived?

In each case, a counterfactual historian would work through the example, seeking to construct a convincing narrative. Think about 'what if?' questions you might ask of an organization you are familiar with.

Many historians treat counterfactuals as trivial, as little more than a parlour game. There is this side to them; some of the counterfactual histories produced may be little more than a fanciful indulgence. Yet, they also make some serious points. They can be used as a heuristic – that is a means of learning – to try and identify what the key factors associated

with a particular strategy issue were. In chapter 11, we discuss decision-making and the current global financial crisis. A counterfactual analysis would seek to pose a number of questions: What if US and UK banks had been regulated more tightly? What if bankers' bonuses were heavily taxed? What if banks had been placed under government control after the Second World War? From this perspective a strategist would seek to identify the central organizational, political and historical processes that could explain why things were the way they were. Trying to anticipate how things might unfold in the future would follow this path. Strategists could use them to explore causation. As Hellekson (2000: 244–5) puts it:

> The alternate history as a genre speculates about such topics as the nature of time and linearity, the past's link to the present, the present's link to the future, and the role of individuals in the history making process. Alternate histories question the nature of history and causality; they question accepted notions of time and space; they rupture linear movement … and they foreground the 'constructedness' of history and the role narrative plays in this construction.

This has a bearing on how we understand strategic decision-making. It provides a means of making connections between decisions and outcomes – however convoluted and tenuous that process may turn out to be. Booth (2003) argues that engaging in counterfactual reasoning may be a means for an organization to gain greater self-knowledge.

reaction: it was envisaged that there was little possibility of change so there was little point in even raising it. In the latter stages, once pollution was on the agenda, US Steel heavily influenced the anti-pollution legislation when legislators sought to have it implemented. Crenson noted that while it was unusual for US Steel to enter the formal political arena, it was nonetheless able to exert a strong influence on the 'scope and direction' of city affairs. Interestingly, he argued that the strong political organization in Gary also played a role in keeping pollution off the agenda. This was because the politicians played a strong brokerage role that restricted political issues to topics such as pay and work conditions. Crenson concluded that decision-making activity was channelled and directed by the process of non-decision-making.

In conclusion, Crenson made a number of points that were insightful for the purposes of studying strategic decision-making:

1 Some strategists in an organization may have the 'ability to prevent some topics from ever becoming issues and to obstruct the growth of emergent issues' (1971: 177).

2 Often strategists with this ability do not actually need to exercise it, but merely gaining the reputation for having such power will be sufficient.

3 Often groups 'who do not actively participate [in decisions] ... may influence their content' (1971: 177).

4 Groups that are subject to the power of the dominant regime may remain invisible and strategically powerless.

5 Strategic decision-making is 'channeled and restricted by the process of non-decision-making' (1971: 178).

The work of non-decision theorists, the Bradford team and Pettigrew tell us a great deal about the mechanics of strategic decision-making. Above all it impresses upon us the importance of power and politics. As Eisenhardt and Bourgeois (1988: 737) put it: 'Most strategic decision processes are ultimately political in that they involve decisions with uncertain outcomes, actors with conflicting views, and resolution through the exercise of power'. Kathleen Eisenhardt and Mark Zbaracki (1992: 27) provide a very useful summary of political perspectives on decision-making in three points:

1 Organizations comprise people with partially conflicting preferences.

2 Powerful people will try to accomplish what they want, as strategic decision-making is ultimately political.

3 Decision-makers and resisters will engage in political tactics such as co-optation, coalition formation and the select use of information to enhance their power.

More controversial decisions tend to be more political; this is because, simply put, there is more at stake. Politics are usually accompanied by a certain degree of conflict and, in the case of an organization setting its strategy, disagreements might be wide-ranging. For instance, key executives might disagree with one another as to the importance of a decision and the direction in which a firm is going (see Chapter 7).

RISK, BUREAUCRACY AND DECISIONS

In the case study on the Cuban missile crisis we saw the way in which the military – through following protocols – almost forced Kennedy into launching an air strike against the Soviet missile installations. In our coverage of Lindblom's ideas of incrementalism, we saw a model of strategic decision-making being promulgated that edged forward slowly, based on consensus. An implication of this is that a decision made sets an organization on a path dependency that will lead that organization to make a particular subsequent decision almost by default. Bachrach and Baratz (1970: 42) characterize such a situation as one of 'decisionless decisions'. They provide the following example:

> President Truman's 'decision' to order an atomic attack on Hiroshima in August 1945 was totally foreordained: although he and his top advisors were debating pros and cons of the policy choice to the last moment, the technical arrangements were so complete that a decision to call it off was all but impossible. (Bachrach and Baratz, 1970: 42)

This is a fascinating point. At what stage is an organization – or a group of strategists – committed to a particular decision? It is said that one of the first things that a venture capitalist does, when making a new investment, is to plan an exit strategy: if the venture goes sour, how can it be exited as painlessly as possible? Of course, often decisions that can have huge ramifications get taken at various operational stages of an organizational project. One such example was the *Challenger* disaster in 1986.

The 1986 Space Shuttle disaster: risky technology and decision-making

Diane Vaughan, Professor of Sociology at Columbia University, wrote a classic account of the American Space Shuttle disaster. It had important implications for decision-making. By the mid-1980s Space Shuttle flights had become routine, a point that was symbolized by a non-astronaut – an American school teacher, Christa McAuliffe – being included as part of the crew. Tragically, the Space Shuttle exploded after take off, killing all on board. The *Challenger* disaster tarnished, irrevocably, NASA's iconic status within American culture.

The inquiry reports that followed the tragedy all highlighted that the explosion was more than just a technical error, pointing to deep-seated decision-making failings in NASA. In the extensive media coverage that followed the publication of these reports this message was lost and media pundits focused their attention on middle managers making poor decisions. Media attention zoomed in on the failure of an O-ring (a rubber component on the rocket booster of the Space Shuttle), something that had been allowed to happen by a series of dubious middle management decisions. In particular, the media concentrated on protests made by engineers on the eve of the launch. The source of the engineers' discontent was their opinion that air temperatures were too low to launch the shuttle. The media also focused on the NASA middle managers' decision to proceed with the launch despite there being problems with the O-rings. It was argued by the media that the NASA managers' chief concern was to meet their production schedule by launching the shuttle. Therein, according to popular imagination, lay the problem: 'good' engineers being stymied by 'bad' managers.

Blaming specific individuals is a convenient way of promulgating quick-fix solutions – that is, fire or move the managers concerned – and it distracts attention from broader organizational problems. As Vaughan (1996: 393) put it: 'As long as we see organizational failures as the result of individual actions our strategies for control will be ineffective, and dangerously so'. Vaughan asserts that in the process of looking retrospectively at a past event, there is a tendency to change history such that it becomes consistent with the present. The solution to an historical problem is rendered such that it seems self-evident, thus implying that the organization should have been able to anticipate and deal with an error in advance. Vaughan characterizes such a situation as a case of retrospective fallacy. She argued that the conventional wisdom on the shuttle disaster was erroneous, largely because it failed to understand NASA's culture.

Vaughan's book studied decision-making in NASA in the years preceding the disaster. With the first flight of the shuttle, engineers discovered the O-ring was damaged, something which, in theory, should not have happened. It was decided this damage constituted an 'acceptable risk', because, if the primary O-rings failed, the backup one would function. The engineers developed a theory of how the O-rings functioned, which was subsequently supported by their tests. Inexorably, however, the engineers accepted greater levels of risk. While each decision was made individually, over time the cumulative effect was such that the custom and practice of NASA became increasingly risky. Of course, the Space Shuttle was a highly innovative design and NASA employees were accustomed to encountering

Normalization of deviance occurs when a lower standard of performance is accepted over a period of time such that, gradually, that lower standard becomes the 'norm'. Usually, the acceptance of the lower standard occurs because of pressure (from the budget, schedule, etc.) making the expected standard difficult to maintain. Often the intention is to revert to the higher standard when pressure eases. However, the deviation appears to work OK so it is likely to be repeated when similar stressful circumstances arise in the future. Over time, people no longer see what they are doing as a deviation from expected standards and fail to see their actions as deviant. These actions have become normal.

and fixing problems. What took place in NASA was, therefore, part of a general normalization of deviance, whereby problems were regarded as routine.

The normalization of deviance, *inter alia*, comprises dealing with mixed signals, weak signals and routine signals:

- *Mixed signals* highlighted a potential danger, followed by signs that all is well – thus convincing engineers that they had diagnosed, corrected and solved the problem – and the risk was acceptable.

- *Weak signals* were unclear or involved an improbable occurrence, which the engineers thought would have little chance of recurring.

- *Routine signals* were events that happened frequently, leading to the establishment of a method of assessing and responding to the event – for instance, the O-ring eroded after each flight. This came to be regarded as an acceptable risk. The routine nature of the problem led the engineers to conclude that the erosion of the O-ring was not a danger, but that they understood the problem and instituted a new procedure to ensure safety: the key thing was to ensure the O-ring was properly positioned.

Political pressures contributed to the shuttle disaster, in particular through the introduction of greater accountability, which, in turn, changed NASA's organizational culture. By the 1980s there were three different logics of action at play within NASA's culture:

1 *Technical culture.* The original Apollo space programme had established a culture of engineering excellence, which combined professional expertise with a practical 'getting one's hands dirty' approach. All engineering problems were subject to extensive quantitative analysis and testing.

2 *Political accountability.* The Apollo programme had, in effect, received generous funding, with government largesse lavished on the project. By the early 1980s, the climate had changed and NASA struggled to obtain funding for the shuttle programme. The director of NASA sold the programme to government on the basis it would pay for itself by offering commercial flights to space. This was misleading, given the technology was still very much in a developmental phase.

3 *Bureaucratic accountability.* The production of rockets and spacecraft changed to the extent that it increasingly relied upon contractors for the supply of component parts (a Space Shuttle consisted of 60 million components). The changed nature of production expanded the bureaucracy required to oversee it. In addition to this, the Reagan government, with its emphasis on small government, imposed greater accountability criteria on NASA. These two factors combined to increase the number of rules to be followed and the bureaucracy necessary to administer these rules.

The launch of a shuttle was governed by a procedure (bureaucratic accountability) that followed a time line for lift off (political accountability), which often eroded the technical culture of NASA. Despite NASA being under economic strain, adhering to the schedule was its overriding concern (the budget was based on an over-optimistic launch rate for shuttles). Unless the engineering data decided a component posed a threat to the safety of a mission, any delay was out of the question. While there were many delays with shuttle launches, within the culture of NASA these had to be for scientific reasons backed up by hard, quantitative data. Hunches or intuition were not accepted as a valid rationale. Cognisant of the innovative design of the shuttle combined with the mysteries of nature, NASA engineers followed all the rules. As Vaughan (1997: 90) puts it: 'If they followed all the rules, all the procedures then they had done everything they could to reduce residual risk and to assure safety'.

The fateful launch decision took place through a teleconference in which contractor engineers, from Thiokol, a contractor based in Utah, and managers, from the Kennedy Space Center in Florida and the Marshall Space Center in Alabama, participated in deciding whether to launch or not. In total 34 people were present at the teleconference. The meeting was convened at 8.15pm so they could make a decision before 12.30, when the shuttle was due to be refuelled. If a decision was taken before 12.30 not to launch, NASA would avoid the expensive process of de-tanking the shuttle. This was an instance of political accountability intervening in the process. Of course, the meeting was convened according to bureaucratic precedent. Around the table, there was a shared cumulative base of engineering knowledge. However, the meeting was not routine as there were three unusual variables:

1 The air temperature on the proposed launch day was much lower than normal.

2 While teleconferences were normal, a face-to-face meeting was usually held a fortnight earlier. This had not taken place, in this instance.

3 It was the first time that the Theiokal engineers had argued for a launch not to take place.

The 8.15pm starting time for the meeting caught many of those attending off-guard. Unusually for NASA, things were unfinished and preparations for the meeting were a little rushed. The engineering data highlighted a number of inconsistencies. There were, however, mixed signals: the engineers felt that 53 degrees Fahrenheit was the minimum temperature at which a shuttle could launch, as this was the lowest temperature a previous shuttle had been launched at and the O-ring had been the most damaged. Confusingly, the second most damaged O-ring was launched at a higher temperature. The 'hard data' were therefore inconclusive. That the engineers felt that 53 degrees was the lowest temperature at which a shuttle could be launched was based on qualitative data, which in the 'hard science' culture of NASA cut little ice.

The teleconference was set up to be adversarial: the Marshall managers, adhering to the demands of political accountability, had a schedule to keep, and they engaged, as usual, in a critical interrogation of the engineering evidence. The meeting reached an impasse. The Thiokol engineers took a break to consult. In the absence of more data they were unable to mount a stronger case. Bureaucratic accountability was manifest: even in an unusual situation all of the participants observed the normal rules, which had been designed with safety in mind. The adversarial contestation – by managers – of the engineers' analyses upheld procedure. Protocol dictated who could speak and at what point – something that effectively silenced many of the more junior staff – as well as the formal roles that were to be fulfilled by managers and engineers, respectively. The rituals and procedures for a formal launch were designed to ensure that everything possible had been done to ensure safety. Infamously, the launch took place and the *Challenger* Space Shuttle was engulfed in a ball of flame. All on board lost their lives.

Unsurprisingly, in the aftermath of the tragedy there was public anger, grief and a great deal of finger pointing. Those present at the teleconference blamed each other or agonized over what they could, or perhaps, should have done. Attention focused on the physical fault and the role middle management had played in ignoring the warning from the engineers. This, of course, shielded senior decision-makers from blame. As Vaughan points out, these senior decision-makers were party to political bargains, they set goals, allocated resources, and declared the shuttle programme operational while it was still very much an experimental technology characterized by high levels of unpredictability. While those at the teleconference made the fateful decision, they did so under parameters set by senior decision-makers who were far away from that meeting.

Learning from this case, Vaughan (1997) advocated that in situations of 'risky work':

1　'Top administrators must take responsibility for mistakes, failure and safety by remaining alert to how their decisions in response to environ-mental contingencies affect people at the bottom of the hierarchy who do risky work' (1997: 17). While accidents and errors will always happen in organizations, Vaughan advocated not just looking at the immediate result of the human error, but also extending the analysis to those who design the conditions in which people work.

2　Strategies have deferred results – often harmful effects will become clear long after the senior strategists responsible for policies have left the organization.

3　In the politics of blame that accompany disasters, very often the powerful are protected, while more junior individuals in the organization will get 'scapegoated'.

4　Strategies must have realistic goals and be backed up by the necessary resources.

5　Strategic decisions to change organizations must be accompanied by an evaluation of the likely effects of the changes on safety.

6　Top strategists must be familiar with the difficulties, dangers and risks of their own workplace; otherwise, they can succumb to the 'myth of infallibility'. In NASA, there was a large gap between senior strategists and those that worked on operational issues. Consequently, the senior strategists failed to understand the risks taken – through cuts in budgets – following their declaration that the shuttle was operational.

7　Plan for the worst case scenario – make sure a strategy has a post-disaster plan in place.

8　Culture: organizational cultures are complex and often subtle and difficult to read. Try to understand how employees follow particular rules and violate others during routine work conditions.

9　Interpret signals in the organization: 'In decision-making all participants should be alert to the categories of mixed, weak, routine and strong signals and how they influence others' interpretation of a situation, and therefore, how those others respond' (1997: 99).

10　Make sure all relevant information gets into the conversation – try to develop the conditions for polyphony.

11　Normalization of deviance – it is important that strategists seek to avoid the inexorable expansion of the bounds of what constitutes an acceptable risk.

12　Appreciation of risk is central to organizations that deal with hazards.

With hindsight the *Challenger* disaster would never have happened. The engi-neers' recommendation would have been accepted and the shuttle would not have been launched. All so easy. To use the old cliché, hindsight's vision is always 20:20. As R. K. Betts, an international relations scholar, puts it: 'Strategies can be judged looking backward, but they must be chosen looking forward' (2000: 8). A unifying characteristic of the sections above is that the various insights into decision-making all share a sense of the strategists knowing why they were making a particular decision. Part of this relates to drawing lessons from the past using relevant counterfactuals.

STRATEGIC DECISIONS MAKE THE MANAGER WHO MAKES STRATEGIC DECISIONS

Strategy, as it is wrapped up in the specifics and particulars of making decisions, is largely arrived at through talking through options, framing issues, specifying non-issues and implicitly drawing the boundaries around areas of non-decision-making. As such:

> Strategy talk is not innocent. It is a powerful rhetorical device. It frames issues in particular ways and augments instrumental reason; it bestows expertise and rewards on those who are 'strategists'; and its military connotations reinforce a patriarchal orientation to the organization of work. In doing so, strategy demonstrates managerial rationality and legitimizes the exercise of power. (Levy, Alvesson and Willmott, 2001: 90; cited in Diefenbach, 2009: 47)

Actually, strategy does more than Levy and colleagues suggest. It not only legitimizes specific exercises of power, but also becomes the institutionalized condensation of power relations as mobilizations of bias are built into decisions, operations and organization. As Diefenbach (2009: 47 – italics in original) suggests, '*strategic decisions are not only made by powerful managers – strategic decisions make managers powerful*'. Managers are made powerful through the making of strategies which, as a performative act, as something they will do when they decide what the strategy will be and communicate it to others in decisions, symbolizes them as powerful irrespective of the agendas shaped, non-decisions made, issues included and excluded, which will only serve to entrench some specific powers while whittling away at others. Those powers that are limited will be both particular powers of specific managers whose capabilities are deemed less strategic, or less than strategic, as well as the general power of discursive representation and marginalization: the ways in which specific rationalities, specific rationalized myths, are legitimated and embedded while others are dislodged or excluded. These are the rationalities and myths that touch on

> controversial topics which go against the interests of powerful stakeholders; they do not engender support, they do not fit with the prevailing culture, they are not considered acceptable for discussion, so they are quietly sidestepped or suppressed or dropped. (Miller, Hickson and Wilson, 2002: 80)

Strategies and strategic decision-making represent the current state of structured play in any organization – they show the current institutionalization of top management team interests. They are today's condensation of a ceaseless managerial struggle for the control of agendas, a promotion of interests and the silencing or over ruling of opponents' rival strategies.

SUMMARY AND REVIEW

Strategic decision-making lies at the heart of strategy-making, with decisions being the very stuff of strategy. For some rationalists, decision-making in effect took on the status of a science. Information was collected and a cost–benefit calculus was applied. Such a view of decisions – while widely practised in government and organizations – became the subject of derision in most academic circles. At the fore was Nobel Laureate Herbert Simon, who steamrollered through the prevailing wisdom of rational choice. Simon's belief in science, however, was as unshakeable as the rationalists he sought to displace, but he wanted to treat decision-makers as they were and not as they appeared in economics textbooks. His major contribution was to introduce the related concepts of bounded rationality and satisficing to the decision-making literature. This shifted the debate considerably and became the new locus for discussions around decision-making. Fellow travellers were March, Cohen and Olsen – they pushed things a little further. Decisions were made not just according to bounded rationality, but also with a heavy slug of chance added into the mix. The memorably titled garbage can is as relevant today as it was when it was first showcased in the early 1970s. While this scholarship was flourishing, Charles Lindblom was undertaking a critique of rational planning techniques. His work shared many resonances with Simon's, and he advocated a disjointed incrementalist approach to decision-making. As he put it: look at how decisions are actually made, not how they should be made. In the space of a decade the debate on decision-making had changed significantly. This debate was still largely oriented around displacing rationalist notions – not because rationalism was bad *per se*, but rather because it imploded under the cognitive and informational requirements it demanded of its practitioners.

From stage left came a body of scholarship that sought to understand decision-making as being more about the operation of power and politics. Important research identified not only the way in which decisions were made, but also how they were kept off the agenda. Consequently, to understand strategy-making it is crucial to be able to analyse how and why particular decisions are made. For decisions determine what is attempted by an organization and what sets it on a specific path dependency. As important as the decisions made are those that are not made, those issues that remain non-issues, which might, in counterfactual terms, reasonably have been considered. There is more to decision-making than simply imperative behaviour.

EXERCISES

1 Having read this chapter you should be able to say in your own words and provide an example of what the following key terms mean:
   - Bounded rationality
   - Satisficing
   - Garbage can
   - Action generators
   - Sporadic decisions
   - Fluid decisions
   - Constricted decisions
   - Non-decisions
   - Relevant counterfactual
   - Normalization of deviance
   - Counterfactual history.

2 You have been commissioned to advise the government on rational decision-making. In particular, if is keen to develop a methodology for making decisions rationally. Prepare an A4 sheet of paper advising the government on how to make a rational decision.

3 Summarize the central arguments Herbert Simon made against the rational planning approach. Provide examples to illustrate your answer.

4 To what extent, if any, do you agree with Charles Lindblom's assertion that when it comes to decision-making, organizations just 'muddle through'?

5 Provide a summary of an instance of garbage-can decision-making. What specifically were the characteristics of the decision that led to your describing it as an example of garbage-can decision-making?

6 Andrew Pettigrew's (1972) article in *Sociology* describes the importance of gatekeepers to the decision-making process. Advise how you would empirically establish whether someone was a gatekeeper in an organization. What sorts of things would you look for?

7 Write a short two-page report summarizing the implications of the *Top Decisions* study for strategists.

8 Watch the movie *The Damned Utd*. Critically evaluate why Brian Clough was fired after 44 days in charge of Leeds United FC. Research a sports league of your choice (such as, Barclays Premiership, *Serie A*). How many managers/coaches have been fired over the last three years and what were the reasons given for their dismissal?

9 Eisenhardt and Bourgeois (1988: 760) make the following proposition: 'the greater the use of politics within the top management team, the poorer the performance of a firm'. Critically evaluate this statement.

10 Devise a research plan for studying non-decisions. How can you study whether non-decision-making is going on?

11 Prepare a 10-minute presentation outlining how decision-making processes contributed to the Space Shuttle *Challenger* disaster.

12 Critically evaluate Diane Vaughan's 12 lessons from the Space Shuttle *Challenger* disaster. To what extent are they applicable to modern strategy-making?

13 'Of course power is exercised when A participates in the making of decisions that affect B. Power is also exercised when A devotes his energies to creating or reinforcing social and political values and institutional practices that limit the scope of the political process to public consideration of only those issues which are comparatively innocuous to A. To the extent that A succeeds in doing this B is prevented, for all practical purposes, from bringing to the fore any issues that might in their resolution be seriously detrimental to A's set of preferences' (Bachrach and Baratz, 1970: 7). Discuss the importance of this statement for understanding strategic decision-making. Provide an example from the press or your own experience when this has occurred.

ADDITIONAL RESOURCES

1 Our companion website is the best first stop for you to find a great deal of extra resources, free PDF versions of leading articles published in Sage journals, exercise, video and pod casts, team case studies and general questions and links to teamwork resources. Go to www.sagepub.co.uk/cleggstrategy. Good journals to consult for thinking about strategic

decision-making are *Human Relations*, *Organization Studies* and *Strategic Organization*.

2 Consult Niall Ferguson's (1997) *Virtual History*, London: Papermac. Prepare a report on (a) The circumstances in which you might use counterfactual history, and (b) apply it to an organization you are familiar with.

WEB SECTION

Visit the *Strategy* companion website at www.sagepub. co.uk/cleggstrategy

1 More detail about the Copenhagen Climate Change Summit is available at : http://www.denmark.dk/en/menu/Climate-Energy/COP15-Copenhagen-2009/cop15.htm

2 The online resource www.strategytube.net that the authors produced in tandem with this book is a great resource.

LOOKING FOR A HIGHER MARK?

Reading and digesting these articles that are available free on the companion website www.sagepub.co.uk/cleggstrategy can help you gain deeper understanding and, on the basis of that, a better grade. Each of these articles amplifies understanding of how counterfactual analysis can be used.

1 Maielli, G. (2007) Counterfactuals, Superfactuals and the Problematic Relationship between Business Management and the Past, *Management & Organizational History*, 2: 275–94.

2 MacKay, R. (2007) What If? Synthesizing Debates and Advancing Prospects of Using Virtual History in Management and Organization Theory, *Management & Organizational History*, 2: 295–314.

3 Toms, S. and Beck, M. (2007) The Limitations of Economic Counterfactuals: The Case of the Lancashire Textile Industry, *Management & Organizational History*, 2: 315–30.

United Nations Climate Change Conference 2009

Chris Carter

At the time of writing this book world leaders were convening in Copenhagen to try to agree a climate treaty. Summits are fascinating from the point of view of the study of strategic decision-making. By their very nature, the issue under consideration is likely to be an important one; equally, there are likely to be a range of competing perspectives and interests relating to the issue being discussed at the summit. Climate change is particularly controversial. The previous climate treaty, Kyoto 1992, went unratified by major economies, including the United States; consequently, it had little legitimacy and more than anything became a symbol of the willingness of the United States as a global superpower, to ignore the will of the global community. That said, signatories to the Kyoto Treaty had legally committed themselves to various cuts in emissions. Kyoto was directed at developed countries and did not apply to developing countries. For many years prior to the summit the US government had been a 'climate change sceptic', casting doubt on the veracity of the claims that humankind was causing the earth's climate to change. Anthony Giddens (2009) points out that while only a tiny rump of scientists hold such views, they are given disproportional coverage in the media. This may stem from influential lobbying on the part of climate change sceptics, the predilections of media moguls, or the dynamics of different journalists wanting to take divergent positions on a subject. Most environmental scientists are, however, convinced that climate change is being caused by human activity. Naturally there is a wide range of varying predictions as to the extent of climate change and the effects this will have on the planet. This is, of course, unknowable, although the projections range from the deeply worrying through to the downright apocalyptic.

Pre-summit

There had been a number of pre-meetings, in Bangkok, Barcelona and Bonn, before December 2009, which saw representatives from 192 countries, including 115 leaders, convene at Copenhagen. Teams of negotiators from each of the countries worked for a fortnight prior to the leaders arriving. It was touted as one of the most important summits of the last hundred years. Yvo De Boer, Chief Negotiator for the United Nations, asserted at the outset of the summit that 'Copenhagen will only be a success if there is significant and immediate action'. In the media, expectations were high. Any attempt to tackle climate change in a serious way will, inevitably, change the way in which people live: fuel prices will go up, travel will change, air-conditioning will be heavily taxed, and the amount of material possessions people can consume will reduce. In short, the whole model for industrial manufacturing will have to alter (Lovelock, 2006). Such changes are unlikely, in the short term, to be popular with voters, owners or the shareholders of large corporations. For these reasons it was doubtful whether any major agreement was ever likely. Going into the negotiations, the major players in the European Union wanted a reduction of emissions by 50 per cent by 2050 (some influential members, such as Germany, wanted this raised to 80 per cent) and a legally binding treaty. Small island countries, especially ones likely to be submerged out of existence, advocated large reductions in emissions, a policy supported by some Latin American countries. Around a hundred countries wanted a commitment not to allow temperatures to rise more than 1.5°C. Both China and India were more sceptical, wanting more modest targets to be adopted. Developing countries, in general, wanted some changes to an economic system of trade that was hugely disadvantageous to them. At the outset of the summit, outside of the media hyperbole, commentators were measured in what could reasonably be expected from the summit.

The summit

Early on at the summit there were leaks of information. In particular, notes emerged referring to a document being prepared clandestinely by a small group of wealthy countries. They were annoyed that this had been revealed; in turn, the developing countries were furious that deals were going on behind closed doors and at meetings they had been excluded from. Rancour pervaded the summit. Leaks continued throughout, adding to the feeling of distrust and uncertainty, while, late in the

(Continued)

(Continued)

summit, the negotiations stalled. The Chinese, who had forged a powerful alliance with India, in effect wanted to prevent any measures that would stop their ability to expand economically. In the eyes of the European Union, 'they wrecked the negotiating process'. At the beginning of the summit, Su Wei, their Chief Negotiator, interrupted Connie Hedergaard, the Danish chair of the meeting, a move interpreted in some quarters as questioning the legitimacy of the hosts of the conference.

An emergency meeting was convened by a small number of countries and attended by country leaders and their advisers, though interestingly, and in a breach of diplomatic protocol, the Indian and Chinese leaders did not attend, sending advisers instead. At one point, Wen Jiabao, the Chinese Premier, walked out of the conference. The Danish chair had provoked the conference to such an extent that behind the scenes a delegation from Australia, the UK and the United States met to discuss the removal of Connie Hedergaard from her post as chair of the conference.

On 15 December this led to a loss of five hours of negotiation time when Connie Hedegaard called a 'timeout' to try and cool negotiations down. The African delegation were particularly suspicious that the conference was being used to suspend the Kyoto Protocol, thus relieving developed world signatories of their statutory obligations to reduce emissions. Hedegaard's proposal to call a meeting for 50, out of 192, countries incensed many of the developing world nations. The media were reporting that, in general, no progress had been made in the previous 10 days. The British Prime Minister, Gordon Brown, arrived two days earlier than anticipated, to meet with Australian Prime Minister, Kevin Rudd, to try and formulate a way out of the impasse. Hedegaard warned the media: 'In these very hours we are balancing between success and failure. Success is within reach. But I must also warn you. We can fail'. A South African representative captured the mood of many countries well: 'No-one wants to be the country to be accused of collapsing the talks but we fear a political settlement that is contrary to our interests may be imposed without real consultation'.

On 16 December, Hedegaard resigned as chair, being replaced by Lars Rasmussen, the Danish Prime Minister. Officially, this was explained as a procedural change, as Rasmussen was more appropriate as a head of government to deal with other heads of government; unofficially, Hedegaard was said to be unhappy with the content of the 'Danish text', and African countries were also said to have complained that she favoured the wealthy Western countries in her chairing style. Considerable disquiet was expressed about the apparently heavy-handed treatment of climate activists. Mainstream environmental groups were being prevented from entering the conference, which led to accusations that the conference was silencing civil society. British Prime Minister Gordon Brown feared that the talks were about to collapse.

The 17 December was mired in gloom. British Environment Minister, Ed Miliband, warned the talks were veering towards 'farce', while Australian Prime Minister Kevin Rudd feared 'a triumph of inaction over action'. German Chancellor Angela Merkel was downcast in her address to the German Parliament, prior to travelling to Copenhagen. The negotiations were deadlocked. Much of the dispute was over the attempt by the Western industrialized countries to replace the Kyoto Treaty with an agreement that reflected the new economic and political realities for the world, most particularly the emergence of China and India as major economic powers. When the summit looked as though it was on the brink of collapse, the US Secretary of State, Hilary Clinton, announced a proposal to create a fund of $100 billion per annum to help developing world countries combat climate change.

On Friday 18 December media headlines screamed that the summit was in disarray and the talks could collapse at any moment. Thirty countries had put their name to an accord, but Bolivia, Venezuela, Nicaragua, Sudan and Saudi Arabia were threatening to veto this, which would have led to a complete failure of the summit. The so-called Danish text – an agreement between 30 countries – which, it is alleged, was going to be produced at the last minute to try to force an agreement, was counteracted by a counter-text produced by developing countries (the G77 plus China). There was an impasse. It was hoped President Obama's arrival would help find a way out of the deadlock.

After intense negotiation, late nights and high drama, an accord, brokered by President Obama and Premier Wen Jiabao, was announced. The accord, which had gone through eight previous drafts prior to its agreement, acknowledged the scientific case for not allowing temperatures to rise more than 2°C this century ('The increase in global temperature should be below 2°C'). Countries agreed in principle

(Continued)

(Continued)

for the need to reduce carbon emissions ('Parties commit to implement individually or jointly the quantified economic-wide emissions target for 2020 as listed in appendix 1 (US – reduction of 14–17% from 2005 levels; EU – 20–30% reduction from 1990 levels; Japan – 25% from 1990 levels; Russia – 15–25% from 1990 levels'). It was mooted that countries should try and cooperate to reduce emissions and that developing countries were at a disadvantage ('We should co-operate in achieving the peaking of global and national emissions as soon as possible, recognising that the time frame for peaking will be longer in developing countries'). In addition to this, a recommendation was made for the investigation of a 'cash for forests' deal, whereby countries were paid not to deforest their land ('Substantial finance to prevent deforestation; adoption; technology development and transfer and capacity').

Reactions to the summit

Immediately after the summit, various leaders lined up to tell the gathered media that the accord was 'meaningful', 'a vital first step'. President Obama stated 'We've come a long way but we have much further to go', while Prime Minister Gordon Brown described it as a 'start'. President Sarkozy acknowledged: 'the text is not perfect ... if we had no deal, that would mean two countries as important as India and China would be freed from any type of contract'. China was upbeat: 'The meeting had had a positive result, everyone should be happy'; similarly, the Indian government was positive: 'We can be satisfied that we were able to get our way ... India came out quite well in Copenhagen'. In contrast, Brazil described the summit as 'disappointing'. Also, various critics lined up to condemn the accord. One of the participants, Lumumba Di-Aping, who was Chief Negotiator for the G77, complained: '[the accord shows] the lowest level of ambition you can imagine. It's nothing short of climate change scepticism in action. It locks countries into a cycle of poverty forever'.

Some participants expressed dismay that key points had disappeared from the text of the accord during the day: the desire to have a new treaty, superseding Kyoto; and a deadline for the agreement of the treaty. Outside of the formal meeting, NGOs lined up to criticize the outcome of the Copenhagen

Summit. In particular, the lack of specific measures or plans to ensure that the temperature did not rise about 2°C was criticized. African and other countries that had lobbied for an agreement that the climate could not rise above 1.5°C were dismayed. Some of the developing world delegates criticized the organization by the Danes, in particular their tactic of convening a small group of powerful countries to draft an accord to be agreed by everyone. The Danes retorted that some countries were getting too concerned about the process of the meeting rather than focusing on achieving a desired outcome. Critics were not impressed: a spokesman for the NGO Greenpeace likened Copenhagen to a crime scene, while a US spokesman with Friends of the Earth argued: 'This toothless declaration, being spun by the US as a historic success, reflects contempt for the multi-lateral process and we expect more from our Nobel-prize winning President'.

Questions

1   Identify instances where non-decision-making took place at the Copenhagen summit.

2   How do you think Charles Lindblom would have understood the summit?

3   Apply the concepts of bounded rationality and satisficing to the case study.

4   Which of the types of decision-making identified by the Bradford studies are evident in the case study?

5   Conduct some further research into the summit. Study a developed government (an OECD country), a developing country and an NGO. Compare and contrast their views of the summit. What did they, in your view, set out to achieve? To what extent were they, in your view, successful in this endeavour? How, following the summit, did they account for the summit? What does this exercise tell us about the different rationalities relating to how countries view climate change?

6   Imagine you are advising a future climate change summit. In light of your knowledge of decision-making, how would you advise the summit to be organized to obtain a successful outcome?

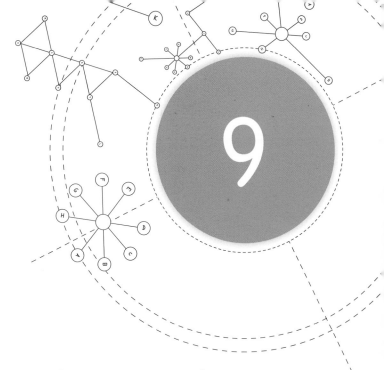

Organizational Politics and Strategy

Mandates, winners and losers

LEARNING OBJECTIVES

By the end of this chapter you will be able to:

- Appreciate the importance of organizational politics in the strategy process

- Grasp the importance of political skill for successful strategic management

- Realize the importance of social capital for strategic managers

- See the strategy process through the lens of the different dimensions of power

- Understand what the main contours of micro-politics are likely to be, especially in multinational corporations

- Analyse the centrality of mandates for strategic politics

- Appreciate the role that power, legitimacy, resources and centrality play in strategy

INTRODUCTION

Like Robert Burns' mouse in the poem, we often devise schemes or strategies that
go askew (the literal translation of the Scots 'Gang aft agley'). Some recent 'best laid
schemes' that have figured widely in the news include the very evident malfeasance
of Enron and Harry Madoff. Both Enron and Madoff had well-laid schemes from
which they had been getting rich and also had been getting away with for many years.

In this chapter we want to look at how schemes can go awry not just because
of unforeseen externalities – the ploughman in Burns' poem – but also because
of internalities: the rats in the ranks of organizations rather than the mice in the
fields. *Rats in the Ranks* (Anderson and Connolly, 1996) is a documentary film
about the election of the mayor of a council by councillors. In *cinéma vérité*, we
see the deals done to make friends of enemies' enemies; the alliances that are
constantly shifting, the enunciation of principles cloaked in self-interest and the
interests of the citizens being treated as a side issue to the question of who gets
which spoils. In short, we can see organizational politics at work in strategy.

An organizational situation where the outcomes achieved are driven by organizational politics and self-interest may seem a long way from representations of the
cool, calm and rational world of strategy – but it is not. Strategy is irremediably
political. Options get taken up; others are rejected; futures are desired while some
scenarios are rejected; arguments are put forward and data marshalled; moves are
surreptitiously made and blocked, as a result of which some proposals will wither
while others flourish. And behind every proposal stands those who are making
them. And they make these proposals not from a position of benign neutrality and
benevolence, but always from a position of interest.

INTERESTS AND STRATEGY

That there are different interests at work in any organization is evident.

Business organizations are composed of different relations of production,
between owners of capital and those hired to maximize returns on capital, management and the employees hired to deliver services and products that will sell to
clients and customers in various markets. For many observers of business strategy

Organizational politics: the use
of organizational resources,
such as knowledge, position
or networks, to engage in
actions that are strategically
self-interested.

Interests can be defined
in terms of the relations
between actors, discursive
rationalities and the structural
positions they occupy.
The same person, when
they are a young junior
manager, will have different
interests, expressed in terms
of different rationalities,
from their mature CEO self;
production managers will
differ in their interests and
rationalities from marketing
managers, and so on.

the key relation has been seen as that between the actual owners of capital and those charged with its day-to-day control and the application of effort to maximize that capital. Non-business organizations differ only in that the stewardship of their resources is in different hands: the relations of power between different actors and interests are no less significant – think of *Rats in the Ranks*.

The separation between ownership and control has long been a staple topic for business students. At its core is a simple question: if the owners of a company do not have charge of its day-to-day business how can they be sure that their interests are being served? Berle and Means first formulated the question in 1932 in their book *The Modern Corporation and Private Property*. They framed the question in the wake of the Wall Street crash of 1929 when many fortunes based on ownership of shares in leading US companies disappeared as the market collapsed and depression ensued. In more recent times the question has been reframed as one of principal and agency. The shareholders are the principals in a business; they own the capital that they place at the disposal of the business in return for an entitlement to any profits or losses accruing to them. As the shareholders are many and varied and are generally not engaged in the running of the business, agents who, theoretically, act on behalf of the principals manage the business.

Now the problem can be phrased quite simply: what mechanisms can be designed that will induce managers to maximize stock, and thus shareholder, value? The answer to this question seems simple: link CEO and top management team pay more and more closely to the company's performance in the stock market. That way the interests of principals, the shareholders and the agents, the CEO and managers, would be closely aligned. CEOs and top management teams become remunerated in part – indeed in large part in many cases – through the mechanism of stock options or through performance-related pay which tracks share prices. The reasoning is that it is in the interests of stockholders for the stewards of their capital to be stockholders or at least to have a significant part of their earnings aligned with stock valuations.

There are problems with this approach, however. Businesses may produce valuations on the stock exchange but this is not their prime activity. It is a side effect of the way they are capitalized. Their prime activity is to deliver goods and services such as automobiles or mortgages. A company might develop a very successful product, raising the stock value. Once that product is launched, and the stock adjusts upwards, the success of that product, while it may be profitable and stable over the long term, may not necessarily be sufficient to drive the stock up further. So other strategies are needed to maintain growth in the share price and keep on delivering returns to existing and new shareholders. As a result, executives are tempted (or pressured) to make decisions that will not necessarily be good for long-term stability or profitability, but will increase the next quarter's stock price.

STRATEGIC INTERESTS AND MICRO-POLITICS

Strategic interests are not just something that a person is interested in, such as football or ballet. These might be something that you would discuss with mates at work, but such shared or different interests would not compel them, necessarily, to ally with or oppose you over some issue. Interests link rationalities, actors and relations with strategies.

A **strategic interest** emerges when there is something at issue, which divides opinions, on which people will take sides. Dominant interpretations of strategic interests will tend to be represented as those that are legitimate for the firm or organization, even against resistance from other representations.

You may be interested in a promotion or a larger salary. When you act in self-interest – to gain a promotion – you may be astute enough to realize that the best way to do so is under the guise of a **strategic interest**. To the extent that you can tie up your self-interests with emergent strategic projects, then your interests can be presented as entirely legitimate, as something inherently organizationally rational even if, coincidentally, these are self-interested. Organizational strategies can easily be divisive because they always have the potential to make some people winners and others losers.

WHAT DO YOU MEAN?

Aligning personal interests with strategic interests

Where differences surface as competing arguments about issues they must be couched not in personal terms but in terms of different expressions of interest. The expression of different interests is typically accomplished as embedded in distinct disciplinary knowledge, sub-unit organization and other real features of the organizations, but is accomplished through Machiavellian skills and capabilities. When personal interests can be represented as if they are strategic interests we have a successful Machiavellian strategy (Machiavelli, 1961). A contemporary book by Robert Greene and Joost Elffers (1998) has updated Machiavelli (and others) into *The 48 Rules of Power*. The rules are fairly self-explanatory so we have reproduced them here:

1 Never outshine the master
2 Never put too much trust in friends: learn how to use enemies
3 Conceal your intentions
4 Always say less than necessary
5 So much depends on reputation: guard it with your life
6 Court attention at all costs
7 Get others to do the work for you, but always take the credit
8 Make other people come to you, use bait if necessary
9 Win through your actions, never through argument
10 Infection: avoid the unhappy and unlucky

11 Learn to keep people dependent on you
12 Use selective honesty and generosity to disarm your victim
13 When asking for help, appeal to people's self-interest, never to their mercy or gratitude
14 Pose as a friend, work as a spy
15 Crush your enemy totally
16 Use absence to increase respect and honor
17 Keep others in suspended terror: cultivate an air of unpredictability
18 Do not build fortresses to protect yourself: isolation is dangerous
19 Know who you're dealing with: do not offend the wrong person
20 Do not commit to a anyone
21 Play a sucker to catch a sucker: seem dumber than your mark
22 Use the surrender tactic: transform weakness into power
23 Concentrate your forces
24 Play the perfect courtier
25 Recreate yourself
26 Keep your hands clean
27 Play on people's need to believe to create a cultlike following
28 Enter action with boldness
29 Plan all the way to the end
30 Make your accomplishments seem effortless
31 Control the options: get others to play with the cards you deal
32 Play to people's fantasies
33 Discover each man's thumbscrew
34 Be royal in your own fashion: act like a king to be treated like one
35 Master the art of timing

(Continued)

(Continued)

36 Disdain things you cannot have: ignoring them is the best revenge

37 Create compelling spectacles

38 Think as you like but behave like others

39 Stir up waters to catch fish

40 Despise the free lunch

41 Avoid stepping into a great man's shoes

42 Strike the shepherd and the sheep will scatter

43 Work on the hearts and minds of others

44 Disarm and infuriate with the mirror effect

45 Preach the need for change, but never reform too much at once

46 Never appear perfect

47 Do not go past the mark you aimed for: in victory, learn when to stop

48 Assume formlessness

The dysfunctionality of many of these rules, in strategic terms, can be seen in James Foley's (1991) film of David Mamet's play, *Glengarry Glen Ross*. The competitive and cutthroat behaviour of this office of real estate agents, based on the mantra of ABC (Always Be Closing), demonstrates how toxic such rules might be in practice.

The main problem with following the 48 rules is that if everyone did so, most organizations would soon become such a complex story of covert operations, with each individual not being what they seem, that there would be strategic fragmentation, chaos and discord! Overall, it is too individualistic an account of how power operates in strategic times. While different managers will have different strategic interests that they will deploy in the occasions that present themselves in opportunities to exercise power over others negatively, they will maximize their chances of success not only through the immediate knowledge that they possess or can command, and through duplicity, but also, more positively, through networks of social relations, which they can draw from familial, peer and other relations; in other words, from their social capital.

All organizations contain diverse knowledge and many different disciplines. All strategy proposals mobilize specific knowledge claims. Implicitly, strategy is a roadmap to success. Ideally, it should coordinate diverse knowledge based in disciplines such as accounting, marketing, production, etc. What happens in practice when strategy is being formulated is that those who are repositories of these different types of knowledge will compete to be more compelling in their claims than rivals with different capabilities. Internal 'tournaments' occur in organizations in which proposals are based on specific spheres of competency, functional responsibilities and disciplinary knowledge. Political skill in mobilizing support is essential if capabilities are to be translated into strategy.

It is evident from the ever-decreasing tenure of many CEOs and members of top management teams (see Chapter 7) that political pressure for performance in the short term tends to stifle longer term strategic thinking in organizations (see Hambrick and Fukotomi, 1991). Under the pressure of competitive performance, differences and divisions can sometimes end up being viscerally personal: a failure to perform as expected means a loss of position, even if softened by attractive severance packages.

Political skill is an essential prerequisite of the strategic managers' job. It entails using knowledge astutely and procedurally in a manner that best serves the strategic interest one is seeking to advance.

STRATEGY AS A POLITICAL GAME

Interests and action

Business involves a relation between interests and actions, connected by strategies formulating actions to realize these interests; thus, Pettigrew (2002) suggests that the strategy process in organizations always entails decisions that will be political. Politics may be defined as the mobilization of support for a position, decision or action (Crick, 2004: 67). A change in strategy can mean a change in politics. Such decisions are 'likely to threaten the existing distribution of organizational resources as represented in salaries, in promotion opportunities, and in control of tasks, people, information, and new areas of business' (Pettigrew, 2002: 45). What do organizational politics arise from, according to Pettigrew?

1 Structural divisions in the organization between different component elements and identities, and the different values, affective, cognitive and discursive styles associated with these.

2 The complexity and degree of uncertainty attached to the dilemma that strategy seeks to address.

3 The salience of issues for different actors and identities in the organization.

4 The external pressure coming from stakeholders or other actors or organizations in the environment.

5 The history of past politics in the organizations in question.

Consequently, organizational politics are absolutely central to the strategy process, as Buchanan and Badham (2008) argue. Organizations are often lived and experienced as a series of 'turf wars' between the different branches, divisions, departments, occupations and cultures located within these: each strategically interested part seeks to protect its own turf and sometimes attack that of others; thus, organizations should be conceived as arenas in which many and varied war games will be in play, with the rules of the game constantly shifting and frequently unclear, and always overlapping. According to Pettigrew (2002: 47), organizational politics are fundamentally concerned with the management of meaning. Actors in these political relations seek to legitimate the ideas, values and demands that they espouse while simultaneously denying or decrying those they seek to oppose. Thus, power is ultimately deployed in games of organizational symbolism.

Power characterizes all social relations as each of us seeks to make others do what we would want them to do. In doing so we seek to subject these others to our will – we seek to make others objects of our will. Because we are all engaged in these power relations we are always potentially both subjects and objects of power.

What is at stake in political struggles in strategy are organizational power relations. The idea of power relations is an essential tool for understanding strategy because power is not something you have or possess. You cannot be pictured with or without it. Power is always relational. You may have the power to do certain things but that power means nothing if it is something that everyone can do. It only begins to be organizationally meaningful when the relations of organizational power enable you to do certain things that others may be restricted from doing. Organizational power involves a relation in which you can get another person not only to do something, but also to do it in a manner that accords with your expressed intentions as to how it should be done: in a word – organization.

Organizing conceived as a verb, and organizations, used as a noun, are complex means for stabilizing power relations between people in order to achieve some goal(s). Essentially, all organizations are tools of a particular kind – tools designed to get others to do things in the service of goals that, in the absence of that organization (noun and verb), they might not otherwise do. Organizations are always, first and foremost, tools of and for power. Organizations are, among many other things, devices for distributing and stabilizing power relations.

Power is wrapped up in myths, beliefs, language and legend – the stuff of organizational culture. Those managers in organizations who are not politically skilled will fail. The underlying purpose of politics involves mobilizing support for particular actions by reconciling different interests and values. Thus, skill must be used to influence decisions, agendas and participation in organizational politics.

Political competence means being the kind of manager who can get things done, despite resistance, because they are skilled at political games (Bacharach, 2005: 93). Only politically skilled managers can be successful strategists.

Power relations are typically thought of as being distributed spatially in organizations: up, down and across the organization. Power relations are the circuitry through which organizational decisions flow. At key nodal points power relations will be concentrated. Some of these key nodal points will occur when:

1   Subgroups in organizations form coalitions to try and frame issues in decision-making according to their preferences (Cyert and March, 1963).

2   Critical contingencies of the organization, which change when the environment changes (Hickson et al., 1971; Salancik and Pfeffer, 1977), are controlled by particular expertise in the organization, located in different departments, divisions or skills.

3   Organizational power relations are institutionalized into systematic relations of hierarchy and lateral interdependence. Doing this, creating a formal structure of authority, seeks to stabilize how the organizational decision-making structures and procedures are framed (Boeker, 1989; also see Boeker, 1992; 1997) by stabilizing the decision-making on key offices, roles, responsibilities and relations (Clegg, 1989).

By design, business organizations are hierarchical social systems in which relations of command and domination, obedience and subordination, are normatively framed in ways that seek to establish these relations as authoritative. However, neither authority nor decision-making are guarantees against the instability and dynamism that power relations can sometimes unleash.

Power relations that are relatively stable over long periods of time 'impair organizational change as a response to declining performance' while 'top management teams with greater tenure differences among executives are more likely to engage in strategic change overall, and particularly in the face of performance decline' (Mitsuhashi and Greve, 2004: 125). Where power is strongly held and formally codified in organizational relations, rigid strategies will tend to result, whereas power differences in top management teams will create more fluid strategies, according to Mitsuhashi and Greve's (2004: 125) research on Japanese robotics and shipbuilding firms.

YOU CAN DOWNLOAD…

Hitoshi Mitsuhashi and Henrich R. Greve's (2004) Powerful and Free: Intraorganizational Power and the Dynamics of Corporate Strategy, *Strategic Organization*, 2(2): 107–32, from the book's website at www.sagepub.co.uk/cleggstrategy

Game stakes

What is often at issue in organizational relations of power and politics are battles either to keep things the same or to change. Usually these are two sides of the same coin: those who want to keep things the same will usually do so because the current situation suits their interests; those who want change will believe it is in their interests to do so. Change is expected of new senior appointments for instance; at such times it is not politically healthy to be seen as too dedicated to a predecessor's schemes and strategies. They are very likely to be changed. Of course, such politics are usually tricked out and expressed in terms of organizational rather than sectional interests, in order to appear organizationally legitimate. Legitimacy is aided when contingencies change in the environment that will favour one set of interests over another because they are better able to deal with the issues that the new contingencies create.

Intra-organizational power often reflects inter-organizational dependencies and is adjusted, albeit in fits and starts, when environmental changes alter the pattern of interdependence (Hickson et al., 1971; Pfeffer and Salancik, 1974; Boeker, 1989; Donaldson, 1999).

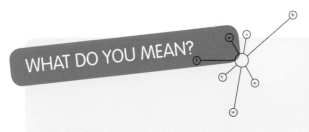

WHAT DO YOU MEAN?

Changing contingencies; changing politics and power

Once the problems in developing a continental marketing strategy in the United States had been resolved by the 1920s, the following decade saw the emergence of contingencies for which a knowledge of finance was most appropriate. Having constructed national continent-wide companies, the key question was how to manage and control them in a disciplined fashion.

New situations required new solutions. CEO disciplines shifted overwhelmingly from marketing to finance as new combinations of power/knowledge and the new disciplinary mechanism of management (budgetary) control were forged and hardened at the apex of businesses (Fligstein, 1987).

The circulation of different power/knowledge elites has continued (Ocasio and Kim, 1999; Thornton and Ocasio, 1999). Shifts of power will usually represent shifts in vested interests, associated strategies and resource allocations. Certain power/knowledge combinations, such as financial accounting rather than marketing, become represented in the 'inner circles' (Useem, 1986) of power relations. Such a representation both symbolically positions certain forms of knowledge at the heart of power relations and systematically skews agendas and mobilizes bias in terms of the bounded rationalities of those combinations of power/knowledge.

Over time the effects of different representations of power/knowledge can be quite dramatic, especially at those moments when events challenge the existing biases in action with contingencies that existing representations have failed to interpret adequately. Think of the reliance on complex finance algorithms in Wall Street banking prior to the global financial crisis and their blindness to the risks of defaulting on sub-prime mortgages in the real world.

Strategy as a game of power and resistance

It is often the case that organizations and their strategy are represented as merely the achievement of technical rather than political exercises, a matter of getting the models right, feeding in the right data and seeing what should be done. Nothing could be further from the truth. Strategy is irremediably political, as we have established.

In Mintzberg's (1983; 2002) terms, business organizations are arenas in which the games that unfold are games of politics and strategy is the sum of all the interconnected games with more or less politically skilled players involved in them (Crozier and Friedberg, 1980). The metaphor of a game suggests sports. Sports, as we know, have codes or rules.

Rules in business are not quite like those in sport. A sports code is constituted by its rules. You know whether it is a game of soccer or rugby by the shape of the ball, by whether it can be handled or not, whether there is a goalkeeper, the design of the posts, and the rules followed and interpreted by the referee. These all shape the arena of action – the game that unfolds on the field of play.

In business power games the rules are neither neutral nor independently arbitrated by a referee with a clear understanding of the rulebook. In business all actors will have strategic interests but some will have more strategies at their disposal than others with which to further their interests. And, as far as the referee goes, the most powerful people will usually blow the whistle, interpret and create the rules, as well as declare others offside. Some of the games that get played in business as Mintzberg has identified them include:

1 *Sponsorship games,* when powerful elites in the organization seek to use strategy to sponsor those who are their clients, those who are loyal (or so they think) to them in the organization.
2 *Alliance-building games* played among peers who implicitly seek reciprocal support.
3 *Budgeting games,* where the objective is to secure resources to one's strategic interest and deny these to the strategic interest of others.
4 *Expertise games,* where participants seek to position their expertise as the strategic key to the strategy dilemma – 'it's a marketing issue' says the marketing representative, while the production managers see the solution in production terms.

Where these games are being played we may say that micro-politics are at work (Dörrenbächer and Gepert, 2009: 200). These micro-political games are sometimes played face to face, in the open; sometimes they will be refereed, according to rules, while other times they will be played in ways that are quite covert, deliberately violating the rules.

> Micro-politics are the strategic attempts to exert a formative influence on social structure and relations in local settings.

The extent to which micro-politics can be conducted as covert operations depends on the degree to which micro-political actors operate in zones about which elites have little or no knowledge. Where strategy formulation requires the elites to have access to resources and knowledge that they do not have in their grasp, that they do not know or understand, then those who do have detailed knowledge are in a potentially powerful position.

All organizations have micro-politics. Such politics strive to 'secure options, realize interests and to achieve success through efforts that are often but not exclusively motivated by interests or individual career plans of key actors' (Dörrenbächer and Gepert, 2009: 200). Organizations are many things, to many people: for shareholders a source of shareholder value; for rank and file employees a job; for managers an opportunity to build a career, earning substantial salary and options packages, as well as a springboard to move on up or out.

A strategy, once conceived, struggles to come into being through processes of micro-politics. The process of struggle is one of political change – getting others to do things that they would not otherwise do. It must engage the self-consciousness of those it seeks to change inasmuch as it must capture the imagination and energies of those whom it seeks to enrol to enact it. All strategies will see some ideas and their bearers assume more or less importance in local politics and these matters of esteem will effect relations between people as well as their self-conceptions. Struggles around and over strategy will always be creative, as new identities, self-understandings, social relations and products, goods and services are created. Strategic struggles will then occur through communicative action constructed in terms of plans, documents, models, commands and reports: there is always a 'discursive' element to strategy and usually many artefacts, such as vision and mission statements. Changes in strategy are a matter of setting categories loose: think of the BCG's 'cash cows' or 'dogs', or SWOT analysis with its 'strengths', 'weaknesses', 'opportunities' and 'threats'.

Representing changes in strategy as a response to a changing environment, or changes in technology, is a familiar power/knowledge strategy. Sometimes the two discourses of a changing technology and a changing business environment will get tangled up with each other. Such was the case in the strategy for transforming the public service broadcaster, the Australian Broadcasting Corporation (ABC), in the1990s.

The strategic politics of digitalization at the Australian Broadcasting

Image 9.1 ABC logo

Corporation

Digital technologies and increasing globalization were bundled up together in a number of strategic reforms of the ABC during the 1990s, aimed at creating a more entrepreneurial and flexible organization. It was a style of organization that was at some distance from the older, public sector rhetoric of the ABC with its largely unionized workforce. Not surprisingly, the two main unions resisted the changes but so did a social movement organization known as the Friends of the ABC.

In resisting the newly strategically reformed and refocused ABC these bodies *creatively appropriated the dominant categories* that had been used to promulgate strategic change at the ABC as the discourses of the global and digital new media environment. However, they used these new and now dominant categories to oppose elements of the change programme. Not only did they do this, but they also identified elements in the new media environment with which they could agree, which they *surfaced as a shared discourse,* and sought to demonstrate that other elements of strategy could undercut these shared values. Finally, they *revived some old core values* of the ABC that positioned it as a sphere in which one was safe from the blandishments of commercialism, commercials and a market-share mentality. Doing this led to some strategic reverses for the ABC board as well as a reinvigoration of the very public service ethos that the reforms seemed bent on destroying.

Untangling strategic change at the ABC over the 1990s and into the 2000s requires an analysis of how power/knowledge relations are constituted as both central strategic initiatives of power and the forces of resistance that confront them. The strategic outcomes represent a negotiated order that is highly contingent on the dynamics of power and resistance (Fleming and Spicer, 2007).

Question

1 Analyse the impact of digital technologies and increasing globalization on broadcasters in your national domain. (As well as Fleming and Spicer's (2007) work you may also find Castells' (2009) *Communication Power* useful.)

One thing is evident from the analysis that Fleming and Spicer make of the ABC: proponents of strategy must persuade others to its course; as such there is always a discursive element to any strategy and discourses are inherently politically unstable. All discourses consist of signifiers that constitute categories that the strategists will seek to advance and fix in the organizational or public consciousness as if they were normal, natural or the best way to do things. Consequently, the best way to resist a strategy is not to negate it entirely: it is to leverage some of its meaning and categories away from the positions that the strategists have assumed through posing counter-discourses, counter-uses. The politics of strategy most often entail the politics of meaning.

The politics of strategy do not take place on a metaphorical level playing field. The strategic centre is invariably more privileged than those who would resist it. Strategy has the potential to change the relations of meaning between an organization's members; for these people it is both a community-building device as it unites, but it is also a white-anting strategy, something that gnaws away at the grounds of others' legitimacy and respect, dividing organizations. Strategy entails a *power to* get things done, but it can only ever achieve this power if it is able simultaneously to exercise *power over* the many others required to implement it. To each of the methods that a strategist might use to ensure compliance, there is always an answer. Strategy might seek to coerce others into compliance but the others can always refuse. There are many ways of refusing, ranging from outright non-compliance to puzzled bemusement at one's inability to quite grasp what it is that needs to be done differently.

THE DIMENSIONS OF POWER

It has been argued that power has three dimensions and that these dimensions can be seen at work in the strategy process (Lukes, 1974; 2006; Hardy, 1994). The first dimension is that of formal decision-making. This is where strategy is explicitly made and adopted. At this level strategy is discursively formulated in terms of improving effectiveness. You are getting others to do what they have not done previously because it will enable the organization to be more effective. Whatever is proposed has to be proposed in these terms.

The first dimension of power where you get others to do what they would not otherwise do is just the tip of the strategy iceberg: underlying it is the second dimension that must address issues of non-decision-making. Non-decision-making occurs where issues are constrained to the legitimate and politically safe, where agendas are constructed with a tacit acknowledgement that certain issues will not be addressed. Often this is a major constraint on strategy-making. Everyone knows what are the CEO's 'sacred cows' and 'pet concerns'. No one will openly propose a strategic change that would question these. As a result, they remain non-issues and not matters for decision-making and hence do not enter onto the agenda. Because of this, if the strategy team want to change these non-issues they will have to move very subtly, politically. Strategically powerful people, such as CEOs, especially when new to posts, will create strategic change through changing processes, so they will also usually have a good understanding of non-decision-making. Marginal or excluded voices can be admitted to deliberations; issues left off agendas can be affirmed and placed there; new members eager for change can be placed on committees that in the past have been conservative or resistant. To facilitate these changes new perspectives will have to be introduced in ways that will legitimate them: the most usual way is to get the consultants in. If they are one of the big firms they will cost a lot of money and produce a convincing report that is able to utter the unutterable and introduce new perspectives.

The third dimension of power concerns those things that are so fundamentally accepted that they seem just to be the 'existing order of things' (Lukes, 1974: 24), the underlying values, preferences, cognitions and perceptions, what we have earlier encountered as the deep assumptions of strategy, that define one as a member of good standing in a particular community of practice or organization. Changing these is difficult *and* politically risky: it entails organization-wide shifts in values and working practices. There have to be interventions into accepted practices, debates about them, definite change proposals for which support must be secured. Agendas will often be covert and people will be manipulated.

While ideological and symbolic bases of power will usually function as a tacit resource for the strategically powerful, as we saw in the ABC case, they can also be leveraged against dominant understandings because symbolic meanings can be seized on, hooked up with projects of resistance and come to take on quite distinct meanings to those initially taken for granted. The third dimension of power is associated with attempts to legitimize some claims and delegitimize the claims of others by managing meaning. If strategic elites are successful then they will use these meanings to anchor and secure their positions. However, meanings can always be cut adrift from their moorings and used to question and resist the status quo. The third dimension of power often entails the use of rational myths that legitimate existing power positions through a recourse to dominant discursive devices, such as science, rationality or tradition. These devices can just as easily be used to advance strategy as resist it.

Institutionalized myths will often take on an artefactual form: the wisdom of the 'Sage of Omaha' (Warren Buffett), for instance, is delivered through his annual letters to Berkshire Hathaway's shareholders, which are eagerly awaited and widely read both by them and the world's business press. Buffett's investment philosophy is that if he cannot understand something, he will not invest in it (a myth that many collateralized debt obligations issuers might have done well to institutionalize). Such views are regularly communicated via the newsletter.

QUESTION TIME?

Power's dimensions

The first dimensional view of power focuses on key decisions and views power as something intended, deliberate and casual – getting someone to do what they would not otherwise do.

Can you think of any strategic changes that have clearly operated at this level – trying to get people to do what they otherwise would not do?

_____
_____
_____
_____

The second dimension of power focuses on decision arenas and agendas, looking especially at things that do not happen – the non-decisions and non-issues that traverse every organization that no one raises or questions.

Can you think of any strategic changes that have clearly operated at this level – where people were constrained by the non-decisions and non-issues that framed an agenda?

_____
_____
_____
_____

The third dimension of power deals with how those things that routinely happen are deeply embedded in rationalized myths, such as tradition, science or rationality.

Can you think of any strategic changes that have clearly operated at this level – where rationalized myths shaped what it was possible to say and excluded other things as impossible?

_____
_____
_____
_____

STRATEGY AS THE INSTITUTIONALIZATION OF MYTH

Strategy seeks to position dominant myths about the organization in the consciousness of its members, customers and stakeholders – 'We try harder', the strategy slogan of Avis, is one such myth. What does it mean? How can it be assessed? When you arrive at the airport or railway station and want to hire a car, does Avis really 'try harder'?

Myths can function as a culture, embodying potential unobtrusive control mechanisms, where shared norms and values guide actions. In such circumstances culture may seek to achieve many of the things usually left to rules and structures. Such rules and structures, of course, are equally an embodiment of political relations, shaping the nature of reporting, interactions, duties, responsibilities, and so on. Often, the structures and rules that an organization adopts are chosen because they reflect symbolically powerful devices that are well understood in the institutional environment. They help grant legitimacy to an organization because of their respectability.

One of the sure signs of strategic success is when a company's strategy is represented as entirely rational and something for which there is no alternative. If stakeholders can be persuaded to believe this, then there is no need for further organizational politics around the strategy process.

Power can work strategically without consciously seeming to do so when we enter the sphere of values, traditions, cultures and structures of an institution such as a profession. Professions will routinely supply managers to organizations but simultaneously they will also introduce specific means of decision and control, such as accounting practices, into them. In turn, such practices will entail a specific calibration of reporting relations, data collection and analysis, which then become powerful and highly unobtrusive ordering devices in businesses and organizations. They are a form of what Foucault (1979) identifies as disciplinary power – where power is embedded in the taken-for-granted routines that are a normal part of the everyday round of work. Such disciplinary power shapes what members can and cannot do without it necessarily being a matter for their conscious deliberation.

Strategy, of course, is such a discipline as Foucault identifies, argue Knights and Morgan (1991). It bestows world-making powers on some managers by empowering them with certain skills and strategic responsibilities that legitimate the dimensions of power that they wield. At the same time, it places other managers far from the strategy discourse and less well positioned in the changing circuitry of power, positioning them where they can hardly affect its dimensions directly, and may be able to do so only indirectly, through resistance.

We often think of resistance to a strategy as something 'dysfunctional', something that is bad for the strategy. However, whatever resistance is organized can only serve to further the categories of the strategy-makers, insofar as it must engage with these terms, if only to resist them. Further, resistance can be used to engender a more vigorous application of the strategy. Resistance serves as a warrant for further strategic application. Failure makes strategy appear even more necessary. Should organization members resist the strategy in ways that suggest they are not *au fait* with it, such resistance merely serves to demonstrate the necessity of further strategic discipline in order to make them knowledgeable – and empowered rather than resistant – subjects.

Effectively empowered subjects know how to do and say what is required strategically; resistant subjects, if they are to be effective, must equally know how to do and say what is required strategically – and must then say and do it to advance their strategic interests rather than those enshrined in the official strategy (as did the Friends of the ABC in Fleming and Spicer's (2007) account). Effectively empowered people have political skill, and political skill is a definite prerequisite of managerial success. Once again, we can see the unity of power/knowledge.

It is important to realize that any successful strategy will be premised not just on knowledge – data, information and advice – but also on power. A successful strategy requires synergistic power/knowledge because power is based on knowledge, uses knowledge, reproduces knowledge and occasionally transforms knowledge, as the dynamics of power and resistance reshape what can be locally taken for granted as strategy. Power and knowledge play out in a field of forces that is decentralized, relativistic, ubiquitous and unstable. The assumptions of the centre will never necessarily prevail; any strategic exercise of power from the centre is likely to generate its own resistance, and such resistance is capable of transforming both power and strategy. It is these processes that make strategy work: power is only effective to the extent that it is engaged in a struggle with some form of resistance. As Foucault (1980) suggests, power works in large part through its failures: without some resistance to power there would be no rationale for the constant attempt to impose it. Thus, resistance has an impact to the extent that it wields a degree of power, as Fleming and Spicer (2007: 6) suggest.

POLITICS AND COMPLEX ORGANIZATIONS

All large organizations are complex by definition. They have more extensive divisions of labour, a greater number of reports to authorities and are often structured as complex divisional structures.

Multinational corporations

Complexity is multiplied when the organization in question works across national boundaries – when it is a multinational corporation (MNC).

A multinational corporation (MNC) involves operations with subsidiary companies in multiple countries.

Think of international business operations where there is a significant spatial separation of core from peripheral business units. There will be geographical, political, socio-economic, cultural and religious boundaries separating the core from the peripheral actors and action. Not only will there be extensive politics around who controls and has access to what resources, but there will also probably be quite different understandings of the rules of the games to be negotiated between participants.

On occasions political games can become quite complex and multilayered. They can also become quite intense conflicts from which victors will emerge. Sometimes the combatants, albeit often uneasily, will enter into a treaty. Uneasy treaties can often lead to shaky alliances as political forces regroup, perhaps to fight another day. Often, however, the struggles will be so vicious that the losers will exit or be forced from the organization, such as when a top management team that resisted the takeover victors are 'let go'. People in organizations that cannot manage their power relations will end up spending more time fighting each other than seeking to find a common purpose against competitor organizations. Only very large organizations or those with no competition can survive sustained complex politics for long.

Organizational politics are rarely a question of winner takes all; more usually compromises have to be made and coalitions and alliances formed. Coalitions represent the hitching together of different individual or collective strategic interests, such as in a department or division, in a form of an alliance that is specific to particular issues and their extensions.

An alliance is a mechanism that links diverse, more or less central and peripheral actors, interests and strategies. Alliances entail a process of convergence of interests via a transaction between supralocal and local actors, in political science terms, and these adapt easily to discussions of strategy (Kalyvas, 2006: 383).

Alliances are, for everyone involved in them, a means rather than an end. The point of an alliance is to achieve something or other. Negotiations between political coalitions create the ordering of goals in organizations (March, 1962). These negotiations can criss-cross organizations: they may occur at the departmental level, around specific strategic projects or over specific strategic issues. Interests that might align on one occasion will not necessarily cohere on another. Sometimes the issues, although seemingly small, can derail much larger strategic projects: for instance, where a sub-unit is defiantly against adopting some new technology that the company has bought in which the sub-unit had no hand in developing – sometimes referred to as the *not-invented-here syndrome* (Katz and Allen, 1982).

Strategies decided at the centre may order goals but they cannot always ensure their implementation in far-flung corners of the organizational empire. Sometimes the strategic centre of an organization can be at a great distance, in knowledge terms, from those places where implementation occurs; this often happens in organizations that have subsidiaries and a strong central direction. The blocking, modifying and avoiding of central directives is sometimes a way of maintaining the discretion to adapt, creatively, what might not otherwise work locally (Sharpe, 2001; Becker-Ritterspach, Lange and Lohr, 2002; also see Dörrenbächer and Gepert, 2009: 203).

To look at strategy as it is formulated at the centre is to look only at the centripetal controls: we need also to consider the centrifugal forces (Morgan, 2001). Recognizing that organizations, especially where they are large, complex and multinational, will be simultaneously subject to centripetal control and centrifugal forces, should ensure that we recognize the reality of strategic interests and micropolitics in the making of strategic practices. What is at issue is how certain practices become crucial in determining what is considered to be a strategic interest. Some actors will have micro-political skills that ensure certain positions are blocked and certain others advanced in terms of the strategic agenda (Johnson et al., 2003).

Central corporate political strategies that seek to affect the public policy environment in a favourable way (Baysinger, 1984) are a major part of the strategy arsenal. Vernon (1971) suggested that, strategically, MNCs with substantial investments would seek to influence host-country government policies to protect earnings and produce a favourable regulatory environment in legal areas such as immigration, trade and investment. This will especially be the case at a time of initial entry into a country (e.g. Vernon, 1971; Fagre and Wells, 1982; Kim, 1988; Dunning, 1993; Grosse, 1996).

The choice of political strategies depends on the bargaining power of MNC subsidiaries compared with that of the host country (Blumentritt, 2003). For much of the twentieth century the 'Banana Republics' of Central America, of which Guatemala was the most notorious, were countries run by corrupt governments for the United Fruit Company, often in cahoots with the CIA (see www.mayaparadise.com/united fruit_company.htm). On the whole, government–business relations today tend to be more subtle than this extreme case, consisting of lobbying, the funding of parties, the sponsorship of representatives, public relations campaigns, the sponsoring of legislative initiatives, and so on. Canada, for instance, has one of the highest percentages of foreign-owned business inside its borders, mostly US owned, but given the robustness of Canadian political institutions, the potential for their corruption is very low.

Boddewyn and Brewer (1994) argue that host governments represent both strategic risks and opportunities: governments may appropriate value from MNCs but they can also protect it (e.g. Boddewyn, 1975; 1988; 1993; Moran, 1985; Rugman and Verbeke, 1993; Eden and Molot, 2002).

MNCs and mandates

Any MNC comprises a highly complex configuration of ongoing micro-political power conflicts at different levels. Social actors and groups inside and outside the firm interact with each other and create temporary balances of power. Sometimes external organizations can succeed in changing organizational mandates. Think of the role of activist civil society organizations shaping pharmaceutical company testing procedures on animals, or their impact on mining companies' interactions with indigenous communities (Morgan and Kristensen, 2006: 1473).

Mandates are tasks that are assigned to subsidiaries by headquarters or that are acquired independently by the subsidiary, which have a specific time and content limitation placed on them, and which frame the internal division of labour within an MNC.

Mandate change: who wins when good intentions prevail? The soccer ball case

Image 9.2 'Soccer ball'

This is a seemingly 'feel-good' story about a major mandate change wrought in an industry by media, NGO and industry stakeholders. It concerns the basic tool of the world's most popular game: the soccer ball. The majority of the world's hand-stitched soccer balls are produced in Sialkot, Pakistan (Cummins, 2000: 4, 27). Until relatively recently, most of these balls were hand-stitched by child workers. On 6 April 1995, a CBS news documentary showed that the soccer ball suppliers employed child labour in dark and dank one-room workshops. The CBS report was picked up by other mass media around the world. In 1996, a campaign against the exploitation of child labour was launched. By 1997 manufacturers in the global soccer ball industry announced a project to eliminate child labour in collaboration with carefully selected civil society NGO partners. The industry successfully positioned itself, in the eyes of the Western media and consumers at least, as a constructive actor working to remove the bane of child labour while preserving the Sialkot soccer ball manufacturing cluster. However, the benefits for children were questionable and the majority of women had to drop out of the workforce. The unintended consequences of removing child labour from the manufacture of these balls and thus preserving the brand value of the global business names that marketed the balls were a loss of income, a disruption to family life and the withdrawal from work of women, effects that were never given significance by NGOs, the industry or the Western media. The child labour was reduced – but at what cost?

Question

1 Analyse the case using a micro-politics perspective: who do you think were the winners and who were the losers, and why do you think this?

For your information, the image of a soccer ball is taken from a site maintained by Oswego City School District Regents Exam Prep Center which is designed to teach children about maths: the soccer ball, we are told, is composed of a combination of pentagon and hexagon faces. This shape is called a buckyball after Richard Buckminster Fuller, who invented the geodesic dome. In reality, the soccer ball is not truly a polyhedron since the faces are not really flat. The faces tend to bulge slightly due to the amount of stuffing in the ball and the pliable nature of the leather. The site can be found at http://www.regentsprep.org/regents/math/geometry/GG2/RegularSolids.htm

YOU CAN DOWNLOAD...

The full story in Farzad R. Khan, Kamal A. Munir and Hugh Wilmott (2007) A Dark Side of Institutional Entrepreneurship: Soccer Balls, Child Labour and Postcolonial Impoverishment, *Organization Studies*, 28: 1055–77, from the book's website at www.sagepub.co.uk/cleggstrategy

Mandates relate directly to the control of resources and the steering of potential actions; hence, mandates bestow different propensities for exercising power in internal relations within MNCs (Cyert and March, 1963; Pfeffer and Salancik, 1974; Birkinshaw and Ridderstråle, 1999). When mandates change there is immense potential for conflict within MNCs because the relative power relations of the different subsidiaries and the centre will change in consequence. Any change can be simultaneously a process of downgrading and upgrading: as one subsidiary shifts to more or less demanding tasks, all others will change relatively in their relations with each other and the centre (Dörrenbächer and Gamelgaard, 2006). Shifts in these relativities can translate directly into changes in status, careers and incomes, things that are often hard fought for.

MNCs often seek to legitimate mandate changes by making a competition of them: bids framed in terms of a change mandate are invited from subsidiaries within the MNC as well as from organizations outside (Birkinshaw and Lingblad, 2005). Competition to deliver on the decisions made legitimates the outcomes. To justify such MNC testing of options it can be claimed that open competition offers the best chance of adapting to market pressures, meeting emergent standards or enhancing shareholder value. All these legitimating claims work well – even when there may be other reasons at work, such as whittling a subsidiary down or obtaining greater control over it. Mandate changes offer subsidiaries an opportunity to enhance their strategic importance for the MNC. Subsidiaries are not just passive receivers of such mandate changes. Claims for mandate change can be made equally from subsidiaries as from the centre, perhaps in response to claims of changing market imperatives or customer relations, while the covert agenda may be to secure and improve their relative position.

The strategic options open to an MNC are always framed within specific contextual factors:

- *Host-country contextual factors*. These are determined by the national institutions, economic structures, resources and foreign investment policies of the country that is host to the investments made.

- *Subsidiary contextual factors*. These are determined by the resources and capabilities at a subsidiary's disposal. The crucial element, according to the resource-based view of the firm (Barney, 1991), is the extent to which the subsidiary controls the inimitable resources that bring added value and are hard to substitute.

- *Headquarters' contextual factors*. In dealing with any specific subsidiary, what are the headquarters' options? If the subsidiary is inimitable, they may be few; dealing with substitutable subsidiaries or outsource companies swings the balance of power in mandated change towards the MNC.

The balance of power does not always lie with the centre, with the MNC headquarters. As Dörrenbächer and Gamelgaard (2006: 209) suggest, 'a career-oriented subsidiary manager', especially an expatriate, may well manage to decline mandate requests from headquarters where they calculate that there is a career advantage in doing so. The loyalties of expatriates will usually differ from those of host-country nationals or third-country nationals, with the assumption usually being made that expatriates are more loyal to headquarters (Harzing, 1999).

Host-country nationals' loyalties tend be regarded as allying more with the fortunes of the subsidiary. Consequently, it has been argued that third-country nationals will be more balanced in their outlook on the micro-politics of subsidiary/headquarters relations. These dynamics have a significant qualifying effect on more structural and deterministic explanations: actors' micro-strategies can accelerate or impede central projects and their reasons for pursuing the strategies they choose may not align at all with the assumptions made at headquarters.

In MNCs the majority of politics around the strategy process will relate to mandated change in headquarters/subsidiary relations (Crozier and Friedberg, 1980; Dörrenbächer and Gamelgaard, 2006: 206). Typically, at headquarters level, one would expect board members, the strategy team and selected functional managers to be involved; as adversaries to the changes being mandated, one would expect to find subsidiary managing directors and their appropriate functional managers.

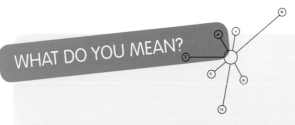

Political dynamics in action

Dörrenbächer and Gamelgaard (2006: 210–12) provide a short story that nicely illuminates micro-political dynamics.

A German engineer managed a German automobile company's French subsidiary. He greatly expanded its technical expertise and sought to utilize the expanded knowledge resources better through additional financial investment. The request was blocked at headquarters because the company was increasingly focusing on short-term increases in shareholder value that such an additional investment would jeopardize. The engineer's approach was based on technical improvements to a flexible manufacturing system through R&D that both added and cost value. However, the company was moving away from its roots in German engineering excellence and closer to a shareholder value model: it had different rationalities and the clash produced considerable conflict. The engineer did not lose totally and was able to maintain the flexible production system.

The strategy of imposing conformance with a central financial performance-related strategy is often used by headquarters to discipline subsidiaries; depending on the degree of development in locally embedded resources and networks, such as technical expertise and R&D, subsidiaries may follow a successful subversive strategy and create a space for a more autonomous and local strategy (Morgan and Kristensen, 2006).

Other parties will surround subsidiary managers with strategic interests:

- Significant shareholders seeking a more efficient exploitation of their assets in the business through changing the international cost, service and regulatory environments.
- Trade unions, who will resist measures that run against the strategic interests of those members they represent.
- Government agencies seeking to secure investment opportunities.
- Non-government agencies with a remit to protect specific strategic interests, such as the environment or child labour.
- Suppliers, for whom the changes will represent hard-to-comply-with specifications.
- Customers who may be dissatisfied with the changes made to a favourite brand, product or service.

How subsidiary managers might manage or ignore these local pressures may not be a matter for calculation at the supralocal level of the corporate centre, but it can pose real struggles and challenges for local actors. Often these struggles and challenges will not be recognized at the centre and the inability to manage them conveniently will be seen as a sign of local failure rather than of the complexity of local environments.

THE POLITICS OF STRATEGY AND STRUCTURE IN DIFFERENT CONTEXTS

Top team managers obviously have strategic choices but these choices will be constrained by the structures they inherit and are embedded within (Donaldson, 1987;

Robins, 1993; Amburgey and Dacin, 1994). Researchers who relate structure to strategy see the relationship occurring over the long term, as Whittington (2002: 123) notes. Managers may stick with dysfunctional structural arrangements for some time.

Structurally, in terms of multidivisional MNCs there is a consensus that accounting and finance managers will favour divisional structures because these consolidate financial control as the key mechanism. Likewise, engineering and production managers will tend to distrust and resist divisional structures because they abstract from the materiality of making things, while sales and marketing managers will tend to support such structures because they favour sales expansion and diversification. Family-owned businesses and bank-controlled firms will also tend to oppose divisional structures as lessening control (Whittington, 2002: 124, citing Cable and Dirrheimer, 1983; Palmer et al., 1993).

Once leading firms in an industry have adopted a divisional structure, other firms are more likely to follow suit in what is called a process of mimetic **institutional isomorphism** (Fligstein, 1987; Palmer et al., 1993; Kogut and Parkinson, 1998).

Legitimacy is an important variable in strategy terms but what is legitimate can vary from one societal context to another. For instance, many of the generalizations made about strategy flow from US examples.

Whitley (1994a) argues that it is the dominance of models of financial markets and professional management in Anglo-Saxon contexts that has favoured the development of divisional structures. Elsewhere, in bank-controlled capitalism in Germany, state-controlled capitalism in France (Whitley, 1994b; 1999), in the dominance of Japanese or Korean conglomerate capitalism or the Chinese family business form in much of Asia (Hamilton and Biggart, 1988; Clegg, 1990), structures militate against the adoption of this strategic model.

There are suggestions that, rather than being alternative models, the contra-examples represent time-lagged observations, at least with respect to Europe, as convergence on the US model is occurring, albeit at a rate of uneven development (Whittington, 2002: 125). The extent to which the global financial crisis of 2008–9 will have devalued US models is a germane point: certainly, President Sarkozy's enthusiasm for them has reduced greatly in favour of the French model he once pledged to make more American.

All models of the MNC (Hedlund, 1986; Ghoshal and Bartlett, 1990; Forsgren, Holm and Johanson, 1995) suggest that the practices of foreign subsidiaries are

> **Institutional isomorphism** is where organizations become more similar because they converge through managerial choice on models and practices that are widely regarded as legitimate. The sources of convergence have been represented as mimetic – or imitations – of culturally valued models; normative, where the structuring is a result of professional norms shaping practice; and coercive, where regulation requires certain forms and practices to be adopted – think of Equal Employment Opportunity (EEO) offices.

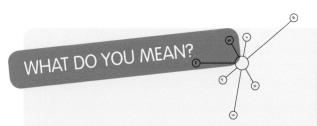

WHAT DO YOU MEAN?

Subsidiaries, power and legitimacy in strategy

The more legitimacy subsidiary powers can accrue to their actions, the greater the probability of their being engaged in corporate decisions (Mitchell, Agle and Wood, 1997). However, their very distance from strategic centres makes this difficult. MNC strategic managers are often far removed from subsidiaries, culturally, geographically and in terms of time zones.

What is a clear strategic plan at headquarters becomes much more confusing if the specificity of all the national regulations, policies, norms and infrastructure systems that the firm is engaged in have to be factored in. Where subsidiaries are only loosely committed to the firm or

(Continued)

(Continued)

where practices are believed to deviate from parent company objectives, they will fail to secure legitimacy.

Bouquet and Birkinshaw (2008: 481) observe the following examples of cases where alliances between local and supralocal actors will be difficult to accomplish:

1 Some countries have levels of corruption that clash with norms of acceptable behaviour in the larger MNC system (Alvaro, 2006; Doh et al., 2003; Rodriguez, Uhlenbruck and Eden, 2005; Uhlenbruck, et al., 2006). Recent reports of corruption in the Karzai administration of Afghanistan would be a case in point.

2 Other countries have an investment climate that is unattractive to foreign investors (Kessing, Konrad and Kotsogiannis, 2007); for instance, where there are unstable political conditions (Henisz, 2000), such as many of the countries in Africa (Harbeson, 1995) and other resource-poor countries that struggle to attract investments, let alone value-added activities, from multinationals.

3 Subsidiaries that operate at the periphery of the world economy (Harzing and Noorderhaven, 2006), where activities are misunderstood or perceived to be of little significance (Galunic and Eisenhardt, 1996; Brown, 2004; Prahalad, 2004); for instance, those that have few location-specific advantages (Dunning, 1981), or are located in relatively depressed industrial areas (Dawley, 2007).

4 Small or youthful operations can rarely demonstrate a proper track record (Birkinshaw, 1999), or are constrained by relatively small market sizes, limited purchasing capacities, inadequate infrastructures.

Subsidiaries that seek to improve their local standing in the MNC and host nation will need to be able to demonstrate that they can deliver corporate objectives and plans; provide strategic information and knowledge on local competitive developments; and generate innovations that can be spread through the global corporate empire. Subsidiaries that cannot exploit these sorts of resources will be unlikely to exercise much power in the web of MNC relations.

YOU CAN DOWNLOAD...

The full story by Cyril Bouquet and Julian Birkinshaw (2008) Managing Power in the Multinational Corporation: How Low-Power Actors Gain Influence, *Journal of Management*, 34(3): 477–508, from the book's website at www.sagepub.co.uk/cleggstrategy

constrained by different contextual rationalities to those of the supralocal MNC (Geppert, 2002; Geppert, Williams and Matten, 2003):

● Subsidiaries have to adapt to the institutional factors and national business systems characterizing the markets in which they operate (Rosenzweig and Nohria, 1994; Geppert and Matten, 2006; Geppert and Williams, 2006).

● Subsidiaries have to find ways to translate corporate ideals into a tangible set of local practices that can effectively bridge the expectations of the head office, if they are to exert any influence on MNC decisions.

● Without legitimacy, subsidiaries will have little influence on corporate decisions (Westney, 1993; Kostova and Zaheer, 1999; Tempel et al., 2006).

● Not only must subsidiary managers seeking to engage in the MNC's central circuits of power have legitimacy, but they must also, according to the VRIN model, have some control over resources that are scarce, not substitutable, in demand in the centre and competitively sought elsewhere.

It is not just subsidiary interests that have to be considered in terms of MNC relations with their subsidiaries:

● Governments in both host and home countries will want to accrue as much value as they can from MNCs in terms of tax, investments, employment and knowledge production and minimize as much as possible any disutility that the MNC activities might create, such as pollution, despoliation or social upheaval. As resources with which to bargain they can use whatever location-specific resources they have available, such as talent pools, natural resources or infrastructure.

● External stakeholders, such as civil society bodies and NGOs, will usually want to ensure that local resources are not unduly exploited, whether labour, the environment, or political and social capital. The resources that they can use include their ability to mobilize public opinion and communicate specific messages about specific firms, and their legitimacy in doing so.

Where subsidiary companies can develop unique bundles of resources and capabilities that are particularly in demand, according to the VRIN model (Birkinshaw and Hood, 1998a; 1998b) they can enter into significant positions in MNC circuits of power. To do so they must make themselves more central by becoming more interlinked in MNC networks, because it is centrality that makes resources valuable, not just having them.

SUMMARY AND REVIEW

To represent strategy as a practice that is entirely rational and without politics is one of the most political ways in which to represent it. It is also one of the most common – and the most fraudulent. The strategy process is always irremediably political, especially when it claims not to be!

Strategy spawns discourses in which interests are paramount, in which politics surround and envelop it: where politics shape what are taken to be the interests of the organization; in which self-interests can be aligned, or others' interests; be misaligned, to these strategic interests; and in which other organizations, such as governments or allied organizations, can be enrolled and translated into strategically interested and aligned partners.

In all organizations much of the politics of strategy will emerge around the practice of mandate changes, especially in MNCs. Strategy always concerns setting a direction and keeping to it against unforeseen resistance and events. Setting a direction and steering it in a complex organization of many different powers and knowledge is always going to be a political activity. This is why strategy, conducted well, is not for the faint-hearted: it produces tough, hard and sometimes robust politics, in which there are winners and losers.

EXERCISES

1 Having read this chapter you should be able to say in your own words what the following key terms mean:

- Organizational politics
- Strategic interest
- Political skill
- Social capital
- Power
- Multinational corporation (MNC)
- Mandate
- Power/knowledge
- Resistance
- Discourse.

2 What are some of the chief power games that occur around the strategy process?

3 Why are MNCs especially likely to be sites of struggle over strategy?

4 How would you seek to secure support for a mandated change?

5 Why are power/knowledge mutually implicated?

6 Looking at Michal Smith's account of 'Politics and Strategy', especially Chapter 3, the 'Art of the possible', on www.strategytube.net, how does Michael suggest that we can produce positive politics around the strategy-making process?

ADDITIONAL RESOURCES

1 Our companion website is the best first stop for you to find a great deal of extra resources, free PDF versions of leading articles published in Sage journals, exercise, video and pod casts, team case studies and general questions and links to teamwork resources. Go to www.sagepub.co.uk/cleggstrategy

2 A good book on political struggles in organizations is Peter Fleming and Andre Spicer's (2007) *Contesting the Corporation: Struggle, Power, and Resistance in Organizations*, Cambridge: Cambridge University Press.

3 Another useful resource is the second edition of David Buchanan and Richard Badham's (2008) *Power, Politics and Organizational Change: Winning the Turf Game*, London: Sage, which explores in far more detail than we are able in this chapter the intricacies and details of the many power games that occur in organizations.

4 Cynthia Hardy's (1994) *Managing Strategic Action*, London: Sage, has a good section on the role of power in approaches used to mobilize change in Part II of the book, especially her own Chapter 13, 'Power and politics in organizations'.

5 Paula Jarzabkowski's (2005) *Strategy as Practice*, London: Sage, presents a particular perspective on strategy research known as 'strategy-as-practice', which seeks to understand strategy through a close scrutiny of what is done in the various sites of the strategy process. Organizational politics are implicit throughout her account.

6 Probably the most interesting case study of power in and around organizations in recent years is Bent Flyvbjerg's (1998) *Rationality and Power: Democracy in Practice*, Chicago: University of Chicago Press, researched in the arena of urban planning in the town of Aalborg in Denmark. It presents a complex picture of the overlapping strategic and self-interests shaping the civil society of the good citizens of Aalborg. It is the best analysis of the practices of the strategy process that we know.

7 The documentary film *Rats in the Ranks* is a wonderful insight into the strategy of politics: see the

excellent notes on the movie available at www.filmaust.com.au/programs/teachers_notes/3895 Ratsinthe Ranks.pdf. The film itself can be ordered from http://shop.abc.net.au/browse/product.asp?productid=735644. It was directed by Robin Anderson and Bob Connolly and broadcast on ABC TV in 2001 as well as being distributed by them.

8   The film *12 Angry Men*, directed by Sidney Lumet (1957), with Henry Fonda, provides an excellent insight into how strategic argument can sway decision-making.

9   Oliver Stone's (1987) film *Wall Street* portrays a compelling character, Gordon Gecko, as the epitome of a financial strategist wholly wedded to the interests of making the deal and making money from it, someone with only one interest and no sense of contextual obligations.

WEB SECTION

Visit the *Strategy* companion website at www.sagepub.co.uk/cleggstrategy

1   The online resource www.strategytube.net that the authors produced in tandem with this book is a great resource: look in particular at the video of Case Study 8 where Michael Smith talks about politics and strategy. Look especially at the 'study questions' for this case. They are designed to complement and extend this chapter.

2   Logging on to the Strategy-as-Practice website provides you with an opportunity to subscribe to a lively community in which many interesting papers are posted. It is free – just go to www.s-as-p.org.

3   The following site contains the comparison between sport and business with which we opened the chapter: www.rotman.utoronto.ca/rogermartin/the Atlantic.pdf

LOOKING FOR A HIGHER MARK?

Reading and digesting these articles that are available free on the companion website www.sagepub.co.uk/cleggstrategy can help you gain deeper understanding and, on the basis of that, a better grade:

1   Farzad R. Khan, Kamal A. Munir and Hugh Willmott (2007) A Dark Side of Institutional Entrepreneurship: Soccer Balls, Child Labour and Postcolonial Impoverishment, *Organization Studies*, 28: 1055–77. A fascinating account of how good intentions can lead to bad outcomes.

2   Cyril Bouquet and Julian Birkinshaw (2008) Managing Power in the Multinational Corporation: How Low-Power Actors Gain Influence, *Journal of Management*, 34: 477–508. The article provides a conceptual integration and synthesis of the literature on power and influence in MNCs. It concentrates on the situation facing, and the strategies pursued by, low-power actors within the MNC network. It is an exhaustive repository of current references.

3   Hitoshi Mitsuhashi and Henrich R. Greve (2004) Powerful and Free: Intraorganizational Power and the Dynamics of Corporate Strategy, *Strategic Organization*, 2(2): 107–32. The article is a very detailed statistical study of the horizontal and vertical dimensions of organizational power structures' influence on the dynamics of corporate strategy in the Japanese robotics and shipbuilding industries.

The 1998 Australian waterfront dispute: different strategic interests, different strategies, different weapons

Stewart Clegg

Australia, as an isolated island continent, is heavily dependent on its ports to be competitive in international trade. At the time that the waterfront dispute took place, approximately 70 per cent of Australia's imports and 78 per cent of exports traded through its ports. During 1997 research into productivity concluded that these ports were uncompetitive compared with best practice benchmarks overseas. Charges were higher, productivity lower and service less reliable, while marine service and port infrastructure charges were two to three times greater than at overseas ports.

The waterfront workers were organized into the Maritime Union of Australia, which ran a virtually closed shop on the docks: only union members were able to work. After a new Conservative federal government was elected in 1996, industrial relations were changed in such a way that this weakened the rights of unions to bargain collectively on behalf of the workforce. Individual rather than collective contracts – Australian Workplace Awards – were encouraged. These were vehemently opposed by the trade unions.

One of the largest stevedoring firms on the waterfront was Patricks. Its strategic interest was in increasing productivity. To do this, however, if had to change much of the customary practice that previous generations of employers and managers had allowed to become embedded on the docks as a result of union pressure. How to do it?

The strategy was simple. On 8 April 1998, the Patrick Stevedoring Company declared itself insolvent. The existing unionized workforce was issued with immediate redundancy notices and locked out. Private security guards were hired by Patricks to evict and ensure employees were not allowed access. The government's industrial relations minister made a statement supporting the company. The company in turn cited a lack of productivity and profit as the reason for its actions as well as a desire to 'clean up' the waterfront.

The security guards were not just keeping union labour locked out. Despite Patrick's 'insolvency' the docks remained fully operational, manned by workers who had contracts with a labour-hire company owned by the same people as the recently announced insolvent Patrick Company. These contracts were non-union and had markedly worse conditions attached to them compared with the union contracts. A section of the new workforce turned out to be ex-armed forces personnel who had been previously recruited and trained in Dubai in advance of the strategic change.

There were confrontational scenes relayed in the media: security guards with fierce dogs and faces masked by balaclavas and angry unionists picketing and demonstrating against the 'scab' labour. Meanwhile, the union took their case to the Federal Court, which found in favour of the union, determining that the company had deliberately restructured its corporate structure with the sole intent of dismissing its unionized workers. Supported by the government, Patricks appealed against this decision but was overruled, eventually by the High Court of Australia. The full bench of the High Court found in the union's favour: the company's corporate restructuring was a device to rid the company of its unionized workforce.

In June 1998 the union and Patricks negotiated a new agreement: it specified voluntary redundancies, the introduction of some casual labour and the contracting-out of some jobs; in addition, smaller work crews, longer regular hours, company control over rostering, and productivity bonuses for faster loading were introduced. The union retained the ability to represent maritime workers while the company achieved significant changes to work practices. The non-union workers were made redundant and while some of the ex-military men did quite well out of their stint on the waterfront, others claimed to have been cheated out of wages due to them.

References

Check out Google – when we did, we found about 74,900 hits for *Australian waterfront dispute 1998*
Also see:
André Spicer, John W. Selsky and Julian Teicher (2002) Paradox in Symbols and Subjects: The Politics of Constructing the Wharfie in S. R. Clegg et al. (eds), *Management and*

(Continued)

(Continued)

Organizational Paradoxes, Amsterdam: Benjamins, pp. 87–118.

John W. Selsky, André Spicer, and Julian Teicher (2003) Totally Un-Australian! Discursive and Institutional Interplay in the Melbourne Port Dispute of 1997–98, *Journal of Management Studies*, 40: 1729–60.

Question

1 Using the references suggested as well as an extensive Web search, identify the different strategic interests of the different players involved in the strategic change and identify what micro-politics were at work. What were the major strategies involved? Who won?

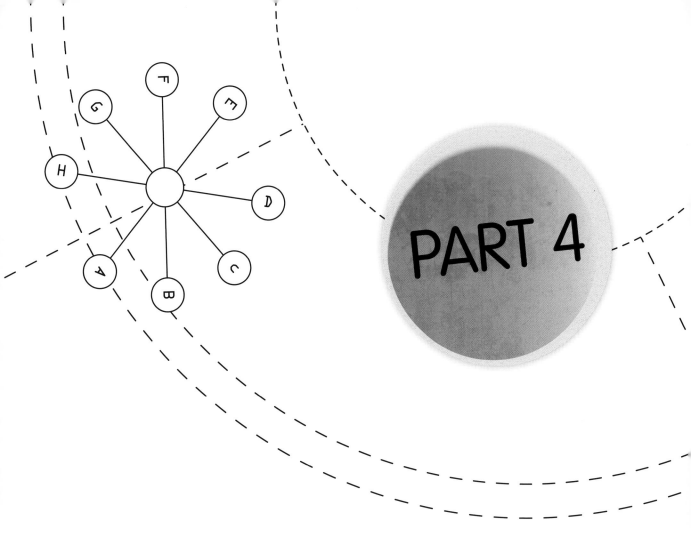

Global Strategies

10 International and collaborative strategies

11 Financialization, risk and accountability

12 Globalization and strategy

10

International and Collaborative Strategies

Multinationals, alliances, networks

LEARNING OBJECTIVES

By the end of this chapter you will be able to:

- Explain the rationale for internationalization
- Define multinational corporations and distinguish internationalization strategies
- Define collaborative strategies and understand their importance
- Discuss the advantages and disadvantages of collaborative strategies
- Distinguish between different types of collaboration and understand their nature
- Explain why collaboration and competition sometimes go hand in hand
- Realize the critical role of partner selection, contracting and governance for collaboration

---

BEFORE YOU GET STARTED . . .

Politeness is the poison
of collaboration.

(EDWIN LAND)

INTRODUCTION

We have learned in previous chapters that a firm seeks competitive advantage by leveraging its resource base, branding its products and services, and positioning these products and services cleverly against competitors in well-defined markets. However, a firm's access to important strategic resources resides increasingly outside its organizational boundaries with alliance partners, subsidiaries and suppliers around the globe. Companies are using such international linkages and strategic alliances more and more because they can open the door to new business opportunities at less cost, and with greater speed and lower risks than traditional supplier relationships, mergers and acquisitions, or even internal growth initiatives. As a result, organizations expand globally to become multinational corporations (MNCs) and they increasingly engage in collaboration – they form alliances and join networks of organizations to combine resources and develop capabilities with external partners so that these partnerships contribute to the achievement of strategic objectives.

The word collaboration comes from the Latin *co* meaning 'with' and *labore* meaning 'to work', so it means 'to work together'.

Stopford and Wells (1972) studied the internationalization strategies of 187 of the largest US-based companies. They found that those organizations adopted different ways to structure their global expansion at different stages. In the early stages of global activities firms tend to establish an international division to handle the early limited volume of foreign sales and range of products being sold internationally. As sales of the limited range of products expand, and the product range does not grow accordingly, the firms tend to move to managing by an area structure, while firms that develop additional product lines tend to adopt a world wide product division structure. When both foreign sales and foreign product diversity are high, firms tend to adopt a matrix structure. However, all these design choices are deeply constrained by the previous histories and contexts of the firms in question.

Moreover, the choices for structuring organizational relationships to expand internationally range widely from very loosely arranged contractual partnerships, for instance for the purpose of a regional joint marketing campaign, to equity-based joint ventures or even mergers and acquisitions, for example to produce jointly products for a local market. In this chapter we will explore further why and how firms grow into MNCs and what the role of associated collaborative strategies is in developing a competitive advantage for the partnering organizations.

WHY COLLABORATE?

One reason that organizations will seek alliances includes accessing resources such as, for example, knowledge for product and service innovation (Powell, Kogut and Smith-Doer, 1996); accordingly, firms such as IBM and Cisco collaborate by combining their specific expertise and creating new products and services that offer more integrated IT network solutions for corporate clients (e.g. Tsai, 2001).

Another motivation for firms to collaborate is to learn from each other. General Motors, for example, entered into a joint venture with Toyota in the United States in 1984 to co-manufacture small cars in California using Toyota's lean production methods. While this gave General Motor's managers and technical staff the opportunity to learn lean manufacturing methods from their inventor, Toyota had a chance to test their production methods that were so successful within the Japanese context on a traditional US workforce. General Motors was able to increase productivity and Toyota learned about US labour management practices, which proved particularly useful when Toyota opened its first manufacturing facilities in the United States a few years later. The initial collaboration led to another. Between 1999 and 2006 GM and Toyota collaborated again. This time the objective was to generate scale economies. Both companies spread their investments over more units by jointly designing a new car and its production facilities.

Another reason for firms to collaborate is to gain access to strategically important markets. A classic example is JVC, the Japanese manufacturer of entertainment equipment, which in the 1980s had a superior video recorder design and manufacturing capability but needed relationships with various European manufactures, such as Thorn-EMI, Telefunken and Thomson, to access the fragmented European market.

Finally, collaboration can help overcome trade barriers. For example, many Western companies that sought to enter the Chinese market in the early 1990s were only able to do so by finding local partners and setting up a joint venture that was located in China and produced goods and services by making substantial use of local resources and suppliers. While foreign companies invested capital and supplied the technology, they also gained local knowledge and, more important, the ability to get around import quotas.

WHY BECOME AN MNC?

Kogut (2002: 266) suggests that expanding internationally improves firm performance by providing an enhanced incentive for firms to invest in intangible assets, such as copyrights, patents, trademarks and brand loyalty, as well as intellectual property intangibles such as know-how and knowledge. Perhaps most important of all is the accrual of human capital – experienced personnel familiar with local ways of doing business in the MNC who can translate this knowledge globally and learn while doing so. The contemporary MNC is best seen as a network of subsidiaries (Kogut, 2002), linked through networks and global collaborative initiatives.

Three factors, of *location* or *comparative advantage*, *capital markets* and the mode of entry for *internalization*, have become the basis of a model that is widely used in the international business literature. The theory of foreign direct investment is also known by the acronym of OLI theory to signify its core elements of *ownership*, *location* and *internalization* (Dunning, 1980; 1998; 2000). Although these elements are useful in thinking about why companies enter multinational markets, they are not especially helpful for theorizing about how mature MNCs, with major global operations, make strategic choices.

Market factors

According to Buckley (2003: 699), MNCs

are perfectly placed to exploit the differences in international integration of markets. The existence of regional goods and services markets enables firms to exploit economies of scale across several economies. Differential labour markets enable costs to be reduced by locating the labour-intensive stages of production in cheap labour economies.

The result is that for these MNCs horizontal integration is assisted by 'regional goods and services markets, vertical integration by differentiated labour markets and distribution of key raw materials. Strategic trade and foreign direct investment can be seen to take place within this framework' (2003: 699). Top-level strategic managers of global organizations typically seek:

- Unrestricted access to resources and markets throughout the world.
- The freedom to integrate manufacturing with other operations across national boundaries.
- Coordination and control of all aspects of the company on a worldwide basis.
- A maximization of shareholder value.
- A minimization of tax liabilities by establishing corporate headquarters in low-tax regimes such as the Dutch Antilles or the Cayman Islands.
- Low levels of government regulation in the markets in which they operate.

From a strategic point of view, diversification into new territories is principally a means for gaining a competitive advantage. It has been suggested that international diversification is more likely to occur when:

- Firms possess high endowments of intangible resources such as knowledge (Delgado-Gomez, Ramirez-Aleson and Espitia-Escuer, 2004; Nachum and Zaheer, 2005).
- Firms are in information-intensive industries seeking intangible resources such as knowledge – when Western technology firms enter places such as Bangalore, India (Hitt et al., 2006).
- Firms' top management teams have an elite education, a lower average age and greater international experience (Sambharya, 1996; Tihanyi et al., 2000; Wally and Becerra, 2001; Herrmann and Datta, 2005).
- Firms are owned by institutional investors, professional investment funds and pension funds.

Comparative advantage

To have a successful strategy for entry into a foreign market – one that is not in the home territory of the business in question – means that the enterprise must be better at doing what it is doing than other businesses that already do what it does and are domiciled in the country in question as well as being able do it profitably. Comparative advantage might come into play: for instance, Afghanistan is well suited to growing poppies and has a population used to producing opium for processing into heroin with local social institutions, such as powerful regional warlords represented in the Afghan government, that enable the crop to flourish and be traded internationally, despite its stigma.

Comparative advantage may explain a few things about strategy in areas of primary production where the raw materials are simply not globally available just anywhere, but outside of these special cases it does not explain much. Comparative advantage is not merely a result of national factor endowments: it is not the clean air, alpine valleys and peaks of Switzerland that make it an especially well-endowed country for a global and secretive banking industry. In this case, as in many others, it is the development of social institutions that provide the comparative advantage. And these social institutions grew out of the strategies of the banks, from the Middle Ages onwards, in building trust and a climate of secrecy and security.

Efficiency

MNCs must be able to do what they do more efficiently and effectively than local non-MNCs. Several 'things' that they do have been suggested in the literature (Buckley, 2003) in terms of deviations from models of perfect competition:

- *Deviations from perfect competition in goods markets.* Product differentiation, marketing skills, administered pricing.
- *Deviations from perfect competition in factor markets.* Access to factors such as knowledge, capital and skill, especially as these are embodied in managerial expertise.
- *Economies of scale due to vertical integration.* These enable unit costs to be dramatically reduced and standardization to be practised, further driving down costs.
- *Overcoming governmental regulations.* Moving inside national territories allows firms to accord with local laws that might limit their capacity to trade as outsiders.

In general, the advantages that attach to multinational operations include:

- Superior organizational and strategic attributes in producing goods and services that can be readily implanted in new contexts.
- Oligopolistic positioning in the advanced economies, enabling the development of the most sophisticated product improvement cycles, through economies of scale, research and development, and innovation, competitive pricing and branding (Bartlett and Ghoshal, 1987; 1989).
- Reduced transaction costs (Williamson, 1975; 1979; 1981; 1985; 1991).

Institutional factors

Sorge (2005: 5) suggests that the 'relative prices of factors of production and transport costs will induce enterprises on the whole to substitute direct investment abroad for exporting'. Hence, convertible and flexible floating exchange rates make it more probable that firms will globalize – but, given the frequency of currency movements and their unpredictability, these factors also make globalization risky – especially if substantial fixed asset investments are required in other currency blocks.

Economists would say that movements associated with the capital market in a regime of flexible exchange rates produce market imperfections and uncertainty that make transnational organization possible; otherwise, local firms would always be winners due to what sociologists would call their 'embeddedness' – their deep immersion in local laws, institutions, cultures, norms, etc. Local embeddedness is something that every transnational has to overcome because, at least initially, it is this that has produced the customer preferences of their prospective consumers.

Firms will only adopt transnational strategies where they expect to make a profit – for which there can never be any guarantees. They may, sensing risk, prefer to license a local business or export rather than be challenged. Of course, these strategies pose other risks as many business have found: once the local firm has built up knowledge that was proprietary, it may well become a rival in that and other markets – an experience not unknown to foreign investors in China.

STRATEGIES FOR MNCS

Arbitrage is the practice of profiting from differences in costs and process across borders – basically buying where prices are lowest, selling where prices are greatest and using international operations as a means of reducing tax liabilities in countries with high-tax regimes and concentrating profits in low-tax regimes and losses in high-tax regimes. Sometimes this is referred to as a strategy of transfer pricing. Arbitrage also occurs when MNCs are able to exploit exchange rate movements profitably by switching production into cheaper currencies.

The key element in developing a global strategy is arbitrage. To be able to exploit the global opportunities for profit that arbitrage offers, an MNC needs strategies that will enable it to have maximal flexibility in locating production, know-how and knowledge, as well as the ability to react rapidly to threats and opportunities. Reactive ability will be limited by the necessity of abiding by the rules of the states in which firms invest because they are not always so liquid that they can easily move.

Arbitrage is also facilitated by different state administrations competing for foreign direct investment. If the local state does not provide what the global investor requires, mobile capitalism can threaten simply to exit the scene and set up where the benefits sought can be ensured.

The national diversity of operations has become a source of advantage, an advantage that Kogut (2002: 265) refers to in terms of 'embedded options'. A further distinction can be made between 'across-country' and 'within-country' options. Across-country options refer to the arbitraging of borders, such as shifting production, arranging tax accountabilities or transferring innovations from one country to another. How economically successful these across-country strategies are is highly variable since the conditions of arbitrage that prevail at a decision point may not prevail when the strategy comes to maturity. Within-country options, on the other hand, refer to establishing a platform, such as brand recognition, from which later investment strategies can develop.

There are at least five different models of internationalization strategies that enable arbitrage in different ways.

Decentralized federation; multinational strategy

According to Bartlett and Ghoshal (1995), this is the typical European model of multinationalization that developed between the wars. The decentralized federation was seen to characterize an era of tariff protection and quotas; to get round these, firms would establish different national subsidiaries to produce inside the protectionist regimes. These flows of trade, people and capital were basically devised to get around the obstacles to more global flows that states erected. In an era of primitive communications technologies subsidiaries thrived with a great deal of autonomy, constrained largely by personal relations and financial controls. The end result was a portfolio of different national subsidiaries within which local learning was largely contained. Moreover, due to constrained resources sourced locally, the ability to respond to local markets may be limited. Also, decisions may be made wholly in terms of local relevancies, which may not always serve the interests of the centre. For instance, there may be a duplication of effort as each periphery replicates functions locally, on a small and more costly scale, with a degree of resistance to innovations from rival centres in the federation.

Coordinated federation; international strategy

The postwar era was characterized by widespread US penetration of European and other markets with technologically more sophisticated products than were available elsewhere. Typically, these companies were professionally managed by trained MBAs using sophisticated management control systems. The result was highly centralized management. The flow was largely one way, of Americanization as globalization. Centralist assumptions about where innovation and ideas came from and went to became widespread. While efficiency, in terms of standardization, might be advanced by this model, it limited the opportunities for local learning feeding back to the parent organization. Also, functional management becomes dominant at the local level because of its key transmission role in translating central company skills, knowledge and capabilities.

Centralized hubs; global strategy

For Japanese firms that internationalized from the 1970s onwards, the idea of continuous improvement was at the heart of strategy. Japanese firms emphasized quality, cost and feature advantages. They were able to offer more features, at a better quality, and for less cost, due to a tight central control of product development, procurement and manufacturing, as well as an extensive use of new managerial approaches such as just-in-time manufacturing, delegated *ringi-ko*[1] decision-making, and an innovation culture closely tied to the shopfloor and to a management which was highly loyal to the company that employed it (Clegg, 1990). At least initially an export-based model of growth led this strategy, although, by the 1980s, many Japanese firms were establishing overseas subsidiaries in countries such as India, the UK and the United States, giving rise to a whole literature on Japanization (Elger and Smith, 1994). In these organizations the flows were still largely one way; although talented locals might aspire to middle management positions within Japanese corporations in the national sphere of operations, the chances of their career ever taking them to the centres of corporate power in Japan were extremely remote. The employment practices of the internal labour market, recruitment of cohorts from specific universities and the intangible elements of Japanese culture meant that expatriates were extremely unlikely to gain access to the inner sanctums.

Knowledge and learning tended to be tightly coupled in Japanese core organizations. The most powerful managers in such a structure of management tend to be the product divisional managers, because they play the key role in product development and innovation, the engine of the whole system. Hence, power tends to be less disaggregated around the peripheries than might initially appear to be the case because the product divisions are centralized in the hubs – and in the case of Japanese organizations, the centralization will be reinforced by culture, as it is rare for non-Japanese managers to move from the peripheries and gain these positions in the core. In addition, these factors limit the ability of the organization to be able to respond to signals from the periphery, whose legitimacy and urgency may be difficult to transmit to a hard-pressed and insular central management.

Capital markets impose performance requirements that lead to continuous organizational restructuring. Within multinationals local managers are pressured

---

[1]The term *'ringi-ko'* refers to a model for decision-making that is developed from interpersonal process mechanisms into a series of decision stages, from which consensus evolves. The decision process is iterative, reverting to previous stages, until the issues blocking a consensus are resolved.

to conform to the expectations of their home context while also being subjected to the transfer of practices from the MNC. The head office managers will transfer practices, people and resources to subsidiaries in order to try and maintain control and achieve objectives while local subsidiaries may resist these transfers or develop them in their own interests. Frequently, the implication in the strategy literature is that these things are achieved fairly effortlessly, as structural adjustments; other writers, whose analysis we prefer, suggest otherwise.

Morgan and Kristensen offer a powerful corrective to some of the overly rationalistic and economistic views in the international business, strategy and multinationals literature:

> [T]he MNC as a totality may be seen as a highly complex configuration of ongoing micro-political power conflicts at different levels in which strategizing social actors/ groups inside and outside the firm interact with each other and create temporary balances of power that shape how formal organizational relationships and processes actually work in practice. Institutions enter into these processes, firstly as co-constitutors of the set of actors/groupings and their mutual roles and identities, secondly as forms of restriction on the choices actors make, thirdly as resources that empower actors and finally as rule-givers for the games that emerge. (2006: 1473)

This puts a very different spin on strategy from the view that it is something that is decided at the hub and then distributed to the peripheries. The multinational and its senior management will strive for coherent practices and procedures globally; to do so they will use devices such as benchmarking procedures that measure factors such as size of the workforce, profitability, inventory, productivity, and so on. Best practice establishes the hurdles that the peripheral and subsidiary organizations are supposed to exceed. A failure to achieve hurdles can see facilities moved from lower to higher performing subsidiaries. These strategies can be buttressed by capital investment decisions, about resources such as financial, knowledge and reputational capital.

Subsidiaries and peripheries are not always passive vessels: they do not always wait to see what gets poured into them or is denied them. The extent to which they are able to resist central strategies and translate them depends on the extent to which they are variants of one or other models of national business systems. Hall and Soskice (2001) characterize these respectively as 'coordinated market economy' versus 'liberal market economy'. In the coordinated market economies, including much of continental Europe and Japan:

> [E]mployees … tend to have high skills and expectations of consultation and involvement in the workplace. Transfers that threaten these skills or are introduced without consultation are likely to be resisted where they threaten existing patterns of authority and the division of labour. Where transfers are potentially more positive for the subsidiary, it is likely that local actors will be more likely to absorb and adapt to these processes than accept them wholesale. (Morgan and Kristensen, 2006: 1474)

By contrast, liberal market economies will be characterized by more conflict and employees with lower levels of skill formation and organizationally weak links into local networks with less capacity for an organized resistance that is capable of translating central imperatives into local practices. Morgan and Kristensen (2006) discuss the different dynamics of these two situations in terms of the hurdle and capital investment strategies of the core actors. The central circuits of capital for firm strategies frame these relations, especially in the liberal market economies where the stable bank control of assets is rare compared with the situation in coordinated market economies such as those of Germany or Japan.

In the Anglo-American economies of the United States and the UK players in capital markets will closely monitor firms' performance in terms of share price.

YOU CAN DOWNLOAD…

Glenn Morgan and Peer Hull Kristensen's (2006) The Contested Space of Multinationals: Varieties of Institutionalism, Varieties of Capitalism, *Human Relations,* 59: 1467–90, from the book's website at www.sagepub. co.uk/cleggstrategy

Failing to meet expectations leads to swift falls in share prices. Senior managers will engage in power games in which institutional investors will set the norms for achieving certain levels of performance (see Lazonick and O'Sullivan, 2000; Williams, 2000; Golding, 2001; Froud et al., 2006). Market discipline pressures will prevail. Senior central managers' ability to reduce costs and increase efficiency in subsidiary and peripheral organizations, in terms of strategies that the key market players understand (see Froud et al., 2006), is vital if share values are to be maintained. Subsidiary managers will either push performance pressure down through the organization in terms of a combined strategy of cutting costs and raising productivity and profits, or will seek to translate them into the local context in ways that are positive in that context.

Headquarters of US and Anglo-Saxon firms can play subsidiaries off against each other so they will compete in a race to increase benchmarks, profit and productivity and to cut costs. One consequence is that global firms in liberal market business systems will frequently restructure and implement change programmes through acquisitions, sell-offs, joint ventures and suchlike. By contrast, those firms in coordinated market economies such as Germany and Japan will be much less likely to be subject to these pressures as their share portfolio tends to be far more stable, and the capital markets less predatory, because of institutional devices such as cross-cutting shareholdings and bank ownership, held in stable patterns. In these situations, as Kono and Clegg (1998) discuss with reference to Japan, longer range planning is far more normalized.

Matrix organizations; binary strategy

The matrix organization, an idea that first emerged in the 1950s in the United States' aerospace industry, attempts to achieve the benefits of both project and functional forms of organization (Galbraith, 1971). Many organizations have adopted various types of matrix structures (Sayles, 1976). By definition, the matrix is a grid-like organizational structure that allows a company to address multiple business dimensions using multiple command structures. In order to ensure that people focus simultaneously on two or more organizational forces, a system of dual reporting relationships is put in place. It is an attempt to structure flows where they are directed within the organization as a global enterprise.

Matrix structures focus on the binaries of regional market share as well as product lines. Companies form matrix structures when they need to have a simultaneous emphasis on two or more of functional, divisional and geographical activities. Davis and Lawrence (1977) define a matrix as any organization that employs a multiple command system that includes related support mechanisms and associated organizational culture and behaviour patterns. The principles of matrix structures have been applied widely in organizations, such as engineering-oriented firms that do business through a number of distinctive projects (Khandwalla, 1977).

In the mid-1970s GE's aircraft engine business applied a two-boss matrix to achieve technical excellence. Many other companies formed matrix structures similar to those of GE. However, some of the companies failed a few years after the matrix was formed. Anderson (1994) states that in the 1970s the power sharing that worked efficiently for missile projects did not transfer well to major appliance projects. Kotter (1996), who researched more than 100 companies in the 1980s, found that few of the change efforts had been successful; some had been utter failures, and most had fallen somewhere in between, with a distinct tilt towards the lower end of the scale. Minor disagreements could blow up into major turf wars, characterized by conflict and confusion over who should be responsible for what; information logjams, because of the multiple reporting channels and a loss of accountability due to international barriers of time, distance, language and culture.

Integrated network; transnational strategy

A fully transnationalized organization will differ from each of the previous four models. It develops multidimensional perspectives, distributed interdependent capabilities, and flexible integrative processes. In an integrated network there is no definite centre–periphery relation but rather more overlapping relations between elements in the network. Each individual centre might be a champion for a particular global competency, process, product or knowledge within the overall network. Relatively autonomous centres are able to translate local issues and concerns into meanings that can be widely distributed in flows of information around the network; having a high degree of standardization of business models connecting the different elements in the network ensures a coordinative capacity for managing system-wide responses with local calibrations.

Creating an effective integrated network will mean finely tuned global politics capable of balancing specific country management against global product division managers and functional managers in key strategic areas. Where this can be achieved, viable national units will play a global role in the network by being the champion for particular responsibilities. In consequence, worldwide interdependence of the network increases as a mechanical division of labour is implemented whereby each element depends on other elements for essential mechanisms in the integrated network. Thus, distributed specialized resources and capabilities develop; there is a rich flow and translation of components, products, resources, people and meaning among the interdependent units, and a distributed network of coordination and cooperation in an environment of shared decision-making.

The risks with the integrated network model are evident: the system can be overwhelmed by the complexity of flows. As flows become normalized within routines focused on one particular set of strategic contingencies, such as functions, geographic units or product specialization, they must not become incapable of rapid switching as strategic contingencies change either within or between the elements being integrated. Top management will need to be focused on centralization, formalization and socialization as three interdependent management processes. Centralization will require strategically managed interventions from time to time; formalization will mean developing procedural mechanisms that must evolve with individual national and management roles; while socialization means that the organization must constantly be aware that it is managing a complex multiculturalism, in terms of both national and intra-organizational differences. Clearly, there is ample room for political misadventure in such a complex balancing of powers, cultures and management devices.

Some networks take on many of the characteristics of organizations, such as One World or Star Alliance, the airline alliances, which are branded and recognized as organizations. They have common symbols, logos, joint marketing and a card to unite all members (Mintzberg et al., 2003: 124–37). Raab and Kenis (2009) suggest that for people working in such networks, there is an interplay of individual, organizational and network identities, in which organizational and network identities can be developed to a different degree. In franchises, for instance, as a network strategy, the network identity overdetermines the organizational identity of the franchise in question; this rarely happens in other kinds of network, such as airline alliances. Not all networks are stable: occasional goal-directed, consciously created, bounded and governed networks that form for a purpose and then dissolve have been less discussed in the literature (Provan, Fish, and Sydow, 2007). Especially, where networks are formed to extend organization capabilities when confronted with fluid customer preferences (Prahalad and Ramaswamy, 2003), they are often created for a limited duration and dissolved at a certain date or after reaching the previously set goal.

Provan and Kenis (2008) suggest that there are three different forms of governance of networks: they can be self-governing, directed by the lead organization, or subject to a network administrative organization. The self-governing network offers the most interesting strategy because it has the potential to grow new roots and branches rapidly.

In light of those internationalization strategies, it is not surprising that collaboration and network-dependent revenues for some of the largest global companies have been growing extensively in recent years (e.g. Gulati, 1998; Harbison et al., 2000; Margulis and Pekar, 2001; Park and Zhou, 2005). IBM considers about one-third of its total revenue to be related to more than 90,000 business partners worldwide, and Cisco, with more than 13,800 partners, generates about 80 per cent of its sales through alliances. Although perhaps not all these alliances can be considered strategic, many will have strategic implications, be they in the form of long-term R&D joint ventures including equity stakes or in the form of loosely agreed marketing partnerships to increase sales in the short term.

It becomes clear that the single firm no longer competes without being embedded in a complex and constantly growing network of partnerships. Moreover, the portfolio of allies may be continuously changing due to firms' shifting requirements for resources. Alliance partners will therefore realize that organizational boundaries can become more fluid and volatile. It is this inter-organizational context and the embedded individual alliances that have a considerable effect on the strategic performance of organizations. Hence, a firm's capacity to manage its collaborative activities successfully represents a critical strategic ability in increasingly globalized, competitive and quickly changing market environments.

There are many strategic as well as practical aspects of inter-organizational collaboration that are important for partners to consider when getting involved with alliances and networks. To begin with, firms have to assess whether or not collaboration is a viable strategy to gain access to important resources, then they have to find suitable partners, negotiate terms and conditions, implement governance structures, processes and policies, choose and integrate the alliance management team and team members, and ultimately know when best to exit the partnership. In what follows we will look more closely at different aspects of collaborative strategies, exploring various types of alliances and the means that firms can use to manage their multiple relationships with alliance partners.

MINI CASE STUDY

Star Alliance: a global partnership of airlines

In 1997, a group of five world-class airlines got together to create something never seen before – an alliance that brought together networks, lounge access, check-in services, ticketing and dozens of other services to improve the travel experience for passengers. Today, Star Alliance is a truly global network of airlines; it was the first airline alliance to offer its customers worldwide reach and a superior travel experience. Its members in 2009 included Air Canada, Air China, Air New Zealand, ANA, Asiana Airlines, Austrian, bmi, Egyptair, LOT Polish Airlines, Lufthansa, Scandinavian Airlines, Shanghai Airlines, Singapore Airlines, South African Airways, Spanair, SWISS, TAP Portugal, Turkish Airlines, THAI, United and US Airways. Regional member carriers enhance the global network, including Adria Airways (Slovenia), Blue1 (Finland) and Croatia Airlines. Air India, Continental Airlines

(Continued)

(Continued)

and TAM have been announced as future members. Overall, the Star Alliance network offers more than 18,100 daily flights to 975 destinations in 162 countries, which means easier travel and quicker connections.

However, while Star Alliance was the first multi partner alliance in the airline industry, it did not remain the only one for very long. Rivalry among large constellations took off when American Airlines and British Airways launched the Oneworld alliance in February 1999. Among the founding members of this group were also Canadian Airlines, Cathay Pacific and Qantas. In September 1999, Finnair and Iberia joined, and later Japan Airlines, LAN, Malev and Royal Jordanian, resulting in 675 destinations being served today, with access to more than 500 airport departure lounges, joint frequent-flyer benefits, products and other corporate solutions. The overall strategy for Star Alliance as much as for Oneworld is to make the travel experience smoother. Member airlines are located closer together in airports and are introducing new technologies and building common facilities at airports, coordinating schedules and installing connection teams for faster transfers.

Most of the alliance activities of Star Alliance are coordinated thought Star Alliance Services GmbH, a jointly managed organization based in Frankfurt, Germany. The operational team of about 75 employees from more than 25 different countries manage a portfolio of alliance products and services, develop new offerings for the partners and manage the Star Alliance brand.

The benefits for partners of the Star Alliance are many. For example, partners are able to optimize their network through an extended 'hub and spoke' system, in which the main airports in a country serve as hubs through which passengers are channelled from and to various spokes that connect the hub to the final destinations. For example, Lufthansa passengers have access to Honolulu, Atlanta, Seattle and other US cities by flying United via the Chicago hub. Similarly, United does not fly from Munich to Frankfurt, but Lufthansa does. Hence, alliance partners have access to millions of new customers and are able to increase sales and subsequent load factors while at the same time building customer loyalty through a smoother transfer. Another major benefit for alliance partners is to combine purchases and increase buyer power. Star Alliance partners combined purchase of goods and services – excluding aircraft – amounts to about $15 billion annually. By jointly sourcing fuel, IT hardware, advertising media, network bandwidth, telecommunications, aircraft parts, in-flight service material and tyres partners can realize enormous efficiencies.

Questions

1 What are the advantages of collaborating in the airline industry and what are the disadvantages?

2 How can a partnership such as the Star Alliance be managed effectively?

3 How do the two main competing airline alliances Start Alliance and Oneworld differ? Go to www.staralliance.com and www.oneworld.com and compare the two.

DEFINING STRATEGIC ALLIANCES – KEY BENEFITS AND LATENT ISSUES

Strategic alliances are commonly defined as purposive linkages between organizations (Kale, Singh and Perlmutter, 2000) that cover collaborations involving an exchange, a co-development or a sharing relationship (Gulati, 1995).

Strategic alliances can include strategic supplier relationships, minority stakes, joint ventures, cross-licensing arrangements, joint marketing agreements or research consortia; however, they exclude mergers and acquisitions, franchising, cooperation internally within firms and simple licensing agreements.

Our view of alliances suggests that they have a number of defining features:

1 An alliance brings two or more individual organizations together.

2 An alliance requires these parties to be interconnected in some way with resource dependencies.

3 Interconnectedness involves reciprocal relations.

4 An alliance strives to define itself through consistent goals, interests or values.

5 In an alliance there is an assumption that the individual parties maintain at least some level of autonomy.

As we have seen in Chapter 9, in the discussion of organizational politics, collaboration is a mechanism that always has to balance the supralocal against the local, the centre against the periphery, the core against the marginal. There are always political costs as well as benefits to be had from alliances. Accordingly, strategic alliances represent arrangements that have emerged or have been purposefully established to leverage the partners' resources and capabilities with the strategic intent of enhancing strategic performance. Beyond the partners' contributions of resources and capabilities, alliances involve structures that facilitate a collaborative interaction among partners. Various studies have contributed to a better understanding of these and many other aspects of alliance management in various types of collaborations, in a range of industries, across numerous cultures or regions, and from many different theoretical perspectives. Alliance research and practice has developed considerably in the last decade.

Some of the key benefits a firm may seek to realize from engaging in collaboration include reducing risk, entering new markets more easily, obtaining new knowledge and realizing operational synergies:

- *Reducing risk.* Alliances can help partners minimize or control risk because they imply that two or more organizations work together and share, for example, an investment in crucial technologies, knowledge and production facilities.

- *Entering markets.* Alliances are a way for firms to overcome obstacles that restrict entry to new markets, thereby expanding faster globally, while keeping costs down. Collaborating with local partners can help surmount the regulations regarding entry modes that are imposed by the host government. It can also be a means of obtaining essential information about local customers, distribution networks and suppliers.

- *Gaining knowledge.* A firm may be able to gain access to knowledge and expertise that it lacks via a strategic alliance. Learning from alliance partners can help build capabilities within the alliance and be transferred to other parts of the organization.

- *Achieving synergy.* The complementary strength of alliance partners combined with the above advantages can result in synergies that allow for more efficient and effective use of resources and, thereby, provide a source for competitive advantage.

Despite these potential benefits and the evident and increasing importance of alliances, their outcome has not always been satisfactory. Many alliances have not accomplished their objectives (Parkhe, 1991; Ellis, 1996; Pearce, 1997; Hennart, Kim and Zeng, 1998). Alliance partners can end up wasting valuable time and resources trying to understand each other, even before the actual collaboration starts.

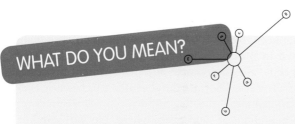

WHAT DO YOU MEAN?

Why do alliances fail?

An alliance between Ford and Fiat in 1995 failed due to managerial complexities that neither partner was able to overcome. After more than a year of discussing a wide range of proposals, they realized that they could not agree on the management structure necessary to launch the alliance. The differences in management and operational structures were so severe that Ford and Fiat decided it was impractical to enter into a cooperative relationship.

In 1992 IBM, Toshiba and Siemens announced an alliance to design and manufacture 256-megabit

(Continued)

(Continued)

chips, which required a high level of interaction among the partners. Despite the strong economic interest of the partners, the alliance was unsuccessful, due to high coordination costs. The economic potential was overshadowed by difficulties in coordinating the three culturally very distinctive firms: IBM perceived Toshiba as excessively group oriented and Siemens as overly concerned with the costs and details of financial planning.

In fact, in the last decade there have been repeated reports suggesting up to 50 per cent of alliances fail to satisfy the set objectives of collaborating partners. A study by the management consulting firm PricewaterhouseCoopers (Rea, 2004) revealed that half of the senior executives who were interviewed considered alliances vital to their business, and that the number of alliances they engaged in was growing substantially. However, while the understanding and use of alliances has clearly improved, executing a successful alliance is not without its difficulties. Over half of the survey respondents either did not know whether their organization's alliances were meeting their performance goals, or admitted that fewer than 50 per cent succeed.

Difficulties with alliances arise as a result of various issues:

- When partners are unable to match resources and align cultures, decision-making processes and systems in the alliance team (Kale et al., 2000).
- When they are unable to create trusting relationships (Ariño et al., 2005).
- When they have to manage conflict (Doz and Hamel, 1998) and when interpersonal ties need to be cultivated (Hutt et al., 2000).
- When there is a need to handle rivalry and managerial complexity (Park and Ungson, 2001; Sampson, 2005).
- When methods of dealing with environmental change differ (Mitchell and Singh, 1996).

Alliance governance concerns the agreements between alliance partners regarding the integration of their interests, the use of combined resources and their relationship.

As elaborated in Chapter 7, the central approach for organizations seeking to avoid and deal with political problems and conflicts is through the establishment of governance structures and mechanisms for the collaboration.

The mechanisms, structures and practices of governance that alliance partners establish to direct their partnerships are at the core of alliance management. These influence many aspects of collaborative activities that can enable and bind partners and alliance managers by framing regulations and practices designed in order to protect mutual interests. It is mastery in designing good governance that enhances the strategic performance of alliances and overall collaborative strategies.

Organizations will differ greatly in their ability to deal successfully with their alliance portfolio (Dyer, Kale and Singh, 2001). IBM and Cisco, for example, are known for their excellent alliance management capabilities. Both companies have collaborated successfully on various occasions: for example, since 2004 they have been providing customers with on-demand voice solutions and have subsequently been ranked number one and two in a study of preferred Internet Protocol telephony solution providers (Yankee Group, 2004). Their superior alliance management capabilities are reflected in processes and structures such as dedicated alliance functions/teams, and specific alliance control and management processes that support the management of alliances. They are good at alliances because they take care to manage alliance relationships.

Success in one domain is no guarantee of success elsewhere. Notwithstanding its track record of purposefully crafted alliance management capabilities, IBM has a record of alliance failures too. For example, in 1990 it collaborated with Apple to compete against Microsoft and Intel but a few years later the alliance vanished without any significant achievements. Hence, good alliance management capabilities take time and experience to develop, and they are not solely sufficient to warrant the superior performance of alliance relationships. Indeed, it is impossible to isolate one comprehensive explanation of strategic alliance performance if by 'explanation' we mean to make accurate predictions of performance. However, it is possible to identify those distinct features and mechanisms of collaborative strategies and their management that add to alliance performance.

MINI CASE STUDY

UPS

In September 2009, UPS, the worldwide delivery service, and The UPS Foundation announced that they would jointly support a multi-year, multimillion-dollar initiative to improve the capabilities of relief organizations to respond to global emergencies. The effort involves a commitment of up to $9 million in the form of substantial financial grants, in-kind services and the deployment of logistics expertise supporting some of the world's most respected relief organizations, including the American Red Cross, UNICEF, the World Food Programme, CARE and the Aidmatrix Foundation.

'This broad strategy for global disaster preparedness and response extends well beyond traditional financial support,' said Ken Sternad, President of The UPS Foundation. 'We are combining our supply chain expertise, our assets and linking our key partners to enable more effective response to global emergencies.'

Hundreds of millions of lives are affected by natural disasters and humanitarian emergencies. According to UNICEF, in the last decade an estimated 20 million children have been forced to flee their homes and more than 1 million have been orphaned or separated from their families as a result of these tragedies. 'If UPS can impact even a small percentage of these disasters that are happening daily somewhere around the world, this initiative will have been a success,' added Sternad.

In launching the initiative, UPS and The UPS Foundation announced major donations to organizations committed to disaster preparedness and relief. They include:

- A $500,000 cash and in-kind donation to the American Red Cross to provide logistics, shipping and warehouse support, enabling it to preposition supplies strategically and more effectively respond to the needs of those affected by disasters.

- A two-year, $1 million commitment to the US Fund for UNICEF, including a grant to strengthen UNICEF's emergency response capacity for its disaster preparedness programme in the Asia–Pacific region.

- Collaboration support for CARE and Aidmatrix to establish integrated and standardized supply-chain management systems.

- Expansion of the UPS commitment to the Logistics Emergency Teams (LETs) initiative that provides logistics experts to the World Food Programme. LETs operate in support of the United Nations Logistics cluster following natural disasters and consist of logistics experts who deploy within 48 to 72 hours for three to six weeks in the aftermath of major natural disasters. Twenty UPS employees will be trained and available globally as LETs responders.

- A $250,000 grant to Aidmatrix to help fund the international expansion of the organization's transportation aid relief programme. UPS is matching this grant with $250,000 in donated transportation.

Founded in 1951 and based in Atlanta, Georgia, the UPS Foundation's major initiatives include programmes that support community safety, non-profit effectiveness, economic and global literacy, environmental sustainability and diversity. The UPS Foundation pursues these initiatives by identifying specific projects where its support can help produce a measurable social impact. In 2008, The UPS Foundation donated $46.9 million to charitable organizations worldwide (source: www.businesswire.com, accessed 24 September 2009 at www.businesswire.com/news/home/20090924005530/en).

Questions

1 What type of collaboration is described in the case? What are the benefits for participants?

2 How is this collaboration different to more straightforward business collaborations?

3 What are the strategic advantages of this type of alliance?

THE ALLIANCE CHOICE – TO MAKE, BUY OR ALLY

In most cases of organizational or market development, a firm can grow organically, through internal growth (*to make*), by purchasing necessary assets and capabilities in the marketplace via a merger with or acquisition of another firm (*to buy*), or by collaborating (*to ally*) with one or more firms. Hence, deciding to employ an alliance is a key strategic choice. While there is a range of potential benefits, a key criterion that can make a firm choose 'to ally' is the shortage of critical resources within the current reach of the firm. Madhok and Tallman (1998) suggest four factors to consider:

1 A lack of the necessary internal capabilities and assets that, with some reorganization, would permit pursuing the new strategic direction without adding new resources.

2 The unavailability of needed resources for purchase in the open marketplace, usually because they are skills and capabilities that are tied to organizations and therefore difficult to transfer.

3 The high cost or risk associated with purchasing a firm that has the necessary resources because the actual competency can be hidden by other activities or an outright acquisition might drive off the very human and group assets that are critical for the strategy.

4 Benefits of collaboration, such as evading extensive organizational integration following a merger or acquisition and the preservation of critical assets and strategic flexibility.

Hence, the decision to make, buy or ally is predominantly aimed at what are constituted as being organizational capabilities rather than tangible assets. The firm either creates new competencies itself, buys them (usually through acquiring another firm or a unit of another firm), or obtains them through some extended contractual arrangement – an alliance. The decision regarding the choice of an alliance strategy, hence, focuses on gaining access to tacit organizational knowledge and capabilities rather than simple commodities or hard assets that can be found in the marketplace but that, typically, do not offer a significant advantage, because they are available to anyone else who can afford to buy them.

Additional factors to consider in constituting collaborative strategies are speed, risk and access to capital. Forming an alliance is likely to be faster than establishing a fully owned start-up organization, and less expensive and less risky than an acquisition. A firm that collaborates may also be able to leave assets and capital available for other purposes, while at the same time alliances may reduce the exposure of capital and assets to a risk of loss, for example when investing in unpredictable markets.

Finally, the decision to collaborate can be even more significant in the international context. The global environment contains a diversity of knowledge embedded in national systems of innovation. Firms face disadvantages from a lack of local knowledge relating to social, political and economic conditions in foreign markets (Beamish, 1994). Hence, as opposed to organic internationalization, collaboration has in the last decades been a preferred way for many organizations of dealing with the lack of knowledge about foreign local environments and entry into such markets.

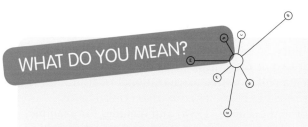

Strategic performance at the inter-organizational level

A strategic performance of alliances occurs as a function of the partners' ability to create value. The ability to create value rests on the set of unique resources and capabilities of the alliance. According to the RBV perspective (see Chapter 3) two distinct mechanisms – resource picking and capability building – are proposed about how firms create economic rents (Barney, 1986).

Resource picking means that managers gather information and analysis to outsmart the resource market in picking resources, similar to the way that a fund manager tries to outsmart the stock market in picking stocks. Capability building means managers design and construct organizational systems to enhance the productivity of resources that the firm acquires.

The two mechanisms are not mutually exclusive, that is firms will usually apply both of them (Makadok, 2001). Taken into the alliance context, value similarly results from the partners' search and selection processes (picking the winning resources) and the innovative configuration and deployment of new resource combinations (jointly building new capabilities).

The capabilities that reside within the relationships, the structures, mechanisms, processes and procedures that enable the leverage of pooled resources and their innovative recombination, contribute collectively to the performance of these collaborative ventures and, ultimately, the creation of superior rents. Accordingly, the two value-creating mechanisms can lead to additional sources of competitive advantage, increased efficiency and the leverage of new business opportunities.

ALLIANCE ORGANIZATION – CONTRACTUAL AGREEMENTS AND GOVERNANCE

Alliances can take various forms, from long-term R&D joint ventures with equity stakes to loosely agreed short-term marketing partnerships. The organization and functioning of alliances, however, are usually established through the contractual agreements and governance forms that have been put in place. Ariño and Reuer (2006) stress the distinct differences of contracting and governance in alliances. While the contract is concerned with the allocation of risks and trading gains resulting from exchanges between cooperating partners, governance refers to the institutional context in which the collaboration takes place. Research on alliance governance for alliances has, hence, largely been based on a distinction between equity and non-equity arrangements. A number of authors would argue that equity alliances provide partners with more managerial control than non-equity alliances by virtue of the establishment of an administrative hierarchy that allows them to exercise a right of control (Hennart, 1988; Pisano, 1989).

- *Equity alliances*, such as joint ventures, involve the creation of a separate, new organizational entity. Joint venture partners provide financial capital and other resources to the newly created firm, which typically has its own management team reporting to a board composed of representatives from the joint venture partners. Equity ownership is associated with greater control under the assumption that more equity ownership provides a partner with more voting power. Shared equity ownership might also be expected to align the incentives of partners, thereby creating mutual interests that will reduce the need for control (Oxley, 1997).

● *Non-equity alliances* are based on contractual agreements and entail any form of cooperative relationship between two or more firms. The agreement can be more or less formalized and either will emerge from the interactions of two or more firms or as the result of purposefully establishing a collaborative organizational relationship. Non-equity alliances are seen as being more akin to arm's-length transactions (Contractor and Lorange, 1988) and include, for example, long-term supply relationships, licensing arrangements and distribution agreements.

The distinction between equity and non-equity alliances does not, on its own, account for the many different types of alliance governance that firms employ to manage their partnerships. For example, Reuer and Ariño (2002) suggest that contractual agreements can change extensively with different forms of governance. Contractual arrangements in alliances are influenced by: aspects such as trust or relational quality (Wang and Nicholas, 2005); the specificity of alliance related investments (Reuer, 2005); and the purpose and type of alliance (Lui and Ngo, 2005).

Alliance contracts also differ in their complexity given varying environmental, situational and behavioural conditions. A common difference is made between contracts that are implicit and those that are explicit:

● *Explicit contracts* in alliances determine the roles and responsibilities of each party, the allocation of decision rights, the ownership structure, the arrangements for different unforeseen events and the policies for a communication and determination of conflicts. The contract also encompasses regulations on various legal matters, such as for example confidentiality and non-disclosure agreements or ownership and licensing of intellectual property rights.

● *Implicit contracts* between partnering organizations are not always covered or enforceable by law, but by mutual interest of the collaborating parties; this includes, for example, trust or the desire to maintain a valuable relationship.

YOU CAN DOWNLOAD...

Steven S. Lui and Hang-Yue Ngo's (2005) The Influence of Structural and Process Factors on Partnership Satisfaction in Interfirm Cooperation, *Group & Organization Management*, 30: 378–97, from the book's website at www.sagepub.co.uk/cleggstrategy

When designing an alliance contract, the partnering organizations are usually faced with the fact that the more specific and complex the contract, the less room there is for opportunistic behaviour of the contract partners in the face of unforeseen events and, according to Ariño and Reuer (2004), the more costly it is to write it.

To manage the alliance jointly firms will usually agree on a shared structure, an assigned management or a delegated arrangement. In a shared management agreement, each partner fully and actively participates in managing the alliance. This type of arrangement is not easy to implement because it usually requires a high level of coordination and comprehensive agreements among parties. In contrast, under an assigned arrangement, one partner assumes primary responsibility for the operations of the alliance, which avoids the conflict and slowdowns that may be associated with a shared structure. Finally, under a delegated arrangement, which usually only applies to equity alliances or joint ventures, the partners agree not to get involved in ongoing operations and delegate management control to the joint venture itself. Executives may be hired from outside the operations to run the alliance, or may be transferred from the parent company, but in either case will have real power and autonomy in decision-making.

Joint ventures

A joint venture is an entity owned by multiple parent firms that is legally distinct from the parent firms. More broadly, it is an entity formed by two or more independent firms that choose to carry out an activity jointly rather than pursuing the project individually or by merging or acquiring entire business units. Joint ventures differ from mergers and acquisitions in that the entity has access to only a limited set of each partner's activities or operations, and there is no change in the control of the parent firms, which remain as independent firms with their own strategic goals and business interests.

While a non-equity strategic alliance requires no financial stake by participants, and is in general a much less rigid agreement, a joint venture encompasses a broad range of operations from a merger, such as set-ups to cooperation for particular functions, including research and development, production or distribution. The focus is generally upon the purpose of the entity and not the type of entity, meaning that a joint venture may be a corporation, a limited liability company, a partnership or other legal structure depending on a number of constraints such as tax and liability regulations.

One commonly cited motive for the formation of a joint venture is knowledge acquisition. A joint venture can be a vehicle to acquire specialized knowledge that would otherwise be very costly to acquire in a market-based transaction. Companies also use joint ventures to pool together their resources to obtain synergies in production or marketing, or gain efficiencies through vertical relationships. A joint venture can be an effective structure to permit a firm to enter into a new geographical market. This motive is common to many international joint ventures where barriers to entry and cross-cultural difficulties can make entry by foreign firms difficult and very costly.

A joint venture can be managed in three ways: parent companies can jointly manage the venture, one parent can manage the venture alone, or an independent team of managers can be hired to run it. Particularly when partners choose an equal ownership and management structure, a joint venture can be unstable. When, for example, two partners each hold a 50 per cent interest in equity and the cash flow that is generated by the joint venture, subsequent shared decision-making, and the possibility of frequent negotiation or bargaining, can make the concept of control in a joint venture elusive.

Joint ventures are typically broader in scope and will have a longer duration than other types of strategic alliances. Yet, the duration of a joint venture is on average five years, with the most frequent reason for termination being the acquisition of the joint venture by one of the partners or the failure of the joint venture (30 to 61 per cent). Joint ventures involving government partners are seen as particularly risky, showing a higher incidence of failure than their private sector counterparts, and, overall, any joint venture faced with a situation of highly volatile demand or rapid change has a very low chance of success.

TYPES OF COLLABORATION

Strategic rational

There are various ways of further classifying the type of alliance beyond the equity/non-equity criterion. As suggested by Barney and Hesterly (1996), alliances are usually motivated by the partnering firms' strategic intents, such as a focus on exploiting economies of scale; gaining a low-cost entry into new markets; learning to enhance a firm's knowledge base; managing uncertainty, costs and risks; or facilitating tacit collusion. Hence, a further classification of alliance type may follow the strategic rationale underlying the formation of the alliance and the subsequent level of mutual commitment to the alliance by partnering firms:

- A *sales alliance*, for example, occurs when two or more companies agree to go to market together to sell complementary products and services. This is perhaps the most common form of alliance. Consider the case of a bank and an insurance company. The insurance company may offer to make an exclusive offer available to only the bank's customers if it includes the offer along with the next bank statement that is sent out. While the bank gains through offering a good deal to its customers, the insurance company benefits through increased customer numbers, and customers gain through receiving an exclusive offer.

- Another type of alliance is the *solution-specific alliance* where two or more companies decide jointly to develop and sell a specific marketplace solution. Consider the earlier mentioned case of IBM and Cisco, which jointly provide business customers with on-demand voice solutions.

- Finally, in a *geographic alliance* two or more companies will come together jointly to market or co-brand their products and services in a specific geographic region. In many cases, alliances between companies will involve two or more of the above types of alliances. For example, with the strategic aim focused on selling solution-specific products to a particular region, there can be an overlap with respect to the aforementioned types of classifying alliances.

Completeness of contract

Another way of classifying alliances is according to the completeness of the partner's mutual contractual agreements:

- *Comprehensive alliances*, for example, involve the participants' agreement to perform multiple stages of the process by which goods and services are brought to market. Because this type of alliance requires that firms engage across multiple functional areas such as finance, production and marketing, comprehensive alliances are often based on complex contractual agreements or structured as joint ventures. While comprehensive alliance agreements are probably the fastest growing form of strategic alliances, these can be difficult to arrange.

- *Functional alliances*, on the other hand, are less complex and will have a narrower scope involving collaboration, for example in only a single functional area of the business. Typically, functional strategic alliances will include production alliances, marketing alliances, financial alliances and R&D alliances.

- In a *production alliance* two or more firms will each manufacture products or provide services in a shared or common facility. Production alliances can also be in the form of technology *cross-licensing* agreements where trademarks, intellectual property and trade secrets are licensed to a partner firm. While this is a low-cost strategy to enter foreign markets, the downside of cross-licensing is the potential loss of control over the technology as well as possible exploitation.

- Hence, firms may agree on *production licensing*, which only allows a partner to manufacture and sell a certain product. Usually each licensee will be given an exclusive geographic area. Compared with building a firms' own manufacturing facilities and distribution networks, production alliances are a lower risk strategy to expand the reach of a firm's products and services.

- In a *marketing alliance* two or more firms will share marketing expertise or services. Typically, this type of agreement involves one partner introducing its products or services into a market in which the other partner already has a presence. Affiliate online marketing, for example, has grown over recent years, with the most successful online retailers such as Amazon using it to great effect.

● An *investment alliance* involves firms that collaborate to reduce the financial risks associated with a project. The risk may be reduced when financial contributions towards the project are shared or when one partner provides the bulk of the financing while the other partner provides special expertise or makes other kinds of contributions.

● A *research and development (R&D) alliance* involves an agreement whereby the partners commit to undertake joint research to develop new products or services. This type of arrangement has evolved as a result of short technology lifecycles and high R&D costs.

● A *public–private partnership* (PPP) is a special type of alliance that involves one or more privately owned firms and a government organization. This type of collaboration occurs, for example, because a firm may be pulled into an alliance with a government if the country in question does not permit wholly owned foreign operations or is a centrally planned economy. Another important motivation for PPPs is their potential to achieve significant cost reductions in the delivery of services for governments (e.g. Worenklein, 2003). In fact government contracting with the private (or non-profit) sector is now regarded as the second most common form of public service delivery (Brown and Pitoski, 2003). PPPs have spread globally, and many governments now use them to deliver services, as an important strategy in both developed and developing economies, sponsored both by regional and national governments, as well as supranational organizations, including the International Monetary Fund and the World Bank. In a context where international financial rating agencies assess national and sub-national governments' economic performance, and influence the resulting investment decisions on the basis of governments' capacity to maintain a balanced budget, PPPs are very attractive because they deliver services while minimizing public indebtedness. PPPs, as a preferred strategy towards this end, potentially enhance governments' international and domestic standing.

MINI CASE STUDY

Hazel Dooney – not a hard sell

Hazel Dooney is one of the Asia–Pacific region's most controversial young female artists. According to the *Australian Financial Review*, she 'walks the razor's edge between respect and celebrity in today's artworld' (September 2006). Her work has been exhibited at shows in Australia, the United States, the UK and Japan and is included in private,

corporate and institutional collections around the world. In her widely read personal blog, Self Vs. Self (www.hazeldooney.blogspot.com), Hazel writes thought-provokingly and provides further information about her work and the market dynamics in the arts industry. In a comment on her involvement with auction houses she gives a great example of an informal, but very valuable collaboration in the arts:

(10 October 2009) On Friday, the Head of Art at a respected Australian auction house, Menzies Art Brands, emailed to tell me that two more of my early works have been consigned for a sale

(Continued)

(Continued)

on December 16. Later, we spoke on the phone about the condition of the paintings, their history, and more generally, about the archival properties of enamel paint. A couple of years ago, my opinions about my own work were dismissed by a rival auction house. Now my insights and expert knowledge are sought by senior staff members at all that sell my work – and these days, my work is included in nearly every major auction of Australian art. When my work is offered by Christie's, in London, I'm in regular contact with their staff – a number of whom follow this blog.

The first time I ever had anything to do with an auction house was when Menzies Art Brands emailed me for permission to reproduce my work in their print and online catalogues. If I hadn't been representing myself, I wouldn't have heard a word. The staff were surprised when I went to the sale preview to check the condition of the work for a collector who was interested in buying it and they were gob-smacked when I emailed additional, useful background information. However, it didn't take them long to 'get' it. Now, the information I send is included in the print catalogue, where my work is always given prominence.

My independence from the traditional primary market has had only positive effects on the regard for my work – and me – in the secondary market, where the financial value of even the most famous artists' works and reputations are tested in public. The idea that artists who manage themselves aren't taken seriously in this market is as dead as the Dodo. No matter what old-school commercial galleries keep telling us, contact between independent artists and even the largest auction houses is not just accepted – it's welcomed. Auction houses recognise that artists who understand the function of auctions and who care not only about the condition of work offered for sale but also about contributing to its long-term value are a resource that enhances their efforts.

Remember, too, artists don't make any money on the sale of work through the auction house, which is usually acting on behalf of collectors who insist on anonymity even from the artist. However, we work together on the basis that the interests of the auction house, the collector and the artist are parallel. Commercial galleries do their damnedest to discredit artists who work outside the traditional system – the so-called primary market – because they believe a lack of complete control will undermine the influence (such as it is) they exert on their collector base and their income. It's a shortsighted and stupid attitude. As collaborations between artists and auction houses are demonstrating – look at Damien Hirst's incredible pre-crash marketing and sales coup with Sotheby's – the benefits for galleries who work with artists on equal terms far outweigh the meagre risks.

Questions

1 How would you characterize the type of collaboration described in the case?
2 What are the benefits for the artist, owners, collectors and auction houses by collaborating in the way described?
3 How is value created through collaboration in this case?

HAZEL DOONEY, 2001. HIGH GLOSS ENAMEL ON CUSTOM-MADE BOARD, 100CM × 150CM. © HAZEL DOONEY (WWW.HAZELDOONEY.COM). USED WITH PERMISSION.

Image 10.1   Sex Drugs Whatever

Overall, different forms and types of strategic alliances are a more common and economically important form of cooperation than, for example, mergers and acquisitions. Where these alliances are between firms that might also be competitors in some other spheres, then they are sometimes referred to as examples of co-opetition.

ALLIANCE LIFECYCLE

The process of forming an alliance is complex, involving at least two, and perhaps many more, already complex organizations, as partners or owners. Depending on previous and existing transactions, relationships, skills, strategies and various other contextual conditions, any description of such a process must be seen as stylized and frequently violated. In reality, the process of collaboration is likely to be compressed in some stages, extended in others, simultaneous when predicted to be sequential, and otherwise unwilling to be placed on a neat timeline. However, the evolution of an alliance can be explained using the concept of an alliance lifecycle. The idea of the alliance lifecycle makes reference to separate stages of collaboration and the role of the partners and alliance managers at each stage. These lifecycle stages can be defined ranging from two stages of pre-incorporation and post-incorporation for joint ventures (Newbury and Zeira, 1997) to an 11-stage model (Parkhe, 1996). Dyer and his colleagues (2001) discuss five alliance phases: alliance business case development; partner assessment and selection; alliance negotiation and governance; alliance management, and alliance assessment and termination (see Table 10.1). Spekman and co-authors (1998) captured the emergence, growth and dissolution of alliances in seven stages: anticipation, engagement, valuation, coordination, investment, stabilization and decision.

From a strategic perspective, alliance formation stages (including, for example, anticipation, engagement and valuation) represent the partnering firms' resource picking, whereas alliance management stages (including, for example, coordination, investment and stabilization) represent capability building within the alliance. Alliance lifecycles, whether they consist of two, four, five or eleven stages, reflect managerial processes that account for differences in managerial behaviour and the changing role and influence of the alliance manager over time. Accordingly, the successful functioning of alliances has different requirements during different evolutionary stages.

TABLE 10.1 Stages in alliance formation

Foundation		*Development*		*Maturity*		*Termination*	
The alliance is in the formative stage – partners are just beginning to understand each other's needs and objectives		The alliance is growing closer – partners have developed mechanisms to coordinate efforts and align goals and objectives		The alliance is strong – partners have a common view of business and are managing joint affairs to mutual satisfaction		The alliance is mature – it is beginning to show some signs of strain due to changes in goals and/or market conditions	
Anticipation	Engagement	Valuation	Coordination	Investment	Stabilization	Decision	End
Pre-alliance competitive needs and motivation emerge	High-energy, strategic potential, goal congruence	Focus on analysis, financial issues, business case	Focus on operations, division of work and parallel activities	Commitment and reallocation of resources, broadening of scope	Focus on maintenance, assessment of value and partner contribution	Strategic evaluation and decision of future direction	The alliance has ended
Business Case	Selection	Negotiation and Governance	Alliance Management			Alliance Assessment and Termination	

SOURCE: BASED ON DYER (2001) AND SPEKMAN (1998)

Alliance foundation

Once the decision to collaborate has been made, a firm will start to consider partners. Geringer (1991) suggests that the alliance foundation stage is critical since partner choice influences resource availability and the viability of the alliance. At this stage real costs will begin to be incurred, as the focal firm approaches potential partners to evaluate their true value and mutual fit. Hence, search costs can vary widely, depending on the experience of the firm, the complexity and specificity of the assets that are involved, the number of possible partners and related concerns.

A number of factors can influence the firm's choice for or against a potential partner. Das and Teng (1999) suggest that fit between partners can be either complementary or supplementary. Complementary fit implies sharing distinct resources, for example in alliances between large firms with access to capital and market know-how and small innovative firms. Supplementary fit, on the other hand, implies pooling matching resources to reduce costs and improve efficiencies. In another study on partner search and selection criteria, Hitt et al. (2000) find that firms in developed markets often emphasize unique competencies and local market knowledge as criteria for partner choice. Hence, the selection of an unskilled partner, or a partner with incompatible systems, or a partner that is unwilling to expose its critical assets will not add value to the alliance, but will still be costly. Other studies also suggest that alliances between strong firms are likely to be successful while alliances between strong and weak firms or between weak firms tend to fail (Bleeke and Ernst, 1991). Thus, the identification of strong and capable partners is critical.

Another important aspect in the alliance foundation stage is the assessment of the integrity of a potential partner. Gathering information about partner integrity is important since moral hazard concerns that can arise from opportunistic behaviour by a partner can lead to unforeseen costs and alliance failure (Balakrishnan and Koza, 1993). A related aspect to consider is the extent to which the partner's goals are compatible (Das and Teng, 1999). Difficulties in identifying genuine strategic objectives will increase due to their changing nature over time. Hence, the network of prior alliances often serves as an information guide in the choice of potential partners (Gulati, 1995). A partner may, therefore, be preferred due to prior relationships or ties that have demonstrated both strategic and operational fit.

When a partner is selected the subsequent negotiation of contractual agreements and governance models (see earlier in this chapter) must balance the inherent requirement for control with the advantages of flexibility in order to take full advantage of collaboration and its anticipated strategic benefits. The contradiction of the negotiation task is that the more organizationally embedded and tacit the resources are that the partners hope to share, the greater the potential value of the alliance, but the more difficult it is to negotiate a complete contract. Prior ties can mean that there is a degree of trust between the partners; however, the ambiguity that is part of sharing complex resources also makes contractual negotiations difficult and the agreement of coordinating mechanisms more complex. The successful final outcome of the foundation stages is the choice of an appropriate partner and an agreed alliance contract that in some way determines the governance of the partnership.

Development and maturity

The next stage of the alliance process involves developing, monitoring and managing the ongoing partnership, the operational stage eventually determines the success or failure of the partnership. Given the high failure rate of alliances that has been reported in the management literature over the past decade (of up to 50 per cent), this stage is without doubt the most difficult to master. However, there are many organizations that collaborate successfully. Researchers who studied both alliance failures and successes suggest that experience and dedicated alliance management functions within the parent firms (Kale, Dyer and Singh, 2002), comprehensive contracts and good governance (Poppo and Zenger, 2002), a suitable contribution of resources (Robins, Tallman and Fladmoe-Linquist, 2002), the right balance of control and ownership, compatible organizational cultures, and mutual knowledge exchange and learning enhance the chances of successful and long-lasting collaborations.

Further aspects that alliance partners should consider include the agreement of procedures to deal explicitly with conflict between partners (Doz, 1996) and cross-cultural differences (Kale et al., 2000). Kogut (1988), for example, suggests that greater cultural distance increases the propensity for alliance formation since he found that in global joint ventures cultural differences between a firm's home country and the foreign location in which it is operating lead to a greater rate of contractual governance modes as opposed to equity ownership. While in such a context a non-equity alliance is generally more difficult to operate (Almeida, Grant and Phene, 2002), the required local knowledge might be bound up with the country's context and can only be accessed through a partner who is also embedded in the context. In addition, relying on the local context, alliance partners can develop important skills including staffing, trust building, resolving conflicts, transferring resources and know-how, training and renegotiating agreements that are part of managing the partnership at this stage (Simonin, 1999). Moreover, to build cohesive and high-performing alliances it is recommended to employ dedicated alliance management teams that are responsible for creating a strategic alignment, a shared governance system and managing interdependencies between the firms (Bamford, Ernst and Fubini, 2004). Similarly, a dedicated strategic alliance function that coordinates all alliance-related activity within each partner organization can help institutionalizing processes and systems to teach, share and leverage prior alliance management experience and know-how throughout the company (Dyer et al., 2001).

Overall, agreeing a good contract and building superior alliance management skills can help avoid considerable losses through alliance strategies. Contracts need not be comprehensive, especially if previous relationships and related levels of inter-organizational trust compensate for more complex agreements; however, alliance management capabilities at both the alliance level and the organizational level are the key to successfully implementing alliance strategies. During the development and maturity stages of the alliance lifecycle, alliance partners will generally seek longevity and stability, in order to fulfil the objectives of the original alliance strategy. However, even successful alliances may need to undergo changes as the relationship evolves, which leads to the last stage, the termination of the alliance.

Termination

Serapio and Cascio (1996) suggest that knowing when and how to exit an alliance is critical to a firm's achieving collaborative objectives without compromising other competitive aspects of its operations. Hence, alliance termination usually occurs due to the achievement of the alliance objectives, but also because partners realize

Competency traps lead firms to fall unconsciously into an adherence to routines and a denial of the need for change. They lead them to rely on past successful processes that may no longer be optimal.

that they were not able to manage complementary resources, create anticipated synergies or adjust to changing circumstances, evolving roles or the changing inter firm relationship. Other authors (Simonin, 1999) also assert that organizations that do not prepare exit strategies in time may either fall into **competency traps** or find that their collaborators are ready to exit when they are not.

It is, hence, important to understand how the alliance evolves over time, how the partner's relative contribution changes, and the original deal, even if profitable, might become no longer good enough (Zajac and Olsen, 1993). Alternatively, the reevaluation of the collaboration and adjustments in its structure and objectives by renegotiating the agreement can lead to new and better results. In fact, some authors suggest that a repetitive sequence of negotiation, commitment, execution stages (Ring and Van de Ven, 1994) and associated learning and subsequent adjustments (Doz, 1996) advances the collaboration through, for example, alterations to contracts, governance structures and monitoring mechanisms (Reuer, Zollo and Singh, 2002). Yet another option is the acquisition of the alliance partner (Vanhaverbeke and Noorderhaven, 2002). In this case one partner clearly considers full control of alliance assets and know-how by integrating the alliance into the organization as the best way to achieving strategic advantage.

Alliance termination does not mean that the alliance has failed to deliver its outcome; if the objectives of the alliance are accomplished or a changing market or evolving capabilities have made the venture no longer rational, then termination is the preferred outcome. Similarly, if the alliance has greater value for one partner than the other, for example due to differential learning, changing strategies, new opportunities or simply different assessments of value, then an acquisition is a good outcome too. Finally, only when an economically viable partnership is terminated because of distrust, disagreements, impatience or other relational issues can it be considered as an alliance failure. Firms that build their partnerships on experience, contractual mechanisms for renegotiation, mediation or arbitration, organizational units with specific responsibilities for maintaining relationships, and the like, will contribute to a better understanding of potential and actual alliance issues and more effective solutions to alliance agreements that might no longer be a good fit. While the termination of a particular contractual agreement may not mean the end of the alliance, renegotiation, termination and acquisition must be recognized as logical steps in the lifecycle of collaborative strategies.

QUESTION TIME?

1 What are the characteristics of different stages of the alliance lifecycle?

2 Under which circumstances is the acquisition of an alliance partner a good idea?

3 What can firms do to increase the possibility of alliance success?

COLLABORATING THROUGH POLYPHONY

Collaboration requires communication – but with whom? Typically, strategy-making has been an elite pastime, but there are some suggestions that the better strategies will be those that are most inclusive and broadly based in terms of collaboration; in other words, collaboration that is polyphonic.

The idea of polyphony refers to the many voices that constitute organizational strategy. Organizationally, polyphony is always present, even though it might be silenced by a dominant discourse. We cannot take the absence of dissent for the moral authority of a genuine legitimacy in which all of those concerned will assent to everything.

Strategies for organizations are discursively constructed and reconstructed through language: they are spoken, written, embodied and otherwise encoded and recorded. Organizations, and those within them, are narratological, according to Brown (2000). Integral to the sensemaking process is the way in which organizational actors will seek to craft and reproduce narratives that are both robust and inscribed with a claim to verisimilitude. Usually, in most organizations, there is a persistent polyphony that shapes organizational reality. While organizations may well be scripted through missions, strategies and so forth (Barry and Elmes, 1997), there are too many directors (i.e. finance, marketing, human resources) for only one script to be followed. Organizations are an arena in which multiplicities of simultaneous and discontinuous dramas occur, the sense of which we make up as we go along, using familiar cues, props and plots.

Organizational polyphony is a major resource for innovation and development, such that when top management produces homogenizing grand narratives they can hinder and eradicate, rather than enable, organizational success. As organizations are powerfully constituted and constantly enacted through languages, a mutual deconstruction of meaning rather than its closure through a grand narrative is thus the precondition of change. Such a mutual deconstruction of meaning entails a translation of terms from the one to the other, from the many possibilities to the central strategy.

This translation can be understood as a form of mediation between different and contradicting languages and the realities they constitute. It has the power of *invention*: during its unfolding it modifies and changes both languages. It is the driving force behind organizational change and development. Like (jazz) improvisation, translation is a play that implicitly changes the grammar and the words (see Hatch, 1999; Zack, 2000; Kamoche, e Cunha and da Cunha, 2002). Jazz improvisation can be described as a curious and hesitating way of exploring and exploiting new patterns while old ones proceed. Like translating, it is a movement from the known and established to the new and yet unknown. In order to do so improvisers and translators both follow a particular process – they carefully vary existing patterns and look for new venues emerging and evolving during improvising. Like improvisation, translation helps us linguistically 'to maintain the images of order and control that are central to organizational theory and *simultaneously* introduce images of innovation and autonomy' (Weick, 1998: 548). Translation reflects on the past, 'original' text while exploring new implications in a process in which the ongoing action can still make a difference. The process produces not so much a right or wrong translation – although some may work better than others in specific contexts – because every single attempt can be a point of departure for a new understanding. Translation is always provisional (Benjamin, 1982: 74), on the way to making sense, constituting strategy from different perspectives.

While more conservative theorists would argue for a strong hand that needs to direct organizational strategy and prevent it from chaos, the concept of translation offers an alternative position: it builds on polyphony, but simultaneously suggests a way of managing it by translating between different languages that constitute organizations. Translation, thus, offers a constructive way of dealing with differences.

Translation does not imply speaking on behalf of other people, as we have seen. Speaking for others implies defining a common ground and identifying a common perspective. Of course, this exercises power since differences might get lost while someone claims to represent an issue better than the people directly affected by it. Translation works on a different level: it does not identify or unify but takes the differences between languages and tries to deal with them in a constructive way. It does not speak for someone else but repeats what someone has said in a different language. The translator does not become the author but stays in the background. Of course, this is still a powerful process, but rather than claiming to represent a standpoint for others, the translator has to explore different ways of linking languages between different people. Whereas speaking for someone else implies knowing their position and expressing it accurately, translation is a much more hesitating and improvisational process. There can never be something like a perfect translation: it is always a 'provisional way of coming to terms with the foreignness of languages' (Benjamin, 1982: 75). The language of translation never fits perfectly; rather, it moves, folding and unfolding, enveloping and developing, and, with every single move, there (dis)appears a new, yet hidden reality. Far from

MINI CASE STUDY

Video Case Study – translating the City of Sydney

Alan Cadogan says, 'the consultation never stops'. Alan leads the City of Sydney's Strategy Unit and also led the Sustainable Sydney 2030 project – Sydney's long-term vision for a sustainable future. What he refers to is the continuous practice of interacting with multiple stakeholders in the strategy formulation process. When defining Sydney's vision for the future the council engaged in a process of intense consultation with its people and included a range of other agencies, partners, consultants as well as the neighbouring councils and a team of Sydney's best minds in urban planning, architecture and design. Over 12 months the internal strategy team and an expert consortium hosted more than 30 community forums, round-table discussions, business forums and City Talks; received more than 15,000 website visitors, and more than 2000 comments over the phone. People of all ages and backgrounds expressed that they wanted an environmentally sustainable city, one in which people can feel at home and yet connected to the world; a city whose thriving economy positions it as a global centre of excellence, while supporting a rich and creative culture. People want a city that continues to respond, adapt to and manage the issues and challenges of climate change and a global economy. Further down the track, when implementing strategy, the collaboration continues. Alan emphasizes that coordinating and managing collaboration is at times difficult but more effective

in the long term. A key to success is to build trustful personal relationships. Since many activities within a city are different from what business organizations deal with, it is at times a challenging entity to organize. The City of Sydney's internal strategy team had to gain expert knowledge in areas such as sustainable energy supplies to enable and encourage implementation at all levels. Watch the video and answer the following questions.

Questions

1 A range of partnering organizations' objectives motivates collaboration. What are typical reasons to engage in collaborative strategies and why does collaboration seem to be the better option?

2 The City of Sydney pursues a collaborative approach for designing and implementing the city's vision for the future. What are the roles of stakeholder consultation and involvement for the development and success of collaborative strategies? Give examples from the video.

3 Collaboration can take many different forms ranging from loose information sharing to joint organizations with equity stakes and formal contracting. Discuss different forms of collaborating and their advantages and disadvantages for the partnering organizations.

4 The ongoing management of alliance relationships is a key to successful collaboration. What are some elements of successful alliance management that are mentioned in the case study? What other elements can you think of?

5 How can strategy formulation as a collaborative effort help in implementing the strategy?

transporting a clear-cut message from one point to another, translation creates a bridge between differing language games that shape organizational reality, deferring to both of them. As the video case study of the City of Sydney's strategy demonstrates, polyphony can be a powerful tool in developing strategy (see www. strategytube.net).

ALLIANCING AND THE FUTURE PERFECT STRATEGY

One form of alliance that has been rapidly developed in recent years is known as alliancing. Here the stress is less on the governance structure and more on the creation of appropriate processes. Alliancing builds on polyphony – but it also seeks to ensure that it is a disciplined polyphony that is tightly coupled. This coupling is achieved by an extreme sensitivity towards projects as something to be accomplished and completed.

We first came to know about alliancing in the context of preparations for the Sydney 2000 Olympics (Pitsis et al., 2003, from which the following account is taken). A decision to undertake a major project in the runup to the Sydney 2000 Olympics was taken as a part of the NSW Government Waterways Project in May 1997, designed to clean up NSW rivers, beaches and waterways. Cleaning up the waters of Sydney Harbour was seen as a priority for the Olympics in 2000 given that the 'eyes' of the world would be on the city in just over three years time. The proposal sought to capture sewerage overflows that occurred during Sydney's sub-tropical storms, when storm water backs up the sewage system and overflows into the harbour, bringing in not only raw sewage but also street detritus such as litter, syringes and dog faeces. The main detail of the project was to build approximately 20 km of tunnel in the sandstone under very affluent areas north of Sydney Harbour.

At the time of commencement, relatively little was known about the ground conditions and the tunnel had not been designed. Given the tight time frame, the availability of tunnel boring machines (TBMs) was critical, as these had to be sourced on a sub-contract from elsewhere in the world. The first stage of the project, of about 18 months, involved a detailed exploration and design phase. Without this, the contractual risks arising from latent conditions would have been unacceptable to any government client. That made completion in an extraordinarily short period of time vital, obviating against a conventional strategic planning process; instead, a constant process of thinking through the future perfect was implemented. The process comprised imagining a future and then seeking to realize it, subject to constant revision, an approach that seemed inductively to fit Schütz's (1967) conception of the future perfect.

The degrees of ambiguity and uncertainty inherent in the project were high because of the deadline, the lack of engineering information, the lack of information about the characteristics of major pieces of technology (the TBMs) and also the characteristics of the communities affected by the project. Because of the more than usual degree of uncertainty, the project was to be managed in a unique way. Instead of a tender process, where the entire project has to be specified in advance and those specifications made public for community comment, Sydney Water invited expressions of interest from companies willing to enter an alliance to deliver the project. The specifications were only 28 pages in length (unheard of in conventional construction where the bill of works and associated contractual documents can run into many thousands of pages). As the project would involve concurrent engineering, much of the design was unspecified. Specified in detail were the agreed principles that the partners were to commit to as the means for resolving issues within the alliance. These differed markedly from traditional detailed construction contracts with the prospect of arbitration when agreement broke down. A typical approach to selecting partners for the alliance was followed (cf. Stiles and Oliver, 1998), choosing the partners on the basis of their commitment to the process envisaged.

Having thought of the usual way of doing things, with the usual problems that this might entail, with worst and best case parameters, the project partners then set about trying to think of extraordinary ways of creating the desired outcome. The outcome was easily encapsulated colloquially: 'a lot less shit and rubbish in the harbour' and sparkling blue water for the TV cameras covering Olympic sailing and swimming events, as well as, in the long term, less pollution generally for residents and tourists. The detailed design of the tunnel was commenced by the alliance once it was established in early 1998 through first defining a *Business As Usual (BAU)* case, using conventional scenario planning approaches: the outcome that would be most likely to occur with the project if it was designed and constructed through traditional planning methods, such as reverse scheduling. But the project partners wanted to do much better than this: they wanted breakthrough innovations. The alliance partners sought to imagine the project in terms of outcomes that were so good that everyone benefited: the marine life in the harbour (which was a potent symbol in the project iconography); the residents around the foreshore and above the tunnel route; the local communities with whom they would interact in the process; the Olympics organizers; public works contractors throughout the State of New South Wales; and the employees, contractors and clients themselves – the members of the alliance. An innovative approach to organizational collaboration framed their thinking and action.

Management consultants experienced in large-scale construction projects helped design a project culture. The consultancy assumed that the alliance would only achieve its objectives if staff at all levels shared the same values, believed that the project was 'something special' and had only its ultimate success in mind – rather than sectional strategic interests. The consultant recommended that cohesiveness could be fostered through creating a project culture that was explicitly designed and crafted to encourage shared behaviours, decision-making and values. (The design and functioning of this culture is addressed at greater length in Clegg et al., 2002.) A list of value statements was produced by the PALT (Project Alliance Leadership Team), which comprised the formal statement of the culture: the two core values were striving to produce solutions that were 'best for project' and having a 'no-blame' culture:

- Build and maintain a champion team, with champion leadership, which is integrated across all disciplines and organizations.
- Commit corporately and individually to openness, integrity, trust, cooperation, mutual support and respect, flexibility, honesty and loyalty to the project.
- Honour our commitments to one another.
- Commit to a no-blame culture.
- Use breakthroughs and the free flow of ideas to achieve exceptional results in all project objectives.
- Outstanding results provide outstanding rewards.
- Deal with and resolve all issues from within the alliance.
- Act in a way that is 'best for project'.
- Encourage challenging BAU behaviours.
- Spread the alliance culture to all stakeholders.

The project team sought to exceed *BAU* expectations and achieve outstanding results. In order to do this, they were constantly thinking in the future perfect: what would they have to have done to achieve an outstanding performance across the demanding range of indicators to which they had committed? When contrasted with the more traditional construction methods of the adversarial exploitation of contractual details for profitable advantage – which are not at all oriented to the future perfect, rather more the future imperfect – and the prospect of their ultimate resolution in arbitration, then the uniqueness of the project approach can be grasped.

The basis for the contractor and client benefit was a risk/reward calculation. The project agreement provided for a risk/reward regime based on performance compared with project objectives defined in terms of five key performance indicators (KPIs): not only *cost* and *schedule* – no surprises there – but also *safety, community* and *environment* – which are not usually part of construction KPIs. There was one non-negotiable performance criterion, the completion of the project for use by the Olympics. While the alliance had the responsibility of defining *BAU* objectives in terms of suitable criteria, there was no precedent for a construction project being assessed against such parameters. To ensure independence, external consultants were engaged to review the benchmarks for the non-cost/schedule criteria that had been developed by the alliance. For each area, performance levels, ranging from poor to outstanding, were defined – with the brief being simply to define outstanding through the future perfect – what would an absolutely spotless report card and review of the project require? The specialist consultants also regularly assessed and reported performance against all criteria throughout the project. Success against the non-cost/schedule criteria was critical for project success in both commercial and overall terms and, as such, this area presented the alliance team with significant risks.

There were positive and negative financial outcomes for performance on each of the objectives in the risk/reward process. Financial rewards were payable on a sliding scale for performance above *BAU* to *Outstanding*. All objectives, except cost, had a maximum amount. Financial penalties accrued when performance was below *BAU* and, most importantly, *the performance in any one area could not be traded off against any other area that was represented by the KPIs. Only an outstanding performance against all five KPIs would yield the maximum return*; less than this in any one area would diminish that return and an adverse performance would put the reward at risk as penalty clauses began to bite. To make the future perfect concrete meant constructing something that could be imagined as already complete and subject to audit. Thus, in each area performance processes and outcomes were constructed on which the project would be assessed.

The discipline of collective imagination of a future perfect, framed by the designer culture and bound by the governmental strategies of the KPIs and the risk/reward scheme, tied the loose coupling of the collaboration together, as regularly reported in the monthly PALT meetings. In addition, specific future perfect strategies were routinely used as management devices throughout the project. Three specific means of managing through the future perfect strategy were identified. These means included the creative use of *strange conversations*; the rehearsal of *end games and the practice of workshopping*; and the *projecting of feelings, concerns and issues*. Each of these adds to our knowledge of how the future perfect strategy is possible, and so we shall elaborate on them here.

Strange conversations

It was Karl Weick (1979: 200) who introduced the notion of strange conversations onto the management literature. Weick defined strange conversations as ones where the agenda, process and outcomes were unclear. A great many community meetings were associated with the project: in each of these, the agenda was unclear, the process highly emergent and the outcomes unknown. In these meetings community members were invited to surface anxieties and make suggestions in relation to the project (almost all of which took place beneath the surface, of which they had little knowledge). What they proposed was often a surprise that, in terms of the rationality of the engineers involved in the project, made little sense: for instance, they were concerned about the visual obtrusiveness of the above-ground works; the noise; mud on the roads; the potential loss of access for dogwalkers or for children to play. These were all secondary considerations for the engineers, intent on building the project.

The conversations were initially strange because the premises from which each of the two sides came were so different: initially some tensions occurred in some meetings. But these strange conversations helped to produce creative solutions to many local community relevancies, such as the diagnosis of the aesthetics of the works. One site was diagnosed as 'ugly' in conversations between the project and the community. That the community liaison officers would be addressing aesthetics was not an outcome that had been envisaged prior to these conversations. Often, in the initial meetings, it was unclear what it was that was being discussed, as the talk ranged so widely, in terms of the community members' emotional and aesthetic response to the engineering works. In fact, it was often the case that the eventual outcome informed what it was that the conversations had been about: for instance, once the proposal for the concealment and beautification of one of the sites had emerged, then it crystallized as what had been wanted all along, even though, at the outset, this had not been clear at all. Later in the project community liaison officers found themselves organizing barbecues between community and project members, where more such intriguing conversations occurred.

End games and the practice of workshopping

End games helped concentrate minds on the future perfect strategy in the project. End games occurred frequently, as the project completion was enacted in the future perfect. Here is an example that occurred at the January 2000 meeting, when a project leader reminded everybody of the objectives. He said:

> We know where we want to be, where we want to go, and where we want to finish up. We need to plan the end and work out each step to get there so everything is synchronised. We need ownership over the deliverables at the end of the project. The ultimate project is the built product.

It was the absence of the usual project pre-scoping and its incorporation in a complex bill of works that made the project unique. It was designed as the process unfolded – an unfolding that did not always develop according to expectations. For instance, in March 1999, one project leader exclaimed, 'It comes down to we have lost 10 weeks but we have only been on the job for 26 weeks!' This particular project leader then complained that suggestions being made on how to deal with the slippage were reactive. The project leaders needed to be more proactive in orientation. He seemed to suggest updating their future perfect planned strategies. Implicitly, he said that they should still project the infrastructure as something that would be built by 31 July 2000. At the same time he also suggested that they should plan backwards for the 78 weeks that were left for this particular phase and take into account that they had only accomplished the amount of work budgeted for 16 weeks in the previous 26 weeks. So, while the original planning had been based on 104 weeks, they would now have to plan as if they had never had more than 94 weeks (of which only 78 were now left).

At the August 1999 PALT meeting, where slippage on the completion date was at issue, one of the project leaders used the end game technique to challenge his colleagues to think in future perfect terms:

Look, I'd like not to have a stretched target. Where will we really be in 2 or 4 weeks? Think hard about what you want to be judged on. What are those numbers you want to be associated with? You know that this will come back to you. We will ask you, have these forecasts been met? What will you say?

The answer, which was simply 'We can meet it', was clearly not what he had hoped for:

Don't set a stretched target and miss it. If you cannot meet it, change it now. I mean we are going to have a very serious discussion with government. We will say to them, we need to increase time, increase costs, because you stuffed us up. They will say OK, but cross-examine us first.

He wanted them to project themselves into a future where – as the end game – government agencies would question them and then think backwards towards the present. How would they cope? How would they feel? He knew that the project would be judged by the outcome and wanted them to think backwards from the outcome. A representative of an indirectly linked organization, who only attended that one particular PALT meeting, stated this bluntly:

Well, I can guarantee you PALT members one thing! The Minister will ask what day you will finish, if you are not finishing on the day you said you were going to finish. You will have etched this into stone, on a report and you will be judged on this date!

He was told that there were contingency plans and that working with machinery was, at best, like a lottery. Another project leader also insisted on future perfect thinking at this meeting by asking, 'If we were meeting the Minister tomorrow, what would we say the finishing date would be?' The project leaders responded by agreeing 'OK, by such and such a date we will have had a risk analysis on the schedule done.'

The significance of end games was that they worked as aids for visualization of the future perfect and enabled the PALT to focus on the future perfect they were seeking to construct. One of the key techniques used to maintain this future perfect focus on the end game was workshopping. When it looked as if the project might run over schedule, the PALT team agreed to have a workshop to address the alignment of the five key objectives between headquarters and construction sites (PALT meeting, June 1999). They agreed that by the time of the workshop, one of the project leaders would have met with the programme managers responsible for the key objectives. He would have discussed the alignment of the overall objectives with those of the particular construction sites. Additionally, he would have codified the learning breakthroughs at each construction site, so that they could identify how they had reached their outstanding achievements. Further, he would have discussed the workshop agenda with management consultants and would have arranged a workshop venue. Once again, the PALT engaged in a future perfect strategy.

Projecting feelings, concerns and issues

Although the PALT team were almost all engineers, people with a technical background who were more professionally versed in technical rather than social construction, there was some explicit recognition of the importance of social construction in one aspect of the PALT meetings. The agenda for each meeting had originally contained a section titled 'Projecting Feelings, Concerns and Issues'. We were rather surprised when we first saw this in action: we had not expected such empathetic and social maintenance work from highly professional engineers. Any member could raise anything under this recurring agenda item, with the issue remaining on the agenda until 'it was no longer important or was addressed to the satisfaction of the person who raised the issue in the first place'. The inclusion of this clause was supposed to ensure that future perfect thinking maintained a reality check: if an issue had been constructed in regard to any aspect of the project that was causing concern, then it was reiterated monthly, until it was no longer a matter for concern. While some of these feelings, concerns and issues were quite technical – about scheduling and such like – others concerned more complex community relations.

The technique was significant – it ensured that the future perfect agenda was open and democratic in its projections among the top leadership team. It managed polyphony. It created a space in which emotional aspects of the project could be discussed (Fineman, 1996; Albrow, 1997). Increasingly, the routinized use of the item, which, after a while, became merely a matter for noting rather than action, and was then later abandoned, signalled the limits of future perfect thinking when confronted by community matters that were outside project control.

Both the social and material reality changed in the Olympic project. Materially, a major amenity and piece of infrastructure was developed, while, socially, a shared culture was built to deliver it, around what the researchers came to characterize as a future perfect approach. Most research (e.g. Rollier and Turner, 1994) stresses the quantity and quality of a priori strategies in securing exceptional outcomes. In this project, there were no detailed a priori strategies, other than those constantly reconstructed through the future perfect. Hence, there was no strategic plan other than the frame of the future perfect and the risk/reward scheme that accomplished it. Work was constructed imaginatively on an unfolding basis that continually re-scoped the future perfect without reference to any original guiding design but with reference to a set of criteria on which the entire process would be judged. The project occurred despite the stillbirth of that strategic planning usually done by theoreticians, who will make decisions early on, based on minimal information, yet lock the process into an inevitable and unquestioned future. Instead, the people who had the greatest opportunity to alter the outcomes were those who made the strategy up as they went along; normally they would be locked into protecting the decisions already made for them through tactics that would invariably lead to litigation. Rather than using detailed project scoping and planning to reduce high ambiguity, as is typical of construction (Stinchcombe, 1985), the PALT project leaders sought to reduce it through creating a shared culture that enabled future perfect thinking to flourish in an imaginative process oriented to a broad range of imagined outcomes by which they would hold themselves accountable.

Future perfect thinking worked most smoothly where the planners had most control – that is, control of the technological and material context for future action. When external actors were empowered to question, achieving the future became more difficult. There were pitfalls in allowing for such a voice but not in providing the accompanying responsibility that would increase the potential for a project to become hijacked. While project managers may adumbrate a strong culture they need to avoid being sucked in by its rhetoric and realize that it does not necessarily incorporate all stakeholders.

The client selected its suppliers on the basis of cultural fit and technical competence rather than price; it then defined its needs in performance terms and empowered the team to develop the best solutions possible. In contrast, in the traditional approach strategic planning is finalized with limited information in advance of the project team being selected and the solution is locked in early, thereby limiting creativity during delivery. It represented a shift in strategic decision-making onto the people who could make the difference.

The project grew from just 28 pages, with no design and no clauses, other than an injunction to think in the future perfect and create a much cleaner Sydney Harbour, into a project that delivered what it had set out to do: on time, only slightly over budget, it made Sydney Harbour sufficiently clear that in July 2002, in an ecologically symbolic representation of the success of the project, three 80 tonne whales came into the harbour to frolic under the famous Sydney Harbour Bridge, with the equally famous Opera House behind them, although cynics might remark that the clarity of the water was due to an extensive drought. In living memory whales had never ventured this far into the harbour before: the Olympic dream appeared to have been spectacularly realized.

SUMMARY AND REVIEW

In this chapter we first analysed approaches various underlying motivations for why organizations engage in collaborative strategies. Firms will use alliances to reduce risks, enter new markets, gain knowledge or achieve synergies. Most importantly, though, firms will seek partnerships because they want access to resources that they deem important for creating competitive advantage.

Rather than organically growing capabilities a partnership with another firm promises quick access to such needed factors as knowledge, technology or local markets. However, the benefit of having quick access usually comes with an increased need for coordination. The issues and implications of contractual agreements and subsequent governance for alliance have been discussed in detail and point out how different types of alliances including equity or non-equity alliances, functional alliances or public–private partnerships have different advantages and disadvantages. A firm has to be aware of such structural and contractual choices before entering into negotiations with potential partners. The concept of the alliance lifecycle emphasizes the importance of a stepwise approach and reoccurring negotiations for agreeing the optimal alliance contract, the ongoing operations of alliance management and finally the partner's awareness of when to exit the partnership.

Collaboration can be a complex matter of translation and polyphony, rather than a straightforward linear process, as the example of the City of Sydney strategy demonstrates. Finally, we have concluded by adumbrating the polyphonic approach, and used the case study of the Sydney Olympics infrastructure as a case in point.

EXERCISES

1   Having read this chapter you should be able to say in your own words what the following key terms mean:

  ● Collaboration
  ● Alliance
  ● Strategic alliance
  ● The alliance choice
  ● Alliance governance
  ● Equity alliances
  ● Non-equity alliances
  ● Joint ventures
  ● Different types of alliances
  ● Alliance lifecycle
  ● Polyphony
  ● Future perfect strategy.

2   How would you try and design an alliance?

3   What are the major issues to manage in an alliance?

4   Why and how does the argument from polyphony differ from that which proposes a need for a strong culture?

5   International NGOs (Non-Governmental Organizations) such as Greenpeace or Human Rights International, as well as civil society organizations (CSOs), such as the various anti-globalization movements, also engage with states, transnational corporations and global institutions. Often, the assumption is that these NGOs and CSOs will have contested relations with these other actors; however, this is not necessarily the case. Look at the case study for this chapter and the interview with Steve Shallhorn at www.strategytube.net. How does Greenpeace, as a global CSO, strategically interact with those organizations in which it has a stake?

ADDITIONAL RESOURCES

1   Our companion website is the best first stop for you to find a great deal of extra resources, free PDF versions of leading articles published in Sage journals, exercise, video and pod casts, team case studies and general questions and links to teamwork resources. Go to www.sagepub.co.uk/clegg strategy

2   James Bamford, Benjamin Gomes-Casseres and Michael Robinson's (2003) book *Mastering Alliance Strategy: A comprehensive Guide to Design, Management, and Organization,* San Francisco: Jossey-Bass, is a very pragmatic yet comprehensive collection of best practices for building and managing alliances.

3　Another useful resource is Morten Hansen's (2009) book *Collaboration: How Leaders Avoid the Traps, Build Common Ground, and Reap Big Results*, Boston, MA: Harvard Business School Press. The book provides interesting insights on how some leaders successfully implement collaborative practices and realize better performance for their organizations.

4　Don Tapscott and Anthony Williams' bestselling (2008) book *Wikinomics: How Mass Collaboration Changes Everything*, New York: Portfolio, provides an in-depth analysis of how collaboration has revolutionized business worldwide and how firms have developed the means to harness a collective capability and genius to spur on innovation, growth and success.

5　The full account of the Sydney Olympics project can be found in Pitsis, T., Clegg, S.R., Marosszeky, M., Rura-Polley, T. (2003) 'Constructing the Olympic Dream: Managing Innovation through the Future Perfect', *Organization Science*, 14:5, 574–590.

WEB SECTION

Visit the *Strategy* companion website at www.sagepub.co.uk/cleggstrategy

1　The online resource www.strategytube.net that the authors produced in tandem with this book is a great resource: look at the video of Case Study 10 where Alan Cadogan talks about collaborative strategy development for the City of Sydney.

LOOKING FOR A HIGHER MARK?

Reading and digesting these articles that are available free on the companion web site www.sagepub.co.uk/cleggstrategy can help you gain deeper understanding and, on the basis of that, a better grade:

1　Namgyoo K. Park, John M. Mezias and Jaeyong Song (2004) A Resource-based View of Strategic Alliances and Firm Value in the Electronic Marketplace, *Journal of Management*, 30: 7–27. This study relies on the resource-based view to examine how alliances of e-commerce firms affected firm value in an emerging business sector.

2　Steven S. Lui and Hang-Yue Ngo (2005) The Influence of Structural and Process Factors on Partnership Satisfaction in Interfirm Cooperation, *Group & Organization Management*, 30: 378–97. In this study, the authors investigate the relationship of structure and process with partnership satisfaction in interfirm cooperation.

3　Devi R. Gnyawali, Jinyu He and Ravindranath ('Ravi') Madhavan (2006) Impact of Co-opetition on Firm Competitive Behavior: An Empirical Examination, *Journal of Management*, 32: 507–30. The authors examine how co-opetition affects firms' competitive behaviour.

4　Koen H. Heimeriks, Geert Duysters and Wim Vanhaverbeke (2007) Learning Mechanisms and Differential Performance in Alliance Portfolios, *Strategic Organization*, 5: 373–408. This study assesses the differential performance effects of learning mechanisms in alliance portfolios.

5　Benjamin Gomes-Casseres (2003) Competitive Advantage in Alliance Constellations, *Strategic Organization*, 1: 327–35. In this article the author discusses what determines the profits of an alliance constellation.

6　R. Duane Ireland, Michael A. Hitt and Deepa Vaidyanath (2002) Alliance Management as a Source of Competitive Advantage, *Journal of Management*, 28: 413–46. In this paper the authors examine the management of strategic alliances using the theoretical frames of transactions cost, social network theory and the resource-based view.

7　C. Jay Lambe, Robert E. Spekman and Shelby D. Hunt (2002) Alliance Competence, Resources, and Alliance Success: Conceptualization, Measurement, and Initial Test, *Journal of the Academy of Marketing Science*, 30: 141–58. This research examines the effect of alliance competence on resource-based alliance success.

8　Jeffrey J. Reuer and N. Africa Ariňo (2002) Contractual Renegotiations in Strategic Alliances, *Journal of Management*, 28: 47–68. This study provides an empirical investigation of the incidence and antecedents of contractual renegotiations in strategic alliances.

9　Hong Ren, Barbara Gray and Kwangho Kim (2009) Performance of International Joint Ventures: What Factors Really Make a Difference and How? *Journal of Management*, 35: 805–32. This article presents an in-depth review and critique of previous research on international joint venture (IJV) performance over the past 10 years.

CASE STUDY

Arts collaboration: Menagerie – Contemporary Indigenous Sculpture

Meghan Hay

Menagerie is a collaborative arts project between Object, the Australian Centre for Craft and Design, and the Australian Museum. Throughout 2008 and 2009 these two Sydney-based organizations developed a major touring exhibition of animal-form sculptural works by Aboriginal and Torres Strait Islander artists from across Australia. The resulting exhibition, *Menagerie – Contemporary Indigenous Sculpture*, featured more than 50 outstanding new works by 34 prominent artists, demonstrating the breadth of contemporary indigenous sculptural practice.

The exhibition was presented in Sydney from September to November 2009 in both Object and the Australian Museum's exhibition spaces:

> We had to think about what it might mean for the two spaces. Does one space get all the lizards? Do we go by state? We really wanted a more equitable division, knowing that some visitors may see one space and not the other, and that's what we've tried to achieve says Bliss Jensen, from the Australian Museum.[1] After its Sydney presentation, the exhibition embarked on a two and a half year tour to nine cities around Australia.

Although in the past there has been a sustained public interest in the contemporary paintings of Aboriginal and Torres Strait Islander artists, sculptural works have often taken a back seat. The exhibition put together by Object and the Australian Museum has marked the beginning of a significant new emphasis on current trends within the medium of sculpture. The works are created from a range of materials including fibre, ceramics and wood carving along with some bronze and aluminium casts, and all of the artists selected cover a broad geographical spectrum. 'This significant

---

[1]Interviewed by Joanna Lowry, www.timeoutsydney. com.au/museums/event/12985/menagerie-contemporary-indigenous-sculpture.aspx

exhibition is the most extensive survey of contemporary Indigenous sculpture to tour Australia. Menagerie celebrates the art and culture of Aboriginal and Torres Strait Islander people and demonstrates the sophistication and diversity of Indigenous art, craft and design in Australia,' says Object Director, Steven Pozel.

Not long after its success in Sydney the Australian Museum Foundation announced that it considers *Menagerie* so important that the foundation had decided to purchase the entire collection to ensure that the works remained together permanently and were thereby accessible to the public. Such an acquisition not only sends a very positive message to the artists but also generates significant income directly to artists contributing to both individual communities and the sustainability of the sector generally.

Why has this collaborative effort been so successful? One reason clearly lies within the overall strategic significance of the project and its objectives. *Menagerie* is important because it is one of only a very few exhibitions of this scale to focus exclusively on indigenous contemporary sculptural practices when formerly other forms of indigenous artistic expression like paintings, dance and storytelling have been more commonly featured. Given this gap in the market of exhibition and the strategic opportunity, Object and the Australian Museum aimed to showcase the significance of sculpture within contemporary indigenous art, craft and design.

Other objectives included the celebration of the diversity that Australia's indigenous cultures have to offer by showcasing the work and personal stories of a selection of outstanding artists, the acknowledgement of the importance of people's relationship with animals and the unique and diverse environments that we share with them, to promote a greater understanding of Aboriginal art and culture through integrated educational programmes, and, finally, to create opportunities for indigenous people.

The initiative for *Menagerie* came from Steven Pozel and Brian Parkes, the Director and Associate Director of Object, who knew that Object had the knowledge and ability to conduct the project research, select the artists and the works, produce the publication that would accompany the exhibition and manage a national touring programme. However, the organization was facing some organizational limitations: Object's exhibition space was not large enough to accommodate the expected size of the show, nor did Object have the conservation experience that would be necessary to catalogue

(Continued)

(Continued)

and protect the anticipated works. Knowing that they would need a partner to turn an inspiring idea into reality, Steven and Brian started looking out for potential candidates to collaborate with. With its focus on nature and culture, the availability of significant exhibition space in Sydney in close proximity to Object's location, as well as its notable expertise both in cultural object conservation and in putting together large-scale projects, the Australian Museum was the perfect organization to approach with the *Menagerie* proposal. However, despite a history of cross-promoting shows and co-presenting public programmes, the two arts organizations had never collaborated on a project before.

In 2008, a memorandum of understanding was signed outlining the way in which both organizations would bring their respective strengths to the project. This comprehensive agreement outlined crucial relationship parameters such as the legal structure of the venture, the process for decision-making, and the division of project management responsibilities and cost responsibility, as well as the specific allocation of duties relating to the development, design, production and presentation of the exhibition. Subsequently, during the two-year project development period, other key partnerships developed that supported the dynamic between Object and the Australian Museum.

One example of such a partnership was the one forged with Sydney's Taronga Zoo, which became involved with the creation of an engaging and inspiring children's education programme, one of the key initiatives for the project. While Object and the Australian Museum worked together to create an education kit for primary school students and teachers that would help communicate the skill of the artists, their cultural heritage and their passion for the natural environment, it was the partnership with the famous Sydney-based zoo that brought the learning programme alive. Through this collaboration, primary school students visiting the exhibition at Object would first meet zoo staff outside the gallery who would then introduce the students to living native animals. The children would get to touch the animals and learn about their habitats and their relationship with humans. The students would then spend some time in the gallery, viewing the indigenous sculptural interpretations of similar animals to the ones they had just met, and then have the opportunity to create their own animal sculptures in the gallery space, surrounded by the artists' sculptures. During the two-month exhibition period, over 800 children were able to share this experience in Object's modest, inner-city gallery space.

Overall, audience responses recorded through visitor evaluation surveys in both venues indicated very high levels of visitor satisfaction with the content and nature of the exhibition. More than 100,000 people saw the exhibition while it was in Sydney.

The exhibition has received significant media coverage in each of the cities in which it has been presented thus far. Critical reviews of the show have been overwhelmingly positive. Moreover, through the project, numerous indigenous artists found their work promoted to a national audience and received income in the form of artist and photographic reproduction fees.

Questions

1 Thinking of this collaboration in terms of this chapter, how would you classify it? Why?

2 All alliances involve stakeholders: who were the stakeholders in this case and how did they each receive value from the alliance?

3 What potential downside for the future do you see arising from the alliance for the indigenous stakeholders? How might this be rectified? What difference would you suggest making to the alliance to protect the future interests of the indigenous stakeholders?

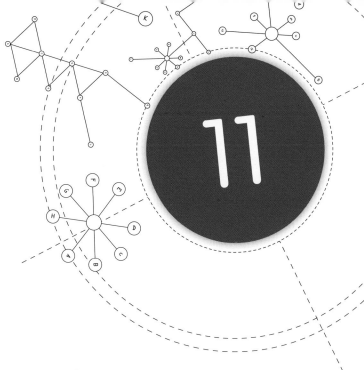

Financialization, Risk and Accountability

Capitalism, economies, crisis

LEARNING OBJECTIVES

By the end of this chapter you will be able to:

- Understand the development of and subsequent crisis in monopoly capitalism
- Comment on the events and ideas that precipitated the rise of neo-liberalism
- Discuss the emergence of the shareholder value movement
- Evaluate the central contours of financialization
- Critically assess the role private equity firms have played in capitalism over the last decade
- Provide an explanation of the causes of the global financial crisis
- Debate the extent to which we live in an audit society
- Assess the ramifications of reactivity to rankings and understand the implications of league tables for strategy-making

(HTTP://WWW.FT.COM/CMS/S/0/51EE3F18-199B-11DF-AF3E-00144FEAB49A.HTML ACCESSED 23RD JULY, 2010)

BEFORE YOU GET STARTED . . .

During the property bubble, when quick profits were
there for the taking, the bankers rushed in, oblivious to the hidden
risks. When the entire system was tottering, the authorities opened the
public purse to prevent a disaster. … That is what makes the current
situation so disturbing. It is not the product of criminality, myopia or
idiocy but of distorted market incentives, misguided government policies
and utopian economic ideas – three things deeply enmeshed in our
financially driven economy.

Money is the lifeblood of the economy, and unless it circulates
readily, the essential economic activities go into the
equivalent of cardiac arrest.

(GILLIAN TETT, 2009: 28)

INTRODUCTION

That we live in a capitalist world is beyond dispute. Many fete capitalism, while for others it is associated with inequality and unfairness. Whatever one's views of capitalism it forms the backdrop against which strategy-making takes place. This is not merely a comment on private sector firms because logics honed in and abstracted from capitalist relations of production also extend to the public sector and NGOs alike. It is important, therefore, for students of strategy to have an understanding of capitalism. Given that most readers of this book will live under capitalist systems, we all have an intuitive sense of how it works. We take for granted its core concepts, such as profits, dividends, bankruptcies, for instance. More than that, however, we understand that economies seem to operate according to a business cycle that moves from boom through to bust. We also understand that capitalism has periods of stability, where everything seems relatively benign, at least to those of us living in the West, followed by periods of crisis, such as has been experienced in recent years. During periods of crisis capitalism has sometimes appeared to be on the brink of collapse, as many thought would be the case after the First World War as well as in the early 1930s and, for a few observers, during a short period in the autumn of 2008.

Economists use the term capital to denote all the economic activity of investment, production, marketing and distribution that organized profit seeking activates. Capital is restless, constantly seeking higher returns, lower costs and new profit opportunities. If we seek to understand the way in which firms relocate their production operations or their call centres to lower cost parts of the world, this is an instance of the logic of capitalism at play. Equally, hospitals deciding not to carry out particular medical procedures because of cost considerations represent a triumph of capitalist logic over the Hippocratic oath, of economic rationalism over social need. Over the last 20 years, for reasons that will be outlined in what follows, the interconnections between the flow of ideas, people and money have intensified, with capital becoming much more footloose.

In this chapter we will deal with the contemporary world in which strategy is articulated; for many the defining feature of this world is the global financial crisis. The current global financial crisis is the latest in a series of crises that have beset capitalism. It is a rude reminder that rhetorically intensive claims made by large organizations need to be subject to critical scrutiny. For instance, the Royal Bank of Scotland (RBS) and HBOS were two organizations that made wild assertions about their success as global banks. For the most part, analysts, government and others were happy to join in the fanfare applauding the financial institutions. Now the reality looks somewhat different.

We will argue that the crisis was, in large part, an effect of strategies of financialization. We will also argue that understanding financialization is of central importance for contemporary strategists. To do so means digesting a fair bit of recent history but we think this is important and necessary because, as has often been remarked, those who do not know history are condemned to repeat it – but the second time around as tragedy. There has been a great deal of forgetting of history in recent times. Both the Asian financial crisis of 1997 and the Enron collapse of 2001 provided indications that all was not well with the global financial system and modes of audit and regulation. Yet these lessons were not heeded; instead they were explained away as anomalies of a system that was otherwise fit for purpose. What is clear now is that these episodes should have sounded serious alarm bells in the finance ministries and boardrooms of the world.

Financialization represents the current stage of capitalism. Capitalism, the most dynamic, creative and innovative system for organizing economic activity that the world has seen, is an evolving project that has become the dominant mode for organizing economies in the contemporary world. The evolution of capitalism has been marked by stages in which different logics have been dominant. Capitalism, as a *dominant* organizational form, has enjoyed little more than 200 years of supremacy, though, of course, it has a much longer history – for instance, Luca Pacioli's *Summa* chronicled the bookkeeping practices of Venetian merchants in the Middle Ages (Sangster, Stoner and McCarthy, 2007). Capitalism has swept away feudalism, outlasted Soviet communism and, in recent years, been embraced by the People's Republic of China. However, there is no such a thing as capitalism *per se*, in a pure sense: there are instead many different kinds of capitalism (Clegg and Redding, 1990); for instance, there is that which is found in the *entrepôt* of South-East Asia, or in the gangster capitalism of the former Soviet Union, or in the welfare capitalism of Scandinavia – these are all quite different from one another. To be a worker, a manager or an investor in these environments means very different things.

The golden age of capitalism

Richard Sennett (2006) points out that for much of its history capitalism has been a highly unstable form, highlighting the way in which mid-nineteenth-century London capitalism was associated with high levels of bankruptcy and unemployment. Further, he argues that it was only in the golden age of Western capitalism – circa 1945 to 1973 – that it was consistently able to deliver high levels of profitability and stability.

A specific organization form was associated with this golden age. Chandler rightly argued that the twentieth century saw the creation of the large, multi-divisional firm. In his seminal work he documented how family firms were bought out or merged to become large organizations. It was during this epoch that much of our modern strategic management emerged. The connections between strategic tools such as Igor Ansoff's product/market growth matrix and the expectation of there being stable markets are clear. Most large-scale organizations were heavily engaged in the production of things, such as automobiles or white goods, which consumers of that period demanded. The relatively benign and stable market conditions meant that large organizations could engage in strategic planning in relatively predictable conditions. Strategic plans became a means of trying to manage and control the future. This era, especially in the 1960s, witnessed the growth of corporate planning as we currently conceive of it.

Baran and Sweezy (1996) characterized this period as one of monopoly capitalism – a period where a small number of large firms experienced growing surpluses. For instance, they document that in the mid-1960s General Motors was highly profitable and accounted for some 1 per cent of US GDP. Large institutional shareholders, such as pension funds or insurance companies, owned these firms, which had long passed out of family ownership. The ownership patterns were comparatively stable: Sennett (2006) found that in the late 1960s large institutional investors, on average, held stock for 4.2 years. The companies they bought stock in were often referred to as 'blue-chip' companies – those that were large and, in general, fairly safe investments. Of course, these companies were no longer run by owner–managers but were instead managed by a new breed: the salaried executive.

Across the Western world the rise of the business executive occurred. Typically, large and powerful institutional stakeholders paid little attention to the actual running of the firms; by common consent this became the domain of executives and strategic managers who were not owners of the business but were charged with creating profitable strategies that maximized shareholder returns. Fund managers of the various investment companies employed a strategy referred to as 'portfolio theory', which advocated holding a range of investments from the very risky, such as start-up ventures, through to the very safe, such as US treasury bonds. Fund managers as portfolio theorists would seek to outperform the market average. Hence, an investment manager who made 1 or 2 per cent above the market average was considered successful. There was a close connection between this form of capitalism and the multidivisional organization. A head office could choose to invest, consolidate or divest assets in a division. Equally, each division would possess an Ansoffian-style strategic plan.

From the early 1970s, when there was a conjunction between the huge US deficits used to finance the Vietnam War with a significant rise in oil costs due to the formation of the OPEC oil-producers cartel in the wake of Israel's victory in the Six Day War, the system of monopoly capitalism founded on stable expectations about the future was undermined. Simultaneous inflation and large-scale increases in unemployment occurred, something that had previously been thought of as mutually exclusive by most economists of the time. As a result of these, new policies were applied from a more purely economically liberal school of economics than the previously dominant Keynesian brand of macro-economics. These policies, associated intellectually with people such as Milton Friedman and politically with Prime Minister Thatcher in the UK and President Reagan in the United States, gave rise to the era of neo-liberal capitalism, based on monetary economics. The central policy device of monetarism is the control of the rate of inflation through control of the money supply.

The triumph of neo-liberal capitalism

Monetarism became the dominant global institutional ideology of those committed to neo-liberalism. There is not an explicit or coherent theory of neo-liberalism (Plant, 2009). Nonetheless, it is a widely used and accepted term with common referents. At its core the ideas of neo-liberalism revolve around a specific conception of the state that regards its primary role as safeguarding the free market and extending that market to the provision of as many goods and services as is possible. Hence, neo-liberalism privileges big business over other concerns and aims to deregulate markets and promote free trade, something that has actively been pursued in the West, leading to the rapid growth of world markets. In the poor South, however, it was very often imposed on the developing world through bodies such as the World Bank or the International Monetary Fund (IMF).

The global nature of economic thought is well illustrated by the case of monetarism: a number of Chilean economists were trained under the tutelage of Professor Milton Friedman, at the University of Chicago. Following the 1973 US-backed coup against the democratically elected Allende government, the Chicago Boys, as they became known, set about redesigning the Chilean economy and society – run by General Pinochet. In economic terms, Chile became a laboratory for Milton Friedman's economic ideas. The results added flesh to his theoretical bones, thus animating a living theory that pugnaciously challenged the Keynesian body of thought and associated policy apparatus.

The journey from Chicago to Chile was just the beginning. As Western economies – especially those of the UK and United States – struggled in the 1970s, in part due to declining international competitiveness but also because of the oil shocks of that era, faith in Keynesian economic orthodoxy began to wane. Monetarist ideas began to gain greater prominence and legitimacy, promising a means of generating economic growth while simultaneously controlling inflation. With the election of Margaret Thatcher in the UK and Ronald Reagan in the United States in 1979, monetarist ideas moved centre stage and began to exert a hegemonic grip on both economic policy and the political imagination, ushering in an age of neo-liberalism where governments privatized, commercialized and generally tried to roll back the frontiers of the state. Assets were freed up and switched to private enterprise, where, it was believed, the discipline of efficient markets would see more effective strategies for their management than the bureaucratically heavy hand of government and the state.

Capitalism enjoyed a long period of stability in the postwar era that the 1970s crisis ended – at least in the Anglo-American context. The postwar political settlement had as its central tenets the full employment, social cohesion and economic growth that Keynesian economics had helped deliver since the 1940s. Monetarists or neo-classical economists rejected Keynesian notions of demand management to maintain full employment. Instead monetarists saw the key element of economic policy to be controlling inflation and leaving the rest, including employment, to the market, which they regarded as the most efficient means of allocating resources. Economic musings, combined with the philosophy of Friedrich Von Hayek, made for a powerful cocktail that was to dominate mainstream economic thinking from the mid-1970s until the most recent global financial crisis.

An intense interest in strategy, as a practice for managers and an academic subject in universities, emerged in the 1970s. One might argue that this was, in part, fuelled by the ongoing sense of crisis that developed at that time. Strategy is, perhaps, a symptom of a larger problem, signalling that all is not well in the corporations and that, unlike in the era of long-range planning, stable markets could not be taken for granted. Old-style strategy no longer seemed to work. Authors such as Michael Porter sought to understand the nature of competition between firms and how their comparative advantages could be assured.

The 1970s became a decade that political economists regarded as one of the periodic 'crises of capitalism'. Rather than large capitalist organizations generating surpluses, they began to lose money and, in turn, large institutional investors saw the value of their assets diminish. Huge amounts of capital were decimated, yet more was devalued as inflation became rampant. The golden age of capitalism had shuddered to a halt. While the claims of various governments to have transformed the economic fortunes of their countries became subject to serious and critical scrutiny, it became clear that the nature of capitalism in the West had changed. Many Western economies that had fallen under the thrall of economic neo-liberalism began a process of deindustrialization and thereby became ever more reliant on the sale of services rather than industrially manufactured products. The modern UK is a typical example: its manufacturing industries have largely disappeared, with the provision of services taking the place of making things. The dominant sector in the UK and elsewhere became the financial services segment of the economy.

FINANCIALIZATION

Fuelled by financial globalization (see Chapter 12) capitalism became footloose, easily switching production from one continent to another. This, in turn, has bolstered the power of finance capital at the expense of the power of organized labour; the process by which this occurs is referred to as financialization.

Financialization refers to the processes through which the logic of finance capital has accrued great power and penetrates increasing parts of the corporate world, in particular, and civil society, more specifically.

Randy Martin defines it thus: 'Financialization integrates markets that were separate, like banking for business and customers, or markets for insurance and real estate. It asks people from all walks of life to accept risks into their homes that were hitherto the province of professionals' (2002: 12).

In terms of strategy, the effects are evident: companies such as Ford and General Motors ceased to make profits from manufacturing cars so much as lending the finance to customers to purchase the cars they produced. The industrial economy in which useful things were made was being overtaken by the financial economy in which capital circulated with increased velocity, creating frenzied movements of currencies and other instruments of exchange. Martin finds that

> as the mass of money available as investment outstrips the amount invested in industrial capacity, through stock markets and their ilk, money seems to be made out of thin air (and disappear back into the same ether). (2002: 192)

The era of monopoly capital, dominated by large industrial corporations that made things, gave way to an economy of signs where the most important signification was capital *per se* and it mattered little what it did so long as it increased in value. The era of neo-liberalism was at hand.

Shareholder value

During the period of transition to a neo-liberal economy questions began to be asked about the quality of senior management. A common critique of management emerged, identifying managers as not necessarily having the same interests as the shareholders on whose behalf they were acting. Economists refer to this as the principal/agency problem. Simply put, this view holds that principals (such as shareholders) have difficulty in controlling the actions of agents (such as senior managers). The corollary is that such agents might act in their own interests with no guarantee that these would be aligned with those of the principals. What does this mean in practical terms? An example would be a chief executive pursuing an aggressive takeover strategy: it might be that the strategy delivers little in terms of extra value to the shareholder, but establishes the CEO as a major business celebrity. As a means of trying to counteract this so-called 'agency problem', accompanied by more general concerns relating to flagging business performance, the shareholder value movement emerged.

The central premise of the shareholder value movement is that business executives should be made far more accountable for the performance of the firms they manage. Following from this, institutional shareholders became far more assertive and aggressive in the demands they made of the companies in which they owned shares:

- Institutional shareholders became more vocal in the press and also at investor meetings.
- The average time a fund held a stock reduced dramatically; in the United States, for instance, this went from 46 months in 1965 to 3.8 months in 2000 (Sennett, 2006).
- Portfolio performance expectations were replaced by more stringent market criteria (instead of accepting that there were different rates of return in different industries, all industries were now under pressure to perform to a market norm).
- Stock prices became the most important measure of performance, displacing the prevailing performance norms, such as price/earnings ratios.

The shareholder value movement placed greater emphasis than ever before on short-term performance. In order to 'incentivize' senior management – or, perhaps, to turn them from mere employees to being part owners of the business – stock options became an increasingly important component of executive remuneration. Shareholder value privileged the notion that the overriding responsibility of senior executives was to deliver value for shareholders. Increases in a company's share price came to be seen as an important measure of firm performance – displacing more traditional measures such as the return on capital employed. The share price being used as a performance measure reflected the short-term view held of firm performance by financial markets: what mattered was that a share could be sold at a profit after a short period of time, rather than laying the foundation for sound growth over time.

MINI CASE STUDY

Enron

Enron is a classic example of a firm using short-term economic results to create the impression of being a hugely successful organization. Enron executives were able to convince Wall Street that they were highly profitable. Enron's share price increased exponentially, attracting more investment. Hard-nosed analysts were seduced by the intense corporate rhetoric of Enron and, to all intents and purposes, suspended their critical faculties. Bonuses in the company were based on increases in the share price, which led to staff engaging in activities that inflated the share price. Accounting sleights

of hand helped facilitate this process: techniques such as *gain-on-sale* accounting, which allowed estimated future profits to be booked in the present, and *off balance vehicles*, which enabled debt to be hidden from the eyes of investors. Both of these accounting techniques led to a surge in the share price. McClean and Elkind (2003) referred to Enron as an 'It company', by which they meant it enjoyed special status on Wall Street, the corporate equivalent of being a Champions League footballer, a film star or a supermodel, perhaps. Indeed Enron was cast as a company of the future. While its own slick public relations operation helped manufacture this image, it was further aided by *Fortune* magazine, case study writers for Harvard Business School and strategy gurus such as Gary Hamel (2000). Institutional investors wanted to purchase Enron stock and invest in Enron projects, bright business school

(Continued)

(Continued)

graduates wanted to work for Enron and governments were keen to be close to Enron. For instance, many commentators have pointed out the close links between the Bush dynasty and Enron. Enron was at the hub of a powerful network that served to reinforce its claims about itself. Enron claimed to have rewritten the rules of finance, and for a time many believed it.

From the vantage point of financialization, Enron created an image of an asset-light, innovation-driven, highly profitable organization. Small wonder Enron's rhetoric proved seductive to investors. That said, many stalwarts of Wall Street were more wary. James Chanos, of Kynos Associates, expressed scepticism towards the Enron model, arguing that using basic investment ratios indicated that Enron's profits were mere fantasy. In March 2001, before Enron's spectacular collapse, Bethany McClean wrote an article in *Fortune* magazine asking whether Enron was overpriced. Her argument was that Enron's accounts were virtually impossible to decipher and it was far from clear as to how Enron actually made its money. Around the same time Jeff Skilling, the Enron CEO, used an expletive to describe an analyst who asked why Enron, unlike other *Fortune*-listed companies, were unable to release an earnings statement with their quarterly accounts. Unfortunately for Skilling, his microphone was still on and his comments were broadcast around corporate America. This was another sign that all was not well with Enron. The company collapsed in the autumn of 2001, it now being obvious that the company was loaded with off-balance-sheet debt and the much praised profitability was little more than fantasy accounting with profit figures plucked out of thin air. The much vaunted model of the new economy collapsed under the weight of its own indebtedness and criminality. Nemesis followed hubris.

Question

1 Research the evolving view of Enron as a successful enterprise, using a quality newspaper. What are the implications for strategists of the changing analysis?

Image 11.1 Wall Street

Karel Williams and his colleagues at the University of Manchester make a number of insightful observations relating to the performance expectations placed on companies:

1 Expectations about the return on capital employed (ROCE) have escalated to the point that managers are asked to 'deliver the undeliverable' (Froud et al., 2000: 80–110).

2 Shareholder value compares firms across different sectors and places similar performance criteria on them, which intensifies the pressure on 'lower performing' industries.

3 Firms that remain listed on the stock exchange are likely to experience far greater pressure from their shareholders over issues of corporate strategy, particularly as they are outperformed by private equity in the short term and as private equity sales yield huge surpluses in the mid-term.

4 Performance is narrowly conceived in financial terms and so strategy becomes increasingly oriented to just these variables, often as they are conceived in the immediate and short term.

5 There will be an intensification of managerial work as managers try and deal with the contradictions of their position as much more exposed in terms of an identification of the contribution they are making to revenue, in companies that can only too easily be sold out from under them if they are judged not to be 'performing'.

Many of these pressures can be seen at work in the case of Enron:

1 Financialization was accompanied with claims of a new and future-oriented way of organizing. Financialization was seen as a harbinger of a world to come, one that superseded the established ways of operating, which became an ideology that many normally hard-nosed analysts bought into almost as a matter of faith.

2 Financialization is often associated with extraordinary rates of return, which, as in the case of Enron, turned out to be fictional.

3 The processes through which profits are made are often obscure and complex. This was the case with Enron's financialization strategies. It should be fairly simple to understand how an organization makes its money. Financialization is often inextricably bound up with a 'crisis of representation' (Macintosh, 2002), where it is far from clear what the financial numbers actually signify.

Enron is the poster book example of an economy of signs at work. Craig R. Littler (2006) argued that downsizing programmes are often associated with the need to send a signal to capital markets that the firm is being efficiently and aggressively managed. We discussed the role of organizational initiatives such as business process reengineering in Chapter 3. Whereas at one time, Littler argued, major restructuring programmes and associated redundancies were taken as a sure-fire sign that a company was in trouble, today they are regarded as being the hallmark of a well-run organization. Simply put, the disruption and restructuring of an organization constitutes *de rigueur* practice in modern corporations. Also, as we learned in Chapter 8, there is now a much higher turnover of senior executives in organizations. The career expectancy of a senior executive has never been shorter. Equally, companies pay far more care and attention to their corporate communications and, as we saw in Chapter 5, pay more attention to branding the firm. Most large companies now also employ lobbyists and PR companies to help manage their relations with important stakeholders. What this points to is a much more impatient and restless capital than existed in the era of monopoly capitalism.

Publicly listed companies are under increasing pressure to maximize their returns for their shareholders. If they fail to impress, they are likely to be taken over or, at least, see a change in the top management team. The media constantly report on what the 'markets think' of a particular issue – such as the outcome of a political election – as if the market was a person with an opinion and a vote. Capital markets are, therefore, very powerful, wielding enormous power. In some ways the discipline exerted by financial markets on companies and on governments is an illustration of governmentality – which sets the rules of the game for companies. Peter Miller and Ted O'Leary (1987) have demonstrated how financial performance measures can be seen as a way of managing at a distance. What they show is that performance expectations from the City or Wall Street can have a disciplining and normalizing effect on senior executives. It constitutes them as governable persons looking for ways to make their numbers. While these strategic pressures were evident throughout the period from the 1970s onwards, they have intensified in recent times with the rise of private equity.

Private equity

YOU CAN DOWNLOAD...

A special issue of the journal, *Human Relations*, 63(9): 1279–1370, September 2010, with four papers that explore the impact of private equity buyouts on work and employment relations from the book's website at www. sagepub.co.uk/cleggstrategy

Before we look at contemporary private equity it is worthwhile to look back at the asset-strippers of the 1970s, when firms such as Slater Walker in the UK were in many important respects the direct ancestors of today's private equity firms. The asset-strippers' approach was to take over a company listed on the stock exchange and break it up, selling off parts and retaining the core business. In the process, they would make huge profits.

An example might be an asset-stripper taking over a brewery that also owned a chain of pubs and a hotel chain. Let us assume it paid £1 billion for the company. The asset-stripper then decided that it only wanted to retain the brewery and, subsequently, sold the chain of pubs for £300 million and the hotel chain for £500 million. By now it just owned the brewery, which was valued at £400 million. This process, in effect, meant that it had paid £200 million for something worth £400 million. Asset-strippers thrived in an era when many companies were international conglomerates – holding a range of different assets – and used historical accounting techniques that seriously undervalued many of their assets, especially land, which was often recorded at cost value rather than present value. Asset-strippers captured the imagination of the business media, especially in the 1980s. Characters such as Lord Hanson, at the forefront of the movement, were generally regarded as being charismatic (as well as publicity hungry) and, for a period, were lauded as breathing new life into industry. Hanson was, reputedly, Mrs Thatcher's favourite businessman. Our illustration above may seem pretty simplistic but it reflected the whole approach, which was, overall, lacking in sophistication. The important part of the operation was to identify those targets whose stock market value was markedly less than their real value.

The recession of the late 1980s and early 1990s put paid to the asset-stripping boom, generally thought to be a practice that had been consigned to the past; however, the noughties saw the emergence and boom of private equity as a variation on the theme. The idea behind private equity is to buy a company listed on the stock market, take it off the stock market, manage it aggressively so as to realize cost savings, and then sell the company after three to five years, thus making a large profit. Unlike asset-strippers, private equity concerns itself not just with buying and selling but also with managing – albeit for a fairly short period. Of course, buying a stock-market-listed company is not cheap and requires large amounts of finance. While relatively low interest rates in the early noughties meant financing was relatively inexpensive, it was the huge availability of credit that prompted the boom in private equity.

Thus, the last 10 years have seen the emergence of a very different type of capitalist organization: the private equity firm. Such firms have excited the media, horrified trade unions and, generally, attracted attention while concomitantly arousing controversy. They have characterized themselves as 'kickass capitalism' and been described by the German Chancellor, Angela Merkel, as locusts. The premise of private equity firms is that they can buy stock-exchange-listed firms and take them off the market, put in more aggressive and 'efficient' managers to run them, and realize additional value. A private equity takeover is often quickly followed by a bout of downsizing and cost cutting.

The ready availability of credit has been accompanied by a dramatic collapse in stock market values, making publicly listed companies cheaper to buy. These factors combined to create profit-making opportunities for private equity firms that manage with hard, lean and mean strategies. In a recent report by the Workplace Foundation, it has been argued 'that private equity firms have been able to extract previously hidden value in the companies they take over' (Thornton, 2007: 22). The privatized capital in private equity becomes altogether more clandestine and open to obfuscation. The reason for this is that private equity firms do not have the same disclosure requirements as stock-exchange-listed firms. By being delisted from the stock exchange, private equity firms are insulated from having to disclose their earnings and profits. Many stakeholders within civil society have argued that this results in an alarming lack of corporate accountability, such that it is very difficult to understand what an organization is up to, how it is funded and what its general sustainability is as an ongoing proposition. Is the value being sucked out of it to service debt and yield a substantial return when it is sold on?

Trade unions, especially, remain concerned that private equity leads to an intensification of work conditions, a reneging of pension agreements and an increased chance of being made redundant. Private-equity-owned firms comprise a significant chunk of the economy, with around 20 per cent of employees in the British private sector being employed by them. The big winners from private equity deals seem to be the private equity capitalists, the finance houses that put together the deals, and the managers that are brought in to run the firms. However, since the onset of the global financial crisis there have been far fewer private equity takeovers. And as we will see, many have struggled to refinance themselves.

Private equity strategy

Private equity strategy was simple: borrow heavily to buy a publicly listed company; take it private; reengineer the business; sell assets; restructure the debt; and, after 3–5 years, float the company on the stock market. This, if all went to plan, would result in huge profits for the private equity firm. The credit crunch has, however, posed many problems for private equity firms. Some of them might yet prove to be insurmountable. The most serious is the complete drying up of funds in the financial markets. Banks lacked the ability or appetite to lend to private equity firms, which left them flailing around attempting to secure new sources of finance.

There is a central question at the heart of private equity: why is it that private equity firms need to refinance? What was wrong with their previous sources of finance? This goes right to the heart of their strategy and business model. Most highly leveraged private equity deals have the provision for a 'bullet payment' – the

YOU CAN DOWNLOAD…

A paper that reviews the key issues involved in the debate about the financialization of the economy, by Andrew Watt and Béla Galgóczi (2009) Financial Capitalism and Private Equity – A New Regime?, *Transfer: European Review of Labour and Research*, 15(2): 189–208, from the book's website at www.sagepub.co.uk/ cleggstrategy repayment of a large amount of the original loan – after five years. Normally, this is of little concern to private equity firms as the business is generally sold on after 3–5 years. In the environment at the time of writing this chapter, many private equity firms have the prospect of bullet payments being triggered hanging menacingly over them. Private equity firms will need to find new ways of refinancing themselves – such as bond issues or even floating themselves on the stock exchange – or may find themselves hoisted on their own petard: losing out in the casino that is modern capitalism.

Much of the hyperbole associated with private equity firms in the heady days of 2006 and 2007 emphasized their superior management prowess, particularly when compared with the management team that had run the businesses beforehand. Private equity could unlock value it was claimed – value that the present team of managers were not capable of generating because they were insufficiently ruthless, avaricious or capable. A recent PricewaterhouseCoopers' report into private equity concluded: 'the burden of debt they are operating under has seriously restricted their ability to carry out their strategy'. In other words, poor business plans and feckless borrowing curtailed the ability of private equity firms to deliver the results they promised.

Private equity has been a notable feature of many economies in recent years, not least those of the UK and the United States. Gorged on debt and now struggling to survive, private equity's future is obscure. Has it ridden the noughties, boom only to be wiped out in the financial tsunami that has followed? Or will it prove more redoubtable, surviving the current crisis to become an enduring part of the economy? What is clear, however, is that capitalism will continue to throw up financially engineered strategies to try and realize higher profits. Equally, private equity, as a movement, crystallized how finance capital thinks companies should look, how they should be run and to whom they should deliver. In this regard, private equity is probably a harbinger of the strategies to come.

STRATEGY AND THE GLOBAL FINANCIAL CRISIS

From buccaneers to bankrupts

The representation of private equity has shifted from depictions of it as run by exciting, self-styled capitalist buccaneers to the buccaneers becoming seen as heavily indebted basket cases. Capitalism's fabled powers of creative destruction have destroyed their strategies. Take Terra Firma, for instance. In 2010 it was skulking around capital markets trying to raise some cash, which stands in sharp contrast to the high-rolling confidence of a few, short years before. The intervening factor has been, of course, the global financial crisis (GFC). The world economy was shaken to its very foundations in the later months of 2008. Indeed, the reverberations will be felt for many years to come. It was a salutary lesson on the extent to which the macro-environment can change abruptly, shattering the received wisdom about the nature of the economy. It was also a rude rebuttal of the notion that the economy could keep on growing.

Early writers on capitalism were fully cognisant of its inherently unstable nature. These lessons need to be learnt once again. Of course, unlike some natural disaster the financial crisis is humanmade, with some of its most respected and venerable institutions playing major roles. Noughties capitalism in the major financial centres of London and New York was characterized by easy credit and lax regulatory regimes. It is worth noting that other countries, notably Australia and Sweden – which brought in tight regulations following its own banking crash in the early 1990s – had significantly tighter financial regimes. In London, the City had traditionally been self-regulating and the 'New Labour' government was very happy to see it booming in order to demonstrate the government's market-friendliness. In many ways the success of the market could be seen as emblematic of their Third Way philosophy. In New York, Wall Street had waged a long campaign to free up its activities, many of which had been limited as a juridical response to the 1929 Wall Street crash. The Glass–Steagall Act – a legacy of the legislative response to the Great Depression – was repealed by the Clinton administration in the late 1990s. Retail banks were now able to engage in much riskier activities.

THE 2008 BANKING CRASH

Financial innovation had flourished during the noughties. To evade international banking regulations, which imposed strict lending limits based on the capital reserves held by a bank, banks developed various means of packaging their loans and selling them on to to third parties. As Gillian Tett put it:

> The J.P. Morgan derivatives team was engaged in the banking equivalent of space travel. Computing power and high-order mathematics were taking the business far from its traditional bounds. (2009: 7)

The combination of 'new finance', information technology and lax regulation made for dramatic changes in the banking market. This process was known as securitization.

While the property market was offering huge returns, for institutional investors such as pension funds, the stock market and bonds offered dismally low returns. In fact, the stock market, in major Western economies, lost nearly half its value in the early noughties in the wake of the dot-com collapse. This was at a juncture where the money markets were awash with cash, as sovereign funds and saver economies, such as China, sought to invest their money. Banks engaged in financial innovations to meet the demand from institutional investors for investments with higher returns. Their chief response was a product known as the collateralized debt obligation (CDO). In some cases, CDOs were being created out of existing CDOs in a product known as the CDO squared! The Bank of America, one of the largest global banks, started to use CDOs for mortgages.

The CDOs constructed out of mortgages were attractive to investors, largely because they comprised so-called sub-prime loans, which attract high rates of interest. The bank that had created the CDO from the sub-prime loans would sell it off in bonds, allowing institutional investors to make good the returns on their investments. A CDO worked as follows:

- A bank obtains monies on the short-term money markets.
- The bank gives a sub-prime investor a mortgage, which they use to buy a house.
- The amount of the mortgage is combined with thousands of other mortgages into a CDO.
- Different tranches of CDO were created – super senior, senior, mezzanine, junior.
- The CDO received a high credit rating from a credit rating agency.

A collateralized debt obligation (CDO) is an investment vehicle which carries a bundle of debt, such as mortgages, loans and other assets. These are then sold to investors comprising other banks, pension funds, sovereign funds, etc.

- Investors put money into the CDO.
- This money is used to repay monies from short-term borrowings that the bank had borrowed in the first place.
- The mortgage repayments flow into the CDO, allowing investors a return on their investment.
- If there is a shortfall in repayments, the super senior will be prioritized with money flowing down through the other grades.

Thus, banks were getting risk off their balance sheets, investors were making good returns, increasing numbers of people were becoming homeowners, and these homes were appreciating in value. This appeared to be a virtuous circle of capital accumulation: everyone, it seemed, was a winner. Sub-prime CDOs went from $80 billion worth of business in 2000 to a colossal $800 billion in 2005. The CDOs were thus fuelling the boom, as the banks did not require capital reserves to back the loans, because the loans were packaged up as CDOs and sold as bonds to investors. The bankers styled themselves as 'Masters of the Universe' and accumulated vast riches in the process of setting up these deals.

The CDOs were investments that attracted high rates of return. They were very attractive to cash-rich banks and other financial institutions across the world. For instance, European banks purchased 40 per cent of CDOs from the United States. The problem was that the assets backing these CDOs were extremely risky. When the sub-prime mortgages began to default, the mortgage repayments ceased and the properties were repossessed. In normal times a repossessed house would be sold by the foreclosing bank for around 70 per cent of its purchase value, and this is what the financial models used by the banks predicted. Sub-prime loans were, however, defying the behavioural patterns ascribed to them by the models: sub-prime borrowers generally bought homes on newly constructed estates where their neighbours were other sub-prime borrowers. Consequently, in some cases 30 per cent of a single street would be repossessed at around the same time, leading to a collapse in the value of property; in some cases the estates became virtually valueless. As bankers began to realize that the 'super senior' CDOs were in fact very risky, the credit ratings began to be downgraded; in turn this led to a further reduction in their value. Many of the banks – such as Citigroup – held 'super senior' CDOs on their own balance sheets, selling the riskier mezzanine and junior funds to investors. This was not a strategy born of conservatism; rather, it was an indicator that by dint of 'super senior' being regarded as a very safe investment, it generated low rates of return. The corollary was that it was unattractive to investors. Everyone was learning, at a cost, that 'super senior' was not the safe investment it seemed. In late 2007, Citigroup announced losses in the region of $10 billion on 'super senior' CDOs. More alarmingly, it also revealed a further $50 billion loss on its balance sheet. The banks that had ramped up their CDOs during the heady days of 2005–6 were now looking very exposed: Merrill Lynch and UBS were both having to write down multi-billion-dollar losses.

What the banks and credit rating agencies had failed to account for was, that unlike in the corporate lending sector where corporate failures take place at different times for different reasons, in the sub-prime mortgage market the defaults were highly synchronized. Thus, the 'normal' finance assumption that only a certain percentage of a loan book will go bad at any one time did not hold. Moreover, it now appears that very few people in each of the banks had a clear overall picture of what was going on in their organization. And furthermore, very few senior executives in the organization understood how the credit default swaps and CDOs actually worked. In fact, you might have more of an idea from reading this chapter than some of the self-styled aristocracy of the banking sector did!

In Chapter 8 we discussed the notion of the normalization of deviance. This is a concept that applies readily to the banks as they became inured to taking greater risks. Part of the blame, without doubt, can be attributed to the remuneration packages that awarded large bonuses for short-term performance. While governments in the UK and United States have regulated banking bonuses through the tax system in the wake of the GFC, this has not stopped the culture of bank bonuses in its tracks. The argument for bonuses is that, unless they are paid, people in financial markets will have insufficient incentive to do their jobs properly. The point is, however, that they were *not* doing their jobs properly – hence the GFC. One consequence of the GFC is that there are a lot of unemployed bankers so bonuses can hardly be due simply for retaining rare talent – this talent is not in short supply. Even as the banks piled up huge losses and were being nationalized the bankers were still enjoying bonuses (see Johnston, 2010). In a memorable phrase, one British politician, Vince Cable, at the time the Liberal Democrat Treasury Spokesman, said: 'RBS rewarding individual bankers is like a football team paying their striker for scoring when they've just been relegated' (Manning, 2010).

Signs of the coming relegation, to continue the metaphor, were evident as early as the end of 2007. Within banking circles it was clear by then that the sector was in trouble. Ironically, this came after a record year of profits for most banks. Steeling themselves for larger losses, banks began to exercise much more caution in relation to each other. More specifically, they were now reluctant to lend to each other in the short-term money markets. A money market in which there are no sellers is not much of a market. It is akin to visiting a fruit market to buy fruit only to find none of the fruit vendors have turned up! So banks needing short-term cash found this increasingly hard to source. This freezing up of money on the short-term money markets had led to the downfall of Northern Rock (a detailed discussion of the collapse of Northern Rock is available on the www.sagepub.co.uk/cleggstrategy website). It was also causing trouble for the banks, as they were running short of capital. Many of the banks sought and gained substantial injections of finance from sovereign funds in developing countries and the Tiger economies of South-East Asia.

Elsewhere in the US, Bear Stearns was encountering difficulties in raising monies on the short-term money markets. In a sense, it was a replay of the problems that had beset Northern Rock a few months previously. In addition, it had been rocked by the failure of its Bear hedge fund in 2007. Commercial investors had started to withdraw their monies from Bear: in 10 days during March 2008, over $10 billion in cash was taken out of the bank (Tett, 2009: 255). It was clear that Bear Stearns was no longer viable as a bank. The Federal Reserve exerted heavy pressure on JPMorgan Chase to intervene and help. JPMorgan Chase had suffered some losses, but these were tiny when compared with its competitors. Its caution in the property market – for which it had been castigated a few years before – was now proving prescient. While JPMorgan had developed the financial innovations behind the current crisis, it was far-sighted in realizing the dangers of applying such instruments to the real estate market. JPMorgan purchased the bank for £250 million ($2 a share, against the $100 it had been trading at the year before), which was backed with a $30 billion Fed guarantee against losses. This was seen as a very low price for Bear Stearns and was shortly after renegotiated with the government, when more liabilities were spotted: in return for government guarantees the price was lifted to $10 a share. The markets briefly rallied on hearing this news; many interpreted it as a decisive move to prevent what they feared could have been a financial meltdown. Monies started to flow once more into the short-term money markets. In many ways this was reminiscent of the 1929 Wall Street crash, where at various junctures the markets rallied and commentators proclaimed the crisis to be over (Galbraith, 1955). By April 2008 it was estimated that $400 billion had been lost from CDOs (Tett, 2009), while the International Monetary Fund speculated that the total losses could be in the region of $1000 billion.

In September 2008 Freddie Mac and Fannie Mae, two large American mortgage providers, were in trouble. They were highly leveraged, lending out large multiples of loans against their asset base, and were seriously undermined by the defaults in the mortgage market. The US government, in effect, nationalized the two mortgage providers. At this juncture the banking sector was descending into crisis, with something akin to a domino effect breaking out.

It is widely agreed that the tipping point in the recent banking crash came when the US government decided not to bail out Lehman Brothers. As an iconic Wall Street bank, Lehman Brothers had been at the forefront of much of the lending that had taken place, with particularly aggressive positions in the sub-prime market. Resonant with Bear Stearns and Northern Rock, Lehman Brothers obtained much of its financing from the short-term money markets. It was struggling to raise funds and investors were withdrawing their assets. Critically, Dick Fuld, its Chairman, failed to seek early help for the bank from potential suitors. Events started to spiral out of control and other bankers simply lost trust in Lehman's balance sheet: in their estimation Lehman was understating its huge exposure defaults on 'super senior' CDOs. Banks were unwilling to trade with Lehman, which, among other things, prompted the Fed to call a meeting about the future of Lehman. The fascinating feature of this meeting – attended by the Fed and all the major American banks and some European ones – was that Lehman Brothers was not actually invited! At it, the bankers divided into groups and went into breakout rooms to discuss various options to save Lehman Brothers. They rejected the idea, mooted by the US government, of forming a consortium to bail out the bank.

Barclays was interested in purchasing the bank, but, following much deliberation, was stymied by the British government who feared, correctly as it transpired, that Barclays' financial position was insufficiently strong to mount a takeover. Discussions went on between Barclays Capital, the UK Financial Services Authority and Hank Paulson. Barclays Capital wanted to make the deal, but the Financial Services Authority was less keen and wary of being railroaded into doing so. When Alistair Darling, the British Chancellor, told Paulson that the deal was off, Paulson told his colleagues that 'the British don't want to import our cancer' (Ross-Sorkin, 2009). Paulson was keen for 'closure' by 7pm on the Sunday evening, because that was when the Asian stock markets opened. He decided to let Lehman Brothers fail. Having pressured JPMorgan Chase to subsume Bear Stearns and having bailed out Freddie Mae and Fannie Mac, he concluded that he was not willing to countenance any further rescues and that an example of the consequences of moral hazard needed to be evident. The decision not to rescue Lehman Brothers was a dramatic one and it sent shock waves not just through the financial community but also through the broader economy and political sphere. On 14 September 2008, Lehman Brothers went into bankruptcy. The world reeled from the shock that an iconic Wall Street institution was being allowed to fail. On the Monday morning, following the bankruptcy announcement, stock exchanges around the world lost a stunning $600 billion in a two-day period.

Tett (2009) likened it to the worst fall in stock values since the Wall Street crash of 1929. In some financial jurisdictions – such as London – the bankruptcy of Lehman Brothers meant that some investors and banks were unable to access their assets. Panic engulfed the financial markets. The next institution to implode was

AIG – the giant American insurer – the organization that had been insuring many of the CDOs. It was massively exposed, holding around $560 billion of 'super senior' CDOs. In 2008 it had written down $43 billion in losses on the CDOS and was in deep trouble.

Finance ministers across the world were shocked that Lehman Brothers was not rescued, with many, usually sober, commentators regarding it as a huge mistake. Their fear was that, in the context of the banking industry, this cataclysmic event could lead to a spate of other banking collapses. Simply put, they now suspected that the *entire* financial system was at risk of breaking down. It was the biggest financial crisis since the 1929 Wall Street crash. Coincidentally, Chairman of the Fed Ben Bernanke's PhD thesis had been an investigation of the banking crisis that followed the 1929 crash, on which the accepted opinion is that the actions of central bankers transformed a recession into a world wide slump, which, among other things, led to the rise of fascism. Lehman Brothers had fallen, Merrill Lynch was in trouble, Morgan Stanley was days away from filing for bankruptcy and Goldman Sachs was not far behind. There were fears that this would cascade beyond Wall Street and that General Electric (GE), the American conglomerate that was heavily involved in financial services, was reputedly in trouble.

At a meeting of the US Treasury, it was noted of these circumstances that 'this is our financial 9/11' (Ross-Sorkin, 2009). Consequently, when it became clear that AIG was teetering on the brink of collapse, Hank Paulson stepped in with a rescue package. This was a complete *volte-face* on his long-espoused policy position of non-intervention. Shortly after this, he put together the controversial 'Troubled Asset Relief Program' (TARP) rescue package for the banks.

The panic crossed the Atlantic to Europe and, in particular, to America's neo-liberal bedfellow: the UK. In the UK, Mervyn King, Chairman of the Bank of England, was temperamentally disinclined to intervene to support banks: he called for 'faith' in the markets. His premise was that intervening encouraged 'moral hazard'. King's rationale was that to rescue a bank would be to indicate to that bank, and others, that they could take wild risks and be bailed out. By allowing banks to fail, it would impress on other banks that they were responsible for the consequences of their strategies. Events in the autumn of 2008 led King to change his mind. While, initially, he felt sub-prime losses would be easily contained, he began to fear for the future of the banks themselves. HBOS, RBS and Barclays were all in serious trouble. The share prices of HBOS and RBS, two of the largest banks in Europe, plummeted. In October 2008, Gordon Brown, the British Prime Minister, announced a bailout package for British banks, which, in effect, constituted a part nationalization of RBS, HBOS and Barclays. Hank Paulson followed suit, in effect part-nationalizing several major US banks.

While we have restricted our story to the UK and the United States, the financial crisis is a global phenomenon. It has visited terrible devastation on some countries, such as Iceland, and exposed the hubris of others, such as Dubai. It has had a devastating effect on the developing world, as the remittances of guest workers have plummeted and foreign direct investment has shrunk.

Neo-liberalism was the dominant ideology in the Anglo-American economies for over 30 years. In a few short months the paradigm collapsed. The notion that markets knew best and were efficient was cruelly exposed as little more than ideological dogma. It is now clear that the much vaunted boom – across many Western countries – was largely due to credit-induced asset bubbles, primarily in real estate. The effects of the banking crash reverberated throughout the economy, with fears of a 1930s-style slump. Unlike in the 1930s, however, governments were heavily interventionist, so much so that Keynes was momentarily back in fashion and

Moral hazard occurs when people are prepared to take greater risks than they would otherwise do because they know they will be protected from the consequences of their own miscalculations should the risk they take prove injurious, dangerous or misguided. This is the case where government effectively insures against risk by bailing out any bank that is judged too big to fail.

governments were pumping large sums of money into the economy. Thirty-five years after the ideas of the architect of the postwar economy – J. M. Keynes – were consigned to the dustbin of history by hawkish neo-liberals, the neo-liberal policy apparatus pulled off a stunning 'U' turn: the neo-liberals were, at least temporarily, losing their religion.

QUESTION TIME?

Joseph Stiglitz is one of the leading contemporary heterodox economists. In 2001 he was awarded the Nobel Prize in Economics. In addition to academic positions, he has also held senior appointments in the World Bank and the Clinton administration. Stiglitz views the financial crisis as having been made in the United States and as being a consequence of the deregulation that has taken place since the Reagan era. Accordingly, poor regulation combined with perverse bonus incentives contributed to the financial crash. In Stiglitz's view it is mistaken to concentrate on the individual actions of actors such as Alan Greenspan or Ben Bernanke – although he is critical of them – as they were acting broadly in line with the central precept of neo-classical economics: markets are efficient. Stiglitz reminds us that a financial sector is not an end in itself but rather has a social function that is fairly straightforward: to allocate capital; manage risk, and run the payments mechanism. All of this should be done at as low a transaction cost as possible.

In contrast Stiglitz reminds us that the financial sector misallocated capital, created risk, put the payments mechanism at risk and did all of this at enormous transaction costs. The booming financial sector, which in the middle of the last decade appeared to be creating so much wealth, was, according to Stiglitz, the sign of a sick economy.

What strategies have been successful in treating this 'sick economy'?

The Chief Economist of the IMF, Oliver Blanchard (2009), had, prior to the crisis, been a prominent advocate of rational utility and expectations models that assumed efficient markets and equilibrium outcomes. In a fine example of analysis after the fact he examined why the crisis had occurred. Four main reasons were identified:

1 Assets had been created, sold and bought that appeared to be much less risky than they actually were. Risk had been systematically underestimated.

2 Securitization strategies had led to the balance sheets of financial institutions becoming littered with complex and hard-to-value assets.

3 Securitization and globalization made the financial market more tightly coupled and connected and also more extensive.

4 Financial institutions financed their portfolios with diminishing amounts of capital, using that capital more efficiently in order to raise the rate of return. Again, the rational expectation proved to be founded on too much optimism, too much belief in equilibrium and too little appreciation of the risk (see Ormerod, 2010: 16–17).

Ormerod reasons, quite correctly in our view, that:

Modern macroeconomics, with its basis in rational agents and rational expectations (RARE), bears a heavy burden of responsibility for the financial crisis. … The discipline provided the intellectual underpinnings for a world in which situations involving risk lead to it being systematically underestimated, and in which situations of genuine uncertainty were not recognised for what they were. (2010: 17)

The RARE view of the world should be fully discredited by the events of the financial crisis. Should be, but 'should' is not the same as 'will be'. We know from the history of science that a lack of alignment between evidently anomalous assumptions and empirical observations can persist for long periods of time due to the commitment that theorists who have invested their intellectual capital in a theory have to those investments – even when bankrupted (Kuhn, 1962). Writing so close to the crisis, it is difficult to see how events will unfold. We will leave that to scenario planners, palm readers and astrologists.

Evidently, there are important lessons to be learnt that include requiring banks to hold larger capital reserves and separating commercial banking from the casino activities of the stock market. What is clear, however, is that it signifies a shift in power away from US capitalism. We started the chapter with a discussion of Baran and Sweezy's (1965) seminal account of monopoly capitalism. They were writing in the mid-1960s, the high noon of US capitalism. They highlighted the way in which major firms – the monopoly capitalists – were seeing ever-larger profits. Their book reported that GM accounted for 1 per cent of US GDP. As a symbol of how the times have been a-changing, note that, 45 years later, GM was in crisis and sought a government bailout. While the US dollar is still the world's reserve currency, the United States is also the most indebted nation. Savings from China, the Far East and the Middle East fund its deficit.

STRATEGY IN A CRISIS

According to Michel Wieviorka (2009), there are two ways to view the financial crisis. The first resonates with the account we have given above, emphasizing the role of sub-prime mortgages, credit default swaps, CDOs and a crisis spreading from the Untied States to the rest of the world. His second perspective, the one that he advocates, connects the financial crisis to the changes that took place in the 1970s that ushered in neo-liberalism. From this perspective, the rise of an economy centred on financial strategies and models and the decline of an economy, in which what was central to capital's reproduction were not just the offer of services but also the provision of materially useful things, explains how the crisis happened.

Prior to 2008 the banks were the central sovereign power of the world capitalist economy: their profits were huge in both the City and Wall Street, and their willingness to supply capital for various activities determined a great deal of corporate strategy. Today, the future of the banking sector is obscure. At the time of finishing this book, many banks, in spite of making large losses, were continuing to pay out large bonuses to executives. It is a curious feature of financial capitalism that performance bonuses can be paid despite record losses! It is unclear whether the global economy is emerging from recession (the so-called U-shaped recession), or is on the brink of a double-dip (the so-called W recession) downturn. Wieviorka (2009), a French social theorist, makes a very relevant and interesting argument for strategists in relation to the crisis.

While the conventional view is that it is very difficult to see things clearly when in the midst of a crisis, in contrast, Wieviorka argues that:

- A crisis reveals things, ideas and processes that were not previously apparent in the 'normal' status quo. Therefore, in the midst of a crisis it is often possible to see things more clearly than in a steady state. For instance, Wieviorka argues that in the financial crisis we can better understand the neo-liberal economic model and its integral problems than before.

● While a crisis brings about devastation and destruction, it can also open
   up the possibility for creativity and innovation. As Wieviorka puts it,
   crisis is a moment when there is an acceleration of interest in new ideas,
   thus allowing new paradigms to develop. He cites the example of GM,
   the iconic US carmaker, which is currently in serious financial difficulty.
   GM basically wants large state subsidies to return to business as usual (i.e.
   producing large quantities of gas-guzzling cars). Wieviorka argues that this
   point of crisis is an opportunity for GM to rethink its business and enter
   a new era, by embracing environmental technologies and desisting from
   the production of SUV 4×4 vehicles. There are some signs that this may
   be happening: GM has sold off Hummer, the most pointless vehicle ever
   marketed for urban transport. Electric cars are being designed. In one of
   those Schumpeterian moments of creative destruction it is evident that
   long-overdue innovations are occurring.

That the Western financial system came close to collapse is well established. The
discussion of the credit crunch above highlights the way in which global finance
is interconnected: savers in China, home-buyers in the United States, regional
banks in the UK and entrepreneurs in Iceland were all tightly connected, albeit
loosely coupled, in what amounted to very few degrees of separation. The crash
revealed that very few people understood the financial system, and those that did
acted out of pure self-interest. The global financial infrastructure lacked transparency, and financial innovations greatly amplified the effects of movements in the
economy.

RISK AND AUDIT

Risk is seemingly endemic to our modern global society. Much of it is produced by
the unanticipated consequences of human action, such as global warming and the
chaos of the financial markets. These are not the result of the failures of modern
institutions so much as their success: global warming related to the vast industrial
achievements of modernity and the chaos of the financial markets related to their
extraordinary capacity to recycle and reproduce capital effectively and properly.
The risks we face in these areas are a result of the success of the practices that we
have institutionalized.

Beck's (2008) theory of world risk society maintains that modern societies are
shaped by new kinds of risks, of which the GFC is an example, that are characterized by three features:

1 *Delocalization.* The causes and consequences of risk are not limited to
   one geographical location or space; they are in principle omnipresent. For
   instance, the GFC might have started in Wall Street but it rapidly spread to
   the UK, Iceland, Ireland, Greece and elsewhere.

2 *Incalculableness.* Risk's consequences are in principle incalculable. The
   risk cannot be extrapolated from past behaviour. There was nothing in the
   financial models being used that predicted the GFC. As Beck (2008: 3) puts
   it, 'colonizing … the future based on probability doesn't work'.

3 *Non-compensation.* The risks are so enormous that they cannot be insured
   or compensated. The trillions of US taxpayer dollars needed to bail out the
   banks, added to the trillions that the banks 'lost', will probably never be
   recouped.

The risks of global modernity, such as the GFC, are contained neither by space nor time: they do not respect national sovereignty and they cannot be contained for the future by a present action. Moreover, because of the complexity of the problems and the length of chains of effect, the assignment of causes and consequences is no longer possible with any degree of reliability. As we said at the outset of the chapter, the GFC was not the result of the actions of a particular group of individuals.

Beck points out that it was, ironically, originally in economics that the discovery of the incalculability of risk was first made. In a famous article in *The Quarterly Journal of Economics*, Keynes (1937) wrote about what he termed 'uncertain knowledge', where no scientific basis exists on which to form any calculable probability whatever, such as futures, and where we simply do not know what the future holds. In this situation, states have had to try and stem the tides of risk, uncertain knowledge and undecidability where they can. In terms of the GFC this has resulted in what Beck (2008: 5) refers to as 'a state socialism for the rich', the costs of which are placed on the shoulders of the poor – nationally and globally:

> The market is not what economists made and make us believe, the answer, the saviour to all our problems, but a threat to our existence. We have to learn fast that modernity is urgently in need of reflexive market regulations, more than that, of an international constitution to negotiate conflicts over answers to global risks and problems – built on consensus between parties, nations, religions, friend and foe. Of course, this may not happen. But suddenly it is common knowledge that this is the precondition of survival. All this is part of the reflexivity generated by risk, by the anticipation of catastrophe. I cannot think of any power inducing, enforcing such a global learning process in such a short period of time. Be careful: not catastrophe does this. The catastrophe is the moment of (total) destruction. The anticipation of catastrophe does it. Manufactured uncertainty, global risk is, highly ambivalent, paradoxically also a moment of hope, of unbelievable opportunities – a cosmopolitan moment. (2008: 7)

The perverse and negative cosmopolitanism of the GFC connected millions of peasant labourers toiling in Chinese factories to the strategies of financialization that emerged out of the Chicago School of Economic to transform corporate strategies. A GFC was not supposed to happen. The unknown unknowns of future systematic catastrophes hidden in the normalized practices of risk taking were supposed to be controlled by the audits made by the ratings agencies. The ratings agencies had rated the system and its institutions as fundamentally sound. Audits failed, however, to reveal the real state of affairs.

Strategists would have had less faith in the power and accuracy of ratings agencies if they had read a book by an ex-Plymouth Argyle football player who had studied Frankfurt school philosophy at the Universities of Oxford and Cambridge, before training as an accountant. Swapping football for academia, Mike Power became a professor at the London School of Economics to then become the Director of the *Centre for the Analysis of Risk and Regulation (CARR)*. While Power acknowledges that the rise of auditing in society in quantitative terms is not, in itself, remarkable, there has nonetheless been an explosion of the idea of the 'audit'. He coined the term the *audit society* to reflect the explosion in checking, ranking and auditing evident from the 1990s onwards. He notes that the problematic for every society is to decide on the relationship between how much should be checked up on and how much to trust.

Think about the world in which we live. We have become obsessed with rankings. If you have ever completed a review for Tripadvisor, or rated sellers on eBay or Amazon, then you have participated in an audit process. Consequently, new agencies – complete with audit processes – emerged to produce trust and comfort through their rankings. League tables are produced about hospitals, universities, business schools, cities and even hotels. Lists are everywhere. The *Independent* even has a list of the best sex toys – presumably audited!

Power argues that the function audits perform is to produce trust and comfort. In recent times, at least in the UK (but his thesis almost certainly has a wider applicability), checking up increasingly takes the form of an audit. While the idea of auditing comes from financial accounting, it has a much broader applicability. The university you are studying in has almost certainly been audited for the quality of its teaching, its research, its access policy, perhaps its environmental credentials, as well as many other things. The business school you are studying in has quite likely been through an accreditation for Equis or AASCB or will be planning to do so; the claim of being audited by these agencies is that it helps business schools learn more about how and what they are doing. The fact that they have been accredited inspires trust and comfort, especially among fee-paying students. The criticism of such bodies is that they standardize management education – through the promotion of an homogeneous approach to business schools. A further point is that bodies such as Equis and AASCB are self-anointed arbiters of what constitutes a good business school. That they were not appointed or elected by business schools or government has not deterred them from casting their judgement upon business schools.

A society wedded to auditing trusts such audits to produce what are taken to be truths about organizations, however arbitrary their representations of reality might actually be. If Tripadvisor ratings are critical of a hotel and rank it bottom in a city, you are probably not going to stay there, at least if you have consulted the rankings. Equally, if a hospital were to be rated badly, would you go there for an operation? And if a business school is rated low, would you choose to study your Master's or MBA there?

We are not arguing against auditing *per se*. Imagine an organization or society where nothing was checked: chaos would reign in such a place; but, equally, think about what an organization or society would be like where everything was checked. Such a society would surely collapse under the weight of its own bureaucratic apparatus. An example of this, perhaps, would be some of the regimes that formed the Soviet Bloc in the second half of the twentieth century. For instance, Anna Funder, an Australian author, notes in *Stasiland*, an account of life in the German Democratic Republic (GDR), that in the 40 years of its existence the GDR managed to create more written records than in the entire history of the German-speaking peoples!

According to Power, since the 1980s the term audit has become commonplace and is applied in a wide array of different contexts. The popularity of the term has been accompanied by the emergence of a range of different audit bodies – checking up on schools, hospitals, universities, and so on. Power asks 'Is there a systematic trend towards the extreme case of a society engaged in constant checking and verification?' (1997: 4). Of course, the desire to check up on things requires a systematic practice. Enter financial auditing. Power notes, with some irony, that at the very time when the financial audit as a set of practices was in crisis, through the numerous scandals that have engulfed it and the accountancy profession over the last decade, its central ideas were picked up and applied in many other different contexts. Financial auditing has provided the model that has influenced the design of auditing practice in many other fields.

Credit rating agencies, such as Moody's and Standard and Poor's, for example, are essential for the sale of a bond. The agencies' scale of ratings – from AAA for an issuer of unimpeachable creditworthiness, to the Cs and Ds for issuers of highly speculative or defaulted securities that are often called junk bonds – formed the basis of the capital markets. A triple-A rating was a prerequisite for the pooled structured investment vehicles (SIVs) that invested the City's and Wall Street's surplus cash. But how were these ratings made on SIVs that were subsequently rapidly to unravel as worthless? When auditing becomes alchemy we should become very worried. The role of financial auditing by the credit rating agencies was central to the financialization strategies that led to the GFC. Without them, the strategies of financialization would not have been possible.

Auditing is central to strategy-making in other ways as well. Often, at the front of every strategy there will be a smooth website with a statement of mission, vision and values. Having designated a vision, mission and value statement, an audit of operations enables an independent check on whether or not there is a consistency of purpose and action throughout an organization. Auditing becomes the means with which organizations can turn their operations into a vast panopticon, opening up their innards and actions to deep scrutiny. Of course, no audit can ever tell whether the strategy is a good one; all it can do is tell whether or not it is being systematically complied with and whether or not its standards are being met.

Accountancy is a powerful profession and has provided a heavy ideational influence on audit practice. The appeal of audits rests in their capacity to create quantities out of qualitative phenomena. This allows benchmarking between different organizations. So while auditing has its origins – and derives its legitimacy – from the financial audit, the idea has travelled far.

Like so many of the issues discussed in this book, the transformations that were taking place in the 1980s were crucial in ushering in a new era, one where old certainties were no longer trusted. Auditing was the primary tool of the credit rating agencies that were supposed to evaluate objectively the risks of the various financial strategies that were afoot. Clearly, auditing failed and the unknown unknowns triumphed. Nonetheless, the numbers produced were such that they created trust, faith and a sense of security. Numbers are so powerful in our world. They define company profits, government budgets are framed using them, and you will almost certainly be graded in this strategy module through a number. They possess a power that words often do not.

RANKINGS AND REACTIVITY: HOW PUBLIC MEASURES RECREATE SOCIAL WORLDS

Building on Power (1997), Espeland and Sauder (2007: 1) note that: 'In the past two decades demands for accountability, transparency, and efficiency have prompted a flood of social measures designed to evaluate the performances of individuals and organizations'. Their interest is in how various rankings have emerged and the effects they have. They call this process one of commensuration – the way that qualitative phenomena were transformed into a quantity. In particular, they want to understand the actions of those who are subject to the ranking process. Consider the following: if you know that you, or your organization, are subject to some sort of ranking process, will this alter your behaviour? Espeland and Sauder's assertion is that actors are reflexive – meaning they are self-aware and thoughtful about the situation they find themselves in – and will try and perform well in rankings. They refer to this as **reactivity**.

Rankings of organizations construct a social reality that is then taken to represent how these organizations relate to each other. As we have seen above, Espeland and Sauder highlighted the way in which law schools were ranked. The concepts of reactivity and self-fulfilling prophecy make it clear that there were two forms of reactivity that impacted on the rankings (see 'What do you mean?' box overleaf).

'Although definitions of **reactivity** vary across approaches, the basic idea is the same: individuals alter their behavior in reaction to being evaluated, observed, or measured' (Espeland and Sauder, 2007: 6).

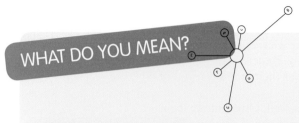

WHAT DO YOU MEAN?

What do rankings do?

In a paper in the *American Journal of Sociology*, Espeland and Sauder (2007) study the *US News and World report* (USN) ranking (www.top-law-schools.com/rankings.html) of accredited US law schools. USN is a newspaper and its ranking began as a simple exercise in providing information to potential students. In the intervening years it has become 'the definitive ranking of law schools virtually monopolizing legal education' (Espeland ad Sauder, 2007: 7), and both potential students and employers take it seriously. It is seen to signal the relative quality of a law school. Their study was interested in capturing the reactivity of the law schools to the ranking. This is foremost a story of strategy: how do the law schools react to the rankings? And how do they strategize?

The authors suggest there are two forms of reactivity:

1   *Self-fulfilling prophecy*. This is where the USN rankings outline the expectations of what a law school should look like, which are then conformed to by people. One feature of the rankings is that they magnify tiny differences, such that there may be very little difference between being, for example, 9th in the rankings and 21st. Yet in people's minds this represents a substantial difference. Over time this difference can become entrenched. A second feature is that historical reputation counts in the present: past evaluations can colour the current reputation and ranking of a law school. Third, if a ranking gets linked to a school's budget, granted from its university, this can, in effect, mean that it only has the budget to maintain its position in the ranking, as it might be very expensive to move up to the next level. Finally:

> law schools respond to the conception of legal education that is embedded in rankings factors. Rankings create self-fulfilling prophecies by encouraging schools to become more like what rankings measure, which reinforces

the validity of the measure. Rankings impose a standardized, universal definition of law schools which creates incentives for law schools to conform to that definition'. (Espeland and Sauder, 2007: 15)

2   *Commensuration*. The act of commensuration – turning qualitative phenomena into quantities – underpins contemporary society. We are accustomed to hearing about the performance of individuals and organizations in numbers. Think about your own examination performances, for example. The exam that you sit at the end of your strategy module is an instance of commensuration. Espeland and Sauder identify three characteristics of commensuration that can produce reactivity. They are 'its capacity to reduce, simplify, and integrate information; the new, precise, and all-encompassing relationships it creates' among and between departments and schools, and 'its capacity to elicit reflection on the validity of quantitative evaluation' (2007: 16). The first point is that commensuration reduces large amounts of data to a single number in a ranking table: 'Numbers circulate more easily and are more easily remembered than more complicated forms of information' (2007: 18). The second point is that commensuration builds a common relationship between entities by comparing them on the same metric. Simultaneously, it differentiates between different entities – it creates a set of relations between them, that is a better law school, a worse law school, an average school. The third point is to reflect on what the numbers produced in the act of commensuration actually mean. Espeland and Sauder illustrate that the producers of the USN rankings see what they produce as a 'real' account of relations between different schools, future students regard them as the 'truth', while staff in the schools themselves think 'rankings misrepresent their schools in harmful ways. Their deeper knowledge of their school and the effects of rankings, and their experience in helping generate the numbers they often see as arbitrary and only superficially connected to practices at their school' (2007: 21).

What were ranking's effects? The implication is that prospective students make decisions based on the rankings, employers make hiring decisions on the basis of the ranking, and law schools make strategic decisions on the basis of the rankings:

> Over time, law schools learned that rankings were fateful, that people made important decisions using rankings, and schools began to invest heavily in improving rankings. This reinforced rankings' impact and legitimacy and set in motion the self-fulfilling prophecies described above. Commensuration exacerbated patterns of self-fulfilling prophecies. (Espeland and Sauder, 2007: 24)

Important strategic implications follow from Espeland and Sauder's (2007) work. Where firms, university schools and departments and other organizations are being ranked, the important question is how the organizations in question react to the rankings they receive. Three strategic reactions are evident:

1 *Maximize rankings by reallocating resources*. With this strategy the focus is on what the rankings measure and value and, accordingly, targeting resources at them. Here we see that rankings privilege certain factors as key performance indicators, even if existing strategies were not focused on them. For instance, in the law schools that Espeland and Sauder (2007: 25) researched there were 'sharp increases in spending on merit scholarships and marketing one's law school to other law schools'.

2 *Redefine work and policies in a strategic reorganization*. If the rankings are not delivering the verdict that the strategist desires, then look at what is being rewarded in the rankings and try to imitate it. This involves what sociologists call institutional isomorphism: seeking to copy those admired elements of other similar organizations in one's environment. The USN rankings often led to changes in the way in which a law school is organized in order for it to try and rise up the rankings, with changes occurring most frequently in the 'careers services, admissions, and the dean's office' (Espeland and Sauder, 2007: 27). These areas were most likely because it was here that the key performance indicators for the ratings were being managed. In relation to career services, their finding was that much more time was spent on tracking alumni to check up on their salaries and career progress, as these were measured by the USN rankings. The cost of this was in spending less time providing careers advice and support to existing students, as this was not valued in the USN ranking. Espeland and Sauder (2007) found that the power of the USN ranking was such that whereas in the past Law Schools admissions staff used their professional judgement in offering a place on a course, increasingly places were being offered if potential entrants conformed with what was measured and valued by the law schools, such as high grades. The USN rankings increasingly redefined what it was to be a dean of a school – a strong performance and moving up the rankings were often rewarded with bonuses or promotions, while a poor performance in the rankings could lead to resignations or sackings.

3 *Gaming rankings*. Espeland and Sauder (2007: 29) argue that various strategies can be used to try and boost organizations' standing in the rankings. The main one is 'gaming', the manipulation of rules and numbers to manage appearances without making substantive changes to what the rules and numbers are supposed to depict.

The study discussed above is an illustration of an example of a ranking system having considerable power within a field of activity. The power of rankings was such that it led, wittingly or otherwise, to a fundamental reshaping of law schools in the United States. Of course, not all league tables have such power, and some may be used as a rough guide, or even completely dismissed as banal and point-less. Nonetheless, a strategist needs to understand the potential implications of the rankings they are subjected to, especially for the way in which they, in effect, produce truth and reality about an organization. The implication is that a strate-gist needs to engage in realpolitik and game playing to respond in ways that make the organization look better through the numbers – even if the underlying reality barely changes.

MINI CASE STUDY

Ranking your school

In recent years, a number of rankings have been produced relating to business schools. They include rankings such as the *Financial Times* ranking for MBAs, *Guardian* newspaper subject listings for undergraduate courses in manage-ment in the UK, as well as the RAE rankings for research. More generically, there are the *Busi-ness Week* rankings, while in Australia there are the *Australian Financial Review Boss Magazine* ratings.

Questions

Choose the rankings that your school has been involved in and investigate:

1 The process of commensuration involved in producing the rankings.

2 The extent to which the rankings act as a self-fulfilling prophecy.

3 The reactivity engaged in by your school in trying to climb up the rankings. To what extent, for example, did your school attempt to seek to maximize rankings by reallocating resources, redefining work and policies, or engaging in gaming? (You might need to check out web-sites and news releases and maybe interview one or two faculty and administrators.)

Rankings are a fascinating phenomenon. Two of us (Chris and Martin) have written on strategy and city league tables. What we were interested in was the way in which city league tables functioned and the 'reactivity' of city managers. City league tables purport to measure such things as the quality of life when living in a city, the ease of doing business, and so on. Some are focused more on lifestyle, while others are more concerned with economic issues. City league tables, such as Anholt or WCCI, are published annually and will list the 'best' cities, according to the criteria they have set. You might have come across them, announcing the best or worst place to live. Unlike the USN law school rankings discussed above, they do not possess the same sort of power. Many city managers will merely dismiss them as irrelevant or unimportant. Some, however, will take them more seriously and seek to try to get the city they work for to rise further up a league table. Kornberger (2010) talks about the importance some city managers in Edinburgh paid to the league tables, trying to build the city's brand and see it ascend the league table.

In summary, league tables do the following:

1 *League tables reduce qualities to a quantity*. This is akin to Espeland and Sauder's notion of commensuration. In the context of a city it means identifying particular categories and then measuring them. For instance, in the influential WCCI city index global commerce is defined as compris-ing six key attributes (placed in parentheses is the relative weight that each

dimension contributes to the overall score): legal and political framework (10 per cent); economic stability (10 per cent); ease of doing business (20 per cent); financial flow (22 per cent); business centre (22 per cent); and knowledge creation and information flow (16 per cent). As the report explains: 'Collectively these six dimensions are meant to cover the key functional characteristics of a city considered to be among the world's Centers of Commerce'. Each of these dimensions comprise various factors that can be measured. For instance, one of the 'knowledge creation and information flow' measures is the number of MBA programmes in a city. Data are collected on the various measures and a score is derived for a city. Thus, qualitative features about a city are turned into a quantity.

2 *League tables create connections between very different entities.* What is the relationship between Paris and Edinburgh, or Sydney and Vienna? No obvious relationships exist between the different cities but once a league table containing them all is brought into existence, they can be compared against each other. Thus a league table, measuring particular things, creates an order between different cities by rendering them comparable.

3 *League tables stimulate competition.* League tables are produced periodically; in the case of the city league tables they are generally produced annually. Integral to the logic of a league table is the premise that there is movement within the table, that is cities can go up and down.

4 *Once competition is accepted, individual players need a strategy to play the game.* When a league table is created, participants take that seriously and it creates a need for an organization to have a strategy with which to compete.

5 *League tables have important power effects.* Assuming league tables are taken seriously, they can have important effects in framing the criteria on which organizations compete.

In corporate organizations we see echoes of the ranking strategy at work when CEOs such as Jack Welch argue that GE should not remain in any business in which it is not number 1 or 2. Rankings are an extreme outcome of strategy: there can only ever be one number 1, or 10 in the top 10. If getting there is the goal of strategy then most organizations in any well-populated field will be losers not winners, indeed, strategies, while promising to create winners, will much more easily produce losers. With different organizations' strategies seeking to achieve excellence in competition with each other there are bound to be more losers than winners. Thus, the value of any strategy will always be compromised by the rankings that pre-exist their production and which will survive after the strategy has been formulated.

YOU CAN DOWNLOAD...

An article that suggests that the financial and economic crisis that began in the United States in 2008 indicates the start of a systemic crisis of neo-liberal capitalism, by Kotz, D. M. (2009) The Financial and Economic Crisis of 2008: A Systemic Crisis of Neoliberal Capitalism, *Review of Radical Political Economics*, 41(3): 305–17, from the book's website at www.sagepub.co.uk/cleggstrategy

SUMMARY AND REVIEW

That strategy is central to organizational life is the central proposition of this book. Overwhelmingly, the strategies of recent times have been associated with financialization, which have come to function for many corporate organizations as the dominant rationality, in large part because the flows of capital, the lifeblood of a capitalist system, depended on having financially persuasive strategies. Bearing the name of strategy, a particular form of rationality was made up, one that was very good at rationalizing and sanctioning itself in the name of the 'bigger picture', the 'mission', 'the future', and other heroic images. The financial authorities controlling the flows of capital rationalized particular versions of their rationality as what must be done – in the name of strategy. Thus, in this chapter we have encountered the consequences of global financialization for organizational strategies: the shift to private equity, the dominance of capital flows, the inefficiency of the market, and the wholesale nationalization of failed enterprises that has resulted. We have investigated risk, unknown unknowns, audit and rankings, and demonstrated that none are quite what they might appear to be. The consequences of this chapter should be cautionary for those who are or seek to become strategists. The very strategies that make you rich can also make you poor. One might say the same thing about freedom as one would say about wealth: the very things that once were supposed to have made us free now hold us captive.

EXERCISES

1 Having read this chapter you should be able to say in your own words what the following key terms mean:

- Financialization
- Collateralized debt obligation
- Monopoly capital
- Neo-liberalism
- Asset stripping
- Shareholder value
- Private equity
- Futures
- Options
- Moral hazard
- Risk
- Audit
- Ratings
- Reactivity
- Self-fulfilling prophecy
- Commensuration.

2 To what extent is strategy a rational science?

3 Research the rhetoric behind the 'new economy'. What was it and what were its central claims?

4 Critically evaluate the arguments for and against private equity firms.

5 Research the private equity buy out of Manchester United Football Club by the Glaser family. Discuss how the deal was financed and why it is controversial.

6 What constraints does private equity finance place on strategy-making?

7 Could the global financial crisis have been averted? If so, which agencies would have to have done things differently and what would these have been?

8 Critically evaluate the governmental response to the global financial crisis in a country of your choice.

ADDITIONAL RESOURCES

1 Our companion website is the best first stop for you to find a great deal of extra resources, free PDF versions of leading articles published in Sage journals, exercise, video and pod casts, team case studies and general questions and links to teamwork resources. Go to www.sagepub.co.uk/cleggstrategy

WEB SECTION

Visit the *Strategy* companion website at www.sagepub.co.uk/cleggstrategy

1 The London School of Economics and Political Science maintains some excellent podcasts on its web pages at www.lse.ac.uk/resources/podcasts/publicLecturesAndEvents.htm. Of particular interest for this chapter are the following:

- Jimmy Stewart Is Dead – Ending the World's Ongoing Financial Plague with Limited Purpose Banking Speaker: Professor Laurence J. Kotlikoff Chair: Professor Christopher Polk
  This event was recorded on 17 February 2010 in the New Theatre, East Building. Let's call a spade a spade. Today's financial system, with its limited liability, insider rating, political kickbacks, director sweetheart deals, non disclosure, and internal corporate raiders, was built for hucksters – hucksters who systematically manufactured and sold trillions in fraudulent securities, grabbed hoards of loot, and left the public to pick up the pieces.

● 21st Century Challenges: how global crises provide the opportunity to transform the world

Speakers: Professor Lord Anthony Giddens, Professor David Held, Professor Mary Kaldor, Professor Danny Quah
Chair: Professor Henrietta L. Moore

This event was recorded on 16 February 2010 in the Old Theatre, Old Building.
The world now confronts crises that are unique in their global character. Distinguished LSE experts argue that these crises provide an opportunity to transform the world and to build the capacity to respond to extreme global challenges.

2 There is a special issue of the journal, *Human Relations*, 63(9): 1279–1370, 2010, with four papers that explore the impact of private equity buyouts on work and employment relations. In particular, the paper by Suzana B. Rodrigues and John Child (2010) Private Equity: The Minimalist Organization and the Quality of Employment Relations (pp. 1321–42), is worth consulting.

LOOKING FOR A HIGHER MARK?

Reading and digesting these articles that are available free on the companion web site www.sagepub.co.uk/cleggstrategy can help you gain deeper understanding and, on the basis of that, a better grade:

1 Watt, A. and Galgóczi, B. (2009) Financial Capitalism and Private Equity – A New Regime?, *Transfer: European Review of Labour and Research,* 15(2): 189–208, provides a sound and interesting supplementation to your learning about private equity.

2 The statistical effects of the GFC on world trade are evident in Holland, D., Barrell, R., Fic, T., Hurst, I., Liadze, I., Orazgani, A. and Pillonca, V. (2009) The World Economy: The Global Financial Crisis and Collapse in World Trade, *National Institute Economic Review,* 208(1): 9–16.

3 An article that might not be what budding strategists would want to read – but they probably should – is by Kotz, D. M. (2009) The Financial and Economic Crisis of 2008: A Systemic Crisis of Neoliberal Capitalism, *Review of Radical Political Economics,* 41(3): 305–17.

Private equity unplugged: EMI, 2007–9

Chris Carter

The record industry has undergone tremendous changes in the last decade or so, largely due to the shift in format of music from the compact disc to on line downloads. For instance, 163.4 million CDs were sold in the UK in 2004; by 2007 sales had plummeted to 138.1 million. Some pundits have likened the changes, brought about by digital media, to an Industrial-Revolution-style shift in the record industry. Falling sales have led to a decline in the profitability of the large record companies, which until recently were modern-day leviathans in the music industry. EMI, a leading British record company, and the third largest music group in the world, was for some time seen as vulnerable, partly because it had relatively little presence in the large US market. Employing 5500 people in 2007, its recent financial performance had been dismal; it issued two profit warnings and suspended dividend payments in the financial year to 31 March 2007, in which it made a loss of £263.6 million.

In March 2007, EMI turned down a takeover bid of 260p a share from Warner Music, the American entertainment giant. In May 2007, the EMI board announced that it had received offers of interest from a number of private equity firms. Later that month, the board announced that it was opening the financial accounts for potential suitors to conduct their own analyses of the firm. A number of private equity firms – One Equity Partners, Cerberus Capital and Fortress – were reputed to be interested in EMI, as were Warner Music. At the end of May, Terra Firma, a private equity firm, made an offer of £4 billion[1] or 265p per share that the board recommended shareholders accept. Ironically, the previous year the board had rejected offers of 310p and 320p per share, respectively.

By August 2007, immediately prior to the onset of the global financial crisis, Terra Firma, after a few last-minute uncertainties over funding, took control

---

[1]Different figures have been quoted for the total costs of the purchase of EMI. These range from £2.4 billion through to £4 billion. We use the higher figure in this chapter, as it is the one most frequently cited.

of EMI with £2.6 billion of the deal being financed by the US-based Citigroup. Guy Hands, the Chief Executive of Terra Firma, stated: 'The initial focus will be to maximise the value of the significant assets in EMI's publishing business and to realise the digital opportunity in recorded music.' EMI's business comprised its publishing division, selling printed sheet music and, more importantly, its back catalogue, where the revenues, from radio royalties and sales, were very stable, and from selling newly recorded music. Many well-known contemporary artists – Coldplay, Radiohead, Robbie Williams, Kylie Minogue – were signed to EMI, and it also owned a back catalogue that included some of the greats in pop and rock history, such as The Beatles, Blur, David Bowie, Paul McCartney, Pink Floyd, the Rolling Stones and Queen. Terra Firma aimed to restructure EMI for the digital age.

The back catalogue provided a steady income from royalties when tracks received airplay on the radio or television. Citigroup had planned to securitize this income, selling bonds on the basis of projected future income streams from this part of the business. Normally, a range of financial investors would have queued up to buy the bonds issued. With the freezing of financial markets, this was no longer an option.

With one exception the previous executive team were removed and a new team brought in, including John Birt, the controversial former Director General of the BBC. Music industry insiders no longer ran the organization. In November 2007, EMI announced that it was going to change the way in which it managed its music business and was going to take a harder nosed approach, including sacking 'unproductive' artists. In addition, expenses, such as the reputed £200,000 per annum that EMI was spending on 'candles and flowers' for offices, were to be cut. (The term 'flowers' is understood in music accounting circles to cover a number of stimulants to the imagination that might help accentuate creativity, not all of which can be put in vases.) Various stories of rock 'n' roll excess were leaked and circulated in the business press, some of which were worthy of the satirical movie *Spinal Tap*. Consequently, Terra Firma claimed that it aimed to reduce costs by £100 million a year. The changed approach to management at EMI provoked considerable criticism: the band Radiohead cited Terra Firma's lack of knowledge of the music industry as the key reason for their not signing a new recording contract with the label. As Ed O'Brien (2007), the band's guitarist, put it:

(Continued)

(Continued)

EMI is in a state of flux. It's been taken over by somebody who's never owned a record company before, Guy Hands and Terra Firma, and they don't realise what they're dealing with. It was really sad to leave all the people [we've worked with]. But he wouldn't give us what we wanted. He didn't know what to offer us. Terra Firma doesn't understand the music industry.

That this was the case has recently been indicated by a legal action. EMI sought to 'unbundle' music that had in the past been contracted for vinyl and then for CD distribution as individual tracks for digital downloading, rather than only distributing them in their original album format. One of their bands, Pink Floyd, had recorded the second best selling albums in the catalogue, after The Beatles, almost all as complete 'concept' albums. Their 1999 contract, agreed well before iTunes and digital developments, explicitly forbade unbundling. Pink Floyd sued EMI/Terra Firma for breaching their contract and won the UK High Court battle, thus preventing their record label EMI from selling individual songs online. The judge agreed that the contract contained a clause to 'preserve the artistic integrity of the albums'. Hence, another profit line was closed off to the beleaguered company.

Radiohead famously made their *In Rainbows* album available on the Web, for which people donated what they thought it was worth as they downloaded it. Between 1.2 and 1.8 million people are estimated to have done so. For some this highlighted a turning point in the music industry – one that threatened to erode the historic power of the record companies. Whatever the future of the major labels, Radiohead's actions pulled into sharp focus the crisis facing the music industry: as music became digital and moved to the Web it fuelled piracy, but also created a new distribution channel that had the potential to erode the power of the major labels. Accordingly, music industry commentators noted that well-known bands no longer needed major labels, while up-and-coming bands could avoid the exploitative contracts often associated with the industry through distributing their music on the Web.

Radiohead's departure from EMI aroused considerable attention. Other artists were also reported to be unsure about the present state of the record company and were reputed to be considering their futures. Robbie Williams apparently went on strike while producing his new album. Williams' manager stated:

We're led to believe there is going to be a new and wholesale cutback in staff. Tony Wadsworth [a long-standing EMI executive] has left, we understand other long-serving employees will be leaving too. We won't deliver an album to a company where we don't know what their structure will be or how they will handle things.

In contrast, Guy Hands, Chief Executive of Terra Firma, saw people within the music industry labouring under the following misapprehensions:

1 That hit records will cover all expenses and make a profit.

2 That mergers between record labels will produce sufficient economies of scale to deliver profits.

3 That experts in particular genres of music know what will sell in the marketplace. He pointed out that 85 per cent of record releases make no money and 35 per cent of signed artists never release a record. In his view, artists needed to do more to make their money.

The disagreements between well-known artists and Terra Firma continued. In many respects it can be seen as a clash between the logic of finance capital and that of creative musicians. This took a step further when in early 2008 EMI announced that it was shedding 2000 employees (around a third of the workforce). In addition, cuts in marketing, administration and artist advances were announced as part of a 'revolutionary strategy' to deliver value. Perhaps the most radical part of this strategy was Terra Firma's announcement that it was aiming to take power away from the artist and repertoire (A&R) staff. A&R staff sign bands to record labels. They are generally obsessed with music and in touch with particular music scenes. Traditionally, within the music industry, A&R people have been hugely influential, and are widely seen as pivotal to a successful record label. To Terra Firma, the A&R staff seemed an unprofessional bunch and it sought to make signing bands more 'business-like', as opposed to the more 'intuitive' methods used by A&R staff. As Guy Hands put it: 'What we are doing is taking the power away from the A&R guys and putting it with the suits – the guys who have to work out how to sell music.' For their part, music industry insiders and musicians thought that Terra Firm, simply put, did not understand the music business: it just did not get it.

Terra Firma's acquisition of EMI took place a few months prior to the credit crunch. Part of its original plan would have included using the profitable publishing wing of the business to refinance the original purchase. Citibank would have securitized EMI's

(Continued)

(Continued)

debt, swapping some of it for equity – thus reducing the costs of lending. In the wake of the financial crisis, however, no investors were interested in buying EMI's debt. The credit crunch meant that banks were unable or unwilling to refinance EMI, especially Citibank, which was hit particularly hard. As a private equity buyout, EMI was servicing a huge debt of around £2.6 billion. The inability to refinance was contributing to its costs, as the cost of financing was higher than anticipated.

The first year of Terra Firma's ownership of EMI was a rocky one. Major artists such as Radiohead, Paul McCartney and the Rolling Stones left the label. The reorganization looked to exploit its back catalogue through rereleases, digital remasters and various compilation albums. In addition, it hired in a high-profile digital director from Google and a 'hit maker' from Universal Music. More modest successes included Brian Wilson, late of the Beach Boys, returning to the label. In July 2008, a year after the acquisition, Elio Leoni-Sceti, an Italian marketing executive, was appointed to run the recording business. He was hired from Reckitt-Benckiser, a British consumer goods company specializing in cleaning products. In July 2008, Guy Hands claimed that in the first year under Terra Firma ownership the financial performance of the firm had improved dramatically, with a £100 million profit being generated. Financial analysts in the media were less sure, regarding the purchase of EMI as a mistake. In October 2008, the annual profit figures were released: the overall losses for the year were a colossal £757 million. Closer inspection of these figures revealed that the net financing costs were £520 million. Servicing the estimated £2.6 billion loan from Citigroup was causing problems for EMI. Citigroup itself was in trouble, with its loans, in effect, being underwritten by the US government.

The bad news continued into 2009 and it was reported that Guy Hands, had written off £1.2 billion of Terra Firm's investment in EMI. It was announced that he was standing down as Chief Executive of Terra Firma (though remaining Chairman), to concentrate on turning around the investments held by the private equity firm. At the fore was EMI. Bad publicity continued to mount at EMI: veteran 'progressive' rockers Pink Floyd sued, claiming their royalties had been miscalculated; Joss Stone also expressed her desire to buy out of her contract and leave EMI. In an attempt to generate revenues, EMI achieved some success in releasing material from its back catalogue. EMI dubbed 09/09/09 'Beatles Day', releasing both a box set and remastered albums across the world. The company, though, was straining under the dead weight of the estimated £2.6 billion debt it was trying to service.

In late 2009 there was serious discussion as to whether EMI would default on its debt schedules. Much hinged on its operational performance, which industry insiders seemed to think was going well. The debt was reviewed every six months and relations between Citibank and Terra Firma were deteriorating with the reviews. Under the covenant of the debt, EMI needed to make sure that this was no more than a certain multiple of its earnings, the corollary being that Terra Firma's source of funds was under constant scrutiny and vulnerable to recall. It was with this in mind that Terra Firma was desperate for capital injections and was trying to interest investors in taking a stake in EMI. Such an entreaty was hardly attractive given the parlous circumstances the company was in. EMI was on the brink and Citigroup, reputedly, was lining up potential buyers.

In early 2010 at the time of writing, the situation remained bleak at EMI, despite improvements in the financial performance of the company – especially in the, hitherto troubled, recording part of the business which realized a £298 million pre-interest profit in 2009. Nonetheless, EMI was threatened by a financial sword of Damocles as the combination of massive interest charges, a £1.2 billion financial write-down and the costs of restructuring transmogrified an operating profit into an earth-shattering £1.75 billion loss. In 2010, this was reputed to be the largest loss ever made by a private equity company. Under the legal covenants of its loans with Citigroup, Terra Firma was obligated to raise £105 million to avoid surrendering EMI to the bank. Matters were complicated further by Guy Hands taking out a lawsuit against Citigroup for, in effect, furnishing him with poor advice as to the true value of EMI. While the future of EMI, at the time of writing, hangs in the balance (there are stories circulating that it is planning to sell the iconic Abbey Road studios) it is worth reflecting on the broader implications of private equity.

Question

1 Private equity appeared to be a sure-fire get-rich-quick scheme in the noughties. But as the case demonstrates, things do not always work out that way. What are the main lessons about strategy that you can draw from this case?

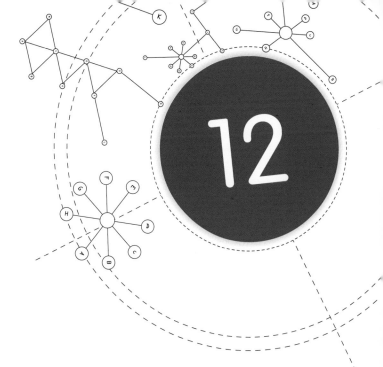

Globalization and Strategy

Convergence, divergence, glocalization

LEARNING OBJECTIVES

By the end of this chapter you will be able to:

● Define globalization
● Identify several of the common misconceptions about globalization
● Grasp the different approaches to internationalization and globalization
● Understand the phenomenon of being 'born global'
● See the limits to discourses of corporate social responsibility
● Understand why businesses try to develop global strategies
● Explain what global strategies are typically used as well as the strengths and weaknesses of each

---

BEFORE YOU GET STARTED . . .

I would define globalization as the freedom for my group of companies to invest where it wants when it wants, to produce what it wants, to buy and sell where it wants, and support the fewest restrictions possible coming from labour laws and social conventions.

(PERCY BARNEVIK, PRESIDENT OF THE ABB INDUSTRIAL GROUP)

INTRODUCTION

Globalization can be thought of as worldwide integration in virtually every sphere, achieved principally through the international diversification of goods, services and processes across the borders of global regions and countries into different geographical locations or markets. Globalization involves increasing liquidity and multidirectional flows of people, material things and immaterial significations, as well as the structures that they flow through, around and over, that act as barriers to increasing liquidity.

The quote from Barnevik suggests that globalization means only one thing: an unfettered freedom to profit. Some writers would agree: Micklethwait and Wooldridge (2000) also see globalization as an unfettered freedom, working not just for multinationals but also for people more generally: globalization, they suggest, produces an economy close to a liberal's utopia. Economically, it is one where rational individuals armed with perfect information acquired from the Internet are able to pursue their interests relatively free of governments and geographical obstacles: people whose interest is primarily in getting what they want for the cheapest price possible.

The International Monetary Fund, in defining globalization, pays particular attention to trade and financial flows, as well as the movements of people and technologies across international borders. Trade, usually thought of as entailing the physical transfer of goods from one place to another in a very material sense (on ships, trains, trucks and aircraft), refers increasingly to the movement of immaterial things, of 'liquid modernity' in the form of downloads, capital and culture. Financial flows are the most immediate, liquid and virtual manifestation of globalization.

Globalization is more than just economic liberalization and financialization, however, even though that was a key element in the models that prevailed until the global financial crisis of 2008, because globalization transforms social relations (think of Facebook) not just business relations. Moreover, anti-globalization groups are as likely to use the technologies of globalization, such as the Internet and mobile phones, to articulate protests against it as proponents. Looked at this way, we need to address globalization as a long-term process of transformation that is contradictory, uneven and eventful, just as likely to be resisted as celebrated (Morgan, 2009).

Analytically, Ritzer (2010: 2) identifies globalization as 'a transplanetary process or set of processes involving increasing liquidity and the growing multidimensional flows of people, objects, places, and information as well as the structures they encounter and create that are barriers to, or expedite, those flows'. It is generally agreed that globalization intensifies social relations over ever-greater distances, linking different and previously separated peoples and locales, transforming the spatial and temporal organization of social relations and transactions, premised on global flows of power, people, ideas and things, with the result that the world is simultaneously compressed and experience of, and in it, is intensified. From this perspective, globalization is a relational process perhaps better thought of as globalizing, as a verb, rather than as a noun, because there may be nothing that corresponds to it; simply, it is a process rather than a thing, as we will go on to argue.

GLOBALIZATION

Almost all the basic strategy models for thinking about globalization derive from North American and European assumptions about the internationalization of business. Hence, they tend to be rather ethnocentric, seeing globalization as a Western 'conquering' of the world. There are good historical auspices for this view of the world as something to conquer, because it has been a part of the North's dominant myth making ever since the Euro-Asian world expanded greatly as a result of the voyages of discovery in the fifteenth century, of which Columbus's is the best known. The idea that the world 'out there' was waiting to be conquered has been both instrumental in developing imperial worldviews in Europe and North America and latterly in European and American business, as a constitutive part of competitive strategy.

The translation of political imperialism into contemporary commercial globalization is usually seen as a late twentieth-century phenomenon, although there is an argument that says that the world economy in the early twentieth century was almost as globalized as it is now, even if the mechanisms of globalization differed – the telegraph instead of the Internet, for instance. From this perspective, globalization is just internationalization speeded up and in no way differs from processes that have been characteristic of much of past human history. For instance, the age of colonialism, by the end of the nineteenth century, had produced a remarkably globalized world, one in which global trade flowed through schemes of imperial preference with currencies readily exchangeable because of the gold standard. Admittedly, it ended in carnage and autarchy with the First World War and the Depression of the 1930s, giving rise to the Second World War.

Pro-globalizing arguments stress that as steamships, railways, trucks, automobiles and jet aircraft gave way to the Internet as the major communication device, its distinctive modes of communication make the present wave of globalization different from the past because information now travels at the speed of light.

Fervent fans of globalization are usually referred to as 'globalists' or 'hyperglobalizers': however, they are balanced by a group of writers whom we can refer to as 'sceptics'. While the globalists see globalization as a done deal, covering virtually the whole globe, the sceptics point to the fact that not only are great swathes of the world's population barely incorporated into the global arena, but also there are many obstacles and barriers to globalization erected by various interests: states and their governments; domestic industrial players, keen to protect themselves from global competition; trade unions, equally keen to ensure that the price of labour in the labour market is not cheapened and weakened by too global a flow of poor people who will enable unscrupulous employers to cut labour costs. Globalists would point out that it is no longer possible to be a sceptic when the global risk society spreads with no regard to borders; that the carbon footprint of the most globally advanced nations is warming the planet for even the poorest people on it.

It is possible even for sceptics to concede that, as a result of vastly more efficient agro-businesses, the planet is able to sustain a population of 6½ billion, which has doubled in the last 30 years, and that the huge growth in business has in part contributed to this increased population by providing more and better jobs and an improved availability of foodstuffs. However, more does not mean equal shares: the benefits are hardly distributed evenly. For instance, the United States consumes nearly 40 per cent of the planet's resources such as food, oil and timber, but contains only 6 per cent of the global population, of whom 30 per cent are obese from consuming too much (OECD Health Data, 2005: www.nationmaster.com/graph/hea_obe-health-obesity, accessed 18 February 2010). That is one reason why many critics of globalization claim that it is really an 'Americanization'.

Globalists argue that globalization has created the liberalization of global markets and the design of a 'flat' or 'borderless' world – where flat and borderless are metaphors for an open market, conceived as a levelling of opportunities for all who compete in it. Yet, as critics are quick to point out, there is no inevitability about liberalization: it can just as easily go into reverse as forward motion, and many of the elements of national responses to the global financial crisis of 2008 suggest that we are currently in reverse on some fronts, such as the US Congress' response in inserting protectionist clauses into House Bills.

While globalization increases the ubiquity of objects, practices and experiences in increasingly homogenized, standardized and convergent modes, not everyone around the globe eats the same industrially produced foods, watches the same movies and wears the same global chain-store-produced clothes. Globalization does not mean that local cultural differences are obliterated. Globalization mingles and mashes up cultures, with hybrids being the result: it produces Bollywood-inspired Oscar winners such as *Slumdog Millionaire*; makes curry the English national dish; and sees the *jihab* become a garment of affirmation – or protest and subjection, depending on perspective and politics – worn around the world.

Globalization is not just Westernization by another name – or, more specifically, the process of Americanization. Most of the manufactured goods and fashions that spread the materiality of globalization are produced by workers in China – a notionally communist state that sits at the centre of the global capitalist economy. For Western radicals, globalization might mean immiseration in Asian sweatshop factories; on the other side of the planet, in China, globalization may be the means of leaving the wretchedness of rural life behind as new factory jobs are created.

Globalization entails the translation of objects, practices and experiences in space and time. Translation is an open and unfolding process in which meanings shift with each new translation. Globalization entails harmonization and the assimilation of national and local cultures as well as their destruction and debasement.

- *Harmonization* emerges as the same retail chains, brands, malls and fashions can be found wherever one goes in the world: in the ubiquitous malls of the world many of the same brands, designs and chains will be found irrespective of whether one is in Mexico or Macau.

- *Assimilation emerges* when cultures blend and condense, creating new hybrids and experiences in old cultures. Examples can be found in the restaurants of many of the world's global cities.

- *Destruction* is wrought most especially on people of the 'Fourth World' – the world of indigenes whose lands were subject to expropriation by settlers globalizing from elsewhere, as in the United States and Australia.

- *Debasement* can be seen in the 'packaging' of local culture, such as that of Hawaii or other parts of Polynesia, as a curiosity for foreigners who are jetted in and jetted out with a frequency that breeds bizarre entertainment rituals with little or no cultural authenticity.

A few companies are truly global – they span the globe with their presence virtually everywhere. They are an important part of the effective infrastructure of globalization. But often they do so not as independent entities but through a strategy of broad-based alliances and networks. They leverage localization from their globalization – in a synergy some analysts refer to as *glocalization* – through cross-investments and partnerships with national, regional and local companies that deliver a deeper penetration of global markets.

Strategies for glocalization constantly have to steer between a tendency to play to a set of values and beliefs that are believed to be widely shared around the world – the traditional basis for economies of scope and scale – and also be alert to the existence of highly specific values and beliefs that differentiate particular identities globally. The latter are typically based on specificities of geography, history and culture – especially religion – that mean there can never be a wholly globalized model of a global culture for a global world. Globalization is always flowing in new directions with unanticipated results. Trying to sell a product globally means paying careful attention to the context and, where necessary, retooling it in terms of local sensitivities. Sometimes this can be done crudely and will create a bigger backlash than the original globalizing model might have done. In August 2009 Microsoft was lambasted for Photoshopping a black man into a (mostly) white man in an advertisement for the Polish market – mostly, because it forgot to make his hands white! This was not a smart move: in trying to play to the perceived conservatism of Polish culture Microsoft simply made itself look strategically stupid and racist.

BORN GLOBAL

The globalization of enterprise need not be developmental and need not be the end point of internationalization strategies. There are firms that are 'born global'. The topic of 'born global' has attracted a lot of attention in recent years. In the past the international business strategy literature suggested that internationalization occurred as a result of an evolutionary model, in which internalization was the outcome of a move from exports, to joint ventures, to fully owned operations (Johanson and Vahlne, 1977). Most of this literature focused on large and multinational organizations, as we saw in chapter 10.

The concept 'born global' was first used in Rennie's (1993) Australian report for McKinsey & Co, and it has been widely used and discussed together with similar concepts, such as, for example, International New Ventures (McDougall, Shane and Oviatt, 1994; Oviatt & McDougall, 1994). The basic point is that it is not necessary to have evolved into a large firm to internationalize. E-commerce companies operating in a virtual domain can overcome spatial and temporal barriers to undertake international operations quickly and cheaply.

A number of factors can be identified as contributing to the phenomenon of firms being 'born global', including more global market conditions, new developments in transportation and communication technologies, especially the Internet, and an increase in the available numbers of people with international experience. Additionally, as we can see in the following case study, born-global firms may produce standardized products but operate in a highly specialized niche.

MINI CASE STUDY

Born global: Infomedia

Infomedia Ltd is a publicly listed Australian company that has become a leading supplier of electronic parts catalogues for the global automotive industry. The company is headquartered in Sydney and has support centres in Melbourne, Europe, Japan, Latin and North America.

This born-global company first expanded into international markets by partnering with other businesses, before distributing more of its product itself through wholly owned subsidiaries. As is typical for born-global enterprises, its customers dragged Infomedia into the world market. Today, Infomedia's electronic parts catalogues have become the global standard for the automotive industry, shipping to more than 50,000 dealers in over 160 countries and 25 languages.

Current Chairman Richard Graham, who emigrated from the United States with experience in

(Continued)

(Continued)

technology and computer hardware sales, founded Infomedia in January 1990. Graham initially distributed other parties' software under the name of Infomagic, but later decided to transform his business into a software development company.

The seed of Infomedia was Graham's purchase of the intellectual property for Apple software that enabled the conversion of automotive microfiche and books into user-friendly, digitized catalogues for electronic parts. The inventor of this software, Wayne Sinclair, joined Infomedia as its lead program engineer.

Infomedia soon secured its first client, Ford Motor Company Australia, and by December 1990 had developed its first product: Microcat. While others in the market were selling hardware and software packages on five-year contracts, Infomedia offered monthly subscriptions with no obligation to continue purchasing. Subsequent Australian clients were acquired through Nissan and Daihatsu.

Infomedia's first export opportunity arose in 1996, when Ford invited the company to attend a meeting with Ford Europe. The challenge for Infomedia was quickly to produce a catalogue in 17 languages and to beat large competitors. Graham decided to show Ford Europe what Infomedia could do, so he flew part of his team to Europe, where working from different countries they pulled the product together and made their first export sale in September 1997.

Infomedia's first international success was critical in several respects. First, it marked the beginning of the company's profitability. Second, it vindicated the generous and crucial assistance that Infomedia had been receiving from Austrade. Third, it initiated Infomedia's partnering with distributors (Clifford Thames in Europe and the United States, DHL in Europe). Fourth, the company's relationship with Ford propelled it in succeeding years into Japan, Canada, the United States and then all of Ford's emerging markets.

Infomedia's rapid international expansion meant that it went from having a distribution of 19 markets, mainly in Europe, to over 100 worldwide. In 2002, Infomedia completed its first foreign acquisition: a division of US technology services company EDS. This acquisition gave Infomedia a licence to serve General Motors, which it combined with its previously obtained licence to serve Toyota.

By 2004, Infomedia's growth and development was prompting it to shift away from its original business model of third-party distribution towards direct dealings with original equipment manufacturers (OEMs). Infomedia was increasingly finding that automobile manufacturers wanted to talk to it directly.

In July 2004 Infomedia established a new entity in Europe to manage directly its in-country relationships with the OEMs. In September 2005 the company also established an entity in North America to do the same. All European customer service is performed in Sydney headquarters, which operates two shifts in a call centre that covers business hours across all the international time zones.

So what have been the key determinants of Infomedia's international success? According to CEO Gary Martin, Infomedia's competitive edge can be attributed to its superior technology, its low-cost and agile production and its Australian foundation.

While competitors produced on IBM-compatible PCs, Infomedia made use of Apple Macintoshes. These allowed for better catalogue design and search capacity, as well as language switching without rebooting.

Additionally, Infomedia demonstrated that it could operate at a lower cost and faster turnaround of product than competitors. Indeed, Infomedia has had to educate one of its major distributors, which was used to a much more leisurely turnaround. In Martin's words: 'Distributor education is always a big one.'

Finally, Infomedia has taken advantage of its Australian origin. On the one hand, Infomedia can draw on Australian businesses' reputation of being somewhat rough but highly effective. On the other hand, being based in Australia's time zone and in multicultural Sydney enables Infomedia to employ a multilingual workforce that operates globally tomorrow, today.

Question

1 Identify a case of a 'born-global' company, similar to Infomedia, from your own country. What are the key factors in the case that have enabled it to be born global?

Google is relatively new, wholly global, with a philosophy that *You can make money without doing evil*. Is Google the precursor of future born-global and born-good companies? Maybe the new wave of global businesses can be more socially accountable than their predecessors because they carry no historical baggage (although we should note that Google for quite some time bowed to the command by the Chinese state that they block some sites for Chinese consumption, and has now moved out of China because of the political pressure).

UNEVEN GLOBALIZATION; UNEVEN RISK

The globalization of markets in goods and services is not as well developed as this is in capital. Although most people in 'the West' have the literacy, money and Internet access to order any book from Amazon or book a cheap online air ticket, this would not be the case for many people in Africa or Asia. For many, it is the externalities of globalization that impinge most evidently on their lives. Global markets fuel rapacious behaviour and unsustainable strategies, the risks of which cannot be contained. Pollution flows globally: the smoke from Malaysia's burning forests (burnt by illegal loggers clearing rare first-growth hardwoods for export markets) drifts over Singapore impairing the quality of the air and the health of its citizens; Chernobyl's toxic poison drifted far from the Ukraine over Central and Northern Europe. Given the risks that people face from irresponsible economic activity and business, there is today a burgeoning strategic push for corporate social responsibility (CSR).

Adopting **corporate social responsibility (CSR)** implies that an organization is ecologically reflexive; that it cares about its carbon footprint; strives to measure it; and seeks to minimize it strategically. One reason for the growth of CSR is a realization that so many corporate strategies that aim to sell more things to those who have effective demand – who can afford them – have an ethical dimension that is rarely addressed and that they are not sustainable business models for the planet and *everyone* on it. What makes the corporation successful can diminish the health of people and the planet even as it provides them with more of what those with an effective demand apparently want. To the extent that these strategies are unsustainable, in ecological terms they destroy the habitat of the planet. For many countries and companies the impetus to be green is not as great as the impetus to continue profiting from existing forms of business, irrespective of their negative externalities. For some organizations, the realization that green strategies can mean less waste and thus the more efficient exploitation of those resources consumed has led their top management team to a commitment to sustainability, at least where costs can be cut; where they might be increased it is often another matter.

Early studies of sustainable organizational practices were characterized by their appeal to the ethical principles by which organizations should guide their ecological actions. Until the 1990s, empirical examples of pro-active environmental practices in firms were extremely scarce (Fischer and Schot, 1993). More recently, the necessity of working with the rules that currently guide managerial action by incrementally incorporating bio-centric values into these rules, which, over time, will, it is argued, result in better environmental practices in organizations. Such approaches have been characterized as **ecological modernization strategies**. From an ecological modernization perspective all strategy should be oriented to seeing that current modes of production and consumption are redesigned according to ecological principles (Spaargaren and Mol, 1992; Mol and Spaargaren, 1993; Mol, 1995; Yearley, 2007). The sheer efficiency of modern systems of production could be significantly improved by using knowledge in a strategically reflexive fashion. Weizsäcker, Lovins and Lovins (1997), for instance, propose that in many industrial sectors it is possible to double wealth at the same time as the use

Corporate social responsibility (CSR) has been defined by the European Commission (2005) as exisiting when companies integrate 'social and environmental concerns in their business operations and in their interactions with their stakeholders on a voluntary basis'.

Ecological modernization strategies suggest that economic and technological win–win solutions – gaining less pollution and more profits through a more efficient use of resources – can ameliorate harmful environmental effects.

of resources could be halved – in mathematical terms, by a factor of four. Because these achievements would be based on the incorporation of ecological principles, such as resource efficiency and dematerialization, into current industrial practices, they would represent processes of ecological modernization. Where these strategies would make most difference is obvious: global corporations are the dominant agents within the world economy and it is here that strategic change must begin.

Proponents of ecological modernization argue that rather than dismantling the foundations of industrial societies, the only viable alternative is to solve the ecological crises – the continuous burdening of the sustenance base of the planet – by fully exploring the potential of wealth creation. This would be done through the use of one central source of the dynamism of modernity: the *reflexivity* of knowledge appropriation. The use of rational capabilities should allow us to install a process of continuous revaluation and redesign of modern institutions as a key element of all strategies. Over time, systems of production and consumption would be redefined according to ecological requirements, as well as economic and technical ones. The intensification of reflexive strategy would, ultimately, allow modern organizations and societies to redefine the rules governing the economy, as well as its social extensions.

Such a view is quite appealing. Maintaining modern institutions is an alluring argument for those who benefit from the current state of affairs in highly industrialized societies. This is why critics of ecological modernization theory see it as another neo-liberal ideology in *green* camouflage that does not challenge tendencies towards monopolistic organization (with no competitive spurs to perform in ecologically better terms), social inequality, and the appropriation and exploitation of nature. The theory of ecological modernization, critics argue, apparently ignores the institutionalization of doubt, the disenchantment of science and the endangering characteristics of modern science and technology (Mol, 1995; Beck, 1997; see also Orsato and Clegg (2005) for further elaboration).

Strategically, business enterprises are both the responsible agents for the promotion of environmental reform and sufficiently powerful to be able to make such promotion (Hawken, 1993; Hawken et al., 1999). It is this realization that has seen a substantial literature develop on CSR and strategy. Banerjee (2007: 16–18) sees the following elements as implicit in firms that commit to CSR:

- A commitment to reporting a firm's social performance in some ways, through audit, social impact analaysis and social reporting. Often what is measured is perceptions rather than actual performance.

- Exceeding expectations of minimal obligations; going above and beyond what is legally required in positive ways, in terms of worker and community welfare.

- Discretionary behaviour constituted by codes of conduct that are not legally binding but statements of policy and intent in regard to various nominated categories of stakeholders.

CSR has become a global phenomenon in recent times. Global institutions such as the United Nations (UN), International Labour Organization (ILO), World Bank and International Monetary Fund (IMF), and the G8, frame the institutional rules of the global economy. These are largely neo-economically liberal. Within this frame the idea of stakeholder capitalism has developed to complement that of shareholder capitalism. From the classical neo-liberal perspective the idea that companies might have stakeholders other than shareholders can be dangerously subversive (Friedman, 1962). Nonetheless, it has grown in popularity. From this perspective the firm comprises a constellation of interests competing for managerial attention; interests are identified with stakeholders, and the task is to manage stakeholders.

One consequence of the enhanced legitimay of CSR is that a focus purely on shareholder wealth maximization is no longer a default business option. Progressive and values-based organizations are now embracing the notion of CSR by considering non-shareholder stakeholders' concerns and publishing external corporate social reports. The publication of such reports is motivated by desires to legitimize business operations with various constituents in society (Deegan, 2002; Deegan, Rankin and Tobin, 2002), to enhance corporate reputation (Owen et al., 2000; Owen, Swift and Hunt, 2001) and reduce corporate risks. It is not only in the West that CSR is fashionable; it is also being introduced with increased frequency in non-Western countries. Social reporting in developing countries is mainly driven by 'outside' forces. Such forces include instructions from head office based in Western developed countries, the influence of international agencies such as the ILO and World Bank, and the coercive conditions from international buyers imposed on the developing country companies supplying goods and services to the Western market. Social accounting techonology is being exported to the developing countries via multinational companies based in Western developed countries.

There are both broad and narrow accounts of stakeholders. Broadly, any group or individual affected by the organization's objectives can be considered a stakeholder (Freeman, 1984). Narrower conceptions try to rank stakeholders in terms of the risk, and the types of risk, that they bear. Stakeholder approaches are essentially:

- *Descriptive*. Stakeholders are who they are described as being – or not being – as management constitutes them. Evident activist stakeholders might thus be excluded as illegitimate.

- *Instrumental*. Stakeholder management can be lauded as a performance criterion, perhaps as a part of 'triple bottom line'. There is no clear evidence, however, that stakeholder management affects firm performance in positive economic terms (Margolis and Walsh, 2003).

- *Normative*. The focus is on some ethical conception of what should and should not be done to whom by corporate agents: what is permissible depends totally on the moral compass being used to steer conceptions. These can often differ markedly between organization agents and those who constitute themselves as stakeholders, especially NGOs and CSOs.

Organizations such as Greenpeace clearly seek to make a difference to corporate practice by drawing attention to organizational misbehaviour – corporate behaviour that is undesirable. By doing so Greenpeace has become a major advocate for CSR, even though NGOs and advocacy groups do not have the power to ensure companies and other organizations conform to corporately socially responsible behaviour (Clegg and Clegg, 2008). They can engage firms in dialogue, enter into partnerships and help frame codes of conduct, but these often legitimate the companies as much as they change their behaviour, and the activist organizations then run the risk of being co-opted. Meanwhile, companies may gain credence for being corporately socially responsible while not being required to document the basis on which these claims are made; their good reputational management might even help them avoid effective legislation. While companies might make their profit-making more sustainable, their efforts may have little or no, or even an adverse, impact on the communities whose resources they mine, farm, fish and manufacture, or to whom they market (Banerjee, 2007: 145–7).

Banerjee (2007: 149), drawing on the Framework Convention on Corporate Accountability prepared for the Johannesburg Earth Summit (Bruno and Karliner, 2002), suggests that if firms are to become really corporately socially responsible they must accept:

- Mandatory corporate reporting requirements on environmental and social impacts, and a process for prior consultation with affected communities including an environmental and social impact assessment and complete access to information.

- Extended liability to directors for corporate breaches of environmental and social laws and corporate liability for breaches of international laws and agreements.

- Rights of redress for citizens, including access for affected people anywhere in the world to pursue litigation, provisions for stakeholders legally to challenge corporate decisions and legal aid mechanisms to provide public funds to support such challenges.

- Community rights to resources, including indigenous people's rights over common property such as forests, fisheries and minerals.

- Veto rights over developmental projects and against displacement and rights to compensation for resources expropriated by corporations.

- Sanctions against corporations for breaching these duties including suspending stock exchange listings, fines and (in extreme cases) revoking the corporation's charter or withdrawal of limited liability status.

Overall, it is doubtful that established corporations, effectively institutionalized in a legacy of exploitative organizational behaviour and misbehaviour, can become wholly socially responsible, let alone socially accountable, on their own. Past traditions loom nightmarishly large on their present actions, even when these are well intentioned. There has been a dark side to the translation of forms of European-originated organization, practice and knowledge into universal categories (Chakrabarty, 2000), from the mercantilism of the East India Company onwards. Nonetheless, the Enlightenment and the spread of a rights-based reason are strong and powerful weapons to wield against those corporations not committed to enlightening their own operations. Liberalism, as heir to the Enlightenment, offers the possibility of its basic respect for individual rights being translated into more enlightened practice by using the categories of liberalism to reform its practice. What is required is a shift from CSR to corporate social accountability and innovation premised on establishing the rights of those who constitute the corporately excluded. The forces of globalization, suggests Banerjee (2007: 149), can be harnessed to the promotion of social justice.

GLOBALIZING FLOWS

In the previous section we noted how unsustainable business produces pollution that cannot be contained – it flows through the air, in rivers and oceans, despoiling lives and environments far from its source, with no respect for national boundaries. Pollution is not the only thing that flows; in fact, the whole of globalization can be conceived of as something flowing. Indeed, rather than be thought of as a thing, globalization may be better thought of as a relational process; hence, it is better to think of it as globalizing – as a verb, rather than as a noun.

The main organizers of globalizing, above all, are the major corporations that own and control assets in more than one country. It is their strategies of investment, production, marketing, contracting and employment that frame globalization. There are about 80,000 such firms in the world today, accounting for over 70 per cent of world trade. In 2005 total transnational foreign direct investment amounted to over $974 billion.

While finance is obviously globalized – think of the global financial crisis of 2008 – labour markets are largely not globalized, except in quite restricted and specific sectors. For the vast majority of workers the labour market is national: if there were a global market in labour a lot more people from Africa, the Middle East, Latin America and Asia would be free to move to 'the West' rather than resorting to expensive people-smugglers and risky journeys to gain admission. Western interests largely skew the global political economy, especially in labour.

If labour is relatively constrained in its movement, capital is much more unfettered. Financial systems control the supply and value of the underlying key commodity for business, which, of course, is capital. Globalizing, as a process of interdependence in markets, is most advanced in financial markets. The effects of the global financial crisis (GFC) of 2008 seem to suggest that a very high degree of global integration has been achieved if we look at the speed with which the sub-prime crisis unravelled – with global consequences, especially in the North Atlantic economies.

It is evident that qualitatively different phenomena have been progressively globalizing in an uneven development, translating various materialities, practices and concepts from one place to many others. Globalizing occurs through the translation (Czarniawska and Sevón, 2006) of innovations from one place to another. In contemporary times, globalizing increasingly occurs through immaterial forms such as financial innovation – immaterial forms that have substantial material consequences – and it is these that are currently typically referred to as globalization and will provide the major focus here.

Today, virtually the whole world economy as a market is incorporated into a world system dominated by a capitalism based on what Simmel (2004) called the philosophy of money. Mediated by money, exchange can be subject to impersonal and precise division and manipulation and the measurement of equivalents. Flows of capital promote seemingly rational calculations and, while they further the rationalization that is characteristic of modern economy and society, they can also, by virtue of their immateriality and capacity for invention, innovation and translation, morph into ever-new forms of representation that are increasingly liquid and weightless. In globalizing, shapes and forms will shift rapidly, flows will abruptly change and liquid phenomena will fix neither in time nor space. Continuous flux is the apparent norm and, although all senses of time are always relative and plural, not absolute, the dominant flows of time associated with digital immediacy become dominant globally.

Presence and immediacy hasten the adoption of dominant discourses as they can flow anywhere and everywhere simultaneously. Globalizing modernity has flowed through a specific set of conduits or channels in which a number of assumptions about what comprised efficient organization came to shape structural orthodoxy in the era of neo-liberal hegemony. As Colado (2008) argues, more than merely a globalization of economic forms but a globalization of whole forms of life has occurred. Contemporary globalizing and organizing occurs at its core through four major systems of tightly coupled flows.

GLOBALIZING FINANCE, PROCUREMENT, PEOPLE, AND COMMUNICATION

We use Clegg's circuits of power model to analyse the four flows. With this model we can conceive of the flows as moving analytically through the three distinct circuits of power: episodic power, dispositional power and facilitative power (Clegg, 1989, where the model was first developed in Chapter 8). Each circuit plays a distinct role in globalizing flows: episodic power relations change the notions of social relations, the standing conditions necessary to express them consistently, and the social relations through which they are expressed; dispositional power structures change relations of social integration (and disintegration); while facilitative power moves through the circuit of system integration (and disintegration) where innovations and inhibitions in techniques and disciplinary practices flow. The model is a heuristic that we will apply to each of the four main types of flow characterizing globalizing.

Financial flows

The liberalization of the financial system that took place in the 1980s, accelerating through the 1990s, together with the digital revolution in information technology (IT), led to the widespread use of new financial instruments, such as junk bonds, leveraged buyouts and collateralized debt obligations, which became de rigueur as finance capital took on a hyper-real quality in the era of neo-liberalism's dominance, an era marking the fusion of neo-classical economics and political

FIGURE 12.1
Financial flows

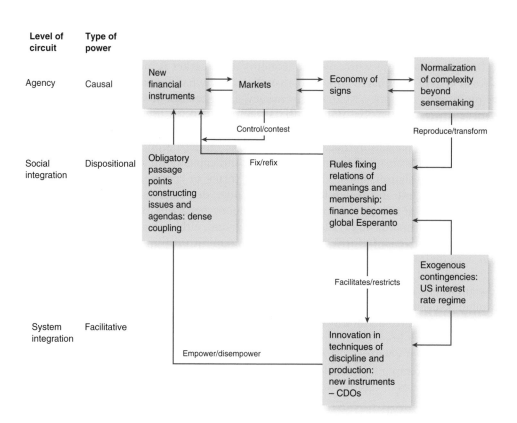

liberalism's joint adherence to the privileging of the individual subject and their liberties as the focus for analysis. Of course, the other side of the neo-liberal coin was an anti-regulation and anti-state pose with programmes that practised deregulation, privatization and the externalization of unavoidable costs, such as ecological despoliation and pollution to the developing world (Colado, 2006). Domestically, taxation reform invariably favoured the elites, while elsewhere liberalisms remedies for capitalism's ills would apply harsh regimes of transition from welfare to work for the poor. Naomi Klein (2007) refers to it as a shock therapy that creates little but destroys much.

The financial system has achieved an unprecedented degree of autonomy, becoming dominated by an economy of signs representing capital flows rather than an economy of things (Harvey, 1992: 194). It became concentrated in circuits and networks that were skewed in terms of the key nodal points (Clegg, 1989) towards the few truly global cities, in which global corporate organizations and their citizens are headquartered, such as New York, London, Tokyo. It is the boards of the firms in top-tier global cities who control the global distribution of capital, technology, knowledge, labour skills, natural resources and consumer markets. Typically, they have greater range and resources than the national states over whose territories their business interests run, except where those states exercise a monopoly or oligopoly control over a key resource base, such as the OPEC states.

Globalizing neo-liberalism places hurdles and barriers around marginal forms of materiality, creating special trading and export zones in much of the developing world as spaces tightly regulated to which access or egress is tightly controlled. Ong (2006) refers to these sites as spheres of exception in which graduated sovereignty is practised. Capital, not citizens or the state, shapes the rules in these zones. The firms are highly competitive on price but for other criteria such as sustainability, human development, and liberty, equality and fraternity in all their dimensions, typically they do not give a damn (see Klein, 2000; Banerjee, 2008).

Globalizing neo-liberalism furthers the integration of financial markets, collapsing the importance of local time and creating instantaneous financial transactions in loans, securities and other innovative financial instruments that shape the 'electronic herd' (Friedman, 1999) of bond, currency and foreign direct investment. The deregulation and internationalization of financial markets created a new competitive spatial environment (Harvey, 1992: 161). Globally integrated financial markets increased the speed of information flows and the rapidity and directness of transactions. Instantaneous financial trading means that shocks felt in one market communicate immediately around the world's markets, as with the example of the US sub-prime loans. The tight coupling of the world's financial system, and its subsequent chaos, limited nation-states' ability to control capital flows and hence fiscal and monetary policy (see Chapter 11).

Procurement flows

Activities that can be performed anywhere, such as call centre work, or the processing of basic accounting data, the interpretation of radiological data, or the preparation of a manuscript for publication, can be digitized and located in a much cheaper labour market. Wherever material or immaterial matter to be worked on can be easily moved around the world, then the outsourcing of labour can cheapen its production. Such work can be organized globally so that it flows 24/7. Outsourcing also occurs when an organization such as a business or a hospital (which can sometimes overlap with tourism – for example medical tourism when wealthy people fly to countries where health care costs are much

FIGURE 12.2
Procurement
flows

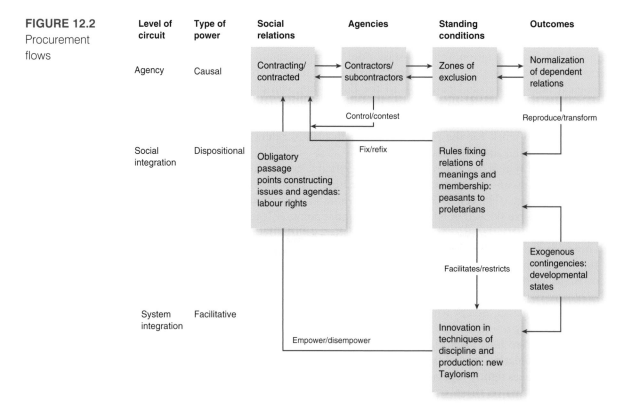

MINI CASE STUDY

Sneaker manufacturing, anti-globalization and global supply chains

The CEO of a global sports good brand has called you in. The strategy of the company consists of paying very high sponsorship fees to sporting global superstars to wear, endorse and advertise your products; designing the goods in design studios in three of the world's major cities (Los Angeles, Tokyo and London); and manufacturing them in subcontracted global supply chains in the Far East, in China, Indonesia and Malaysia mostly.

As a result of anti-globalization campaigns, coordinated through the global justice movement, the brand stores are being targeted by protestors throughout the world. They are complaining that the brand's supply chains employ child labour and that they are ignoring the fair-labour agreements with suppliers.

In addition, one of the global superstars that advertises your product has taken an indefinite break from the sport because there have been some very lurid revelations about his adulterous relations with a large number of 'showgirls', cocktail waitresses and other young women.

Liberal opinion in your core markets is turning against your company. The good reputation of the company and brand is diminishing; the good that the company does in spreading employment opportunities in the Third World is not being communicated as the sweatshop message is overwhelming any communication of the positive things, and the good relations that the company has had with various stakeholders are threatened as moral outrage mounts against the rock 'n' roll lifestyle of the brand ambassador – who had hitherto enjoyed a squeaky-clean and controlled reputation.

What should be your strategy to combat these pressures, which are hitting the share price of the company, while at the same time maintaining the strategic success of the brand?

(Continued)

(Continued)

Suggestions: you should spend some time scouring the Web to become familiar with the strategies and claims of anti-globalization movements and the responses of actual companies to them with respect to their outsourcing strategies.

In addition, consult Pekka Aula and Saku Mantere's (2008) *Strategic Reputation Management* – and then look at Subhabrata Bobby Banerjee's (2007) *Corporate Social Responsibility: The Good, The Bad and The Ugly*.

Finally, you might also consider some recent well-publicized cases in the press of errant sports stars: the name Tiger Woods perhaps comes to mind.

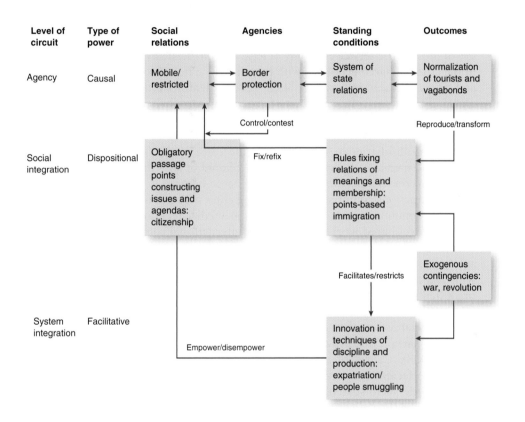

FIGURE 12.3
People flows

lower for surgical procedures) or the military (much of the work of the war in Iraq has been outsourced to companies such as Halliburton) seeks to cheapen the costs of its activities by arranging for some elements of these to be done more cheaply by specialists in these activities. While outsourcing may increase corporate profit, it can lessen corporate control – the most spectacular case of this is occurring at the time of writing with the recall of over 8 million Toyota vehicles worldwide because of safety issues with a subcontract-supplied accelerator pedal (see Figure 12.2).

People flows

When the 2009 GFC hit China there were news reports of millions of employees returning by train to the interior of China from the trading zones of the coastal cities, which are at the heart of the global Chinese economy. These workers had come in their millions to be transformed from peasants into proletarians in one generation.

YOU CAN DOWNLOAD...

Richard Locke, Matthew Amengual and Akshay Mangla's (2009) Virtue Out of Necessity? Compliance, Commitment, and the Improvement of Labor Conditions in Global Supply Chains, *Politics & Society*, 37 (3): 319–51, from the book's website at www.sagepub.co.uk/cleggstrategy

They were one of the most significant internal migrations in history. Elsewhere, one of the reasons why cities such as Mexico City, Sao Paulo or Mumbai are so large is that they act as magnets, both attracting global and national capital to invest in them and pulling in previously peasant labour to work in the opportunities created by that capital or to survive in the interstices of 'demodernity' (Zermeño, 2005).

Adapting Ritzer (2010), we can distinguish between different types of global flows of peoples. Tourists hardly need explanation: they are the liquid mass of consumers armed with passports and credit cards for whom national borders afford mere pauses to their flow through the world of events, spectacles, conferences, places and people.[1] These elites are easy to spot: on the one hand those who are highly skilled and educated and employed in global organizations; on the other hand, and sometimes closely related through their dependence on the expertise of those in the service economy of legal and financial advice, the entrepreneurs of the criminal narco-economy, with the celebrity elites of football, popular music and cinema situated in between. Sklair (2002) identifies different fractions in the global elite: the *corporate fraction* of executives of global corporations and their comprador affiliates; the *state fraction* of elite politicians and public servants as well as NGO elites; the *technical fraction* of professionals sent by their employers to foreign subsidiaries or headquarters; the *consumerist fraction* of merchants, traders and media executives; and the most liquid of all – the *criminal fraction* of global arms traders, people smugglers and narco-barons.

These fractions comprise the globalizing elites who not only partake in similar forms of communication, sharing common media, technologies and messages, but also have shared work experiences in international companies and organizations, working and living in global financial and economical centres. Expatriates are the most liquid human element in these global elites if only because they flow with and are shaped by globalizing capital. While globalizing is not exclusively organized by elites from North American-dominated institutions, it is significant that multinational financial institutions, governments and markets all recruit individuals socialized in elite centres of higher learning, through business schools, such as Wharton, that are *de facto* schools of finance capitalism (Khurana, 2007; Clegg, 2008). Cadres of neo-classically trained economists, imbued with neo-liberalism, facilitate extensive networks of governed interdependence because they provide socio-spatially dispersed and strategically positioned agents in a project linked through institutional associations and normative agreement (Pusey, 1991; Konings, 2008). The GFC, as has been often remarked, is an indictment of the financialization of the business school elites as a project centred on the MBA.

The prominence and wealth of financial centres in the high period of late modernity, from the 1980s onwards, deepened links between national elites and institutions of higher education, ensuring the reproduction of the 'financial man'; individuals, mostly male, embedded in a moral community and organizational system that motivated them to enrich themselves, their corporation and, from the perspective of state elites, be able to advance core national interests (Walter, 2005). Business schools, especially the *Financial Times* elite, were at the core of this activity.

Vagabonds are occasionally seen in the airports of the great cities, sometimes sleeping in and around the facilities. Sometimes these people are in limbo, lacking the accreditation that could send them elsewhere; other times, they are local people who merely sleep near where they work because they are homeless or far from home. The most evident vagabonds are the asylum seekers that one sees on the news as they huddle at points of entry to the global world, seeking to get in, or

---

[1]When not in transit they are able to outsource and transfer activities to some other agency as an economic transaction: for instance, families that hire chauffeurs, nannies, gardeners, cooks, domestics, etc., are outsourcing domestic labour that might, in other circumstances, be done, literally, in-house, by family members.

are apprehended as they try to sail, walk or truck into global centres. Sometimes it is their bodies that are found as a testament to another failed attempt to enter the global world, when, occasionally, they tumble out of the sky falling from stowaway positions on the landing gear of the giant aircraft that, for some, make global tourism possible. Vagabonds enhance the lifestyles of elite fractions through their labours. Often these people will be recruited from the ranks of the illegal immigrant population, working in the shadows of the informal economy.

Communication flows

Ever since *The German Ideology* (Marx and Engels, 1845/1968) there has been a conviction that the most fundamental form of power lies in the ability to shape the human mind. Effectively, this has been the territory of Steven Lukes' conception of power ever since his 'radical view' burst on the scene (1974; 2005). Communication and its control is thus at the heart of this modality of power. Power is neverending in its struggles, operating at every level of and in all types of social practice, and including relational, asymmetric, resistance-inducing *power to* as well as *power over*; hence, there is always power and resistance.

Lukes' (2006) radical power flows through what Appadurai (1996) terms mediascapes. These are the forms of communication shaped through the digital processes of mass and mass self-communication, such as social networking, which are central to resistance because they act as conduits for alternative and dominant discourse construction in contemporary times. The mediascape is where images of identity, selfhood and otherness thrive. While the rise of mass self-communication makes the privatization of the digital commons a profitable sphere for those commanding networked and network-making power, the space constituted through its messages is a wild, anarchic space, in which all sorts of new pluralities of ideas

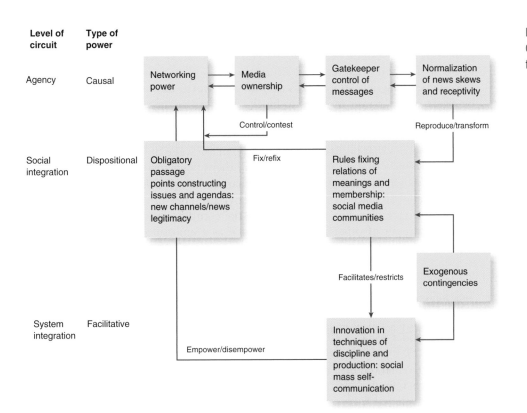

FIGURE 12.4
Communication flows

may and do circulate, with subversive, resistant effects. Think of the role of social media in building internal political opposition to the current Ahmadinejad regime and its clerical supporters in Iran.

Networks are increasingly objects for a contemporary analysis of global power, laced together as multiple, overlapping, open and socio-spatially interactive systems comprising interconnected nodes. Communication flows through these nodes have been revolutionized since the development of digital technologies, creating the global network society in its interactions and exchanges with, as well as its marginalization of, already existing societal sites, cultures, organizations and institutions of various types. The nodes configure power relations: again, think of the role of mobile phones and text messaging in organizing various mass oppositional mobilizations around the world in recent times. But they are articulated in and often against states.

Just as companies such as News Corp are creating global media industries, there are other elements of the new technologies that are delivering quite different solutions to the need to communicate. The capabilities embedded in the diffusion of Internet mass communication have created a form of born-global enterprise that Castells (2009: 55) sees as based on mass self-communication. Increasingly, for younger, better educated people everywhere, these forms of mass self-communication are becoming the dominant form of social networking, working, finding things out, being entertained, accessing information, reading, viewing, listening to media, and so on. The emergence of Web 2.0 and Web 3.0, the cluster of technologies, devices and applications that support the proliferation of social spaces on the Internet due to increased broadband capacity, innovative open-source software and enhanced motion graphics and interfaces, has produced SMS, blogs, vlogs, pod casts, wikis and tweets as the new systems of mass self-communication. While global in reach these are local in origin; for instance, Mandarin is fast becoming a major language globally as the number of wireless users in China outstrips those in the United States. As Castells (2009: 69) notes, wireless communication is now the delivery platform of choice for many kinds of digitized games, music, images, news, data, and representations of self-interests and activities, offering a perpetual connectivity with like-minded others both near and far.

Putting these systems of flows together, firms can enter new markets, and exploit technological and organizational advantages, as well as reduce business costs and risks, developing new strategies as they do so. Clearly, these strategies will need to be aware of the power of states to block or otherwise have an impact on them – think of the banks in the wake of the GFC – as well as the ease of organization of counter-strategies by outsiders – here, think of the swarming and destruction of bank properties that occurred, symbolically, in the wake of the GFC.

Organizations that do manage to put all these flows together on a truly global scale are known as transnationals rather than multinationals because they extend beyond national space in their routine activities. They are able to exert control either through ownership and/or through the coordination and control of operations, as a result of other mechanisms, such as a multisubsidiary form based on capital interdependency.

Mass self-communication can potentially reach a global audience, through message carriers such as YouTube, Facebook or an email list. The media that diffuse it may be a personal computer, or a mobile phone wirelessly connected via the Internet to the World Wide Web. The content is self-communication because the message is self-generated, the receivers are self-directed and the retrieval of specific messages from the World Wide Web and electronic communication networks is self-selected. It represents the many connecting with the many.

GLOBAL STRATEGIES: CONVERGENCE, DIVERGENCE OR TRANSLATION?

As we have remarked on a number of occasions in this book, the strategy literature has overwhelmingly North American roots; indeed, some authors suggest that it initially developed from somewhere as specific as Harvard University (Galan and Sanchez-Bueno, 2009).

The multidivisional, increasingly multinational, organization was seen as the pinnacle of a universal model of corporate evolution for all advanced economies based on Chandler's (1962) initial framework. As Spicer (2006: 1467) notes, 'The debate about organizational globalization is split between those who argue that organizational logics *converge* on a single Anglo-American model, and those who contend that organizational logics continue to *diverge* into national types'.

Many recent studies, especially in what is known as the business systems literature (Whitley, 1992; 1994a; 1994b; 1999) and related theory (Djelic, 1998; Hall and Soskice, 2001), argue that there is divergence as well as convergence, although the convergence literature is the longest established viewpoint (Kogut, 2002; Teece, 1993). National, or contextual, differences in terms of business practices, in this perspective, are seen to influence how firms develop with respect to strategy and structure. Against the regional differences between varieties of Anglo-American, European and Asian capitalism identified by the business systems literature, many writers in strategy still maintain that the 'universalistic' theories of strategy and organization associated with Chandler (1962), Channon (1973) and Dyas and Thanheiser (1976) are applicable in Europe, as argued by the work of Mayer and Whittington (1999) and Whittington and Mayer (2000).

In an important contribution to the debate about globalization and strategy Spicer (2006) has argued that we should reject the dichotomy of the *convergence* and *divergence* approaches. Instead he argues that globalization entails the *transformation* of organizational logics.

To be implemented any mandated change needs to accrue legitimacy. The process of legitimization involves far more than merely developing an agreed strategy at the top level of the organization that the strategy team regards as appropriate or desirable: it also means implementing it, even against resistance from stakeholders.

Implementation is complex and difficult in any MNC because it is an internally differentiated set of intra-organizational and extra-organizational linkages in which resources are constantly being exchanged. The complexity of the networks makes it difficult for any nodal point in the network to know where the most critical resources reside. As Bouquet and Birkinshaw (2008: 485) note:

> new technology can bring power to its inventor, but only to the extent that it can be brought to the attention of people who, through their direct and indirect connections, can facilitate its identification and deployment to other parts of the corporation. (Andersson, Forsgren, & Holm, 2007; Andersson & Pahlberg, 1997)

Those closer to the centre are more readily able to achieve such a bringing to attention compared with those further out in the periphery (Prahalad and Doz, 1987).

The greater the degree of both the corporate embeddedness of a subsidiary, as well as its degree of external embeddedness in its host nation, the more probable it will be that it has a more advanced mandate within an MNC.

The fact that a strategic mandate may be set centrally does not necessarily minimize the creative and positive resistance of the margins, suggest Bouquet and Birkinshaw (2008: 491). Subsidiaries can:

- Develop new products or bid for new corporate investments.
- Build their profile through stronger relationships with other parts of the global company.
- Most radically, seek to 'break the rules of the game' (Markides, 2000).

The capacity for subsidiaries to break the rules of the game depends on the structural relations that prevail within corporate empires. A great deal of corporate action in an MNC is simultaneously decentralized *and* linked to corporate strategy. Local actors will use the resources that the MNC provides to seek local advantages over local rivals, while the MNC will use the locals to tap into networks and mobilize resources that it would not otherwise access.

YOU CAN DOWNLOAD...

Jose I. Galan and Maria J. Sanchez-Bueno's (2009) Strategy and Structure in Context: Universalism versus Institutional Effects, *Organization Studies,* 30(6): 609–27, from the book's website at www.sagepub.co.uk/cleggstrategy

Legitimacy has been defined as 'a recognized perception or assumption that the actions of an entity are desirable, proper, or appropriate within some socially constructed system of norms, values, beliefs, and definitions' (Suchman, 1995: 574).

Convergence thesis

Convergence theorists argue that organizational logics are becoming increasingly similar. Organizational logics are the outcome of different strategies; they are sense-making frames that provide understandings concerning what is legitimate, reasonable and effective in a given context (Guillén, 2001: 14; see also Biggart, 1991: 222–4; MacDuffie, 1995; Biggart and Guillén, 1999). When strategy is aligned with action it produces a shared organizational logic. Typically, organizational logics are thought of in terms of an implicit business systems model, because, suggests Spicer (2006), they tend to be embedded in shared spaces, such as the nation-state (Granovetter, 1985). Some argue that this is because of the functional efficiency of certain strategy/structure models (Donaldson, 1999; 2000; 2001); others argue that it is an outcome of processes of institutional isomorphism, where because dominant and prestigious models are dominant and prestigious they are widely imitated – not because they are necessarily efficient but because they are held in high regard.

The factors that are seen to be leading to convergence are creating a 'disembedding' of MNCs from national space and witnessing them being reembedded into a global space (Giddens, 1990). A number of factors are seen to be driving this disembedding:

1. Real-time technology (Castells, 1996).
2. Volatile capital flows that circumvent the reach of nation regulation (Strange, 1996).
3. Geographically homogeneous consumer demand across the globe (Levitt, 1983).
4. Pressures from international standards (Brunsson and Jacobsson, 2001) on how an enterprise should be managed to ensure 'quality'; how enterprises should deal with the environmental impact of their operations; how they should manage their risks, knowledge and the complaints made against them; how they should keep their accounts and ensure regulatory compliance and probity in other ways (Higgins and Hallström, 2007).
5. Increasing homogeneity of the nation-state form, the professions and scientific reason (Meyer et al., 1997).

Because they are subject to these convergent pressures, firms become increasingly disconnected from national economies (Ohmae, 1990; 1995) and a largely US-inspired model of organizational relations that legitimates shareholder governance, short-term antagonistic employment relationships, short-term price-driven buyer–supplier relations and individual training (Hall and Soskice, 2001) is adopted. The strategy/structure researchers seem to favour this model, drawing equally on cultural learning as the decisive factor in divergence, in which unique institutional advantages will assert themselves, and a form of determinism in which the functional efficiencies of US models see them emerging as dominant.

From the early 2000s convergence models came under increasing attack as first Enron, WorldCom and others, and then the GFC of 2008–9, destroyed trillions of dollars of value and millions of jobs. The GFC was linked to increased incentivization and financialization because these gave business strategists good self-interested reasons for focusing on acts that improved share prices, irrespective of anything else. If for no other reason, the logic of convergence seems to have been severely weakened by the delegitimation of the dominant models for convergence.

It is not only dominant models that have been delegitimated. By the mid-2000s there were new players on the strategy block: the BRIC countries of Brazil, Russia, China and India, all of which had departed in various ways from the US model, with the central-government-controlled China doing so most evidently. With new players also came new approaches to strategy. After the collapse of the US financial industry signalled by Bear Stearns, Lehman Brothers and Merrill Lynch, US business models seems to have lost most of their legitimacy, and with the BRIC countries growing in influence, there are other evident models available for global strategy. Thus, Spicer suggests that the process of globalization is marked less by either convergence or divergence but by transformation: strategic business models do circulate globally and firms do sometimes try to impose the same model on their global operations or these models are copied by competitors and best practice benchmarkers elsewhere, in other countries, although in the process the strategies get transformed.

Divergence thesis

The divergence approach argues that economic transactions are embedded in long-term relationships that involve obligation, trust and reciprocity (Granovetter, 1985). These relations are shaped by nationally specific factors, such as structures of ownership, buyer–supplier relations, labour relations and legal infrastructure (Hall and Soskice, 1999). Consequently, divergent state institutions, such as national industrial relations and tax systems, the financial system, skill development and control, and culturally specific values such as trust and authority relations, will produce divergent, nationally specific organizational logics (Whitley, 1999). Many empirical studies document that organizational logics differ markedly across advanced capitalist economies (Wade, 1990; Whitley, 1992; Fligstein and Freeland, 1995; Storper and Salais, 1997; Fligstein, 2001; Guillén, 2001).

Kostova and Zaheer (1999) argue that multinational subsidiaries experience 'institutional duality'. On the one hand, headquarters pressure them to adopt their desired practices while the subsidiary is pressurized by its host context to follow local practices. Thus, it has to deal with a double and conflicting set of legitimation expectations about strategy. The greater the 'institutional distance' between the home and host countries, the more dualism will be experienced (Xu and Shenkar, 2002) and the more likely host influences will prevail (Morgan and Kristensen, 2006).

Most divergence theorists do not deny globalizing tendencies but do not see them as strong enough to eradicate specific features of nationally embedded business systems (Whitley, 1999: 117–36), although some argue that globalization will exacerbate nationally specific organizational logics (e.g. Hall and Soskice, 1999) because nationally specific advantages can function as unique competencies in the global market (Biggart and Guillén, 2001). The fact that most Japanese people live in small apartments meant that when it came to the miniaturization of domestic electronic components, such as hi-fi systems, firms had a considerable advantage over those in cultures such as the United States, in which suburban sprawl and larger dwellings were the norm.

Business systems researchers stress the distinctiveness of different cultural contexts, seeing these as formed by local embedded political and other institutions. The recent GFC has added fuel to the fires of the ongoing debates. Capelli (2009), for instance, notes the ascendance and dominance of the US business model for most of the twentieth century. At its core were a number of assumptions: corporate ownership and managerial control as opposed to family ownership, more often found in Europe and in Chinese family businesses, for instance; large-scale mass production methods, rather than more flexible production; open markets and informal oligopolies in contrast to the more formal cartels that were common in Europe and to a lesser extent in Asia; multidivisional form structures, compared with more informal organizational family-based business; and a form of workplace-based collective bargaining with largely instrumental – rather than political – trade unions. As Capelli notes, these business arrangements were both imposed on the defeated powers after the war (although with strong national characters, we might say) and spread through example and learning.

Translation thesis

Globalization need not result in the convergence or the continued divergence of organizational logics but a process of transformation, hybridization (Abo, 1994) and translation (Czarniawska-Joerges and Sévon, 1996). Spicer (2006) notes that such translations occurred when Japanese total quality management moved into the United States (Abo, 1994), when North American scientific management and British human relations moved into Israel (Frenkel and Shenhav, 2004; Frenkel, 2005) and when North American corporate governance moved into Germany (Buck and Shahrim, 2005). In each case, what was being globalized changed as it was adopted *in situ*.

While the decade of the 1980s may be said to have been the decade of learning from Japan (Kono and Clegg, 1998; 2001), in the 1990s and the new century US models were reinvented in terms of 'financialization' of value and 'flexibility'. The former meant the ascendancy of models of shareholder value and the 'incentivization' of executives through stock options and other financial packaging; the latter, the network model that emerged from California's Silicon Valley from the 1980s onwards, was seen by many commentators as indicative of future strategy. If one compares it with the corporate US model whose heyday flourished in the 1950s and the 1960s, there are quite sharp contrasts (Table 12.1).

The core of the Silicon Valley model is its project basis that depends for its success on a ready pool of known, mobile and highly technologically qualified labour that can learn and move fast (Saxenian, 1994; Bahrami and Evans, 1995; Casper, 2007). The project form is also encouraged by the role that venture capital

TABLE 12.1   Contemporary US project versus corporate models

Silicon Valley model	*Corporate US model*
Highly flexible small-firm start-ups able to reconfigure rapidly the nature and organization of core activities and skills	Large size
Limited diversification	Diversified divisions
Rapid commercialization and speed to market of new products and services, exploiting niches and discontinuous innovations, with strategic competition against existing capabilities – including those of the innovating organization	The mass production of standardized goods, mass marketed and distributed to largely homogeneous mass markets
Shallow hierarchies	An extensive hierarchy of managerial controls
Extensive network linkages externally	Systematic centralized managerial coordination and control of the disaggregated elements of development, production and marketing
Knowledge workers and creative industry employees controlled by culture rather more than structure with the culture being focused on 'can-do' and 'change', not unionized	A largely proletarianized and relatively deskilled workforce, unionized
Highly responsive to rapid changes in markets and technologies with highly skilled knowledge workers and knowledge networks focused on particular projects that can be rapidly developed and terminated	High development of mechanization limiting flexibility and favouring long production cycles

(Continued)

TABLE 12.1 *(Continued)*

Silicon Valley model	Corporate US model
● Value delivered through start-up focus so that those who are on the ground floor can get rich quick with initial public offerings (IPOs) that deliver equity ownership, with informed venture capital supporting start-ups	● Value delivered through a strong focus on cost reductions through capital intensity (downwardly), flexible labour markets and outsourcing to suppliers who could be beaten down on price
● Workers who move fluidly from project to project rather than building organizational careers, who are able to operate in highly dynamic and uncertain environments	● Lifetime employment in the model of the 'organization man'
● Clustering of related industries and firms in ecological proximity to one another, and to major technology-based universities, creating a 'hot-house' talent pool	● Extensive supply chains and subcontracting with contracting largely based on 'at-length' hard-money contracts

plays: risks could be spread and realized with relatively low transaction costs. The strategy is one of backing ideas that will disrupt, reconfigure or create markets, forming projects to develop them and rapidly realizing gains or moving on quickly. These project-based knowledge networks seem to be quite specific to certain sectors of business activity, such as highly knowledge specific and highly trained technological expertise in areas such as IT, biotechnology and nanotechnology. Moreover, they rely on a specific kind of infrastructure of defence contracting, large pharmaceuticals or a sophisticated health-based industry ready to buy-in innovation, and research-based universities with private, state or a mix of funding to supply the knowledge-based personnel.

Factors inhibiting the further development of project-based knowledge networks include the collapse of the hyperflexible financial markets of the noughties in 2008–9, when slicing and dicing financial instruments became the major technology of the highly creative financial industry, largely learnt in accounting, finance and economics classes at leading business schools. It is increasingly likely that states will steer away from an excessive reliance on financial innovation as the engine of growth for national economies. This could have consequences for the development of future strategy, to the extent that the strategy field has become a subordinate part of those quantitative discourses that assumed the existence of efficient markets and saw strategy largely in terms of developing tools for pricing options and other derivatives.

Increasingly, as Hitt et al. (2006) argue, knowledge and innovation are being outsourced internationally; moreover, new firms from emerging market countries are increasingly diversifying into international markets. Companies such as the Indian conglomerate Tata, through its subsidiary Corus, now own and control significant overseas assets, such as British steel mills.

YOU CAN DOWNLOAD…

Michael A. Hitt, Laszlo Tihanyi, Toyah Miller and Brian Connelly's (2006) International Diversification: Antecedents, Outcomes, and Moderators, *Journal of Management*, 32: 831–67, from the book's website at www.sagepub.co.uk/clegg strategy

FUTURES OF GLOBALIZATION?

Global power relations have a structural architecture, expressed in terms of spatial and temporal orderings, focused on the extraction and appropriation of value conceived in terms of various logics that are themselves an expression of power.

The GFC was the product of economically dominant forms of neo-liberal capitalism and its specific techniques and technologies of infrastructural power and private enrichment were used to advance the shared goals of hegemonic states, financial institutions and the flows of decomposing and recomposing organizations globally. These could be thought of as centripetal pressures shaping global organizations. Yet, there are also centrifugal pressures.

Neo-economic liberals wanted to limit the role of government as a strategic imperative and let the markets decide. The consequence has been that the state has stepped in to clear up the chaos and mess that an unbridled market in financial strategies created. While at one level some observers see this as an increase in the power of the state, we should be cautious about drawing such a conclusion. The neo-liberal agenda of the marketization of as many elements of everyday life as possible always required the state to transform established institutions, reforming them through markets – or, in health, education, welfare and other areas, through quasi-markets. The ultimate paradox, then, is that a view determined to let markets rip has destroyed itself and the markets it created. Little legitimacy attaches any more to financialization but, as Gray (2010: 11) argues, in rescuing the market in countries such as the UK and the United States, if not Australia, financialization also eroded the state, by burdening it with such an onerous level of debt that we might well speak today, once more, of the fiscal crisis of the state (O'Connor, 1973).

While globalizing financialization outsources and flattens the world of business, literally and metaphorically, states still manage national spaces that are traversed by national media, national enterprises, national procurement, especially in relation to military requirements, and nationally organized labour movements. The intersection of globalizing flows with these islands in the stream is likely to ensure essentially contested processes, with states as formidable obstacles that sometimes will be capable of diverting dominant flows. Nowhere is this more evident than in the rise of China.

CHINA

It is a rarely acknowledged aspect of all transitions from pre-modernity to modernity, from a society dominated by feudal agrarianism to one dominated by industry, that they have all been based, in part, on an historical access to massive resources at minimal cost to the state: European powers via the colonies; the United States by exploiting a virtually empty continent and a bountiful supply of forced and free labour; the Soviet Union through collectivization and state capitalism. In China three factors have combined to create the conditions of the current transition: the state owns all the land; it controls an endless supply of cheap (and repressed) labour; it has easy access to global raw materials both from foreign direct investments in Africa and through open markets in Australia and Latin America. Meanwhile, China, as the most significant creditor state, is the source of massive capital inflows into the United States, servicing its indebtedness, in part to consume the global flow of commodities that are produced in China.

It is China that exercises centrifugal force in the post-GFC world. For Jacques (2009: 29) China's rise signifies the end of 'western universalism' and the beginning of 'the age of contested modernity' or what Dussel and Colado (2006) refer to as the condition of transmodernity. For Hutton (2007a) 'China's economic and social model is dysfunctional. It is not just corrupt and environmentally dangerous. It is wildly unbalanced and lacking in innovation'. That is, perhaps, a tad too totalizing. China over the past 30 years has seen considerable functional, political and social pressure (Oliver, 1992) for the deinstitutionalization of Maoist norms aiding the development of a new hybridity (Gamble, 2010). One endogenous element in this hybridity has been the development of an indigenous organizational ecology based in part on firms that are 'highly diversified and are organizationally segmented into separately managed units' (Hamilton, 1996: 291–2) based on webs of countless personal relationships, rather than a framework of organizations (Fei, 1992: 32; see also Yeung, 2000). In rural areas this Chinese network model of social relations, *chaxegeju*, has proven to be dynamic in terms of business development and, contra Hutton, innovation (at least organizational innovation). For example, in Wenzhou, by 1990 more than 3000 families were involved in producing lighters through more than 700 private family businesses, with a division of labour between them. Their costs diminished and they entered the world market, to outcompete Japanese and South Korean firms. There are numerous such highly competitive, family-based networks, usually clustered in a geographic area, with high flexibility and low costs, and also, increasingly, high levels of knowledge and technology. In the rural area of Shengzhou, by 2002 more than 1000 family-based firms made 250 million neckties a year. In two years they invested about $22 million in new technologies and collaborated with European designers and quality experts, enabling them to deliver ties to the big fashion houses, such as Armani. They collaborate with the fashion industry on design via software over the Internet and make new products from new designs in 24 hours (see *Harvard Business Review* [2004] on 'Doing Business in China'). Of course, in a country whose provinces are larger than most European countries, and whose large cities are much larger than their European counterparts, it is virtually impossible to generalize.

More traditional indices of innovation are also indicative of changing times. Zhang et al. (2010) present data showing that the amount of Intellectual Property registered through patents is both changing in form and increasing in number in China. It is becoming less a matter of imitation and more genuinely innovative; in fact, it is a Chinese company, Huawei Technologies, that is now the number one filer of patents under the Patent Cooperation Treaty, and while the number of patents filed globally declined by 4.5 per cent in 2009, in China they increased by almost 30 per cent.

As well as endogenous sources of institutional innovations, exogenous innovations translated through strategic alliances with Western multinational firms are crucial sources of technology, capital and market resources for the transformation of Chinese family enterprises into more open structures integrated into the production networks of core global countries (Zhang and Van Den Bulcke, 2000: 142). Firms are evolving from a simple familial model in which they are subcontractors to more complex network modes of organization. The familial form is being transformed by the employment of a growing stratum of professional middle managers. University graduates are being employed in larger numbers than hitherto, mainly in product development and design departments and in technical positions. Liaison with universities is being cultivated to access research and development facilities and to ensure access to the best and brightest technical graduates. In consequence, day-to-day control of manufacturing operations is being delegated (Chan and Ng, 2000). With day-to-day operations under the control of professional managers, the owners are able to focus their attention on business development opportunities either independently or with US, European and Japanese partners whose branded goods they have been manufacturing for several years. New business development opportunities include the key long-term objective of developing own-branded products for the mainland, US and European markets. With few exceptions, however, China's brands are at present globally unknown, with the exception of brands that are bought in (Table 12.2).

TABLE 12.2   Best Chinese brands, 2009

		Brand value ($ BILLIONS 2006)	Revenue ($ BILLIONS 2005)	Net Income ($ BILLIONS 2005)
1	China Mobile	35.51	30.46	6.71
2	Bank of China	10.29	24.14	3.25
3	China Constr. Bank	8.53	16	5.9
4	China Telecom	4.01	21.22	3.5
5	China Life	4.01	12.23	1.16
6	Ping An	1.63	8.11	0.53
7	China Merchants Bank	1.63	3.59	0.46
8	Moutai	1.32	0.43	0.14
9	Bank of Communications	0.93	6.73	1.15
10	Lenovo	0.77	12.99	0.03
11	Netease	0.56	0.2	0.11
12	Gome	0.48	2.26	0.06
13	ZTE	0.43	2.7	0.16
14	Wuliangye	0.34	0.7	0.1
15	Air China	0.33	4.43	0.3
16	Changyu	0.29	0.21	0.04
17	Vanke	0.20	1.24	0.17
18	Gree	0.19	2.28	0.06
19	China Netcom	0.15	10.93	1.74
20	China Overseas Property	0.13	0.88	0.19

SOURCE: WWW.BUSINESSWEEK.COM/GLOBALBIZ/CONTENT/AUG2006/GB20060825_342949.HTML ACCESSED 14 MARCH 2010, USED WITH PERMISSION.

WHAT DO YOU MEAN?

New patterns of global ownership

China and India are the strongest emerging markets; consequently both outward/inward foreign direct investment (FDI) from/to them is significantly on the rise. For example, the cumulative FDI inflows to India since 2000 and up to July 2009 amounted to $100.33 billion and the outward FDI reached a record high of $15 billion (see www.india-briefing.com/news/fdi-india-crosses-us100-billion-threshold-1181.html/). For China, while in 2008 global FDI fell by around 20 per cent, outward FDI from China nearly doubled. This disparity is likely to continue as China invests even more overseas. China's FDI outflows took off in the noughties as a result of the government's adoption and promotion of a 'go global' policy aimed at

(Continued)

(Continued)

establishing the country's national champions as international players. Having averaged only $453 million a year in 1982–9 and $2.3 billion in 1990–9, the out flows rose to $5.5 billion in 2004, $12.3 billion in 2005, $17.6 billion in 2006 and $24.8 billion in 2007. Preliminary figures for 2008 show a rise to $40.7 billion. If financial FDI (not counted before 2006) is included, the 2008 total was $52.2 billion, nearly double the $26.5 billion in 2007 (see Davies, 2009). Defining internationalization as 'the crossing of national boundaries in the process of growth' (Buckley and Ghauri, 1999: ix), means that China is currently the most active internationalizing economy among the developing countries.

Both India and China have institutional contexts in which the government and its agencies have been important in steering development (Dunning and Narula, 1996). Fairly recently, in both India and China, a number of firms have begun to internationalize; as global players in international markets they are developing the capacity to organize their overseas operations systematically and seeking to integrate their existing practices into new acquisitions (e.g. Hansen, 2005; *The Economist*, 2006). Both Indian and Chinese capitalism display elements of what has been referred to in the literature as 'late development', an argument initially applied to Japan and subsequently to the emergent economies of East Asia, notably Taiwan, South Korea, Hong Kong and Singapore. Latecoming firms within these countries engaged in outward investment to gain knowledge of practices in technology and business in the more developed economies (Matthews, 2002: 471). Building on initial competitive advantages, such as low labour costs, the firms developed higher value products to move into more sophisticated markets – classic cases being Korean firms such as LG and Samsung. International investment is a means of addressing initial competitive disadvantages for firms in such economies.

Despite the organizational network innovations that may be producing them, Chinese brands are not known globally for their uniquely innovative or creative content: largely they are 'me-too' brands or have been bought in, such as Lenovo. As Hutton (2007b: 4) states:

> China must become a more normal economy, but the party stands in the way. Chinese consumers need to save less and spend more, but consumers with no property rights or welfare system are highly cautious. To give them more confidence means taxing to fund a welfare system and conceding property rights. That will mean creating an empowered middle class who will ask how their tax renminbi are spent. Companies need to be subject to independent accountability if they are to become more efficient, but that means creating independent centres of power. The political implications are obvious.

The changing reality of BRIC (Brazil, Russia, India and China) investment globally limits the applicability of much of what we accept as knowledge about globalization strategies because so much of this knowledge has been based on large manufacturing firms situated in the United States. We do not know if this knowledge is applicable everywhere else where there is high institutional distance between home and host countries and it would be sociologically surprising if it were. Firms going abroad need to gain legitimacy in the new markets they enter. Being foreign can be a liability, especially when the institutional distance between home- and host-country institutions is large, where languages, religions, laws, cultures, folkways, norms and mores all differ sharply. For instance, situations where the political imperatives of a one-party state dominate all other institutions, including legal processes, lend themselves to widespread opportunities for foreign businesses to land in trouble. Where there is a huge and impenetrable bureaucracy to circumnavigate in order to do business the risk of taking shortcuts that line some importuning official's or intermediary's pockets is always present. Practices that might be effective in the local context do not look so good if held up to governance standards in the home base (see van Iterson and Clegg (2008) for the case of the Australian Wheat Board and Saddam's Iraq; the same provisos hold for high-profile cases in China (Rio Tinto) and India (Lockheed), while the problems of an absence of due process and natural justice are legion in Russia, where out-of-political-favour plutocrats can be easily imprisoned if the state deems it necessary).

SUMMARY AND REVIEW

Globalization is an essentially contested concept – there is considerable divergence of opinion and analysis of its effects. Evolutionary models of globalization are being questioned; firms can be born global and globalization may be better seen in terms of globalizing – processes associated with global flows of finance, people, procurement and communication. Some analysts see corporate social responsibility speeding globally as part of ecological modernization. The dominance of North American theories, models and practices of strategy has given rise to a significant degree of debate about whether or not these are culturally embedded and politically dominant models or really the best way of organizing global business. The jury is still out on this, but it is notable that the business systems literature would seem to suggest that the US models have a fairly limited remit and that, in the wake of the global financial crisis, US models will be likely to have diminished legitimacy, especially in so far as they have elements of financialization implicit in them. While the US models work well for the Anglo-Saxon liberal market economies, their purchase is far weaker for the coordinated market economies. As new models emerge from the BRIC countries it is even less likely that we will be able to see strategic convergence. Even in the Anglo-Saxon economies change seems to be afoot, as Indian and Chinese firms, in particular, have expansionist inward investment strategies, so that the future is increasingly likely to be one of interim alliances, nimble networks and flexible projects. In many ways the emergent industries being built around mass self-communication industries would seem to suggest that the future of globalization might well entail a global mixture of globalization and glocalization and some new technologies of social relations transforming power relations.

EXERCISES

1   Having read this chapter you should be able to say in your own words what the following key terms mean:

- Globalization
- Globalizing
- Multidivisional form
- Ecological modernization
- Multinational corporations (MNCs)
- Transnationals
- Decentralized federation
- Centralized hubs
- Flows

- Venture capital
- Project-based knowledge networks
- Corporate social responsibility
- US century
- Chinese family businesses.

2   Who are the major actors in developing ideas for the strategy process and in what ways do they do so?

3   Why are transnationals especially likely to be sites of struggle over strategy?

4   Norsk Hydro is a global transnational. According to Svein Richard Brandtzaeg, Executive Vice President Aluminium Products and board member of Norsk Hydro, how do you go about constructing a global strategy? (See www.strategytube.net)

ADDITIONAL RESOURCES

1   Our companion website is the best first stop for you to find a great deal of extra resources, free PDF versions of leading articles published in Sage journals, exercise, video and pod casts, team case studies and general questions and links to teamwork resources. Go to www.sagepub.co.uk/cleggstrategy

2   There is a fascinating exchange of views about the US models of strategy and business in the wake of the global financial crisis in *Academy of Management Perspectives*, 23(2), May 2009.

3   Good novels about global strategy, wrapped up in a thriller format, are the Millennium trilogy of novels of Stieg Larsen (2008a; 2008b; 2008c): *The Girl with the Dragon Tattoo, The Girl Who Played with Fire* and *The Girl Who Kicked the Hornets' Nest*. They consist of the unravelling of corporate crime by hacking into computers. The accounts of finance and strategy are very believable.

WEB SECTION

Visit the *Strategy* companion website at www.sagepub.co.uk/cleggstrategy

1   The online resource www.strategytube.net that the authors produced in tandem with this book is a great resource: look in particular at the video Case Study 8 where Svein Richard Brandtzaeg talks about the management of change. Look especially at the 'study questions' for this case. They are designed to complement and extend this chapter.

2   There is an excellent video on Corporate Social Innovation, documenting the strategies followed by a number of companies to be both innovative in

capturing new opportunities and to aid socially responsible development. See: http://www.youtube.com/watch?v=17-rfo3k1DAO&feature=player_embedded.

3 A very useful site for this chapter is www.sociology.emory.edu/globalization

4 The Interbrand/Business Week China Brands list can be found in a slide format at http://images.businessweek.com/ss/06/08/china_brands/index_01.htm

LOOKING FOR A HIGHER MARK?

Reading and digesting these articles that are available free on the companion website www.sagepub.co.uk/cleggstrategy can help you gain deeper understanding and, on the basis of that, a better grade:

1 One paper that usefully reviews the arguments for and against the convergence versus divergence models of strategy – whether the US models are ones that the rest of the world is evolving towards – is by Jose I. Galan and Maria J. Sanchez-Bueno (2009) Strategy and Structure in Context: Universalism versus Institutional Effects, *Organization Studies,* 30(6): 609–27.

2 Another useful resource is a paper by Michael A. Hitt, Laszlo Tihanyi, Toyah Miller and Brian Connelly (2006) International Diversification: Antecedents, Outcomes, and Moderators, *Journal of Management*, 32: 831–67. It is an extensive review of the past 20 years of research on the causes, consequences and correlates of firms going global.

3 A very interesting paper has been written by Glenn Morgan and Peer Hull Kristensen (2006) The Contested Space of Multinationals: Varieties of Institutionalism, Varieties of Capitalism, *Human Relations*, 59: 1467–90.

CASE STUDY

Shell

David Bubna-Littic and Crelis Rammelt

Introduction

In an era in which the average life expectancy of a multinational corporation – Fortune 500 or its equivalent – is between 40 and 50 years, according to de Geus (1997), Shell has exceptional longevity, for a company its size. Shell's history can be traced back to the 1890s, when it sold oil for lamps in the Far East (Shell was named after the fact that seashells were used as money in the Far East), while the Dutch founders imported kerosene from Sumatra. From 1906 Shell's primary business has been the worldwide production and marketing of oil and petroleum.

In 1907, the British Shell Transport and Trading Company merged with the Royal Dutch Petroleum Company to form the Royal Dutch Shell Group. It grew to become the main supplier of fuel and TNT for the British Army during the First World War. The postwar depression forced Shell to reduce its staff, and the Second World War led to the destruction of a lot of its properties. The return of peace, however, brought a renewed demand for oil products (Royal Dutch Shell, 2009a). Shell thereby became one of the 'seven sisters' (Sampson, 1975).

How green is Shell?

In October 2002, a group of engineering students visiting Royal Dutch Shell's (hereafter Shell) research and technology headquarters in Amsterdam were told how, every second, 300 would cars refuel at one of Shell's 58,000 service stations. Shell is best known for its oil exploration and production, but it delivers a much wider range of products, including gas and power, oil products and chemicals (Royal Dutch Shell, 2002). The students were also told that renewable technologies and hydrogen had become some of Shell's more recent and fast-growing business pillars. At this point, an inquisitive student asked the speaker to elaborate on the relative size of investment in the different pillars, but was given no answer. Seven years later in an interview with George Monbiot in early 2009, Shell's Chief Executive, Jeroen van der Veer, was

repeatedly asked (15 times) a similar question: 'What is the value of your annual investments in renewable energy?' In refusing to answer, van der Veer explained that 'those figures are misused and people say it is too small' (Monbiot, 2009a).

Only a few months later, the question had lost much of its relevance. Speaking at the Anglo-Dutch group's annual strategy briefing, van der Veer revealed that Shell was planning to drop all new investments in wind, solar and hydrogen energy. Shell was fighting to maintain its core oil and gas business in the face of a more than $100 slide in the price of crude oil since the summer of 2008 (Pagnamenta, 2009). Shell's retreat from renewable energy investments is indicative of a global trend; the International Energy Agency warns that the global financial crisis has hit renewable energy investments particularly hard and investments fell by about one-fifth in 2009 compared with the previous year (Keller, 2009). This raises serious concerns for the future, not just in terms of ecological sustainability, but also in terms of Shell's own ability to face the approach of 'peak oil'.

Peak oil

Apart from the period of the oil crises in the 1970s, there was always enough production to ensure low oil prices up to the beginning of the twenty-first century. The price as of July 2008 is drastically different in nature from those of the past, which were politically induced. The rise is caused by the increasing difficulty for production to keep up with an exponentially growing demand. This trend is likely to be of a long-term nature (Tsoskounoglou, Ayerides and Ayerides, 2008).

'Peak oil' is defined as the point at which the rate of extraction exceeds the discovery of new supplies, with considerable economic and political consequences for energy-hungry countries reliant on oil for everything from energy through pharmaceuticals to agricultural fertilizers. Exact predictions vary, starting as early as 2012 or 2023 (Arnott, 2008; Tsoskounoglou et al., 2008). Even Shell forecasts a plateau of supply as production moves to more difficult oil resources (Arnott, 2008).

Shell is one of the three largest, privately owned oil companies in the world (Beale and Fernando, 2009). It operates in over 100 countries and employs about 102,000 people (Royal Dutch Shell, 2009b). In the United States alone, 22,000 employees work for Shell's affiliate, the Shell Oil Company (Royal Dutch Shell, 2009c). In 2008, Shell's total revenue was over $458 billion (Royal Dutch Shell, 2009b), and

(Continued)

(Continued)

it was ranked first on the Global 500's list of most profitable companies (with Exxon Mobil in second position) (CNN, 2009). Albeit with some fluctuation, it seems that two world wars have had little impact on the global expansion of this corporate giant.

The oil shocks of 1974 and 1979, on the other hand, did change the industry by providing an incentive to diversify (Grant and Cibin, 1996). Shell undertook this by setting up new joint ventures and developing new competencies (such as those mentioned in the introduction, including early investments in renewable energy), and adopting new approaches to long-term strategic planning (Kolk and Levy, 2001). Several other events are also said to have had some impact on the company's overall direction: the 1989 oil pipe leakage at the Shell Stanlow refinery; the 1995 debacle surrounding the proposed sinking of the Brent Spar oil platform;[1] and the media coverage of human rights violations in Nigeria in the late 1990s.[2] According to Skodvin

---

[1]In 1995, after research into the possible environmental, cost and safety concerns Shell decided to sink a decommissioned oil storage rig called Brent Spar in the Atlantic Ocean off north-west Scotland. However, this decision caused a great deal of controversy, and Greenpeace, who opposed the deep-water disposal of the Spar, staged an occupation of the rig in order to prevent this from happening. The media coverage of this event led to a greater public opposition to Shell's plan. At first, Shell tried to defend its decision, but in the end it decided to go along with public opinion (Zyglidopoulos, 2002); the Brent Spar was towed to shore for dismantlement and recycling. Independent studies later conducted proved that Shell's initial plan for deep-water disposal was the environmentally correct option. Greenpeace was forced to apologize after it was revealed that its scientific studies were flawed. The improvement of Shell's image has been helped by Greenpeace's admission of errors in the technical details.

[2]The story of Shell's environmental degradation of the Niger River Delta, particularly through gas flares, and its complicity in the events leading to the execution of Ken Saro-Wiwa and eight colleagues, has been told many times. Those events became worldwide symbols of corporate complicity in human rights abuses, and led to mass campaigns against Shell and a massive PR headache for the company. In 1958, Shell discovered and developed a major oil reserve in the home of the Ogoni people, among the poorest in Nigeria. Starting in 1990, Ogoni activists, led by

and Skjoerseth (2001), these events led to a strategic reorganization in the direction of:

- greater transparency;
- corporate social/environmental responsibility.

Transparency

The idea that corporations have a duty to disclose non-financial information emerged in the 1970s, initially focusing on environmental reporting, but gradually including human resource productivity, human rights violations and civic participation. During this time, the term stakeholder began to emerge alongside shareholder in discussions on corporate disclosure (Carduff, 2003). Both Exxon and Texaco published environmental reports in 1990, while the two European companies followed a few years later: BP in 1995 and Shell in 1997 (Kolk and Levy, 2001).

Halfway through the 1990s, Shell had come under public attack by special interest groups regarding environmental concerns and human rights violations following the controversies in Nigeria and with the Brent Spar. The company's new chairman heralded a transition from a closed to a more open culture (Kolk and Levy, 2001). It has been argued that, with this transition, Shell was able to reduce false claims by providing non-financial performance measures through its website and other forms of media to pre-empt claims made by special interest groups (Carduff, 2003). For example, it has been suggested that much of the controversies and social discontent surrounding the Brent Spar incident could have been avoided by being more transparent in an open dialogue with 'stakeholders'.

Shell has also been accused of 'green washing' and 'blue washing', or using deceptive practices to present an environmentally and socially responsible

---

writer Ken Saro-Wiwa, protested against what they believed to be serious environmental degradation. The violence eventually resulted in the 1995 execution of Saro-Wiwa and several other activists. Since then, Shell has faced several lawsuits for complicity in human rights abuses, for a $1.5 billion pollution claim from the Nigerian Parliament and for unprecedented misconduct. Gas flaring in Nigeria has not yet been stopped. Shell Chief Executive Jeroen van der Veer explains that 'you need infrastructure, pipelines to transport the gas, to a power station for instance. This has been difficult in Nigeria, safety reasons. We hope this will be resolved soon'.

(Continued)

(Continued)

public image of an organization that distorts or exaggerates its actual practices.

Green washing

In 2007, the UK's independent advertising watchdog, the Advertising Standards Authority (ASA), upheld a complaint against an advertisement by Shell in which the oil company claimed that its waste carbon dioxide was used to grow flowers (Judge and Leroux, 2009). The ad featured an oil refinery with flowers emerging from the chimneys (see picture below) (Tibbetts, 2008):

> If only we had a magic bin that we could throw stuff in and make it disappear forever. What we can do is find creative ways to recycle. We use our waste CO_2 to grow flowers. And our waste sulphur to make super strong concrete. Real energy solutions for the real world.

According to Shell, the intention was to raise awareness about the environmental consequences of producing and using energy: 'Most people understand that, and see there is a role here for producers and users of energy alike, with governments needing to establish sensible frameworks' (Edlund, 2007). The ASA[3] nonetheless said that the ad suggested that Shell used all its waste carbon dioxide to grow flowers, when it was shown that only 0.325 per cent of its emissions were used in this way (Judge and Leroux, 2009).

In 2008, Shell was prosecuted again for an ad claiming that its $10billion investment in the

Athabasca Oil Sands Project in Alberta, Canada, was a contribution to a sustainable energy future (Pearce, 2009) (see picture below). The WWF complained that extracting low-grade bitumen from tar sands is highly inefficient and destroys huge tracts of virgin forest (Hickman, 2008). Overall, the emissions from mining, refining and burning tar sands are 3–10 times greater than those for conventional oil: 'Their extraction cannot be described as a sustainable process and for Shell to claim otherwise was wholly misleading,' said the WWF (Pearce, 2009; Vidal, 2009).

In its defence, Shell maintained that new technology was reducing pollution from the oil sands project. Shell quoted a critical WWF report which rated its Muskeg River Mine as one of the least damaging coal-tar sands projects because it sought to limit emissions of nitrogen oxide, sulphur dioxide and organic compounds (Hickman, 2008). Contributing towards sustainable development, said Shell, 'meant helping to meet the world's growing energy needs in economic, social and environmentally responsible ways, and that in all their operations they integrated economic, environmental and social considerations into their business decision-making' (Vidal, 2009). ASA nevertheless ruled that the ad had breached the rules on substantiation, truthfulness and environmental claims. Shell should not have used the word 'sustainable' for its tar sands project and a second scheme to build North America's biggest oil refinery. Both projects would lead to the emission of more greenhouse gases (Hickman, 2008). In early 2009, Shell explained that oil sands only produce 15 per cent more CO_2 than the classic production of crude oil: 'Also, going for oil sands means less coal production in the world, and coal is even more CO_2 intensive than oil' (Monbiot, 2009a; Monbiot, 2009b).

Van der Veer acknowledged that Shell is 'very big in oil and gas and … so far relatively small in

[3]In advertising, an industry self-regulation body sets codes, called the Committee of Advertising Practice, and these codes are policed by the ASA.

(Continued)

(Continued)

alternative energies' and stated that advertising only about alternative energy activities and not about the 90 per cent other activities would be dishonest. When asked if Shell intended to return to that kind of advertising, van der Veer replied: 'Probably not ... I'm very much "keep your feet on the ground, tell them who you are and explain why you are who you are"' (Monbiot, 2009a).

Blue washing

Recently, 'blue washing' has emerged as a common practice among certain transnational companies. Blue refers to the colour of the UN flag. Many of the same companies that pioneered 'green washing' are now wrapping themselves in the UN flag and claiming to be champions of UN values such as human rights and poverty elimination. Shell's catchphrase of this ideology is 'Profits & Principles – Does there have to be a choice?' (CorpWatch, 2002).

In response to the pressures that Shell experienced around its operations in Nigeria during the mid-1990s, when it was being associated with human rights violations committed by the government of General Abacha against the Ogoni people, it changed its statement of business principles to recognize its responsibility for human rights. Shell was one of the first companies to recognize the relevance of international human rights standards, referring to the Universal Declaration of Human Rights in its policy documents and reports (Friends of the Earth International, 2003): 'Without the tyres of the rich men, the poor would not have such nice shoes. Without the shoes of the poor man, the tyres would probably be left in nature. Thus respect the poor man, rich man and nature' (Royal Dutch Shell, 2002). Shell writes that local communities must see concrete benefits from the oil and gas produced beneath their feet. The Niger Delta shows vividly how important it is to meet this challenge.

Shell's capital expenditure on social development is among the highest in absolute value within the petroleum industry, demonstrating its concern with the impact of its operations on society (Chang and Yong, 2007). A study by the ethics management rating firm Management & Excellence (M&E) rated Shell as the world's most ethical oil company. This must, however, be seen in the context of the oil industry as a whole – Exxon Mobil, for example, has been linked to possible human rights abuses in Chad, Cameroon and, more seriously, Aceh (Beale and Fernando, 2009):

While I applaud Shell for investing in wind technology, their human rights record is deplorable beyond our imaginations. When Shell is ready to have a human conscience then we as consumers will start to have some trust in their deeds and they won't have to spend so much on greenwashing.

This quote is not from a Greenpeace campaign leaflet, but from *Meeting the Energy Challenge* (Royal Dutch Shell, 2002), the third instalment in a disarmingly candid annual series of sustainability reports from Shell (Joyce, 2003). Friends of the Earth published several 'alternative annual reports' presenting case studies from a few of the many countries, towns and suburbs that have been damaged by Shell's environmental and social failures (Friends of the Earth International, 2002; 2003; 2004). These suggest that Shell fails to respond to community concerns unless and until its bad practices are brought to public attention. And even when Shell comes under public scrutiny, such as in Nigeria, Durban, South Africa and Port Arthur, Texas, it often fails to act, or does not act in good faith (Friends of the Earth International, 2003).

In 2000, the Nigerian government established the Niger Delta Development Commission (NDDC) to coordinate development in the region. Shell's contribution to development in Nigeria was $330,000 in 1989 and rose to $68.9 million in 2004 to the NDDC. Shell claims that 70 per cent of its invesments are classed as being sustainable. However, NGO groups have criticized the selection and timeframe of the studies being conducted to verify Shell Nigeria's claims of community development projects' success (Beale and Fernando, 2009). Friends of the Earth suggested that Shell has benefited from the billions of dollars of oil in Nigeria. 'If Shell wants to put US$69 million into community development, why doesn't it set up a foundation which has no direct links to the company and let development workers who know what they're doing manage the projects?' asks Friends of the Earth Nigeria (Friends of the Earth International, 2003).

The end of Shell's corporate environmental responsibility?

In 1988, the Intergovernmental Panel on Climate Change (IPCC) began to support claims that humans are contributing to global warming. At first, the Shell Group, particularly its American branch office, Shell Oil, questioned the science (CorpWatch, 2002), but

(Continued)

(Continued)

in the 1990s Shell in Europe began to embrace the idea that a modern global oil company could and should transform itself into a green energy company (Pearce, 2009). Internally, Shell continued to struggle with Shell Oil over the company's choice of climate strategy (Skodvin and Skjoerseth, 2001).

By 1997, when the Kyoto Protocol was proposed, Shell publicly recognized the climate problem. Together with BP, it was one of the first oil companies to adopt a more open stance towards the protocol and to join industry associations and partnerships with environmental non-governmental organizations reflecting this perspective (Kolk and Levy, 2001). In that same year, the Shell Group established a fifth core business – Shell International Renewables – with an investment plan of $0.5 billion over the next five-year period (Beale and Fernando, 2009). On its website it stated: 'Tackling climate change and providing fuel for a growing population seems like an impossible problem, but at Shell we try to think creatively' (Pearce, 2009).

In 2002, however, Corporate Watch attacked the disparity between rhetoric and action on renewable energy sources, and issued Shell with the 'Greenwash Award'. According to the critics, Shell spends less than 1 per cent of its annual investments on renewables (CorpWatch, 2002; Joyce, 2003). In its 'Meeting the Energy Challenge' annual report, Shell bases its sustainability strategy on seven core principles: generating robust profitability; delivering value to customers; protecting the environment; managing resources; respecting and safeguarding people; benefiting communities; and working with stakeholders (Royal Dutch Shell, 2002). The achievements in profitability and shareholder value remain significantly more substantial than those principles at the end of the scale (Joyce, 2003).

Shell's Head of Sustainable Development Mark Weintraub explains that '[i]t's important to view these numbers in context. We're talking here about markets at very different levels of development. ... Renewables provide just one percent of the world's energy, and our investment goes mainly into R&D and developing new business models – very early stage stuff'. Moreover, although the relative investment is low, the impacts are high: 'Shell currently produces 13 percent of the world's solar panels, for example. ... We will get there with renewables, but we're talking decades rather than a few years' (Joyce, 2003).

In the following years, Shell seemed to continue its move towards environmental corporate responsibility, although not without criticism. In 2004, for example, it adopted a self-imposed greenhouse gas (GHG) emission reduction target of 5 per cent lower emissions in 2010 than in 1990 (Beale and Fernando, 2009). In the Netherlands, Shell played a role in voluntary emission trading, proposed to counter regulation (Kolk and Levy, 2001). Nevertheless, the operating GHG emission reductions achieved by Shell were said to be a tiny fraction of the emissions produced by the end use of its products (Jones and Levy, 2007). In that same year, Shell opened the world's largest grid-connected solar park (Pearce, 2009). Moreover, in anticipation of the 2010 European Commission targets under the Kyoto Agreement, Shell invested in an ethanol refinery that converts residual biomass (*The Economist*, 2004).

In 2005, according to Jones and Levy (2007), Shell committed to invest more than $1 billion in renewable energy but critics argued that the investment was miniscule in comparison with its core oil and gas operations and in the context of a company with a market capitalization of around $163 billion. The investment represented about 1 per cent of total capital investment in the period 2001–5 (Refocus, 2006). In early 2006, Shell announced record profits of £13 billion for the previous financial year, and reemphasized its commitment to alternative energy by announcing significant new developments in biofuels and wind, solar and hydrogen power (Refocus, 2006).

Shell claimed that its strategy was to become a world leader in the production of wind-powered energy (Boiral, 2006). Graeme Sweeney, Executive Vice President of Shell Renewables, said:

> Much of our current investment goes into wind, because this sector shows the best prospects for becoming a substantial business in the near term. This is followed by our activities in hydrogen, which accounts for about a fifth of the capital investment into alternative energy. In solar, which has been a major impetus for us, we are refocusing our efforts onto next generation technology, thin-film technology, which we regard as highly promising. (Refocus, 2006)

In the period 1997–2006, Shell invested more than $500 million in photovoltaic energy developments (Boiral, 2006). By 2007, the Anglo-Dutch oil

(Continued)

(Continued)

giant had an established position as the world's largest marketer of biofuels, as well as the leading developer of advanced biofuels technology (Chang and Yong, 2007). Shell also reported that '45% of our total oil and gas production in 2008 was natural gas, the cleanest-burning fossil fuel'. However, critics claim that natural gas is at best an incremental improvement over oil and, at worst, a distraction from the real challenge of moving our economies beyond fossil fuels (CorpWatch, 2002). Finally, other renewables – wave, current and tidal energy, for instance – are constantly scanned for new technologies, but have not been considered viable (Refocus, 2006).

Goldman Sachs's intangibles research team make annual assessments of global energy and mining companies, ranking companies on the basis of sustainability factors, financial returns and access to new resource reserves. In 2007, Shell was ranked one of the leaders in all three categories (Engardio et al., 2007). Throughout the 1990s and early 2000s, Shell clearly invested in alternative forms of energy. While the exact proportion compared with its core oil business investments is unclear, there is no doubt that Shell is first and foremost a petrochemical company. According to its own figures for the 2003–8 period, Shell invested $1.7 billion in renewable energy and projects to reduce CO_2 emissions – just over 1 per cent of its $150 billion investment budget over the same period. It also spent $148 million on social investment programmes in 2008 (Royal Dutch Shell, 2009b). In comparison, the company recorded $1.7 trillion in company sales and $126.8 billion in net profit for the same period (Renewable Energy Focus, 2009).

Whatever we feel about the data, 2008–9 marked a radical shift in Shell's investments in renewables. In 2008, Shell pulled out of what would be the world's largest offshore wind farm in the Thames Estuary. The company claimed at the time that it was going to concentrate its renewables business in the United States, but in 2009 that plan was quietly dropped (Pearce, 2009). In early 2009, van der Veer announced that Shell was planning to drop all new investment in wind, solar and hydrogen energy. 'I don't expect them to grow much at Shell from here, due to portfolio fit and the returns outlook compared to other opportunities,' he said, speaking at an annual strategy briefing. In an update on Shell's new strategy, Linda Cook, Head of Shell Gas and Power, told reporters: 'We do not expect material amounts of investment in those areas going forward. They continue to struggle to compete with the other investment opportunities we have in our portfolio' (Renewable Energy Focus, 2009). Instead, Shell would focus its remaining renewable energy investments on biofuels, where it is conducting research into 'second-generation' fuels, so far with little commercial success. According to Cook, 'It's now looking like biofuels is one which is closest to what we do in Shell' (Renewable Energy Focus, 2009). Shell also said that it will maintain its spending on carbon capture and storage projects in Germany, the Netherlands, Norway, Canada, Australia and the United States – most of which also receive significant government support (Pagnamenta, 2009).

Greenpeace Executive Director John Sauven said that, with this shift, Shell had 'rejoined the ranks of the dirtiest, most regressive corporations in the world. ... After years of proclaiming their commitment to clean power, they're now pulling out of the technologies we need to see scaled up if we're to slash emissions' (Pagnamenta, 2009).

From a strategic point of view, Shell's past investments in sustainability in a number of ways raise several important and related questions.

1. In the context of the recent global financial crisis and its substantial drop in profits, did Shell's strategy require a mid-course correction?

2. In the context of falling oil prices, did the drop in economic viability of its investments in renewable energy reveal a more fundamental set of societal relations that emphasize private over collective interests?

3. Do these societal power relations call into question the power of management ultimately to determine strategy?

4. Shell's claims regarding long-range planning can be seen as part of more general rhetoric of management rationality. Strategy theory downplays the self-interested and short-term concerns of the capital markets, which ultimately limit any management's ability to control the direction of a corporation's strategy. Moreover, the loosely coupled, systemic and impersonal nature of management's relationship to the owners of corporations complicates questions of agency. The complexity of the relationship allows management to play in the margins, but ultimately this only assists in the manufactured consent of a credulous public. Can we realistically expect any corporation operating

(Continued)

(Continued)

in Shell's particular context of governance and market competition to act differently?

5   Are Shell's investments in renewable energy more indicative of public pressure to be seen to be doing something about its broader environmental impacts, rather than an aspect of a broader strategic rationality which anticipates the need for forgoing current profits that externalize the costs of the negative environmental impacts of its activities and the need for radical change for a sustainable future?

Discussion

Shell's experience has a number of implications for the analysis of long-term strategic planning. As mentioned, the oil crises of the 1970s led Shell to think about new approaches to long-term strategic planning. In 1985, Shell economist Pierre Wack (Wack, 1985; Taylor, 1987) suggested that:

> From studying evolution, we learn how an animal suited to one environment must become a new animal to survive when the environment undergoes severe change. We believed that Shell would have to become a new animal to function in a new world. Business as usual decisions would no longer suffice.

In his bestselling book *The Living Company*, ex-Shell Planning Coordinator Arie de Geus (1997) reported on research that assessed the 'genetic material' of 27 firms, as old and as large as Shell, to determine what had allowed them to survive over time. A major trait common to these companies' was their sensitivity to their environment[4] (Fulmer, Gibbs and Keys, 1998), which Shell initially developed through the use of long-term strategic planning tools, such as 'Forecasting'[5] and 'Environmental Scanning.'[6] Plans based on forecasts from history

---

[4]Other identified traits were: possession of a strong sense of identity, tolerance of new or different ways of thinking or acting (often associated with decentralization), and a conservative approach to financing.

[5]Forecasting is generally undertaken by extrapolating past trends into the future. In 1965, Shell introduced its 'Unified Planning Machinery' designed to look ahead six years. Later, 'Horizon Year Planning' was adopted to provide a forecast of 15 years.

[6]Strategic planning, according to de Geus (1997), should include a model for detecting and responding to

can be accurate when times are stable. However, Shell began to realize that, since the world business environment is often turbulent and volatile, it had to develop an alternative tool for looking at the future (Brenneman, Keys and Fulmer, 1998). Graham Galer and Kees Van der Heijden say, 'Sophisticated decision-making and forecasting alone fail to perceive unexpected influences that come at a project "sideways" (Galer and Van der Heijden, 1992; Brenneman et al., 1998).

It was believed that scenario planning allowed Shell to be more prepared for the 1973 oil crisis and to sell off its excess oil supplies before the worldwide glut developed in 1981. The US-based affiliate Shell Oil Company clung tenaciously to mental models that included confidence in a cost of $30 for a barrel of oil, and, consequently, did not do as well (Ginter and Duncan, 1990). After this turbulent period, Wack observed: 'We now want to design scenarios so that managers question their own model of reality and change it when necessary so as to come up with strategic insights beyond their mind's previous reach' (Wack, 1985; Taylor, 1987).

The aim of scenarios was, however, not just to protect the business, but also to discover new strategic options (Ginter and Duncan, 1990). The purpose of Shell's global scenarios was thus to provide a background against which business strategies may be formulated and tested, discursively identifying trends and discontinuities that could be significant for Shell's businesses in the future. Scenarios are not necessarily always realized, as unanticipated changes may lie outside the scenarios, and events may take an entirely different direction, but the logic behind scenario analysis is that even when events do take an unexpected direction strategists will recognize elements discussed in these scenarios and have a familiarity with the issues that provides them with key strategic insights. Shell usually drafts two scenarios. One of the pair of scenarios developed

---

what he terms 'weak signals' in the (system's) environment and thus managing strategic surprise. For Shell in the 1970s, the scope was to look at economic, political and social developments. Forecasting included scenarios for up to 20 years. Although not much is known about the history of Shell's scanning group, it too is obviously conscious of ongoing attempts to enhance corporate management's environmental perceptions (Thomas, 1980).

(Continued)

(Continued)

at any time represents a no-growth, recessional future and the other one an evolutionary growth future. Companies usually prefer growth to recession (Ketola, 1998).

The scenarios created by Shell in 1989 paid special attention to the natural environment because those issues had just become acute as a result of Chernobyl, the *Exxon Valdez* oil spill in Alaska and Shell's own Stanlow leakage (Ketola, 1998). The scenario pair for 1992–2020 concentrated more on geopolitics because of the recent breakdown of the Soviet Union. Shell backed out of the environmentally progressive scenario, which called for international collaborative efforts to address environmental concerns. Instead, and as a result of the detailed analysis of the financial consequences of the implications, Shell showed a preference for a scenario where businesses would deal with the environment through market forces and self-regulation (Ketola, 1998).

Following the Brent Spar incident, consumer boycotts were organized in European countries, and sales dropped, particularly in Germany. Whereas Shell's previous scenarios did not consider this type of social engagement, they currently envisage substantial public pressure about globalization and the environment, which translates into political pressure (Kolk and Levy, 2001).

In 2008, Shell outlined two possible routes in its new 'Scenarios to 2050' (Royal Dutch Shell, 2008):

1 In the first route, nations rush to secure energy resources for themselves, fearing that energy security is a zero-sum game, with clear winners and losers. Policy makers pay little attention to curbing energy consumption, supplies run short and GHG emissions are not addressed until major shocks trigger political reactions. Too little too late? You bet.

2 The second (preferred) scenario is more positive. Coalitions emerge to take on the challenges of economic development, energy security and environmental pollution through cross-border cooperation. National governments introduce efficiency standards, taxes and other policy instruments to improve the environmental performance of buildings, vehicles, and transport fuels.

There seems to be a mismatch between the logic behind Shell's strategic processes and what is presented to the public by the scenario programme.

The scenarios outline the necessity for thinking about long-term environmental concerns; however, despite its compelling logic, Shell has directly contradicted the conclusions by cutting its investments in hydrogen and renewable energy. Even if this is a temporary reaction to the crisis, it casts doubt on the long-term 'strategic rationality' of Shell's actions and begs the question of when these strategic anticipatory activities will be resumed. A deeper question is: what place do these scenarios have in terms of the realized strategy Shell's?

Sustainable development: a serious goal, or just a catchphrase?

In the 1970s, emerging environmental concerns about the limits of our global environmental resources were not shared by the oil industry. For some time, the belief has been that the more a non-renewable resource such as oil is extracted and consumed, the cheaper it becomes. By investing profits in technical innovation, previously untapped oil reserves become accessible and cost effective. More recent concerns have arisen in relation to the impacts of industrial pollution, particularly on the planet's climate, but also on local ecosystems and human health. This appears to have been acknowledged by Shell. In a 2002 report, it stated that over the next 50 years, '[g]lobal energy demand is expected at least to double and energy producers will need to seek ways of meeting those needs, whilst minimising the effect on the environment and doing business in a socially responsible manner' (Royal Dutch Shell, 2002).

In 2006, van der Veer said: 'In 20 years or 30 years, alternative energies will start to play a key role. My wish, my ambition for this company is that if we can make at least one alternative energy a major business, then I think we have done well' (Cummins and Williams, 2006; Chang and Yong, 2007). During that year, a range of advertisements about Shell's intentions showed up: 'The world wants more energy, the planet wants less pollution', 'One energy company is going further to make hydrogen a reality', 'How can we produce more energy but lower carbon emissions?' (Monbiot, 2009b).

It might be contended that these commitments demonstrate that Shell has a long-term strategy intended to differentiate the company from more defensive competitors and to anticipate the rising

(Continued)

(Continued)

pressure against large industrial emitters (Boiral, 2006). On the other hand, it could also mean that Shell's acknowledgement of its corporate environmental (and social) responsibilities is just rhetoric and that the (limited) investments in activities related to the social and ecological concerns are a result of public pressure, with the aim of improving the firm's credibility and legitimacy, as well as to obtain reliability and participation in discussions about future energy strategies (Kolk and Levy, 2001). Shell (Royal Dutch Shell, 2002) stated that '[o]ur commitment to contribute to sustainable development is not a cosmetic public relations exercise. We believe that sustainable development is good for business and business is good for sustainable development'. Shell posits that tackling climate change is 'the pro-growth strategy' (Pickard and Mackenzie, 2009).

A significant change in the corporate landscape has been the diffusion and increasing legitimacy of this type of 'win–win' discourse articulating the compatibility of environmental and business interests. In 2007, *Business Week* asked readers to 'Imagine a world in which eco-friendly and socially responsible practices actually help a company's bottom line. It's closer than you think' (Engardio et al., 2007). CERES optimistically suggests that companies in the vanguard no longer question how much it will cost to reduce GHG emissions, but how much money they can make from doing it (Jones and Levy, 2007). BP, for example, became an ardent defender of the Kyoto Protocol and committed to cutting its GHG emissions by 10 per cent before 2010, based on 1990 levels. The Gulf of Mexico 2010 Deepwater oil spill, however, presented another face of BP, in which engineering corners were cut with ecologically catastrophic consequences. In 2002, company managers announced that the objective was reached eight years earlier than planned, without additional costs (Boiral, 2006). Clearly, the context for strategy-making will have changed with the $20 billion or so of claims expected against BP. Shell has repeatedly emphasized that the investments in renewables are not public relations stunts, but involve long-term business decisions that need to become profitable (Kolk and Levy, 2001).

It has been suggested that if a company does not invest in sustainability, it could suffer from costly setbacks from environmental disasters, political protests and human rights or workplace abuses.

It is argued that the growing clout of watchdog groups making use of the Internet is one important factor. New environmental regulations also play a powerful role (Engardio et al., 2007).

The win–win and win–lose dichotomies, however, remain simplistic. The long-term relationship between environmental and business concerns depends on many factors, including corporate management, technologies and processes, firm size, market structure, expected return on investments, and so on. Understanding these factors is difficult as they are embedded in a political, social and scientific context that can vary from one sector or one region to another (Boiral, 2006).

For Shell, investments in renewable energy cost money; they have been very limited in the past and recently cut altogether. In the absence of subsidies or other incentives, companies are likely to be concerned with the loss of a competitive edge and it is not surprising that Shell hopes for a governance framework to implement better environmental standards in the entire sector in its latest scenario (see above). In an interview, van der Veer explains: 'if we find something that is good for the consumers, then we will put big money behind it' (Monbiot, 2009b). Shell's strategy is determined by the nature of the game. The rules are set out by governments who decide the general framework of the energy mix, and corporations, such as Shell, can only do 'the best possible job within such a framework', relying ultimately on getting a better reputation and thus more customers (Monbiot, 2009a). This places the locus of a sustainable strategy outside of Shell and thus avoids taking responsibility on the basis that corporations are passive players who must wait upon governments or market pulls. This downplays corporations' ability to influence government, which David Korten (1995) claims 'means that it is corporations that dominate people and their governments'.

Shell's short-term immediate concerns in the global financial crisis illustrate that regardless of whether they are conceived as window-dressing or not, its social and ecological expenditures were the first to go. This has long-term implications. Shell is said to be running the risk of making investments in activities and measures that may turn out to be futile and unnecessary unless a common regulatory regime for GHG emissions

(Continued)

(Continued)

is established. However, if it does not invest, Shell also runs the risk of not having positioned itself in time to capture a valuable market share in potential future markets for both renewable energy and international trading in GHG emissions (Skodvin and Skjoerseth, 2001).

Understanding the inconsistencies in Shell's strategic logic

While Shell has been a strong advocate of sustainability, it also been involved directly and indirectly in activities that can be considered to be in conflict with the principles of sustainability. This indicates ambiguity within the organization.

In 1989, the UN created the Intergovernmental Panel on Climate Change (IPCC). Shortly after the first meeting, Shell joined the newly created Global Climate Coalition (GCC) made up of companies and trade associations that have strongly opposed the enforcement of limits on GHG emissions (Boiral, 2006). This is not surprising, following the precedent of the 1987 Montreal Protocol for the control of ozone-depleting substances. Compared with the United States, European industry was far less aggressive in responding to the issue (Jones and Levy, 2007). In 1998, Shell left the GCC. Some suggest that it did so because the coalition's positions became unpopular (Skodvin and Skjoerseth, 2001; Jones and Levy, 2007). The GCC was finally deactivated in 2002, after its mission was fulfilled and the United States withdrew from the Kyoto Protocol in 2001 (Skodvin and Skjaerseth, 2001; Jones and Levy, 2007).

In 2007, Shell joined the US Climate Action Partnership (UCAP), a coalition of major businesses and environmental organizations advocating mandatory caps and trade. UCAP appears to be attempting to shape the emerging emissions regime in anticipation of future regulations (Jones and Levy, 2007).

The American Petroleum Institute (API) is another research institute opposing the US ratification of Kyoto, in which the American branch offices of companies like Shell and BP Amoco are also still members. In 1998, it distributed a video titled *Fuelless: you can't be cool without fuel*. It was intended to provide teachers and students with materials on the vital role of oil and natural gas in modern life. An API memo leaked to the media in 1998 shed light on the motivation for targeting schools (David, 2006):

'Informing teachers/students about uncertainties in climate science will begin to erect barriers against further efforts to impose Kyoto-like measures in the future.'

In 2009, a plan by the US oil industry to deploy thousands of workers in rallies protesting against imminent climate change legislation exposed splits within the API as some members – including Shell – also belong to UCAP, which supports President Obama's environmental policies (Pickard and Mackenzie, 2009). API core members, such as Exxon Mobil, warned that the legislation could put businesses employing millions of workers 'at a disadvantage' with competitors, but not all members were convinced. The contradiction inherent in the simultaneous membership of both lobbying groups (API and UCAP), which have incompatible objectives, reveals something fundamentally important about the nature of corporate agency. This schizophrenic behaviour by Shell and other oil giants may seem to be duplicitous, but it might also reflect assumptions about how corporates enact their power in a global economy.

These actions show that corporate strategy can include both proactive and resistive strategic actions. Strategic actions can be initiated by different parts of a corporation at different times or be focused on specific activities or certain organizational aspects without recourse to how well this fits within a general strategic logic. The commitment to global warming is also strongly driven by the dominant image, social legitimacy and mimetic forces at play in a particular moment in time (Boiral, 2006). Moreover, within a large multinational bureaucracy like Shell, it is hard to imagine that there is an internally consistent view on matters of sustainable development. Halfway through the 1990s, for example, there were efforts within Shell to bring the US-based Shell Oil Company, which obstructed Shell's corporate position on the climate change issue, more in line with corporate policies (Kolk and Levy, 2001).

Inconsistencies in relation to social sustainability have also been recorded. Friends of the Earth reports regularly on a range of unethical practices by Shell around the world (see the section on blue washing). In 2003, it warned that Shell is working to destroy what little credibility it has by lobbying against an important UN standard, *Norms on the Responsibilities of Transnational Corporations and Other Business Enterprises with Regard to*

(Continued)

(Continued)

Human Rights (Friends of the Earth International, 2003).

Questions

1 Reading the case carefully, analyse it in strategic terms from the following perspectives:

(a) Strategic decision-making perspectives (Chapter 7)

(b) Resource-based view (Chapter 3)

(c) Political perspective (Chapter 9)

(d) Innovation perspective (Chapter 10)

2 Using Shell as a representative example, analyse the role that the business community has played in shaping the system of global governance and relations between states, businesses and NGOs. To what extent is Shell willing to undertake measures consistent with supporting a fragmented and weak policy regime, while at the same time taking political action to create, shape and preserve that compromised regime in the territories in which it operates?

3 Using the Shell case as indicative, in what ways is a corporate commitment to sustainability meaningful?

REFERENCES

Aaker, D. A. (1996) *Building Strong Brands*, London: Simon & Schuster.

Aaker, D. A. and Joachimsthaler, E. (2002) *Brand Leadership*, London: Simon & Schuster.

Abbott, A. (1988) *The System of Professions: An Essay on the Division of Expert Labour*, Chicago: Chicago University Press.

Abercrombie, N., Hill, S. and Turner, B. S. (1980) *The Dominant Ideology*. Thesis, London: Allen & Unwin.

Abo, T. (1994) *Hybrid Factory*, New York: Oxford University Press.

Abrahamson, E. (1996) Management Fashion, *Academy of Management Review*, 21(1): 254–85.

Abrahamson, E. and Freedman, D. H. (2006) *A Perfect Mess: The Hidden Benefits of Disorder. How Crammed Closets, Cluttered Offices, and On-the-Fly Planning Make the World a Better Place*, London: Weidenfeld & Nicolson.

Abramson, J. (2009) *Minerva's Owl: The Tradition of Western Political Thought*, Cambridge, MA: Harvard University Press.

Albrow, M. (1997) *Do Organizations Have Feelings?* London: Routledge.

Allison, G. T. (1969) Conceptual Models and the Cuban Missiles Crisis, *American Political Science Review*, LXIII(3): 689–718.

Allison, G. T. (1971) *Essence of Decision*, Boston, MA: Little, Brown.

Almeida, P., Grant, R. and Phene, A. (2002) Knowledge Transfer through Alliances: The Role of Culture. In M. Gannon and K. Newman (eds), *Handbook of Cross Cultural Management*, Oxford: Blackwell.

Alvaro, C. C. (2006) Who Cares about Corruption? *Journal of International Business Studies*, 37(6): 807–22.

Alvesson, M. (1993) Organizations as Rhetoric: Knowledge-Intensive Firms and the Struggle with Ambiguity, *Journal of Management Studies*, 30(6): 997–1015.

Alvesson, M. (1994) Critical Theory and Consumer Marketing, *Scandinavian Journal of Management*, 10(3): 291–313.

Alvesson, M. and Willmott, H. (1995) Strategic Management as Domination and Emancipation: From Planning and Process to Communication and Praxis. In P. Shrivastava and C. Stubbart (eds), *Advances in Strategic Management: Challenges from Outside the Mainstream*, Greenwich, CT: JAI Press.

Amabile, T. and Conti, R. (1999) Changes in the Work Environment for Creativity during Downsizing, *Academy of Management Journal*, 42(6): 616–29.

Amburgey, T. L. and Dacin, M. (1994) As the Left Foot Follows the Right: The Dynamics of Strategic and Structural Change, *Academy of Management Journal*, 37(6): 1427–52.

Anderson, C. (2006) *The Long Tail: Why the Future of Business Is Selling Less of More*, New York: Hyperion.

Anderson, R. and Connolly, B. (1996) *Rats in the Ranks*. Documentary Film. Australia: Film Australia and Arundel Productions.

Anderson, R. E. (1994) Matrix Redux, *Business Horizons*, 37(6): 6–10.

Andersson, U. and Pahlberg, C. (1997) Subsidiary Influence on Strategic Behaviour in MNCs: An Empirical Study, *International Business Review*, 6(3): 319–34.

Andersson, U., Forsgren, M. and Holm, U. (2007) Balancing Subsidiary Influence in the Federative MNC: A Business Network View, *Journal of International Business Studies*, 38(5): 802–18.

Andrews, K. (1989) Ethics in Practice, *Harvard Business Review*, September–October: 99–104.

Ansoff, H. I. (1965) *Corporate Strategy: An Analytic Approach to Business Policy for Growth and Expansion*, New York: McGraw-Hill.

Ansoff, H. I. (1991) Critique of Henry Mintzberg's 'The Design School': Reconsidering the Basic Premises of Strategic Management, *Strategic Management School*, 12(6): 449–61.

Appadurai, A. (1996) *Modernity at large: Cultural Dimensions of Globalization*. Minneapolis: University of Minnesota Press.

Arend, R. J. and Bromiley, P. (2009) Assessing the Dynamic Capabilities View: Spare Change Everyone? *Strategic Organization*, 7(1): 75–90.

Argyris, C. (1990) *Overcoming Organizational Defences*, Boston, MA: Allyn and Bacon.

Argyris, C. and Schon, D. (1978) *Organizational Learning: A Theory of Action Perspective*, Reading, MA: Addison Wesley.

Ariño, A. and Reuer, J. J. (2004) Alliance Contractual Design. Barcelona, *IESE Business School Working Paper* No. 572.

Ariño, A. and Reuer, J. J. (2006) *Strategic Alliances: Governance and Contracts*, London: Palgrave Macmillan.

Ariño, A., de la Torre, J. and Ring, P. S. (2005) Relational Quality and Inter-personal Trust in Strategic Alliances. *European Management Review*, 2: 15–27.

Arnott, S. (2008) UK Companies Urge Steps to Head Off Global 'Oil Crunch', *The Independent*, Thursday, October 30. http://www.independent.co.uk/news/business/news/uk-companies-mge-steps-to-head-off-global-oil-crunch-9785, accessed 13 September 2010.

Ashby, W. R. (1956) *An Introduction to Cybernetics*, London: Chapman & Hall.

Augier, M. and Teece, D. (2008) Strategy as Evolution with Design: The Foundation of Dynamic Capabilities and the Role of Managers in the Economic System, *Organization Studies*, 29(8/9): 1187–208.

Aula, P. and Mantere, S. (2008) *Strategic Reputation Management*, London: Routledge.

Avolio, B. J., Bass, B. M. and Jung, D. I. (1999) Re-examining the Components of Transformational and Transactional Leadership Using the Multifactor Leadership Questionnaire, *Journal of Occupational & Organizational Psychology*, 72(4): 441–62.

Avolio, B. J., Walumbwa, F. O. and Weber, T. J. (2009) Leadership: Current Theories, Research, and Future Directions. *Annual Review of Psychology*, 60: 421–49.

Bacharach, S. (2005) *Get Them on Your Side: Win Support, Convert Skeptics, Get Results*, Avon, MA: Platinum.

Bachrach, P. and Baratz, M. (1970) *Poverty and Power: Theory and Practice*, Oxford: Oxford University Press.

Baden-Fuller, C. and Stopford, J. M. (1992) *Rejuvenating the Mature Business: The Competitive Challenge*, New York: Routledge.

Bahrami, H. and Evans, S. (1995) Flexible Re-Cycling and High-Technology Entrepreneurship, *California Management Review*, 37(3): 62–89.

Bain, J. S. (1956) *Barriers to New Competition*, Cambridge, MA: Harvard University Press.

Bain, J. S. (1968) *Industrial Organization*, New York: Wiley.

Balakrishnan, S. and Koza, M. (1993) Information Asymmetry, Adverse Selection and Joint Ventures, *Journal of Economic Behaviour and Organization*, 20(1): 99–118.

Balogun, J. and Johnson, G. (2004) Organizational Restructuring and Middle Manager Sensemaking, *Academy of Management Journal*, 47(4): 523–49.

Balogun, J. and Johnson, G. (2005) From Intended Strategies to Unintended Outcomes: The Impact of Change Recipient Sensemaking, *Organization Studies*, 26(11): 1573–601.

Bamford, J.D., Gomes-Casseres, B. and Robinson, M.S. (2003) *Mastering Alliance Strategy: A Comprehensive Guide to Design, Management, and Organization*, San Francisco: Jossey-Bass.

Bamford, J., Ernst, D. and Fubini, D. (2004) Launching a World-Class Joint Venture, *Harvard Business Review*, 82(2): 90–100.

Band, W., Leaver, S. and Rogan, M. A. (2008) *CRM Best Practices Adoption*, New York: Forrester Research.

Banerjee, S. B. (2007) *Corporate Social Responsibility: The Good, the Bad and the Ugly*, Cheltenham: Edward Elgar.

Banerjee, S. B. (2008) Necrocapitalism, *Organization Studies*, 29(12): 1541–63.

Baran, P. and Sweezy, P. (1965) *Monopoly Capital: An Essay on the American Social and Economic Order*, New York: Monthly Review Press.

Barkema, H. G. and Pennings, J. M. (1998) Top Management Pay: Impact of Overt and Covert Power, *Organization Studies*, 19(6): 975–1003.

Barker, J. R. (1993) Tightening the Iron Cage: Concertive Control in Self-managing Teams, *Administrative Science Quarterly*, 38: 408–37.

Barnard, C. (1938) *Functions of the Executive*, Cambridge, MA: Harvard University Press.

Barnett, W. and McKendrick, D. (2004) Why Are Some Organizations More Competitive Than Others? Evidence from a Changing Global Market, *Administrative Science Quarterly*, 49(4): 535–71.

Barney, J. (1986) Strategic Factor Markets: Expectations, Luck, and Business Strategy, *Management Science*, 32(10): 1231–41.

Barney, J. (1991) Firm Resources and Sustained Competitive Advantage, *Journal of Management*, 17(1): 99–120.

Barney, J. (1995) Looking Inside for Competitive Advantage, *Academy of Management Executive*, 9(4): 49–61.

Barney, J. and Arikan, A. (2006) *The Resource-Based View: Origins and Implications*. In M. A. Hitt, R. E. Freeman and J. S. Harrison (eds), *The Blackwell Handbook of Strategic Management*, Oxford: Blackwell, pp. 124–88.

Barney, J. and Hesterly, W. S. (1996) Organizational Economics: Understanding the Relationship between Organizations and Economic Analysis. In S. R. Clegg, C. Hardy and W. R. Nord (eds), *Handbook of Organization Studies*, Thousand Oaks, CA: Sage, pp. 115–47.

Barry, D. and Elmes, M. (1997) Strategy Retold: Toward a Narrative View of Strategic Discourse, *Academy of Management Review*, 22(2): 429–52.

Bartlett, C. and Ghoshal, S. (1987) *Managing Across Borders: The Transactional Solution*, Harvard Business School Press, 28(Summer): 7–17.

Bartlett, C. and Ghoshal S. (1989) *Managing Across Borders: The Transnational Solution*, London: Hutchinson Business Books.

Bartlett, C. and Ghoshal, S. (1995) *Managing Across Borders: The Transnational Solution*, Boston, MA: Harvard Business School Press.

Bass, B. M. (1985) *Leadership and Performance Beyond Expectation*, New York: Free Press.

Bass, B. M. (1998) *Transformational Leadership: Industrial, Military, and Educational Impact*, Mahwah, NJ: Lawrence Erlbaum Associates.

Bass, B. M. and Avolio, B. J. (1993) Transformational Leadership: A Response to Critiques. In M. M. Chemers and R. Ayman (eds), *Leadership Theory and Research: Perspectives and Directions*, New York: Academic Press, pp. 49–80.

Bass, B. M. and Avolio, B. J. (1995) *MLQ – Multifactor Leadership Questionnaire* (2nd edn), Redwood City, CA: Mind Garden.

Bass, B. M. and Avolio, B. J. (1997) *Full-range of Leadership Development: Manual for the Multifactor Leadership Questionnaire*, Palo Alto, CA: Mind Garden.

Baudrillard, J. (1988) *Jean Baudrillard, Selected Writings*, ed. M. Poster, Stanford, CA: Stanford University Press.

Baudrillard, J. (1993) *The Transparency of Evil: Essays on Extreme Phenomena*, London: Verso.

Bauerschmidt, A. and Chrisman, J. J. (1993) Strategies for Survival in the Microcomputer Industry: 1985–1989, *Journal of Management Inquiry*, 2(1): 63–82.

Baysinger, B. (1984) Domain Maintenance as an Objective of Business Political Activity: An Expanded Typology, *Academy of Management Review*, 9(2): 248–58.

Beale, F. and Fernando, M. (2009) Short-termism and Genuineness in Environmental Initiatives: A Comparative Case Study of Two Oil Companies, *European Management Journal*, 27(1): 26–35.

Beamish, P. (1994) Joint Ventures in LDCs: Partner Selection and Performance, *Management International Review*, 34: 60–75.

Beattie, A., Luce, T., Guha, K. and Guena, F. (2009) Obama Gets Tough on Executive Pay, *The Financial Times*, 04 February 2009, http://www.ft.com/cms/s/0/06bao88-f2b7-11dd-abe6-00007afd2ac.html, accessed 23 September 2010.

Bechky, B. A. (2003) Sharing Meaning across Occupational Communities: The Transformation of Understanding on a Production Floor, *Organization Science*, 14(3): 312–30.

Beck, U. (1997) *The Reinvention of Politics: Rethinking Modernity in the Global Social Order*, Cambridge: Polity Press.

Beck, U. (2008) Risk Society's Cosmopolitan Moment, Lecture at Harvard University – 12 November 2008, http://docs.google.com/viewer?a=v&q=cache:lQ5Vu-FXpIEJ:www.labjor.unicamp.br/comciencia/files/risco/AR-UlrichBeck-Harvard.pdf+beck+risk+society+and+financial+crisis&hl=en&gl=au&sig=AHIEtbQ8Ehs2-oysj-rV8agqxm4v3WSdwQ, accessed 2 March 2010.

Becker-Ritterspach, F., Lange, K. and Lohr, K. (2002) Control Mechanisms and Patterns of Reorganization in MNCs. In M. Geppert, D. Matten and K. Williams (eds), *Challenges for European Management in a Global Context – Experiences from Britain and Germany*, Basingstoke: Palgrave, pp. 68–95.

Beckman, S. L. and Barry, M. (2007) Innovation as a Learning Process: Embedding Design Thinking, *California Management Review*, 50(1): 25–56.

Belliveau, M. A., O'Reilly III, C. A. and Wade, J. B. (1996) Social Capital at the Top: Effects of Social Similarity and Status on CEO Compensation, *Academy of Management Journal*, 39(6): 1568–93.

Benjamin, W. (1982) The Task of the Translator: An Introduction to the Translation of Baudelaire's Tableaux Parisiens. In H. Arendt (ed.), *Illuminations*, London: Fontana/Collins.

Berglund, J. and Werr, A. (2000) The Invincible Character of Management Consulting Rhetoric: How One Blends Incommensurates while Keeping Them Apart, *Organization*, 7(4): 633–55.

Berle, A. A. and Means, C. (1932) *The Modern Corporation and Private Property*, New York: Commerce Clearing House.

Berrone, P. (2008) Current Global Financial Crisis: An Incentive Problem, University of Navarra, *IESE Business School Occasional Paper*, OP–158.

Berry, L. (1983) *Relationship Marketing, Emerging Perspectives on Services Marketing*, Chicago: American Marketing Association, pp. 25–8.

Berry, L. (1995) Relationship Marketing of Services: Growing Interest, Emerging Perspectives, *Journal of the Academy of Marketing Science*, 23(4): 236–45.

Berry, L. and Parasuraman, A. (1991) *Marketing Services*, New York: Free Press.

Bessant, J. and Tsekouras, G. (2001) Developing Learning Networks, *AI and Society*, 15(2): 82–98.

Bessant, J., Kaplinsky, R. and Morris, M. (2003) Learning Networks, *International Journal of Technology Management and Sustainable Development*, 2(1): 19–28.

Betts, R. K. (2000) Is Strategy an Illusion? *International Security*, 25(2): 5–50.

Bevan, J. (2001) *The Rise and Fall of Marks and Spencer*, London: Profile Books.

Biggart, N. (1991) Explaining Asian Economic Organization: Towards a Weberian Economic Perspective, *Theory and Society*, 20(2): 199–232.

Biggart, N. and Guillén, M. F. (1999) Developing Social Organization and the Rise of the Auto Industries of South Korea, Taiwan, Spain, and Argentina, *American Sociological Review*, 64(5): 722–47.

Birkinshaw, J. (1999) The Determinants and Consequences of Subsidiary Initiative in Multinational Corporations, *Entrepreneurship Theory and Practice*, 24(1): 9–36.

Birkinshaw, J. and Hood, N. (1998a) Multinational Subsidiary Evolution: Capability and Charter Change in Foreign-owned Subsidiary Companies, *Academy of Management Review*, 23(4): 773–95.

Birkinshaw, J. and Hood, N. (1998b) *Multinational Subsidiary Evolution and Subsidiary Development*, New York and London: Macmillan and St. Martin's Press.

Birkinshaw, J. and Lingblad, M. (2005) Intrafirm Competition and Charter Evolution in the Multibusiness Firm, *Organization Science*, 16(6): 674–86.

Birkinshaw, J. and Ridderstråle, J. (1999) Fighting the Corporate Immune System: A Process Study of Subsidiary Initiatives in Multinational Corporations, *International Business Review*, 8(2): 149–80.

Birkinshaw, J., Bessant, J. and Delbridge, R. (2007) Finding, Forming and Reforming: Creating Networks for Continuous Innovation, *California Management Review*, 49(3): 67–84.

Birkinshaw, G., Hamel, G. and Mol, M. (2008) Management Innovation, *Academy of Management Review*, 33(4): 825–45.

Blake, R. R. and Mouton, J. S. (1964) *The Managerial Grid*, Houston, TX: Gulf Publishing.

Blandard, O. (2009) Sustaining a Global Recovery, Finance and Development 26(3), http://www.imf.org/external/pubs/ft/andd/2009/09/blanchardindex.html, accessed 25 May 2010.

Bleeke, J. and Ernst, D. (1991) The Way to Win in Cross-Border Alliances, *Harvard Business Review*, 69: 127–35.

Blumentritt, T. P. (2003) Foreign Subsidiaries' Government Affairs Activities: The Influence of Managers and Resources, *Business & Society*, 42(2): 202–33.

Boddewyn, J. (1975) *Corporate External Affairs: Blueprint for Survival*, New York: Business International Corporation.

Boddewyn, J. (1988) Political Aspects of MNE Theory, *Journal of International Business Studies*, 19(3): 341–63.

Boddewyn, J. (1993) Political Resources and Markets in International Business: Beyond Porter's Generic Strategies, *Research in Global Strategic Management*, 4: 83–99.

Boddewyn, J. and Brewer, T. L. (1994) International-Business Political Behavior: New Theoretical Directions, *Academy of Management Review*, 19(1): 119–43.

Boeker, W. (1989) The Development and Institutionalization of Subunit Power in Organizations, *Administrative Science Quarterly*, 34(3): 388–410.

Boeker, W. (1992) Power and Managerial Dismissal: Scapegoating at the Top, *Administrative Science Quarterly*, 37(3): 400–21.

Boeker, W. (1997) Strategic Change: The Influence of Managerial Characteristics and Organizational Growth, *Academy of Management Journal*, 40(1): 152–70.

Boiral, O. (2006) Global Warming: Should Companies Adopt a Proactive Strategy? *Long Range Planning*, 39(3): 315–30.

Boje, D. M. (1991) The Storytelling Organization: A Study of Story Performance in an Office-Supply Firm, *Administrative Science Quarterly*, 36(1): 106–26.

Boje, D. M. (1995) Stories of the Storytelling Organization – A Postmodern Analysis of Disneyland as Tamaraland, *Academy of Management Journal*, 38(4): 997–1035.

Boland, R. J. and Collopy, F. (2004) *Developing Capability, Managing and Designing*, Palo Alto, CA: Stanford University Press.

Bolman, L. G. and Deal, T. E. (2001) *Leading with the Soul*, San Francisco, CA: Jossey-Bass.

Bonzo Dog Doo Dah Band (1967) Cool Britannia, *Gorilla*, London: Liberty Records.

Booth, C. (2003) Does History Matter in Strategy? The Possibilities and Problems of Counterfactual Analysis, *Journal of Management History in Management Decision*, 41(1): 96–104.

Bouquet, C. and Birkinshaw, J. (2008) Managing Power in the Multinational Corporation: How Low-Power Actors Gain Influence, *Journal of Management*, 34(3): 477–508.

Bourdieu, P. (1973) Cultural Reproduction and Social Reproduction. In R. Brown (ed.), *Knowledge, Education and Cultural Change*, London: Tavistock, pp. 71–112.

Bourdieu, P. (1984) *Distinction: A Social Critique of the Judgement of Taste*, Cambridge, MA: Harvard University Press.

Bourdieu, P. (1990) *The Logic of Practice*, trans. R. Nice, Stanford, CA: Stanford University Press.

Bourdieu, P. (1996) *The State Nobility*, Cambridge: Polity Press.

Bourdieu, P. and Passeron, C. J. (1977) *Reproduction in Education, Society and Culture*, London: Sage.

Bourdieu, P. and Wacquant, L. J. D. (1992) *An Invitation to Reflexive Sociology*, Chicago: University of Chicago Press.

Bourdieu, P., Boltanski, L. and de St Martin, M. (1973) Les Strategies de Reconversion, *Social Science Information*, 12(1): 61–113.

Bowers, D. G. and Seashore, S. E. (1966) Predicting Organizational Effectiveness with a Four Factor Theory of Leadership, *Administrative Science Quarterly*, 11(2): 238–63.

Boyatzis, R. E. (1982) *The Competent Manager*, New York: Wiley.

Brandenburger, A. and Nalebuff, B. (1995) The Right Game: Use Game Theory to Shape Strategy, *Harvard Business Review*, 73(4): 57–71.

Bray, D. W., Campbell, R. J. and Grant, D. L. (1974) *Formative Years in Business: A Longterm AT&T Study of Managerial Lives*, New York: Wiley.

Breene, R. T. S., Nunes, P. and Shill, W. E. (2007) The Chief Strategy Officer, *Harvard Business Review Reprints*, http://www.accenture.com/NR/rdonlyres/0EF340C8-ECAC-4A45-87CA-0B8EE06A120B/0/CSO.pdf, accessed 24 November 2009.

Brenneman, W. B., Keys, J. B. and Fulmer, R. M. (1998) Learning across a Living Company: The Shell Companies' Experiences, *Organizational Dynamics*, 27(2): 61–70.

Brown, A. D. (2000) Making Sense of Inquiry Sensemaking, *Journal of Management Studies*, 37(1): 45–75.

Brown, A. D. and Starkey, K. (2000) Organizational Identity and Organizational Learning: A Psychodynamic Perspective, *Academy of Management Review*, 25(1): 102–20.

Brown, J. S. (2004) Minding and Mining the Periphery, *Long Range Planning*, 37(2): 143–51.

Brown, T. (2009) *Change by Design: How Design Thinking Transforms Organizations and Inspires Innovation*, New York: Harper Collins.

Brown, T. and Pitoski, M. (2003) Managing Contract Performance: A Transaction Costs Approach, *Journal of Policy Analysis and Management*, 22(2): 275–97.

Bruno, K. and Karliner, J. (2002) *Earth Summit Biz: The Corporate Take-over of Sustainable Development*. Oakland, CA: Food First Books.

Brunsson, N. (1994) *The Organization of Hypocrisy: Talk, Decisions and Actions*, Chichester: Wiley.

Brunsson, N. and Jacobsson, B. (2001) *A World of Standards*, New York: Oxford University Press.

Buchanan, D. and Badham, R. (2008) *Power, Politics, and Organizational Change*, London: Sage.

Buck, T. and Shahrim, A. (2005) The Translation of Corporate Governance Change across Nations: The Case of Germany, *Journal of International Business Studies*, 36(1): 42–61.

Buckley, P. (2003) *Globalization and Multinational Enterprise*. In D. Faulkner and A. Campbell (eds), *The Oxford Handbook of Strategy*, Oxford: Oxford University Press.

Buckley, P. J. and Ghauri, P. N. (1999) *The Internationalization of the Firm*, London: Thomson.

Bunch, D. S. and Smiley, R. (1992) Who Deters Entry? Evidence on the Use of Strategic Entry Deterrence, *Review of Economics and Statistics*, 74(3): 509–21.

Burgelman, R. A. (1983) A Process Model of Internal Corporate Venturing in the Diversified Major Firm, *Administrative Science Quarterly*, 28(2): 223–44.

Burgelman, R. A. (1991) Intraorganizational Ecology of Strategy Making and Organizational Adaptation: Theory and Field Research, *Organization Science*, 2(3): 239–62.

Burns, J. M. (1978) *Leadership*, New York: Harper & Row.

Burt, R. S. (1992) *Structural Holes: The Social Structure of Competition*, Cambridge, MA: Harvard University Press.

Burt, R. S. (2000) The Network Structure of Social Capital. In B. M. Staw and R. I. Sutton (eds), *Research in Organizational Behavior*, New York: Elsevier, pp. 345–423.

Burt, R. S., Hogarth, R. M. and Michau, C. (2000) The Social Capital of French and American Managers, *Organization Science*, 11(2): 123–47.

Butler, R. (1990) Decision-Making Research: Its Uses and Misuses. A Comment on Mintzberg and Waters: Does Decision Get in the Way? *Organization Studies*, 11(1): 11–16.

Byrne, J. A. (1999) *Chainsaw: The Notorious Career of Al Dunlap in the Era of Profit-At-Any-Price*, New York: HarperCollins.

Cable, J. and Dirrheimer, M. J. (1983) Hierarchies and Markets: An Empirical Test of the Multidivisional Hypothesis in West Germany, *International Journal of Industrial Organization*, 1(1): 43–62.

Camillus, J. C. (2008) Strategy as a Wicked Problem, *Harvard Business Review*, 86(5): 98–106.

Canback, S. (1998) The Logic of Management Consulting (Part One), *Journal of Management Consulting*, 10(2): 3–11.

Capelli, P. (2009) The Future of the US Business Model and the Rise of the Competitors, *Academy of Management Perspectives*, 23(2): 5–10.

Carduff, K. (2003) Review: The Value Reporting Revolution: Moving Beyond the Earnings Game, *Research in Accounting Regulation*, 16: 285–8.

Carlile, P. R. (2002) A Pragmatic View of Knowledge and Boundaries: Boundary Objects in New Product Development, *Organization Science*, 13(4): 442–55.

Carlile, P. R. (2004) Transferring, Translating, and Transforming: An Integrative Framework for Managing Knowledge across Boundaries, *Organization Science*, 15(5): 555–68.

Carr, N. G. (2007) The Ignorance of Crowds, Strategy and Business Change, www.StrategyandBusiness.com/article07204?gko=6c4ad, accessed 23 September 2010.

Carter, C. and Mueller, F. (2002) The Long March of the Management Modernisers: Ritual, Rhetoric and Rationality, *Human Relations*, 55(11): 1325–54.

Carter, C. and Mueller, F. (2006) The Colonisation of Strategy: Financialisation in a Post-Privatisation Context, *Critical Perspectives on Accounting*, 17(8): 967–85.

Carter, C., Clegg, S. R. and Kornberger, M. (2008a) *A Very Short, Fairly Interesting and Reasonably Cheap Book about Studying Strategy*, London: Sage.

Carter, C., Clegg, S. R., and Kornberger, M. (2008b) S-A-P: Zapping the Field, *Strategic Organization*, 6(1): 107–112.

Carter, C., Clegg, S. R. and Kornberger, M. (2008c) Strategy as practice, *Strategic Organization*, 6(1): 83–99.

Casciaro, T. and Lobo, M. S. (2005) Competent Jerks, Lovable Fools, and the Formation of Social Networks, *Harvard Business Review*, June: 92–9.

Casey, C. (1995) *Work, Self and Society: After Industrialism*, London: Routledge.

Casper, S. (2007) How Do Technology Clusters Emerge and Become Sustainable? Social Network Formation and Inter-firm Mobility within the San Diego Biotechnology Cluster, *Research Policy*, 36(4): 438–55.

Cassani, B. and Kemp, K. (2003) *Go: An Airline Adventure*, London: Time Warner.

Castells, M. (1996) *The Rise of the Network Society*, London: Blackwell.

Castells, M. (2009) *Communication Power*, Oxford: Oxford University Press.

Catmull, E. (2008) How Pixar Fosters Collective Creativity, *Harvard Business Review*, September 2008.

Chakrabarty, D. (2000) *Provincializing Europe: Postcolonial Thought and Historical Difference*, Princeton, NJ: Princeton University Press.

Chan, K. B. and Ng, B. K. (2000) Myths and Misperceptions of Ethnic Chinese Capitalism. In K. B. Chan (ed.), *Chinese Business Networks: State Economy and Culture*, Singapore: Prentice Hall, pp. 286–302.

Chandler, A. D. (1962) *Strategy and Structure: Chapters in the History of the American Industrial Enterprise*, Cambridge, MA: MIT Press.

Chandler, D. P. (2000) *A History of Cambodia*, Boulder, CO: Westview Press.

Chang, Y. and Yong, J. (2007) Differing Perspectives of Major Oil Frms on Future Energy Developments: An Illustrative Framework, *Energy Policy*, 35: 5466–80.

Channon, D. (1973) *The Strategy and Structure of British Enterprise*, London: Macmillan.

Chappell, C., Rhodes, C., Tennant, M., Solomon, N. and Yates, L. (2003) *Reconstructing the Lifelong Learner*, London: Routledge.

Charan, R. and Tichy, N. M. (1998) *Every Business Is a Growth Business*, New York: Times Books/Random House.

Chesbrough, H. W. (2006) *Open Business Models: How to Thrive in the New Innovation Landscape*, Boston, MA: Harvard Business School Press Books.

Chesbrough, H. W. and Appleyard, M. M. (2007) Open Innovation and Strategy, *California Management Review*, 50(1): 57–76.

Chia, R. (2000) Discourse Analysis as Organization Analysis, *Organization*, 7(3): 513–18.

Chia, R. and Mackay, B. (2007) Post-Processual Challenges for the Emerging Strategy-as-Practice Perspectives; Discovering Strategy in the Logic of Practice, *Human Relations*, 60(1): 217–42.

Child, J. (1972) Organizational Structure, Environment, and Performance: The Role of Strategic Choice, *Sociology*, 6: 1–22.

Christensen, C. (1997) *The Innovator's Dilemma*, Boston, MA: Harvard Business School Press.

Clark, D. N. (1997) Strategic Management Tool Usage: A Comparative Study, *Strategic Change*, 6(7): 417–27.

Clark, E. (2004) Power, Action and Constraint in Strategic Management: Explaining Enterprise Restructuring in the Czech Republic, *Organization Studies*, 25(4): 607–27.

Clark, K. B. and Fujimoto, T. (1991) *Product Development Performance*, Boston, MA: Harvard Business School Press.

Clark, P. (2000) *Organizations in Action*, London: Routledge.

Clark, T. and Fincham, R. (2002) Introduction: The Emergence of Critical Perspectives on Consulting. In T. Clark and R. Fincham (eds), *Critical Consulting: New Perspectives on the Management Advice Industry*, Oxford: Blackwell, pp. 1–18.

Clausewitz, C. von (1976) *On War*, ed. and trans. M. Howard and P. Paret, Princeton, NJ: Princeton University Press.

Clegg, S. R. (1989) *Frameworks of Power*, London: Sage.

Clegg, S. R. (1990) *Modern Organizations: Organization Studies in the Postmodern World*, London: Sage.

Clegg, S. R. (2008) Relationships of Ownership, They Whisper in the Wings ..., Review Article of Khurana, R. (2007) *From Higher Aims to Hired Hands: The Social Transformation of American Business Schools and the Unfulfilled Promise of Management Education*, Princeton, NJ: Princeton University Press, *Australian Review of Public Affairs*, March 2008, http://www.australianreview.net/digest/2008/03/clegg.html, accessed 4 September 2009.

Clegg, S. R. and Hardy, C. (1996) Representations. In S. R. Clegg, C. Hardy and W. Nord (eds), *Handbook of Organization Studies*, London: Sage, pp. 676–708.

Clegg, S. R. and Haugaard, M. (eds) (2009) *The SAGE Handbook of Power*, London: Sage.

Clegg, S. R. and Redding, S. G. (eds) (1990) *Capitalism in Contrasting Cultures*, Berlin: de Gruyter.

Clegg, S. R., Courpasson, D. and Phillips, N. (2006) *Power and Organizations*, London: Sage.

Clegg, S. R., Kornberger, M. and Pitsis, T. (2008) *Managing and Organizations: An Introduction to Theory and Practice* (2nd edn), London: Sage.

Clegg, S. R., Kornberger, M. and Rhodes, C. (2004) When the Saints Go Marching In: A Reply to Sturdy, Clark, Fincham & Handley, *Management Learning*, 35(3): 341–4.

Clegg, S. R., Pitsis, T., Rura-Polley, T. and Marosszeky, M. (2002) Governmentality Matters: Designing an Alliance Culture of Inter-organizational Collaboration for Managing Projects, *Organization Studies*, 23(3): 317–37.

Clegg, W. E. and Clegg, S. R. (2008) Corporate Social Responsibility. In S. R. Clegg and J. E. Bailey (eds), *International Encyclopedia of Organization Studies*, Thousand Oaks, CA: Sage, pp. 302–5.

Clifton, R. (2003) Introduction. In R. Clifton and J. Simmons (eds), *Brands and Branding*, London: Profile Books, pp. 1–10.

CNN (2009) Global 500: Annual Ranking of the World's Biggest Companies from *Fortune* Magazine, http://money.cnn.com/magazines/fortune/global500/2009/, accessed 8 December 2009.

Coase, R. (1988) The Nature of the Firm: Origin, Meaning, Influence, *Journal of Law, Economics, and Organization*, 4(11): 3–47.

Cohen, M. D., March, J. G. and Olsen, J. P. (1972) A Garbage Can Model of Organizational Choice, *Administrative Science Quarterly*, 17(1): 1–25.

Coleman, J. S. (1988) Social Capital in the Creation of Human Capital, *American Journal of Sociology*, 94 (Supplement): S95–S120.

Colgate, M. R. and Danaher, P. J. (2000) Implementing a Customer Relationship Strategy: The Asymmetric Impact of Poor versus Excellent Execution, *Journal of the Academy of Marketing Science*, 28(3): 375–87.

Collinbridge, D. and Douglas, G. (1984) Three Models of Policy Making: Expert Advice in the Control of Environmental Lead, *Social Studies of Science*, 14(3): 343–70.

Collins, D. (2007) *Narrating the Management Guru: In Search of Tom Peters*, London: Routledge.

Collins, D. (2008) Has Tom Peters Lost the Plot? A Timely Review of a Celebrated Management Guru, *Journal of Organizational Change Management*, 21(3): 315–34.

Collinson, D. (1994) Strategies as Resistance: Power, Knowledge and Subjectivity. In J. M. Jermier, W. R. Nord and D. Knights (eds), *Resistance and Power in Organizations: Agency, Subjectivity and the Labour Process*, London: Routledge, pp. 25–68.

Conner, K. R. and Prahalad, C. K. (1996) A Resource-Based Theory of the Firm: Knowledge versus Opportunism, *Organization Science*, 7(5): 477–501.

Contractor, F. J. and Lorange, P. (1988) *Cooperative Strategies in International Business*, Lexington, MA: Lexington Books.

Cook, J. and Brown, J. S. (2002) Bridging Epistemologies: The Generative Dance between Organizational Knowledge and Organizational Knowing. In S. Little, P. Quintas and T. Ray (eds), *Managing Knowledge*, London: Sage, pp. 68–101.

Cooks, D. (2008) The Contribution Revolution: Letting Volunteers Build Your Business, *Harvard Business Times*, 86, October, pp. 60–69, http://www.ft.com/cms/s/o/424b268a-f6ff-11dd-8alf.000077afd2ac.html, accessed 23 September 2010.

Cool, K., Dierickx, I. and Jemison, D. (1989) Business Strategy, Market Structure and Risk-Return Relationships: A Structural Approach, *Strategic Management Journal*, 10(6): 507–22.

Cooper, R. G. (1998) Benchmarking New Product Performance: Results of the Best Practices Study, *European Management Journal*, 16(1): 1–17.

Coriat, B. and Weinstein, O. (2002) Organizations, Firms, and Institutions in the Generation of Innovation, *Research Policy*, 32(2): 273–90.

Corley, K. G., Harquail, C. V., Pratt, M. G., Glynn, M. A., Fiol, C. M. and Hatch, M. J. (2006) Guiding Organizational Identity through Aged Adolescence, *Journal of Management Inquiry*, 15(2): 85–99.

CorpWatch (2002) Greenwash + 10, *The UN's Global Compact, Corporate Accountability and the Johannesburg Earth Summit*, San Francisco, CA: CorpWatch.

Courpasson, D. (2000) Managerial Strategies of Domination: Power in Soft Bureaucracies, *Organization Studies*, 21(1): 141–61.

Courpasson, D. (2009) We Have Always Been Oligarchs: Business Elites in Polyarchy. In S. R. Clegg and C. Cooper (eds), *The SAGE Handbook of Organizational Behaviour, Volume 2: Macro Approaches*, London: Sage, pp. 424–55.

Cox, A. (2009) Barclays Executives Must Wait Longer for Bonuses, *Financial Times*, February 2009, http://ft.com/cms/s/0/ede5bfae-f7dc-11d-a284-000077b07658.html, accessed 23 September 2010.

Cray, D., Mallory, G., Butler, R., Hickson, D. and Wilson, D. (1991) Explaining Decision Processes, *Journal of Management Studies*, 28(3): 207–322.

Crenson, M. (1971) *The Un-Politics of Air Pollution*, Baltimore, MD: Johns Hopkins University Press.

Crick, B. (2004) *Essays on Citizenship*, New York: Continuum.

Croft, G., Larsen, P. T. and Parker, G. (2009) Ex-HBOS Chiefs Accused over Risk Controls as Bankers Offer Apologies, *Financial Times*, 11 February 2009, http://www.ft.com/cms/s/0/36a29afa-f7dd-a284-000077b07658.html, accessed 23 October 2010.

Crozier, M. (1964) *The Bureaucratic Phenomenon*, London: Tavistock.

Crozier, M. (1976) Comparing Structures and Comparing Games. In G. Hofstede and M. Sami Kassem (eds), *European Contributions to Organization Theory*, Amsterdam: Van Goreum, pp. 193–207.

Crozier, M. and Friedberg, E. (1980) *Actors and Systems: The Politics of Collective Action*, Chicago: University of Chicago Press.

Cummings, S. (2002) *Recreating Strategy*, London: Sage.

Cummings, S. and Daellenbach, U. (2009) A Guide to the Future of Strategy? The History of Long Range Planning, *Long Range Planning*, 42: 234–63.

Cummins, C. and Williams, M. (2006) Shell's Chief Follows Simple Goals, *The Wall Street Journal*, 17 January 2006.

Cummins, E. (2000) *The Pakistan Soccer Ball Stitching Industry (Public Document)*, Islamabad: Save the Children Fund.

Cunha, M. P. e. and Da Cunha, J.V. (2008) Managing Improvisation in Cross Cultural Virtuous Teams, *International Journal of Cross Cultural Management*, 1(2): 187–208.

Cusamano, M. A. and Gawer, A. (2002) The Elements of Platform Leadership, *Sloan Management Review*, 43: 51–8.

Cyert, R. M. and March, J. G. (1963) *A Behavioral Theory of the Firm*, Englewood Cliffs, NJ: Prentice-Hall.

Czarniawska, B. (1997) *Narrating the Organization*, Chicago: Chicago University Press.

Czarniawska, B. (2008) Alterity/Identity Interplay in Image Construction. In D. Barry and H. Hansen (eds) *The SAGE Handbook of New Approaches in Management and Organization*. London: Sage, pp. 49–67.

Czarniawska, B. and Sevón, G. (2006) *Global Ideas: How Ideas, Objects and Practices Travel in the Global Economy*, Malmö and Copenhagen: Liber and CBS Press.

Czarniawska-Joerges, B. and Sevón, G. (1996) *Translating Organizational Change*, Berlin: De Gruyter.

Dalt, R. L. and Weick, K. E. (1984) Towards a Model of Organizations as Interpretation Systems, *Academy of Management Review*, 9(2): 284–95.

Damanpour, F. (1991) Organizational Innovation: A Meta-Analysis of Effects of Determinants and Moderators, *Academy of Management Journal*, 34(3): 555–90.

Danneels, E. (2002) The Dynamics of Product Innovation and Firm Competences, *Strategic Management Journal*, 23(12): 1095–122.

Das, T. and Teng, B. (1999) Managing Risks in Strategic Alliances, *Academy of Management Executive*, 13(4): 50–62.

D'Aveni, R. (1994) *Hypercompetition*, New York: Free Press.

Davenport, T. (2009) How to Design Smart Business Experiments, *Harvard Business Review*, 87(2): 68–76.

David, L. (2006) Science à la Joe Camel, *Washington Post*, November 26, http://www.washingtonpost.com/wp-syn/content/article/2006/11/24/AR2006112400789.html, accessed 13 September 2010.

Davies, K. (2009) *While Global FDI Falls, China's Outward FDI Doubles*, Vale Columbia Center on Sustainable International Investment, Columbia FDI Perspective No. 5, May 26, www.vcc.columbia.edu/documents/DaviesPerspective-Final.pdf, accessed 20 November 2009.

Davis, G. F. and Useem, M. (2002) Top Management, Company Directors, and Corporate Control. In A. Pettigrew, H. Thomas and R. Whittington (eds), *Handbook of Strategy and Management*, London: Sage, pp. 233–59.

Davis, G. F., Yoo, M. and Baker, W. E. (2003) The Small World of the American Corporate Elite, 1982–2001, *Strategic Organization*, 1(3): 301–26.

Davis, S. M. and Lawrence, P. R. (1977) *Matrix*, Reading, MA: Addison-Wesley.

Dawley, S. (2007) Fluctuating Rounds of Inward Investment in Peripheral Regions: Semiconductors in the North East of England, *Economic Geography*, 83(1): 51–73.

De Certeau, M. (1984) *The Practice of Everyday Life*, trans. by S. Randall, Berkeley, CA: University of California Press.

De Chernatony, L. (2002) Would a Brand Smell Any Sweeter by a Corporate Name? *Corporate Reputation Review*, 5(2/3):114–32.

De Cock, C. (2009) Jumpstarting the Future with Fredric Jameson: Reflections on Capitalism, Science Fiction and Utopia, *Journal of Organizational Change Management*, 22(4): 437–49.

De Geus, A. (1997) *The Living Company: Growth, Learning and Longevity in Business*, London: Nicholas Brealey.

Deal, T. E. and Kennedy, A. A (1982) *Corporate Cultures: The Rites and Rituals of Corporate Life*, Reading, MA: Addison-Wesley.

Deegan, C. (2002) The Legitimising Effect of Social and Environmental Disclosures – A Theoretical Foundation, *Accounting, Auditing and Accountability Journal*, 15(3): 282–311.

Deegan, C., Rankin, M. and Tobin, J. (2002) An Examination of the Corporate Social and Environmental Disclosures of BHP from 1983–1997: A Test of Legitimacy Theory, *Accounting, Auditing and Accountability Journal*, 15(3): 312–43.

Delgado-Gomez, J., Ramirez-Aleson, M. and Espitia-Escuer, M. (2004) Intangible Resources as a Key Factor in the Internationalisation of Spanish Firms, *Journal of Economic Behavior and Organization*, 53(4): 477–87.

Denning, S. (2004) Telling Tales, *Harvard Business Review*, May: 1–9.

Desarbo, W. S. and Grewal, R. (2007) An Alternative Efficient Representation of Demand-Based Competitive Asymmetry, *Strategic Management Journal*, 28(7): 755–66.

Desarbo, W. S. and Grewal, R. (2008) Hybrid Strategic Groups, *Strategic Management Journal*, 29(3): 293–317.

Desarbo, W. S., Grewal, R. and Wang, R. (2009) Dynamic Strategic Groups: Deriving Spatial Evolutionary Paths, *Strategic Management Journal*, 30(13): 1420–39.

Diderot, D. and d'Alembert, G. (eds) (1751) *Encyclopedie ou Dictionnaire des Sciences, des arts et des Metiers*, Paris: Briasson.

Diefenbach, T. (2009) *Management and the Dominance of Managers: An Inquiry into Why and How Managers Rule Our Organizations*, London: Routledge.

Dierickx, I. and Cool, K. (1989) Asset Stock Accumulation and Sustainability of Competitive Advantage, *Management Science*, 35(12): 1504–11.

Dillon, J. (2003) The Use of Questions in Organizational Consulting, *Journal of Applied Behavioral Science*, 39(4): 438–52.

Djelic, Marie-Laure (1998) *Exporting the American Model: The Postwar Transformation of European Business*, Oxford: Oxford University Press.

Dodgson, M. (2000) *Management of Technological Innovation*, Oxford: Oxford University Press.

Dodgson, M., Gann, D. and Salter, A. (2005) *Think, Play, Do: Technology, Innovation and Organization*, Oxford: Oxford University Press.

Doh, J. P., Rodriguez, P., Uhlenbruck, K., Collins, J. and Eden, L. (2003) Coping with Corruption in Foreign Markets, *Academy of Management Executive*, 17(3): 114–27.

Donaldson, L. (1987) Strategy and Structural Adjustment to Regain Fit and Performance: In Defence of Contingency Theory, *Journal of Management Studies*, 24(1): 1–24.

Donaldson, L. (1999) *Performance-Driven Organizational Change: The Organizational Portfolio*, Thousand Oaks, CA: Sage.

Donaldson, L. (2000) Design Strategy to Fit Strategy. In E. Locke (ed.), *Handbook of Principles of Organizational Behaviour*, Oxford: Blackwell, pp. 291–303.

Donaldson, L. (2001) *The Contingency Theory of Organizations*, Thousand Oaks, CA: Sage.

Donaldson, T. and Dunfee, T. W. (1995) Towards a Unified Conception of Business Ethics: Integrative Social Contracts Theory, *Academy of Management Review*, 19(2): 252–75.

Dörrenbächer, C. and Gammelgaard, J. (2006) Subsidiary Role Development: The Effect of Micro-political Headquarters – Subsidiary Negotiations on the Product, Market and Value-added Scope of Foreign-owned Subsidiaries, *Journal of International Management*, 12(3): 266–8.

Dörrenbächer, C. and Gepert, M. (2009) Micro-political Strategies and Strategizing in Multinational Corporations: The Case of Subsidiary Mandate Change. In L. A. Costannzo and R. B. MacKay (eds), *Handbook of Research on Strategy and Foresight*, Cheltenham: Edward Elgar, pp. 200–18.

Dougherty, D. (2004) Organizing Practices in Services: Capturing Practice-based Knowledge for Innovation, *Strategic Organization*, 2(1): 35–64.

Dougherty, D. (2006) Organizing for Innovation in the 21st Century. In S. R. Clegg, C. Hardy, W. R. Nord and Lawrence, T. (eds), *Handbook of Organization Studies* (2nd edn), London: Sage. pp. 598–617.

Dougherty, D. (2008) Bridging Social Constraint and Social Action to Design Organizations for Innovation, *Organization Studies*, 29(3): 415–34.

Dougherty, D. and Hardy, C. (1996) Sustained Product Innovation in Large, Mature Organizations: Overcoming Innovation-to-Organization Problems, *Academy of Management Journal*, 39(5): 1120–53.

Doz, Y. L. (1996) The Evolution of Cooperation in Strategic Alliances: Initial Conditions or Learning, *Strategic Management Journal*, 17(Special Issue): 55–83.

Doz, Y. L. and Hamel, G. (1998) *Alliance Advantage*, Boston, MA: Harvard Business School Press.

Doz, Y. L. and Kosonen, M. (2008) The Dynamics of Strategic Ability: Nokia's Rollercoaster Experience, *California Management Review*, 50(3): 95–118.

Dror, Y. (1968) *Public Policymaking Re-examined*, San Francisco: Chandler.

Drucker, P. F. (1988) The Coming of the New Organization, *Harvard Business Review*, 66(1): 45–53.

Dunning, J. H. (1980) Toward an Eclectic Theory of International Production, *Journal of International Business Studies*, 11(1): 9–31.

Dunning, J. H. (1981) *International Production and the Multinational Enterprise*, London: Allen & Unwin.

Dunning, J. H. (1993) *Multinational Enterprises and the Global Economy*, New York: Addison-Wesley.

Dunning, J. H. (1998) Location and the Multinational Enterprise: A Neglected Factor, *Journal of International Business Studies*, 29(1): 45–86.

Dunning, J. H. (2000) The Eclectic Paradigm as an Envelope for Economic and Business Theories of MNE Activity, *International Business Review*, 9(1): 163–90.

Dunning, J. H. and Narula, R. (eds) (1996) *Foreign Direct Investment and Governments: Catalysts for Economic Restructuring*, London: Routledge.

Durkheim, E. (2002) *Suicide: A Study in Sociology,* trans. from the French by J. A. Spaulding and G. Simpson (ed.), with an introduction by G. Simpson, London: Routledge.

Dussel, E. and Ibarra Colado, E. (2006) Globalization, Organization and the Ethics of Liberation, *Organization*, 13(4): 489–508.

Dutton, J. E. and Dukerich, J. E. (1991) Keeping an Eye on the Mirror: Image and Identity in Organizational Adaptation, *Academy of Management Journal*, 34(3): 517–44.

Dyas, G. and Thanheiser, H. (1976) *The Emerging European Enterprise*, London: Macmillan.

Dyer, J. H., Kale, P. and Singh, H. (2001) How to Make Strategic Alliances Work, *MIT Sloan Management Review*, 42(4): 37–44.

Eden, L. and Molot, M. A. (2002) Insiders, Outsiders and Host Country Bargains, *Journal of International Management*, 8 (4): 359–88.

Edlund, B. (2007) *Our Response*, London and Amsterdam: Royal Dutch Shell plc, p. 2.

Edwards, R. (1979) *Contested Terrain: The Transformation of the Workplace in the Twentieth Century*, New York: Basic Books.

Eisenberg, H. (1997) Reengineering and Dumbsizing: Mismanagement of the Knowledge Resource, *Quality Progress* 30(5): 57–64.

Eisenhardt, K. (1999) Strategy as Decision-Making, *Sloan Management Review*, 40(30): 65–92.

Eisenhardt, K. and Bourgeois, L. (1988) Politics of Strategic Decision-Making in High-Velocity Environments, *Academy of Management Journal*, 31(4): 737–70.

Eisenhardt, K. and Martin, J. L. (2000) Dynamic Capabilities: What Are They? *Strategic Management Journal*, 21(10/11): 1105–21.

Eisenhardt, K. and Zbaracki, M. (1992) Strategic Decision-Making, *Strategic Management Journal*, 13(Special Issue): 17–37.

Elger, T. and Smith, C. (eds) (1994) *Japanization? The Transnational Transformation of the Labour Process*, London: Routledge.

Ellis, C. (1996) Making Strategic Alliances Succeed, *Harvard Business Review*, 74(4): 8–9.

Emirbayer, M. and William, E. M. (2005) Bourdieu and Social Work, *Social Service Review*, 79(4): 689–724.

Engardio, P., Capell, K., Carey, J. and Hall, K. (2007) Beyond the Green Corporation: Imagine a World in which Eco-friendly and Socially Responsible Practices Actually Help a Company's Bottom Line. It's Closer than You Think, *Business Week*, 4019: 50.

Eriksson, P. and Lehtimäki, H. (2001) Strategy Rhetoric in City Management: How the Presumptions of Classic Strategic Management Live On, *Scandinavian Journal of Management*, 17: 201–23.

Espelend, W. (1998) *The Struggle for Water: Politics, Rationality and Identity in the American South-West*, Chicago: Chicago University Press.

Espelend, W. and Sauder, M. (2007) Rankings and Reactivity: How Public Measures Recreate Social Worlds, *American Journal of Sociology*, 113(1): 1–40.

Etzioni, A. (1967) Mixed Scanning: A Third Approach to Decision-Making, *Public Administration Review*, 27(5): 385–92.

Evans, P. and Wolf, B. (2005) Collaboration Rules, *Harvard Business Review*, 83(7/8): 96–104.

Ezzamel, M. and Willmott, H. (2004) Rethinking Strategy: Contemporary Perspectives and Debates, *European Management Review*, 1(1): 43–8.

Ezzamel, M. and Willmott, H. (2008) Strategy as Discourse in a Global Retailer: A Supplement to Rationalist and Interpretive Accounts, *Organization Studies*, 29(2): 191–217.

Fagre, N. and Wells, L. T. (1982) Bargaining Power of Multinations and Host Governments, *Journal of International Business Studies*, 13(2): 9–24.

Fama, E. F. (1980) Agency Problems and the Theory of the Firm, *Journal of Political Economy*, 88(2): 288–307.

Fei, X. T. (1992) *From the Soil: The Foundations of Chinese Society*, trans., Introduction and Epilogue by G. G. Hamilton and W. Zheng, Berkeley, CA: University of California Press.

Feldman, M. and Pentland, B. (2003) Reconceptualizing Organizational Routines as a Source of Flexibility and Change, *Administrative Science Quarterly*, 48(1): 94–118.

Ferguson, N. (1997) *Virtual History: Alternatives and Counterfactuals*, London: Papermac.

Ferguson, N. (2008) *The Ascent of Money: A Financial History of the World*, Harmondsworth: Penguin.

Fiedler, F. E. (1967) *A Theory of Leadership Effectiveness*, New York: McGraw-Hill.

Fiedler, F. E. (1986) The Contribution of Cognitive Resources to Leadership Performance, *Journal of Applied Social Psychology*, 16: 532–48.

Fiegenbaum, A. and Thomas, H. (1990) Strategic Groups and Performance: The US Insurance Industry, 1970–1984, *Strategic Management Journal*, 11(3): 197–215.

Fincham, R. (1999) The Consultant–Client Relationship: Critical Perspectives on the Management of Organizational Change, *Journal of Management Studies*, 36(3): 335–51.

Fineman, S. (1996) Emotion and Organizing. In S. Clegg, C. Hardy and W. Nord (eds), *Handbook of Organization Studies*, London: Sage, pp. 543–64.

Fiol, C. (2001) Revisiting an Identity-based View of Sustainable Competitive Advantage, *Journal of Management*, 27(6): 691–9.

Fischer, K. and Schot, J. (1993) *Environmental Strategies for Industry: International Perspectives on Research Needs and Policy Implications*, Washington, DC: Island Press.

Fleischmann, E. A. (1953) The Description of Supervisory Behaviour, *Personnel Psychology*, 37(1): 1–6.

Fleming, P. and Spicer, A. (2007) *Contesting the Corporation: Struggle, Power, and Resistance in Organizations*, Cambridge: Cambridge University Press.

Fligstein, N. (1987) The Intraorganizational Power Struggle: Rise of Finance Personnel to Top Leadership in Large Corporations, 1919–1979, *American Sociological Review*, 52(1): 44–58.

Fligstein, N. (2001) *The Architecture of Markets: An Economic Sociology of Twenty-first-Century Capitalist Societies*, Princeton, NJ: Princeton University Press.

Fligstein, N. and Freeland, R. (1995) Theoretical and Comparative Perspectives on Corporate Organization, *Annual Review of Sociology*, 21(1): 21–43.

Flyvbjerg, B. (1998) *Rationality and Power: Democracy in Practice*, Chicago: University of Chicago Press.

Foley, J. (Director) (1991) *Glengarry Glen Ross* [motion picture], United States: GGR.

Ford, J. and Ford, L. (1995) The Role of Conversations in Producing Intentional Change in Organizations. *Academy of Management Review*, 20(3): 541–70.

Forsgren, M., Holm, U. and Johanson, J. (1995) Division Headquarters Go Abroad: A Step in the Internationalization of the Multinational Corporation, *Journal of Management Studies*, 32(4): 475–91.

Foss, N. (1996) Knowledge-Based Approaches to the Theory of the Firm: Some Critical Comments, *Organization Science*, 7(5): 470–6.

Foss, N. and Eriksen, B. (1995) Industry Capabilities and Competitive Advantage. In C. A. Montgomery (ed.), *Evolutionary and Resource-Based Approaches to Strategy*, Boston, MA: Kluwer.

Foucault, M. (1972) *The Archaeology of Knowledge*, Trans. A. M. Sheriden-Smith, London: Tavistock.

Foucault, M. (1979) *Discipline and Punish*, Harmondsworth: Penguin.

Foucault, M. (1980) *Power/Knowledge: Selected Interviews and Other Writings 1972–1977*, edited by C. Gordon, New York: Pantheon Books.

Francis, D., Bessant, J. and Holoday, M. (2003) Managing Radical Organization Transformation, *Management Decision*, 44(1): 77–90.

Freeman, C. and Soete, L. (1979) *The Economics of Industrial Innovation* (3rd edn), London: Pinter.

Freeman, R. E. (1984) *Strategic Management: A Stakeholder Approach*, Boston, MA: Pitman.

French, J. and Raven, B. H. (1959) The Bases of Social Power. In D. Cartwright (ed.), *Studies of Social Power*, Ann Arbor, MI: Institute of Social Research, pp. 150–67.

Frenkel, M. (2005) The Politics of Translation: How State-Level Political Relations Affect the Cross-National Travel of Management Ideas, *Organization*, 12(2): 275–301.

Frenkel, M. and Shenhav, Y. (2004) From Americanization to Colonization: The Diffusion of Productivity Models Revisited, *Organization Studies*, 24(9): 1537–61.

Friedman, M. (1962) *Capitalism and Freedom*, Chicago: University of Chicago Press.

Friedman, T. (1999) *The Lexus and the Olive Tree*, London: HarperCollins.

Friedrich, C. (1937) *An Introduction to Political Theory*, New York: Harper and Row.

Friends of the Earth International (2002) *Failing the Challenge: The Other Shell Report*, London: Friends of the Earth International.

Friends of the Earth International (2003) *Behind the Shine: The Other Shell Report*, London: Friends of the Earth International.

Friends of the Earth International (2004) Lessons Not Learned: *The Other Shell Report*, London: Friends of the Earth International.

Frings, K. V. (1997) Rewriting Cambodian History to 'Adapt' It to a New Political Context: The Kampuchean People's Revolutionary Party's Historiography (1979–1991), *Modern Asian Studies*, 31(4): 807–46.

Froud, J. and Williams, K. (2000) Shareholder Value and Financialisation: Consultancy Promises, Management Moves, *Economy & Society*, 29: 80–110.

Froud, J., Johal, S., Leaver, A. and Williams, K. (2006) *Financialization and Strategy: Narrative and Numbers*, London: Routledge.

Fulmer, R. M., Gibbs, P. and Keys, J. B. (1998) The Second Generation Learning Organizations: New Tools for Sustaining Competitive Advantage, *Organizational Dynamics*, 27(2): 7–20.

Furrer, O., Thomas, H. and Goussevskaia, A. (2008) The Structure and Evolution of the Strategic Management Field: A Content Analysis of 26 Years of Strategic Management, *Research International Journal of Management Reviews*, 10(1): 1–23.

Galan, J. and Sanchez-Bueno, M. (2009) Strategy and Structure in Context: Universalism versus Institutional Effects, *Organization Studies*, 30(6): 609–27.

Galbraith, J. (1971) Matrix Organization Designs, *Business Horizons*, 14(1): 29–40.

Galbraith, J. K. (1955) *The Great Crash 1929*, London: Hamish Hamilton.

Galer, G. and van der Heijden, K. (1992) The Learning Organization: How Planners Create Organizational Learning, *Marketing Intelligence & Planning*, 10(6): 5–12.

Galunic, D. C. and Eisenhardt, K. M. (1996) The Evolution of Intracorporate Domains: Divisional Charter Losses in High-Technology, Multidivisional Corporations, *Organization Science*, 7(3): 255–82.

Gamble, J. (2010) Transferring Organizational Practices and the Dynamics of Hybridization: Japanese Retail Multinationals in China, *Journal of Management Studies*, 47(4): 705–32.

Gardner, N. (2009) Resurrecting the 'Icon': The Enduring Relevance of Clausewitz's *On War*, *Strategic Studies Quarterly*, 3(1): 119–33.

Garfinkel, H. (1967) *Studies in Ethnomethodology*, Englewood Cliffs, NJ: Prentice-Hall.

Gartner Group (2003) CRM Success is in Strategy and Implementation, Not in Software, *www.gartner.com*, accessed 28 April 2010.

Gavetti, G. and Levinthal, D. A. (2004) The Strategy Field from the Perspective of Management Science: Divergent Strands and Possible Integration, *Management Science*, 50(10): 1309–18.

Geletkanycz, M. A. and Hambrick, D. C. (1997) The External Ties of Top Executives, *Administrative Science Quarterly*, 42: 654–81.

Geppert, M. (2002) Change Management Approaches in MNCs: A Comparison of Sensemaking and Politics in British and German Subsidiaries, *Management Research News*, 25(8–10): 58.

Geppert, M. and Matten, D. (2006) Institutional Influences on Manufacturing Organization in Multinational Corporations: The Cherrypicking Approach, *Organization Studies*, 27(4): 491–515.

Geppert, M. and Williams, K. (2006) Global, National and Local Practices in Multinational Corporations: Towards a Sociopolitical Framework, *International Journal of Human Resource Management*, 17(1): 49–69.

Geppert, M., Williams, K. and Matten, D. (2003) The Social Construction of Contextual Rationalities in MNCs: An Anglo-German Comparison of Subsidiary Choice, *Journal of Management Studies*, 40(3): 617–41.

Geringer, M. (1991) Strategic Determinants of Partner Selection Criteria in International Joint Venture, *Journal of International Business Studies*, 22(1): 41–63.

Geroski, P. A. (1995) What Do We Know about Entry? *International Journal of Industrial Organization*, 13(4): 421–40.

Ghoshal, S. and Bartlett, C. A. (1990) The Multinational Corporation as an Interorganizational Network, *Academy of Management Review*, 15(4): 603–25.

Giddens, A. (1990) *The Consequences of Modernity*, Oxford: Polity Press.

Giddens, A. (1991) *Modernity and Self-identity: Self and Society in the Late Modern Age*, Cambridge: Polity Press.

Giddens, A. (2009) *The Politics of Climate Change*, Cambridge: Polity Press.

Ginter, P. M. and Duncan, W. J. (1990) Macroenvironmental Analysis for Strategic Management, *Long Range Planning*, 23(6): 91–100.

Gioia, D. A. (1992) Pinto Fires and Personal Ethics: A Script Analysis of Missed Opportunities, *Journal of Business Ethics*, 11: 379–89.

Gioia, D. A. and Chittipeddi, K. (1991) Sensemaking and sensegiving in strategic change initiation, *Strategic Management Journal*, 12(6): 433–48.

Glazer, B. and Strauss, A. (1967) *The Discovery of Grounded Theory*, Chicago: Aldine.

Gnyawali, D. R., He, J. and Madhavan, R. (2006) Impact of Co-operation on Firm Competitive Behavior: An Emperical Examination, *Journal of Management*, 32: 507–30.

Golding, T. (2001) *The City: Inside the Great Expectations Machine*, Harlow: Pearson Education.

Gomes-Casseres, B. (2003) Competitive Advantage in Alliance Constellations, *Strategic Organization*, 1: 327–35.

Gomez, P. Y. and Korine, H. (2008) *Entrepreneurs and Democracy: A Political Theory of Corporate Governance*, Cambridge: Cambridge University Press.

Gonzales, L. (2003) *Deep Survival: Who Lives, Who Dies, and Why: True Stories of Miraculous Endurance and Sudden Death*, New York: W. W. Norton.

Gordon, R. and Grant, D. (2005) Knowledge Management or Management of Knowledge? Why People Interested in Knowledge Management Need to Consider Foucault and the Construct of Power, *Tamara: Journal of Critical Postmodern Organization Science*, 3(2): 1–12.

Gordon, R., Clegg, S. and Kornberger, M. (2009) Embedded Ethics: Discourse and Power in the New South Wales Police Service, *Organization Studies*, 30(1): 73–99.

Gouldner, A. W. (1954) *Patterns of Industrial Bureaucracy*, New York: Free Press.

Govindarajan, V. and Trimble, C. (2005a) Building Breakthrough Businesses within Established Organizations, *Harvard Business Review*, 83(5): 56–68.

Govindarajan, V. and Trimble, C. (2005b) Organization DNA for Strategic Innovation, *California Management Review*, 47(3): 47–76.

Grandy, G. and Mills, A. J. (2004) Strategy as Simulacra? A Radical Reflexive Look at the Discipline and Practice of Strategy, *Journal of Management Studies*, 41(7): 1153–70.

Granovetter, M. (1985) Economic Action and Social Structure: The Problem of Embeddedness, *American Journal of Sociology*, 91(3): 481–510.

Grant, R. M. (1991) The Resource-Based Theory of Competitive Advantage: Implications for Strategy Formulation, *California Management Review*, 33(3): 114–35.

Grant, R. M. (1996) Toward a Knowledge-Based Theory of the Firm, *Strategic Management Journal*, 17(Winter Special Issue): 109–22.

Grant, R. M. (2003) Strategic Planning in a Turbulent Environment: Evidence from the Oil Majors, *Strategic Management Journal*, 24(6): 491–517.

Grant, R. M. (2007) *Contemporary Strategy Analysis* (7th edn), Oxford: Blackwell.

Grant, R. M. (2009) *Contemporary Strategy Analysis* (6th Edn), Oxford: Blackwell.

Grant, R. M. and Cibin, R. (1996) Strategy, Structure and Market Turbulence: The International Oil Majors, 1970–1991, *Scandinavian Journal of Management*, 12(2): 165–88.

Gray, J. (2010) The Contradictions of Neo-liberalism, *Australian Financial Review*, 5 March: 11.

Green, M. (2010) Yours Gratefully, *Australian Financial Review*, 19 March.

Greene, R. and Elffers, J. (1998) *The 48 Laws of Power*, London: Viking/Penguin.

Greene, S. (2008) Funds Say They Did All They Could to Warn Banks, *Financial Times*, 8 February 2009, http://www.ft.com/cms/s/0/6488979a-f4f2-11dd-9e2e-0000779fd2ac.html, accessed 23 September 2010.

Greve, H. R. and Mitsuhashi, H. (2007) Power and Glory: Concentrated Power in Top Management Teams, *Organization Studies*, 28(8): 1197–221.

Grint, K. and Case, P. (1998) The Violent Rhetoric of Re-engineering: Management Consultancy on the Offensive, *Journal of Management Studies*, 35(5): 557–77.

Grint, K. and Case, P. (2000) Now Where Were We? BPR Lotus Eaters and Corporate Amnesia. In D. Knights and H. Willmott (eds), *The Re-Engineering Revolution: Critical Studies of Corporate Change*, London: Sage.

Gronroos, C. (1995) Relationship Marketing: The Strategy Continuum, *Journal of the Academy of Marketing Science*, 23(4): 252–4.

Grosse, R. (1996) International Technology Transfer in Services, *Journal of International Business Studies*, 27(4): 781–800.

Grove, A. S. (1996) *Only the Paranoid Survive*, New York: Doubleday.

Guillén, M. F. (2001) *The Limits of Convergence: Globalization and Organizational Change in Argentina, South Korea, and Spain*, Princeton, NJ: Princeton University Press.

Gulati, R. (1995) Social Structure and Alliance Formation Pattern: A Longitudinal Analysis, *Administrative Science Quarterly*, 40(4): 619–42.

Gulati, R. (1998) Alliances and Networks, *Strategic Management Journal*, 19(4): 293–317.

Habermas, J. (1971) *Knowledge and Human Interests*, London: Heinemann.

Haddock, R. and Jullens, J. (2009) The Best Years of the Auto Industry Are Still to Come, *Strategy+Business*, 55(Summer): 1–12.

Hagel, J. (1999) The Coming Battle for Customer Information. In D. Tapscott (ed.), *Creating Value in the Network Economy*, Boston, MA: Harvard Business School Press, pp. 159–71.

Hall, P. and Soskice, D. (2001) *Varieties of Capitalism: The Institutional Foundations of Comparative Advantage*, Oxford: Oxford University Press.

Hall, R. (1993) A Framework Linking Intangible Resources and Capabilities to Sustainable Competitive Advantage, *Strategic Management Journal*, 14(8): 607–18.

Hambrick, D. C. and Finkelstein, S. (1987) Managerial Discretion: A Bridge between Polar Views of Organizational Outcomes in Research. In L. L. Cummings and B. M. Staw (eds), *Organizational Behavior*, Greenwich, CT: JAI Press, pp. 369–406.

Hambrick, D. C. and Fukotomi, G. D. S. (1991) The Seasons of a CEO's Tenure, *Academy of Management Journal*, 16(6): 719–42.

Hambrick, D. C. and Mason, P. (1984) Upper Echelons: The Organization as a Reflection of its Top Managers, *Academy of Management Review*, 9(2): 193–206.

Hamel, G. (1996) Strategy as Revolution, *Harvard Business Review*, 74(7): 69–82.

Hamel, G. (2000) *Leading the Revolution*, London: Penguin.

Hamel, G. (2006) The Why, What and How of Management Innovation, *Harvard Business Review*, 84(2):72–83.

Hamilton, G. G. (1996) *Asian Business Networks*, Berlin: De Gruyter.

Hamilton, G. G. and Biggart, N. W. (1988) Market, Culture, and Authority: A Comparative Analysis of Management and Organization in the Far East, *American Journal of Sociology*, 94(Supplement): 52–94.

Hammer, M. and Champy, J. (1993) *Reengineering the Corporation: A Manifesto for Business Revolution*, London: Harper Business.

Hansen, F. (2005) International Business Machine, *Workforce Management*, July: 37–46.

Hansen, M. (2009) *Collaboration: How Leaders Avoid the Traps, Build Common Ground, and Reap Big Results*, Boston, MA: Harvard Business School Press.

Harbeson, J. (1995) *Africa in World Politics: Amid Renewal, Deepening Crisis*. In J. Harbeson and D. Rothchild (eds), *Africa in World Politics: Post-Cold War Challenges*, Boulder, CO: Westview Press, pp. 3–20.

Harbison, J. R., Pekar, P. J., Viscio, A. and Moloney, D. (2000) *The Allianced Enterprise: Breakout Strategy for the New Millennium*, Los Angeles: Booz Allen & Hamilton.

Hardy, C. (1994) *Managing Strategic Action: Mobilizing Change: Concepts, Readings, and Cases*, London: Sage.

Hardy, C., Palmer, I. and Phillips, N. (2000) Discourse as a Strategic Resource, *Human Relations*, 53(9): 1227–48.

Harvard Business Review (2004) *Doing Business in China*, Boston, MA: Harvard Business School Press.

Harvey, D. (1992) *The Condition of Postmodernity*, Oxford: Blackwell.

Harzing, A. W. (1999) *Managing the Multinationals: An International Study of Control Mechanisms*, Cheltenham: Edward Elgar.

Harzing, A. W. and Noorderhaven, N. (2006) Geographical Distance and the Role and Management of Subsidiaries: The Case of Subsidiaries Downunder, *Asia Pacific Journal of Management*, 23(2): 167–85.

Hatch, M. J. (1999) Exploring the Empty Spaces of Organizing: How Improvisational Jazz Helps Redescribe Organizational Structure, *Organization Studies*, 20(1): 75–100.

Hatch, M. J. and Schultz, M. (2001) Are the Strategic Stars Aligned for Your Corporate Brand? *Harvard Business Review*, February: 128–34.

Hatch, M. J. and Schultz, M. (2008) *Taking Brand Initiative: How Companies Can Align Strategy, Culture, and Identity through Corporate Branding*, Jossey-Bass: San Francisco.

Hawken, P. (1993) *The Ecology of Commerce: A Declaration of Sustainability*, New York: HarperCollins.

Hawken, P., Lovins, A. and Lovins, L. H. (1999) *Natural Capitalism: Creating the Next Industrial Revolution*. Boston, MA: Little, Brown.

Hedlund, G. (1986) The Hypermodern MNC: A Heterarchy? *Human Resource Management*, 25(1): 9–35.

Heimeriks, K. H., Duysters, G. and Vanhaverbeke, W. (2007) Learning Mechanisms and Differential Performance in Alliance Portfolios, *Strategic Organization*, 5: 373–408.

Helfat, C. E. and Peteraf, M. A. (2009) Understanding Dynamic Capabilities: Progress along a Developmental Path, *Strategic Organization*, 7(1): 91–102.

Hellekson, K. (2000) Towards Taxonomy of the Alternate History Genre, *Extrapolation*, 41(3): 248–56.

Henderson, B. D. (1989) The Origins of Strategy, *Harvard Business Review*, November–December: 139–43.

Hendry, J. (2000) Strategic Decision-Making, Discourse, and Strategy as Social Practice, *Journal of Management Studies*, 37(7): 955–77.

Henisz, W. J. (2000) The Institutional Environment for Multinational Investment, *Journal of Law Economics and Organization*, 16(2): 334–64.

Hennart, J. F. (1988) A Transaction Cost Theory of Equity Joint Ventures, *Strategic Management Journal*, 9(4): 361–74.

Hennart, J. F., Kim, D. J. and Zeng, M. (1998) The Impact of Joint Venture Status on the Longevity of Japanese Stakes in US Manufacturing Affiliates, *Organization Science*, 9(3): 382–95.

Herek, G., Janis, I. and Huth, P. (1987) Decision-Making During International Crises: Is Quality of Process Related to Outcome? *Journal of Conflict Resolution*, 31(2): 203–26.

Herrmann, P. and Datta, D. (2005) Relationships between Top Management Team Characteristics and International Diversification: An Empirical Investigation, *British Journal of Management*, 16(1): 69–78.

Hess, R. L., Jr, Ganesan, S. and Klein, N. M. (2003) Service Failure and Recovery: The Impact of Relationship Factors on Customer Satisfaction, *Journal of the Academy of Marketing Science*, 31(2): 127–45.

Heugens, P. M. A. R. and Mol, M. J. (2005) So You Call That Research? Mending Methodological Biases in Strategy and Organization Departments of Top Business Schools, *Strategic Organization*, 3(1): 117–28.

Hickman, M. (2008) Shell Rebuked for 'Greenwash' over Ad for Polluting Oil Project, *The Independent*, 13 August 2008, http://www.independent.co.uk/environment/green-living/shell-rebuked-for-greenwash-over-ad-for-polluting-oil-project, accessed 13 September 2010.

Hickson, D. J., Butler, R. J., Cray, D., Mallory, G. R. and Wilson, D. C. (1986) *Top Decisions: Strategic Decision-Making in Organizations*, San Francisco: Jossey-Bass.

Hickson, D. J., Hinings, C. R., Lee, C. A., Schneck, R. E. and Pennings, J. M. (1971) A Strategic Contingencies Theory of Intra-Organizational Power, *Administrative Science Quarterly*, 16(2): 216–29.

Higgins, J. W. and Hallström, K. (2007) Standardization, Globalization and Rationalities of Government, *Organization*, 14(5): 685–704.

Hill, S. and Rifkin, G. (2000) *Radical Marketing: From Harvard to Harley, Lessons from Ten that Broke the Rules and Made it Big*, New York: HarperCollins.

Hill, T. and Westbrook, R. (1997) SWOT Analysis: It's Time for a Product Recall, *Long Range Planning*, 30(1): 46–52.

Hirsch, F. (1976) *The Social Limits to Growth*, London: Routledge and Kegan Paul.

Hitt, A. M., Dacin, M. T., Levitas, E., Arregle, J.-L. and Borza, A. (2000) Partner Selection in Emerging and Developed Market Contexts: Resource-Based and Organizational Learning Perspectives, *Academy of Management Journal*, 43(3): 449–67.

Hitt, M., Tihanyi, L., Miller, T. and Connelly, B. (2006) International Diversification: Antecedents, Outcomes, and Moderators, *Journal of Management*, 32(6): 831–67.

Hodgkinson, G. and Wright, G. (2002) Confronting Strategic Inertia in a Top Management Team: Learning from Failure, *Organization Studies*, 23(6): 949–77.

Hodgkinson, G., Whittington, R., Johnson, G. and Schwarz, M. (2006) The Role of Strategy Workshops in Strategy Development Processes: Formality, Communication, Co-ordination and Inclusion, *Long Range Planning*, 39(5): 479–96.

Hogg, M. A. and Terry, D. J. (2000) Social Identity and Self-categorization Processes in Organizational Contexts, *Academy of Management Review*, 25(1): 121–40.

Holland, D., Barrell, R., Fic, T., Hurst, I., Liadzro, I., Orazgari, A. and Pillonca, V. (2009) The World Economy: The Global Financial Crisis and Collapse in World Trade, *National Institute Economic Review*, 203(1): 9–16.

Hooley, G., Greenley, G., Fahy, J. and Cadogan, J. (2001) Market-Focused Resources, Competitive Positioning and Firm Performance, *Journal of Marketing Management*, 17(5/6): 503–20.

Hooley, G., Piercy, N., Saunders, J. and Nicoulaud, B. (2007) *Marketing Strategy and Competitive Positioning*, London: Prentice Hall.

House, R. J. (1971) A Path–Goal Theory of Leader Effectiveness, *Administrative Science Quarterly*, 16(3): 321–39.

Howard, A. and Bray, D. W. (1988) *Managerial Lives in Transition: Advancing Age and Changing Times*, New York: Guilford Press.

Howell, J. and Hall-Merenda, K. (1999) The Ties that Bind: The Impact of Leader–Member Exchange, Transformational and Transactional Leadership, and Distance on Predicting Follower Performance, *Journal of Applied Psychology*, 84(5): 680–94.

Human, S. E. (2009) Emergent Theory. In S. R. Clegg and J. R. Bailey (eds), *International Encyclopaedia of Organization Studies*, London: Sage, pp. 425–6.

Hunt, M. S. (1972) Competition in the Major Home Appliance Industry, PhD dissertation, Harvard University, Cambridge, MA.

Hunt, S. and Lambe, C. (2000) Marketing's Contribution to Business Strategy: Market Orientation, Relationship Marketing and Resource-Advantage Theory, *International Journal of Management Reviews*, 2(1): 17–43.

Huston, L. and Sakkab, N. (2006) Connect and Develop: Inside Procter and Gamble's New Model for Innovation, *Harvard Business Review*, 84, March: 58–66.

Hutchins, E. (1991) Organizing Work by Adaptation, *Organization Science*, 2(1): 14–39.

Hutt, M. D., Stafford, E. R., Walker, B. A. and Reingen, P. H. (2000) Case Study: Defining the Social Network of a Strategic Alliance, *Sloan Management Review*, 41(2): 51–62.

Hutton, W. (2007a) *The Writing on the Wall: China and the West in the 21st Century*. London: Little, Brown.

Hutton, W. (2007b) New China, New Crisis, *Observer*, 7 January: 4. http://www.guardian.co.uk/business/2007/jan/07/bookextracts.china, accessed 13 September 2010.

Ibarra Colado, E. (2006) The Ethics of Globalization. In S. R. Clegg and C. H. Rhodes (eds), *Management Ethics: Contemporary Contexts*, London: Routledge.

Ibarra Colado, E. (2008) Neoliberalism and Organization. In S. R. Clegg and J. R. Bailey (eds), *International Encyclopedia of Organization Studies*, Vol. 3, London, Sage, pp. 959–63.

Ind, N. (2001) *Living the Brand*, London: Kogan Page.

Iyer, B. and Davenport, T. H. (2008) Reverse Engineering Goggle's Innovation Machine, *Harvard Business Review*, 87(4): 59–68.

Jackall, R. (1988) *Moral Mazes: The World of Corporate Managers*, New York: Oxford University Press.

Jackson, B. (2000) *Management Gurus and Management Fashions: A Dramatistic Inquiry*. London: Routledge.

Jacques, M. (2009) *When China Rules the World: The Rise of the Middle Kingdom and the End of the Western World*, Harmondsworth: Allen Lane.

Jarzabkowski, P. (2003) An Activity Theory Perspective on Continuity and Change, *Journal of Management Studies*, 40(1): 23–56.

Jarzabkowski, P. (2004) Strategy as Practice: Recursiveness, Adaptation and Practices-In-Use, *Organization Studies*, 25(4): 529–60.

Jarzabkowski, P. (2005) *Strategy as Practice: An Activity-Based Approach*, London: Sage.

Jarzabkovski, P. and Spee, A. P. (2009) Strategy as Practice: A Review and Future Directions for the Field, *International Journal of Management Reviews*, 11(1): 69–95.

Jarzabkowski, P. and Whittington, R. (2008) Hard to Disagree, Mostly, *Strategic Organization*, 6(1): 101–6.

Jensen, M. C. and Meckling, W. H. (1976) Theory of the Firm: Managerial Behaviour, Agency Costs and Ownership Structure, *Journal of Financial Economics*, 3(4): 305–60.

Jensen, T., Sandström, J. and Helin, S. (2009) Corporate Codes of Ethics and the Bending of Moral Space, *Organization*, 16(4): 529–45.

Johanson, J. and Vahlne, J. (1977) The Internationalization Process of the Firm – A Model of Knowledge Development and Increasing Foreign Market

Commitments, *Journal of International Business Studies*, 8(1): 23–32.

Johnson, G. (1987) *An 'Organization Action' Approach to Strategic Management*, Manchester: Manchester Business School.

Johnson, G., Langley, A., Melin, L. and Whittington, R. (2007) *Strategy as Practice: Research Directions and Resources*, Cambridge: Cambridge University Press.

Johnson, G., Melin, L. and Whittington, R. (2003) Guest Editors' Introduction: Micro Strategy and Strategizing: Towards an Activity-Based View, *Journal of Management Studies*, 40(1): 3–22.

Johnson, G., Scholes, K. and Whittington, R. (2008) *Exploring Corporate Strategy*, London: Pearson.

Johnston, P. (2009) The Curse of the Banking Bonus Culture, *The Daily Telegraph*, February 3. www.telegraph.co.uk/comment/columnists/philipjohnston/4560657/The-curse-of-the-banking-bonus-culture.html, accessed 28 February 2010.

Jones, C. A. and Levy, D. L. (2007) North American Business Strategies Towards Climate Change, *European Management*, 25(6): 428–40.

Jones, L. B. (1996) *Jesus CEO: Using Ancient Wisdom for Visionary Leadership*, New York: Hyperion.

Joyce, M. (2003) Not Just an Exercise in Greenwash, www.ethicalcorp.com/content.asp?ContentID=756, accessed 7 December 2009.

Judge, E. and Leroux, M. (2009) Advertising Regulators Get Tough over 'Greenwash', *Times Online*, http://www.timesonline.co.uk/tol/business/industry-sections/media/article5645A78.ece, accessed 13 September 2010.

Jung, D. I. (2001) Transformational and Transactional Leadership and Their Effects on Creativity in Groups, *Creativity Research Journal*, 13(2): 185–97.

Jung, D. I. and Avolio, B. J. (1999) Effects of Leadership Style and Followers' Cultural Orientation on Performance in Group and Individual Task Conditions, *Academy of Management Journal*, 42(2): 208–19.

Jung, D. I. and Sosik, J. J. (2002) Transformational Leadership in Work Groups: The Role of Empowerment, Cohesiveness, and Collective-Efficacy on Perceived Group Performance, *Small Group Research*, 33(3): 313–37.

Jung, D. I., Chow, C. and Wu, A. (2003) The Role of Transformational Leadership in Enhancing Organizational Innovation: Hypotheses and Some Preliminary Findings, *Leadership Quarterly*, 14(4–5): 525–44.

Kadushin, C. (1995) Friendship among the French Financial Elite, *American Sociological Review*, 60: 202–21.

Kale, P., Dyer, J. and Singh, H. (2002) Alliance Capability, Stock Market Response, and Long-term Alliance Success: The Role of the Alliance Function, *Strategic Management Journal*, 23(8): 747–67.

Kale, P., Singh, H. and Perlmutter, H. (2000) Learning and Protection of Proprietary Assets in Strategic Alliances: Business Relational Capital, *Strategic Management Journal*, 21: 217–37.

Kalyvas, S. N. (2006) *The Logic of Civil War*, Cambridge: Cambridge University Press.

Kamoche, K. and e Cunha, M. P. (2001) Minimal Structure: From Jazz Improvisation to Product Innovation, *Organization Studies*, 22(5): 733–64.

Kamoche, K., e Cunha, M. P. and da Cunha J. V. (2002) *Organizational Improvisation*, London: Routledge.

Kanter, R. M. (1992) *The Challenge of Organization Change: How Companies Experience It and Leaders Guide It*, New York: Free Press.

Kanter, R. M. (2002) Strategy as Improvisational Theatre, *Sloan Management Review*, 43(2): 76–81.

Karmark, E. (2005) Living the Brand. In M. Schultz, Y. M. Antorini, and F. F. Csaba (eds), *Corporate Branding: Purpose/People/Process*, Copenhagen: Copenhagen Business School Press, pp. 103–25.

Karpen, I. O. and Bove, L. L. (2008) Linking S-D Logic and Marketing Practice: Toward a Strategic Service Orientation, *Otago Forum II*, Dunedin, New Zealand.

Kärreman, D. and Rylander, A. (2008) Managing Meaning through Branding: The Case of a Consulting Firm, *Organization Studies*, 29(1): 103–25.

Katz, R. S. and Allen, T. (1982) Investigating the Not Invented Here Syndrome: A Look at the Performance, Tenure and Communication Patterns of 50 R&D Project Groups, *R&D Management*, 12(1): 7–19.

Kauffman, S. (1995) *At Home in the Universe*, New York: Oxford University Press.

Keck, S. L. and Tushman, M. L. (1993) Environmental and Organizational Context and Executive Team Structure, *Academy of Management Journal*, 36(6): 1314–44.

Keleman, M. and Peltonen, T. (2001) Ethics, Morality and the Subject: The Contribution of Zygmunt Bauman and Michel Foucault to 'Postmodern' Business Ethics, *Scandinavian Journal of Management*, 17(2): 151–66.

Keller, G. (2009) Energy Agency Warns of Falling Investment, www.google.com/hostednews/ap/article/qM5gBTdaBU8nEVPmO1Rilk2YdA0KZ0QD9BSLMMO0, accessed 7 December 2009.

Kellerman, B. (2004) *Bad Leadership*, Boston, MA: Harvard Business School Press.

Kennedy, R. and Schlesinger, A. (1999) *Thirteen Days: A Memoir of the Cuban Missile Crisis*, New York: W. W. Norton.

Kenny, G., Butler, R., Hickson, D. G., Cray, D., Mallory, G. and Wilson, D. (1987) Strategic Decision-Making: Influence Patterns in Public and Private Sector Organization, *Human Relations*, 40(9): 613–31.

Kerr, S. and Jerminer, J. M. (1978) Substitutes for Leadership: Their Meaning and Measurement, *Organizational Behavior and Human Performance*, 22(3): 375–403.

Kessing, S. G., Konrad, K. A. and Kotsogiannis, C. (2007) Foreign Direct Investment and the Dark Side of Decentralization, *Economic Policy*, 49: 6–70.

Ketchen, J. D. J., Combs, J. G., Russell, C. J., Shook, C., Dean, M. A., Runge, J., Lohrke, F. T., Naumann, S. E., Haptonstahl, D. E., Baker, R., Beckstein, B. A., Handler, C., Honig, H. and Lamoureux, S. (1997) Organizational Configurations and Performance: A Meta-Analysis, *Academy of Management Journal*, 40: 223–40.

Ketola, T. (1998) Why Don't the Oil Companies Clean Up Their Act? The Realities of Environmental Planning, *Long Range Planning*, 31(1): 108–19.

Kets de Vries, M. F. R. (1991) *Organizations on the Couch: Handbook of Psychoanalysis and Management*, San Francisco, CA: Jossey-Bass.

Kets de Vries, M. F. R. and Miller, D. (1986) Personality, Culture and Organization, *Academy of Management Review*, 11: 266–79.

Keynes, J. M. (1937) The General Theory of Employment, *Quarterly Journal of Economics*, 52(1): 209–23.

Khan, F. R., Munir, K. A. and Willmott, H. (2007) A Dark Side of Institutional Entrepreneurship: Soccer Balls, Child Labour and Postcolonial Impoverishment, *Organization Studies*, 28: 1055–77.

Khandwalla, P. (1977) *The Design of Organizations*, New York: Harcourt Brace Jovanovich.

Khurana, R. (2007) *From Higher Aims to Hired Hands: The Social Transformation of American Business Schools and the Unfulfilled Promise of Management Education*, Princeton, NJ: Princeton University Press.

Kim, W. (1988) The Effects of Competition and Corporate Political Responsiveness on Multinational Bargaining Power, *Strategic Management Journal*, 9(3): 289–95.

Kim, W. C. and Mauborgne, R. (1999) Creating New Market Space: A Systematic Approach to Value Innovation Can Help Companies Break Free from the Competitive Pack, *Harvard Business Review*, 76: 83–93.

Kim, W. C. and Mauborgne, R. (2004) Blue Ocean Strategy, *Harvard Business Review*, 81: 76–85.

Kim, W. C. and Mauborgne, R. (2005) *Blue Ocean Strategy*, Cambridge, MA: Harvard Business School Press.

Kjonstad, B. and Willmott, H. (1995) Business Ethics: Restrictive or Empowering? *Journal of Business Ethics*, 14(6): 445–64.

Klein, N. (2000) *No Logo: Taking Aim at the Brand Bullies*, Toronto: Knopf.

Klein, N. (2007) *The Shock Doctrine: The Rise of Disaster Capitalism*, New York: Metropolitan Books.

Knights, D. (2002) Writing Organization Analysis into Foucault, *Organization*, 9(4): 573–93.

Knights, D. and Morgan, G. (1991) Corporate Strategy, Organizations, and Subjectivity: A Critique, *Organization Studies*, 12(2): 251–73.

Knights, D. and Morgan, G. (1995) Strategy under the Microscope: Strategic Management and IT in Financial Services, *Journal of Management Studies*, 32(2): 191–214.

Kogut, B. (1988) Joint Ventures: Theoretical and Empirical Perspectives, *Strategic Management Journal*, 9(July/August): 319–32.

Kogut, B. (2002) International Management and Strategy. In A. Pettigrew, H. Thomas and R. Whittington (eds), *Handbook of Strategy and Management*, London: Sage.

Kogut, B. and Parkinson, D. (1998) Adoption of the Multidivisional Structure: Analyzing History from the Start, *Industrial and Corporate Change*, 7(2): 249–73.

Kogut, B. and Zander, U. (1992) Knowledge of the Firm: Combinative Capabilities, and the Replication of Technology, *Organization Science*, 3(3): 383–97.

Kolk, A. and Levy, D. (2001) Winds of Change: Corporate Strategy, Climate Change and Oil Multinationals, *European Management Journal*, 19(5): 501–9.

Konings, M. (2008) The Institutional Foundation of US Structural Power in International Finance: From the Re-emergence of Global Finance to the Monetarist Turn, *Review of International Political Economy*, 15(1): 35–61.

Kono, T. and Clegg, S. R. (1998) *Transformations of Corporate Culture: Experiences of Japanese Enterprises*, De Gruyter Studies in Organization, No. 83, Berlin and New York: De Gruyter.

Kono, T. and Clegg, S. R. (2001) *Trends in Japanese Management*, London: Palgrave.

Kor, Y. and Mahoney, J. (2004) Edith Penrose's (1959) Contributions to the Resource-Based View of Strategic Management, *Journal of Management Studies*, 41(1): 183–91.

Kornberger, M. (2010) *The Brand Society*, Cambridge: Cambridge University Press.

Kornberger, M., Carter, C. and Clegg, S. R. (2006) Rethinking the Polyphonic Organization: Managing as Discursive Practice, *Scandinavian Journal of Management*, 22(1): 3–30.

Kortein, D. (1995) *When Corporations Rule the World*, San Francisco: Berrett-Koehler.

Kostova, T. and Zaheer, S. (1999) Organizational Legitimacy under Conditions of Complexity: The Case of the Multinational Enterprise, *Academy of Management Review*, 24(1): 64–81.

Kotter, J. (1996) *Leading Change*, Boston, MA: Harvard Business School Press.

Kotter, J. P. (1982) *The General Managers*, New York: Free Press.

Kotz, D. M. (2009) The Financial and Economic Crisis of 2008: A System Crisis of Neoliberal Capitalism, *Review of Radical Political Economics*, 41(3): 305–17.

Kuhn T. S. (1962) *The Structure of Scientific Revolutions*, Chicago: University of Chicago Press.

Kumar, V. and Petersen, J. A. (2005) Using a Customer-Level Marketing Strategy to Enhance Firm Performance: A Review of Theoretical and Empirical Evidence, *Journal of the Academy of Marketing Science*, 33(4): 504–19.

Laine, P. M. and Vaara, E. (2007) Struggling and Subjectivity: A Discursive Analysis of Strategic Development in an Enginnering Group, *Human Relations*, 60(1): 29–58.

Lam, C.-Y. (2009) To What Extent is the Japanese Government Able to Steer the Nation's Economy in the Digital Age? PhD thesis, University of Technology, Sydney.

Langley, A. (1990) Patterns in the Use of Formal Analysis in Strategic Decisions, *Organization Studies*, 11(1): 17–45.

Langlois, R. and Foss, N. (1997) *Capabilities and Governance: the Rebirth of Production in the Theory of Economic Organization*, DRUID Working Papers 97–2, DRUID, Copenhagen Business School, Department of Industrial Economics, and Strategy/Aalborg University, Department of Business Studies.

Lanzara, G. F. (1998) Self-Destructive Processes in Institution Building and Some Modest Countervailing Mechanisms, *European Journal of Political Research*, 33(1): 1–39.

Larsen, P. T. and Cox, A. (2009) Barclays Bankers Braced for Bonus Cuts, *The Financial Times*, 6 February 2009, www.ft.com/cms/s/0/4480cca8-f48e-11dd-8e76-0000779fd2ac.html, accessed 23 September 2010.

Larsen, S. (2008a) *The Girl With The Dragon Tattoo*, London: MacLehose/Quercus Press.

Larsen, S. (2008b) *The Girl Who Played with Fire*, London: MacLehose/Quercus Press.

Larsen, S. (2008c) *The Girl Who Kicked the Hornets' Nest*. London: MacLehose/Quercus Press.

Latour, B. (2005) *Reassembling the Social: An Introduction to Actor-Network-Theory*, Oxford: Oxford University Press.

Lazonick, W. and O'Sullivan, M. (2000) Maximizing Shareholder Value: A New Ideology for Corporate Governance, *Economy and Society*, 29(1): 13–35.

Learned, E. P., Christensen, C. P., Andrews, K. P. and Guth, W. (1969) *Business Policy*, Homewood, IL: Irwin.

Levitt, T. (1983) The Globalization of Markets, *Harvard Business Review*, 61(3): 92–102.

Levy, D. L. (1994) Chaos Theory and Strategy: Theory, Application, and Managerial Implications, *Strategic Management Journal*, 15(Special Issue): 167–78.

Levy, D. L. Alvesson, M. and Willmott, H. (2001) Critical Approaches to Strategic Management, Paper Presented to the *Critical Management Studies Conference*, Conference Stream: Strategy, 11–13 July 2001, Manchester.

Levy, D. L., Alvesson, M. and Willmott, H. (2003) Critical Approaches to Strategic Management. In M. Alvesson and H. Willmott (eds), *Studying Management Critically*, London: Sage, pp. 92–109.

Liebeskind, J. (1996) Knowledge, Strategy and Theories of the Firm, *Strategic Management Journal*, 17(Winter Special Issue): 93–107.

Likert, R. (1967) *The Human Organization: Its Management and Value*, New York: McGraw-Hill.

Lilley, S. (2001) The Language of Strategy. In R. Westwood and S. Linstead (eds), *The Language of Organization*, London: Sage, pp. 66–88.

Lindblom, C. (1959) The Science of Muddling Through, *Public Administration Review*, 19(2): 79–88.

Lindblom, C. (1979) Still Muddling, Not Yet Through, *Public Administration Review*, 39(6): 517–26.

Lipczynski, J., Goddard, J. and Wilson, J. S. O. (2009) *Industrial Organization: Competition, Strategy and Policy*, (3rd edn), London: Financial Times/Prentice Hall.

Littler, C. (2006) Corporate Comets or Typical Trajectories?: Corporate Dynamics in the 1990s, *Critical Perspectives on Accounting*, 17(5): 627–55.

Loche, R., Arnegual, M. and Mangla, A. (2009) Virtue out of Necessity? Compliance, Commitment, and the Improvement of Labour: Conditions in Global Supply Chains, *Politics & Society*, 37(3): 314–51.

Lounsbury, M. and Ventresca, M. (2003) The New Structuralism in Organizational Theory, *Organization*, 10(3): 457–80.

Lovelock, J. (2006) *The Revenge of Gaia*, London: Allen Lane.

Lu, S. S. and Ngo, H.-Y. (2005) The Influence of Structural and Process Factors on Partnership Satisfaction in Interfirm Cooperation, *Group & Organization Management*, 30: 378–97.

Lui, S. S. and Ngo, H.-Y. (2005) The Role of Trust and Contractual Safeguards on Cooperation in Nonequity Alliance, *Journal of Management*, 30(4): 471–85.

Lukes, S. (1974) *Power: A Radical View*, London: Macmillan.

Lukes, S. (2005) *Power: A Radical View* (2nd edn), London: Palgrave Macmillan.

Lumet, S. (Director) (1957) *12 Angry Men* [motion picture], United States: Orion-Nova Productions.

Lury, C. (2004) *Brands The Logo of the Global Economy*, New York and London: Routledge.

MacClean, M., Harvey, C. and Chia, R. (2010) Dominant Corporate Agents and the Power Elites in France and Britain, *Organization Studies*, 31(3): 327–48.

MacDuffie, J. (1995) Human Resource Bundles and Manufacturing Performance – Organizational Logics and Flexible Production Systems in the World Auto Industry, *Industrial and Labour Relations Review*, 48(2): 197–221.

Machiavelli, N. (1961) *The Prince*, Harmondsworth: Penguin.

Macintosh, N. (2002) *Accounting, Accountants and Accountability: Poststructural Positions*. London: Routledge.

Mackay, R. (2007) What if? Synthesizing Debates and Advancing Prospects of Using Virtual History in Management and Organization Theory, *Management and Organizational History*, 2(2): 295–314.

Mackenzie, D. (2006) *An Engine, not a Camera: How Financial Models Shape Markets*, Boston: MIT Press.

Madhok, A. and Tallman, S. B. (1998) Resources, Transactions and Rents: Managing Value through Interfirm Collaborative Relationships, *Organization Science*, 9(3): 326–39.

Maguire, S., Hardy, C. and Lawrence, T. (2004) Institutional Entrepreneurship and Emerging Fields: HIV/AIDS Treatment Advocacy in Canada, *Academy of Management Journal*, 47(5): 657–79.

Mahmood, I. P. and Rufin, C. (2005) Government's Dilemma: The Role of Government in Imitation and Innovation, *Academy of Management Review*, 30(2): 338–60.

Mahoney, J. T. and McGahan, A. M. (2007) The Field of Strategic Management within the Evolving Science of Strategic Organization, *Strategic Organization*, 5(1): 79–99.

Makadok, R. (2001) Toward a Synthesis of the Resource-Based and Dynamic-Capability Views of Rent Creation, *Strategic Management Journal*, 22(5): 387–401.

Malefyt, T. and Moeran, B. (2003) Introduction: Advertising Cultures – Advertising, Ethnography and Anthropology. In T. D. Malefyt and B. Moeran (eds), *Advertising Cultures*, Oxford: Berg, pp. 1–34.

Manning, C. (2010) RBS Backlash as Bonus Culture Continues Despite Losses, www.mirror.co.uk/news/ top-stories/2010/02/26/taxpayers-loss-3-6billion-traders-bonus-1-3billion-115875-22070843/, accessed 28 February 2010.

Mantere, S. (2005) Strategic Practices as Enablers and Disablers of Championing Activity, *Strategic Organization*, 3(2): 157–284.

Marceau, J. (2008) Innovation. In S. R. Clegg and J. R. Bailey (eds) *The International Encyclopaedia of Organizations*, Thousand Oaks, CA: Sage, pp. 670–3.

March, J. G. (1962) The Business Firm as a Political Coalition, *Journal of Politics*, 24(4): 662–78.

March, J. G. (1966) The Power of Power. In Easton, D. (ed.), *Varieties of Political Theory*. Englewood Cliff, NJ: Prentice-Hall

March, J. G. (1978) Bounded Rationality, Ambiguity, and the Engineering of Choice, *Bell Journal of Economics*, 9(2): 587–608.

March, J. G. (1988) The Technology of Foolishness. In J. G. March (ed.), *Decisions and Organization*s, Oxford: Blackwell, pp. 253–65.

March, J. G. (1991) Exploration and Exploitation in Organizational Learning, *Organization Science*, 2(1): 71–87.

Marchand, R. (1998) *Creating the Corporate Soul: The Rise of Public Relations and Corporate Imagery in American Big Business*, Los Angeles: University of California Press.

Marcuse, H. (1964) *One Dimensional Man*, Boston, MA: Beacon Press.

Margolis, J. D. and Walsh, J. P. (2003) Misery Loves Company: Rethinking Social Initiatives by Business, *Administrative Science Quarterly*, 48(2): 268–305.

Margulis, M. S. and Pekar, P. (2001) *The Next Wave of Alliance Formations*, Los Angeles: Houlihan, Lokey, Howard and Zukin.

Markides, C. (2000) *All the Right Moves: A Guide to Crafting Breakthrough Strategy*, Vol. 1, Boston, MA: Harvard Business School Press.

Martin, J. (2002) *Organizational Culture: Mapping the Terrain*, Thousand Oak, CA: Sage.

Martin, J., Feldman, M. S., Hatch, M. J. and Sitkin, S. B. (1983) The Uniqueness Paradox in Organizational Stories, *Administrative Science Quarterly*, 28: 438–53.

Martin, R. (1988) Truth, Power, Self: An Interview. In L. H. Martin, H. Gutman and P. H. Hutton (eds), *Technologies of the Self: a seminar with Michel Foucault*, Amherst, MA: University of Massachusetts Press, pp. 9–15.

Martin, R. (2002) *Financialization of Everyday Life*, Philadelphia: Temple University Press.

Marx, K. and Engels, F. (1845/1968) *The German Ideology*, Moscow: Progress Press.

Mason, E. (1939) Price and Production Policies of Large-Scale Enterprise, *American Economic Review*, 29(1): 61–74.

Mason, E. (1949) The Current State of the Monopoly Problem in the US, *Harvard Law Review*, 62: 1265–85.

Matthews, J. A. (2002) Competitive Advantages of the Latecomer Firm: A Resource-Based Account of Industrial Catch-up Strategies, *Asia Pacific Journal of Management*, 19(4): 467–88.

Matthews, J. A. (2010) Lachmannian Insights into Strategic Entrepreneurship: Resources, Activities and Routines in a Disequilibrium World, *Organization Studies*, 31(2): 219–44.

Mayer, M. and Whittington, R. (1999) Euro-Elites: Top British, French and German Managers in the 1980s and 1990s, *European Management Journal*, 17(4): 403–8.

McClean, B. and Elkind, P. (2003) *The Smartest Guys in the Room*, London: Penguin.

McClelland, D. C. and Boyatzis, R. E. (1982) Leadership Motive Pattern and Long-term Success in Management, *Journal of Applied Psychology*, 67(6): 737–43.

McDougall, P. P., Shane, S. and Oviatt, B. M. (1994) Explaining the Formation of International New Ventures, *Journal of Business Venturing*, 9(6): 469–87.

McGee, J. and Thomas, H. (1986) Strategic Groups: Theory, Research and Taxonomy, *Strategic Management Journal*, 7(2): 141–60.

McGivern, C. (1983) Some Facets of the Relationship between Consultants and Clients in Organization, *Journal of Management Studies*, 20(3): 367–86.

McIntyre, K. (1996) Geography as Destiny: Cities, Villages and Khmer Rouge Orientalism, *Comparative Studies in Society and History*, 38(4): 730–58.

McKinlay, A. (2002) The Limits of Knowledge Management, New Technology, *Work and Employment*, 17(2): 76–88.

McLean, M. and Harvey, C. (2006) *Business Elites and Corporate Governance in France and the UK*, Basingstoke: Palgrave Macmillan.

McNamara, G., Deephouse, D. L. and Luce, R. A. (2003) Competitive Positioning within and across a Strategic Group Structure: The Performance of Core, Secondary, and Solitary Firms, *Strategic Management Journal*, 24(2): 161–81.

McNulty, T. and Pettigrew, A. (1999) Strategists on the Board, *Organization Studies*, 20(1): 47–74.

Merton, R. K. and Barber, E. (2004) *The Travels and Adventures of Serendipity*, Princeton, NJ: Princeton University Press.

Meyer, J. and Rowan, B. (1977) Institutionalized Organizations: Formal Structure as Myth and Ceremony, *American Journal of Sociology*, 83(2): 340–63.

Meyer, J., John, B., George, M. and Francisco, O. (1997) World Society and the Nation State, *American Journal of Sociology*, 103(1): 144–8.

Michelli, J. (2007) *The Starbucks Experience: 5 Principles for Turning Ordinary into Extraordinary*, New York: McGraw-Hill.

Micklethwait, J. and Wooldridge, A. (2000) *A Future Perfect: The Challenge and Hidden Promise of Globalization*, London: Crown Business.

Miles, R. E., Snow, C. C and Miles, G. (2007) The Ideology of Innovation, *Strategic Organization*, 5(4): 423–35.

Miller, D. (1990) *The Icarus Paradox: How Exceptional Companies Bring about Their Own Fall*, New York: HarperCollins.

Miller, J. and Muir, D. (2004) *The Business of Brands*, Chichester: John Wiley & Sons.

Miller, P. and O'Leary, T. (1987) Accounting and the Construction of the Governable Person, *Accounting, Organizations and Society*, 12: 235–66.

Miller, S. J. and Wilson, D. C. (2006) Perspectives on Organizational Decision-Making. In S. R. Clegg, C. Hardy, T. Lawrence, and W. Nord (eds), *Handbook of Organization Studies* (2nd edn), London: Sage, pp. 469–85.

Miller, S. J., Hickson, D. J. and Wilson, D. C. (2002) Decision-Making in Organizations. In G. Salaman (ed.), *Decision-Making for Business*, London: Sage, pp. 74–92.

Mills, C. W. (1956) *The Power Elite*, Oxford: Oxford University Press.

Miner, J. B. (1965) *Studies in Management Education*, Atlanta, GA: Organizational Measurement System Press.

Mintzberg, H. (1973) *The Nature of Managerial Work*, New York: Harper & Row.

Mintzberg, H. (1978) Patterns in Strategy Formation, *Management Science*, 24(9): 934–48.

Mintzberg, H. (1983) *Power In and Around Organizations*, Englewood Cliffs, NJ: Prentice-Hall.

Mintzberg H. (1989) *Mintzberg on Management: Inside Our Strange World of Organizations*, New York: Free Press.

Mintzberg, H. (1990) The Design School: Reconsidering the Basic Premises of Strategic Management, *Strategic Management Journal*, 11(3): 171–95.

Mintzberg H. (1994) The Fall and Rise of Strategic Planning, *Harvard Business Review*, 74(2): 107–14.

Mintzberg, H. (2002) The Organization as a Political Arena. In S. R. Clegg (ed.), *Central Currents in Organization Studies II: Contemporary Trends*, London: Sage, pp. 50–69 (originally published in (1985) *Journal of Management Studies*, 22(2): 133–54).

Mintzberg, H. (2004) *Managers Not MBAs: A Hard Look at the Soft Practice of Managing and Management Development*, San Francisco: Berrett-Koehler.

Mintzberg, H. and McHugh, A. (1985) Strategy Formation in an Adhocracy, *Administrative Science Quarter*, 30(2): 160–97.

Mintzberg, H. and Waters, J. A. (1985) Of Strategies, Deliberate and Emergent, *Strategic Management Journal*, 6(3): 257–72.

Mintzberg, H., Lampel, J., Quinn, J. and Ghoshal, S. (2003) *The Strategy Process: Concepts, Contexts, Cases* (4th edn), Upper Saddle River, NJ: Prentice-Hall.

Mintzberg, H., Raisinghani, D. and Theoret, A. (1976) The Structure of 'Unstructured' Processes, *Administrative Science Quarterly*, 21(2): 246–75.

Misumi, J. and Shirakashi, S. (1966) An Experimental Study of the Effects of Supervisory Behaviour on Productivity and Morale in a Hierarchical Organization, *Human Relations*, 19: 297–307.

Mitchell, R. K., Agle, B. R. and Wood, D. J. (1997) Toward a Theory of Stakeholder Identification and Salience: Defining the Principle of Who and What Really Counts, *Academy of Management Review*, 22(4): 853–86.

Mitchell, W. and Singh, K. (1996) Survival of Businesses Using Collaborative Relationships to Commercialize Complex Goods, *Strategic Management Journal*, 17(3): 169–96.

Mitroff, I. I. and Denton, E. (1999) *A Spiritual Audit of Corporate America*, San Francisco: Jossey-Bass.

Mitsuhashi, H. and Greve, H. R. (2004) Powerful and Free: Intraorganizational Power and the Dynamics of Corporate Strategy, *Strategic Organization*, 2(2):107–32.

Mizruchi, M. S. (1996) What Do Interlocks Do? An Analysis, Critique, and Reassessment of Research on Interlocking Directorates, *Annual Review of Sociology*, 22(4): 271–98.

Mol, A. P. J. (1995) *The Refinement of Production: Ecological Modernization Theory and the Chemical Industry*, Utrecht: Van Arkel.

Mol, A. P. J. and Spaargaren, G. (1993) Environment, Modernity and the Risk-Society: The Apocalyptic Horizon of Environmental Reform, *International Sociology*, 8(4): 429–59.

Monbiot, G. (2009a) Shell's Game, www.monbiot.com/archives/ 2009/01/06/shells-game/, accessed 7 December 2009.

Monbiot, G. (2009b) George Monbiot meets ... Jeroen van de Veer, *The Guardian*, 6 January 2009, http://www.youtube.com/watch?v=MqUfuYM74, accessed 13 September 2010.

Moran, T. (1985) Multinational Corporations and the Developing Countries: An Analytical Overview. In T. Moran (ed.), *Multinational Corporations: The Political Economy of Foreign Direct Investment,* Lexington, MA: D. C. Heath, pp. 3–24.

Morgan, G. (2001) The Multinational Firm: Organizing Across Institutional and National Divides. In G. Morgan, P. H. Kristenssen and R. Whitley (eds), *The Multinational Firm: Organizing Across Institutional and National Divides*, Oxford: Oxford University Press, pp. 1–24.

Morgan, G. (2009) Globalization, Multinationals and Institutional Diversity, *Economy and Society*, 38(4): 580–605.

Morgan, G. and Kristensen, P. (2006) The Contested Space of Multinationals: Varieties of Institutionalism, Varieties of Capitalism, *Human Relations*, 59(11): 1467–90.

Morgan, R. and Hunt, S. (1994) The Commitment-Trust Theory of Relationship Marketing, *Journal of Marketing*, 58(3): 20–38.

Morris, E. (2003) *The Fog of War* [Motion picture], www.errolmorris.com/film/fow.html, accessed 29 April 2010.

Mueller, F., Sillince, J., Harvey C. and Howorth, C. (2004) A Rounded Picture is What We Need: Rhetorical Strategies, Arguments and the Negotiation of Change in All Hospital Trusts, *Organization Studies*, 25(1): 85–103.

Munir, K. and Phillips, N. (2005) The Birth of the 'Kodak Moment': Institutional Entrepreneurship and the Adoption of New Technologies, *Organization Studies*, 26(11): 1665–87.

Munro, I. (1992) Codes of Ethics: Some Uses and Abuses. In P. Davies (ed.), *Current Issues in Business Ethics*, London: Routledge, pp. 97–106.

Murray, R., Caulier-Grice, J. and Mulgan, G. (2010) *The Open Book of Social Innovation*, London: NESTA.

Nachum, L. and Zaheer, A. (2005) The Persistence of Distance? The Impact of Technology on MNE Motivations for Foreign Investment, *Strategic Management Journal*, 26(8): 747–67.

Nag, R., Hambrick, D. C. and Chen, M. J. (2007) What is Strategic Management, Really? Empirical Induction of a Consensus Definition of the Field, *Strategic Management Journal*, 28(9): 935–55.

Nath, D. and Gruca, T. S. (1997) Convergence across Alternative Methods for Forming Strategic Groups, *Strategic Management Journal*, 18(9): 745–60.

Nelson, R. (2005) *Technology, Institutions, and Economic Growth*, Cambridge, MA: Harvard University Press.

Nelson, R. R. and Winter, S. G. (1982) *An Evolutionary Theory of Economic Change*, Cambridge, MA: Belknap Press of Harvard University Press.

Nelson, R. R. and Winter, S. G. (2002) Evolutionary Theorizing in Economics, *Journal of Economic Perspectives*, 16(2): 23–46.

Newbury, W. and Zeira, Y. (1997) Generic Differences between Equity International Joint Ventures (EIJVs), International Acquisitions (IAs) and International Greenfield Investment (IGIs): Implications for Parent Companies, *Journal of World Business*, 32(2): 87–102.

Nonaka, I. and Takeuchi, H. (1995) *The Knowledge-Creating Company: How Japanese Companies Create the Dynamics of Innovation*, Oxford: Oxford University Press.

Nurmi, R. (1988) Knowledge-Intensive Firms, *Business Horizons*, May–June: 26–32.

Nutt, P. (1999) Surprising but True: Half the Decisions in Organizations Fail, *Academy of Management Executive*, 13(4): 75–90.

O'Brien, E. (2007) Radiohead: 'EMI don't understand the music biz', http://www.tourdates.co.uk/news/11759-radictead-emi-dont-Understand-the-musk-biz, accessed 5 April 2009.

Obama, B. (1995) *Dreams from My Father: A Story of Race and Inheritance*, New York: Three Rivers Press.

Obama, B. (2006) *The Audacity of Hope: Thoughts on Reclaiming the American Dream*, New York: Crown.

Ocasio, W. and Kim, H. (1999) The Circulation of Corporate Control: Selection of Functional Backgrounds of New CEOs in Large US Manufacturing Firms, 1981–1992, *Administrative Science Quarterly*, 44(3): 532–62.

O'Connor, J. (1973) *The Fiscal Crisis of the State*, New York: St. Martin's Press.

OECD (Organization for Economic Co-operation and Development) (1997) *National Innovation Systems*, Paris: OECD.

Ohmae, K. (1990) *The Borderless World*, London: Collins.

Ohmae, K. (1995) *The End of the Nation State*, New York: Free Press.

Olins, W. (2003) *On Brand*, London: Thames & Hudson.

Oliver, C. (1992) The Antecedents of Deinstitutionalization, *Organization Studies*, 13(4): 563–58.

Oliver, D. and Roos, J. (2005) Decision-Making in High-Velocity Environments: The Importance of Guiding Principles, *Organization Studies*, 26(6): 889–913.

Olsen, J. P. (1976) Choice in an Organized Anarchy. In J. G. March and J. P. Olsen (eds), *Ambiguity and Choice in Organizations*, Bergen: Universitetsforlaget, pp. 82–139.

Ong A. (2006) *Neoliberalism as Exception: Mutations in Citizenship and Sovereignty*, Durham, NC and London: Duke University Press.

O'Reilly, C. A. and Tushman, M. L. (2004) The Ambidextrous Organization, *Harvard Business Review*, April: 74–81.

Orlikowski, W. J. (2002) Knowing in Practice: Enacting a Collective Capability in Distributed Organizing, *Organization Science*, 13(4): 249–73.

Ormerod, P. (2010) The Current Crisis and the Culpability of Macroeconomic Theory, *21st Century Society*, 5(1): 5–18.

Orr, J. (1996) *Talking about Machines: An Ethnography of a Modern Job*, Ithaca, NY: Cornell University Press.

Orsato, R. and Clegg, S. R. (2005) Radical Reformism: Towards Critical Ecological Modernisation, *Sustainable Development*, 13(4): 253–67.

Orwell, G. (2002) *Homage to Catalonia*, Harmondsworth: Penguin.

Osborn, R. N. and Hagedoorn, J. (1997) The Institutionalization and Evolutionary Dynamics of Interorganizational Alliances and Networks, *Academy of Management Journal*, 40(2): 261–78.

Oviatt, B. M. and McDougall, P. P. (1994) Toward a Theory of International New Ventures, *Journal of International Business Studies*, 25(1): 45–64.

Owen, D. L., Swift, T. A., Humphrey, C. and Bowerman, M. (2000) The New Social Audits: Accountability, Managerial Capture or the Agenda of Social Champions, *European Accounting Review*, 9(1): 81–90.

Owen, D. L., Swift, T. and Hunt, K. (2001) Questioning the Role of Stakeholder Engagement in Social and Ethical Accounting, Auditing and Reporting, *Accounting Forum*, 25(3): 264–82.

Oxley, J. E. (1997) Appropriability Hazards and Governance in Strategic Alliances: A Transaction Cost Approach, *Journal of Law, Economics and Organization*, 13(2): 387–409.

Pagnamenta, R. (2009) Anger as Shell Reduces Renewables Investment, *Times Online*, http://business.timesonline. co.uk/tol/business/industry-sectors/natural-resources/ article5927869.ece, accessed 13 September 2010.

Paine, L. (1994) Managing for Organizational Integrity, *Harvard Business Review*, March–April: 106–17.

Palmer, D. A. and Barber, B. (2001) Challengers, Elites and Owning Families: A Social Class Theory of Corporate Acquisitions in the 1960s, *Administrative Science Quarterly*, 46(1): 87–120.

Palmer, D. A., Jennings, P. D. and Zhou, X. (1993) Late Adoption of the Multidivisional Form by Large US Corporations: Institutional, Political, and Economic Accounts, *Administrative Science Quarterly*, 38(1): 100–31.

Paret, P. (1992) *Understanding War: Essays on Clausewitz and the History of Military Power*, Princeton, NJ: Princeton University of Press.

Park, N. K. and Mezias, J. M. and Song, J. (2004) A Resource-Based View of Strategic Alliances and Firm Value in the Electronic Marketplace, *Journal of Management*, 30: 7–27.

Park, S. H. and Ungson, G. (2001) Interfirm Rivalry and Managerial Complexity: A Conceptual Framework of Alliance Failure, *Organization Science*, 12(1): 37–53.

Park, S. H. and Zhou, D. (2005) Firm Heterogeneity and Competitive Dynamics in Alliance Formation, *Academy of Management Review*, 30(3): 531–54.

Parker, C. and Nielsen, V. L. (2009) Corporate Compliance Systems: Could They Make Any Difference? *Administration and Society*, 41(1): 3–37.

Parker, G. and Thomas, D. (2000) Former Executives Face Bonus Grilling, http://www.ft.com/0b55e60ea-f648-11dd-a9ed-0000779fd2ac.html, accessed 23 September 2010.

Parker, M. (2002) *Against Management: Organisation in the Age of Managerialism*, Cambridge: Polity Press.

Parkhe, A. (1991) Interfirm Diversity, Organizational Learning, and Longevity, *Journal of International Business Studies*, 22(4): 579–601.

Parkhe, A. (1996) International Joint Ventures. In B. J. Punnett and O. Shenkar (eds), *Handbook for International Management Research*, Cambridge, MA: Blackwell.

Paroutis, S. and Pettigrew, A. (2007) Strategizing in the Multi-Business Firm: Strategy Teams at Multiple Levels and over Time, *Human Relations*, 60(1): 91–135.

Payne, A. (2006) *Handbook of CRM: Achieving Excellence in Customer Management*, Oxford: Butterworth-Heinemann.

Payne, A. and Frow, P. (2005) A Strategic Framework for Customer Relationship Management, *Journal of Marketing*, 69(4): 167–76.

Pearce, F. (2009) Greenwash: Shell Betrays 'New Energy Future' Promises, *The Guardian*, http://www.guardian. co.uk/environment/2009/mar/26/fred-pearce-greenwash-shall-exxon, accessed 23 July 2010.

Pearce, J. and Zahra, S. (1991) The Relative Power of CEOs and Boards of Directors: Associations with Corporate Performance, *Strategic Management Journal*, 12(2): 135–53.

Pearce, R. J. (1997) Toward Understanding Joint Venture Performance and Survival: A Bargaining and Influence Approach to Transaction Cost Theory, *Academy of Management Review*, 22(1): 203–25.

Penrose, E. (1959) *The Theory of the Growth of the Firm*, London: Wiley.

Penrose, E. (2009) *The Theory of the Growth of the Firm*, with an introduction by C. Pitelis, Oxford: Oxford University Press.

Perrow, C. (1984) *Normal Accidents: Living with High Risk Technologies*, New York: Basic Books.

Peters, T. (2003) *Re-Imagine! Business Excellence in a Disruptive Age*, London: Dorling Kindersley.

Peters, T. (2005) *Design: Innovate, Differentiate, Communicate*, New York, Dorling Kindersley.

Peters, T. and Waterman, R. (1982) *In Search of Excellence: Lessons from America's Best Run Companies*, New York: Harper & Row.

Pettigrew, A. (1972) Information Control as a Power Resource, *Sociology*, 6(2): 187–204.

Pettigrew, A. (1973) *The Politics of Organizational Decision-Making*, London: Tavistock.

Pettigrew, A. (1985) *The Awakening Giant*, Oxford: Basil Blackwell.

Pettigrew, A. (1992) On Studying Managerial Elites, *Strategic Management Journal*, 13(2): 163–83.

Pettigrew, A. (2002) Strategy Formulation as a Political Process. In S. R. Clegg (ed.), *Central Currents in Organization Studies II: Contemporary Trends*, London: Sage, pp. 43–9 (originally published in (1977) *International Studies of Management and Organization* 1: 78–87).

Pettigrew, A. and McNulty, T. (1995) Power and Influence in and around the Boardroom, *Human Relations*, 48(8): 845–73.

Pettigrew, A. and McNulty, T. (1998) Sources and Uses of Power in the Boardroom, *European Journal of Work and Organizational Psychology*, 7(2): 197–214.

Pettigrew, A., Thomas, H. and Whittington, R. (eds) (2006) *Handbook of Strategy and Management*, London: Sage.

Pettinger, L. (2004) Brand Culture and Branded Workers: Service Work and Aesthetic Labour in Fashion Retail, *Consumption Markets & Culture*, 7(2): 165–84.

Pfeffer, J. (1972) Size and Composition of Corporate Boards of Directors: The Organization and its Environment, *Administratve Science Quarterly*, 17(2): 218–28.

Pfeffer, J. (1981) *Power in Organizations*, Marshfield, MA: Pitman.

Pfeffer, J. (1992) *Managing with Power: Politics and Influence in Organizations*, Boston, MA: Harvard Business Review Press.

Pfeffer, J. and Fong, C. T. (2002) The End of Business Schools? Less Successful than Meets the Eye, *Academy of Management Learning & Education*, 1(1), www.aomonline.org/Publications/Articles/BSchools.asp, accessed 21 March 2010.

Pfeffer, J. and Salancik, G. R. (1974) Organizational Decision-Making as a Political Process: The Case of a University Budget, *Administrative Science Quarterly*, 19(2): 135–51.

Phillips, W., Lamming, R., Bessant, J. and Noke, H. (2006) Discontinuous Innovation and Supply Relationships: Strategic Alliances, *R&D Management*, 36(4): 451–61.

Pickard, J. and Mackenzie, K. (2009) US Oil Industry Split as Leaked Memo Reveals Lobbying Plan, *Financial Times*, 15 August.

Pine, B. and Gilmore, J. (1999) *The Experience Economy*, Boston, MA: Harvard Business School Press.

Pisano, G. (1989) Using Equity Participation to Support Exchange: Evidence from the Biotechnology Industry, *Journal of Law, Economics and Organization*, 5(1): 109–26.

Pitelis, C. N. (2007) A Behavioral Resource-Based View of the Firm: The Synergy of Cyert and March (1963) and Penrose (1959), *Organization Science*, 18(3): 478–90.

Pitelis, C. N. (2009) The Co-Evolution of Organizational Value Capture, Value Creation and Sustainable Advantage, *Organization Studies*, 30(10): 1115–39.

Pitelis, C. N. and Teece, D. J. (2009) The (New) Nature and Essence of the Firm, *European Management Review*, 6(1): 5–15.

Pitsis, T., Clegg, S. R., Marosszeky, M. and Rura-Polley, T. (2003) Constructing the Olympic Dream: A Future Perfect Strategy of Project Management, *Organization Science*, 14(5): 574–90.

Plant, R. (2009) *The Neoliberal State*, Oxford: Oxford University Press.

Pondy, L. (1978) Leadership as a Language Game. In M. W. McCall and M. M. Lombardo (eds), *Leadership: Where Else Can We Go?*, Durham, NC: Duke University Press, pp. 87–99.

Pondy, L. R. and Mitroff, I. I. (1979) Beyond Open Systems Models of Organizations. In B. M. Staw (ed.), *Research in Organizational Behavior*, Greenwich, CT: JAI Press, pp. 3–39.

Poppo, L. and Zenger, T. (2002) Do Formal Contracts and Relational Governance Function as Substitutes or Complements? *Strategic Management Journal*, 23(8): 707–25.

Porac, J. F. and Thomas, H. (1994) Cognitive Categorization and Subjective Rivalry among Retailers in a Small City, *Journal of Applied Psychology*, 79(1): 54–66.

Porac, J. F. and Thomas H. (2002) Managing Cognition and Strategy: Issues, Trends and Future Decision. In T. H. Pettigrew and R. Whittington (eds), *Handbook of Strategy and Management*, London: Sage, pp. 165–81.

Porac, J. F., Thomas, H., Wilson, F., Paton, D. and Kamfer, A. (1995) Rivalry and the Scottish Knitwear Producers, *Administrative Science Quarterly*, 40(2): 202–27.

Porch, D. and Wirtz, J. J. (2002) Surprise and Intelligence Failure, *Strategic Insights*, www.ccc.nps.navy.mil/si/sept02/homeland.asp, accessed 12 December 2009.

Porter, M. E. (1980) *Competitive Strategy*, New York: Free Press.

Porter, M. E. (1985) *Competitive Advantage: Creating and Sustaining Superior Performance*, New York: Free Press.

Porter, M. E. (1996) What Is Strategy? *Harvard Business Review*, 74(6): 61–78.

Porter, M. E. (2008) The Five Competitive Forces that Shape Strategy, *Harvard Business Review*, 86(1): 78–93.

Porter, M. E. and Kramer, M. R. (2006) Strategy and Society: The Link between Competitive Advantage and Corporate Social Responsibility, *Harvard Business Review*, 84(12): 78–92.

Porter, M. E., Takeuchi, H. and Sakakibara, M. (2000) *Can Japan Compete?*, London: Macmillan.

Postrel, V. I. (1997) The Peters Principle – Interview with Tom Peters, *Reason*, October, http://findarticles.com/P/articles/mi_m1568/is_n5_v29/ai_20521295/, accessed 20 August 2007.

Powell, T. C. (2001) Competitive Advantage: Logical and Philosophical Considerations, *Strategic Management Journal*, 22(9): 857–88.

Powell, W. W., Koput, K. W. and Smith-Doer, L. (1996) Interorganizational Collaboration and the Locus of Innovation in Biotechnology, *Administrative Science Quarterly*, 41(1): 116–45.

Power, M. (1997) *The Audit Society*, Oxford: Oxford University Press.

Prahalad, C. K. (2004) The Blinders of Dominant Logic, *Long Range Planning*, 37(2): 171–9.

Prahalad, C. K. and Doz, Y. L. (1987) *The Multinational Mission*, New York: Free Press.

Prahalad, C. K. and Hamel, G. (1990) The Core Competence of the Organization, *Harvard Business Review*, 68(3): 79–91.

Prahalad, C. K. and Ramaswamy, V. (2003) The New Frontier of Experience Innovation, *Sloan Management Review*, 44(2): 12–18.

Prahalad, C. K. and Ramaswamy, V. (2004a) Co-creating Unique Value with Customers, *Strategy & Leadership*, 32(3): 4–9.

Prahalad, C. K. and Ramaswamy, V. (2004b) *The Future of Competition: The Co-creating of Unique Value with Customers*, Boston, MA: Harvard Business School Press.

Priem, R. L. and Butler, J. E. (2001) Is the Resource-Based 'View' a Useful Perspective for Strategic Management Research?, *Academy of Management Review*, 26(1): 22–40.

Provan, K. G. and Kenis, P. (2008) Modes of Network Governance: Structure, Management, and Effectiveness. *Journal of Public Administration Research and Theory?*, 18(2): 229–52.

Provan, K. G., Fish, A. and Sydow, J. (2007) Interorganizational Networks at the Network Level: A Review of the Empirical Literature on Whole Networks, *Journal of Management*, 33(3): 479–516.

Prusak, L. (1997) *Knowledge in Organizations (Resources for the Knowledge-Based Economy)*, Oxford: Butterworth–Heinemann.

Pullen, A. (2009) Identity. In S. R. Clegg and J. R. Bailey (eds), *International Encyclopaedia of Organization Studies*, London: Sage, pp. 630–4.

Pullen, A. and Linstead, A. (2005) *Identity and Organization*, London: Routledge.

Pusey, M. (1991) *Economic Rationalism in Canberra: A Nation-Building State Changes Its Mind*. Cambridge: Cambridge University Press.

Putnam, R. D. (1976) *The Comparative Study of Political Elites*, Englewood Cliffs, NJ: Prentice-Hall.

Quinn, B. J. (1978) Logical Incrementalism, *Sloan Management Review*, 20(1): 7–19.

Raabl, J. and Kenis, P. (2009) Towards a Society of Networks: Empirical Developments and Theoretical Challenges, *Journal of Management Inquiry*, 18(3): 198–210.

Ramani, G. and Kumar, V. (2008) Interaction Orientation and Firm Performance, *Journal of Marketing*, 72(1): 27–45.

Ramos-Rodríguez, A. R. and Ruíz-Navarro, J. (2004) Changes in the Intellectual Structure of Strategic Management Research: A Bibliometric Study of the Strategic Management Journal, 1980–2000, *Strategic Management Journal*, 25(10): 981–1004.

Rao, H. (2009) *Market Rebels: How Activists Make or Break Radical Innovations*, Princeton, NJ: Princeton University Press.

Ray, T. and Little, S. (2005) *Managing Knowledge: An Essential Reader* (2nd edn), London: Sage, in association with the Open University Press.

Rea, A. (2004) *The CFO's Perspective on Alliances: Growth, Risk, and Measurement*, Boston, MA: CFO Publishing Corp.

Refocus (2006) Belief in RE: View from the Top at Shell Renewables, *Refocus*, 7(2): 60–3.

Reinartz, W. and Kumar, V. (2000) On the Profitability of Long-Life Customers in a Noncontractual Setting: An Empirical Investigation and Implications for Marketing, *Journal of Marketing*, 64(4): 17–35.

Reinartz, W., Krafft, M. and Hoyer, W. (2004) The Customer Relationship Management Process: Its Measurement and Impact on Performance, *Journal of Marketing Research*, 41(3): 293–305.

Reinartz, W., Thomas, J. and Kumar, V. (2005) Balancing Acquisition and Retention Resources to Maximize Customer Profitability, *Journal of Marketing*, 69(1): 63–79.

Renewable Energy Focus (2009) Shell Withdraws from Wind and Solar – Focuses on Biofuels, *News/Roundup*, May/June.

Rennie, M. W. (1993) Global Competitiveness: Born Global, *McKinsey Quarterly*, 4(1): 45–52.

Reuer, J. J. (2005) Avoiding Lemons in M&A Deals, *MIT Sloan Management Review*, 46(3): 15–17.

Reuer, J. J. and Ariño, A. (2002) *Contractual Heterogeneity in Strategic Alliances*, IESE Working Paper No. D/482, http://

ssrn.com/abstract=462302 or doi:10.2139/ssrn.462302, accessed 29 April 2010.

Reuer, J. J., Zollo, M. and Singh, H. (2002) Post-Formation Dynamics in Strategic Alliances, *Strategic Management Journal*, 23(2): 135–51.

Ries, A. and Trout, J. (2001/1982) *Positioning: The Battle for Your Mind*, New York: Warner.

Ring, P. and Van de Ven, A. (1994) Developmental Processes of Cooperative Interorganizational Relationships, *Academy of Management Review*, 19(1): 90–118.

Rittel, H. W. J. and Webber, M. M. (1973) Dilemmas in a General Theory of Planning, *Policy Sciences*, 4(2): 155–69.

Ritzer, G. (1993) *The McDonaldization of Society*, Thousand Oaks, CA: Pine Forge Press.

Ritzer, G. (2004) *The Globalization of Nothing*, Thousand Oaks, CA: Pine Forge Press.

Ritzer, G. (2010) *Globalization: A Basic Text*, London: Wiley-Blackwell.

Robins, J. A. (1993) Organization as Strategy: Restructuring Production in the Film Industry, *Strategic Management Journal*, 14(2): 103–18.

Robins, J. A., Tallman, S. and Fladmoe-Lindquist, K. (2002) Autonomy and Dependence of International Cooperative Ventures, *Strategic Management Journal*, 23: 881–902.

Roddick, A. (2005) *Business as Unusual: The Triumph of Anita Roddick*, London: HarperCollins.

Rodrigues, S. B. and Child, J. (2008) *Corporate Co-Evolution: A Political Perspective*, Oxford: Wiley–Blackwell.

Rodrigues, S. B. and Child, J. (2010) Private Equity, the Minimalist Organization and the Quality of Employment Relations, *Human Relations*, 63(9): 1321–1342.

Rodriguez, P., Uhlenbruck, K. and Eden, L. (2005) Government Corruption and the Entry Strategies of Multinationals, *Academy of Management Review*, 30(2): 383–96.

Rollier, B. and Turner, J. A. (1994) Planning Forwards by Looking Backwards: Retrospective Thinking in Strategic Decision-Making, *Decision Science*, 25(2): 169–88.

Romme, A. G. L. (2003) Making a Difference: Organization as Design, *Organization Science*, 14(5): 558–73.

Romme, A. G. L. and Endenburg, G. (2006) Construction Principles and Design Rules in the Case of Circular Design, *Organization Science*, 17(2): 287–97.

Roos, J. and Victor, B. (1999) Towards a New Model of Strategy-Making as Serious Play, *European Management Journal*, 17(4): 348–55.

Roos, J., Victor, B. and Statley, M. (2004) Playing Seriously with Strategy, *Long Range Planning*, 37(6): 549–68.

Rose, N. and Miller, P. (1992) Political Power beyond the State Problematics of Government, *British Journal of Sociology*, 43(2): 173–205.

Rosenzweig, P. M. and Nohria, N. (1994) Influences on Human Resource Management Practices in Multinational Corporations, *Journal of International Business Studies*, 25(2): 229–51.

Ross-Sorkin, A . (2009) *Too Big to Fail: Inside the Battle to Save Wall Street*, London: Allen Lane.

Royal Dutch Shell (2002) Meeting the Energy Challenge, *The Shell Report,* London and Amsterdam: Royal Dutch Shell, p. 52.

Royal Dutch Shell (2008) Shell Energy Scenarios to 2050 webchat, www.shelldialogues.com/event/shell-energy-scenarios-2050-webchat, accessed 8 December 2009.

Royal Dutch Shell (2009a) The History of Shell – About Shell, www.shell.com/home/content/aboutshell/who_we_are/our_history/dir_our_history_14112006.html, accessed 8 December 2009.

Royal Dutch Shell (2009b) Shell at a Glance – About Shell, www.shell.com/home/content/aboutshell/at_a_glance/, accessed 8 December 2009.

Royal Dutch Shell (2009c) Shell at a Glance – United States, www.shell.us/home/content/usa/aboutshell/at_a_glance/shell_us_glance.html, accessed 8 December 2009.

Rughase, O. G. (2006) *Identity and Strategy: How Individuals' Visions Enable the Design of a Market Strategy that Works*, London: Elgar.

Rugman, A. M. and Verbeke, A. (1993) *Generic Strategies in Global Competition*. In A. M. Rugman and A. Verbeke (eds), *Research in Global Strategic Management: Global Competition Beyond the Three Generics*, Vol. 4, Greenwich, CT: JAI Press, pp. 3–15.

Rugman, A. M. and Verbeke, A. (2002) Edith Penrose's Contribution to the Resource-Based View of Strategic Management, *Strategic Management Journal*, 23(8): 769–80.

Rumelt, R. P. (1979) *Strategic Management: A New View of Business Policy and Planning*, Boston, MA: Little, Brown.

Rumelt, R. P. (1984) Toward a Strategic Theory of the Firm. In R. Lamb (ed.), *Competitive Strategic Management*, Englewood Cliffs, NJ: Prentice-Hall, pp. 556–70.

Rumelt, R. P. (1991) How Much Does Industry Matter? *Strategic Management Journal*, 12(3): 167–85.

Rust, R., Lemon, K. and Zeithaml, V. (2004) Return on Marketing: Using Customer Equity to Focus Marketing Strategy, *Journal of Marketing*, 68(1): 109–27.

Sacks, H. (1992) *Lectures on Conversation*, Volume I and II, edited by G. Jefferson with an Introduction by E.A. Schgloff, Oxford: Blackwell.

Sacks, H., Schegloff, E. and Jefferson, G. (1974) A Simplest Systematics for the Organization of Turn-taking for Conversation, *Language*, 50(4): 696–735.

Sadler, P. (2003) *Leadership* (2nd edn), London: Kogan Page.

Salaman, G., Storey, J. and Billsberry, J. (2005) *Strategic Human Resource Management: Theory and Practice*, London and Milton Keynes: Sage and The Open University.

Salancik, G. and Pfeffer, J. (1977) Who Gets Power – and How They Hold onto It: A Strategic-Contingency Model of Power, *Organizational Dynamics*, 5(3): 3–21.

Sambharya, R. (1996) Foreign Experience of Top Management Teams and International Diversification Strategies of US Multinational Corporations, *Strategic Mangement Journal*, 17(9): 739–46.

Sampson, A. (1975) *The Seven Sisters: The Great Oil Companies and the World They Shaped*, New York: Viking Press.

Sampson, R. C. (2005) Experience Effects and Collaborative Returns in R&D Alliances, *Strategic Management Journal*, 26(11): 1009–31.

Samra-Fredericks, D. (2003) Strategizing as Lived Experience and Strategists' Everyday Efforts to Shape Strategic Direction, *Journal of Management Studies*, 40(1): 141–74.

Samra-Fredericks, D. (2004a) Managerial Elites Making Rhetorical and Linguistic 'Moves' for a Moving (Emotional) Display, *Human Relations*, 57(9): 1103–43.

Samra-Fredericks, D. (2004b) Understanding the Production of 'Strategy' and 'Organization' through Talk amongst Managerial Elites, *Culture and Organization*, 10(2): 125–41.

Samra-Fredericks, D. (2005) Strategic Practice, 'Discourse' and the Everyday Interactional Constitution of 'Power Effects', *Organization*, 12(6): 803–41.

Sangster, A., Stoner, G. and McCarthy, P. (2007) Lessons for the Classroom from Luca Pacioli, *Issues in Accounting Education*, 22(3): 447–57.

Savage, M. and Williams, K. (2008) Elites: Remembered in Capitalism and Forgotten by Social Sciences. In M. Savage and K. Williams (eds), *Remembering Elites*, Oxford: Blackwell, pp. 1–24.

Saxenian, A. (1994) *Regional Advantage: Culture and Competition in Silicon Valley and Route 128*, Cambridge, MA: Harvard University Press.

Sayles, L. R. (1976) Matrix Management: The Structure with a Future, *Organizational Dynamics*, 5(2): 2–17.

Schattschneider, E. (1960) *The Semi-Sovereign People*, New York: Holt, Rinehart and Winston.

Schein, E. H. (1988) *Process Consultation, Volume I: Its Role in Organization Development*, Reading, MA: Addison-Wesley.

Schein, E. H. (1997) *Organizational Culture and Leadership* (2nd edn), San Francisco: Jossey-Bass.

Schein, E. H. (1999) *Process Consultation Revisited: Building the Helping Relationship*, Reading, MA: Addison-Wesley.

Schein, E. H. (2002) Consulting: What Should It Mean? In T. Clark Fincham (ed.), *Critical Consulting: New Perspectives on the Management Advice Industry*, Oxford: Blackwell, pp. 21–7.

Schmalensee, R. (1982) Antitrust and the New Industrial Economics, *American Economic Review*, 72 (May): 24–8.

Schrage, M. (2000) *Serious Play: How the Worlds Best Companies Simulate to Innovate*, Boston, MA: Harvard Business Press.

Schultz, M. and Hatch, M. J. (2005) Building Theory from Practice, *Strategic Organization*, 3(3): 337–48.

Schultz, M., Antorini, Y. M. and Csaba, F. F. (2005) Corporate Branding: An Evolving Concept, In M. Schultz, Y. M. Antorini and F. F. Csaba (eds), *Corporate Branding: People/Purpose/Process*, Copenhagen: Copenhagen Business School Press, pp. 2–22.

Schumpeter, J. (1975) *Capitalism, Socialism and Democracy*, New York: Harper.

Schutz, A. (1967) *The Phenomenology of the Social World*, Evanston, IL: Northwestern University Press.

Scott, J. (1982) *The Upper Classes: Property and Privilege in Britain*, London: Macmillan.

Scott, J. (1991) Networks of Corporate Power: A Comparative Assessment, *Annual Review of Sociology*, 17: 181–203.

Scott, J. (1996) *Stratification and Power: Structures of Class, Status and Command*, Cambridge: Polity Press.

Scott, J. (2001) *Power*, Cambridge: Polity Press.

Scott, J. (2008) Modes of Power and the Re-conceptualization of Elites. In M. Savage and K. Williams (eds), *Remembering Elites*, Oxford: Blackwell, pp. 27–43.

Scott, R. W. (1995) *Institutions and Organizations*, Thousand Oaks, CA: Sage.

Seidl, D. (2007) General Strategy Concepts and the Ecology of Strategy Discourses: A Systematic-Discursive Perspective, *Organization Studies*, 28(2): 197–218.

Self, P. (1975) *Econocrats and the Policy Process: The Politics and Philosophy of Cost–Benefit Analysis*, London: Macmillan.

Selsky, J., Spicer, A. and Teicher, J. (2003) Totally Un-Australian: Discursive and Institutional Interplay in the Melbourne Port Dispute of 1997–98, *Journal of Management Studies*, 40(7): 1729–60.

Seo, M.-G. and Creed, W. E. D. (2002) Institutional Contradictions, Praxis and Institutional Change: A Dialectical Perspective, *Academy of Management Review*, 27(2): 222–47.

Sennett, R. (2006) *The Culture of the New Capitalism*. New Haven, CT and London: Yale University Press.

Serapio, M. and Cascio, W. (1996) End Games in International Alliances, *Academy of Management Executive*, 10(1): 62–74.

Sewell, G. (1998) The Discipline of Teams: The Control of Team-Based Industrial Work through Electronic and Peer Surveillance, *Administrative Science Quarterly*, 43(2): 397–428.

Sharpe, D. R. (2001) Globalization and Change: Organizational Continuity and Change within a Japanese Multinational in the UK. In G. Morgan, P. Kristensen and R. Whitley (eds), *The Multinational Firm: Organizing across Institutional and National Divides*, Oxford: Oxford University Press, pp. 196–222.

Shaw, G., Brom, R. and Bromley, P. (1998) Strategic Stories: How 3M is Rewriting Business Planning, *Harvard Business Review*, 76(5): 41–50.

Shen, W. and Cannella, A. Jr, (2002) Power Dynamics within Top Management and Their Impacts on CEO Dismissal Followed by Inside Succession, *Academy of Management Journal*, 45(6): 1195–206.

Shenhav, Y. (2003) The Historical and Epistemological Foundations of Organization Theory: Fusing Sociological Theory with Engineering Discourse. In H. Tsoukas and C. Knudsen (eds), *The Oxford Handbook of Organization Theory*, Oxford: Oxford University Press, pp. 183–209.

Sheth, J. and Parvatiyar, A. (1995) Relationship Marketing in Consumer Markets: Antecedents and Consequences, *Journal of the Academy of Marketing Science*, 23(4): 255–71.

Shin, S. J. and Zhou, J. (2003) Transformational Leadership, Conservation and Creativity: Evidence from Korea, *Academy of Management Journal*, 46(6): 703–15.

Short, P. (2004) *Pol Pot: The History of a Nightmare*, London: John Murray.

Shrivastava, P. and Schneider, S. C. (1984) Organizational Frames of Reference, *Human Relations*, 37(10): 795–807.

Sillince, J. (2006) The Effect of Rhetoric on Competitive Advantage: Knowledge, Rhetoric and Resource-Based Theory. In S. R. Clegg, C. Hardy, W. R. Nord, and T. Lawrence (eds), *The Sage Handbook of Organization Studies* (2nd edn), London: Sage. pp. 800–813.

Simmel, G. (2004) *The Philosophy of Money*. London: Routledge and Kegan Paul.

Simon, H. A. (1956) Rational Choice and the Structure of the Environment, *Psychological Review*, 63(2): 129–38.

Simon, H. A. (1957) A Behavioral Model of Rational Choice. In *Models of Man, Social and Rational: Mathematical Essays on Rational Human Behavior in a Social Setting*, New York: Wiley.

Simon, H. A. (1969) *The Sciences of the Artificial*. Cambridge, MA: MIT Press.

Simon, H. A. (1978) Rational Decision-Making in Business Organizations, *Nobel Memorial Lecture*, 8 December 1978, http://nobelprize.org/economics/laureates/1978/simon-lecture.pdf, accessed 9 November 2010.

Simon, H. A. (1985) Human Nature in Politics: The Dialogue of Psychology with Political Science, *American Political Science Review*, 79(2): 293–304.

Simonin, B. L. (1999) Ambiguity and the Process of Knowledge Transfer in Strategic Alliances, *Strategic Management Journal*, 20(7): 595–623.

Sklair, L. (2002) *Globalization: Capitalism and Its Alternatives*, Oxford: Oxford University Press.

Skodvin, T. and Skjærseth, J. B. (2001) Shell Houston, We Have a Climate Problem!, *Global Environmental Change*, 11(2): 103–6.

Smircich, L. and Morgan, G. (1982) Leadership: The Management of Meaning, *Journal of Applied Behavioural Studies*, 18: 257–73.

Smith, A. (1977/1776) *An Enquiry into the Nature and Causes of the Wealth of Nations*, Chicago: University of Chicago Press.

Smith, M. and Higgins, W. (2000) Cause-Related Marketing: Ethics and the Ecstatic, *Business & Society*, 39: 304–22.

Soderbergn, S. (Director) (2008) *Che: Part One* [motion picture], United States: Estudios Picasso.

Sogson, M. (2000) *The Management of Technological Innovation*, Oxford: Oxford University Press.

Sorenson, T. (1965) *Kennedy*, New York: Harper & Row.

Sorge, A. (2005) *The Global and the Local: Understanding the Dialectics of Internationalization*, Oxford: Oxford University Press.

Sosik, J. J., Kahai, S. S. and Avolio, B. J. (1998) Transformational Leadership and Dimensions of Creativity: Motivating Idea Generation in Computer Mediated Groups, *Creativity Research Journal*, 11(2): 111–22.

Sosik, J. J., Kahai, S. S. and Avolio, B. J. (1999) Leadership Style, Anonymity, and Creativity in Group Decision Support Systems, *Journal of Creative Behavior*, 33(4): 227–57.

Spaargaren, G. and Mol, A. (1992) Sociology, Environment and Modernity: Ecological Modernization as a Theory of Social Change, *Society and Natural Resources*, 5(4): 323–44.

Spee, A. P. and Jarzabkowski, P. (2009) Strategy Tools as Boundary Objects, *Strategic Organization*, 7(2): 223–32.

Spekman, R., Forbes, T. M., Isabella, L. A. and Magavoy, T. C. (1998) Alliance Management: A View from the Past and a Look to the Future, *Journal of Management Studies*, 35(6): 747–72.

Spence, A. M. (1977) Entry Capacity, Investment, and Oligopolistic Pricing, *Bell Journal of Economics*, 8(2): 534–44.

Spencer, B., Peyrefitte, J. and Churchman, R. (2003) Consensus and Divergence in Perceptions of Cognitive Strategic Groups: Evidence from the Health Care Industry, *Strategic Organization*, 1(2): 203–30.

Spender, J.-C. (1989) *Industry Recipes*, Oxford: Blackwell.

Spicer, A. (2006) Beyond the Convergence–Divergence Debate: The Role of Spatial Scales in Transforming Organization Logic, *Organization Studies*, 27(10): 1467–83.

Spicer, A., Dunfee, T. and Bailey, W. (2004) Does National Context Matter in Ethical Decision-Making? An Empirical Test of Integrative Social Contracts Theory, *Academy of Management Journal*, 47(4): 610–22.

Spicer, A., Selsky, J., Teicher, J. and Clegg, S. R. (2002) Paradox in Symbols and Subjects: The Politics of Constructing 'The Wharfie'. In S. R. Clegg, J. V. da Cunha and M. P. e Cunha (eds), *Management and Organization Paradoxes*, Amsterdam: Benjamins, pp. 87–118.

Srinivasan, R. and Moorman, C. (2005) Strategic Firm Commitments and Rewards for Customer Relationship Management in Online Retailing, *Journal of Marketing*, 69(4): 193–200.

Star, S. L. and Griesemer, J. R. (1989) Institutional Ecology, 'Translations' and Boundary Objects: Amateurs and Professionals in Berkeley's Museum of Vertebrate Zoology, 1907–39, *Social Studies of Science*, 19(4): 387–420.

Starbuck, W. H. (1983) Organizations as Action Generators, *American Sociological Review*, 48(1): 91–102.

Starbuck, W. H. (1992) Learning by Knowledge-Intensive Firms, *Journal of Management Studies*, 29(6): 713–40.

Starbuck, W. H. (1993) Strategizing in the Real World, *International Journal of Technology Management*, 8(1/2): 77–85.

Stevens, B. (1994) An Analysis of Corporate Ethical Code Studies: 'Where Do We Go From Here?', *Journal of Business Ethics*, 13(1): 63–9.

Stiles, R. M. and Oliver, M. (1998) Anecdotes from Alliancing, *New Zealand Petroleum Conference Proceedings*, www.med. govt.nz/crown_minerals/1998_pet_conference/stiles/index. html, accessed 14 September 2000.

Stinchcombe, A. L. (1985) Project Administration in the North Sea. In A. L. Stinchcombe and C. A. Heimer (eds), *Organization Theory and Project Management: Administering Uncertainty in Norwegian Offshore Oil*, Norway: Norwegian University Press.

Stogdill, R. M. (1974) *Handbook of Leadership: A Survey of Theory and Research*, New York: Free Press.

Stone, O. (Director) (1987) *Wall Street* [motion picture], United States: Twentieth-Century Fox.

Stonehouse, G. and Snowdon, B. (2007) Competitive Advantage Revisited: Michael Porter on Strategy and Competitiveness, *Journal of Management Inquiry*, 16(3): 256–73.

Stopford, J. M. and Wells, L. T. (1972) *Managing the Multinational Enterprise: Organization of the Firm and Ownership of the Subsidiaries*, New York: Basic Books.

Storper, M. and Salais, R. (1997) *Worlds of Production: The Action Frameworks of the Economy*, Cambridge, MA: Harvard University Press.

Strange, S. (1996) *The Retreat of the State: The Diffusion of Power in the World Economy*, Cambridge: Cambridge University Press.

Stross, R. (2008) *Planet Google: How One Company is Transforming Our Lives*, London: Atlantic Books.

Sturdy, A. (1997a) The Consulting Process: An Insecure Business? *Journal of Management Studies*, 34(3): 389–413.

Sturdy, A. (1997b) The Dialectics of Consultancy, *Critical Perspectives on Accounting*, 8(5): 511–35.

Sturdy, A., Clark, T., Fincham, R. and Handley, K. (2004) Silence, Procustes and Colonization: A Response to Clegg et al.'s 'Noise, Parasites and Translation: Theory and Practice in Management Consulting', *Management Learning*, 35(3): 337–40.

Styhre, A. (2001) Kaizen, Ethics, and Care of the Operations: Management after Empowerment, *Journal of Management Studies*, 38(6): 795–810.

Suchman, M. C. (1995) Managing Legitimacy: Strategic and Institutional Approaches, *Academy of Management Review*, 20(3): 571–610.

Sull, D. (1999) Why Good Companies Go Bad, *Harvard Business Review*, July–August: 42–52.

Szilagyi, A. D. and Schweiger, D. M. (1984) Matching Managers to Strategies: A Review and Suggested Framework, *Academy of Management Review*, 9(4): 626–37.

Tapscott, D. and Williams, A. D. (2006) *Wikinomics: How Mass Collaboration Changes Everything*, New York: Portfolio.

Taylor, A. J. P. (1977) *How Wars Begin*, New York: Atheneum.

Taylor, J. R. and Van Every E. J. (2000) *The Emergent Organization: Communication as Its Site and Surface*, Mahwah, NJ: Lawrence Erlbaum and Associates.

Taylor, L. P. (1987) Management: Agent of Human Cultural Evolution, *Futures: The Journal of Forecasting and Planning*, 19(5): 513–25.

Teece, D. A. (1993) The Dynamics of Industrial Capitalism: Perspectives on Alfred Chandler's Scale and Scope (1990), *Journal of Economic Literature*, 31(1): 199–225.

Teece, D. J., Pisano, G. and Shuen, A. (1997) Dynamic Capabilities and Strategic Management, *Strategic Management Journal*, 18(7): 509–33.

Tempel, A., Edwards, T., Ferner, A., Muller-Camen, M. and Wachter, H. (2006) Subsidiary Responses to Institutional Duality: Collective Representation Practices of US Multinationals in Britain and Germany, *Human Relations*, 59(11): 1543–70.

ten Bos, R. (1997) Business Ethics and Bauman Ethics, *Organization Studies*, 18(6): 997–1014.

ten Bos, R. (2000) *Fashion and Utopia in Management Thinking*, Amsterdam and Philadelphia: John Benjamin.

ten Bos, R. (2004) The Fear of Wolves: Anti-Hodological Ruminations about Organizations and Labyrinths, *Culture and Organization*, 10(1): 7–24.

ten Bos, R. and Willmott, H. (2001) Towards a Post-Dualistic Business Ethics: Interweaving Reason and Emotion in Working Life, *Journal of Management Studies*, 38(6): 769–94.

Tett, G. (2009) *Fool's Gold: How Unrestrained Greed Corrupted a Dream, Shattered Global Markets and Unleashed a Catastrophe*, London: Abacus.

The Economist (2004) Industrial Biotechnology: Field of Dreams, *The Economist*, 7 April: 78.

The Economist (2006) Tata and Corus – Steely Logic, *The Economist*, 28 October: 90–1.

Thomas, J. B. and McDaniel, R. R. (1990) Interpreting Strategic Issues: Effects of Strategy and Information-Processing Structure of Top Management Teams, *Academy of Management Journal*, 33(2): 286–306.

Thomas, L. G. and D'Aveni, R. (2009) The Changing Nature of Competition in the US Manufacturing Sector, 1950–2002, *Strategic Organization*, 7(4): 387–431.

Thomas, P. (1998) Ideology and the Discourse of Strategic Management: A Critical Research Framework, *Electronic Journal of Radical Organization Theory*, 4. http://www. mngt.waikato.ac.nz/research/ejrot/vol4_1/thomas.pdf, accessed 25 March 2010.

Thomas, P. S. (1980) Environmental Scanning – The State of the Art, *Long Range Planning*, 13(1): 20–8.

Thorne, L. and Saunders, S. (2002) The Socio-Cultural Embeddedness of Individuals' Ethical Reasoning in Organizations (Cross-Cultural Ethics), *Journal of Business Ethics*, 35(1): 1–14.

Thornton, P. (2007) *Inside the Dark Box: Shedding Light on Private Equity*, London: Workplace Foundation, http://www.theworkfoundation.com/assets/docs/

publications/56_private_equity.pdf, accessed on 23 July 2010.

Thornton, P. H. and Ocasio, W. (1999) Institutional Logics and the Historical Contingency of Power in Organizations: Executive Succession in the Higher Education Publishing Industry, 1958–1990, *American Journal of Sociology*, 105(3): 801–43.

Tibbetts, G. (2008) Record Complaints over 'Greenwashing', *The Daily Telegraph*, http://www.telegraph.co.uk/earth/earthnews/3340705/Record-complaints-over-greenwashing.html, accessed on 09 November 2010.

Tichy, N. M. (1997) *The Leadership Engine: How Winning Companies Build Leaders at Every Level*, New York: Harper Business.

Tidd, J. and Bessant, J. (2009) *Managing Innovation: Integrating Technological, Market and Organizational Change*, Chichester: Wiley.

Tihanyi, L., Ellstrand, A., Daily, C. and Dalton, D. (2000) Composition of the Top Management Team and Firm International Diversification, *Journal of Management*, 26(6): 1157–67.

Tilly, C. (1991) Domination, Resistance, Compliance … Discourse, *Sociological Forum*, 6(3): 593–602.

Toms, S. (2010) Value, Profit and Risk: Accounting and the Resource-Based View of the Firm, *Accounting, Auditing and Accountability Journal*, 23(5): 647–70.

Tom, S. and Beck, M. (2007) The Limitations of Economic Counterfactuals: The Case of the Lancashire Textile Industry, *Management of Organizational History*, 2(2): 315–30.

Townley, B. (1993) Foucault, Power/Knowledge and Its Relevance for Human Resource Management, *Academy of Management Review*, 18(3): 518–45.

Townsend, P. (1971) Won't Get Fooled Again on The Who's *Whos Next* CD, Polydor Records.

Treacy, M. and Wiersema, F. (1995) *The Discipline of Market Leaders*, Reading, MA: Addison-Wesley.

Tsai, W. (2001) Knowledge Transfer in Intraorganizational Networks: Effects of Network Position and Absorptive Capacity on Business Unit Innovation and Performance, *Academy of Management Journal*, 44(5): 996–1004.

Tsoskounoglou, M., Ayerides, G. and Ayerides, E. (2008) The End of Cheap Oil: Current Status and Prospects, *Energy Policy*, 36(10): 3797–806.

Tsoukas, H. (1994) From Social Engineering to Reflective Action in Organizational Behaviour. In H. Tsoukas (ed.), *New Thinking in Organizational Behavior*, Oxford: Butterworth–Heinemann, pp. 1–22.

Tsoukas, H. (1996) The Firm as a Distributed Knowledge System: A Constructionist Approach, *Strategic Management Journal*, 5(4): 289–301.

Tushman, M. L. and O'Reilly, C. (1996) Ambidextrous Organizations: Managing Evolutions and Revolutionary Change, *California Management Review*, 38(4): 8–30.

Uhlenbruck, K., Rodriguez, P., Doh, J. and Eden, L. (2006) The Impact of Corruption on Entry Strategy: Evidence from Telecommunication Projects in Emerging Economies, *Organization Science*, 17(3): 402–14.

Urry, J. (2007) *Mobilities*, London: Sage.

Usdiken, B. (1987) Book Review: David J. Hickson, Richard J. Butler, David Cray, Geoffrey R. Mallory, and David C. Wilson: Top Decisions – Strategic Decision-Making in Organizations 1986, *Organization Studies*, 8(2): 187–8.

Useem, M. (1986) *The Inner Circle: Large Corporations and the Rise of Business Political Activity in the US and UK*, Oxford: Oxford University Press.

Useem, M. and Davis, G. F. (2002) Top Management, Company Directors and Corporate Control. In A. Pettigrew and H. Thomas (eds), *Handbook of Strategy and Management*, London: Sage, pp. 232–60.

Useem, M. and Karabel, J. (1986) Pathways to Top Corporate Management, *American Sociological Review*, 51(2): 184–200.

Vaara, E. (2002) On the Discursive Construction of Success/Failure in Narratives of Post-Merger Integration, *Organization Studies*, 23(2): 213–50.

Vaara, E., Kleymann, B. and Seristö, H. (2004) Strategies as Discursive Constructions: The Case of Airline Alliances, *Journal of Management Studies*, 41(1): 1–35.

Vaara, E., Tienari, J., Pickkari, R. and Santti, R. (2005) Language and Circuits of Power in a Merging Multinational Corporation, *Journal of Management Studies*, 16(3): 333–47.

Van de Ven, A., Polley, D., Garud, R. and Venkatarman, S. (1999) *The Innovation Journey*, Oxford: Oxford University Press.

Van der Heijden, K. (2005) *Scenarios: The Art of Strategic Conversation* (2nd edn), Chichester: Wiley.

Van Iterson, A. and Clegg, S. R. (2008) The Politics of Gossip and Denial in Inter-organizational Relations, *Human Relations*, 61(8): 1117–37.

Van Maanen, J. (1991) The Smile Factory: Work at Disneyland. In P. Frost, L. Moore, M. Louis, C. Lundberg, and J. Martin (eds), *Reframing Organizational Culture*, Newbury Park, CA: Sage, pp. 58–76.

Vanhaverbeke, W. and Noorderhaven, N. G. (2002) Competition between Alliance Blocks: The Case of the RISC Microprocessor Technology, *Organization Science*, 22(1): 1–30.

Vargo, S. and Akaka, M. (2009) Service-Dominant Logic as a Foundation for Service Science: Clarifications, *Service Science*, 1(1): 32–41.

Vargo, S. L. and Lusch, R. F. (2004) Evolving to a New Dominant Logic for Marketing, *Journal of Marketing*, 68(1): 1–17.

Vargo, S. L. and Lusch, R. F. (2008) Service-Dominant Logic: Continuing the Evolution, *Journal of the Academy of Marketing Science*, 36(1): 1–10.

Vaughan, D. (1996) *The Challenger Launch Decision: Risky Technology, Culture, and Deviance at NASA*, Chicago: Chicago University Press.

Vaughan, D. (1997) The Trickle-Down Effect: Policy Decisions, Risky Work and the Challenger Tragedy, *Californian Management Review*, 39(2): 80–102.

Venkatesan, R. and Kumar, V. (2004) A Customer Lifetime Value Framework for Customer Selection and Resource Allocation Strategy, *Journal of Marketing*, 68(4): 106–25.

Verganti, R. (2006) Innovating through Design, *Harvard Business Review*, 84(12): 114–22.

Vernon, R. (1971) *Sovereignty at Bay*, New York: Basic Books.

Victor, B. and Cullen, J. (1988) The Organizational Bases of Ethical Work Climate, *Administrative Science Quarterly*, 33(1): 101–25.

Vidal, J. (2009) Shell Rapped by ASA for 'Greenwash' Advert, *The Guardian*, 13 August 2008.

Vis, D. A. (2005) *The Google Story*, New York: Bantam Dell.

Wack, P. (1985) Scenarios: Unchartered Waters Ahead, *Harvard Business Review*, September–October: 73–89.

Wade, R. (1990) *Governing the Market*, Princeton, NJ: Princeton University Press.

Wally, S. and Becerra, M. (2001) Top Management Team Characteristics and Strategic Changes in International Diversification: The Case of US Multinationals in the European Community, *Group and Organization Management*, 26(2): 165–75.

Walter, A. (2005) Understanding Financial Globalization in International Political Economy. In N. Philips (ed.), *Globalizing Political Economy*, Palgrave Macmillan, Basingstoke, pp. 141–64.

Wang, Y. and Nicholas, S. (2005) Knowledge Transfer, Replication and Learning in Non-Equity Alliances: Operating Joint Ventures in China, *Management International Review*, 1: 45(2005).

Warglien, M. and Masuch, M. (1995) *The Logic of Organizational Disorder*, Berlin: De Gruyter.

Warren, R. (1993) Codes of Ethics: Bricks without Straw, *Business Ethics: A European Review*, 2(4): 185–91.

Watkins, M. D. and Bazerman, M. H. (2003) Predictable Surprises: The Disasters You Should Have Seen Coming, *Harvard Business Review*, 81(3): 72–80.

Watt, A. and Galgoczi, B. (2009) Financial Capitalism and Private Equity – A New Regime?, *Transfer European Review of Labour and Research*, 15(2): 189–208.

Weaver, G. R., Treviño, L. K. and Cochran, P. L. (1999a) Integrated and Decoupled Corporate Social Performance: Management Commitments, External Pressures, and Corporate Ethics Practices, *Academy of Management Journal*, 42(5): 539–53.

Weaver, G. R., Treviño, L. K. and Cochran, P. L. (1999b) Corporate Ethics Practices in the Mid-1990's: An Empirical Study of the Fortune 1000, *Journal of Business Ethics*, 18(3): 283–94.

Weick, K. E. (1979) *The Social Psychology of Organizing* (2nd edn), New York: Addison-Wesley.

Weick, K. E. (1995) *Sensemaking in Organizations*, Thousand Oaks, CA: Sage.

Weick, K. E. (1998) Introductory Essay: Improvisation as a Mindset for Organizational Analyses, *Organization Science*, 9(5): 543–55.

Weick, K. E. (2001) *Making Sense of the Organization*, Malden, MA: Blackwett.

Weick, K. E. (2004) Rethinking Organizational Design. In R. J. Boland and F. Collopy (eds), *Managing as Designing*, Stanford, CA: Stanford Business Books, pp. 36–53.

Weick, K. E. (2008) Sensemaking. In S. R. Clegg and J. R. Bailey (eds), *The International Encyclopedia of Organization Studies*, Thousand Oaks, CA: Sage, pp. 1403–1406.

Weick, K. E. and Westley, F. (1996) Organizational Learning: Affirming an Oxymoron. In S. R. Clegg, C. Hardy and W. R. Nord (eds), *Handbook of Organization Studies*, Thousand Oaks, CA: Sage, pp. 440–58.

Weick, K. E., Sutcliffe, K. M. and Obstfeld, D. (2005) Organizing and the Process of Sensemaking, *Organization Science*, 16(4): 409–21.

Weizsäcker, E., Lovins, A. B. and Lovins, L. H. (1997) *Factor Four: Doubling Wealth – Halving Resource Use*: Sydney: Allen & Unwin.

Wernerfelt, B. (1984) A Resource-Based View of the Firm, *Strategic Management Journal*, 5(2): 171–80.

Wernerfelt, B. (1995) The Resource-Based View of the Firm: Ten Years After, *Strategic Management Journal*, 16(3): 171–5.

Werr, A. (1999) *The Language of Change: The Roles of Methods in the Work of Management Consultants*, Stockholm: Stockholm School of Economics.

Werr, A., Stjernberg, S. and Docherty, P. (1997) The Functions of Methods of Change in Management Consulting, *Journal of Organizational Change Management*, 10(4): 288–307.

Westley, F. (1990) Middle Managers and Strategy: Micro-Dynamics of Inclusion, *Strategic Management Journal*, 11(5): 337–51.

Westney, E. (1993) Institutionalization Theory and the MNE. In S. Ghoshal and E. Westney (eds), *Organization Theory and the Multinational Corporation*, New York: St. Martin's Press, pp. 53–76.

Whitley, R. (1992) *European Business Systems: Firms and Markets in Their National Contexts*, London: Sage.

Whitley, R. (1994a) Dominant Forms of Economic Organization in Market Economies, *Organization Studies*, 15(2): 153–82.

Whitley, R. (1994b) The Internationalization of Firms and Markets: Its Significance and Institutional Structuring, *Organization*, 1(1): 101–24.

Whitley, R. (1999) *Divergent Capitalisms: The Social Structuring and Change of Business Systems*, Oxford: Oxford University Press.

Whitley, R., Thomas, A. and Marceau, J. (1981) *Masters of Business: Business Schools and Business School Graduates in Britain and France*, London: Tavistock.

Whitt, J. A. (1982) *Urban Elites and Mass Transportation: The Dialectics of Power*, Princeton, NJ: Princeton University Press.

Whittington, R. (1993) *What Is Strategy – and Does It Matter?*, London: Routledge.

Whittington, R. (1996) Strategy as Practice, *Long Range Planning*, 29(5): 731–5.

Whittington, R. (2002) Corporate Structure: From Policy to Practice. In A. Pettigrew, H. Thomas and R. Whittington (eds), *Handbook of Strategy and Management*, London: Sage, pp. 113–28.

Whittington, R. (2003) The Work of Strategizing and Organizing: For a Practice Perspective, *Strategic Organization*, 1(1): 119–27.

Whittington, R. and Mayer, M. (2000) *The European Corporation: Strategy, Structure, and Social Science*, Oxford: Oxford University Press.

Wiersma, M. F. and Bantel, K. A. (1992) Top Management Team Demography and Corporate Strategic Change, *Academy of Management Journal*, 25(1): 91–121.

Wiersema, M. F. and Bird, A. (1993) Organizational Demography in Japanese Firms: Group Heterogeneity, Individual Dissimilarity, and Top Management Team Turnover, *Academy of Management Journal*, 36(5): 996–1025.

Wierviorka, M. (2009) Sociology and the Financial Crisis: Which Crisis and Which Sociology?, *Centre for the Study of Global Governance and Department of Sociology Public Lecture*, Wednesday 25 Novemeber, London School of Economics.

Williams, K. (2000) From Shareholder Value to Present-day Capitalism, *Economy and Society*, 29(1): 1–12.

Williamson, O. (1975) *Markets and Hierarchies: Analysis and Antitrust Implications*, New York: Free Press.

Williamson, O. (1979) Transaction Cost Economics: The Governance of Contractual Relations, *Journal of Law and Economics*, 22(2): 233–61.

Williamson, O. (1981) The Economics of Organization: The Transaction Cost Approach, *American Journal of Sociology*, 87(3): 548–77.

Williamson, O. (1985) *The Economic Institutions of Capitalism*, New York: Free Press.

Williamson, O. (1991) Strategizing, Economizing, and Economic Organization, *Strategic Management Journal*, 12 (Special issue): 75–94.

Wilson, D. (1982) Electricity and Resistance: A Case Study of Innovation and Politics, *Organization Studies*, 3(1): 119–40.

Wilson, D., Butler, R., Cray, D., Hickson, D. J. and Mallory, G. (1986) Breaking the Bounds of Organization in Strategic Decision Making, *Human Relations*, 39(2): 309–32.

Winter, S. G. (1987) Natural Selection and Evolution. In J. Eatwell, M. Milgate and P. Newman (eds), *The New Palgrave: Dictionary of Economics*, (Vol. 3), Basingstoke: Palgrave, pp. 614-17.

Winter, S. G. (2004) Specialized Perception, Selection and Strategic Surprise: Learning from the Moths and Bees, *Long Range Planning*, 37(2): 163–69.

Wipperfürth, A. (2005) *Brand Hijack: Marketing Without Marketing*, New York: Portfolio.

Wirtz B. W., Mathieu, A. and Schilke, O. (2007) Strategy in High Velocity Environments, *Long Range Planning*, 40: 295–313.

Wissema, H. (2002) Driving through Red Lights: How Warning Signals are Missed or Ignored, *Long Range Planning*, 35(5): 521–39.

Wittgenstein, L. (1968) *Philosophical Investigations*, Oxford: Blackwell.

Worenkelin, J. J. (2003) The Global Crisis in Power and Infrastructure: Lessons Learned and New Directions, *The Journal of Structured and Project Finance*, 9(1): 7–11.

Xu, D. and Shenkar, O. (2002) Institutional Distance and the Multinational Enterprise, *Academy of Management Review*, 27(4): 608–18.

Yankee Group (2004) *Managed Security Services Survey*, Boston, MA: Yankee Group.

Yearley, S. (2007) Globalization and the Environment. In G. Ritzer (eds), *Blackwell Companion to Globalization*, Oxford: Blackwell, pp. 393–53.

Yeats, W. B. (1921) The Second Coming. In *Michael Robartes and the Dancer*, Dublin: Cuala Press.

Yeung, W.-C. H. (1994) Transnational Corporations from Asian Developing Countries: Their Characteristics and Competitive Edge, *Journal of Asian Business*, 10(4): 17–58.

Yeung, W.-C. H. (2000) The Dynamics of Globalization of Chinese Business Firms. In H.-W. C. Yeung and K. Olds (eds), *Globalization of Chinese Business Firms*, Basingstoke: Macmillan, pp. 75–104.

Yoo, Y., Boland, R. J. and Lyytinen, K. (2006) From Organization Design to Organization Designing, *Organization Science*, 17(2): 215–29.

Young, G., Smith, K. G. and Grimm, C. M. (1996) Austrian and Industrial Organization Perspectives on Firm-level Activity and Performance, *Organization Science*, 7(3): 243–54.

Yukl, G. A. (1989) *Leadership in Organizations*, Englewood Cliffs, NJ: Prentice-Hall.

Yukl, G. A. (2001) *Leadership in Organizations* (5th edn), Upper Saddle River, NJ: Prentice-Hall.

Yukl, G. A. and Falbe, C. M. (1991) The Importance of Different Power Sources in Downward and Lateral Relations, *Journal of Applied Psychology*, 76(3): 416–23.

Zack, M. H. (2000) Jazz Improvisation and Organizing: Once More from the Top, *Organization Science*, 11(2): 227–34.

Zajac, E. J. and Olsen, C. P. (1993) From Transaction Cost to Transactional Value Analysis: Implications for the Study of Interorganizational Strategies, *The Journal of Management Studies*, 30(1): 131–45.

Zald, M. N. and Ash, R. (1966) Social Movements Organizations: Growth, Decay, and Change, *Social Forces*, 44(3): 327–41.

Zander, I. and Zander U. (2005) The Inside Track: On the Important (But Neglected) Role of Customers in the Resource-Based View of Strategy and Firm Growth, *Journal of Management Studies*, 42(8): 1519–648.

Zeitlin, M. (1974) Corporate Ownership and Control: The Large Corporations and the Capitalist Class, *American Journal of Sociology*, 79(5): 1073–119.

Zermeno, S. (2005) *La desmodernidad Mexicana y las alternativas a la violencia y a la exclusion en nuestros dias*, Mexico: Oceano.

Zhang, G., An, X., Lu, J. and Zhang, G. (2010) China's IP System Comes of Age, *Managing Intellectual Property: The Global Magazine for Intellectual Property Owners, Supplement – China IP Focus 2010, 8th Edition*, http://www.managingip.com/Article.aspx?ArticleID=2460070, accessed 27 April 2010.

Zhang, H. and Van Den Bulcke, D. (2000) Internationalization of Ethnic Chinese-Owned Enterprises: A Network Approach. In H.-W. C. Yeung and K. Olds (eds), *Globalization of Chinese Business Firms*, Basingstoke: Macmillan, pp. 126–49.

Zyglidopoulos, S. C. (2002) The Social and Environmental Responsibilities of Multinationals: Evidence from the Brent Spar Case, *Journal of Business Ethics*, 36(1/2): 141–51.

INDEX

3M 142
Abbott, Andrew 109
Abrahamson, Eric 108
Abramson, Jeffrey 7
accountability 284, 359–90
action generators 270–3
action orientation 4–5
Actor-Network Theory (ANT) 158, 227
adaptive practices 218–22, 224
AIG 375
airlines 154–5, 172
    budget 272–3
    Star Alliance 330, 331–2
alliance-building games 301
alliances 278, 306–7, 322, 332–55
    development and maturity 344–5
    formation 343
    foundation 344
    lifecycle 343–6, 355
    organization 337–9
    termination 345–6
alliancing 349–55
ambidextrous organizations 198,
    200, 202
American Express 160–1
Americanization 393–4
Ansoff, Igor 16–17, 118, 122, 361
Apple 190, 194, 202, 243, 334
    CRM 159
    iPod 98, 159
Appleyard, 204–6
arbitrage 326
Ariño, Africa 337, 338
Arizona water politics 102–3
Arthur Andersen 115–16
Asian financial crisis 361
assets, RBV 84–5
asset specificity 61
asset-strippers 368
asymmetry of information 51
AT&T 170
audit 378–81, 386
Australian Broadcasting Corporation (ABC)
    301–2
automobile industry 55–6
    see also individual companies
    brands 163–4, 165, 169
    collaboration 323, 333
    complementors 63
    core competencies 95
    employee power 64
    incremental innovation 192
    innovation 185–6, 200
    strategic groups 65
    value capture 100

Bacharach, Peter 279–80, 282
Bain, Joe S. 49
Baratz, Morton 279–80, 282
Barclays 374, 375
Barnard, Chester 261
Barney, Jay 84, 85, 86, 87–8, 90–1, 136

barriers to entry 50, 62, 98
Barry, David 141, 143
Bear Stearns 373
Beck, Ulrich 378–9
behavioural segmentation 155
Benetton 169
Berle, Adolph Augustus 239, 240, 295
binary strategy 329
black box 103, 133
Blanchard, Oliver 376
boardrooms 243–4, 249
Body Shop 72, 160
Boje, David 111
'born globals' 395–7
Boston Consulting Group 53
boundary objects 152, 232–3
bounded rationality 19, 198, 261–3
Bourdieu, Pierre 226
Bourgeois, Louis 277–8, 282
Bradford studies 275–7
brand-driven strategy 166–72
brands 34, 149–81
    capital 163–5
    equity 162
    formation 163–5
    identity 161–5, 169–70, 173–4, 176–7
    leadership 169
    value capture 100
BrandsExclusive 78–82
Brown, Tim 195, 196
budgeting games 301
bullet payment 369–70
Burberry 162
bureaucracy 282–7
bureaucratic accountability 284
Burgelmann, R. A. 33, 224
Bush, George W. 271
Business As Usual (BAU) 350, 351
business environment
    competitive performance 48–82
    macro- 53–6
business process reengineering (BPR) 104–7
Butler, John 95, 96, 97
Butler, Richard 261

Café Society 113
Cambodia, strategic vision 41–4
Camillus, John C. 21–3
Canon 94
capabilities 10–11
    dynamic 98–100
    RBV 86–7, 89–92
    repertoire 101
capitalism 359–90
Caulier-Grice, Julie 208–9
cause-related marketing 160–1
centralized hubs 327–9
Challenger disaster 283–6
Chandler, Alfred 15–16, 118, 361
Chesbrough, Henry 204–6
chief strategy officers (CSOs) 4–5
China 414–17

Chittipeddi, Kumar 138–9
Christensen, Clayton M. 188–9
Cirque du Soleil 212
Cisco 331, 334
Citigroup 372, 388, 390
Clark, Peter 95, 101, 201, 218
Clausewitz, Karl von 6, 8–9
Clegg, Stewart 41–4, 402
closed model of innovation 206
clusters, innovation 206–7
coalitions 306–7
Coase, Ronald 85
cognition 19, 36
    mode 139
cognitive maps 140, 145
Cohen, Michael D. 33
collaborative strategies 321–58
collateralized debt obligation (CDO)
    371–2, 375
commensuration 381, 382
communication flows 407–8
company-based elites 229
comparative advantage, MNCs 323, 324–5
competency traps 346
competitive advantage 76
    core competencies 93–5
    evolution 19–20
    generic strategies 69
    innovation 183–212
    narrative 142
    RBV 96, 97
    resources 18
    sustainability 91–2
    sustainable 52–3, 97, 136, 151
    value chain 66–9
    VRIN model 87–8
competitive attractiveness 59–63
competitive performance 47–82
competitive positioning 153–8, 176
competitive rivalry, intensity 62
complementors 63, 64
complexity theory 23–5, 36
complex organizations,
    politics 306–10
comprehensive alliances 340
consensus strategy 128
constitutive approach 260
constraining innovation 198–9
constricted decisions 276
consultants 232–42
contingency model 222
contracts
    alliances 337–9, 345, 355
    completeness 340–2
control of strategy 237–42
convergence 410–11
coopetition 63, 342
coordinated federation 327
coordinated market economy 328
core competencies 93–5
corporate codes 246–9
corporate governance 238, 240–2

corporate planning 9
corporate social responsibility (CSR) 397, 398–400
correctness 132
Corrs Chambers Westgarth 171–2
cost cutting, BPR 105–7
cost focus strategy 71–2
cost leadership 69–70, 72, 74
counterfactuals 280–1
creative destruction 187–90
creativity 194–200
credit rating agencies 380–1
Crenson, Matthew 280–2
critical theory 160
Cuban missile crisis 267–70, 282
Cultural Revolution 24
culture 135–7
    alliances 345
    brands 171
    decision-making 284
    globalization 394
customer relationship management (CRM) 158–61
customers
    bargaining power 60–1
    insider track 203
    intimacy 74
    relationship 151, 158–61, 176, 179–81, 194
decentralized federation 326
decisionless decisions 282
decision-making 259–92
deep assumptions 133, 135
delegated management agreement 338
deliberate strategy 26, 126–9
Dell 73, 74, 75
demographic segmentation 155
Denning, Steve 111
Descartes, René 119
design thinking 194–200
differentiation 69, 70–1, 74
differentiation focus strategy 71–2
'dirty hands' 7–8
disabling strategic practices 217–18, 219–21
disciplinary power 305
discourse, strategy as 143–4, 145
discursive struggles 28
Disneyland 172–3
disruptive technologies 187–90
divergence 411
diversification 49–50, 91, 324
division of labour 123
Doc Martens 164
dominant ideology thesis 14
dominant logic 19
dominant strategy paradigm 15–18
Dooney, Hazel 341–2
dot-com boom 63
double loop learning 134
Dougherty, Deborah 197–8, 210
downsizing 106–7, 233, 367
Dukerich, Janet 139–40
Dunlap, Al 'Chainsaw' 106
Dutton, Jane 139–40
dynamic capabilities, RBV 98–100

eBay 203
ecological modernization strategies 397–8
economic influences, PESTEL analysis 54, 55
economic rent 52, 90–3, 97–8
efficiency, MNCs 325
Eisenhardt, Kathleen 277–8, 282
elites 226–30
Elmes, Michael 141, 143

embedded mobility 229
embeddedness 325
emergent strategy 26, 126–9, 145, 218
EMI 388–90
employees, power 64, 93
enabling innovation 198, 199
enabling strategic practices 217–18, 219–21
end games 352–3
energy, innovation 198, 199, 210
Enron 115–16, 174–5, 245–6, 361, 365–6, 367, 410
entrepreneurial strategy 127
entrepreneurship
    institutional 201
    RBV 97–8
environment
    CSR 397
    globalization 397–400
    innovation 200–7
    PESTEL analysis 54–5
    Shell 422–9
environmental modelling 10–11
equity alliances 337, 338, 355
Espeland, Wendy 102–3, 261, 381–3
ethics 7–8, 160–1, 246, 247–9
evolutionary perspective 19–20, 36, 190
expertise games 301
explicit contracts 338
explicit knowledge 103–4, 109, 236
externalization, knowledge 109
Ezzamel, Mahmoud 143, 145, 260

fashion 78–82, 162
feedback, wicked problems 22
feed forward, wicked problems 22
feelings, alliancing 353–5
financial crisis 35, 361, 370–9, 394, 401, 410
    corporate governance 241–2
    evolutionary perspective 20
    flows 405, 408
financial flows 402–3
financialization 359–90, 411, 413–14
Five Forces Model 12, 14–15, 59–63, 64, 75, 76, 90
flows, globalizing 400–8
fluid decisions 276
fluidity 197, 198, 210
focus strategies 71–2, 74
foolish playfulness 191, 192
Ford 30, 119–20, 169, 185, 333, 396
foreign direct investment 323, 326, 401
Foss, Nicolai 96
Foucault, Michel 143–4, 305, 306
frames of reference 19
free markets 85
Friedman, Milton 362, 363, 403
functional alliances 340, 355
future perfect 349–55

games 299–303
garbage-can-type decision-making 33, 266–7
gatekeepers 274
General Motors 200, 323, 362, 377
general public, power 64
generic strategies 69–73, 75, 76
geographic alliance 340
geographic segmentation 155
Gioia, Dennis A. 30, 138–9
Glazer, Barney 125
global financial crisis see financial crisis
globalization 391–430
    uneven 397–400

global strategies 319–430
    financialization, risk and accountability 359–90
    globalization 391–430
    international and collaborative 321–58
glocalization 394–5
goods-dominant (G-D) logic 152
Google 118, 135, 147–8, 202, 396–7
governance 215–58
    alliances 337–9, 355
    collaboration 334
government policy 50
Govindarajan, Vijay 207–8
Grant, Robert 84, 89, 92
Grateful Dead 193
grounded theory 125–6
Grove, Andrew 63

Hamel, Gary 23–4, 36, 93–5, 174
Harvard Business School 25
HBOS 361, 375
Hewlett Packard 191
high-velocity environments 191–2, 277–8
Hobbes, Thomas 6, 8
homogeneous markets 57
horizontal relations 48, 53
HSBC 124, 167
humanization 125
Humphrey, Albert 17
hypercompetition 58, 76
hypocrisy 249

IBM 331, 333–4
ICI 128, 274
IDEO 195, 196
ideological strategy 127
IKEA 70, 73–4, 98
implementation 29
implicit contracts 338
imposed strategy 128
improvisation 192–3
incremental discontinuities 192–3
incremental innovation 184, 191, 192–3
incrementalism 26, 282
industrial organization (IO) 48–51, 65, 76
industry shakeouts 63
Infomedia 395–6
information and communication technology (ICT), innovation 202, 203
information technology
    CRM 159
    dot-com boom 63
    knowledge management 109–10
ING 166–8
innovation 183–212
    China 415
    environments 200–7
    experiments 207–8
    as strategic driver 75–6
insider track 203
institutional entrepreneurship 201
institutional factors, MNCs 325–6
institutional innovation 200–1
institutional isomorphism 311
integrated networks 330–2
integrity 197, 198, 199, 210, 344
intelligibility 132–3
interests 28, 294–9
internalization
    knowledge 109
    MNCs 323
international strategies 321–58

Internet
    BrandsExclusive 78–82
    innovation 202, 203
    mass self-communication 408
    online markets 58–9
Intranets 110, 112–13
investment alliance 341
isolating mechanisms 65, 86
isomorphism 311

Japan 14–15, 327, 329
Jarosch, Daniel 78
Jarzabkowski, Paula 129–30
Johnson & Johnson 163
joint ventures 337, 338–9, 345
JPMorgan Chase 373
just-in-time strategy 193
JVC 323

Keynes, J. M. 375–6, 379
key performance indicators (KPI) 351
King, Mervyn 375
Knights, David 143
knowledge 83–116
    explicit 103–4, 109, 236
    management 104–13
    mining 110
    RBV 95–6
    tacit 103–4, 109, 111, 236, 336
knowledge-based organizations 103–4
knowledge-based resources 87
knowledge economy 107–8
Kodak 201
Kuhn, Thomas 9, 11

labour, globalization 401, 405–7
Landes, David 107–8
leadership, role 222–4
league tables 384–5
learning networks 206–7
learning organizations 134
legal influence, PESTEL analysis 55
legitimacy 311–12, 409
LEGO 174, 197
Lehman Brothers 241, 374–5
liberal market economy 328
Lindblom, Charles 263–6, 282, 288
lineage of strategy 6–9
Littler, Craig R. 367
Lusch, Robert 152

McDonald's 164, 173
Machiavelli, Niccolò 6–8, 9
McHugh, Alan 33
McKinlay, Alan 109–10, 112
McNamara, Robert 25, 119–20
McNulty, Terry 243–4, 249
macro-environment 53–6, 76
management fashion 108
management innovation 206–7
managerialism 15, 34, 151, 158
mandates, MNCs 307–10, 312
Mantere, Saku 217, 221–2, 232
Marceau, Jane 183
market factors, MNCs 323–4
marketing 149–81
marketing alliance 340–1
marketing strategy 150
market segmentation 153–8, 176
market structure 57
Marks & Spencer 89, 229, 251–8
Martin, Joanne 136–7, 163
Martin, Randy 364
Martin, Roger 238

Mason, Edward S. 49
mass self-communication 408
matrix organizations 329
MBA 230–2
Means, Gardiner 239, 240, 295
mediascapes 407–8
Menagerie 357–8
mergers and acquisitions 13, 91, 336
Meyer, Claus 67
microfinance 208–9
micropolitics 295–7, 301, 307–10
Microsoft 135, 186, 187, 190, 395
military 64, 119–20, 271
military strategy 9
Mintzberg, Henry 26, 28–9, 33, 121–6, 129,
    143–5, 192, 261, 300, 301
mixed signals 284
mobility barriers 65
monetarism 363
monopolies 57
monopoly capitalism 362, 364, 377
moral hazard 375
Mountbatten, Lord Louis 216
Mulgan, Geoff 208–9
multinational corporations (MNCs) 306–14,
    322–55, 410–11
Murray, Robin 208–9

narrative 27
    knowledge management 111
    strategy as 140–4
NASDAQ index 108
national innovation system 206–7
Nelson, Sidney 19
neo-classical economics 85, 104, 363
neo-liberalism 362–4, 375–6, 377, 386, 398,
    402–3, 405, 413
network-based mobility 229
new entrants threat 61
new industrial organization (NIO)
    theories 51
New York Port Authority 139–40
Nike 165, 173
Nonaka, Ikujiro 109
non-decision-making 279–82, 287, 303
non-equity alliances 338, 345, 355
normalization of deviance 284, 373
Northern Rock 373
not-invented-here syndrome 307

objective approaches 143
oligopolies 57–8
OLI (ownership, location and
    internalization) 323
Olsen, Johan P. 33
open innovation networks 204–7
open-source model 203–4
open strategy 204–6
operational excellence 74
organization 10–11, 13
organizational decision-making 274–5
organizational improvisation 192–3
organizational memory 106–7
organizational metaphysics 234, 236–7
organizational politics 293–317
organizational retooling 234, 235
organizational surgery 233–5
organizational therapy 234, 235–6
'organization man' 9
organization theory 85, 199
Orr, Julian E. 111, 134
outsourcing 68, 95, 233, 403
ownership 237–42
    global 416–17

Page, Larry 147
paradigmatic perspective 9–13
pattern, Mintzberg 124
Penrose, Edith 17–18, 85–6, 203
people flows 405–7
performance 10–11, 47–82, 278
    inter-organizational 337
    key indicators 351
    S–C–P 49–52, 59–60, 76
perspective, Mintzberg 123
PESTEL (Political, Social, Technological,
    Environmental and Legal) analysis 54–5,
    56, 76, 90
Peters, Tom 24–5, 136, 194–5
Pettigrew, Andrew 128–9, 143, 243–4, 249,
    274–5, 297–8
pharmaceutical industry, KM 112–13
Pina e Cunha, Miguel 41–4
Pixar 195–6
planned strategy 127
planning 9, 120–6, 129, 138,
    218, 221–2
platforms 185, 186, 187
ploy, Mintzberg 124
pluralism 245
Police Service 248
political accountability 284
politics 34, 213–317
    decision-making 267–70
    marketing 150
    performance 278
    PESTEL analysis 54, 55
    storytelling 111–12
    targeting 153
pollution 397, 400
Pol Pot 41–4
polyphony 346–9, 355
Porter, Michael 18, 50, 84, 118, 184, 363
    Five Forces Model 12, 14–15, 59–63, 64,
        75, 76, 90
    generic strategies 69, 71
    innovation 194
    strategic positioning 73
    value chain 66, 68–9
position, Mintzberg 124
positional goods 176
positioning 153–8, 176
power 34
    communication flows 407–8
    dimensions 303–4
    politics 298–313
Power, Mike 379–80, 381
power relations 27, 28, 217–21, 225
    boardrooms 243
    politics 298–9
practice, strategy as 26–7, 36,
    129–34, 217
Prahalad, C. K. 93–5, 202–3
preparedness 34
Priem, Richard 95, 96, 97
principal/agency problem 364
private equity 368–70, 386, 388–90
process
    Pettigrew 128–9
    strategy as 117–45
process innovation 75, 184
process strategy 127–8
Procter & Gamble 204
procurement flows 403–5
product demand 49
product differentiation 49, 50
product innovation 75, 184
production alliance 340
production licensing 340

product leadership 74
product market approach 90–1
profitability, industry structure 18
property-based resources 87
psychographic segmentation 155
public–private partnership (PPP) 341, 355

quantitative analysis 5
Quinn, Brian J. 26

radical innovation 184
railways 16
Ramaswamy, Venkat 202–3
Ramsey, Gordon 93, 186
rankings 379–86
rational agents and rational expectations
    (RARE) 375–6
rational choice models 119–20, 263–4
rational discontinuities 190–2
rationalism 25–6, 34, 118–21, 142–3
rationalist approach to innovation 191
rationality 272
rational planning 218, 221–2
RBS 361, 375
reactivity 381, 382
Reagan, Ronald 362, 363
recursive approach 218–21
Redzepi, René 67
Rego, Arménio 41–4
relevant counterfactual 280–1
reliability 185
remuneration 238, 295
    bankers 241–2, 373
    financial crisis 373
repertoires 101–2, 201
replicability 92
research and development alliance 341
resistance 300–3, 305
resource-based view (RBV) 17–18,
    83–103, 113, 118
    criticisms 95–8
    culture 136
resources, alliances 336
Restaurant Noma 66–8
Reuer, Jeffrey J. 337, 338
revolutionary perspective 18, 20–3, 36
rightsizing 233
risk 359–90
    decision-making 282–7
    management 242
    uneven 397–400
ritual elements 28
Ritzer, George 175, 176, 392, 406
'root' approach 264
routines, evolution 19
routine signals 284
Rumelt, Richard 261

sales alliance 340
Saligna 205
Samra-Fredericks, Dalvir 131–3
Samsung 120–1
satisficing 263
Sauder, Michael 381–3
Schein, Edgar 133, 135, 233
Schumpeter, Joseph 187, 201
self-fulfilling prophecy 382
Sennett, Richard 361, 362
sensegiving 29, 137–40
sensemaking 29, 137–40
September 11 2001 31–2
serendipity 33–4
service-dominant (S-D) logic 152–8, 176
shared management agreement 338

shareholders
    power 64
    value 364–8
Shell 420–30
Silicon Valley model 411–12
Sillence, John 95, 96–7
Simon, Herbert 194, 261–3, 288
sincerity 132
single loop learning 134
Skype 75
Smith, Adam 101, 175
Snowdon, Dave 104
soccer balls 308
social capital 226–7
social context 28
social distance 227
social influence, PESTEL analysis 54, 55
social innovation 208–9
socialization, knowledge 109
solution-specific alliance 340
Southwest Airlines 70
specialization 156
Spee, Andreas P. 129–30
Spicer, André 409, 410, 411
sponsorship games 301
sporadic decisions 275–6
stakeholder capitalism 398–9
stakeholders
    MNCs 313
    wicked problems 22
Star Alliance 330, 331–2
Starbuck, Bill 121, 271
Starbucks 153–4
state, sixth force 63–4
Stiglitz, Joseph 376
storytelling 111–12, 113, 140, 142
strange conversations 351–2
strategic alliances 332–5
strategic champions 217, 220–2, 232, 249
strategic change 138–9, 225
strategic choice theory 225
strategic groups 65–6, 76
strategic improvisation 192–3
strategic interest 295–7
strategic leadership 223
strategic planning 120–6, 129
strategic positioning 73
strategy-as-practice (s-as-p) 26–7, 36, 129–34,
    217
strategy as narrative 27
Strauss, Anselm 125
structural poses 101–2
structure–conduct–performance (S–C–P)
    approach 49–52, 59–60, 76
structured investment vehicles (SIVs) 381
subjective approaches 143
substitute products, threat 61–2
substitutors 63
successive limited comparison
    approach 265
suppliers
    bargaining power 61
    M&S 89
supply conditions 49
surprise 29–32, 36
sustainable competitive advantage 52–3, 97,
    136, 151
Swatch watches 200
SWOT (strengths, weaknesses, opportunities
    and threats) analysis 17, 120, 301
Sydney 348, 349–55

tacit knowledge 103–4, 109, 111, 236, 336
Takeuchi, Hiro 109

targeting 153–8, 176
tautology, RBV 96–7
technical culture 284
technology
    innovation 190
    PESTEL analysis 54, 55
Telemig 173
TELESTAR 179–81
Terra Firma 388–90
Tett, Gillian 371, 374
Thatcher, Margaret 362, 363, 368
theory of the firm 96
Toms, Steven 95, 96
top-down control systems 15
top management 215–58
total quality management (TQM) 160
Toyota 164, 323, 403
trade barriers 323
trade unions 64, 369
transactional leadership 223–4
transferability 92
transformational leadership 223
translation
    collaboration 347–9, 355
    globalization 412–13
transnational strategy 330–2
transparency 92, 421
Trimble, Chris 207–8
truth 132–3

ultimate values 14
umbrella strategy 127
unconnected strategy 128
uniqueness paradox 163
unitarism 245
United Nations Climate Change Conference
    290–2
UPS 335

value
    capture 100–1
    chain 66–9, 75, 76
    co-creation 201–4
    creation, RBV 100–1
value-creating disciplines 74, 76
values, culture 135
Vargo, Stephen 152
Vaughan, Diane 283–6
vertical integration 49–50
vertical relations 48, 53
virtuality 113
VRIN model 87–8, 96, 312

Wall Street crash 371, 375
Wal-Mart 25
Waterman, Robert 136
weak signals 284
Weber, Rolf 78
Weick, Karl E. 30, 135, 137–8, 351
Wernerfelt, Birger 17, 90
Westley, F. 30
Whittington, Richard 130–1
wicked problems 21–3, 36
Wieviorka, Michel 377–8
Wikipedia 203
Williams, Karel 367
Willmott, Hugh 143, 145, 260
Winter, Richard 19
workshopping 352–3

Xerox 190, 191

Zbaracki, Mark 282
zero-sum game 64